Empowering the 21st Century Professional School Counselor

Jackie M. Allen, Editor

Counseling Outfitters

Counseling Outfitters, LLC

Empowering the 21st Century Professional School Counselor

10   9 8 7 6 5 4 3 2 1

Counseling Outfitters, LLC
P.O. Box 1208
Ann Arbor, MI 48106-1208

Cover photograph by Garry R. Walz, Ph.D.

We selected the sunrise photo for the cover because it reflects the futuristic tone of the text, the dawn of a new day, and bright goals to work toward.

Library of Congress Cataloging in Publication Data

Allen, Jackie.

Empowering the 21st Century Professional School Counselor/Jackie M. Allen
          p.cm.

Includes bibliographical references and index

ISBN 13: 978-0-9795668-2-0 (alk. Paper)

Empowering the 21st Century
Professional School Counselor

Table of Contents

Section I. Professional Issues:
What it Means to be a Professional School Counselor

Section II. Leadership Issues and Challenges: School Counselors Leading Educational Reform

Section III. Skill Building: School Counselors as Practitioners

Foreword

It goes without saying that our actions as counselors are driven by what we know. As our knowledge increases, so, too, do the types and quality of interventions we can use to help our clients and students. Even the best counselors display gaps in their knowledge; and today's counselors face an exceptionally tough challenge in keeping up to date not only because of the increasingly complex problems that our clients/students present, but also because of the rapid development of new programs and practices brought about by new technologies and an increasing emphasis on research and program evaluation.

The largest ever effort devoted to enhancing the knowledge of educators at all levels and in all settings has been the U.S. Department of Education's ERIC program. It has stimulated the systematic collection and dissemination of information and resources to all persons interested in education. During the 38-year tenure of the ERIC Clearinghouse on Counseling and Student Services (ERIC/CASS), a large number of publications and information digests were developed and made available specifically for practicing counselors in a wide variety of positions and settings. One of the most popular publications was School Counseling: *New Perspectives & Practices*, edited by Dr. Jackie M. Allen. It was the enthusiastic acceptance and widespread use of this monograph that led us to encourage Dr. Allen to produce a new edition that speaks to the challenges and issues in school counseling today.

The task of identifying and recruiting authors to contribute chapters that provide up-to-date, practical information on the wide variety of topics today's professional school counselor has to address was a daunting one. However, we believe Dr. Allen was exceedingly successful in meeting the challenge. In producing her new edition, she incorporated two special features to insure the substance and relevance of the book. First, she insured substance by recruiting a group of highly experienced authors who are recognized experts on the topics of their chapters. Second, she insured relevance to current school counseling situations by pairing counselor educators with practicing school counselors to co-author most of the chapters.

Dr. Allen further increased the usefulness of the monograph by having the authors produce a set of discussion questions at the end of their chapters. This feature makes the book especially valuable as a resource for school counselor education courses. It also helps individual readers reflect on the contents of the chapters and consider how they might apply the new information in their own school counseling programs. The result is a volume covering the critical issues in school counseling in the 21st century. It contains information worth knowing that can make a difference in how a school counselor performs his/her work. It is unusual in its breadth and coverage of practical information that school counselors need to know.

We want to note also that, as the publisher of the book, we have followed the same practice we used in producing books for ERIC/CASS. By that, we mean that we have allowed the authors to "speak in their own words." As a result, you will find that some of the chapters are in a non-traditional format (e.g., one is in an interview style) and others are in a conversational format. In those, you will feel as if the authors are speaking directly to you. We hope you will find this variation interesting and enjoyable.

So, enjoy! We recommend this book without reservation. It's a "good read" – and a book that will benefit both you and your students.

Garry R. Walz, Ph.D.
Jeanne C. Bleuer, Ph.D.
Counseling Outfitters, LLC

Dedication

This book is dedicated to the future school counselors who will provide the leadership for the 21st century. Graduate students and new school counselors will set the pace for school counseling in the decades to come. The counselor educators, counseling experts, and school counselors who have written these chapters with the intent of informing and inspiring future generations want to share their knowledge and experience with the pathfinders of the 21st century in an effort to empower, improve, and assist school counseling to find its proper place in the educational community.

Jackie M. Allen, Editor
University of La Verne

Preface

Jackie M. Allen

School counselors in the 21st century continue to be on the front lines of educational change. With the growing number of dropouts, tight budgets, national legislation setting the bar for academic success, the growing emotional and social issues young people face, career and employment concerns, and the every day challenge of providing efficacious school counseling services and programs, school counselors seek empowerment for their lives and their jobs.

This book has been designed to provide all those who read it, whether in a school counseling class or in their office or home, a resource on current topics in school counseling that will empower school counselors with knowledge, practices, and personal development tips to serve the young people in our schools throughout the nation. This book is unique in that teams of counselor educators and practicing school counselors were invited to submit chapters on current topics. The collaboration of counselor educators and practicing school counselors gave experiential credibility to the chapters. In addition, some counseling experts added valuable information to complete the requested chapter topics.

The book is divided into four sections:

I. Professional Issues and Challenges-School Counselor as Professional
II. Leadership Issues and Challenges-School Counselor as Leader
III. Skill Building-School Counselor as Practitioner
IV. Care for the Care Giver-School Counselor Taking Care of Self

The first section is comprised of chapters including the professional issues of: planning for the future, law and ethics, mentoring models, grant writing, and school counselor research. Futurists Sheri & Curly Johnson have written a thought-provoking chapter on "The Future for School Counselors in 2025: Who Will Decide?" School counseling ethics expert and 2006-2007 ASCA President Carolyn Stone discusses "The Complications and Complements of Ethics and Law in Counseling." Jeannine Studer, Betty Ann Domm, and Sue Clapp explain how to do "Mentoring Through Supervision." In

preparing school counselors to go out into the field, Suzy Thomas and Laurel Edgecomb have put together a unique program linking graduate students with school counselors in the field in their chapter on "Mentoring Models: Preparing School Counselors for the Future." Keeping school counselor programs funded is a big concern, which Debbie Vernon and Steve Rainey tackle with creative ideas in "Money Matters: Grant Writing and Funding Your Counseling Program." The very future of the profession may depend on our ability to demonstrate our accountability; Lonnie Rowell shares an innovative program in California in his chapter "School Counselors and Research: A Missing Link in Professional Identity?"

Leadership issues and challenges form the theme of the second section of the book. School counselors are increasingly called upon to provide leadership in student support services and are challenged to provide leadership in their own school and in the local school system. Regina Schaefer and Donna Cleman start this section off with a challenging chapter on "School Counselors Leading Change." Collaboration, a notable counselor leadership function, is discussed by Kathy Emery and Suzy Thomas in "Collaboration Strategies to Enhance the Relationships Between School Counselors and the School Community." Two 21st century phenomena in school counseling are the American School Counselor National Model and the Support Personnel Accountability Report Card. John Carey, with Natalie Kosine, Brian Mathieson, and Jason Schweid has developed an instrument for "Assessing Readiness to Implement the ASCA National Model for School Counseling Programs." Mr. SPARC, Bob Tyra, created a clever dialogue with coauthor William Welcher in "The Support Personnel Accountability Report Card (SPARC): A Practitioner and Consultant Share Perspectives." Former ASCA presidents Brenda Melton and Janice Gallagher prepare the school counselor for taking a leadership role in implementing staff in-service training with "From Planning to Practice: Instituting Effective Professional Development." Introducing school counselors to new Individual with Disabilities Education Act 2004 concepts, John Brady and Jackie Allen conclude the section with "Response to Intervention-What School Counselors Need to Know."

School counselors are always looking for ways to

build their skills and/or add new skills to be the best they can be. The third section of the book is dedicated to skill building to enhance the school counselor as practitioner. The 17 chapters in this section cover a wide variety of areas from counseling techniques to the application of computer technology in school counseling, career development, and student study teams. Charleen Alderfer and Mark S. Kiselica emphasize working with families in "Expanding the Therapeutic Repertoire of School Counselors: Family Systems Counseling with Children and Adolescents in Educational Settings." Kelly Collins and Gerald Chandler share techniques on a current topic of high importance in "Working with Students of Deployed Family Members." A unique look at the developments of brain-based learning as they apply to school counseling is found in the chapter "Brain-Based Learning" by Jackie M. Allen. The next four chapters deal with crisis issues in school counseling: "Suicide Prevention: Things the Counselor Must Know," by Deborah Kimokeo, Rosemary Rubin, and Nancy Schubb; "Self Injury: Understanding and Providing Assistance to Students Who Self-Mutilate," by Chris Simpson and Samuel K. Bore; "Working With the Victims of Extreme Crises," by Cheri Lovre; and "Crisis Intervention and the School Counselor: A Case Study," by Michael Pines, Brandon Dade, and Samar Yassine.

What would we do in the 21st century without computers? Computer literacy has often been a real challenge for school counselors. Our next group of authors have accepted that challenge and not only improved their personal computer literacy, but want to help other school counselors get on board. Contributors are: Russell Sabella and Theresa Stanley, with a tremendous chapter," School Counseling and Technology: An Overview"; Sally Gellardin and Marilyn Harryman, with the message of "Staying Current: Using Cybertools to Reach More Students"; and ACA's 2006-2007 President Marie Wakefield with Cynthia J. Rice emphasizing "The Impact of Cyber-Communication on the Personal, Social, and Emotional Growth of Today's Youth."

For the future of America's students, career development is an important part of their secondary and post secondary education and one of the three areas in the ASCA standards. To set the stage, Linda Kobylarz and past NCDA President Martha Russell explain the National Career Development Guidelines in "Career Development: Foundation for Student School Success and Post Secondary Transition." Robert Chope stresses "How Families Can Become Career Developers." Suzy Mygatt Wakefield and Deborah Crapes discuss "Helping Unfocused Kids and At-Risk Kids with Career Planning." Phil Jarvis and Michael Gagitano explore the possibilities of "The Real Game Series: Helping Students Imagine Their Future." Stanford professor John Krumboltz and Stephanie Eberle provide a thoughtful and student-focused chapter on "School Counselors Are In Charge of Learning." Jackie Allen elaborates on the role of the school counselor in "Career Education for Special Education Students." This section on skill building is completed with the chapter from David Kopperud, Betty Collia Ibarra, and Stephen McPherson on "Using Student Study Teams and School Attendance Review Boards to Improve Attendance, Graduation Rates, and Academic Performance."

The final section of the book provides provocative ideas and useful information for school counselor personal growth, self-care, career exploration, and retirement. Lee Richmond and Debbie Margulies provide a thought-provoking chapter on "Spirituality and School Counseling." Doris Rhea Coy and Stephanie Zimmermann help school counselors keep their day and their life in control with "Time Management and The School Counselor." The last four chapters give school counselors ideas for enhancing their personal and professional lives and preparing for a meaningful retirement. Gail Uellendahl, Mary Rennebohm, and Lisa Buono team together to share the experiences of "Counseling Abroad: Using Your Skills in the World." Jackie Allen and Penelope Black present "Writing for Professional and Personal Enjoyment." Robert Hansen and William Welcher provide "Food For Thought: Investigating A School Counselor Career Ladder or Pathways." And, finally, two very energetic and successful retired counselors, Mary Honer and Winifred Strong, write about "Retirement: An Option to Live a 'Passion' of Your Life."

It is hoped that the reader will find many chapters of interest and will enjoy the experiences, thoughts, ideas, and challenges presented by this wonderful group of counselors who have shared their expertise and experiences and written chapters with you, the reader, in mind, to empower you in your school counseling practice.

About the Editor

Jackie M. Allen, Ed.D, is a nationally certified counselor, nationally certified school counselor, a California licensed Marriage Family Therapist, and certificated in clinical neuropsychology. She has been an educator for over 35 years. She has worked as an English and Spanish teacher in middle school, as a high school counselor, an elementary bilingual school psychologist, and an education programs consultant in student support services for the California Department of Education. Currently Dr. Allen is an associate professor at the University of La Verne, La Verne, California, and chair and founder of the school psychology credential and master's program at that institution.

Active in state and national organizations, Dr. Allen is a former president of the American School Counselor Association, served two terms on the American Counseling Association Governing Council, and has served in other numerous positions for national counselor organizations. She has served as president of the California School Counselor Association, president of the California Association for Counseling and Development, president of the California Women's Caucus, and currently is president of the California Association of Counselor Educators and Supervisors and the Counselor Educator/Supervisor Representative for the California Association of School Counselors, Inc. She has served as the California Association of School Counselors' representative on the State Attendance Review Board and has been the chair of the California Alliance of Pupil Personnel Service Organizations. She was appointed to the Little Hoover Commission Children's Mental Health Advisory Committee and worked on the Mandated (Child Abuse) Reporter Training Development Ad Hoc Committee developing guidelines for Child Abuse Reporter Training in California. She recently worked on the committee to develop California School Counselor Standards. She is the Co-Chair of the H. B. McDaniel Foundation. She is a member of the Board of Institutional Review for the California Commission on Teacher Credentialing. She has been honored with the Clarion Model Award for service and leadership, H. B. McDaniel Individual Award for statewide work in counseling and psychology (2003) and an H. B. McDaniel Foundation Hall of Fame inductee (2005).

Dr. Allen is an accomplished presenter to national and international forums, presenting across the United States and in Australia, Argentina, Canada, China, Costa Rica, England, Greece, Ireland, Lithuania, Netherlands, Puerto Rico, Russia, Spain, Viet Nam, Thailand, and the Virgin Islands. Her research and writing interests include advocacy for accountability, action-oriented research, Response to Intervention, student support service models and program evaluation, the child in crisis in the classroom, neuropsychological and bilingual assessment, career counseling for the special needs student, and brain-based learning.

Dr. Allen is the editor of *The California School Counselor* newsmagazine and originator and editor of the California Association of School Counselors annual Monograph. She has authored and co-authored numerous documents and articles including *Local Proactive Counseling Leadership Compendium*, the *Action-Oriented Research Desk Guide for Professional School Counselors, School Counseling: Collaborating For Student Success, Counseling the Special Needs Student, Addressing Fragmentation-Building Integrated Services For Student Support*, and the *Professional School Counselor: Decision-Making Facilitator and Agent of Change*. She is editor of the popular book: *School Counseling: New Perspectives and Practices*.

About the Authors

Charleen Alderfer, Ed.D., is an associate professor and coordinator of the Marriage and Family Therapy Program in the Department of Counselor Education of The College of New Jersey. She is a former President of the New Jersey Association for Marriage and Family Therapy. (Chapter 13)

Jackie M. Allen, Ed.D., is an associate professor and Chair of the School Psychology Credential and Master's Preparation Program at the University of La Verne, La Verne, California and is a former school counselor, school psychologist, and Past President of ASCA. She is the editor of *The California School Counselor* newsmagazine and originator and editor of the California Association of School Counselors annual Monograph. She serves as the President of the California Association of Counselor Educators and Supervisors and the CASC Counselor Educator/Supervisor Representative. (Chapters 12, 15, 28, and 33)

Penelope Black, Ed.D., is a high school counselor at Birmingham High School in Van Nuys, California. She is a member of the California Counselor Leadership Academy and has served as the CASC Los Angeles Area Representative. (Chapter 33)

Samuel K. Bore, M.Ed., is a counselor at Madison High School in Dallas, Texas while also pursuing his doctorate in Counseling at Texas A & M University-Commerce. His previous experience includes working with self-injuring adolescents/teenagers in middle school settings. (Chapter 17)

John Brady, Ph.D., is an associate professor in the School of Education at Chapman University where he coordinates the school counseling graduate program. He is a former school psychologist, special education administrator, and family therapist. His interests are in developing collaborative consulting relationships in the schools. (Chapter 12)

Lisa Buono, M. S., is a clinical faculty member in the School of Education at California Lutheran University, Thousand Oaks, where she also coordinates field experiences for both school and college student personnel candidates. She recently delivered online instruction to future school counselors in Micronesia. (Chapter 32)

John C. Carey, Ph.D., is the Director of the National Center for School Counseling Outcome Research, School of Education, University of Massachusetts, Amherst. His research interests include school counseling outcome measurement, school counseling program evaluation, standards-based models of school counseling, and academic interventions to eliminate the achievement gap. He is the 2006 co-recipient of the ASCA Counselor Educator of the year award. (Chapter 9)

Gerald "Jerry" Chandler, Ph.D., is the director of the school counseling program at the University of Central Oklahoma. He has been a school counselor and a psychologist in private practice and has worked in community mental health agencies, psychiatric hospitals, and hospice setting. He has been very active in professional organizations and has served as president of the Oklahoma Counseling Association twice. (Chapter 14)

Robert C. Chope, Ph.D., is Professor and Chair of the Department of Counseling at San Francisco State University. He also counsels privately at the Career and Personal Development Institute in San Francisco. He is a Fellow of NCDA and ACA and has received numerous awards, including the 2002 Robert Swan Lifetime Achievement Award in Career Counseling and the 2004 NCDA Outstanding Career Practitioner Award. (Chapter 24)

Sue K. Clapp, M.S., is a professional school counselor at Halls Middle School in Knoxville, TN. She was recognized by the TN Counseling Association as their 2006 Middle School Counselor of the Year and has been serving as President of the Smoky Mountain Counseling Association (division of TCA) for 2007-2008. She has led state conference sessions about her Character Counts Comprehensive Counseling Program and "How to Start a Peer Mediation Program" in your school. (Chapter 3)

Donna Cleman, M.S., is a middle school counselor in the Temple City Unified School District. In 2003 she was Counselor of the Year for the California Association of School Counselors where she currently serves as Middle School Vice President. She is an adjunct professor at California State University, Los Angeles, and is a founding member of the Los Angeles County Office of Education California Counselor Leadership Network. (Chapter 7)

Kelly Collins, M.A., is a professional school counselor in Midwest City, Oklahoma. She is Executive Director of the Oklahoma School Counselor Association and serves on committees in both ASCA and ACA. Collins was honored as ASCA's Secondary Counselor of the Year in 2003. (Chapter 14)

Doris Rhea Coy, Ph.D., is an associate professor in the Department of Counseling, Human Services, and Social Work at Northern Kentucky University. She is known for her work in the areas of self injurious behavior and bullying. She is a past president of ACA and ASCA and has written over 50 articles and chapters and is the author or co-author of several books. (Chapter 31)

Deborah Crapes, M.A., is a Facilitator and Career Specialist in Spokane Public Schools Career Centers, Havermale High School, Spokane School District, Washington. She is a past president of the Washington Career Development Association.

Brandon Dade, M.S., is the Assistant Principal of Guidance at Alhambra High School. He was employed as a Guidance Counselor at Alhambra High School at the time of the incident described in this chapter. (Chapter 19)

Betty Anne Domm, Ed. S., is a middle school professional school counselor at Cedar Bluff Middle School in Knoxville, Tennessee. She has been a middle school counselor for 20 years and is a former president of the Tennessee School Counselor Association. (Chapter 3)

Stephanie K. Eberle, M.Ed., is the Educational Resources and Client Services Manager at Stanford University's School of Medicine Career Center and an instructor at the University of San Francisco. Her professional interests focus on diversity in the workplace and lifespan transitions counseling. (Chapter 27)

Laurel L. Edgecomb, M.A., is a school counselor in the Martinez, CA, Unified School District, where she works in an elementary and alternative high school. Laurel is also an adjunct faculty member at Saint Mary's College of California, teaching *Solution-Focused Brief Therapy Methods in the Schools*. She is known as an advocate for Solution Oriented Counseling and gives lectures and workshops throughout the Bay Area. (Chapter 4)

Kathy Emery, Ph.D., is the executive director of the San Francisco Freedom School and adjunct lecturer in political science at San Francisco State University.

Kathy is co-author of *Why Is Corporate America Bashing Our Public Schools* (Heinemann, 2002) and *Lessons from Freedom Summer* (Common Courage Press, fall 2008). (Chapter 8)

Janice S. Gallagher, M.Ed., works as a consultant in counseling and education, presenting workshops and staff development programs. She has a background in school counseling, school district administration, and leadership in professional organizations (former President of ASCA, TCA, and TSCA). Her wide range of experience has given her the opportunity to work with a variety of counseling related groups. (Chapter 11)

Michael Gangitano, M.S.W., is a social worker/school counselor at Lee Middle School in Woodland, CA. He has served on the National Advisory Board for *The Real Game Series* and is a member of the steering committee spearheaded by the California Career Resource Network in the creation of the latest version of *The Real Game Series*, *The Real Game California*, and recently completed piloting the program. (Chapter 26)

Sally Gelardin, Ed.D., Adjunct Faculty, University of San Francisco, designed the eLearning Job Search Practitioner (JSP) Training, Job Juggler's Lifelong Employability eCourse, Distance Job and Career Transitions Coach (DJCTC) Training, and a series of Entrepreneur Kits. She teaches the eLearning Career Development Facilitator (eCDF) curriculum, conducts Audio Interviews with Leading Career and Counselor Educators, authored *The Mother-Daughter Relationship* and *Starting and Growing a Business in the New Economy* (NCDA, 2007), and earned the NCDA Merit Award for significant contributions to the field of career development. (Chapter 21)

Robert D. Hansen, Ed.D., is a Professor of Educational Counseling at the University of La Verne. He is the editor of the 2008-09 *Life after High School: Career and College Information for California Students and Their Families*. Prior to being in higher education, he served in five California school districts at the K-12 level as a teacher, counselor, dean, assistant principal, principal, assistant superintendent, and superintendent. (Chapter 34)

Marilyn A. Harryman, M.S., is a counselor educator and supervisor at the University of LaVerne, former counselor coordinator and school counselor, and counselor at the Bay Area Career Center, San Francisco. She is also the producer and host of CCC Live! The Counselor Community Connection KDOL TV and co-author of the *High School Success Guide*. She is a counselor advocate at the Pupil Services Coalition and has been recognized by the Hall of Fame, H. B. McDaniel Foundation and by Inroads as Educator of the Year. (Chapter 21)

Mary Honer, Psych Ed.D., is a retired school psychologist from the Garden Grove Unified School District, CA who is using her expertise in different countries around the world where American or English speaking children are being educated overseas. She has written many articles and also a book: *Missy Fundi, Kenya Girl*, which relates her life story and experiences in East Africa. (Chapter 35)

Betty Collia Ibarra, M.A., is a school psychologist in Kings County Office of Education working for students with special needs in the areas of multiple handicaps, severe developmental delay, severe orthopedic impairment, traumatic brain injury, autism, and deaf and hard of hearing, from preschool to adult. She has worked with bilingual and multicultural students in the state of Arkansas and, more recently, with multicultural assessment in the state of California. (Chapter 29)

Phil Jarvis, B.A., is Vice President and co-founder of the National Life/Work Center in New Brunswick, Canada, and has been a leader in instigating numerous national initiatives that have changed the face of career development in Canada. He is known as the author of the Choices computer-based career exploration program and as a leader in the development and implementation of career resources like *The Real Game*, the *Blueprint for Life/Work Designs* and *Smart Options*. (Chapter 26)

C.D. "Curly" Johnson, Ph.D., is a consultant in the areas of education, counseling, mental health, and business. His career has spanned teaching, counseling, administration, professor, consultant, and author. He is the recipient of several achievement awards from national and state professional associations including PTA, NCDA, CACD, and ASCA's Lifetime Achievement Award. (Chapter 1)

Sharon K. Johnson, Ed.D., is Professor Emeritus of Counselor Education at Cal State University, Los Angeles. Her career includes positions as teacher, counselor, administrator, professor, consultant, and author. She is a past president of the California Association of Counselor Educators and Supervisors, the California Association for Counseling and Development, the Los Angeles chapter of Phi Delta Kappa and in 2007 she was awarded the ASCA Lifetime Achievement Award. (Chapter 1)

Deborah Kimokeo, Ed.D., is the District Crisis Guidance Manager for Davis Joint Unified School District. Her Columbia University dissertation about useful and efficacious guidelines for school-based suicide prevention is available in part via the California Department of Education Counseling and Student Support Division Web site. She is co-author of *"Atomic,"* a conflict resolution simulation curriculum commissioned by the New York Board of Education. (Chapter 16)

Mark S. Kiselica, Ph.D., is a professor in the Department of Counselor Education at The College of New Jersey. He is also the founder and former Coordinator of the ASCA Professional Interest Network on Teenage Parents, and the former Book Review Editor of *The School Counselor* and *Professional School Counseling*. (Chapter 13)

Linda Kobylarz, M.Ed, is an award winning career development consultant at Linda Kobylarz & Associates. She is known for her work helping schools implement holistic, career development programs and was a major contributor to the development of the enhanced National Career Development Guidelines. Kobylarz has served as President of both the Connecticut Counseling Association (CCA) and the Connecticut Counseling and Career Development Association, and is a member of the Board of Directors for the NCDA. (Chapter 23)

David M. Kopperud, M.A., is the chairperson of the State School Attendance Review Board (State SARB) at the California Department of Education. He is known for his role in developing the Model SARB Recognition Program to recognize effective dropout prevention programs and is a major contributor to the School Attendance Review Boards Handbook. (Chapter 29)

Natalie Kosine, Ph.D., is a Senior Research Fellow for the National Center School for School Counseling Outcome Research, School of Education, University of Massachusetts, Amherst. Natalie Kosine has worked in several areas of counseling and psychology in school. She is an assistant professor at the University of Louisville in the Department of Educational and Counseling Psychology where she trains school counselors and engages in research on school counseling and childhood/adolescent risk issues. (Chapter 9)

John D. Krumboltz, Ph.D., is Professor of Education and Psychology at Stanford University. He has worked as a high school counselor and algebra teacher, a research psychologist for the U.S. Air Force, has received a Guggenheim Fellowship, and spent a year as a Fellow at the Center for Advanced Studies in the

Behavioral Sciences. In 2004, ACA designated him a Living Legend in Counseling; and in 2006, he received the Outstanding Achievement Award from the University of Minnesota. (Chapter 27)

Cheri Lovre, M.S., is director of Crisis Management Institute. With a focus on prevention, she has written extensively about and responded to major school crises for over 30 years. Her passion is in helping districts use the "teachable moment" that crisis provides to improve school climate by connecting students to one another in compassion, empathy and understanding. (Chapter 18)

Debbie R. Margulies, M.Ed., is a school counselor in the Baltimore County Public School System. Deborah is the Secondary Vice President of the Maryland School Counselor Association. She loves working with adolescents, especially those who are considered difficult to work with and also enjoys doing group work. (Chapter 30)

Brian W. Mathieson, Ed.D., is a school counselor in Mesa, Arizona. He has run ASCA National Models on several campuses and taught school counselors to implement and evaluate their own programs. He has also served as President of the Arizona School Counselors Association and worked as an adjunct college faculty member. (Chapter 9)

Steve McPherson, B.A., works for Washington Unified School District's Yolo (Continuation) High School and has been a Youth Outreach Specialist and Truancy Officer for 14 years. He is also a junior college and high school football coach, and owns a private coaching school called Peak Performance Sports Services. He has done extensive work supporting foster children and helping other high-risk children find appropriate educational options. (Chapter 29)

Brenda L. Melton, M.Ed., is a school counselor at Lanier High School, San Antonio ISD. A frequent presenter at national and state conferences, Melton has served in numerous leadership positions including ASCA, President (2002-03), and Texas Counseling Association (TCA), President (2007-08). She was named the 1994 Outstanding Counselor of the Year by the TCA. (Chapter 11)

Michael R. Pines, Ph.D., retired from the Los Angeles County Office of Education after establishing and managing the School Mental Health Center where he provided training and technical assistance in mental health prevention and early intervention. He continues to deliver training in suicide prevention to schools and mental health clinicians. (Chapter 19)

John S. (Steve) Rainey, Ph.D., is an assistant professor in the Counseling and Human Development Services program at Kent State University. Following six years as a school counselor in the Dallas, Texas area, he was an assistant professor (Ad Interim) at Texas A&M University-Commerce. His research interests are in the school counseling areas of ethics, supervision, and program development and implementation. (Chapter 5)

Mary Rennebohm, M.S., is a school counselor currently working at the Universal American School in Dubai, UAE. She possesses a Masters degree in Counseling from Western Oregon University, and has spent 16 years working overseas in Europe, Asia, and the Middle East. During her time overseas, she has worked with children from 3- 18 years old. (Chapter 32)

Cynthia J. Rice, M.Ed., has been a school counselor in Hawaii and Las Vegas for the past eighteen years. Although she has K-12 experience in counseling, she has also actively pursued professional development for the past five years. She speaks throughout the country on fun and inspirational behavior management strategies and techniques. (Chapter 22)

Lee J. Richmond, Ph.D., is professor in the Education Specialties Department at Loyola College in Maryland. Past-president of NCDA and ACA, her interest in spirituality has been highlighted in several books and journals, and her specific interest in spirituality and school counseling became apparent when she co-edited, with Chris Sink, the June 2004 special issue of *Professional School Counseling* dedicated to that subject. (Chapter 30)

Lonnie L. Rowell, Ph.D, is an associate professor at the University of San Diego and Director of the Center for Student Support Systems (CS3). He is known for his work in action research and creative solutions to the gap between research and practice in school counseling. In 2006, he was appointed as a Founding Member of the Research Review Committee for the American School Counseling Association's National School Counseling Research Center. (Chapter 6)

Rosemary Rubin, M.S., is a school counselor, secretary of the California Association of School Counselors, and co-chair of the Los Angeles County Child and Adolescent Suicide Review Committee. She served 10 years in the Los Angeles Unified School District (LAUSD) Suicide Prevention Unit and co-authored LAUSD Youth Suicide Prevention Training Manual (Rev) and *Quick Reference Guide*. She currently works as an Organization

Facilitator and chairs the Local District 2 Crisis Team for the Los Angeles Unified School District. (Chapter 16)

Martha M. Russell, M.S., has been providing career delivery services to adults since 1987 as owner of Russell Career Services. Her work has included integrating career development with school counseling, workplace consulting and retirement coaching. She is a past president of NCDA and a NCDA Career Development Facilitator Instructor (CDFI). (Chapter 23)

Russell A. Sabella, Ph.D., is a professor at Florida Gulf Coast University, Fort Myers, Florida. He is known for his contributions in the areas of counseling technology, solution focused brief counseling, and comprehensive school counseling programs. He is former president of ASCA (2003-2004). (Chapter 20)

Regina M. Schaefer, Ed.D., is an associate professor in the College of Education and Organizational Leadership at the University of La Verne. Her school counseling background covers a wide array of experience from Title I counselor in an inner city school to academic college counseling. She is especially interested in the school counselor as change agent and leader within school systems. (Chapter 7)

Nancy A. Schubb, M.A., is a middle school counselor at Los Cerros Middle School, Danville, CA. She is 2008-2009 President of the California Association of School Counselors and passionately advocates for school counselors and students at the local, state, and federal levels. She is on the Board of Directors for the Suicide Prevention Advocacy Network (SPAN) and was instrumental in creating the California Suicide Prevention guidelines. (Chapter 16)

Jason Schweid, M.Ed., is a graduate student in school counseling and a graduate assistant for the National Center for School Counseling Outcome Research, School of Education, University of Massachusetts, Amherst. He is also a *Teach For America* alumnus and has served as a teacher, curriculum writer, and school leader on the border of south Texas and in Harlem, New York. (Chapter 9)

Chris Simpson, Ph.D., is an assistant professor in the Department of Counseling at Texas A&M University-Commerce. He also has a private practice in the Dallas, Texas area where he works primarily with children and adolescents. (Chapter 17)

Theresa Stanley, M.Ed., is a School Counselor at J. Colin English Elementary School in Lee County Florida.

She is a National Board Certified Teacher and enjoys mentoring candidates through the process. (Chapter 20)

Carolyn Stone, Ph.D., has been a counselor educator at the University of North Florida since 1995 where she teaches and researches in the area of school counselors and accountability and legal and ethical issues. Prior to becoming a counselor educator, she spent 22 years as a school counselor and guidance supervisor. She served as ASCA's Ethics Chair for six years prior to serving as ASCA President in 2006-2007. (Chapter 2)

Winifred Strong, M.A., has over 40 years of experience as teacher (elementary through university), school counselor, and consultant/administrator in the field of education. Her work currently includes short-term counseling, consulting projects, and conference workshop leadership. (Chapter 35)

Jeannine R. Studer, Ed. D., is a professor and coordinator of the School Counseling Program at The University of Tennesee, Knoxville. She has published numerous articles and books surrounding the school counselor's role and supervising the school counselor trainee. (Chapter 3)

Suzy R. Thomas, Ph.D., is an associate professor in the Graduate Counseling Program at Saint Mary's College of California and former middle and high school counselor. She is an advocate for school counselors in local, statewide, and regional venues. She has various publications in areas related to school counseling reform and was the 2007-2008 recipient of the School Counselor Advocate Award through the California Association of School Counselors (CASC). (Chapters 4, 8)

Bob Tyra, M.A., is a Project Director with the Los Angeles County Office of Education. In 2001, Bob worked with the California Department of Education and a Guidance Advisory Committee to develop and implement the Support Personnel Accountability Report Card (SPARC) system. He received the 2004 H.B. McDaniel Individual Achievement Award in School Counseling in California. (Chapter 10)

Gail E. Uellendahl, Ph.D., is professor and Director of the Counseling and Guidance Program at California Lutheran University in Thousand Oaks. As a counselor educator, she has prepared hundreds of candidates to work as school counselors and college student affairs professionals. Her most current research focuses on school counseling practices and she has collaborated with local school districts to offer in-service training opportunities to school counselors in practice. (Chapter 32)

Debbie Vernon, Ph.D., has been a school counselor at Hudson Middle School since 2003 and has taught part-time for the Department of Educational Foundations and Special Services at Kent State University since 2005. Her clinical experience spans 16 years in a variety of counseling settings. Her research interests are in the school counseling areas of group work, supervision, ethics, and program development and evaluation. (Chapter 5)

Marie A. Wakefield, M.S., is a 30-year veteran educator. She has worked as an elementary teacher, counselor, Administrative Specialist for Guidance Services, assistant principal, principal. She is currently a doctoral student in school counseling, Past President of the American Counseling Association, and a consultant. (Chapter 22)

Suzy Mygatt Wakefield, Ph.D., is a retired high school counselor and instructor in the Career Development Certificate Program at the University of Washington. She has served as President of the Washington School Counselor Association (1988-89), Washington Career Development Association (2004-2007), and was awarded the Distinguished Service Award by the Washington Counseling Association in 1989 and 2001. She is deeply concerned about the career guidance opportunities provided to students. (Chapter 25)

William (Bill) Welcher, M.A., is a retired school counselor, formerly the head counselor at Sierra Vista High School in the Baldwin Park Unified School District in California. He has lectured at several California universities and at the California School Counselor Leadership Academy on counselor-related issues. He is the recipient of the 2005 California School Counselor of the Year Award. (Chapter 10, 34)

Samar Yassine, M.S., is a guidance counselor at Alhambra High School where she runs grief counseling groups with students. She has also been a volunteer on a telephone crisis counseling line for several years. (Chapter 19)

Stephanie Zimmermann, M.E., is an elementary school counselor in the Dallas Independent School District. In 2006, she received a Ross Trust Scholarship from the American Counseling Association. She was formerly a gifted and talented teacher in Dallas. (Chapter 31)

Section I.
Professional Issues:
What it Means to be a
Professional School Counselor

Chapter 1

The Future for School Counselors in 2025:
Who Will Decide?

C.D. "Curly" Johnson and Sharon Johnson

Abstract

The field of professional school counseling has recently undergone many changes, generating new energy that is bringing school counseling into a leadership role within the educational community. At the same time that programs are in a state of flux, counselors are asking the question: What does the future hold for school counselors? What is predictable is that changes will occur based on many factors that are visible now and many that are not. The purpose of this paper is to provoke thoughts on how we might answer the questions but also to understand the changes and to ensure that professional counselors will create their own future.

Introduction

To create a framework for the future of school counseling, it is useful to look at current changes and how they compel us to plan ahead in a systemic way. To address the myriad of changes facing counselors, the professionals must begin to take charge of their own destiny by becoming actors-- not reactors, in determining professional contributions. Change is never comfortable. Rosabeth Kanter (1983) wrote that before change can occur, individuals must decide what they are willing to give up. To use counselors' professional time in a new way means they will have to give up current professional activities that they might enjoy or tasks they have been assigned by others.

Changes in Our Current World

The following is a sample of conditions in our current world that have already changed the work environment and expectations for school counselors. Each change raises questions that must be answered if school counseling is going to remain viable.

- **Global Economy:** A popular book, *The World Is Flat* (Friedman, 2005) presents a way of thinking about world economics and the trend to move from self-maintenance to world maintenance. Examples of the current environment include outsourcing, immigration, migration, and global

communications. Some of the world's populations are moving from one location to another based on the economics required to maintain a reasonable lifestyle. The United States is the country of choice for many people wanting to migrate from their current situation to the land they perceive as full of promise. U.S. communities are filled with families representing different countries, religions, different values, and most important, different ways of relating to others. Differences in developmental expectations of these immigrant and migrant students affect school cultures. Although the United States was populated with people from many countries from the beginning, never has there been diversity as complex as we now face. *What part does the professional school counselor play in this worldwide change?*

- **Virtual Schooling:** Virtual schooling is here to stay. The growth of distance learning shows that 67% of universities and colleges offer on-line programs. Stanford University has started a virtual high school (Vu, 2006). The International School Organization is now developing virtual schools worldwide. There is a National Virtual School Association. There is a concern about maintaining compulsory attendance in view of the current and future changes in the "place" of learning. There are now 24 states with virtual schools. Utah began in 1993 with the electronic high school. Florida followed with 65,000 students in grades 6 – 12 in virtual schools. The Center for Educational Reform (Wurtzel, 2006) reports that there are 148 cyber charter schools. There are also 67% of colleges and universities with distance education. There is an increase in for-profit educational institutions that are totally virtual schools (distance education). Many in education predict that the current value on a diploma will be lessened with many vying for specific education/training in lieu of a broad education. There is a financial market in this endeavor that is moving businesses to become more involved in education for profit. Is virtual counseling available?

3

Yes, but some say it has not been developed nor researched enough to determine its effectiveness. *Where will the professional school counselor fit in this change from students attending a traditional school building to having a student body that stays at home, in a church, or at other locations? Or, in some cases, when a student has schooling half time at a school building and half at home?*

- **Outsourcing and Tutoring:** In today's current labor market, governed by technology, it is common for phone calls to U.S. companies to be answered in India. The information provided may be limited because of different cultural knowledge or the operator's lack of understanding of the situation, however it is cheaper. There are companies in the United States that offer tutoring in any subject matter for one-fourth the cost to have local tutoring. The tutoring is outsourced to India and other countries. Outsourced tutoring is also being used for courses as diverse as music lessons, math, cooking, and many others (Honawar, 2005). *Where does the professional school counselor of the future fit as this paradigm expands where education occurs both inside and outside of traditional schooling?*

- **Technology:** In a ninth grade geography class in a high school in southern California that was using the 'blackboard' software system, while the teacher was lecturing, one (or more) students were tapping in to a South Africa university's library to get more information on the content being addressed in the class. The information available to students via the computer is unlimited and may well be the warning of the decline of textbooks for current information. Seemingly unlimited information is available, but now the assessment of the source and the application of information are becoming a critical need in education. What once was a school counselor's domain of assisting families to find information on classes, careers, higher education opportunities, financial assistance, and work opportunities is no longer needed. The information is currently free and accessible, on Web sites supplied by companies and colleges. However, skills in applying the information to the individual student's situation may still be needed. Technology is more than personal computers. For today's students, it is interactive TV, streaming, and MP3s, DVDs, microchips and Internet. *How will the professional school counselor's contribution be changed as more information and help is available online and students and parents become more sophisticated in the use of technology?*

- **The virtual phone:** A recent article in the Los Angeles Times listed ten current uses of the cell phones – banking, stock markets, email, text messages, mapping, photographs, video making, instant communication. It was estimated that 90% of the families in the United States have one or more cell phones. Many families have eliminated the single house phone and opt for individual cell phones for each family member. It is possible to use the phones for assistance with school work (test scores) and grades while in class, home, on the bus, or from wherever one is working. Of importance for educators is that many students, even those in elementary school, are "phone use" smart in ways that can affect classroom instruction. Teachers, administrators, and counselors currently carry cell phones to use in contacting a student's parent or guardian for both positive feedback and referrals, i.e., instant school-family contacts. *How can the professional school counselor use this communication tool to support parent involvement in their child's education to ensure each student achieves academically and socially?*

- **Developmental Gaps:** The differences between the values of current students graduating from high school in 2008 and those that will be finishing in 2025 are unknown, but we do know there will be differences. Variations in values have been identified by decades and labeled by numerous writers and journalists (Howe & Strauss, 2000) who coined baby boomers (1945-65), generation X (1965-85) and the millennials (1985-today). Each age and each population has its own way of adjusting to current times. Projections differ but the millennials are leaning toward more emphasis on children and children's needs, tightening of nurture and care, as well as higher family stability. If these projections hold true, it could be great support for what counselors contribute to student achievement, or it could become a burden. Current research (Tonn, 2005) indicates that parent involvement is an important predictor of student success. *What will or can the professional school counselor contribute to* *making an increase in parent involvement a positive change in school environment?*

• **Mandated Testing:** The No Child Left Behind legislation has made the issue of high stakes testing a reality for every educational level (The Education Letter, 2003). The overarching idea is that only through a standardized, written test can the success of a student's education be measured. Although most educators question the premise, it is, and from all indications will continue to be, a way of life. School counselors have traditionally been seen as the educators who have the most training and understanding of test results as they relate to students' career and educational plans. *How can professional school counselors use the drive for accountability, student assessment, and program evaluation to open doors to a variety of additional opportunities for themselves?*

• **School Reforms:** The demand and mandate for reform in education in the United States is present but it is not new; it has been an issue for over 50 years. Virtual schools, technology, and mandated testing all fall within the school reform movement. However, there is also a trend toward decentralizing education, moving toward accountability for student results, small learning communities, and more active and aggressive family involvement. Howe & Strauss (2000) refer to the current parents as "Kamikaze parents." Leadership is evolving away from the traditional military or hierarchal model toward a participative, inclusive management model. *What will the professional school counselor contribute to leadership, positive parent involvement, and student success within the new structures and school cultures?*

• **Other Projected Trends:**
a) A return to local communities;
b) Computer technology in all homes;
c) The return to the traditional family unit, but with both parents employed, ready cooked meals delivered to the home, regular visits to a health center for preventive health care, and family involvement in the schooling of children are a few of the changes that will affect our communities;
d) Education will become decentralized;
e) The world economy will lead to a two-class system;

f) Results orientation will transcend all institutions; and
g) The leadership in education will be participative, inclusive and will be modeled after the learning organization paradigm.

The State of School Counseling

Nationally, budget constraints have led to many cuts in educational resources and programs. A few school districts have eliminated credentialed school counselor positions and use clerical staff (often labeled as advisors or technicians) to perform the basic tasks of enrolling students in appropriate classes, monitoring progress toward graduation, and coordinating the administration of standardized tests. Unfortunately, if administrators are not educated in the contributions of professional school counselors and the resultant benefit to students, they mistakenly believe that advisement is equivalent to a guidance program. This leaves students without an advocate, without professional help in personal matters, without long range educational and career plans, without assistance in solving interpersonal conflicts, and with no instruction in the process of problem-solving and decision-making.

Until recently, there was little professional agreement on the essential contributions expected of school counselors. There were counseling materials for classroom presentations, but no blueprint for how a comprehensive program should be planned and implemented. There was no agreement within the profession that school counselors are responsible to ensure each student in the school acquires specific competencies that are developmentally appropriate. There are now three models being used to build a national consensus on the expectations for professional school counselors: (1) the Comprehensive School Counseling Program (Gysbers & Henderson, 2000); (2) the Results-Based Student Support Program (Johnson, Johnson, & Downs, 2006); and (3) the ASCA National Model: A Framework For School Counseling Programs (American School Counseling Association, 2005). By focusing on how students are different because of guidance (student support) programs, the traditional approach of providing services as needed, is being replaced by a focus on delivering student competencies (knowledge, skills, attitudes) required to become successful in their lives now and in the future.

The Only Way To Go

When asked about his life, General Colin Powell has a favorite new expression: He prefers to look through the front windshield rather than the rear view mirror. "There is nothing I can do about what's in the rearview mirror," he explains, "and if I go fast, that which is behind me will disappear more rapidly." The saying is apt, given that Powell, who turned 69 on April 5, likes nothing better than to get under the hood of a car (his retirement gift from President Bill Clinton was a beat-up 1966 Volvo fixer-upper). (Graham, 2006)

To Exist or to Lead?

The future of professional school counseling lies directly in the hands of the current practitioners, the school and district level student support program administrators, and counselor educators. The future is not waiting; it is exploding in many different directions; and now is the time to take the critical steps needed for school counseling to claim identity as a profession. To move from seeing counseling as a career choice to understanding it as a profession will take many changes. The most important is the personal decision of each counselor to assume responsibility for the students and the results of the program. As a professional, there are no excuses. Either one takes responsibility for self or gives over that responsibility to another, in which case he/she becomes an assistant to the person in charge, carrying out another person's wishes and goals.

It takes a shift in thinking from focusing on processes and activities (things we do) to being accountable for the results we contribute (what we produce). This shift not only must occur for practicing professionals, but also implies changes needed in the counselor education programs that prepare new counselors. For school counseling to become a respected profession, responsibility must be taken to monitor our own profession. Counselors must empower the professional organizations to act as local and national gatekeepers with the responsibility of enforcing an ethical code, setting standards for preparation and maintenance of qualifications, providing professional development training opportunities, as well as all the other requirements of a profession.

To make this shift, Wurtzel (2006) has presented a paradigm of seven elements of professionalism that provide a guide toward becoming a profession. These elements were proposed as a guide to Transform High School Teaching and Learning. We have taken the liberty to use these seven elements to illustrate some tenets for professional school counseling in the next twenty years.

Seven Elements of Professionalism and the Implications for the School Counseling Profession:

1. *The primary duty is to the students through the delivery of student results.* If the efforts of the professionals do not produce planned-for student results, then changes are made immediately. Everything is judged based on the effectiveness of the process in producing student results. Regularly gathering and analyzing data of student success becomes the standard for practice.

2. *School counselors are accountable to their profession.* The profession needs a definition of malpractice, and there is a need for standards and procedures for sanctioning and ultimately ejecting from the profession those who commit malpractice. It is recommended that the profession support an ethics panel that reviews and acts upon referrals of malpractice.

3. *The school counseling profession must have a body of specialized knowledge and agreed upon standards of practice and a specific protocol for performance.* The norms and protocols must be based on evidence of effectiveness in improving student results. Therefore, it is recommended that the profession support research centers established to collect and publish research studies for dissemination to the profession.

4. *Each professional school counselor has a duty to improve her/his own practice on an ongoing basis.* Therefore, the profession should provide regular professional development opportunities and provide a monitoring system to encourage CEU credits at a recommended level. Participation in professional development, coaching, observation and continued learning is considered a part of the job, not an optional activity.

5. *Each professional school counselor has the ability and responsibility to improve common or collective practice in the profession.* Regular roundtable discussions held locally or regionally would provide a vehicle to share readings, experiences, and research on effective practices. Review of professional journals could be shared collaboratively between different professionals (e.g., counselors, school psychologists, social workers). Student support program efforts include working collaboratively with others in an effort to learn from them, to help them learn, and to contribute to the collective knowledge about what works for students.

6. *Each professional school counselor is expected to exercise professional judgment.* Collaborative teams at school and district level could provide input in cases where professional judgment is not clear- serving as an advisement function and for shared learning. Autonomy is not a goal but within the context of professional practice, individual responsibility creates the opportunity for innovation, improvement, empowerment, and commitment.

7. *Each professional school counselor must foster productive student behaviors that lead to successful outcomes.* Collaborative relationships among and between counselors, teachers, parents, community members, administrators, and others have a higher chance of ensuring success for students. However, each counselor has the freedom and responsibility to develop an infrastructure for student success and program improvement. (Ideas adapted from Wurtzel, 2006).

The intent of the following is to suggest ideas to promote serious dialog on school counseling as a profession. The ideas may be familiar, but the dialog within the profession should be considered as a beginning – not an end.

Each counselor and all counselors have responsibility for themselves as professionals, for everything they do and for the results of everything they do. No one can know the future. All we can do is commit ourselves to the primary purpose of our profession, to ensure that each student finds his or her own success. Working within the structure of the educational system motivates the school counselor to drive students toward academic success in the field of their choice, based on the unique goals, interests, talents, and other characteristics of each student. "Professionals need tools to do their work and a work context that allows them to evaluate and improve the effectiveness of their practice." (Cohen & Ball, 1999).

Some Thoughts About How Professional School Counselors Can Face the Future: Building Upon What Is Happening Now and How School Counselors Are Reacting

1. **The professional school counselor of the future must stay current on the use of technology in the schools and by students.** It is increasingly difficult to address current opportunities and concerns proactively or to even stay aware of the uses of new electronic resources that seem to multiply weekly. For example, the picture phone offers an opportunity for distance personal counseling to be an everyday activity. The laptop computers continue to shrink in size and may completely be replaced by hand held devices in the near future. When the current music equipment allows 7500 songs on a very small chip, imagine the quantity of information professionals and others can routinely carry with them. Maybe the future for the professional counselor is to be a walking on-the-spot data resource. It is certain that the students' school identification card will be the size of a charge card and will carry all of her/his school records (and maybe medical records) including a current picture and parent/legal guardian means of contact.

Computer use is no longer a luxury. It is a necessity in today's world and the uses in the near future portend changes in the rituals of families and schools. Computer data bases will replace libraries as we know them today, newspapers will be replaced and delivered on the web 24 hours – 7 days per week, bound school text books may cease to exist and be replaced by online documents. All business transactions will be handled electronically. It seems that every facet of life will be electronically guided.

2. **The professional school counselor of the future must be able to do distance counseling.** As the number of virtual schools continues to evolve in the United States as well as world wide, how will the school counselor in the year 2025 make and maintain personal contact with students? Will there be some way created to guarantee equity in our advocacy responsibility? There may be changes for the student support personnel, as we know it today. School counselors may be assigned to families to advocate for the success of all the children in the family as well as the parents. Although the counselor will still be responsible for the student and parent results, finding a viable means to ensure equity will be the challenge.

3. **The professional school counselors of the future must have a solid educational foundation and supervised internship.** The education of professional counselors must change to conform to what is expected of other licensed professionals. Currently, the counselor education programs vary by colleges and universities in each state and between states. Sometimes the required courses are geared to the

expertise of specific professors or conform to what is popular at the time. The conflict for many years has been whether the expectations are for public school counselors to work with all students and their development tasks or to provide mental health 'therapy' to specific students as needed. Currently, there may be some difficulty in selling any Board of Education on therapy provided for students. The mission of schooling has consistently reinforced the need for student equity and advocacy for school achievement, career planning and preparation to make a successful transition to higher education, and career preparation or employment. Based on today's school leadership education, it is suggested that a standard training foundation for counselor education be adopted nationally to ensure consistency in the knowledge and skills of new counselors.

4. **A School Counselor Career Ladder must be established.** School leaders will have to realign professional assignments in order to provide assistance for home schoolers, for those involved in distance learning, for those in college-high school programs, and for those students attending school in industries and businesses where their parents are working. The concept of a career ladder could be developed for the professional and credentialed school counselor to address differentiated staffing needs. At one time, 14 states offered career ladders for educators, most of which were based on additional graduate course work, not on professional competence. The purpose of a career ladder is to ensure equity for each student as a means to acquire pre-delineated competencies required to enter into an institution of higher learning, career, or employment of choice. The School Counselor Career Ladder proposed is one that is based on academic preparation, internship, and demonstrated specific competencies that will be required as the professional school counselor moves up the ladder. The following is offered as a beginning for future in-depth discussions related to the mission of school counseling.

This sample model consists of five steps or levels:

Level 1: Counselor Intern. The Counselor Intern is a person newly assigned to the guidance program. The intern will possess a bachelor's degree and will have all course work in counselor education with the exception of fieldwork. The intern shall be granted an intern certificate by the State Department of Education. The intern is required to have completed all coursework toward a master's degree with appropriate grade point average. When placed, the intern will spend time learning the school curriculum, the processes that ensure that students (and their parents/guardians) acquire competencies in selecting appropriate courses leading to a selected career and/or higher education. The intern will assist other counselors in their attaining student results. The intern will be supervised by a certificated counselor and a college or university staff member. To proceed to Level 2, the intern will serve two years and will apply for promotion. The promotion will be approved by a panel of counselors.

Level 2: General School Counselor. The general counselor has a master's degree in school counseling and is licensed and/or has a school counseling credential issued by the State Department of Education. The general counselor is the professional that ensures students acquire and use competencies in educational planning and progress toward graduation. This counselor may have contact with parents and collaborates with teachers regarding educational progress. This professional will manage students' portfolio completion, the testing program, parent-teacher conferences, and some staff development programs. This position is held for a minimum of two years. Advancement to Level 3 will be made available when the counselor has completed Level 2 satisfactorily, showing evidence of required competencies and making application for advancement. Advancement will be approved by a panel consisting of Master School Counselors and administrator representatives.

Level 3: School Counselor Specialist. The School Counselor Specialists are the professionals that have acquired advance professional competencies in specific student support areas of student results: Learning Specialist, Career Specialist, Interpersonal Specialist, and Personal (Life Style) Specialist. These Specialists are expected to develop, implement, and evaluate programs that ensure the students acquire and use specific competencies related to the program mission and goals. They will show evidence of having acquired and demonstrated required professional competencies for the specialty.

Level 4: Master School Counselor. The Master School Counselor is the professional who is charged with managing the student results-based program. The requirements for this position include at least two years as a School Counselor Specialist with additional training in personnel management, planning, monitoring program progress, and evaluating program outcomes. This person shall be on an administrator work schedule.

Level 5: Guidance or Student Support Program Administrator. These persons will be credentialed school counselors and will possess an administrator's certificate. They are to administer the total student support program including counselors, school psychologists, social workers, school nurses, and other student support team members.

Distinction or Extinction: We Choose

It becomes clear when speaking with student support professionals that without a blueprint of how the fields of school counseling, psychology, nursing, social work, attendance workers, and other support programs will change to address the future, extinction is guaranteed. Major changes are already occurring that affect the student support programs of the future. (Johnson & Johnson, 2002)

Change is constant; it is sometimes overwhelming and always relentless. Advice on how to adjust to change, new ideas to try, and new paradigms to provide multiple frameworks abound. How can professional school counselors adjust to change; but, more importantly, how can they help students understand and adapt to the changes in every aspect of their lives? Perhaps there is wisdom in the teaching of Tao that advises: "Learn to see things inside out, backwards, upside down." We must learn and model how to take care of ourselves. Living a healthy lifestyle of exercise, nutrition, and relaxation as a balance to the chaos of change in schools helps us address the future more clearly. Yes, change is inevitable; but so is the need for human contact, someone to listen, assistance in problem solving, and having an advocate to champion success for all students.

Discussion Questions

1. What impact does the current interest of students in MySpace, YouTube, Second Life, and other open web sites have on the guidance program?
2. Using the seven elements of professionalism, do you think school counseling meets the criteria to be considered a profession? How can school counselors support the agenda of being a profession?
3. How can the concept of a career ladder be adapted to schools with few counselors?
4. When forming a student support team, whom would you involve and how would you like to work together?
5. What trends do you see developing that cause you concern in relation to school counseling and the mission of school counseling?
6. Given a choice, what specialty would you choose for yourself and how would your specialty benefit students?

References

American School Counselors Association (2005). *The national model: A framework for school counseling programs.* Alexandria, VA: Author.

Cohen, D. K., & Ball, D. L. (1999). *Instruction, capacity, and improvement.* Philadelphia: Consortium for Policy Research in Education, University of Pennsylvania.

Friedman, T. L. (2005). *The world is flat.* New York: Farrar, Straus and Giroux.

Gysbers, N., & Henderson, P. (2000). *Developing and managing your school guidance program.* Alexandria, VA: American Counseling Association.

Education Letter, The. (2003). *Spotlight on high stakes testing.* Cambridge, MA: Harvard Education.

Graham, N. P. (2006, July and August). Staying Powell. *AARP Magazine.*

Honawar, V. (2005, November 9).India is becoming online hub for tutoring US students. *Education Week, 25*(11), 8.

Howe, N., & Strauss, W. (2000). *Millennials rising.* New York: Vintage Books.

Johnson, C., & Johnson, S., (2002). *Building stronger school counseling programs: Bringing futuristic approaches into the present.* Austin, TX: Pro-Ed, Inc.

Johnson, S., Johnson, C., & Downs, L. (2006). *Building a results-based student support program.* Boston: Lahaska.

Kanter, R. R. (1983). *The change masters.* New York: Simon & Schuster, Inc.

Tonn, J. (2005, June 8). Keeping in touch. *Education Week, 24*(39), 30-33.

Vu, P. (2006). *School is just a click away.* Retrieved July 24, 2006, from http://www.stateline.org.

Wurtzel, J. (2006, May). *Transforming high school teaching and learning: A district-wide design.* Washington, DC: The Aspen Institute.

Chapter 2

The Complications and Complements of Ethics and Law in Counseling

Carolyn Stone

Abstract

The myriad of complex issues that school counselors face are often multifaceted and involve both legal and ethical principles. Instead of aiming for black and white answers, counseling professionals continuously strive to develop a certain level of comfort with ambiguity in order to better serve students. Conflicts between the law and ethics are not uncommon, and this leaves counselors to negotiate between legal responsibilities and ethical imperatives. This chapter provides a look at ethical reasoning and understanding of the laws that pertain to the school counselor's work and thus provides counselors a greater level of confidence when struggling with the ambiguous and situational dilemmas common to the school counseling profession.

Introduction

The professions are distinguished from other occupations chiefly because of their specialized skills and knowledge, but also because they are guided by codes of ethics and standards of practice. Codes of practice and guiding principles are used to maintain the professional's credibility.

What constitutes professional behavior is defined by the members of the profession. For example, in school counseling, being active in one's own professional development through active membership in professional organizations, in-service workshops, and professional reading in the current research of the profession are all examples of professional behavior. Ethics are the principles of conduct governing an individual or group; concerns for what is right or wrong, good or bad (Oregon State University, 2006). Ethical codes and behavior are the result of values within a profession or organization and bind those who, by membership, ascribe to them. Ethics provide a general framework for professional conduct. The language in code is aspirational in nature and quite often is broad to cover many possible situations (Remley & Huey, 2002). Counseling professionals continually define and refine their ethical standards and codes to remain current in the norms, customs, and practices of the profession.

The law is the minimum standard that society will tolerate (Remley & Huey, 2002). Law is all the official rules and codes that govern citizens' actions, including the Constitution, statutory laws enacted by the Legislature, case laws established by court decisions, and administrative law as set forth by executive branch agencies (New Jersey Legislature, n.d.). The U.S. Constitution, federal and state statutes, as well as regulatory and case laws are based on precedence or common law.

Common law is judge-made law. Common law also has been referred to as the "body of general rules prescribing social conduct" (Alexander & Alexander, 2005). Because it is not written by elected politicians but by judges, it can be referred to as "unwritten" law. Thus, common law is law set by precedent in court and by interpretation of the constitution and statute law (Georgetown University Law Library, 2001).

Common law often contrasts with civil law systems that require all laws to be written in a code or written collection. Judges look for prior cases that have similar law and facts to the case at hand (precedents) and render a judgment consistent with prior case law (Alexander & Alexander, 2005; L. Colvin, personal communication, January 30, 2005; Duhaime Law, 2004). Laws and their interpretation differ from one geographic location to another (Alexander & Alexander, 2005).

The myriad of complex issues that school counselors face are often multifaceted and involve both legal and ethical principles. For example, confidentiality is an ethical imperative; but, in a number of state statutes, confidentiality is also defined for counseling professionals. It is important to note that ethics established by ethical codes of a profession are not necessarily legal and vice-versa.

Ethical reasoning and understanding of the laws that pertain to the school counselor's work provide counselors with greater confidence when struggling with the ambiguous and situational dilemmas that are common in our profession. Instead of aiming for black and white answers, counseling professionals continuously strive to develop a certain level of comfort with ambiguity in order to better serve students.

Raising awareness reduces risk to the counselor and the student. The more informed counselors are about the law and standards of ethical practice, the more comfortable the counselor is in struggling with the complexities of ethical dilemmas and the fact that there are no clear-cut solutions. Responses to ethical and legal dilemmas are context dependent and recognize that each dilemma requires consideration of areas such as the student's personal history, developmental stages, family situation, and problem-solving abilities.

Conflict in Law and Ethics

Conflicts between the law and ethics are not uncommon, and this leaves counselors to negotiate between legal responsibilities and ethical imperatives. When ethics and law collide, the law supersedes the ethical codes. However, counselors make their professional ethical imperative known and try to advocate for their ethics. The fact that law supersedes should not minimize the critical importance of ethical codes and standards of practice. Counselors can lose their jobs having never broken a single law, but having disregarded their ethical codes or professional standards of practice.

ACA code H.1.b. Conflicts
Between Ethics and Laws

If ethical responsibilities conflict with law, regulations, or other governing legal authority, counselors make known their commitment to the ACA Code of Ethics and take steps to resolve the conflict. If the conflict cannot be resolved by such means, counselors may adhere to the requirements of law, regulations, or other governing legal authority. (ACA, 2005a, p. 19)

An example of a conflict between ethics and law would be when a school counselor receives a subpoena for testimony for confidential information that the counselor received in the context of an individual counseling session. In the vast majority of states, the courts are entitled to the school counselor's testimony because students have not been given privileged communication in the state's legislation. Even though the school counselor has an ethical imperative to respect the student's confidentiality, by law they owe the courts their testimony. The school counselor will work to *get the subpoena quashed or declared null and void; but if the counselor is unsuccessful, he or she testifies.*

The complex nature of practicing in the human services fields means that counseling professionals often face issues without written guidance in law, state department regulations, ethical code, or school board policy. Malpractice, negligence, and student or client privacy rights are a few of the complex issues without a multitude of established principles of law (Levick, 2000) leaving counselors to practice in absence of clear-cut guidelines. Laws are often interpreted during the hearing of a case. Federal courts in each state can interpret the same law in different ways, and the interpretation will remain unresolved until a higher court determines the meaning of the law.

ACA and ASCA Codes of Ethics

The American Counseling Association (ACA) Code of Ethics (2005a) and the American School Counselor Association (ASCA) Ethical Standards for School Counselors (2004) are both attempts by the counseling profession to standardize professional practice for the purpose of protecting students, clients, parents, and the counselor. The ASCA Ethical Standards (2004) are a guide to help us meet the needs of individual situations, but seldom are appropriate for rote application, as it is the context of a dilemma that determines appropriate action. It is only the counselor, in consultation with other professionals, who can determine how to apply an ACA/ASCA standard to further the best interest of her/his client or student. Codes are guides or frameworks that require professional judgment in context to make each standard meaningful. Codes are not intended to provide answers, but are meant to guide.

The ACA Code of Ethics and the ASCA Ethical Standards guide counselors in their ethical responsibility to students, clients, and parents, but do not attempt to provide complete answers. Ethics are situational and have to be considered in context of institutional and community standards, school board policy, and individual circumstances. It is ultimately the responsibility of the counselor to determine the appropriate response for individual students, clients who put their trust in the security of the counseling relationship (Stone & Isaacs, 2002).

The full text of the ACA code of ethics and ASCA ethical standards can be found at these Web sites:

American Counseling Association is http://www.counseling.org and American School Counselor Association is www.schoolcounselor.org.

A Synopsis of ASCA Ethical Standards for School Counselors (2004)

Standard A.1. Responsibilities to Students discusses counselors' responsibilities to students. Under this standard, obligations of respect toward students and their values, encouragement of students, and knowledge of appropriate laws and policies regarding students are enumerated.

Standard A.2. Confidentiality explores the issue of confidentiality and its limits. Although counselors try to maintain confidentiality at all costs, there may be times when it must be breached, as in cases of potential suicide or risk of harm to another person. This standard also discusses the counselor's responsibility in legal matters where confidentiality is breached as a result of a court order. Finally, counselors must also balance the need to maintain confidentiality with their students with the right of parents to be involved in all aspects of their children's lives.

Standard A.3. Counseling Plans concerns counseling plans and the implementation of a counseling program that is comprehensive and supports students' choices for a wide variety of post-secondary education options.

Standard A.4. Dual Relationships discusses counselors' responsibility to remove themselves from dual relationship situations or proceed with extreme caution when such a relationship is unavoidable. This standard also addresses counselors' dual relationships with other school personnel that might harm the counselor/student relationship.

Standard A.5. Appropriate Referrals relates to the appropriate referral of students and parents to outside professionals and guides counselors in the proper referral process.

Standard A.6. Group Work guides the counseling professional who works with students in groups and defines the selection, notification of parents (if necessary) and the expectations of confidentiality for students in this setting.

Standard A.7. Danger to Self and Others discusses the counselor's responsibilities when students are a danger to themselves or others. These situations almost always require a breach of confidentiality, and this standard helps counselors do so while seeking to maintain the highest level of trust and confidence

possible between the student and the counselor.

Standard A.8. Student Records covers the issues of records, both educational and sole-possession records, and gives the counseling professional guidance about the disposition of sole-possession records.

Standard A.9. Evaluation, Assessment and Interpretation deals with the use of assessment instruments and the counselor's role in their administration, interpretation, and use.

Standard A.10. Technology is concerned with the appropriate use of technology.

Standard A.11. Student Peer Support Program concerns itself with the unique responsibilities counselors have to students involved in peer-to-peer programs.

Standard B.1. Parent Rights and Responsibilities requires counselors to respect the inherent rights and responsibilities of parents for their children and endeavors to establish, as appropriate, a collaborative relationship with parents to facilitate the student's maximum development. Counselors must be sensitive to cultural and social diversity among families and recognize that all parents, custodial and non-custodial, are vested with certain rights and responsibilities for the welfare of their children by virtue of their role and according to law.

Standard B.2 Parents/Guardians and Confidentiality instructs counselors to: (1) inform parents of the counselor's role with emphasis on the confidential nature of the counseling relationship between counselor and counselee; (2) provide parents with accurate, comprehensive, and relevant information in an objective and caring manner as is appropriate and consistent with ethical responsibilities to the counselee; and (3) make reasonable efforts to honor the wishes of parents and guardians concerning information that s/he may share regarding the counselee.

Sections C through G are respectively: *Responsibilities to Colleagues and Professional Associates; Responsibilities to the School and Community; Responsibilities to Self; Responsibilities to the Profession;* and *Maintenance of Standards.* This last section discusses the procedure to rectify situations with individuals or groups that are in conflict with the ethical standards.

The standards demonstrate the scope and depth of the role of counselor to school personnel, parents, and students. Members and non-members of ACA and ASCA can find a great deal of information about professional behavior by carefully reading the standards.

Furthermore, professionals in schools can use the standards to improve effectiveness, avoid ethical problems, and escape legal entanglements.

A Synopsis of ACA Code of Ethics and Standards of Practice (2005a)

Section A: The Counseling Relationship addresses important issues in forming, maintaining, and ending the counseling relationship. This section includes guidelines to help counselors keep client welfare foremost and respect client rights. It contains standards that emphasize the importance of respecting diversity and being aware of one's own personal needs and how these can influence the counseling relationship. It provides guidance on how to handle troublesome issues such as dual relationships, fees, and termination. Guidelines for working with multiple clients and the use of computer technology are also included in this section.

Section B: Confidentiality addresses the client's right to privacy of information shared during counseling sessions and of records. Exceptions and limitations to confidentiality are specified; and special considerations in working with minors, families, and groups are addressed. Guidelines are offered for maintaining confidentiality when consulting or conducting research.

Section C: Professional Responsibility contains standards related to competence. It emphasizes the importance of advertising services and credentials in an accurate manner. It also addresses the counselor's responsibilities to the public.

Section D: Relationships with Other Professionals offers guidelines for employer/employee and consultative relationships. This section highlights the importance of respecting and establishing good working relationships with professionals in related mental health professions.

Section E: Evaluation, Assessment, and Interpretation section includes standards on competence to select, use, and interpret tests. Client rights in testing, test security, and proper testing conditions are addressed. This section also includes standards related to the diagnosis of mental disorders.

Section F: Teaching, Training, and Supervision presents guidelines for counselor educators and trainers, counselor preparation programs, and students and supervisees. Guidance is provided on issues such as relationship boundaries, evaluation, and endorsement of students to enter the profession.

Section G: Research and Publication describes research responsibilities, informed consent practices, and the reporting of research results. A wide range of issues is covered from protection of human subjects to ethical procedures in seeking publication.

Section H: Resolving Ethical Issues addresses the responsibility of counselors to know their ethical standards and explains procedures for resolving and reporting suspected ethical violations. (Remley & Herlihy, 2005, p. 11)

Ethical Decision-Making

An ethical dilemma is not a clear-cut breach of the law, but an ambiguous situation from which positive or negative consequences can result and an ethical decision making model can illuminate how the problem should be handled. An ethical decision-making model empowers counselors to make the best choices as they become more comfortable with ethical and legal ambiguity (Remley & Herlihy, 2005).

Laws are open to interpretation, but codes are even more ambiguous and are interpreted differently in the context of each dilemma as there will always be more than one right answer to a complex ethical dilemma. The purpose of an ethical decision making model is to allow school counselors a way to explain their reasoning behind their decision should it be necessary.

Five Moral Principles

Counselors need to develop sound ethical decision-making skills. Kitchener's (1984) five moral principles can serve as a guide to ethical decision-making:

Autonomy refers to promoting students, clients' ability to choose their own direction. The counselor makes every effort to foster maximum self-determination on the part of students, clients.

Beneficence refers to promoting good for others. Ideally, counseling contributes to the growth and development of the student, and whatever counselors do should be judged against this criterion.

Nonmaleficence means avoiding doing harm, which includes refraining from actions that risk hurting students, clients.

Justice, or fairness, refers to providing equal treatment to all people. This standard implies that anyone — regardless of age, sex, race, ethnicity, disability, socio-economic status, cultural background, religion, or sexual orientation is entitled to equal treatment.

Loyalty, or fidelity, refers to staying connected with your students, clients and being available to them to the extent possible. Counselors often carry heavy case loads and loyalty takes on a different dimension than how it may be defined at an agency. Loyalty for the counselor does not necessarily mean we have 50-minute sessions once a week with our students, clients. Staying loyal may include connecting with students, clients by encouraging them to stop by before and after school, visiting them at the bus loading zone or briefly visiting a student's classroom.

Seven-Step Decision-Making Model

The American Counseling Association (ACA) has developed *A Practitioner's Guide to Ethical Decision Making* (2004). The model presents a framework for sound ethical decision-making and incorporates the work of Van Hoose and Paradise (1979), Kitchener (1984), Stadler (1986), Haas and Malouf (1989), Forester-Miller and Rubenstein (1992), and Sileo and Kopala (1993). The practical, sequential, seven-step model has served counselors in all settings. The seven steps in *A Practitioner's Guide to Ethical Decision Making* (ACA, 2004) are:

1. Identify the problem.
2. Apply the ACA Code of Ethics.
3. Determine the nature and dimensions of the dilemma.
4. Generate potential courses of action.
5. Consider the potential consequences of all options; choose a course of action.
6. Evaluate the selected course of action.
7. Implement the course of action.

1. **Identify the Problem**
   Take the necessary steps to gather the facts while weeding out innuendos, rumors, hearsay, and hypotheses.

2. **Apply the ACA and ASCA Ethical Codes and The Law**
   Ask yourself whether your code of ethics or the law offers a possible solution to the problem. Ethical dilemmas are often complex and we will not usually find a definitive answer in the codes or laws. The very nature of an ethical dilemma means there is more than one acceptable answer, so we must apply good judgment by proceeding with all steps of the ethical decision-making model and paying careful attention to seek consultation and supervision.

3. **Determine the Nature and Dimensions of the Dilemma**
   Consider the basic moral principles of autonomy, beneficence, nonmaleficence, justice, and loyalty (Kitchener, 1984) and apply them to the situation. It may help to prioritize these principles and think through ways in which they can support a resolution. Decide which principles apply and determine which principle takes priority for you in this case. In theory, each principle is of equal value, which means it is your challenge to determine the priorities when two or more of them conflict. Review the relevant professional literature to ensure that you are using the most current professional thinking in reaching a decision. Consult with experienced professional colleagues and/or supervisors. As they review with you the information, they may see other relevant issues or offer a new perspective. They also may be able to identify aspects of the dilemma you are not viewing objectively. Consult your state or national professional associations to see if they can help.

4. **Generate Potential Courses of Action and Their Consequences**
   Brainstorm as many solutions as possible. Be creative. If possible, enlist the assistance of at least one colleague to help you generate options. It is helpful to write down the options and also to discuss options with another person.

5. **Consider the Potential Consequences of All Options; Choose a Course of Action**
   Ponder the implications of each course of action for the client, student, for others who might be affected, and for you. List the good and bad consequences of each decision.

6. **Evaluate the Selected Course of Action**
   Considering the information you have gathered and the priorities you have set, evaluate each option and assess the potential consequences for all the parties involved. Ponder the implications of each course of action for the client, for others who will be affected, and for yourself as a counselor. Eliminate the options that clearly do not give the desired results or cause even more problematic consequences. Then decide which combination of options best fits the situation and addresses the priorities you have identified.
   Review the selected course of action to see if it presents any new ethical considerations. Stadler (1986) suggests applying three simple tests to ensure the decision is appropriate. In applying the test of *justice*, assess your own sense of fairness by

determining if you would treat others the same in this situation. For the test of *publicity*, ask yourself if you would want your behavior reported in the press. The test of *universality* asks you to assess whether you could recommend the same course of action to another counselor in the same situation (ACA, 2004).

If the course of action you have selected seems to present new ethical issues, then you'll need to go back to the beginning and re-evaluate each step. Perhaps you have chosen the wrong option or you might have identified the problem incorrectly (ACA, 2004).

If you can answer in the affirmative to each of the questions suggested by Stadler (thus passing the tests of justice, publicity, and universality) and you are satisfied you have selected an appropriate course of action, then you are ready to move on to implementation (ACA, 2004).

7. Implement the Course of Action

Go forward with your decision after you have considered the previous steps. Regardless of your decision there will be risk, but you made the best decision based on the advice and information you had at the time. Counselors cannot practice risk free, but we can reduce our risk and raise our support for students, clients by using ethical reasoning.

Taking the final step in the ethical model can be disconcerting. In a real-life ethical dilemma the final step never will be easy, but by strengthening your confidence through continuous professional development it becomes easier to carry out your plans. After implementing your course of action, it is good practice to follow up on the situation to assess whether your actions had the anticipated effect.

Although the model is presented sequentially, it seldom will occur sequentially when you are tackling an ethical problem in the field.

Nine-Step Decision-Making Model for Schools

Stone (2001) further developed the ACA model by addressing the unique circumstances for counselors who are working in a school setting.

STEPS, an acronym for Solutions To Ethical Problems in Schools (Stone, 2001), adapts the seven steps in the ACA model and extends the conceptual and contextual applications. STEPS is a nine-step model addressing the emotional influences of a problem and considers chronological and developmental appropriateness, as well as parental rights. STEPS helps school counselors negotiate the nuances of ethical dilemmas that come with working in an environment significantly different than those found in agency, community, private, or hospital counseling settings. Counseling is another matter all together when you primarily serve minors who are mandated by law to be in attendance in an environment designed for academic instruction and not counseling.

The nine steps in STEPS: Solutions To Ethical Problems in Schools (Stone, 2001) are:

1. Define the problem emotionally and intellectually
2. Apply the ACA and ASCA ethical codes and the law
3. Consider the students' chronological and developmental level
4. Consider the setting, parental rights, and minors' rights
5. Apply the moral principles (Kitchener, 1984)
6. Determine your potential courses of action and their consequences
7. Evaluate the selected action
8. Consult
9. Implement the course of action

1. Define the Problem Emotionally and Intellectually

- How do your emotions define this problem (your initial reaction)? What does your heart tell you should happen in this case? File this initial reaction away for later reference.
- How does your intellect define the problem - unemotionally, objectively?
- What are the facts? Separate the hearsay, but remember rumors often inform.

It is important to acknowledge your first reaction to the problem. When a student in need comes through the door crying and in pain, our initial reaction generally is, "What can I do to help this student?" This immediate reaction and your supportive instincts will lead you toward a resolution to benefit this student. This emotional reaction is important because it helps us protect our students/clients' confidences. In defining the problem, counselors are careful not to act on emotion without considering the other ethical decision-making steps. Because we care about our students/clients, we don't want to discard the emotional reaction, but use it to guide us with a healthy combination of reason and judgment.

Take the necessary steps to gather the facts while weeding out innuendos, rumors, hearsay, and hypotheses. However, in school settings, we cannot rule out the hearsay or rumors as they are often how counselors discover the truth about situations that involve their students/clients.

2. **Apply the ACA and ASCA Ethical Codes And The Law**
   See previous ACA model.

3. **Consider the Students' Chronological and Developmental Levels**
   How does the student's developmental level impact the dilemma and how you will approach it? This step is critical, yet, it has been left out of decision-making models. A child's age, and the ability to show he or she can make informed decisions, matters. Also, counselors have to remember that the younger and more immature the child, the greater our responsibility to their parents/guardians.

4. **Consider the Setting, Parental Rights and Minors' Rights**
   You must consider the rights of parents to be the guiding voice in their children's lives, especially in value-laden decisions. Clear and imminent danger can take many forms. Parents' rights to be informed and involved when their children are in harm's way must be honored.

   You must consider the dilemma in the context of the school setting. Ethical dilemmas in a school take on a different meaning than ethical issues in other contexts. Students, clients come to school for academic instruction, and when they enter into the personal or emotional arena we cannot discount that this will carry obligations to other educators and to parents.

5. **Apply the Moral Principles**
   See discussion of Kitchener, 1984, above.

6. **Determine Your Potential Courses of Action and Their Consequences**
   See previous ACA model.

7. **Evaluate the Selected Action**
   See previous ACA model.

8. **Consult**
   Discuss your case with a fellow professional, preferably a supervisor, to help you illuminate the issues. When caught in an ethical dilemma it is sometimes difficult to see all the issues clearly. Counselors often have to do their ethical problem-solving on the run. It is not always possible or feasible for counselors to close their office doors, sit with paper and pencil, and follow the ethical decision-making model. Consultation is one step that never should be skipped (Stone, 2001).

   Consulting is such a critical part of ethical behavior

that it is important to establish a network of professionals with whom you can routinely and confidentially consult when situations arise. Counselors need to be constant consumers of legal and ethical information by seeking counsel of colleagues, administrators, supervisors, and school attorneys. The complexity of the legal and ethical world is less daunting and security is enhanced when consultation with other professionals is routine. More importantly, consultation can help counselors provide increased safety and security for students, clients.

9. **Implement the Course of Action**
   See previous ACA model.

Violations of Ethical Codes

Violations of ACA Code of Ethics

When an ethical violation is suspected or occurs, the charged individual's membership can either be suspended or revoked. Any report of an ACA ethical violation must be submitted in writing to the Ethics Committee at the ACA headquarters, where a copy of the complaint and any further evidence is then forwarded to the charged member. The charged member is asked to respond to the complaint and is given the option to request a conference hearing before the committee. All of this information is taken into account and a two-thirds majority vote is needed to make the final decision if there was an ethical violation (ACA, 2005b).

Violations of ASCA Ethical Standards

Non-professional behavior is usually handled through school districts' due process procedures, the courts, principals' annual evaluations of counselors, or other local procedures. Rarely are ethical violations brought to the ASCA Governing Board to address. However, ASCA has developed a means to revoke membership. The ASCA Membership Revocation document allows for members to be expelled for reasons such as failure to pay membership dues or violation of the association's ethical standards. Further, ASCA's Governing Board can also revoke membership for "any other reason deemed...to be in the best interests of ASCA" (ASCA, 2003, p. 1).

The process of membership revocation is straightforward. Individuals must submit in writing, along with the support of other ASCA members, a request to expel a member. The member in question has a right to remediate the situation within a specified period of time and the right to respond to the charges in person, including the option of questioning witnesses. The ASCA Board of Governors must approve the revocation of membership by a two-thirds majority, and the decision of the panel is considered final.

Counselors and the Law

The United States has a federal and state court system, although most cases are decided by state courts (Alexander & Alexander, 2005; Imber & Van Geel, 2004). State courts include: 1) courts of last resort such as the state supreme courts; 2) intermediate appellate courts; 3) courts of general jurisdiction or otherwise known as district, circuit, superior, or juvenile; and 4) courts of limited jurisdiction or otherwise known as small claims courts, probate, and justice of the peace.

The highest court in terms of this body of law is the supreme court of a state, called the Court of Appeals or Supreme Judicial Court in seven states. The states' supreme courts are not considered lower courts even in relation to the Supreme Court of the United States. State supreme courts follow the U.S. Supreme Court's ruling on the meaning of the Constitution of the United States; but the highest court in each state is free to interpret state laws or the state constitution in any way that does not violate principles of federal law (Alexander & Alexander, 2005).

Intermediate appellate courts exist in 38 states to hear appeals from trial court, to review trial court proceedings and to correct errors in the application of law and procedure (Alexander & Alexander, 2005). Courts of general jurisdiction are major courts in which defendants or plaintiffs can appeal to higher courts. About three-fourths of all cases in the Limited Jurisdiction Courts involve traffic offenses (Alexander & Alexander, 2005; Imber & Van Geel, 2004).

The federal court system includes at least one district court in each state with most states having two courts. California, Texas, and New York each have four district courts. These federal courts litigate cases involving citizens of different states and cases involving federal statutes. Appeals go to the district circuit courts of appeals or directly to the Supreme Court of the United States. Beyond the Supreme Court, citizens of the United States have no redress (Alexander & Alexander, 2005; Imber & Van Geel, 2004).

A *plaintiff* or *petitioner* is one who initiates a court action by filing a complaint with the appropriate court. A summons is served on the person(s) that is named as the *defendant*. The next step is the plea. With a plea, the defendant can respond by a denial, by seeking independent relief, or by introducing an affirmative defense (Alexander & Alexander, 2005; Imber & Van Geel, 2004).

Prior to trial, there is a process of discovery in which the attorneys may require: 1) an oral or written deposition; 2) written interrogatories requiring written responses to questions; 3) certain documents or materials; 4) a request to submit a listing of the facts that are not in dispute; and/or 5) a physical or mental examination of one of the parties of the lawsuit (Alexander & Alexander, 2005; Imber & Van Geel, 2004).

The case may be disposed of before going to trial by the judge dismissing the case or a motion for summary judgment if there is no dispute of the facts; and therefore, a trial is not necessary to establish facts. Alternatively, the case may be voluntarily dismissed by the plaintiff, or an out of court settlement may be reached. The vast majority of civil suits are settled out of court (Alexander & Alexander, 2005; Fischer & Sorenson, 1996). If the case goes to trial, it could be heard by a judge or a jury. The plaintiff bears the burden of proof.

Counselors and court testimony are governed by privileged communications which may mean a counselor's student or client can render them incapable of testifying about their counseling communications. However, there is judicial reluctance to extend the privilege to school counselors because of the age of their clients and the setting in which they work (Fischer & Sorenson, 1996). Another problem with privilege is what constitutes counseling. The court's tendency is to interpret privilege statutes for counselors very narrowly (Fischer & Sorenson, 1996). For counselors, counseling takes place everywhere; the playground, the bus loading zone, the hallways. Currently, there are no court cases to give us authoritative guidance on this matter (Fischer & Sorenson, 1996; Stone, 2005). To see how your state addresses the issue of privilege communications visit your state statutes or the Web site http://nccanch. acf.hhs.gov/general/legal/statutes/immunity.pdf.

Counselors can become involved in the law as defendants, plaintiffs, and witnesses. Even though we live in a litigious society, school counselors are rarely sued in the course of doing their job (Parrott, 2001; Remley & Herlihy, 2001; Stone, 2001; Zirkel, 2001). When school counselors are involved in the legal system, it is most likely that they will be called upon to be a witness in a custody battle or child abuse case. Some of the most common cases in which a counselor may become a defendant involve defamation and qualified privilege, abortion or birth control counseling, academic advising, failure to report child abuse, and unauthorized disclosure of information (Fischer and Sorenson, 1996; Stone, 2001).

Constitutional law can be a discussed in two categories, criminal law and civil law. A crime is a wrong against society (Garvey, Aleinikoff, & Farber, 2004; Tribe, 2000). A civil wrong is a wrong against another person that causes physical, emotional, or monetary damage and the plaintiffs can seek compensation. Counselors are more likely to be involved in a civil wrong, malpractice, or other forms of negligence, rather than job-related criminal activity.

An Example of Negligence

Civil wrongs in counseling may involve issues of negligence and malpractice. Negligence is a civil wrong or, in legal terms, a tort in which one person breaches the duty owed to another. Malpractice, on the other hand, is the negligent rendering of professional services (Remley & Herlihy, 2001; Valente, 1998). All four of the following elements must be present for negligence to be proven (Prosser, 1971).

- A duty was owed by the counselor to a client or student or parent/guardian;
- The duty owed was breached;
- There was a sufficient legal causal connection between the breach of duty and the injury; and,
- An injury or damages was suffered and an assessment made.

The following example helps explain the elements of negligence.

A teacher brings you a student's journal to read an entry in which the student discusses dark thoughts that neither you nor the teacher picked up as suicidal ideology. The worst happened and the student, Yolanda, committed suicide the next week. Parents sued you, the teacher, and the school district.

A "duty owed" means that the counselor of a client or student or parent/guardian has a duty to protect a child, anticipate foreseeable danger, and take steps to ensure that the child is protected. The school counselor, as well as the school, can be liable if he or she does not take the necessary precautions in a critical situation (Taylor, 2001).

In the case of Yolanda, the school counselor is held to a higher standard. Because of the school counselor's specialized training in students' personal, social, and emotional needs, the school counselor, even more so than the teacher, should have anticipated the foreseeability of harm and taken measures to safeguard Yolanda. The teacher and the counselor had a duty to protect the student, but the heavier weight of protection lies with the school counselor who should have known that Yolanda might be in trouble.

"The duty owed was breached" means that the standard of care, or what the reasonably competent school counselor would do, must be taken into consideration. In general, school counselors have a duty to provide a reasonable standard of care to all students. In the case of liability, if the counselor fails to do so, the counselor has breached his or her duty (Sherman, 2002).

Yolanda's parents needed to be informed so that they would have a chance to intervene on behalf of their daughter. The breach came when the school counselor dismissed the journal entry as "nothing of concern" and did not ask Yolanda's parents to seek help for her.

There must be a "causal connection" between the school counselor's breach of duty and the injury that the student suffered.

Is there a direct link between the fact that the school counselor and teacher failed to notify Yolanda's parents that their child might be at risk and Yolanda's suicide? In most cases suicide is determined to be an intervening variable, meaning that suicide is a situation that breaks the causal connection. However, in a few cases, Eisel v. Montgomery County Maryland (1991) being one of the more notable ones, suicide was not considered to be an intervening variable.

If a legal duty is established, the plaintiff must then move forward, in order to prove that the injury was the result of the counselor's breach of duty (Taylor, 2001). Liability in negligence cases hinges on causation. Proximate cause refers to the foreseeability of the counselor to predict the harm (Houston-Vega, Nuehring, & Daguio, 1997). The courts are reluctant to hold counselors to the duty owed element of negligence and have rejected the vast majority of negligence cases against counselors (Fischer & Sorenson, 1996). Even if one can prove that the counselor had a legal duty that was breached, there must be an "injury" that is substantial enough to warrant a lawsuit. Normally, a personal-injury plaintiff is entitled to compensation for out-of-pocket expenses such as medical bills and is entitled to damages for pain and suffering (Sherman, 2002).

Injury is apparent in this case and the injury is grievous. Little compares to the death of a child.

Standard of Care

The judgment as to whether or not a breach has occurred with regard to the duty owed is centered on the issues of reasonability and an agreed upon standard of care. Reasonableness includes precautions taken. Another test of whether one has acted reasonably is the potential of harm and the possible magnitude of harm to the victim.

In Yolanda's case, the counselor and teacher believed there was no likelihood of harm. However, as the one person in the school who is supposed to be best trained in the personal, social, emotional arena, the school counselor realizes the level of incidence for suicide among America's youth and understands with each student's expressing dark thoughts the possibility of depression or suicide must be considered. Additionally, in Yolanda's case, the magnitude of the potential harm is without parallel. The consequence of the risk of not calling parents is so great, even in the face of a relatively remote chance of suicide, that could be enough to establish duty (Eisel v Montgomery County Board of Education, 1991, np.).

A malpractice claim requires that the court make a comparison between the acceptable standard of care for the counseling profession and the conduct in question. Malpractice claims often result from a dissatisfaction with services provided, breakdowns in communications between persons, anger with the professional, retaliation, or personal greed, and not from substantiated grievances (Alexander & Alexander, 2005). To determine if the counselor's conduct met the standard of professional care, expert witnesses, people in the counseling profession who review the court documents, render an opinion. Ethical codes, licensing and credentialing bodies both locally and nationally, school board policies, pre-service preparation programs, and continuing professional development all provide pieces of the determination regarding standard of care (Caudill, 2004). The court will use standard of care to determine if the counselor acted as the reasonably competent professional would have acted under the same or similar circumstances (Cottone & Tarvydas, 1998).

Negligence can involve an error in judgment and may not necessarily be intentional, willful, or malicious wrong doing (Alexander & Alexander, 2005).

A malicious, willful, and intentional tort by a counselor is found in *Doe v. Blandford* (2000). A student was abused by a counselor, and her parents brought a complaint against the school district claiming that the defendants were negligent in hiring, failing to supervise, and failing to fire the student's abuser.

The law also recognizes *in loco parentis*, a special relationship between counselors and minor students. This relationship is especially strong in a school setting in which the minor is often under a mandate to attend, and it requires that we offer special consideration to provide a high standard of care that would be expected of a parent.

Conclusion

Ethics in the professions are standards that contain aspects of fairness and duty to the profession and the general public (Title Guaranty & Insurance, Co., n.d.). An understanding of laws and ethical codes informs professionals as to the implications and consequences of their work. Law, the minimum standard that society will tolerate, sometimes conflicts with ethics, at which point the professional school counselor explains his or her ethical imperative and if the situation cannot be resolved, then the counselor follows the law.

School counselors are acting in an ethical way if: they have the student's best interest at heart; they are promoting their student's autonomy and independence; they are trying to do good; they are applying an ethical decision making model; and they are showing their students loyalty and justice.

The ACA Code of Ethics and the ASCA Ethical Standards guide counselors in their ethical responsibility to students and parents, but are not intended to deliver concrete one-size-fits all answers. Ethics are situational and have to be considered in context of institutional and community standards, school board policy, and individual circumstances. All ethical dilemmas require that the counselor carefully consider the context before determining the appropriate course of action for their students or parents.

The unique circumstances of counseling in a school setting require a reevaluation of traditional ethical decision making models. The model Solutions To Ethical Problems in Schools adapts the seven steps in the ACA model and extends the conceptual and contextual applications to more strongly consider the chronological and developmental levels of students as well as the critical consideration of parental rights.

Seeking supervision and consulting are key

elements of any ethical decision making model but especially one that addresses students who are mandated to be in a setting designed for academic instruction. More importantly, consultation and supervision can help counselors provide increased safety and security for students, clients.

Counselors rarely find themselves entangled in a lawsuit in which they are the defendant. In the unlikely event that a lawsuit happens, counselors can stand ready to defend themselves if they followed an ethical decision making model and followed the appropriate standard of care for the profession.

Discussion Questions

1. Discuss your opinion of the premise that a thorough knowledge of the laws, ethical codes, school board policies, and prevailing community standards better prepares the professional school counselor to make tough decisions.
2. What are the elements of negligence? Why is it so difficult to find that a school counselor owes a duty to prevent suicide?
3. You have been told by a student that her friend Rolanda is threatening suicide. When you call Rolanda in, she vehemently denies it and scoffs at the idea that she would ever harm herself. You are convinced and you drop it without discussing it with anyone. Is there an ethical or legal dilemma?
4. Determine if your state extends privileged communication to students in schools. How does the statute read? If your students do not have privileged communication in statutes, is there any language that encourages you to protect their confidences?
5. The prosecution's attorney has subpoenaed you. Is this different from receiving a court order from a judge?
6. Why is it impossible to develop laws, ethical codes, written school board policies, or procedures that cover all the potential situations school counselors might face? How should we proceed, in light of the fact that we cannot always find guidance in laws, codes, or policies for all the situations we face?
7. Discuss how you as a school counselor have an ethical imperative to promote the autonomy of your minor students.
8. What is standard of care? Who is the reasonably competent professional?

References

Alexander, K., & Alexander, D. (2005). *American public school law* (6th ed). Belmont, CA: Thomson West.

American Counseling Association (ACA). (2004). *A practitioner's guide to ethical decision making.* Alexandria, VA: Author.

American Counseling Association (ACA). (2005a). *Code of ethics and standards of practice.* Alexandria, VA: Author.

American Counseling Association (ACA). (2005b). *Policy and procedures for processing complaints of ethical violations.* Alexandria, VA: Author.

American School Counselor Association (ASCA). (2003). *The ASCA national model: A framework for school counseling programs.* Alexandria, VA: Author.

American School Counselor Association (ASCA). (2004). *Ethical standards for school counselors.* Alexandria, VA: Author.

Caudill, C. O. (2004). *Therapists under fire.* Retrieved June 1, 2004, from http://www.cphins.com/riskmanagement/therapists_under_fire.htm

Cottone, R., & Tarvydas, V. (1998). *Ethical and professional issues in counseling.* Upper Saddle River, NJ: Merrill-Prentice Hall.

Doe v. Blandford, 402 Mass. 831, 835, 525 N.E.2d 403 (2000).

Duhaime Law. (2004). *Duhaime's online legal dictionary: Common law.* Retrieved October 15, 2006, from http://www.duhaime.org/dictionary/dict-c.aspx

Eisel v. Board of Education of Montgomery County. 324 Md. 376, 597 A. 2d 447 (Md Ct. App. 1991). Retrieved December 27, 2002, from LexisNexis database.

Fischer, L., & Sorenson, G. P. (1996). *School law for counselors, psychologists, and social workers* (3rd ed.). White Plains, NY: Longman.

Forester-Miller, H. & Davis, T. (1996). *A practitioner's guide to ethical decision making.* Retrieved on February 21, 2005, from http://www.counseling.org/Resources/Code of Ethics/TP/Home/CT2.aspx

Forester-Miller, H., & Rubenstein, R. L. (1992). Group counseling: Ethics and professional issues. In D. Capuzzi & D. R. Gross (Eds.), *Introduction to group counseling* (pp. 307-323). Denver, CO: Love Publishing Co.

Garvey, J., Aleinikoff, A., & Farber, D. (2004). *Modern constitutional theory: A reader* (5th ed.) St. Paul, MN: West Group Publishing.

Georgetown University Law Library. (2001). *Legal research definitions: Common law.* Retrieved October 15, 2006, from http://www.ll.georgetown.edu/tutorials/definitions/common_law.html

Haas, L. J., & Malouf, J. L. (1989). *Keeping up the good work: A practitioner's guide to mental health ethics.* Sarasota, FL: Professional Resource Exchange, Inc.

Houston-Vega, M. K., Nuehring, E. M., & Daguio, E. R. (1997). *Prudent practice: A guide for managing malpractice risk.* Washington, DC: National Association of Social Workers Press.

Imber, M. & Van Geel, T. (2004). *Education law* (3rd ed.). Mahway, NJ: Erlbaum.

Kitchener, K. S. (1984). Intuition, critical evaluation and ethical principles: The foundation for ethical decisions in counseling psychology. *Counseling Psychologist, 12*(3), 43-55.

Levick, M. (2000). Privacy rights of minors. In F. W. Kaslow (Ed.), *Handbook of couple and family forensics: A source book for mental health and legal professionals* (pp. 105119). New York: John Wiley & Sons.

New Jersey Legislature. (n.d.). *Glossary of terms: Law.* Retrieved October 15, 2006, from http://www.njleg.state.nj.us/legislativepub/glossary.asp

Oregon State University. (2006, August). *Definitions of anthropological terms: Ethics.* Retrieved October 15, 2006 from http://oregonstate.edu/instruct/anth370/gloss.html

Parrott, J. (2001, July 9). Are advisors risking lawsuits for misadvising students? *The Mentor: An Academic Advising Journal.* Retrieved January 20, 2002, from www.psu.edu/dus/mentor/

Prosser, W. (1971). *The law of torts.* St. Paul, MN: West Group Publishing.

Remley, T. P., & Herlihy, B. (2001). *Ethical, legal, and professional issues in counseling.* Upper Saddle River, NJ: Merrill-Prentice Hall.

Remley, T. P., Jr., & Herlihy, B. (2005). *Ethical, legal, and professional issues in counseling* (2nd ed.). Upper Saddle River, NJ: Merrill-Prentice Hall.

Remley, T. P., Jr., & Huey, W. C. (2002). An ethics quiz for school counselors. *Professional School Counseling, 6,* 3-11.

Sherman, D. (2002). *Personal injury and negligence claims against a school.* Retrieved October 16, 2006, from http://www.aboutautismlaw.com/suing_a_public_school_for_money_damages.html

Sileo, F., & Kopala, M. (1993). An A-B-C-D-E worksheet for promoting beneficence when considering ethical issues. *Counseling and Values, 37,* 89-95.

Stadler, H. A. (1986). Making hard choices: Clarifying controversial ethical issues. *Counseling & Human Development, 19,* 1-10.

Stone, C. (2005). *School counseling principles: Ethics and law.* Alexandria, VA: American School Counselor Association.

Stone, C. (2001). *Legal and ethical issues in working with minors in schools* [Film]. Alexandria, VA: American Counseling Association.

Stone, C., & Isaacs, M. (2002). Confidentiality with minors: The effects of Columbine on counselor attitudes regarding breaching confidentiality. *The Journal of Educational Research, 96*(2), 140-150.

Taylor, K. R. (2001). Student suicide: Could you be held liable? *Principal Leadership.* Available online at http://findarticles.com/p/articles/mi_qa4002/is_200109/ai_n8962412

Title Guaranty & Insurance, Co. (n.d.). *Glossary: Ethics.* Retrieved October 15, 2006, from http://www.titleguarantynm.com/glossary/glossary_e.asp#E

Tribe, L. (2000). *American constitutional law* (3rd ed.). New York: Foundation Press.

Valente, W. (1998). *Law in the schools* (4th ed.). Upper Saddle River, NJ: Merrill-Prentice Hall.

Van Hoose, W. H., & Paradise, L. V. (1979). *Ethics in counseling and psychotherapy: Perspectives in issues and decision-making.* Cranston, RI: Carroll Press.

Zirkel, P. (2001). Ill advised. *Phi Delta Kappan, 83,* 98-99.

Chapter 3

Mentoring Through Supervision

Jeannine R. Studer, Betty Anne Domm, and Sue Clapp

Abstract

The roles of supervisor and mentor are critical to the school counseling trainee's understanding of the school counseling profession and identity. Receiving supervision by a professional school counselor is one of the most valuable learning experiences individuals training for the profession of school counseling can acquire. This chapter introduces the reader to the roles of the school counselor supervisor and mentor. A discussion of how these roles are similar and how they differ is included along with the shared responsibilities and goals.

Introduction

When I was an intern, my supervisor was awesome! At first I was reluctant to start new activities, but with her support I felt confident, particularly since I knew she would allow me to make mistakes without negative consequences. During the internship she encouraged me to do things I thought I would never have the opportunity or the skills to do. By the time the internship was over, I felt ready to begin my career as a school counselor. What made me feel even more confident was her invitation to call her whenever I needed to discuss a situation or if I had some concerns. At times she would even phone me to check on how I was doing. I don't know what I would have done if I didn't have her support.

The statement above was articulated by a school counseling trainee after he completed his internship experience. Students training for school counseling express eagerness mixed with trepidation as they put their knowledge into practice when they enter their clinical experiences, often known as the practicum and internship. Practicing professional school counselors have a professional obligation to serve as site supervisors for students training to be school counselors.

Although serving as a supervisor is an essential role that has a tremendous impact on how trainees learn about the professional school counselor's role and identity, few practicing school counselors have received training in supervision (Roberts, Morotti, Herrick, & Tilbury, 2001). This information is generally not offered in the master's level school counseling curriculum. As a result, site supervisors at all grades supervise differently, and trainees receive dissimilar experiences.

Generally, the practicum is the last time trainees will receive supervision by a practicing school counselor. Unfortunately, building administrators, who often have little training and knowledge of the school counselor's professional orientation, are usually the supervisors of practicing school counselors. This results in concerns about professional identity, particularly in situations that create ethical dilemmas. It is during this time that novice school counselors yearn for the comfort, security, and advice they had under the protection of their on-site school supervisor who guided them through their training. The role of supervisor and mentor are critical to the trainee's understanding of the school counseling profession and identity. Although the terms "supervisor" and "mentor" seem similar, and in many aspects share similarities, mentoring and supervising are distinctly different (Johnson, 2003).

The word "supervision" is derived from Latin roots meaning "to look over" or "to oversee" (Garthwait, 2005), in which the novice counselor is provided with a greater knowledge of self, the profession, and how he or she assimilates into the school counselor role (Borders & Brown, 2005). Although supervision of school counselors-in-training is not a new concept, what is new are the changing supervisory functions due to societal needs, program expectations, and transformed school counseling programs. Despite the supervisory variables both within and external to the school setting, the relationship between the supervisor and the trainee is regarded as one of the most crucial factors in supervision satisfaction (Ramos-Sanchez et al., 2002), with mentoring as the most crucial factor influencing the relationship (Tentoni, 1995).

A mentor is "a wise and trusted counselor" in which a more experienced individual performs numerous roles such as guide, role model, counselor, consultant, and teacher (Johnson, 2002, as cited in Johnson, 2003). Like supervision, mentoring is not a new concept; what is new is the view of mentoring within a supervisory relationship (Tentoni, 1995). This leads to the question, "What are the similarities and differences between a supervisor and a mentor?" Consider the following scenarios:

1. *Dr. McCarthy, the school counselor program supervisor at a local college, worked closely with the local county supervisor of school counselors in the placement of students who were ready for their clinical experiences. The needs and goals of each of these student trainees were discussed, as were the qualities of the individuals who agreed to serve as site supervisors. After much thought, placements were made. The students were instructed to contact their assigned site supervisor to set up an initial meeting, and to discuss the terms of the clinical experience. Several days later, one of the students tearfully called the program supervisor. Between sobs, the student told her that she made an appointment to meet with her supervisor, and was greeted by the "head of the counseling program." This program head expressed her displeasure at having interns coming into the school who felt that they could "just waltz in and take over the counselor's responsibilities without thinking about how it would take up their time."*

2. *Sue Lang was an experienced, professional middle-school counselor in a rural school that served 600 students in grades 6-8. She was often asked to serve as a supervisor for school-counselors-in-training who were enrolled in a local university program, and she readily agreed whenever she was needed. Because Mrs. Lang was often involved with numerous duties when the trainee arrived, the trainee would pick up his or her assignments that were left with the secretary and would conduct the activities according to the instructions that were included with the packet of assignments. She would meet with the trainee every week for about an hour to discuss concerns, check on progress, and evaluate efforts on reaching contract goals. At the end of the clinical experience Mrs. Lang would evaluate the trainee and discuss her assessment with the program supervisor and the trainee.*

3. *Juan Martinez, eager and ready for his internship experience, interviewed Mr. Kato to determine whether or not their philosophy of counseling was similar, took time to review the school counseling program, and after reflection, requested to be placed with Mr. Kato. During the internship experience Mr. Kato provided a comfortable working relationship in which Juan not only learned about the school counseling profession, but also was surprised to find himself confiding personal concerns, fears, and accomplishments to Mr. Kato. In addition, Juan was astonished when Mr. Kato would regularly ask him to self-reflect on the various situations he encountered in the school setting, gave advice on his resume, and asked pertinent questions regarding personal and career goals. Juan was given periodic feedback throughout the experience that assisted him in reaching his personal and professional goals. As a result, the final evaluation was an honest reflection of his skills, with no surprises in the final assessment. After graduation, Juan would regularly consult with Mr. Kato for advice and continued their professional and personal relationship.*

Based on these scenarios, it is clear that the first individual was neither a mentor nor a supervisor, and did not feel that working with school counselor trainees was part of her role, despite the American School Counselor Association (ASCA) standards that state otherwise. According to Section F. 2.c of the *Ethical Standards for School Counselors*, "the professional school counselor provides support and mentoring to novice professionals" (ASCA, 2004). Although these standards do not specifically define the professional school counselor's role in supervision, the *American Counseling Association Code of Ethics* (2005) explicitly mentions supervision as a professional obligation and responsibility.

In the second scenario, although Mrs. Lang was not always able to meet with her students when they arrived, she provided support and activities, made time to discuss concerns with her trainees, and offered an assessment of their abilities. Mrs. Lang collaborated closely with the program supervisor and made strides in fulfilling her ethical obligation as a supervisor.

In the final situation, Mr. Kato prepared Juan for the profession of school counseling as did Mrs. Lang, but there were several differences in his style. Not only was Mr. Kato a supervisor, he was also a mentor. The purpose of this chapter is to discuss the differences and similarities between the role of the supervisor and mentor, how an individual can be a mentor while serving as a supervisor, and how mentoring benefits the supervisor as well as the trainee.

The Supervisory Role

The term "supervisor" specifies a contractual relationship between the college or university counseling program and an appropriately credentialed, experienced school counselor, with the purpose of guiding the personal and professional growth of trainees (Roberts et al., 2001). An additional responsibility of supervisors is to protect the well-being of the counselees with whom they work (Stoltenberg & Grus, 2004).

Meaningful clinical experiences do not just occur accidentally; they must be nurtured in a comfortable environment with ample opportunities given to the trainee. The supervisor creates a learning environment based on his or her understanding that each trainee progresses at different rates as a result of varied experiences, educational differences, and developmental levels (Cobia & Pipes, 2002). The supervisor is responsible for assessing such things as the trainee's skill with particular types of counselees and other individuals, ability level in classroom management, or skillfulness in conducting new strategies (Hart, 1994). Trainees will require diverse activities and interactions based on these differences (Stoltenberg & Grus, 2004).

Supervisors have a responsibility to form relationships with their trainees. Part of the supervision experience is to support and encourage and to make certain that the trainee feels comfortable asking questions and revealing personal concerns about assignments without fear of a negative evaluation. Supervisors need to be aware of the power differential that is apparent when assuming an evaluator role, and how this factor may influence the supervisee's willingness to express personal goals or concerns. Supervision requires structure in attending to the trainee's performance while maintaining continual contact with the program supervisor. Conversely, mentoring does not require the same structure and vigilance.

The Mentor Role

Mentoring is purposeful and characterized by reciprocity and mutuality as the trainee's career development is nurtured as he or she progresses from a novice to a collegial member of the profession (Johnson, 2003). The act of mentoring is described as one in which best practices are modeled, identified tasks are accomplished, and support and acceptance are given (Tentoni, 1995). The mentor's role is to focus on the trainee's needs and career goals while serving as a confidant by offering a safe, nurturing environment in which the trainee can risk disclosing personal concerns.

Although there is dispute among professionals regarding the constructs that create an effective mentorship role, there is consensus that: (1) emotional and psychological support are essential because of the many doubts new professionals bring to the setting (Tentoni); (2) career and professional development is facilitated through professional socialization and greater awareness of career opportunities (Tentoni); (3) both individuals benefit from the relationship, and; (4) the mentor provides opportunities for the trainee to self-reflect and assess personal growth and goals (Johnson, 2003; Tentoni).

How Are Supervisors and Mentors Similar and Different?

It is not unusual for counselors to bring their personal feelings and thoughts into counseling relationships that may influence their interactions with their counselees. Mentors can facilitate opportunities for trainees to analyze their own feelings, beliefs, and attitudes that they bring into the counselor's role. Unlike a supervisor, a mentor will provide feedback, but may not necessarily be responsible for providing a summative, formal evaluation that could impact grades or employability. Each of these areas is discussed in more detail.

The Role Model as a Shared Responsibility

Mentor	Supervisor
Serves as a role model for the profession. Models ethical and legal behavior.	Serves as a role model for the profession. Discusses, observes, and evaluates trainee's legal/ethical knowledge and behavior.

As the chart above indicates, both the mentor and the supervisor have an awareness of the ASCA ethical guidelines, state laws, district policies and procedures, and ethical decision-making. Making decisions about controversial situations that are routine for the supervisor/mentor may not be as clear to the trainee. Therefore, discussing sensitive cases in which there are no clear-cut answers may improve the trainee's ability to think through ethical dilemmas. Providing structure and direction, observing the professional school counselor counsel, interacting with teachers, consulting with parents, and collaborating with administrators are some of the trainee's preferred activities during the initial stages of supervision. A supervisor can allay some of the trainee's anxiety by introducing him or her to the faculty, students, and administrators. In addition, helping the trainee understand the school structure, policies and procedures, and working relations with other key personnel such as secretaries, custodians, and bus drivers, demonstrates the central role the professional school counselor plays within the academic setting.

Mentors and supervisors caution trainees that teachers are sometimes mistrustful of school counselors due to previous, negative interactions. For instance, if the counselor associates primarily with the administration and is perceived as performing administrative tasks, teachers will be skeptical of how counselors can collaborate and assist them in classroom goal attainment. Likewise, if the counselor does not communicate with the principal and is perceived as working in isolation, administrators may be reluctant to approve new counselor strategies or interventions. A perceptive mentor will demonstrate the collaborative role school counselors play with all professionals in the school through such strategies as eating lunch with different teachers and listening to their concerns, observing and assisting in the classroom, and constantly communicating how the school counselor assists student academic, career, and personal/social growth.

Open communication and mutual contributions help create a trustful environment in which there is a reciprocal exchange of concerns, ideas, and materials. The professional school counselor has a wealth of materials that have been accumulated over the years, and has networked with numerous community agencies. Sharing this information facilitates the trainee's understanding of available resources and the importance of a mutual partnership. Likewise, the trainee can share with the supervisor some of the most current information that has been received in the classroom. For example, many experienced school counselors have not been trained in the ASCA National Model (ASCA. 2003); and, although they may have attended conferences and workshops that discuss the benefits of a comprehensive, developmental model, they may feel they lack the rudimentary knowledge necessary for initiating the transformation process. The trainee may have the ability to assist the supervisor with the information that is needed to begin the initial steps in changing to a developmental program.

Although the supervisory setting may be more reflective of a traditional school counseling program, together the supervisor and trainee may identify activities that fulfill the mission of the school program as well as the spirit of the ASCA National Model. Mutually, the supervisor and trainee can envision how the school counselor can operate in a transformed program, the trainee can experience the counselor's role in a comprehensive school counseling program, and the supervisor may gain a better understanding of how the existing program may be revised to reflect the purpose of the ASCA National Model.

Mentors may prepare trainees for administrative differences when the trainee moves into a position as a school counselor. For instance, a middle school counselor position was available that had previously been held by a counselor who created a negative impression because of her lack of interaction with the faculty and failure to communicate with the administration. When the new school counselor arrived, she was met with negativity and mistrust. The new school counselor sought the advice of her former supervisor, whom she also considered a mentor; and she was able to get materials, lesson plans, and support. From there, her mentor suggested that she "sell" the faculty and principal on her program by presenting current information at faculty meetings, collaborating with the teachers, regularly communicating with her principal, and collecting data to demonstrate how she was able to assist in student academic, career, and personal/social growth. Although these efforts took time, the work was worth it as the teachers eventually regarded her as a key educational resource.

Evaluation as a Shared Responsibility

Mentor	Supervisor
The trainee can risk discussing personal/professional concerns without fear of a negative evaluation. Interpersonal interactions may be necessary in changing the trainee's behavior and attitude that could impair performance.	The trainee's self-disclosure may negatively impact evaluation. The supervisor is a gatekeeper to the profession and holds legitimate power that influences trainee behavior and attitude change.

The supervisor, as a gatekeeper to the profession, has an obligation to provide an honest appraisal of the trainee, a task that supervisors report as one of the most disliked aspects of this role. Mentors, on the other hand, listen to trainee concerns and provide advice and feedback that are separate from the evaluative process. These differences are shown in the chart above.

Too often, the trainee does well academically, but may need additional assistance to develop essential skills. Supervisors frequently handle the evaluator role by giving only positive ratings and disregarding areas that need improvement. This practice does not allow the trainee to be aware of areas that need improvement or to identify strategies to achieve the necessary skills (Michaelson, Estrada-Hernández, & Wadsworth, 2003). When trainees perceive the evaluative process as threatening, they may be reluctant to share concerns or issues they feel may negatively impact their grade. When the site supervisor and program supervisor communicate concerns and are able to identify strategies to remediate concerns, the trainee benefits.

In one situation, the practicing school counselor was concerned not only about her trainee's inability to ask questions and to request assistance, but also her defensive manner when she would discuss the trainee's problematic behaviors. As a mentor, she was aware that corrective feedback was crucial to the trainee's future success. A meeting was held between the supervisors and the trainee, concerns were discussed, and strategies for remediation were outlined. Although the trainee was visibly upset about this feedback, she was able to change her behavior and eventually thanked her site supervisor for caring about her enough to provide her with this information. When an on-going assessment is provided with identified strategies to improve performance, personal and professional growth may lead to increased motivation, self-awareness, and a greater understanding of his or her professional identity.

It is obvious that the supervisor wears many hats and fulfills varied roles, one of which may be the role of mentoring. Because dual relationships can create ethical concerns when roles intersect and conflict, professionals need to be clear as to where one role ends and the other begins - a difficult decision since mentors and supervisors share many characteristics (Aponte, 1994, as cited in Huber, 1994).

Goals as Common Responsibilities

Mentor	Supervisor
Works with trainee on developing and attaining long-term goals. Focuses not only on completing the guidelines of the school counselor program, but also helping the trainee with self-assessment.	Works with trainee on identifying and achieving short-term goals. Focuses on assisting trainees through meeting counselor education guidelines.

The school counseling program has various expectations and requirements. The supervisor needs to be aware of these guidelines and to keep in continual contact with the program supervisor. In addition, each trainee enters the clinical experiences with different experiences, skills, and knowledge. A contract is made that reflects his or her personal and professional goals, the objectives of the training program, and how these goals can meet the needs of the site supervisor. The supervisor will monitor and provide evaluative feedback on how well the trainee accomplished these goals. If additional opportunities arise that would give the trainee extra learning experiences, the contract may be altered to include these new activities. The differences between the supervisor and mentor in attention to goal attainment are described in the chart above.

The supervisor as mentor is also alert to the importance of self-awareness. When the trainee is unaware of his or her own thoughts and feelings that may impair the counseling relationship, the mentor may facilitate self-awareness by asking pertinent questions such as, "What were you thinking when you asked the counselee that question?" "What counselees are most challenging for you?" or "How did you want the counselee to view you?" (Cashwell, 2001). Socratic questioning is another strategy for exploring beliefs and assumptions (Paul, 1990). This approach would ask questions such as, "What are you assuming?" "What are some other assumptions?" "What led you to that belief?" and, "What would change your mind about that belief?"

Once the trainee has completed the clinical experiences, the supervisor is no longer responsible for monitoring and evaluating the trainee's performance. A mentor, however, will continue to work with the trainee on achieving long term goals after the supervision relationship has ended.

A supervisor wearing a mentor hat is advised to initiate the first contact with trainees because former trainees may feel reluctant to contact their mentor for fear of appearing too dependent, needy, or simply feeling as if they are interrupting their busy schedule. At times, mentors may need to invite, encourage, and accompany their former trainees to attend professional development opportunities such as conferences, workshops, and meetings because it is sometimes difficult for students and new professionals to attend a new function without the presence and support of another individual.

Furthermore, when the trainee leaves the clinical training and enters a different school setting or grade level, it may be difficult for the supervisor, now serving as a mentor, to provide the guidance that is required. Different school systems and grade levels often require a new set of expectations that may not be part of the mentor's expertise or background. However, if a strong relationship is formed between the program supervisor and area professional school counselors, networking with other counselors may provide the needed guidance. For example, an elementary school counselor worked with a trainee who eventually graduated and was offered a position in a middle school. The two were in contact throughout the years, but due to life circumstances, eventually lost contact with each other. Several years passed, and the former trainee wanted to contact her former mentor, but was unable to locate her. She called her former counselor professor from the university in which she graduated and was able to reconnect.

Summary

Receiving supervision by a professional school counselor is one of the most valuable learning experiences individuals training for the profession of school counseling can receive. It is during this experience that trainees have the opportunity to connect with a practitioner and to put their classroom knowledge into practice. The experienced professional school counselor works with the school counseling program supervisor in achieving the trainee's goals and program requirements, serving as a role model in demonstrating the ethical and legal requirements of the profession, and evaluating the trainee's performance. In some cases this relationship ends when the clinical experience is over. In other cases, this relationship moves to a more personal level, in which the supervisor takes an interest in the trainee's personal and professional growth. In these instances, the supervisor serves as a mentor. In a mentoring relationship, the trainee's long-term goals are facilitated, and more opportunities are available for self-reflection and professional development. A mentor will also provide a continual assessment of skills and feedback that are separate from the trainee's formal course evaluation.

Discussion Questions

1. Discuss the traits that you possess that would contribute to your role as a supervisor or mentor.
2. Identify the areas in which you feel you would like additional training or experience in order to provide excellent supervision for school counselor trainees.
3. Suppose you are in a mentor/supervisor role and your trainee discloses personal information that you feel may negatively impact his/her counseling relationships. How can you reconcile disclosing this information to the school counseling program supervisor without impairing your relationship with your trainee?
4. What are some of the ways a supervisor/mentor can provide corrective feedback to the trainee without impairing the relationship?
5. List some of the ways a mentor can assist the trainee in connecting with counseling professionals in the community.
6. Identify some of the ways that the school supervisor can assist the trainee become involved with the professional organizations.
7. A novice counselor has taken a new position as a school counselor in an elementary school in which the principal demands that he/she perform administrative duties such as attendance, scheduling, discipline, cafeteria duty, bus duty, and substitute teaching. What are some of the ways a mentor can guide this individual to educate the principal about counseling-related tasks and scope of training?

References

American Counseling Association. (2005). *ACA Code of Ethics*. Alexandria, VA: Author.

American School Counselor Association (2003). *The ASCA national model: A framework for school counseling programs*. Alexandria, VA: Author.

American School Counselor Association (2004). *Ethical Standards for School Counselors*. Retrieved December 22, 2005, from http://www. schoolcounselor.org/content.asp?contentid=173

Borders, L. D., & Brown, L. L. (2005). *The new handbook of counseling supervision*. Mahwah, NJ: Lahaska Press.

Cashwell, C. S. (2001, October). IPR: Recalling thoughts and feelings in supervision. *CYC-Online, 33*. Retrieved January 19, 2005, from http://www.cyc-online/cycol-1001-supervision.html

Cobia, D. C., & Pipes, R. B. (2002). Mandated supervision: An intervention for disciplined professionals. *Journal of Counseling & Development, 80*, 140-144.

Garthwait, C. L. (2005). *The social work practicum: A guide and workbook for students*. Boston: Pearson.

Hart, G. M. (1994). *Strategies and methods of effective supervision*. Greensboro, NC: ERIC Clearinghouse on Counseling and Student Services. (ERIC Document Reproduction Service No. ED372341)

Huber, C. H. (1994). How personal should supervision be? *The Family Journal: Counseling and Therapy for Couples and Families, 2,* 354-356.

Johnson, W. B. (2003). A framework for conceptualizing competence to mentor. *Ethics & Behavior, 13,* 127-151.

Michaelson, S. D., Estrada-Hernández, N., & Wadsworth, J. S. (2003). A competency-based evaluation model for supervising novice counselors-in-training. *Rehabilitation Education, 17,* 215-223.

Paul, R. (1990). *Introduction to Socratic questioning.* Retrieved March 16, 2006, from http://okra.deltastate.edu/~bhayes/socratic.html

Ramos-Sanchez, L., Esnil, E., Goodwin, A., Riggs, S., Touster, L. O., Wright, L. K., Ratanasiripong, P., & Rodolfa, E. (2002). Negative supervisory events: Effects on supervision satisfaction and supervisory alliance. *Professional Psychology:Research & Practice, 33,* 197-302.

Roberts, W. B., Morotti, A. A., Herrick, C., & Tilbury, R. (2001). Site supervisors of professional school counseling interns: Suggested guidelines. *Professional School Counseling, 4,* 208-215.

Stoltenberg, C., & Grus, C. (2004). Defining competencies in psychology supervision: A consensus statement. *Journal of Clinical Psychology, 60,* 771-785.

Tentoni, S. C. (1995). The mentoring of counseling students: A concept in search of a paradigm. *Counselor Education and Supervision, 35,* 32-42.

Chapter 4

Mentoring Models: Preparing School Counselors for the Future

Suzy Thomas and Laurel Edgecomb

Abstract

Mentoring has long been considered an important element of professional practice in many fields, though it has not been as widely practiced within the field of counseling. This chapter reviews the characteristics of successful mentoring relationships, mutual benefits and ethical dilemmas associated with mentoring, and the role of culture and gender. Three innovative approaches to mentoring are presented, including a practicum experience, a format for preparing graduate students to make professional presentations, and a peer consultation group to support alumni practicing in the field of school counseling.

Introduction and Background

Mentoring is a practice that has long been recognized as influential in promoting the success of novices in their newly acquired professional roles (Black, Suarez, & Medina, 2004; Cesa & Fraser, 1989; Eby & Lockwood, 2005; Fagenson, 1989; Johnson, 2002; Johnson & Nelson, 1999; Kirchmeyer, 2005; Kram, 1985; Roche, 1979; VanZandt & Perry, 1992). The earliest written reference to the concept of mentoring can be found in Homer's *Odyssey* (Davis, Little, & Thornton, 1997; Johnson, 2002; Johnson & Nelson, 1999). Mentor was the name of the elder from Ithaca whose job it was to educate and protect Odysseus' son Telemachus.

In academic settings, mentoring has traditionally been defined as a relationship in which a faculty member guides, supports, and challenges a graduate student who is usually younger and less experienced (Johnson, 2002; Johnson & Nelson, 1999; Kram, 1985). Mentor-protégé relationships can occur between faculty and students, between experienced practitioners and students or novices, and between advanced and beginning students in the same training program (Black et al., 2004; Kirchmeyer, 2005).

Mentoring is typically considered to be a less formal relationship than that of teacher-student or supervisor-trainee, although some of the functions are similar (Black et al., 2004; Johnson & Nelson, 1999;

VanZandt & Perry, 1992). Mentoring relationships are traditionally long-term, complex, and intimate (Black et al., 2004; Johnson & Nelson, 1999). Kirchmeyer (2005) conducted a longitudinal study of the effects of mentoring in academic professions and found that the main purpose of mentoring lies in the "political" realm, in that the mentor assists the protégé in learning how to navigate through the social system and improves the protégé's potential for using resources and contacts within the system.

Young, Sheets, and Knight (2005) described mentoring as a combination of art and science; a successful connection involves constant modifications and adaptations to suit individual needs and preferences. In order to be effective, a mentor should possess a love of learning and a commitment to reflective practice (Young et al., 2005). Davis et al. (1997) focused on the teaching and learning essential to the mentoring process, as well as the inevitable "angst" involved in the search for deeper self-understanding for both mentor and protégé.

Although mentoring is widely recognized as a meaningful and desirable professional practice, it is not widely practiced within the field of counseling and counselor education (Black et al., 2004; Cesa & Fraser, 1989; Cronan-Hillix, Gensheimer, Cronan-Hillix, & Davidson, 1986; Johnson, 2002). Black et al. (2004) posit that mentoring may be underutilized because of issues related to lack of structure in the relationship and roles. They propose a four-part model to make the process more systematic. The model begins with mutual self-appraisal, followed by becoming knowledgeable about the roles and process of mentoring, examining a series of questions about the psychosocial and vocational aspects of mentoring, and finally, establishing goals for the mentoring relationship.

The division of mentoring into psychosocial and vocational realms was initially recommended by Kram (1985) and has been used as a framework for describing mentoring relationships ever since (Johnson, 2002; Johnson & Nelson, 1999; Kirchmeyer, 2005; Lankau, Riordan, & Thomas, 2005). Kram conceived of the psychosocial functions in terms of improving protégé competence and sense of identity, and the vocational functions in terms of the coaching and learning opportunities needed for socialization into the career and preparation for advancement.

Much of the research on mentoring took place in fields other than counseling, such as business and teacher education. Since the 1990s, there has been an increase in research on mentoring relationships within the professional realms of counseling, counselor education, and counseling psychology (Black et al., 2004; Colley, 2001; Johnson & Nelson, 1999; Lankau et al., 2005; VanZandt & Perry, 1992).

Characteristics of Successful Mentoring Relationships

The elements of a successful mentoring relationship include synergy and good communication and boundaries between the mentor and protégé, as well as respect for the mentor and a willingness to learn on the part of the protégé (Bressler, 2004; Eby & Lockwood, 2005; Johnson, 2002). Good mentoring relationships include a personal connection as well as a focus on professional development (Johnson & Nelson, 1999). Lankau et al. (2005) studied the effects of similarity and liking in formal mentoring relationships, concluding that having significant similarities was important to both mentors and protégés; liking was not a predictor of mentor-protégé success, while time spent together played a more important role for both parties. Mentoring relationships that involve emotional closeness afford more opportunities for the protégé to advance in the profession by being carefully coached about the norms and social skills needed for success in the field. On the other hand, the aspects of mentoring that include skills and knowledge require mentor competence more than intimacy between mentor and protégé (Kram, 1985). Fagenson-Eland, Marks, and Amendola (1997) found that key ingredients in mentoring relationships include support, assistance with career planning, modeling, and effective communication.

Black et al. (2004) considered mentoring to be an ongoing relationship involving nurturing, modeling, and coaching. They underscored the importance of high ethical standards and clear boundaries, asserting that the primary responsibility for establishing and maintaining these rests with the mentor as the more experienced party. A good mentor is aware of the developmental needs of the protégé, accurately assesses and affirms the protégé's potential and interests, and intentionally models ethical and professional behavior (Davis et al., 1997; Johnson, 2002).

As mentioned before, good communication is a key factor in good mentoring. The mentor, as the more experienced professional, should be able to surface and attempt to resolve conflict or tension and be willing to allow the protégé to leave the mentoring relationship without repercussions if it is not proving productive, or when there is no longer a need for being mentored (Johnson, 2002). Effective mentors also do not attempt to work with too many protégés, in order to be able to devote the time and energy needed to make the relationship successful (Johnson, 2002).

Roche (1979) focused on the professional socialization opportunities available through mentoring relationships. Roche identified several key factors in mentoring relationships in graduate schools, including mutual support, professional development (especially for the protégé), and participating in research together. These factors have also been emphasized by other researchers over time (Black et al., 2004; Cronan-Hillix et al., 1986; Eby & Lockwood, 2005; Fagenson, 1989; Johnson, 2002; Kirchmeyer, 2005; Van Zandt & Perry, 1992). The mentor's role is, in some ways, similar to that of a consultant (Black et al., 2004). Although there exists a power difference in the relationship between mentor and protégé, Black et al. (2004) argue that this disparity becomes less apparent over time as the two individuals begin to relate to each other more as colleagues.

Mentoring and Issues Related to Culture and Gender

In general, a gender or cultural match does not predict a productive mentoring relationship (Bressler, 2004; Brown et al., 1999; Fagenson, 1989; Roche, 1979). Ragins and Cotton (1999), however, found that gender played a role in the effectiveness of the mentoring connection. Traditional mentoring relationships between faculty members and graduate students still reflect a disparity in terms of gender and ethnicity, in that a higher proportion of tenured faculty are White males (Brinson & Kottler, 1993; Johnson, 2002). Mentors need to be competent in working with protégés from diverse cultural backgrounds and aware of the specific needs of female protégés and protégés of color (Brinson & Kottler, 1993; Gilbert, 1985; Kram, 1985). Knowledge, skills, and awareness of the principles of effective cross-cultural counseling should be applied to mentoring relationships where gender or cultural background differences exist. For example, good mentors will be culturally self-aware, open to diverse points of view, and willing to de-emphasize power in the relationship.

Formal and Informal Mentoring Relationships

Researchers have studied both formal and informal mentoring, although more studies have been done on the informal development of mentoring connections (Eby & Lockwood, 2005). Informal mentoring relationships are considered by many to be more effective than formal ones (Cesa & Fraser, 1989; Eby & Lockwood, 2005; Fagenson-Eland et al., 1997; Johnson, 2002; Ragins & Cotton, 1999). In addition, formal training in mentoring is limited (Johnson, 2002). Formal mentoring is also narrower in scope than informal mentoring (Eby & Lockwood, 2005). Formal mentoring programs may decrease the likelihood of the development of a close, personal connection between mentor and protégé; and formally assigned mentors may approach the work with less enthusiasm or motivation (Eby & Lockwood, 2005).

A mismatch between mentor and protégé is one of the most common pitfalls, and mismatch is more common in mentoring relationships that are assigned as opposed to spontaneous (Eby & Lockwood, 2005). Although formal mentoring programs exist, Cesa and Fraser (1989) make the important point that a good match between mentor and protégé often emerges more informally based on similar personalities and interests. Faculty members, for example, may be most likely to become mentors to protégés who remind them of themselves (Johnson, 2002). Cronan-Hillix et al. (1986) argue that a good mentor cannot really be "assigned," and that mentoring may be underutilized partly because protégés have trouble finding a mentor who fits their personal and professional needs.

Johnson (2002), however, argues that the informal way in which mentoring relationships typically develop may actually prevent the practice from being more frequently and fully utilized. Instead, he advocates for "intentional mentoring," which he describes as a multi-faceted approach beginning with guidance and recognition from national organizations such as the American Psychological Association, along with increased attention to creating a culture of mentoring within graduate programs. Intentional mentoring would include faculty training and incentives for the role, formal preparation of protégés in the dynamics of mentoring and strategies for having a successful mentoring experience, and regular evaluation of outcomes.

VanZandt and Perry (1992) recommend soliciting mentors rather than relying on informal avenues for the development of these relationships. They implemented a statewide mentoring program for new school counselors, pairing them with experienced counselors who had been trained in an orientation session that focused on cognitive, developmental, and practical issues in mentoring, as well as self-awareness and role issues for mentors. The program was evaluated by both mentors and protégés, and on a Likert-type scale of 1 (lowest) to 5 (highest), the mean satisfaction score was 4.5 for protégés and 4.7 for mentors. Regular evaluation of the potential benefits and pitfalls of the relationship is recommended (Johnson, 2002). Cesa and Fraser (1989) proposed an evaluation questionnaire to help make the informal mentoring process more systematic and formalized. They designed a questionnaire for graduate student protégés to evaluate their faculty mentors, emphasizing the role of mentoring in producing scholarly literature and the level of personal satisfaction with the relationship.

Mutual Benefits of Mentoring

Researchers have found that the benefits of mentoring are mutual and far outweigh the costs (Blackman, Hayes, Reeves, & Paisley, 2002; Bressler, 2004; Diaz, 2003; Johnson, 2002; Johnson & Nelson, 1999; VanZandt & Perry, 1992). As to the benefits of mentoring, Van Zandt and Perry (1992) found that protégés appreciated having someone available to support them, and that mentors focused on the value of networking and mutual support. Eby and Lockwood (2005) noted learning, support, and assistance with career planning as primary benefits for protégés, while personal satisfaction and increased professional and interpersonal skills were emphasized by mentors.

For protégés, benefits are both professional and personal, relating to improvements in performance as well as job satisfaction (Black et al., 2004; Johnson, 2002; Johnson & Nelson, 1999; Kirchmeyer, 2005; VanZandt & Perry, 1992). Protégés tend to value a match in the realm of personality traits over their perception of the mentor's competence or success within the profession (Cronan-Hillix et al., 1986). Fagenson (1989) found that individuals who had been mentored had higher satisfaction levels and greater career mobility and promotions than those who were not mentored.

For mentors, benefits are associated with a commitment to maintaining currency in the field and a sense of renewal (Black et al., 2004; Eby & Lockwood, 2005; Johnson & Nelson, 1999). Blackman et al. (2002) conducted a qualitative case study evaluation of their eight-year partnership project between counselor educators and counselors and found that key themes for all participants included a feeling of renewal, a greater commitment to ongoing professional development, and an increased sense of community and connectedness.

While mentors primarily seek commitment and competence in their protégés, protégés wish to have mentors who will both challenge them and be patient with them, and who will offer a combination of support and specific guidance (Black et al., 2004). Strategies for enhancing the mentor-protégé relationship include clearly defining the objectives of the collaboration, ensuring that there is a good match between the mentor and protégé, and some structured monitoring of the progress made in the relationship (Eby & Lockwood, 2005).

Ethical Dilemmas in Mentoring

There are a number of potential ethical dilemmas associated with mentoring, many of which arise from the very nature of the relationship itself. Mentoring is a long-term, intimate connection that often develops informally and may involve overlapping roles (Black et al., 2004; Johnson, 2002; Johnson & Nelson, 1999). Because mentoring occurs between professionals with different levels of experience, there is an inherent power difference in the relationship. For example, mentors may exploit their protégés by taking credit for their work or by using them as assistants. Because mentoring is more successful when there is a sense of personal or emotional closeness, the possibility of boundary violations, especially sexual misconduct, becomes an issue of primary concern.

Dual relationships are not typically recommended within the counseling profession (Corey, Schneider-Corey, & Callahan, 2003). Because formal guidance on mentoring is limited (American Psychological Association, 1992), it may be useful to apply some of the key recommendations regarding dual roles between client and therapist (e.g., informed consent, avoiding sexual relationships, attending to issues of power and principles of autonomy, fidelity, and beneficence, etc.) to the mentoring dyad (Corey et al., 2003; Johnson & Nelson, 1999).

Johnson and Nelson (1999) identified the following as areas of ethical concern in mentoring relationships: mentor competence; equal access to and accurate portrayal of mentoring opportunities; power imbalance and the potential for protégé exploitation; dual roles and multiple relationships; and difficulties with termination. They recommend establishing structure within the relationship through informed consent and clear communication. Regular and open evaluation of mentoring experiences may help to prevent some of these abuses (Cesa & Fraser, 1989; Johnson, 2002). Ultimately, it is the responsibility of the mentor and also of the institution to protect the protégé from harm, to navigate the multiplicity of roles, to offer equal opportunities, and to terminate the relationship if it is no longer needed or has become harmful (Black et al., 2004; Davis et al., 1997; Johnson, 2002; Johnson & Nelson, 1999).

Issues for Beginning School Counselors

New school counselors experience a number of common difficulties as they enter the school environment, and these include isolation, lack of mentoring and support, and a general lack of definition regarding the professional induction process (Thomas, 2001). Socialization into the work environment is much more clearly defined in fields other than counseling (Little, 1990; Matthes, 1992; Staton & Gilligan, 2003; Stickel & Trimmer, 1994; Thomas, 2001; VanZandt & Perry, 1992), and mentoring has been heralded as a significant way for novices to become socialized into their professions (Black et al., 2004; Cesa & Fraser, 1989; Eby & Lockwood, 2005; Fagenson, 1989; Johnson, 2002; Johnson & Nelson, 1999; Kirchmeyer, 2005; Kram, 1985; Roche, 1979; VanZandt & Perry, 1992).

The role of the school counselor has been described as increasingly complex in the 21st Century (American School Counselors Association, 2003; Baker & Gerler, 2004; Borders & Drury, 1992; Campbell & Dahir, 1997; Grothaus, 2004). Counselors are called upon to work in collaboration with others (ASCA, 2003; Fischetti & Lines, 2003; House & Martin, 1998; Quealy-Berge & Caldwell, 2004). For example, the American School Counselor Association (ASCA) National Model (2003) highlights the role of the school counselor as a collaborator. Staton and Gilligan (2003) state that it is the responsibility of the counselor education program to prepare future school counselors to work in partnership and collaboration with others. Collaboration can result in increased understanding of one's role, which can be especially useful in the field of school counseling, where role definition continues to be problematic (Baker & Gerler, 2004; Borders & Drury, 1992; Campbell & Dahir, 1997; Paisley & Borders, 1995; Thomas, 2001; VanZandt & Perry, 1992). Collaboration also reduces isolation (Blackman et al., 2002; Staton & Gilligan, 2003; VanZandt & Perry, 1992), but it is a skill that must be taught (Staton & Gilligan, 2003). The most frequently cited barriers to collaboration are perceived lack of time and lack of support from the administration (Staton & Gilligan, 2003).

Any collaborative effort, while potentially valuable, is also time-consuming and labor-intensive, requiring a sustained commitment on the part of all those involved (Black et al., 2004; Blackman et al., 2002; Bressler, 2004; Fischetti & Lines, 2003; Kirchmeyer, 2005). Protégés may complain of neglect or unmet expectations, and mentors may feel unprepared or unqualified for the role (Eby & Lockwood, 2005). Johnson (2002) notes that obstacles to mentoring between faculty members and graduate students include the focus within graduate institutions on publishing, which may occur at the expense of time spent teaching and/or mentoring. In addition, programs that foster a culture of competition rather than collaboration may not cultivate mentoring relationships (Johnson, 2002).

Blackman et al. (2002) point out that mentoring and partnership relationships between counselor educators and practicing school counselors are easy and obvious recommendations, but that the task of implementing and maintaining these relationships in a way that is productive and successful can be challenging and even daunting. However, because technology allows for regular contact via e-mail or telephone, the time required to maintain a mentoring connection can be significantly reduced without compromising the quality of the relationship (Diaz, 2003).

A Review of Three Innovative Approaches to Mentoring

In the field of counseling, mentoring may occur between counselor educators and school counselors or graduate students, between school counselors and counselors-in-training, and between peers (e.g., students, counselors, or counselor educators) with different levels of experience (Black et al., 2004; Kirchmeyer, 2005). This section describes three innovative strategies for involving school counselors in mentoring relationships, beginning with their initial training in the graduate counseling program and extending throughout their professional careers. Each strategy is relatively easy to incorporate into a counselor education program and offers significant benefits to both mentors and protégés.

The first strategy is implemented in the beginning practicum in school counseling and involves first-year graduate students being mentored by 2nd- and 3rd-year students and by practicing school counselors. The second strategy involves a unique approach to preparing graduate students and practicing school counselors for making presentations at professional counseling conferences. This approach most closely mirrors the traditional mentoring that occurs between faculty members and graduate students. The third strategy is the alumni peer consultation group, which provides practicing school counselors with ongoing support and professional development activities, as well as the opportunity to mentor new inductees into the profession.

Each of the strategies is intended to bridge the gap between theory and practice (Blackman et al., 2002; Brott, 1996; Rowell, 2005; Staton & Gilligan, 2003), to make tangible connections between what was learned in the graduate training program and actual practice in the field, and to establish mentoring relationships as an essential element of the professional life of the school counselor. Black et al. (2004) and others (e.g., Johnson, 2002; Johnson & Nelson, 1999) urge counselor educators to establish structured opportunities for mentoring relationships within their graduate training programs, given the tangible benefits for both parties and the current lack of formal mentoring that occurs within the field. Cesa and Fraser (1989) noted that faculty mentors pay less attention to the importance of mentoring in improving student socialization experiences, and they call for more attention in this area. The programs described below focus on the socialization process. Finally, geographic matching tends to make mentoring more successful (Eby & Lockwood, 2005; VanZandt & Perry, 1992), and the programs described below involve mentoring relationships between parties who are in close geographic proximity.

Mentoring in the School Counseling Practicum

Practicum experiences are intended to provide some initial exposure to schools prior to the field placement or culminating internship (Coker & Shrader, 2004; Fischetti & Lines, 2003) The activities of many practicum placements, however, may or may not prove relevant in terms of adequately preparing trainees for the realities of the school counselor's job (Kahn, 1999). As mentioned before, it is far more common that new school counselors do not experience the benefits of structure or support during the induction process (Little, 1990; Matthes, 1992; Staton & Gilligan, 2003; Stickel & Trimmer, 1994; Thomas, 2001; VanZandt & Perry, 1992).

The School Counseling Practicum at Saint Mary's College of California, designed by Suzy Thomas and based on the model developed by Rowell (2005), gives beginning school counseling students practical experience in problem-solving and action research in a school setting. Students shadow school counselors and identify and explore an actual, school-based problem or issue related to school counseling. Using the principles of collaborative action research (Gillies, 1993; Sagor, 1992), students work in teams to create and implement an original assessment tool that addresses the identified problem or issue. Class time is spent processing the shadowing experiences, learning about collaborative action research, and working together to find ways to approach the identified problem or issue. Final team papers are presented to faculty and advanced students at the end of the semester.

The goals of the Practicum are to bridge the gap between theory and practice (Blackman et al., 2002; Brott, 1996; Rowell, 2005; Staton & Gilligan, 2003), to create a culture of collaboration between and among professionals of varying levels of experience (Beale, Copenhaver, Leone, & Grinnan, 1997; Blackman et al., 2002; Clark & Horton-Parker, 2002; Fall & VanZandt, 1997; Fischetti & Lines, 2003; Quealy-Berge & Caldwell, 2004; Rowell, 2005), and to facilitate the socialization process for the new school counselor to include ongoing support and tangible experiences. In addition, the course is designed to promote the value of conducting school-based research and presenting that research within school and professional settings. These goals reflect several of the priorities outlined in the National Model (ASCA, 2003), such as data collection within the Management System and results reports within the Accountability section.

The opportunity to conduct original research on school-based problems while in graduate school is intended to foster a commitment to this practice once the trainee enters the profession. Since school counselors have been called upon to be leaders (House & Martin, 1998), there are some clear benefits to making public presentations that are intended to help students overcome shyness and take on a leadership role through the use of action research. Action research is an especially useful tool within school settings, because research topics emerge from day-to-day problems, and projects are aimed at improving practice. In addition, the research itself can be carried out by the practitioners themselves or in collaboration with counselor educators (Rowell, 2005; Sagor, 1992). We use Sagor's (1992) framework, in which projects initiate, monitor, or evaluate some counseling-related action or program. Many Practicum project topics over the past four years have focused on perceptions of the role of the school counselor and improving understanding among students, teachers, and parents of the purpose of counseling. Other topics include stress among middle school students,

solution-focused strategies for behavioral issues, program evaluations, and needs assessments.

The mentoring component of this course is two-tiered: students are mentored by the practicing school counselors they are shadowing, as well as by the more advanced students in the field experience class. The mentoring relationships that develop between graduate students and school counselors allow both parties to engage in professional reflection, an activity that is recommended (Fischetti & Lines, 2003; Young et al., 2005). Davis (2003) claimed that school counselors place a higher value on work-based learning experiences as opposed to professional development activities, and the Practicum offers tangible opportunities for growth for all parties.

Mentoring should increase a protégé's professional contacts (Kirchmeyer, 2005). Our students have found that the mentoring they experience during the Practicum often helps them to secure a field placement or a job upon graduation. Of course, the fact that mentors are assigned in this course can present some potential problems, as described above. If there is a mismatch in terms of personality, the value of the mentoring experience may be more limited (Cesa & Fraser, 1989; Cronan-Hillix et al., 1986; Eby & Lockwood, 2005). There is abundant evidence that the benefits of informal mentoring relationships outweigh those found in formal ones (Blackman et al., 2002; Bressler, 2004; Diaz, 2003; Johnson, 2002; Johnson & Nelson, 1999; VanZandt & Perry, 1992); however, it is also the case that mentoring is underutilized within the counseling profession (Black et al., 2004; Cesa & Fraser, 1989; Cronan-Hillix et al., 1986; Johnson, 2002). There is a clear call for counselor educators to incorporate mentoring into their programs (Black et al., 2004; Johnson, 2002; Johnson & Nelson, 1999) to improve the socialization process for new inductees.

This course reflects the commitment to "intentional mentoring," as described by Johnson (2002), and the recommendation to solicit and train prospective mentors (VanZandt and Perry, 1992). Mentors from within the field are chosen by Suzy Thomas, who teaches the course. They are recruited for their willingness to spend time with protégés and their curiosity about conducting research on a school-based problem. Mentors are prepared for the role through discussions with the counselor educator, who outlines the types of activities that make Practicum a useful experience for the protégé. The time spent preparing mentors helps to clarify the roles of both parties and has mostly been successful.

For the beginning student, being mentored offers the opportunity to become socialized into the profession in a more structured manner, with built-in support systems and resources. For the advanced student who is about to graduate and enter the field, mentoring beginning students promotes reflection on learning and helps to consolidate or synthesize the graduate school experience. The bulk of the mentoring with the Practicum, however, occurs between practitioners and students. For the school counselor, mentoring graduate students encourages reflective practice and enhances a professional self-concept. For those counselors who passionately love their jobs, there is nothing better than being a mentor for the opportunity of sharing the pleasure and exciting variety of a "typical" workday with a burgeoning prospective counselor. The wonderful irony of witnessing a "typical" counseling workday incorporates the concept of learning to expect the unexpected. The role of a Practicum supervisor is to provide graduate students with the opportunity to observe the counselor's response to the unexpected events that inevitably arise amidst the sessions that were planned.

Laurel Edgecomb is a full-time school counselor, working at Las Juntas Elementary School and Vicente Alternative High School in Martinez, California. At Edgecomb's schools, the Practicum students have the chance to spend 100% of their time with the counselor. The schools' permission forms, sent out at the beginning of the year to parents, include a clause, which states that counselors in training may occasionally observe their child's sessions. This level of direct observation has not happened at every Practicum site, but at Edgecomb's schools, the staff, administration, and counselor are all supportive of a mentoring process that delineates the complete picture of a counselor's day and how integral the counselor is to a healthy school climate.

At Edgecomb's schools, the Saint Mary's College Practicum students are included in every counseling activity, from individual and group sessions, to consultations with the staff, meetings with the principal, and all incidental moments that occur during a counselor's day. Edgecomb's style is Solution Focused, and Practicum students get to witness firsthand the simple yet powerful techniques that help a bully become a leader, let a withdrawn child find her latent joy, and assist a teacher in redefining an ADHD student as "easily fascinated," instead of "easily distracted." Edgecomb has an infectiously positive attitude, which has helped to create an environment where children vie to come to counseling and view "getting to see the counselor" as a reward worth earning with improved behavior.

Edgecomb has also developed an innovative method to assist the Practicum students with processing their day. After visiting the school, they are expected to do a write-up of the interactions of the day (changing students' names to ensure conifidentiality), which they send to Edgecomb via e-mail. She responds to their questions and comments, adds relevant details or background information on various exchanges, and returns the e-mail write-up, with her responses, to all of the Practicum students visiting her site. This way, all of the Practicum students learn from each other, have additional exposure to Solution Focused counseling methods, and develop a more complete picture of the many hats a counselor may wear. Best of all, the graduate students see how a counselor makes a tremendous and immediate difference in the lives of students and teachers, the way an 8-hour day can fly by, and how, at the end of the day, one feels energized, exhilarated, and ready to return to do it all again.

Mentoring through Professional Presentations

Research is lacking on the professional development needs and experiences of school counselors (Grothaus, 2004), and it seems to be the case that school counselors do not regularly read professional literature or conduct their own research (Bauman et al., 2002). Mentoring is considered a key element of professional development (Brott, 1996). One of the roles of mentors is to encourage protégés to engage in professional development activities such as scholarship (Black et al., 2004). Roche (1979), for example, argued that producing research in a collaborative manner is a key ingredient of mentoring in academic settings.

Faculty members in the Graduate Counseling Program at Saint Mary's College of California have developed a unique approach to preparing graduate students and practicing school counselors for making professional presentations by offering them tangible support during each step of the process. Our intent is to instill in students the values and benefits of producing and presenting research while still in graduate school, so that they maintain those activities in their practice as school counselors. We also aim to continue to support them in the same way once they are in the field. The approach was described by Heid, Thomas, and Schubb (2004) and is detailed below.

Step 1: Recruitment of students and the initial meeting. Students are recruited in classes, primarily after they finish their action research projects in the

Practicum and while they are working on their master's projects, to present at an upcoming counselor conference. Alumni who are working as school counselors are also contacted and queried about current "best practices" that they might be able to translate into a presentation. Interested students and counselors are invited to attend a discussion and planning session.

At this initial meeting, participants share their ideas for presentations, and faculty mentor Suzy Thomas works with them to shape each idea into a format that would work for a presentation. Thomas' role is to offer reassurance to the students, who tend to have a high level of anticipatory anxiety and a lack of confidence that their ideas could translate into a professional presentation. In addition, Thomas reviews the steps involved in submitting a proposal, a timeline for the related activities, and background information on the group sponsoring the conference. The intent of this meeting is to demystify the process of making a professional presentation; to frame it as something that is not only possible for students to do, but professionally and personally rewarding; and to reassure students that they will be supported through each step of the experience.

Step 2: Preparation and submission of proposals. Students who have agreed to make a proposal after the initial discussion session also receive assistance with the submission process. Students are given a copy of the proposal form or a link to obtain it online; they develop an initial proposal and send it to Thomas, who edits and evaluates what they have written so that it adheres to the guidelines for submission. Sample proposals are also sent to students via e-mail so that they can see examples of how to write in this manner. Thomas generates an electronic list of potential participants in order to facilitate regular communication and to offer congratulations for each accomplishment, beginning with the step of sending the proposal.

Step 3: Mock presentation with faculty feedback. Once student proposals have been accepted, the next step in this supportive process involves setting up a mock presentation with faculty members as the audience. Each student or team is given constructive feedback by faculty members and the other students after their presentation. In this way, novice presenters can experience a friendly "dry run" with familiar faces in the audience and the promise of helpful feedback aimed at improving the performance, before actually having to give the presentation. This is one of the most important elements in the approach we have developed, and students appreciate the opportunity for structured rehearsal.

Step 4: Faculty attendance at presentation. In addition, faculty members attend student sessions in order to support them during the presentations. It is not uncommon for presenters to be questioned or challenged by audience members, and novice presenters can sometimes take these comments personally or be uncertain about answering questions. Another purpose of faculty presence, then, is to bolster students' confidence to respond, or to speak up for them and protect them in the event that they are unfairly challenged.

Step 5: Follow-up and debriefing sessions. It is also important to help students to reflect on the experience of making a professional presentation, and to offer suggestions for improvement and for continued participation in professional development activities. Some of this debriefing occurs informally at the conference, during break or meal times. Follow-up discussions also occur after the conference, either in person or via e-mail. Participants are given a small gift from the College, to acknowledge their courage and to congratulate them on this significant accomplishment.

The most recent events at which students made presentations included the annual conference of the Western Association of Counselor Educators and Supervisors (WACES), the California Summit on School Counseling, and the Northern California conference of the California Association of School Counselors (CASC). Topics at these events have included suicide prevention, solution-focused counseling tools, consultation methods for working with teachers, how to survive the first year as a school counselor, and a variety of action research projects.

It is our hope that our graduates will continue to produce, discuss, and present meaningful research throughout their careers, and we are glad to make time to support them in these efforts, even after they have begun working as school counselors. The process outlined in this section is obviously time-consuming, as is any worthwhile mentoring activity (Black et al., 2004; Blackman et al., 2002; Bressler, 2004; Fischetti & Lines, 2003; Kirchmeyer, 2005); but, it is also mutually beneficial (Blackman et al., 2002; Bressler, 2004; Diaz, 2003; Johnson, 2002; Johnson & Nelson, 1999; VanZandt & Perry, 1992). For the faculty members, it is a chance to play a role in launching the professional careers of students and graduates; and for the participants, it offers a structured way to step foot into the world of research and to make a commitment to being actively involved in their professional community. This is time well spent indeed.

The Alumni Peer Consultation Group

Alumni groups such as the one developed by Thomas (2005) also offer support in the form of collaboration and mentoring, as well as the promise of ongoing professional development and awareness of key issues and best practices. Mentoring within an alumni peer consultation group can occur between the faculty facilitator and the participants, or between experienced and new members of the group. It has been suggested that, without some type of intervention, school counselors may actually experience a decline in skill level over the years (Grothaus, 2004).

Since, as was pointed out earlier, the induction process tends to be problematic for school counselors (Matthes, 1992; Stickel & Trimmer, 1994; Thomas, 2001), efforts to ease that transition through sustained contact with the graduate institution and with experienced peers should be welcomed by new inductees. The alumni peer consultation group at Saint Mary's College (Thomas, 2005) was designed based on the proven effectiveness of teacher research groups, in which teachers collaborate to improve their practice and develop new approaches to teaching (Castori, 2002; Papale, Castori, & Wilson, 2002). Peer consultation groups have also been used for counselors (Logan, 1997), and the goals of such groups involve a combination of personal and professional support, networking opportunities, and a place to reflect on current issues in the field (Logan, 1997; Thomas, 2005). Blackman et al. (2002) described a similar professional development activity in the project they refer to as "The Collaborative," a school-university partnership in which counselor educators and practicing school counselors meet monthly to engage in professional development, networking, and reflection. In this model, counselor educators also spend time in local schools working with practitioners on school-based problems.

The alumni peer consultation group for school counselors at Saint Mary's College has been in existence for six years, and the group continues to grow every year. The first year, between 4 to 10 alumni attended the meetings; now there are 40 members and 8 to 20 people at the meetings. Members are recruited each year after graduation, when all new graduates are contacted and queried about their interest in participating. Meetings are held 5 times a year, once every other month, in order to maintain a sense of continuity without burdening their already busy schedules. The two-hour meetings are spent as follows: the first hour involves a discussion of a journal article or book chapter sent to members ahead

of time, on topics they identified as important to them; during the second hour, one of the group members makes an informal presentation on a topic of concern to the group, with resources and recommendations for improving skills or awareness in school counseling.

In this way, members have the opportunity to maintain currency with professional literature, to share best practices with one another, and to reduce the isolation commonly felt within the profession of school counseling (Hayes, Dagley, & Horne, 1996; Hayes, Paisley, Phelps, Pearson, & Salter, 1997; Little, 1990; Logan, 1997; Matthes, 1992; Robertson, 1998; Staton & Gilligan, 2003; Stickel & Trimmer, 1994; Thomas, 2001; VanZandt & Perry, 1992). Facilitator Suzy Thomas finds the articles to send to participants, sets the meeting schedule, and sends summaries of previous meetings and reminders of upcoming meetings via e-mail. Hot topics for the group include legal and ethical issues, especially with regard to working with parents; student use and misuse of the Internet; current research on brain development; substance abuse among students and their families; self-mutilation; and working with gay, lesbian, bisexual, and transgender youth.

The format of the group encourages mentoring relationships to emerge, a phenomenon that has increased each year. Since some members have been with the group since its inception in 2000, there are varying levels of work experience; and new members can seek mentoring from those who have been in the field longer. A current focus of the group involves veteran members giving advice to recent graduates about how to navigate their way through their first year as school counselors. Their recommendations focus on building good connections with other members of the school system, being involved in all aspects of school life to promote greater understanding of the role of the counselor, and aligning their work with the National Standards.

Although it is widely assumed that mentoring relationships require a significant investment of time, mentoring can also occur in innovative and less time-consuming ways, such as through regular e-mails to contact groups (Diaz, 2003). This is one tool that the alumni group has begun to use regularly as a way to stay in touch with one another between meetings and to share resources, ask for advice, and offer tips about employment opportunities (Kirchmeyer, 2005).

Alumni groups are easy to implement and present a number of tangible benefits for both the counselor educator and the participants. Although the group is managed by a faculty member, the direction and topics are determined by the participants based on the current issues they are facing in their school settings. Group members report that they are much more likely to read professional literature because it is "assigned" as preparation for the meetings; they also appreciate the opportunity to be supported by their graduate institution and by their peers, and they find the group to be a good source for new information and counseling tools. For the counselor educator, the group offers the chance to stay in touch with the realities of working "in the trenches" and provides valuable information that can be used to modify the school counseling curriculum (Thomas, 2005). The alumni peer consultation group is yet another forum for nurturing mentoring relationships that enhance the professional and personal lives of participants on all sides.

Conclusion

As mentioned previously, collaborative activities often result in an increased commitment to sustaining professional development. It has been assumed that mentoring relationships are time-consuming, more beneficial when informally developed, and difficult to integrate into the culture of graduate schools and other professional settings. This chapter reviewed three innovative approaches to mentoring that can be implemented within the framework of the graduate counseling program to provide avenues for both formal and informal mentoring relationships to develop from the initial stages of graduate school well into the professional careers of school counselors. Since it is clear that mentoring relationships present numerous concrete advantages for both mentors and protégés, it is our hope that graduate programs will attempt to find ways to create mentoring possibilities and that graduate students and practicing school counselors will take advantage of the opportunity to participate in the mutually beneficial practice of mentoring.

Mentoring Tip Sheet

1. This practice can be traced back to "Mentor," the elder from Ithaca who educated and protected Odysseus' son.
2. A main feature of mentoring lies in showing the protégé ways to navigate the social system and maximize resources and contacts.
3. Effective mentors exemplify a love of learning and a commitment to reflective practice.
4. A successful mentoring relationship embodies respect, willingness to learn, helpful communication,

and focuses on both personal and professional development.
5. An experienced mentor is accurate in assessing the protégé's potential and interests and provides modeling and supportive feedback.
6. Mentors need to be competent in working with protégés from diverse cultural backgrounds, aware of the specific needs of protégés of color, and attentive to the differing needs of both genders.
7. Benefits of mentoring include mutual appreciation, networking, feeling supported, personal satisfaction, and increased skills for both mentor and protégé.
8. Individuals who receive mentoring have higher satisfaction levels, greater career mobility, and more promotions than those who are not mentored.
9. Regular and open evaluations of mentoring experiences are invaluable to steer these relationships away from the harm that occasionally may arise due to dual relationships, power imbalances, or potential protégé exploitation.
10. Mentoring experiences for graduate students can range from classroom observations, watching scheduling, doing an action research project, or counseling sessions.
11. The mentors themselves gain from the experience of intentional mentoring; it increases their reflective practice and strengthens their focus on being the best that they can be.
12. Graduate programs should work to find ways to create meaningful mentoring possibilities, so that graduate students, practicing school counselors, and counselor educators can take advantage of the opportunity to participate in this mutually beneficial practice.

Discussion Questions

1. What are some of the advantages and disadvantages of formal versus informal mentoring relationships?
2. In what ways does the experience of being mentored benefit the protégé?
3. How can mentoring be beneficial to the mentor?
4. What are some essential qualities that make a mentoring relationship successful?
5. What are some of the challenges associated with building productive mentoring relationships?
6. What are some ethical issues associated with mentoring? What strategies can be employed to decrease the likelihood of ethical violations in a mentoring relationship?
7. What are some common challenges faced by new

school counselors, and how can mentoring ameliorate some of those difficulties?

8. What are the key components of the Practicum described in this chapter, and how does this approach reflect some of the principles of mentoring? What are the various ways in which mentoring takes place during the Practicum, and how is it mutually beneficial for all participants?

9. What are the key components of the process for making professional presentations described in this chapter, and how does this approach reflect some of the most traditional principles of mentoring?

10. What are the key components of the alumni group described in this chapter, and how does this approach reflect some of the principles of peer mentoring?

References

American Psychological Association. (1992). Ethical principles of psychologists and code of conduct. *American Psychologist, 47,* 1597-1611.

American School Counselors Association. (2003). *The ASCA National Model: A framework for school counseling programs.* Alexandria, VA: Author.

Baker, S. B., & Gerler, E. R. (2004). *School counseling for the twenty-first century* (4th ed.). Upper Saddle River, NJ: Pearson/Merrill Prentice Hall.

Bauman, S., Siegel, J. T., Davis, A., Falco, L. D., Seabolt, K., & Szymanski, G. (2002). School counselors' interest in professional literature and research. *Professional School Counseling, 5*(5), 346-352.

Beale, A. V., Copenhaver, R. C., Leone, S. D., & Grinnan, C. D. (1997). The counselor-in-residence program. *Professional School Counseling, 1*(1), 13-15.

Black, L. L., Suarez, E. C., & Medina, S. (2004). Helping students help themselves: Strategies for successful mentoring relationships. *Counselor Education and Supervision, 44*(1), 44-55.

Blackman, L., Hayes, R. L., Reeves, P. M., & Paisley, P. O. (2002). Building a bridge: Counselor educator-school counselor collaboration. *Counselor Education and Supervision, 41*(3), 243-55.

Borders, L. D., & Drury, S. M. (1992). Comprehensive school counseling programs: A review for policymakers and practitioners. *Journal of Counseling and Development, 70,* 487-498.

Bressler, J. G. (2004). Mentors' perceptions of mentoring relationships: Motivators, costs/benefits, gender, and suggestions for future mentors. *Dissertation Abstracts International Section A: Humanities and Social Sciences,* 66 (1-A). (UMI Order No. AAI3160736)

Brinson, J., & Kottler, J. (1993). Cross-cultural mentoring in counselor education: A strategy for retaining minority faculty. *Counselor Education and Supervision, 32,* 241-253.

Brott, P. E. (1996). The development of school counselor identity. *Dissertation Abstracts International Section A: Humanities and Social Sciences,* 57(12-A). (UMI Order No. AAM9715628)

Brown, M. C., Davis, G. L., & McClendon, S. A. (1999). Mentoring graduate students of color: Myths, models, and modes. *Peabody Journal of Education, 74,* 105-118.

Campbell, C. A., & Dahir, C. A. (1997). *Sharing the vision: The national standards for school counseling programs.* Alexandria, VA: American School Counselor Association.

Castori, P. (2002). *CRESS teacher research facilitators' handbook.* The CRESS Center, School of Education, University of California, Davis.

Cesa, I. L., & Fraser, S. C. (1989). A method for encouraging the development of good mentor-protégé relationships. *Teaching of Psychology, 16*(3), 125-128.

Clark, M. A., & Horton-Parker, R. (2002). Professional development schools: New opportunities for training school counselors. *Counselor Education & Supervision, 42,* 58-75.

Coker, K., & Shrader, S. (2004). Conducting a school-based practicum: A collaborative model. *Professional School Counseling, 7*(14), 263-268.

Colley, H. (2001). Righting rewritings of the myth of the mentor: A critical perspective on career guidance mentoring. *British Journal of Guidance & Counseling, 29,* 177-197.

Corey, G., Schneider-Corey, M., & Callahan, P. (2003). *Issues and ethics in the helping professions.* Pacific Grove, CA: Brooks/Cole.

Cronan-Hillix, T, Gensheimer, L. K., Cronan-Hillix, W. A., & Davidson, W. S. (1986). Students' views of mentors in psychology graduate training. *Teaching of Psychology, 13*(3), 123-127.

Davis, J. (2003). The perceived impact of college preparation and professional development on the performance of the self-reported duties of high school counselors in two New Jersey school districts. *Dissertation Abstracts International Section A: Humanities and Social Sciences, 64*(4-A), 1183. (UMI Order No: AAI3087211)

Davis, L. L., Little, M. S., & Thornton, W. L. (1997). The art and angst of the mentoring relationship. *Academic Psychiatry, 21,* 61-71.

Diaz, R. (2003, January). Take a stand: Be a mentor. *NACAC Bulletin, 3.*

Eby, L. T., & Lockwood, A. (2005). Proteges' and mentors' reactions to participating in formal mentoring programs: A qualitative investigation. *Journal of Vocational Behavior, 67*(3), 441-458.

Fagenson, E. A. (1989). The mentor advantage: Perceived career/job experiences of protégés versus non-protégés. *Journal of Organizational Behavior, 10,* 309-320.

Fagenson-Eland, E. A., Marks, M. A., & Amendola, K. L. (1997). Perceptions of mentoring relationships. *Journal of Vocational Behavior, 51*(1), 29-42.

Fall, M., & VanZandt, C. E. (1997). Partners in research: School counselors and counselor educators working together. *Professional School Counseling, 1,* 2-3.

Fischetti, B. A., & Lines, C. L. (2003). Views from the field: Models for school-based clinical supervision. *Clinical Supervisor, 22*(1), 75-86.

Gilbert, L. A. (1985). Dimensions of same-gender student–faculty role-model relationships. *Sex Roles, 12,* 111-123.

Gillies, R. M. (1993). Action research in school counseling. *The School Counselor, 41,* 69-72.

Grothaus, T. J. P. (2004). An exploration of the relationship between school counselors' moral development, multicultural counseling competency, and their participation in clinical supervision. *Dissertation Abstracts International Section A: Humanities and Social Sciences, 65*(2-A), 419. (UMI Order No: AAI3122328)

Hayes, R. L., Dagley, J. C., & Horne, A. M. (1996). Restructuring school counselor education: Work in progress. *Journal of Counseling and Development, 74,* 378-384.

Hayes, R. L., Paisley, P. O., Phelps, R. E., Pearson, G., & Salter, R. (1997). Integrating theory and practice: Counselor educator-school counselor collaborative. *Professional School Counseling, 1*(1), 9-12.

Heid, L., Thomas, S. R., Schubb, N. (2004). *A mentoring model to aid students in writing and presenting research.* Presentation at the annual meeting of the Western Association of College Admissions Counselors (WACES), Sacramento, CA.

House, R. M., & Martin, P. J. (1998). Advocating for better futures for all students: A new vision for school counselors. *Education, 119*(2), 284-291.

Johnson, W. B. (2002). The intentional mentor: Strategies and guidelines for the practice of mentoring. *Professional Psychology: Research and Practice, 33*(1), 88-96.

Johnson, W. B., & Nelson, N. (1999). Mentoring relationships in graduate education: Some ethical concerns. *Ethics and Behavior, 9,* 189-210.

Kahn, B. B. (1999). Priorities and practices in field supervision of school counseling students. *Professional School Counseling, 3*(2), 128-136.

Kirchmeyer, C. (2005). The effects of mentoring on academic careers over time: Testing performance and political perspectives. *Human Relations, 58*(5), 637-660.

Kram, K. E. (1985). *Mentoring at work: Developmental relationships in organizational life.* Glenview, IL: Scott, Foresman.

Lankau, M. J., Riordan, C. M., & Thomas, C. H. (2005). The effects of similarity and liking in formal relationships between mentors and protégés. *Journal of Vocational Behavior, 67,* 252-265.

Little, J. W. (1990). The mentor phenomenon and the social organization of teaching. In C. B. Cazden (Ed.), *Review of Research in Education* (pp. 297-351). Washington, DC: American Educational Research Association.

Logan, W. L. (1997). Peer consultation group: Doing what works for counselors. *Professional School Counseling, 1*(2), 4-6.

Matthes, W. A. (1992). Induction of counselors into the profession. *The School Counselor, 39,* 245-250.

Paisley, P. O., & Borders, L. D. (1995). School counseling: An evolving specialty. *Journal of Counseling and Development, 74,* 150-153.

Papale, J., Castori, P., & Wilson, J. (Eds.) (2002). *Windows on our classrooms.* The CRESS Center, Division of Education, University of California, Davis.

Quealy-Berge, D., & Caldwell, K. (2004). Mock interdisciplinary staffing: Educating for interprofessional collaboration. *Counselor Education and Supervision, 43*(4), 310-320.

Ragins, B. R., & Cotton, J. L. (1999). Mentor functions and outcomes: A comparison of men and women in formal and informal mentoring relationships. *Journal of Applied Psychology, 84,* 529-550.

Robertson, J. R. (1998). Study groups for counselor professional development. *Professional School Counseling, 1*(4), 59-62.

Roche, G. R. (1979). Much ado about mentors. *Harvard Business Review, 57,* 14-28.

Rowell, L. L. (2005). Collaborative action research and school counselors. *Professional School Counseling, 9*(1), 28-36.

Sagor, R. (1992). *How to conduct collaborative action research.* Alexandria, VA: Association for Supervision and Curriculum Development.

Staton, A. R., & Gilligan, T. D. (2003). Teaching school counselors and school psychologists to work collaboratively. *Counselor Education and Supervision, 42*(3), 162-176.

Stickel, S. A., & Trimmer, K. J. (1994). Knowing in action: A first-year counselor's process of reflection. *Elementary School Guidance & Counseling, 29,* 102-109.

Thomas, S. R. (2001). Beginning high school counselors: A qualitative study of professional socialization and role issues. *Dissertation Abstracts International, 62* (9), 2982. (UMI No. 3026714)

Thomas, S. R. (2005). The school counselor alumni peer consultation group. *Counselor Education & Supervision, 45,* 16-29.

VanZandt, C. E., & Perry, N. S (1992). Helping the rookie school counselor: A mentoring project. *School Counselor, 39*(3), 158-163.

Young, P. G., Sheets, J. M., & Knight, D. D. (2005) *Mentoring principles: Frameworks, agendas, tips, and case studies for mentors and mentees.* Thousand Oaks, CA: Corwin Press, Inc.

Chapter 5

Money Matters – Grant Writing and Funding Your Counseling Program

Debbie Vernon and Steve Rainey

Abstract

An important role for school counselors is that of advocate for resources that are necessary to develop and implement comprehensive programs for the students and families they serve. Grant writing is one way in which school counselors can secure financial resources to develop and maintain school counseling programs. This chapter provides an outline of the grant writing process along with strategies for implementation. A discussion of the potential benefits and challenges encountered is also offered, followed by a discussion of next steps as school counselors explore the world of grant funding. Recommendations for school counselor education programs are also presented.

Introduction

The 21st century professional school counselor is charged with many responsibilities in an ever-changing landscape. In recent years, student achievement mandates and finance reform intended to create accountable and fiscally responsible schools (U.S. Department of Education, 2002) have had a significant impact on this landscape. In the wake of decreased federal, state, and local funding for education, many school districts have resorted to cutting school counseling and mental health services that ultimately support student achievement and development (American Counseling Association [ACA], 2004). Recent reports from the National Center for Education Statistics (U.S. Department of Education, 2005) reported that the national average student to counselor ratio in the United States in the 2003-2004 data year was 488:1. In 15 states, the average well exceeds the national average, let alone the American School Counselor Association's (ASCA, 2003) recommended maximum student to counselor ratio of 250:1.

In light of such changes, school counselors must advocate for resources that are required to maintain comprehensive school counseling programs and related services for the students and families they serve. As change agents, school counselors are in a position to lead the way in seeking additional funding sources that can keep schools safe and minimize risk factors that affect academic achievement. In this chapter, we first discuss the significance of grant writing in a climate of decreasing federal and state dollars appropriated to develop and maintain school counseling programs. Specifically, we address how grant writing fits with ASCA's National Model (2003). An overview of the grant writing process follows, along with strategies for implementation. We also present a discussion of potential benefits and challenges that school counselors may encounter along the way. Finally, the chapter closes with a discussion of next steps school counselors can take to explore the world of external grant funding.

Importance of Grant Writing

In 2003, the American School Counselor Association (ASCA) published *The ASCA National Model: A Framework for School Counseling Programs*. This publication set out to define unifying standards for school counseling programs, including both conceptual principles and a practical model for implementation. In addition, the ASCA National Model (2003) provides a vision of transformation for the school counseling profession as we enter the 21st century. Given the changing landscape of education and its implications for the future, school counselors must seek ways to rise to the challenges associated with funding comprehensive school counseling programs. Grant writing allows school counselors to address the needs of their program and the students they serve (Letsch, 2002). Whether school counselors are seeking funds targeting school counseling program development from the ground up (Foundation) or for specific at-risk populations or direct services to students (Delivery System), grants are available from a variety of sources. These sources may include the federal government, private foundations, or local agencies (Lum, 2005). A resource list is provided at the end of the chapter including Internet links to various grant sources. Since little has been written on the topic of grant writing specific to school counselors, the following sections will provide a description of the grant writing process, the benefits and challenges, and suggestions for additional steps to be taken to further your interest in writing grants for your school counseling program.

A Description of the Grant Writing Process

At first glance, the process of grant writing can be a daunting task for school counselors new to the process. Just mention the topic in a room of school counselors and one can imagine the range of reactions. In most cases, the subject of funding programs, let alone those specific to school counseling, generally elicits some degree of anxiety about the future of funding effective and quality education for all students across the nation. Anxiety also stems from a lack of understanding about the grant writing process itself. In this section, we will describe each step of the grant development process in an effort to provide the reader with a greater understanding and working knowledge of the skills required. Although most grants may not fund an entire school counseling program, federal and state level Departments of Education can provide significant amounts of money to design accountable school counseling program initiatives. For those programs already in place, external funding is also available to supplement existing resources, particularly in targeting academic achievement or focusing on special populations such as violence prevention, or programming for at-risk students (Gysbers & Henderson, 2006).

Grant Planning Stage: Where Do I Start?

The first step in pursuing a grant is to determine goals and develop a basic vision for your program. One way to accomplish this task is to conduct a needs assessment. For an example of a needs assessment, see Brown and Trusty (2005) or Schmidt (2003). According to Ripley, Erford, Dahir, and Eschbach (2003), the needs assessment is a critical component in either identifying the needs of various populations in a school or in establishing the main goals and foci of a comprehensive school counseling program. Whichever rationale fits your need for funding, a needs assessment can help you identify your goals. The more data you have to justify your proposal the better. Funding sources require you to be descriptive and thorough in your explanation of your program goals and objectives. Having a database of data demonstrates that you have done your homework, that you are serious about solving a potential problem in your school, and that your program is a good fit with the mission of the grant source. In short, grant sources want to make sure that their money will be spent effectively and not present a risk to their organization (Letsch,

2002). Depending on the source and scope of your request, you will be asked how many students or people will be affected directly and/or indirectly by your proposed program. When conducting your needs assessment, remember to include various stakeholders and how they may be affected by your program. Stakeholders include students, parents, teachers, administrators, and the community at large (ASCA, 2003).

With the results of your data in hand, the next step involves identifying potential grant sources to fund your program or project. At the federal level, there are many grants available that support school counseling services and related programs (ACA, 2004). The largest grants available are through the *Elementary and Secondary School Counseling Program* (ESSCP), which is a *No Child Left Behind Act* of 2002 (NCLB) initiative (U. S. Department of Education, 2002). Although ESSCP funding decreased to $22 million for FY 2007, grants are made each year to school districts that demonstrate the greatest need or have the most original program proposals (ACA, 2006).

Other sources at the federal level can be located through the Grants.gov Web site, which announces various calls for grant proposals targeting national initiatives such as safe schools, violence, and drug prevention. Funding may also be available through state Departments of Education or other state educational organizations. Those interested in applying for grants are advised to contact the funding agency of interest to ask questions. Examples of successfully funded programs may be available to you for consultation and consideration as you develop your own proposal. Do not be afraid to contact individual districts and/or school counselors who have received grant funding. Often times, their advice can help you with additional ideas for preparing a successful grant application.

State school counseling associations are ideal sources for seeking grant funding. For example the Ohio School Counselor Association (OSCA) offers grants up to $1,000 for innovative programs. At the yearly *All Ohio Counselors Conference*, there is generally a break-out session that addresses how to apply for grants, including examples of successfully funded grant program applications. These presentations provide information and opportunities to ask questions of grant evaluation committee members. The session helps to increase understanding of what is expected and decrease anxiety about applying for grants. This information assisted the first author of this chapter in writing a successful grant proposal for $650 from the Ohio School

Counselor Association (OSCA) in 2005 to provide programming for at-risk students (Vernon, 2006).

There are also many other smaller non-profit organizations and private foundations that have money available to support school counseling programs. Grant money is available to those who are willing to do the research and justify their request. For example, in the first author's school district, mini-grants are available from the local Parent-Teacher Organization (PTO) in amounts ranging from $150 to $500 (Vernon, 2006). These grants are open to teachers and other educational professionals for supplies, curriculum materials, etc. In many cases, mini-grants can help school counselors obtain funding for curriculum materials and other supplies necessary to support their programs. For example, one year the money was used to purchase supplies for small group guidance programs; the next year a television with a built-in DVD and VCR player to be used in our group room was purchased. Larger grants may also be available from the PTO for programs that affect more than one building. For example, grants can be written for district-wide initiatives, such as anti-bullying campaigns, bringing in speakers to present to parents or students, and/or training teachers in intervention and prevention strategies on key issues.

Beyond the school district, school communities can be another rich source of grants. Contacting the school administrative office can help to identify who writes the most grants in a district. This person can provide guidance to a variety of sources and serve as a consultant during the grant seeking process.

As indicated above, there are a number of resources available to school counseling programs seeking grants. A list of resources for potential grant sources is provided at the end of this chapter; however this list is not exhaustive. School counselors who are interested in obtaining funding are encouraged to search a variety of sources to find the source that best matches their program goals with the mission of the funding organization. Once the list of potential sources has been narrowed, the organizations should be contacted and application materials requested. In many cases, the required application materials are accessible through the website of the funding source. It is extremely important that the resources requested are in line with the grant funding source. For example, some grants will not allow requests to pay for additional personnel, but others will. Above all else, it is important to be realistic about what your program or project can reasonably accomplish.

One final suggestion for the planning stage is to remember to seek "buy-in" from key others, meaning all those who may be affected by the grant. The exact process varies from school system to school system and requires special mention because school counselors work with many other educational professionals. Administrators and other stakeholders want to be apprised of any special programming. It is in the best interest of school counseling professionals to work within their systems and to collaborate with key others for easier navigation through the internal approval process before beginning the application process.

Writing the Grant

At this stage, you have defined your school counseling program's needs, identified your grant funding source, and received authorization from appropriate stakeholders within your school community to continue to the writing stage. It is important to familiarize yourself with the application and begin assembling the required support materials. Make note of the deadline, and follow the directions carefully. Allow yourself enough time to write the grant. Most grant applications contain similar sections. These include the following sections: (a) a statement of need; (b) the project goals and objectives; (c) a project description; (d) an actual amount of money requested; (e) a detailed budget for your project; (f) a timeline for implementation; and (g) evaluation procedures and measures. Depending on the grantor, application guidelines may vary. According to Kerney (2005), grant readers are most interested in how well your grant proposal adheres to the guidelines delineated in the application, your attention to each component, and your supply of the information requested by the deadline. Grant sources are also interested in how well the proposal communicates the need for the funding.

Readers of your proposal will have many applications to review. Therefore, it is important to write your application in a manner that is easy to read. That is, it should be written free of jargon, in a clear and concise manner, and with headings for each of the required responses in the application (Letsch, 2002). To ensure you have met these writing suggestions, have others proofread your application and check your math on your budget request before submission of your grant. Failure to address any of these key points may result in rejection of your proposal.

Try to avoid discouragement if your proposal is rejected. In the case of the first author, several first attempts at large grants from community organizations were rejected on the basis of either incomplete information or incorrect addition on the total budget (Vernon, 2006). This did not necessarily mean the proposal idea was bad. Attention to details is part of the proposal evaluation process. Should your proposal be rejected, talk to the grant funding source and ask for feedback on ways to improve your proposal resubmission. Finally, regardless of the outcome, be sure to thank the grantor for considering your proposal (Letsch, 2002).

Implementing the Grant

After what seems like a long waiting period, the much anticipated day comes when the outcome of your grant proposal is received. Once accepted, the grantor will send a packet of information that outlines the requirements for the implementation stage. In many cases, a letter of agreement will have to be signed by the main contact person on the grant and an administrator in your district stating that you agree to implement the grant in accordance with the guidelines outlined by the grantor. Once the signatures are received by the organization, you will receive the funds and can proceed with the implementation of your proposal.

During the implementation stage, there are several key points to consider. First, do what you said you were going to do in your proposal. The timeline you created can help break down the tasks and keep you focused on the steps involved in implementation. Second, make sure you keep good records. This involves both data collection and documentation of expenditures. Maintain all records and materials in a central location. This allows for easy access to materials. Organizing your data and expenditures will help you produce any updates requested by the grant source or other interested stakeholders. Several spreadsheet programs are available to help track data and project expenditures along the way.

A final recommendation is to ask for help if you need it. The 21st century professional school counselor is charged with many responsibilities. In most cases, administration and implementation of the grant proposal is in addition to regular duties. In the case of the first author, someone was needed to help co-lead the group counseling portion of the grant program. Rather than cancel groups due to an unexpected emergency, the district social worker was asked to help. This not only helped implement the grant as proposed, but it also provided services to at-risk students and built additional supports for participants as they transitioned to the high school where the social worker had her office (Vernon,

2006). In addition to in-house support, the grant funding organization can also provide assistance to you if you run into difficulties or have questions along the way. The grantor is interested in your progress and success; so it is important to maintain open communication with the funding source by providing periodic updates.

Final Evaluation of the Grant

After all of the hard work of implementation has concluded, the final task involves providing a final evaluation report to the grant funding source. As the funding period of your grant comes to a close, it is likely that the funding source will send a final evaluation packet to the main contact person. It will include a deadline for submission and an information summary packet. Although the content of the final evaluation will vary by funding source, it typically includes the following: (a) an accounting of your expenditures and original receipts; (b) a summary of goals and objectives including how they were met; (c) a statement of the effectiveness of the project; (d) applicability of your project to other settings; and (e) results of your summative and formative evaluations. According to Letsch (2002), it is important to meet the submission deadline because grant management and dependability are of great importance to the funding source. Your dependability may affect any future applications made to that grant source.

The following grant writing tips should help you in your pursuit of financial support for your counseling program:

Grant Writing Tips

Planning Stage:
1. Identify needs for programming or other resources.
2. Select a funding source that matches your project goals.
3. Keep your project proposal goals simple and realistic. Work with a team.
4. Adhere to the details of the grant application and
5. Follow the guidelines as written.
6. Have extra sets of proofreaders available before you submit the grant.
7. Do not wait until the last minute to submit your grant proposal.

Implementation Stage:
1. Do what you said you were going to do in your grant proposal.
2. Follow your timeline.

3. Collect data along the way.
4. Provide updates to your grant funding source along the way.
5. Track project expenditures and keep copies of receipts.

Evaluation Stage:
1. Have all of your supporting documentation ready to go so that you are not trying to pull it all together at the last minute.
2. Follow the guidelines for submitting your final report as written.
3. Adhere to the deadline for submission of your final report.
4. Remember to thank your funding source for supporting your project.

Short and Long Term Benefits

Beyond simply having more money for the school program, there are other benefits to applying for and receiving grant money. Some of the benefits are relatively short-lived. Obviously, grant money can provide more supplies of a higher quality for programming. When quality supplies and materials are available, programming is more effective, better received, and can reach more students in an efficient manner. Students and faculty recognize when you use highly professional materials. They are more receptive to the content of the programming, and you are perceived as being more professional. With adequate material quality and quantity, your time is used more effectively. Rather than spending time reproducing materials or developing them, you can spend your time implementing your program.

Another short term benefit is that you will be able to try new and innovative programs at no cost to you, your program, or your school. There are many programs available to you for use, but you rarely have the opportunity to try them out without risking large amounts of money. When working within a limited budget, you may be unwilling to spend money on materials that focus on a small, specific population in your school. Grant money can allow you to provide very specific programming to a specific group without damage to your budget.

Other benefits of receiving grant money are more long lasting. The grant writing process requires counselors to evaluate at least a portion of their school counseling program. This evaluation helps to identify areas of student need that may not have otherwise been identified. Going through the grant process also allows school counselors to become more comfortable in conducting this type of assessment. The long term benefit is that once you are more at ease with the process, you are more likely to conduct future assessments. An ongoing needs assessment program will only benefit the students in your school.

A final long term benefit is the perception of school administrators regarding the school counselor who has been able to apply for and receive a grant. Very often, school administrators will view school counselors who successfully obtains grants as being more professional and more committed to their work if they take the initiative to evaluate their program by assessing for needs and take steps to address those needs. Furthermore, if the counselor is able to provide funding through a grant to implement a needed program, the administration will be even more impressed with the counselor's work and the contribution to the comprehensive school counseling program.

Barriers and Challenges to Implementation and How to Address Them

The foremost-cited reason for school counselors' reluctance to evaluate their school counseling programs, a prerequisite for applying for and receiving a grant, is a lack of time (Brown & Trusty, 2005). In order to do the work required to apply for and receive a grant, time must be allotted. Many school counselors work after hours to complete the work. Others have the time provided to them by their administrators. If you are fortunate enough to work on a school counseling team, duties could be divided in a way that would provide you time to work on the grant during your regular work hours. If writing a grant for a project that you alone will be implementing, remember, if you receive the grant, it is an additional responsibility that you are undertaking. If everybody on the team is working on the grant proposal, tasks can be delegated. Be sure to set mini-deadlines along the way, and keep the lines of communication open regarding progress. It is important that the extra tasks associated with the grant process not deter you from moving forward with a request for funding. Many larger districts have personnel whose main duty is to write proposals for grants. If this is your case, all you would have to do is provide the writer the needed information, and they will do much of the work for you.

Another possible barrier is lack of experience and a fear of the process. Addressing this barrier begins with finding appropriate grants for which to apply. We have supplied you with several suggestions of possible sources at the end of this chapter. Worry about whether or not you can write well enough, concern about completing all of the associated paperwork, negotiating the school district bureaucracy, managing money and materials, and other more clerical tasks can sometimes seem overwhelming. Our suggestion is to organize the process step by step. You have overcome these types of challenges as you went through your graduate work and prepared for your first counseling position. Use whatever method worked for you before.

There are also barriers to face once you have received the grant and have implemented the programming. The first author had trouble getting evaluations filled out by parents. She had difficulty finding interested participants, getting original receipts from the district, and funneling money through the purchase order process, which was new to her local school building (Vernon, 2006).

Summary, Conclusions, and Next Steps

Whatever the need, many school counselors are in a unique position to provide leadership as advocates for systemic change. (ASCA, 2003; Bemak, Chi-Ying Chung, & Murphy, 2003; Gysbers & Henderson, 2006; Ripley et al., 2003). As partners in academic achievement, the 21st century professional school counselor can respond to the varied needs of students through developing linkages with resources beyond their own school (Erford, House, & Martin, 2003). As one can see, grant writing is time consuming and challenging; but the benefits far outweigh the challenges.

We were unable to find research on the specific topic of grant writing by school counselors in schools. For those interested in conducting related research, some possible ideas include: (a) counselors' attitudes toward grant writing; (b) how school counseling programs are currently funded; (c) funding sources; and (d) the need for instruction in student advocacy in counselor education programs.

One step in the direction of helping school counselors apply for and receive grant money is by teaching the process to pre-service counselors in counselor education programs. Incorporating a section on grant writing in school counseling courses, possibly at the internship level, may prove to be as beneficial to school counseling programs as any other part of counselor preparation programs. As a course assignment in internship, students could be assigned to find a grant and complete the forms for submission. The instructor and other students could evaluate the quality of the work.

Benefits for the student of this type of assignment include: (1) gaining experience in grant writing; (2) having a grant application completed to be added to their job search portfolio; (3) having a completed application that could possibly be modified and submitted once they have a position; and (4) having an application that they may be able to submit for the school in which they are conducting their internship.

Counselor education programs could also provide instruction to internship supervisors and other local school counselors on the process of grant writing. Universities and state and local school counseling and counselor education organizations could host workshops on grant writing. The opportunities for collaboration between institutions for grant writing instruction are limited only by the participating professionals' imagination.

Scenarios for Discussion
SCENARIO I

Suppose you are an elementary school counselor, the only one in your building. You work approximately 45-50 hours each week, and you have a very limited budget. You are aware that many of your students are latchkey kids, and you want to help them to be safer after school.

1. How would you demonstrate the need for an after-school program?
2. What funding sources would you consider?
3. How would you find the time to do the preliminary work needed?
4. Who within your district could be helpful in the grant writing process?
5. Should you receive the grant, how would you find time and personnel to conduct the program?

SCENARIO II
Suppose you are a high school counselor, and you have three counseling colleagues in the building with you. You have discovered many students in your school have aspirations of attending college; however, their parents did not. These students need support in negotiating the application process and in overcoming any other barriers they may face.

1. How would you propose your idea to your colleagues?
2. If you got agreement from you colleagues, what steps would you put into place in order to move through the grant process?

3. What responsibilities do you foresee, and how would you go about dividing those responsibilities?
4. Who, outside the school district, may be able to provide assistance to you in the application and implementation processes?
5. To whom would you plan to report results?

References

American Counseling Association, Office of Public Policy and Legislation. (2004). *No child left behind: Sources of funding that support school counseling and mental health services.* Alexandria, VA: Author.

American Counseling Association. (2006, June). *Elementary and secondary school counseling program (ESSCP) and FY 2007 federal education funding.* Retrieved July 17, 2006, from http://www.counseling.org/PublicPolicy/PositionPapers.aspx?AGuid=8d08ec97-286e-4b85-ae5c-a053093894d0

American School Counselor Association. (2003). *The ASCA national model: A framework for school counseling programs.* Alexandria, VA: Author.

Bemak, F., Chi-Ying Chung, R., & Murphy, C. S. (2003). A new perspective on counseling at-risk youth. In B. T. Erford (Ed.), *Transforming the school counseling profession* (pp. 285-296). Upper Saddle River, NJ: Pearson Education.

Brown, D. & Trusty, J. (2005). *Developing and leading comprehensive school counseling programs: Promoting student competence and meeting student needs.* Belmont, CA: Brooks Cole.

Erford, B. T., House, R., & Martin, P. (2003). *Transforming the school counseling profession.* In B. T. Erford (Ed.), Transforming the school counseling profession (pp. 1-38). Upper Saddle River, NJ: Pearson Education.

Gysbers, N. C., & Henderson, P. (2006). *Developing and managing your school guidance and counseling program* (4th ed.). Alexandria, VA: American Counseling Association.

Kerney, C. A. (2005, June). *Inside the mind of a grant reader.* Retrieved July 22, 2006, from http://www.techlearning.com/story/showArticle.jhtml?articleID=164300838

Letsch, D. (2002). Catch the cash. *ASCA School Counselor, 40*, 32-35.

Lum, C. (2005). *Getting a grant: Sources of funding and how to pursue them.* Alexandria, VA: American Counseling Association Office of Public Policy and Legislation. (ERIC Document Reproduction Service No. ED484779)

Ripley, V., Erford, B. T., Dahir, C., & Eschbach, L. (2003). Planning and implementing a 21st century comprehensive developmental school counseling program. In B. T. Erford (Ed.), *Transforming the School Counseling Profession* (pp. 63-120). Upper Saddle River, NJ: Pearson Education.

Schmidt, J. J. (2003). *Counseling in schools: Essential services and comprehensive programs.* (4th ed.). Boston: Allyn and Bacon.

U.S. Department of Education. (2002, January). *No child left behind act of 2001* (Public Law 107-110). Retrieved July 19, 2006, from http://www.ed.gov/policy/elsec/leg/esea02/index.html

U.S. Department of Education, National Center for Education Statistics. (2005, October). *United States student-to-counselor ratios* [U.S. Schools Overall]. Retrieved July 17, 2006, from http://www.counseling.org/PublicPolicy/TP/ResourcesForSchoolCounselors/CT2.aspx

Vernon, D. (2006, June). *Grant writing 101.* Paper presented at the meeting of the American School Counselor Association, Chicago, IL.

Resources for Grants

American Counseling Association Web site (Links to Press Room, Public Policy, Resources): http://www.counseling.org/

American School Counselor Association. (2004). *The ASCA national model workbook.* Alexandria, VA: Author.

American School Counselor Association (ASCA) Foundation: http://www.schoolcounselor.org/content.asp?contentid=176

American School Counselor Association Resource Center (members only): http://www.schoolcounselor.org/resources_list.asp?c=15&i=14

Bill & Melinda Gates Foundation: http://www.gatesfoundation.org/Education/

Corporation for Public Broadcasting: http://www.cpb.org/

The Foundation Center: http://fdncenter.org/

The George Lucas Educational Foundation: http://www.edutopia.org/foundation/grant.php

Grants.gov: http://grants.gov/

The National Education Association (NEA) Foundation for the Improvement of Education: http://www.neafoundation.org/

Philanthropy News Digest: http://foundationcenter.org/pnd/

School Grants: http://www.schoolgrants.org/proposal_samples.htm

State School Counselor Associations: http://www.schoolcounselor.org/content.asp?pl=127&sl=179&contentid=179

Target Corporation: http://sites.target.com/site/en/corporate/page.jsp?contentId=PRD03-001818

The U.S. Department of Education: http://www.ed.gov/fund/landing.jhtml?src=rt

The Wallace Foundation: http://www.wallacefoundation.org/WF/GrantsPrograms/FocusAreasPrograms/SchoolCounseling/SchoolCounselingReform.htm

Other Places to Search: local parent-teacher organizations, local school districts, community-based foundations and organizations, professional organizations, local universities, hospitals, and mental health agencies, word of mouth, conferences, talking with various community stakeholders about areas of interest, and local newspapers

Chapter 6

School Counselors and Research: A Missing Link in Professional Identity?

Lonnie L. Rowell

Abstract

The school counseling research summit is a useful tool for strengthening the link between practice and research. This chapter describes experiences with organizing the 2005 California School Counseling Research Summit. The description is grounded in issues of professional identity related to the practitioner-scientist model of professional counselor preparation. Ideas for organizing school counseling research summits are presented along with a discussion of themes that can be addressed through a summit.

Introduction

Little seems to have changed in attempting to address the question posed by Loesch (1988) twenty years ago regarding whether the phrase 'school counseling research' was an oxymoron. Current literature (e.g., Bauman, 2004) continues to discuss the lack of interest in research by school counselors. Even the assertion that the profession itself is at-risk because it lacks solid evidence that school counseling programs "produce positive results for children" (Whiston, 2002, p. 153) seems to have done little to generate a significant response from the school counseling professional community.

Yet, some efforts have been made to address the gap between practice and research in school counseling. Individual researchers, of course, continue to publish scholarly work in *Professional School Counseling*, the field's top peer-reviewed professional journal, in the American Counseling Association's *Journal of Counseling and Development*, and in other journals. As web-based resources proliferate, other means of disseminating new knowledge have emerged and have begun to impact the discussion of the research-practice gap in school counseling. For example, The Center for Outcome-Based Research in School Counseling at the University of Massachusetts Amherst (UMASS) has been a strong advocate for evidence-based practice and the Center's web-based Research Briefs seek to make research "widely available and highlight the implications of the research for school counseling leadership and

practice" (2007). Other approaches to dissemination and to generating broader discussion of the research-practice gap also have emerged. For example, the American School Counselor Association (ASCA) convened research summits in 2003 and 2004 in conjunction with its annual conference to explore the issue of the research-practice gap, and a few states have begun to follow suit with state school counseling research summits (e.g., Arizona School Counselor Association, 2004; Center for Student Support Systems, 2005). Such summits increase interaction between university researchers and school counselors and provide venues for reflection on how best to address the research-practice gap.

National and state-focused school counseling centers also have been established with some of them having a strong research focus. Three university-based centers have been actively involved in disseminating research and other publications that highlight the links between school counseling practice and research (i.e., UMASS' Center for Outcome-Based Research in School Counseling; The University of San Diego's Center for Student Support Systems [CS3]; and, the Iowa School Counseling Research Center [SCRC]). All are fairly new and are in the early stages of their development, although the UMASS center is widely linked to educational, counseling, and university web sites across the country.

In 2003, the Education Trust, in partnership with the MetLife Foundation, established the National Center for Transforming School Counseling (NCTSC). This center focuses on aligning school counseling with the Education Trust's agenda of promoting high academic standards for all students. According to the center's web site, "The NCTSC is a nation-wide network of organizations, state departments of education, school counselor professional associations, institutions of higher education and school districts currently involved in the transforming school counseling initiative. Through the center, the networked sites form a community of influence to transform the field of school counseling into a force for promoting standards-based education reform" (Education Trust, 2007). One of

NCTSC's key objectives is to collect, analyze, and disseminate research on effective school counseling practices.

The centers mentioned are serving as hubs for the collection, organization, and dissemination of information and as points of reference for practitioners to stay informed regarding training and professional development opportunities in their regions, states, and on a national level as well. Such centers often work in conjunction with school-based and other partnership-based projects that serve the school counseling professional community. For example, the Center for Student Support Systems (CS3) established a clearinghouse project in conjunction with the recent addition of $200 million in new program funding for school counseling for grades 7-12 in California. The AB 1802 Clearinghouse Project features AB1802Clearinghouse.com, a web site for student support professionals and school administrators engaged in the implementation of AB 1802. The Clearinghouse was established in partnership with the Los Angeles County Office of Education's California Counselor Leadership Academy. The California Association of School Counselors (CASC) and The Western Association of College Admissions Counseling (WACAC) are co-sponsors of the Clearinghouse web site, and the Clearinghouse operates in cooperation with the California Department of Education. The purpose of the web site is to provide comprehensive, reviewed, updated information on implementation, research, and on-going professional development associated with the Supplemental School Counseling Program established by AB 1802. Projects such as this can encourage innovation in the field and help facilitate communication among practitioners. In the first two months of operation, the AB1802Clearinghouse web site received more than 7,000 hits.

Given the newness of many of the efforts described above, school counseling appears to be in the early stages of an internal transformation. With support from university training programs, interventions and advocacy by high powered groups such as the Education Trust, the diligence and creative efforts of visionary school counseling model developers (e.g., Norm Gysbers, and Sharon Johnson and Curly Johnson), a set of National Standards (ASCA, 2003) and a strong network of national and state professional associations, school counseling may be finding its way towards a stronger sense of itself as a profession. However, the journey needs to include more than simply an awareness of the

need for data or a grudging acceptance of the necessity to add "data-driven" (ASCA, 2003, p. 16) to the descriptors of school counseling programs. Indeed, the school counseling strategy examined in this chapter has to do with the realignment of our understanding of what it means to be a school counselor.

I will seek to interest readers in this realignment through a brief and pragmatic description. To prevent the chapter from drifting into the stratosphere of phenomenology and epistemology, I will ground the discussion in a description of a simple tool to help strengthen school counseling's emergence as a strong and indispensable profession in the American system of education. This tool is the School Counseling Research Summit. A Research Summit is useful in generating dialogue on the research-practice gap and seeking creative solutions to the problems of practitioner disengagement from research. The chapter is based primarily on my experience with organizing a summit in partnership with a state school counseling association. I also draw on communication with colleagues in Arizona regarding their work on a Research summit. The School Counseling Research Summit can be a small, leader-and-state-association focused event (e.g., Arizona) or a large-scale event linked to an emerging strategy for linking universities and school counselors in practitioner-driven research initiatives (e.g., California). Whatever the scope of the event, the two questions examined below can serve as guides in taking the all important first step, that is, being determined to take action within one's state or local area to address the research-practice gap.

The School Counseling Research Summit

Who gathers? By definition, a summit is a gathering of leaders. This was reflected in the ASCA national research summits and the Arizona School Counselor Association Research Summit. The focus was on bringing together school counselor association leaders to hear updates on the state of research in school counseling and to participate in discussions concerning how practitioners might become more involved with research. In the 2005 California Summit, however, a different approach was taken. For this summit, the attention was shifted from established leaders to potential leaders, and from a leadership hierarchy reflected in professional associations to a more horizontal (Friedman, 2006) leader-practitioner model that emphasized empowering school counselors in partnership with counselor educators, researchers, and graduate students in counseling. Through this approach, the California summit gathered more than 250 participants for the day-long event at the University of San Diego's Institute for Peace and Justice.

As will be discussed later, this more democratic approach to convening a summit is not without problems. However, the California planning team wanted to involve a wide range of participants as a way to activate engagement with building a strategic research agenda for school counseling in the state. In this spirit, the goals of the Summit were to begin the process of building an active coalition in California, to highlight the value of action research as a viable tool for school counselors, to share best practices, and to establish a sustainable collaboration among a wide range of individuals concerned about the state of school counseling and school counseling research. The intention was to build a coalition involving university faculty and school counselors around the state and to have this coalition take on a leadership role in identifying statewide priorities for research on the practice of school counseling. There are, of course, many other options for framing the work of a research summit. What seems crucial is to give careful thought to both who the participants will be and what outcomes the organizers are seeking. In some states, a small gathering might be the best way to begin; in others, it may make more sense to try to get as broad a participation as possible, with the understanding that in either scenario there will be a need for follow-up.

How do you plan a summit? The planning process for the California summit was facilitated by staff of the Center for Student Support Systems (CS3). In my capacity as Director of the center, I first approached the California Association of School Counselors (CASC) to see if they would be interested in co-sponsoring and helping to organize a California Summit after attending and presenting at the ASCA summits in 2003 and 2004. In January 2005, the board of CASC voted to co-sponsor the summit and to share organizing responsibilities with CS3. The author agreed to serve as chair of the planning effort. CS3 regularly provides graduate students in school counseling with leadership opportunities related to the center's work, and the summit became one of those opportunities. Two graduate students accepted leadership in the planning and coordinating of the event, and together we developed a plan for moving from concept to reality. A Planning Committee consisting of counselors, counselor educators, and representatives from CASC was assembled and began working by April

2005. An on-line chat space was arranged by one of the graduate students, and most of the committee's planning took place during a series of scheduled on-line meetings. This approach was essential given California's size. There was no possibility for travel to a central meeting place as the Planning Committee had a very limited budget.

To pay for the event, sponsorships were secured from university counselor training programs, the state school counselor association, a local school counselor association, and a local service club with a long record of support for elementary school counseling. In addition, the author received a grant from the University of San Diego's Academic Strategic Priorities Fund that helped pay for a major portion of the summit. Registration fees were kept to a minimum as a way of encouraging significant registration for the summit.

Given the one-day format for the summit and the broad scope of the issue, it was a challenge to decide on the best structure for the day. The basic schedule was 8:45 AM until 5 PM. The event was held in a facility that had a large auditorium (capacity of 300) and numerous breakout rooms. After much discussion and thought, the Planning Committee agreed on the following structure for the day:

- Welcome, Introduction/Overview
- Panel Discussion: Issues in school district use of data
- Panel Discussion: Issues in practitioner use of data
- Breakout sessions – (focused on research-based presentations)
- Panel Discussion: Critical issues in school counseling research
- Luncheon
- Poster Session – (for presentation of graduate student research)
- Work Groups – (focused on aspects of moving forward in addressing the research-practice group – this is where the Planning Committee hoped to build on the momentum generated by the event.)
- Closing Plenary Session (reports from the work groups, sharing regarding how the summit went, summing up the day)

We used the opening session to provide background on the summit, to emphasize the themes for the day, and to address logistical issues. The themes we had chosen were:

- Evidence-based practice and strategic interventions in school counseling
- Establishing an appetite for research in school counseling

- Establishing a California data base for school counseling
- Action research and changing practice in school counseling
- Research on implementing The National Model for School Counseling
- Domain-specific research agendas: Academic Development, Personal/Social Development, and Career Development
- Tools for accountability

These themes emerged from the Planning Committee's on-line conversations. They reflect a fairly diverse set of interests in relationship to the research-practice gap. In our planning work we viewed this diversity as a strength and did not want to narrow down the list. Our intention was to put a lot out on the table and trust that when the gathering took place we would be able to sort out and prioritize the steps that would need to be taken to keep us moving forward.

Discussion

In hindsight, we may have taken on too much with this many themes. Although we did address each of the themes through the breakout sessions, poster session, and work groups, the wide range of background and experience with research forced us to slow down to provide background information at some points and diluted the potential for achieving desired outcomes. Fewer themes may have made it easier for us to focus and to develop a stronger sense of direction for the summit follow-up. Yet, the mix of practitioners, university faculty, and graduate students contributed to a strong sense of collaboration, and interactions among summit participants bridged the interpersonal gaps that are a part of the overall research-practice gap in school counseling. This was very evident during the poster session, which was provided as an opportunity for graduate students and practitioners engaged in research and data-collection-and display projects to present their work. Students from three universities contributed projects as did elementary counselors from one large Southern California district, and counselors, counselor educators, and graduate students mixed freely while viewing the posters and discussing the contents with the presenters.

We had hoped that the Work Group meetings would constitute the nucleus for the follow-up work we wanted to see happen. Each work group was assigned a facilitator or co-facilitators along with at least two notetakers. In the closing plenary meeting, each work group reported out on their efforts and although it seemed that very good discussions had taken place, the diversity of directions brought back to the large group raised many more questions than we had time to answer. However, the notes from all these sessions proved very useful in the planning work done for Summit II, convened in December 2007.

Conclusion

The school counseling research summit can be an important step in bridging the gap between research and practice. The planning of a summit opens up new conversations between and among counselors, counselor educators, and graduate students. The summit event provides an opportunity for reflection and for initiating steps to strengthen the involvement of university counselor training programs with school-based, practitioner-initiated projects, including collaborative action research (Rowell, 2005). A full report on the content of the summit and the outcomes of the working groups and closing plenary session is available from the Center for Student Support Systems (http://www.sandiego.edu /academics/soles/instcenter / studentsupp/). A manuscript examining the summit experience in depth has been submitted for publication (Rowell, Thomas, Valot, & Grewal, in review). The present chapter provides a brief overview of the summit as a tool for bridging the gap between research and practice.

A school counseling research summit is not a quick-fix to the challenges of the research-practice gap. Indeed, there is no such fix. As Brown and Trusty (2005) indicated, the diversity of components in fully implemented school counseling programs confound attempts to show that such programs "are responsible for specific outcomes" (p. 2). Instead, the kind of positive results counselors need to produce may be limited to "strategic interventions aimed at increasing academic achievement" (Brown & Trusty, p. 1), and if this is the case, then school counseling researchers may need to shift their attention away from large scale program implementation (even when such approaches are advocated by ASCA) to smaller scale targeted interventions. This may mean that advocacy for comprehensive guidance and counseling programs, such as the ASCA National Model, will need to rely on strong rationales not necessarily backed up by empirical evidence of their efficacy. In the meantime, the careful work of strengthening the link between practice and research can be attended to at the school-site and school district levels, in part through the efforts of university faculty and school counselors working collaboratively and in part through the efforts of practitioner-researchers who emerge in conjunction with the work of state school counseling summits.

Whatever the outcomes of school counseling research summits, the effort to address the relationship between counseling practice and counseling research will continue to be challenging. Research is a part of the professional identity of counselor educators in large part because the trio of teaching, research, and service defines the role and functions of professors in virtually every field, and faculty in higher education understand that they must divide their work time between the three. For school counselors, however, the situation is different. Many have been trained in master's programs that offer little in the way of integrating a research disposition with clinical knowledge and skills. In fact, in terms of the research orientation of counselor training faculty, Brems, Johnson and Gallucci (1996) found that the research literature of both clinical and counseling psychology was generated by a very small percentage of those designated as professional clinical or counseling psychologists. Thus, it should come as no surprise that most master's level graduates feel disengaged from research.

School counselors may take some comfort in knowing that they are not alone in questioning the relationship between research and practice. Although the benchmark 1949 Boulder Conference on Graduate Education in Clinical Psychology clearly established a model of professional preparation in psychology that emphasized training as scientists and as practitioners (Petersen, 2007), this model has come under criticism from a variety of sources (see, for example, Brems, Johnson, & Gallucci, 1996; Lampropoulos & Spengler, 2002). The scientist-practitioner model was developed during the post-WWII period as psychology flourished in the United States (Petersen, 2007). Since that time, the limitations of the medical model in counseling and clinical psychology, the model on which the scientist-practitioner approach was predicated, have been widely discussed. In the 1990s, an American Psychological Association sponsored group sought to resolve some of the issues and concluded that further research was needed to examine "whether training programs are accurately employing the foundations and assumptions of the model" (Jones & Mehr, 2007, p. 771).

Although in the domain of school counseling practice, research may well be a foreigner, with practitioners showing little inclination to read the formal research of their field or participate in conducting research, there are signs that the situation is beginning to change. Practitioners show awareness of the pressures associated with demands for greater accountability (e.g., Dahir & Stone, 2003; Fairchild & Seeley, 1995; Isaacs, 2003) including calls for the adoption of counseling and guidance models that are evidence-based (Dimmit, Carey, & Hatch, 2007) or results-based (Johnson, Johnson, and Downs, 2006) or data driven (ASCA, 2003). As this awareness continues to evolve, an increase in critical reflection on the relationship between research and practice in school counseling (e.g., Bauman, 2004; Brown & Trusty, 2005) likely will continue as will an intensified search for stronger collaboration between university researchers and practitioners in the field (e.g., Rowell, 2005, 2006;). Whatever directions these reflections might take us in, we will not be able to escape the reality that, as Heppner, Kivlighan, and Wampold (1992) asserted, "To be credible, reliable and effective, a profession must be built on dependable facts or truths" (p. 5). Whatever model or approach is used in furthering developing the credibility, reliability, and effectiveness of school counseling, research will be a part of the effort. Addressing the gap between research and practice will thus remain a critical element in strengthening school counseling as a profession.

Discussion Questions

1) What are some of the steps being taken in addition to school counseling research summits to address the research-practice gap?
2) Discuss the key stakeholders who may need to be included in the planning of a school counseling research summit.
3) Compare the challenges and opportunities of organizing a school counseling research summit in a small state versus a large state (e.g., Texas, New York, California).
4) Discuss the author's assertion that school counseling's future as a profession cannot be separated from addressing the research-practice gap.
5) Describe a scenario for a school district in which research and practice are seriously linked and continuously reflected on. What would this situation look like? How would the linkage be maintained and how would reflection be incorporated into the regular work of school counselors?
6) How would you improve the summit schedule presented by the author? What time would you allocate for the different components of the summit you would design?

7) If you woke up tomorrow and there was no more research-practice gap, how would the work of school counselors be diffcrent in an inner-city high school with a high percentage of students at-risk of academic failure? In a suburban high school with a wealth of resources and a student population that is 95% college bound?

References

American School Counselor Association [ASCA]. (2003). *The ASCA national model: A framework for school counseling programs.* Alexandria, VA: Author.

Arizona School Counselors Association. (2004, November). *Summit packet.* Material presented at the Arizona School Counselors Association Research Summit, Tucson, AZ.

Bauman, S. (2004). School counselors and research revisited. *Professional School Counseling, 7,* 141-151.

Brems, C., Johnson, M. E., & Gallucci, P. (1996). Publication productivity of clinical and counseling psychologists. *Journal of Clinical Psychology, 52*(6), 723-725.

Brown, D., & Trusty, J. (2005) School counselors, comprehensive school counseling programs, and academic achievement: Are school counselors promising more than they can deliver? *Professional School Counseling, 9,* 1-8.

Center for Outcome-Based Research in School Counseling, University of Massachusetts Amherst. (2007). *Research briefs.* Retrieved March 18, 2007, from http://www.umass.edu/schoolcounseling/briefs.htm

Center for Student Support Systems (CS3). (2005, December). *Summit information packet.* Material presented at the California School Counseling Research Summit, San Diego, CA.

Dahir, C. A., & Stone, C. B. (2003). Accountability: A M.E.A.S.U.R.E. of the impact school counselors have on student achievement. *Professional School Counseling, 6,* 214-322.

Dimmitt, C., Carey, J. C., & Hatch, T. (2007). *Evidence-based school counseling: Making a difference with data-driven practices.* Thousand Oaks, CA: Corwin Press.

Education Trust. (2007). *National Center for Transforming School Counseling at The Education Trust.* Retrieved March 18, 2007, from http://www2.edtrust.org/EdTrust/Transforming+School+Counseling/main

Fairchild, T. N., & Seeley, T. J. (1995). Accountability strategies for school counselors: A baker's dozen. *The School Counselor, 42,* 377-393.

Friedman, T. L. (2006). *The world is flat* (Updated and Expanded). NY: Farrar, Straus, and Giroux.

Heppner, P. P., Kivlighan, D. M., Jr., & Wampold, B. E. (1992). *Research design in counseling.* Pacific Grove, CA: Brooks/Cole.

Isaacs, M. L. (2003). Data-driven decision-making: The engine of accountability. *Professional School Counseling, 6,* 288-296.

Johnson, S., Johnson, C., & Downs, L. (2006). *Building a results-based student support system.* Boston: Lahaska Press.

Jones, J. L., & Mehr, S. L. (2007). Foundations and assumptions of the scientist-practitioner model. *American Behavioral Scientist, 50*(6), 766-771.

Lampropoulos, G. K., & Spengler, P. M. (2002). Introduction: Reprioritizing the role of science in a realistic version of the scientist-practitioner model. *Journal of Clinical Psychology, 58*(10), 1195-1197.

Loesch, L. C. (1988). Is "school counseling research" an oxymoron? In G. R. Walz (Ed.), *Building strong school counseling programs:1987 conference papers* (pp. 169-180). Alexandria, VA: American Association for Counseling and Development.

Petersen, C. (2007). A historical look at psychology and the scientist-practitioner model. *American Behavioral Psychologist, 50*(6), 758-765.

Rowell, L., Thomas, S., Valot, B., & Grewal, B. (manuscript in review). The California School Counseling Research Summit: Addressing the gap between practice and research.

Rowell, L. L. (2005). Collaborative action research and school counselors. *Professional School Counseling, 9,* 28-36.

Rowell, L. L. (2006). Action research and school counseling: Closing the gap between research and practice. *Professional School Counseling, 9,* 376-384.

Whiston, S. C. (2002). Response to the past, present, and future of school counseling: Raising some issues. *Professional School Counseling, 5,* 148-157.

Additional Resources

Anderson, G. L., Herr, K., & Nihlen, A. S. (1994). *Studying your own school: An educator's guide to qualitative practitioner research*. Thousand Oaks, CA: Corwin.

Astramovich, R. L., Coker, J. K., & Hoskins, W. J. (2005). Training school counselors in program evaluation. *Professional School Counseling, 9*, 49-54.

Center for Outcome-Based Research in School Counseling, University of Massachusetts Amherst. (2007). *Research briefs*. Retrieved March 18, 2007

Elliott, J. (1991). *Action research for educational change*. Milton Keynes, England: Open University Press.

Gillies, R. M. (1993). Action research for school counselors. *The School Counselor, 41*, 69-72.

Hart, P. J., & Jacobi, M. (1992). *From gatekeeper to advocate: Transforming the role of the school counselor*. New York: The College Board.

Johnson, A. P. (2005). *A short guide to action research*. (2nd ed.). Boston: Pearson.

McTaggart, R. (Ed.). (1997). *Participatory action research*. Albany, NY: SUNY Press.

Ponte, P. (1995). Action research as a further education strategy for school counselling and guidance. *Educational Action Research, 3*, 287-303.

Reason, P., & Torbert, W. R. (2001). The action turn: Toward a transformational social science. *Concepts and Transformations, 6*, 1-37.

Rowell, L. L. (2004). *Guide to collaborative action research in school counseling* (2nd ed.). (Center publications: Center for Student Support Systems). San Diego, CA: University of San Diego.

Sagor, R. (1992). *How to conduct collaborative action research*. Alexandria, VA: Association for Supervision and Curriculum Development.

Section II.
Leadership Issues and Challenges: School Counselors Leading Educational Reform

Chapter 7

School Counselors Leading Change

Regina M. Schaefer and Donna Cleman

Abstract

This chapter reflects the collaboration of a former school counselor, now university professor, who brings to the table her knowledge of proven organizational change theories, with a practicing school counselor, who has recently facilitated the institutionalization of a comprehensive guidance program at her school. The authors examine the eight-step change theory of John Kotter (1996) and draw a direct connection with the process of change that took place in the guidance department at an intermediate school in California. The intent is that this chapter may serve as a guide and springboard for other school counselors contemplating the need for change in their schools.

Introduction

In 2005, I wrote an article entitled "Dragging the Wooly Mammoth: School Counselors Leading Change," (Schaefer, 2005) in which I described a dream which had been shared with me when I was a school counselor in a large, urban high school of 3,000 students. It was a very hot day, and the principal and I were slowly making our way across the library quad toward her office. She was momentarily seeking some solace and understanding amidst the criticism and resistance to change she was experiencing. This highly educated and experienced woman was one in a series of seven administrators who had revolved through the fast moving door of the administration building over an extremely tumultuous period at the school.

She said, almost apologetically, "Regina, I had a most terrible dream last night. I was exerting an enormous amount of energy trying to walk across this quad from the library to the administration building, but I could not even go a few steps. I kept straining and pulling to move myself forward. Exhausted, I finally glanced over my shoulder and realized that I was harnessed to a wooly mammoth which I was expected to drag behind me."

I do not remember my reply on that day; but, in true Jungian style, her dream has stayed with me ever since as a metaphor for the degree of struggle which

often seems to accompany change in systems. Promoting change, even small changes, can seem overwhelming. This is especially true in schools and educational systems encrusted with bureaucratic regulation and longstanding tradition. Formidable obstacles to forward movement abound. The image of an extinct, elephant-like animal being strapped to the back of a lone administrator is a perfect one to express the emotions that are generated when individuals gaze into the face of needed changes within these educational systems.

While the dreamer in this case was a principal, we know that as school counselors we are called forth to be leaders in the schools, to participate in the leadership teams, and to vision better situations for all students. Specifically, we, as school counselors, certainly can relate to the feeling of "tugging" at change processes, like lugging around a nine-ton, extinct animal – a "wooly mammoth."

So what help is available to us as school counselors who wish to improve the lot of our students and of our colleagues? In that first article, I proposed that school counselors, when faced with the daunting task of promoting change, seek help from the world of business administration and organizational theory. The experience of gifted business leaders, masters of organizational change, can be utilized just as nicely in educational settings as they are in business organizations. Why do we as school counselors and educators seek to "reinvent the wheel" of management technique, so thoroughly studied and practiced by business administrators? Why do we not search across disciplines for tools and maps that are already available? As school counselors, are we even aware that change models have been in operation in businesses for centuries and have been tried and tested repeatedly?

Kotter's Eight Step Model for Leading Change

Dr. John P. Kotter, an award-winning expert on leadership at Harvard Business School, is the author of *Leading Change, The Heart of Change, What Leaders Really Do, Matsuhita Leadership, The New Rule*, and other works. Within two years of the publication of his seminal book *Leading Change*, his eight-step formula for leading change was being used by more organizations in North America than any other single change model. In 2002, Dr. Kotter again set forth his model in *The Heart of Change*, this time adding an emphasis on appealing to the emotions of those being asked to change and not purely relying on logical steps to persuade. With the publication of *The Heart of Change* (2002), Dr. Kotter was approached by Dan S.Cohen, of Deloitte Consulting, who then produced a workbook style guide, *The Heart of Change Field Guide* (2005), to accompany that text.

Following is a detailed discussion of Kotter's eight-step formula. For each step, an example from Oak Avenue Intermediate School is provided, thus emphasizing the practical application of Kotter's theory in the world of school counseling.

Step 1. Increase Urgency

"An object at rest or traveling in uniform motion will remain at rest or traveling in uniform motion unless and until an external force is applied."

Sir Isaac Newton

This step deals with inertia. Human beings, as well as school systems, tend to "travel in uniform motion" or "remain at rest" unless acted upon by an outside force. How often have you looked around your school or classrooms and wondered, sometimes silently and sometimes right out loud, " How long are we going to keep on doing this?" Recognize that you are not alone and that you are personally experiencing the "urgency" addressed in Kotter's first step. Dr. Kotter would suggest that what is needed for change is for you to assist others to sense the same necessity or urgency for change that you are experiencing.

Kotter is strong in his belief that those being asked to change must "see" and "feel" the "why," rather than being solely convinced in a logical, analytical way. Writing articles or putting out memos won't do it! Data can help you. It is hard to argue with the facts. The impending visit by an accreditation team is a fertile time to initiate change in an educational system. Persistent insistence by the parent advisory council or community members is also a potent means for creating "urgency."

At Oak Avenue Intermediate School in Temple City, California, the lone counselor had recently finished her Master of Arts degree in school counseling and had been educated in the benefits of a comprehensive school guidance program. In her counselor education program, the notion of providing guaranteed services for all students was introduced. Realizing that the needs of all students were not adequately being addressed at Oak Avenue Intermediate School and knowing that there was a better way to do businesss, she keenly experienced Kotter's "urgency for change" on a daily level. She was aware that the counseling system was disorganized and not as effective as it should have been in reaching all students.

A specific plan for addressing the problem had not been discussed in the district, but there was a suggestion made by district administration that all counselors in the district attend the California Counselor Leadership Academy (CCLA) in Arrowhead, California. Often when one "corner" of an institution or system feels the urgency for change, if voiced, other "corners" will reply with synchronous actions. That was the case in the Temple City Unified School District; and attendance at the Counselor Leadership Academy that year was the Newtonian "external force" which created a shift in direction. It "started the ball rolling."

Step 2. Build the Guiding Team

It is a real temptation for leaders to attempt to push forward a change "Lone Ranger style." There are many reasons for this, but research and excellent management practice warn against going it alone. The 19th century Oxford scholar Benjamin Jowett says it well: "The way to get things done is not to mind who gets the credit for doing them."

An individual school counselor who senses that the need for a change is urgent at his/her school would be well advised to always build a change team. Change initiatives seldom succeed when the initiator works in isolation.

Graduate students, asked why they are pursuing school counseling as a career, often say, "I want to help kids," or "I want to make a difference in the lives of students." In order to assure that this happens, it is essential that the practicing school counselor be skilled in the art of collaboration, knowing how to construct and guide teams to ensure the success of the change efforts, which they may wish to promote.

When constructing a change team, school counselors should assess not only the interest that prospective members of a team have in the change, but also the power factor that each member of the team holds within the district or community. As a group, the members of your team must represent executive level support, have the ability to secure necessary resources for the change initiative, represent wide segments of your school and community, and possess interpersonal skills such as motivation, enthusiasm, and problem-solving.

Be sure that your team does not include too many people (Kotter suggests not more than twelve), so that the business at hand does not become unwieldy. The process of conducting business must not overshadow the initial reason for the team's existence. In some cases, several intersecting teams may be necessary to move your change initiative forward.

In the Temple City Unified School District (TCUSD), a team had already been formed to create the district Support Personnel Accountability Report Card (SPARC). (A detailed discussion of SPARC is presented in Chapter 10 in this book). It was this existing team that transformed into the "change team" for the comprehensive guidance program at Oak Avenue Intermediate School. The change team consisted of two administrators, two counselors, teachers, a school psychologist, and members of the Parent Teacher Student Association (PTSA). At every step of the process, the members of the team reached out and elicited the support of their administration and PTSA. These individuals would be able to secure the community and district support that was necessary for the change effort to proceed.

The team began by asking administrators for help. Giving the highest respect to the effort, administrators attended workshops and conferences with the counselors and learned together with counselors about comprehensive guidance. The counselors and administrators jointly presented the change proposal for instituting a comprehensive guidance program at Oak Avenue Intermediate at a California Counselor Leadership Academy Roundtable meeting.

The change team worked with Drs. Curly and Sharon Johnson (counselor educators and pioneers of results-based counseling theory) throughout the process to ensure that they had a clear model to follow for creating the comprehensive guidance program. Drs. Johnson assisted the team in creating a presentation which the counselors and assistant superintendent showcased with the Board of Education.

The assistant superintendent, in turn, then set up a meeting for the counselors with the new superintendent during her first week on the job. She was so impressed with the efforts that she went to the business office that afternoon and asked if the budget could support two additional counselors right away. The money was found. With that intervention alone, the decreased counselor/student ratio resulted in improved student service.

At this early stage of the change initiative, students were already being directed in a positive way. Team effort works, and the careful construction of a change team sets the stage for success of the change initiative.

Step 3. Get the Vision Right

"A shared urgency for change may push people into action, but it is the vision that steers them in the right direction." (Cohen, 2005)

School counselors, acting as change agents, can find help in creating a vision for the desired change if they look carefully around at artifacts in their school. What is the mission statement for the district or school? During accreditation, what are the "Expected Student Learning Results (ESLRs)?" Are there three or four values that the district has decided to use as touchstones for the year, for example, respect or building resilience? What does the banner over the administration building read? What slogan has the PTSA adopted for the year? Does your desired change have anything to do with improved academic performance, improved attendance, or education of "responsible citizens"? If so, you may have an easier time requesting that diverse segments of the school district line up behind the change.

A common mission that touches the hearts and minds of the parents and board members, administrators, and business owners is essential to successful change efforts. It is often easy to link your change initiative to already existing district or school vision statements. If so, your team is assured that the change effort will already be in alignment with the direction in which the larger system is moving.

At Oak Avenue Intermediate School, the training by Drs. Curly and Sharon Johnson duplicated the third step in Kotter's model. They taught the team that linking a comprehensive guidance program to the district vision was imperative. This was, in fact, the first step in the process. The guidance team was instructed to create a mission statement, which aligned itself with the district mission statement.

As stated and posted throughout the district, "Temple City Unified School District's mission is to provide a rigorous education in a nurturing environment where students are empowered to maximize their learning potential in a diverse setting."

The core values stated by the district are:

- We are student centered and believe all children can learn.
- We work to serve our community.

- We model integrity, honesty, and openness as the basis for all human relationships.
- We respect diversity and differences of opinion.
- We provide safe and orderly school environments.
- We are committed to excellence.

The mission statement formulated by the change team stated, "The counseling and guidance program exists to ensure all students acquire the competencies needed in educational planning, career planning and personal/social development." The counseling vision statement fits perfectly under the umbrella of both the district mission and the directives of the American School Counselor Association National Standards (ASCA, 2005), supplying a double dose of credibility and authority.

A shared vision and common purpose serve as a unifying theme around which to organize disparate factions seeking change within a school district. The common elements of agreement and purpose must be ascertained in order to move forward in a cohesive fashion.

Step 4. Communicate for Buy-In

The fourth step is usually a natural for school counselors. "Communication R' Us" could and should be our motto. After all, the school counseling department is the hub of the school. Administration, teaching staff, and students all make use of the counselors to assist in the formal and informal communication within the school and district.

Once the change team determines the vision for the change initiative, the Paul Reveres (messengers) of the system need to be mobilized. Who are your best communicators within the school? Who communicates best with the parents/guardians, school board, and community leaders? Are they already members of the team? If not, what are the best means (those that have worked in the past) to get the message out to as wide a constituency as possible?

If individuals are not informed of the change, they definitely will not feel a part of it, therefore, lacking even the slightest desire to push it forward. Get the support you need through clear and effective communication of the proposed change.

The entire change team presented the TCUSD Comprehensive Guidance Program proposal to the Board of Education in October 1999. The program was board approved in January 2000. The change vision has been kept in the forefront with regular semi-annual presentations to the Board of Education. One presentation each year coincides with "National School Counseling Week" and serves two functions: to thank those who have supported efforts to expand the comprehensive guidance program and to showcase the gains directly attributable to the change, the initiation of the comprehensive guidance program. Student results are presented to the school board at the end of the year and publicized throughout the district, for example in the SPARC for each school.

Step 5. Enable Action

Once the vision for the change has been accepted and communicated widely, proponents must be enabled to take the actions necessary to "make it happen." Barriers to forward movement can find their origins in the system, in individuals, or "at the top."

Administration must be in support of the initiative. With district and school administrative support, school counselors and the change team can be assured that systemic barriers will be eliminated or minimized. Methods to encourage action within systems may include the use of incentives for those who promote the change and sanctions on "nay-sayers." Performance appraisal based on alignment with the change initiative, and reward and recognition for risk-taking in implementing the change will support the process. With administration, both school and district level, either on your team directly or supporting the change initiative, the school counselors will have a much easier time when leading change.

If individuals are afraid to take the necessary actions to effect the change, sometimes training and the acquisition of new skills is all that is needed. Cohen and Kotter point out that training needs to be at the right time, for the right skills, and using the right approach. (Cohen, 2005, p.120) For example, instead of simply reading about comprehensive guidance, a representative group who will actually be involved in the program might be given adequate release time to visit another district where a model program is up and running.

Seeing the desired change in action is not only educational, but also serves as motivation to improve the way things are done at home. Those who are being asked to change must believe that the change is truly desirable and that they have the capability to enact the changes. Seeing other counselors delivering classroom guidance lessons can encourage those who wish to change. Viewing the guidance curriculum that has been constructed in conjunction with an English or social studies department in another school may allow those who are hesitating to become "believers."

In the Temple City Unified School District, top administrative support was evidenced from the beginning of the process. Proof includes the initial invitation to all counselors in the district to attend the Counselor Leadership Academy and subsequent approval for funding additional counselors after a presentation by the change team. The superintendent obviously understood the change process and the importance of "getting the right people on the bus" (Collins 2001, p.122) and providing adequate resources to those who were spearheading the change initiative.

A second example of district support, which enabled the comprehensive guidance initiative to move forward, was the addition of a job position—Administrative Liaison—to the district organizational chart. The new administrator was to be a formal liaison to the Board of Education and other site administrators. This additional position was added as a direct result of the change team presentation, which set forth the need for a comprehensive guidance program. After his hiring, the new liaison attended all guidance team meetings and arranged dialogue with administration when needed. He also raised significant funding for professional training for all guidance team members.

In addition to the initial financial support by administration, Temple City Unified District has financed ongoing education for the guidance team. This support for training has been a critical component of success for the comprehensive guidance initiative. Yearly visits to the CCLA trainings in Arrowhead, California, have helped the team members understand their task. Equally important, administrators participated in the training sessions right along with the counselors and other support personnel. All of the team members completed training in crisis intervention together, helping to mold the members of the change team into an integrated working unit.

Step 6. Create Short-Term Wins

Do you recall "Counseling Theories 101" in graduate school? Behavior is modified in incremental steps with repetition and intermittent reinforcement. Kotter would suggest that change in systems occurs in the same manner. Recognizing gains in the short-term modifies change in a system. In order to keep the cynics and skeptics at bay and the enthusiastic players on board for the long haul, it is imperative to incorporate short-term wins into the change initiative.

Consider what the first success will be during the change process. Think small! Will the benefit be observable and measurable? How will you use it to celebrate a victory and infuse additional energy into the movement? What are effective rewards for accomplishment in your school? Are luncheons, plaques, certificates, and announcements over the public address system appreciated? Be sure to use the already established means, as well as creative approaches unique to this change initiative to reward forward movement. Remember that "success breeds success."

Each of the schools in the Temple City Unified School District had submitted Support Personnel Accountability Report Cards (SPARCs). In fact, Temple City Unified School District was the only district in the state of California that had all of its schools submit a SPARC. One year, each of the seven schools received an "Academy Award," a "Best in the West," or a "Diamond" award for their SPARCs. This represented a huge success that was directly linked to the furtherance of the change initiative, the comprehensive guidance program. The reason for all the successes that were reported in the SPARCs could be directly linked to the progress with the comprehensive guidance program.

The accomplishments of the year were ritually touted at a spring Board meeting in the Temple City Unified School District, with each school presenting its award to the staff and PTSA. A copy of the winning SPARC was then sent to all district stakeholders. From the annual successes, additional energy and funding grew and was returned to further develop the guidance program.

Step 7. Don't Let Up

"Leaders need to stay focused and demonstrate that they are not easing the pressure to achieve the vision in which they have invested so much energy."(Cohen, 2005, p.164).

In plain terms, this is where persistence, determination, and accountability come into play. What are the benchmarks or outcomes that you established at the beginning? How will the school counselor know that the change is working? Now is the time to continue to monitor, monitor, monitor. Charts, pre- and post-evaluations, histograms, and Power Point presentations can assist in presenting evaluation measures to infuse additional energy for the long haul. Are the students really achieving at a higher level academically? Are more of them attending class? Is the campus actually safer? Why would we let up or rest after small wins if the goal is not completed?

"Don't let up," Kotter's fourth step, is a clear and simple concept. The three words are easy to remember, but action is another story. This is evident from the countless enterprises that have failed because people declared victory prematurely, or because they simply did not maintain momentum" (Cohen 2005, p.173).

Some causes for stopping prematurely when leading change are exhaustion, too fast or too slow a pace with the change, too many changes coming at the staff at once, and the loss of key players. Piloting a program at one school and then celebrating the successes, by expanding the change to other schools within the same district, actually reinforces and infuses momentum. Start small and build.

Here is where the beauty of a theoretical model comes in. When the school counselor who wishes to lead a change initiative already can anticipate difficulties and setbacks, then the change team can address these resistant factors early on and plan accordingly. Sometimes lessons of the everyday workings in a school counseling department cannot be learned ahead of time through book learning in a controlled environment. There is a powerful example of this in the Oak Avenue Intermediate School experience.

After a seemingly successful implementation of the comprehensive guidance program throughout the Temple City Unified School District, there was a change in personnel at both the district and site level. There also was an expansion of personnel throughout the district. The administrative liaison position, mentioned earlier, so critical to the comprehensive guidance program initiative, was eliminated. When there is an unstable environment, in nautical arenas, sailors speak about "battening down the hatches." This is exactly what occurred at Oak Avenue Intermediate. The counselor judged that during that critical period of personnel transition it would be better to concentrate her energies on the comprehensive guidance initiative at her school as opposed to continuing to promote the change throughout the entire district. This worked well and allowed the change process to continue at her school. There was a temptation for the counselor to give up on the whole comprehensive guidance plan. However, because of this counselor's ability to assess, reevaluate, and adjust, the change process proceeded on a smaller scale with renewed energy.

Step 8. Make It Stick

Anyone who has worked for a number of years in education will agree that there is nothing quite so demoralizing as change efforts that require a great deal of time and effort only to reap short term results or to suddenly disappear. Concerning such phenomenon, there exists a common folklore among educators of the "seven- year rule." This "rule" refers to the merry-go-round nature of creative ideas. Every seven years or so, programs, ideas, approaches, such as the "correct" way to teach reading, will re-enter the educational terrain after a prolonged period of dormancy. These "brand-new" ideas are usually marketed by "Lone Ranger" change agents as panaceas. Veteran staff have the organizational memory to avoid this rebound tendency and are thus sometimes stereotyped as change blockers. As you well can imagine, there are only so many times that repeated attempts at short-term change, not anchored in the system, can occur without losing all support from staff and community.

Credibility for school counselors and the change initiative is at stake here, so it is extremely important to take necessary steps to ensure that the new procedure, application, or program for which the team will be lobbying, will continue when you are no longer there. Some methods for securing or anchoring a change into the culture of your school or district are:

1. Wide-spread dissemination of the outcomes of the change initiative
2. Making a direct connection between the successes of the change initiative and the mission statement of the district/school
3. Through the use of comparison data, demonstrating the ways in which the old model was ineffective in achieving the desired results
4. Expecting and carefully receiving criticisms leveled against the change
5. Leading by modeling the new behavior
6. Using anecdotal material and testimonials from staff, parents, or students who have promoted or benefited from the change initiative

At Oak Avenue Intermediate School, as students, parents, teachers, and administration continued to see the positive student results of the comprehensive guidance program, the change initiative continued to thrive and grow. Having regular guidance team meetings and taking the time to discuss issues common to their particular school site strengthened the team. The program was monitored on a regular basis, adjustments made as needed, and success celebrated. At the basis of all of this effort was the common vision that the comprehensive guidance program was affecting lives of countless numbers of students in a positive way.

The discipline of preparing the SPARC on a yearly basis strengthened the cohesiveness of the team and afforded an instrument of self-reflection, evaluation, consistent communication of successes, and subsequent celebration. Proof of the success of the change initiative in the Temple Unified School District is the fact that during years of tight budget constraints, the newly implemented guidance program never suffered cutbacks.

Final Thoughts

Change is predictable and inevitable. For school counselors, the change process is essential to our clients, the students, and their parents/guardians, and to the systems in which we operate. Professional school counselors are educated and dedicated to ways of bettering the systems in which they work. There is a need for school counselors to also learn to cross over the boundaries of particular disciplines in search of guides, research, mentors, and maps to make our school experience easier and more productive. Leadership from the business world can make the change process more explicit, a bit less frightening, and less strenuous.

The next time you sense that you are dragging a "wooly mammoth" behind you in the counseling office, trying to effect a change which you feel is necessary for the good of the students, but getting nowhere by yourself, remember the simplicity of the steps embedded in Dr. Kotter's model for leading change and the wisdom shared by a school counselor at Oak Avenue Intermediate. You may look over your shoulder and recall your ability to crawl out of that harness and follow the lead of others who have outlined and practiced a proven path for making change occur. Good luck!

Discussion Questions

1. List the eight steps of Kotter's model for leading change.
2. Discuss with a partner a time when you felt powerless to move forward to change in a system. Why do you think you felt that way?
3. Which of the eight steps in Kotter's change model do you personally feel would be easiest for you to implement? Which one would be hardest?
4. What kinds of obstacles to change have you experienced in a school system? After reading this chapter, how would you go about overcoming them?
5. As a school counselor, if you were creating a team to implement a comprehensive school guidance program, who would you wish to include on the team?

References

American School Counselor Association. (2005). *The ASCA National Model: A framework for school counseling programs.* Alexandria, VA: Author

Cohen, D. S. (2005). *The heart of change field guide: Tools and tactics for leading change in your organization.* Boston: Harvard Business School Press.

Collins, J. C. (2001). *Good to great: Why some companies make the leap-- and others don't.* New York: Harper Business.

Kotter, J. P. (1996). *Leading change.* Boston: Harvard Business School Press.

Kotter, J. P., & Cohen, D. S. (2002) *The heart of change: Real-life stories of how people change their organizations.* Boston: Harvard Business School Press.

Schaefer, Regina M. (2005, Winter). Dragging the woolly mammoth: School counselors leading change. *The California School Counselor 4*(2), 3, 14.

Chapter 8

Collaboration Strategies to Enhance the Relationships Between School Counselors and the School Community

Kathy Emery and Suzy R. Thomas

Abstract

The ASCA National Standards call upon school counselors to collaborate with the various constituencies in the school community. This chapter discusses several interrelated barriers to collaboration—institutional racism, standardized testing, teacher norms of isolation, the alienation of parents within urban school settings, and the exclusion of students from the decision-making process. In addition to calling upon schools of education and policymakers to provide better training for counselors in these areas, the authors also offer ways in which school counselors can improve their ability to foster collaboration among all members of the school community.

Introduction

... it is impossible to understand the present or prepare for the future unless we have knowledge of the past. . . .
Malcolm X "On Afro-American History"

With counselor/student ratios averaging one to 448 (National Association for College Admission Counseling [NACAC], 2006) and as high as one to 1,660 (Mitchell et al., 2002), school counselors, if they are to be effective specialists in "meeting the needs of students," are going to need help. Perhaps that is why the American School Counselor Association (ASCA) National Model (ASCA, 2003) emphasizes the role of the professional school counselor as collaborator. ASCA defines parents, students, teachers, administrators, and the "community" as the groups with which counselors should be collaborating in order to meet the academic, career, and personal/social needs of students.

In many school settings, however, there is inadequate and unclear communication between and among administrators, school counselors, parents, and students about their respective roles in the school. Lack of communication and mutual understanding has a detrimental effect on the ability of the school to function effectively as a system: it creates misconceptions about roles, animosity between individuals and groups, self-

protectiveness, and suspiciousness of others; it generally impairs the ability of individuals to relate to and work with one another; and it impedes the likelihood of effecting school change.

Current institutions, assumptions, myths, cultural norms, and inequalities are often barriers to effective communication. These obstacles are difficult to address because they have strong roots in the past. Furthermore, the history of the public school system has exacerbated the class, gender, cultural, racial, and ethnic differences between many urban school staffs and the communities they serve. This history has created the parameters within which we operate today. Understanding that the school culture is embedded in a social and political context that has deep historical roots can increase a school counselor's chances of obviating many of the barriers to successful communication and, hence, collaboration.

This chapter discusses several interrelated barriers to collaboration: institutional racism; standardized testing; teacher norms of isolation; the alienation of parents within urban school settings; and the exclusion of students from the decision-making process. In addition to calling upon schools of education and policymakers to provide better training for counselors in these areas, we also offer ways in which school counselors can improve their ability to foster collaboration among all members of the school community.

Institutional Racism

One of the most deeply embedded obstacles to successful collaboration is institutional racism (Fusick & Charkow Bordeau, 2004), the preferential treatment given to members of one group over others within educational, economic, social, and political realms (Axelson, 1999). This is particularly problematic since the vast majority of both school counselors and teachers are White, middle class females; and the vast majority of many urban public school students are poor or working class students of color (Hodgkinson, 1985; Lee, 1995). In 1998, 72 percent of the poor in cities were minority (USHUD, 1998). In 2001, over 70 percent of the nation's

Black students attended predominantly minority schools (Orfield, 2001). According to the NACAC's 2006 *Annual State of College Admission Report*:

> School counseling in the United States is a relatively homogenous profession . . . 87 percent of counselors nationwide are white, non-Hispanic. This is over-representative of the national white non-Hispanic population. According to the Census Bureau, the white population accounts for 62 percent of the U.S. population aged 14-17 . . . African-Americans make up just seven percent of the nation's school counseling corps, while Hispanic-Americans constitute four percent. Both are significantly underrepresented compared to their proportion of the national population. (NACAC, 2006; p. 61)

The cultural divide represented by such data is deep and seemingly intractable because the standards and norms that enforce it have been inherited by successive generations who do not question the origins and purposes of those arrangements (Smith, 2000). Tye (1987) has developed the concept of "deep structure" to address how inherited and unchallenged values, beliefs, and assumptions define the climate of a school. Changes at the level of deep structure are more difficult to achieve because of the powerful, often "unconscious," nature of these norms. The deep structure may be accepted and shared by members of the school setting without question (Elmore, 1995; Oakes, 1992; Tye, 1987).

When a national standard calls upon school counselors to collaborate with parents, the response will depend on how well counselors understand the deep structure in which they are embedded. Historically, White, middle class professionals have made participation in the development of school programs by poor parents of color contingent upon their acceptance of middle class norms, values, and goals (Delpit, 1995; Gilyard, 1991; Greenberg, 1969; Whitfield, 2004). This deal is not made explicitly, nor are many of those who propose it even aware of the underlying quid pro quo. Most often it is woven into the fabric of the tools and assumptions of those trained and employed to serve "disadvantaged" or "at-risk" students (Berlak & Moyenda, 2001; Fine, 1995; Heath, 1983; Perry & Delpit, 1998; Weis, 1985), thereby leading to conflict and misunderstandings between school staff on one hand and parents and students on the other. Fusick and

Charkow Bordeau (2004) defined a student as "... 'at risk' for educational and social failure when his or her potential for becoming a responsible and productive adult is limited by barriers at home, at school, or in the community" (p. 102). Racism is identified as one of these risk factors.

School counselors often do not receive adequate training in multicultural counseling and racism in their professional preparation programs (Durodoye, 1998; Fusick & Charkow Bordeau, 2004; Hobson & Kanitz, 1996; Johnson, 1995). There has been even less focus on this issue within the school counseling specialization than within the larger field of counseling (Constantine, 2002; Holcomb-McCoy, 2005). The work of Helms (1984, 1990), McIntosh (1998), McGoldrick (1998), Sue and Sue (1999), and Sue, Arredondo, and McDavis (1992), among others, has improved understanding of the effects of White privilege within the counseling profession and the articulation of specific multicultural competencies. Constantine (2002) found that awareness of White racial identity and privilege, along with training in multicultural counseling, were key factors in improving school counselors' self-reported levels of competence in working with diverse populations.

Racist attitudes, whether conscious or not, can have a seriously detrimental effect on the emotional, social, developmental, and academic well-being of students (Constantine, 2002; Fusick & Charkow Bordeau, 2004). It thus becomes a matter of professional responsibility and of honoring the overarching principle of client welfare (Corey, Schneider-Corey, & Callahan, 2007) for school counselors to engage in active self-examination and to obtain training through coursework and/or experiential activities (Constantine, 2002; Fusick & Charkow Bordeau, 2004; Holcomb-McCoy, 2005) in order to eliminate barriers to communication and foster effective collaboration among the members of a school's community.

Standardized Testing

One of the areas that both school counselors and school psychologists need to be active in self-examination is the way in which they use standardized tests as a tool to reinforce institutionalized racism. Standardized tests were invented at the turn of the 19th century, ostensibly to remove the bias from sorting working class students into vocational education tracks and middle class students into college preparatory tracks of the newly created comprehensive high schools (Thorndike & Lohman, 1990). And yet, such supposedly unbiased testing has led to the over representation of African-Americans in special education classes, increased within-school segregation and reinforced parent distrust of the school system. The research of Sharon-ann Gopaul-McNicol, Grace Reid, and Cecilia Wisdom (1998) at Howard University provides a case study to illustrate why and how this happens:

Background: Aisha (a pseudonym) is a 14 year old African American girl in the eighth grade who speaks Ebonics and Standard English alternately. Her teacher's records indicated that Aisha was functioning at a fourth-grade level in mathematics and a third-grade level in reading. The teacher felt that a special education program would better address Aisha's academic delays, so she referred Aisha to a psycho-educational evaluator to ascertain which program would be appropriate.

[results of the WISC - III indicated that Aisha had "moderate retardation" and was "eligible for a full-time special education program"]

Ecological Assessment results: . . . In her natural setting, she utilized words such as "dangerous" which she had been unable to define on the written IQ test. Whereas Aisha had been unable to recall as many as seven numbers on the Digit Span sub-test of the Wechsler scales, she could remember all the items on a 10-item grocery list with ease. Equally notable was her ability to perform calculations in basic addition and subtraction in the grocery store, even though she demonstrated no such mathematical aptitude on the WISC -III. . . when she was not penalized for speaking in and filtering her language comprehension through Ebonics, evidence of mental retardation for this child was unfounded. (p. 20)

Research such as this has led the Joint Committee on Testing Practices to warn:

Avoid using a single test score as the sole determinant of decisions about test takers. Interpret test scores in conjunction with other information about individuals (JCTP, 2004, C-5).

In other words, since test scores are inherently imprecise and assumptions about what constitutes intelligence are built into the technology of the test, they must be confirmed by ecological or qualitative, i.e., alternative assessments (Carlson & Lewis, 1993). James Popham (2001) also argues that standardized test scores are inherently imprecise because the tests are built to *sample* knowledge and skills and then teachers make *inferences* about a student's knowledge and skills from the results. The interpretation of test scores depends upon what the teacher and parents know about the student, the curriculum, and the condition of the student and surroundings the day of the test. If a teacher, counselor or psychologist makes unwarranted assumptions about a student, then that interpretation of what the test scores indicate will be equally unwarranted (which raises the legitimate question as to why we are bothering with standardized tests to begin with?).

Why are the ethical and technical guidelines for the use of standardized tests routinely ignored? One reason is because it would take more time, effort, and resources than schools have available. Another reason is that it would undermine the myth that the tests are objective measures, thereby questioning the legitimacy of the existing sorting system (one answer to the "why bother?" question above). Most White middle class school staff, when they were students, scored well enough on tests themselves to have no incentive to question the validity of the tests. They assume what *their* teachers have assumed, that the tests are accurate assessments of ability or achievement (two concepts that have become fused today). Parents and teachers, assuming the professional expertise of the school staff, are forced to accept the same assumptions, which too often leads to distrust and hostility—factors not conducive to engaging in collaboration with school staff.

School counselors who wish to encourage collaboration between White, middle class teachers and working class parents of color must be aware of how test scores have been used historically to support the position of school staff as "experts" while at the same time reinforcing racist and classist assumptions about academic ability. As the stakes attached to standardized testing become higher (e.g., becoming the criteria for funding prioritization, high school graduation, and curriculum selection), the barriers to student success become disproportionately higher for urban students of color. This has placed school counselors in a dilemma. How can they collaborate with the parents of these students and maintain the "professional" identity of the school staff?

This question has become even more pressing to resolve with the recent passage of California's AB 1802, which provides funding for new school counseling positions. A significant portion of the school counselor's time is to be spent working specifically with students who are "at risk" of failing the standardized test for middle school students and/or the California High School Exit Exam. School counselors have always been called upon to work with students in the realm of academic success to some degree (ASCA, 1981, 2003; Campbell & Dahir, 1997). There is debate within the school counseling research community as to whether or not the authors of the ASCA National Model (2003) specifically intend for school counselors to be evaluated based on improved grades and test scores among students (see Brown & Trusty, 2005; Sink, 2005). However, if school counselor effectiveness is to be linked to improved test scores for "at risk" and academically failing students, it is even more essential for school counselors to have a clear understanding of the origins of standardized testing and the connections between these tests and the barrier of institutional racism. If they do not, school counselors may continue to function at times as "gatekeepers," intentionally or unintentionally reinforcing the status quo in terms of inequality in educational opportunity (Constantine, 2002; Constantine, Erickson, Banks, & Timberlake, 1998).

For this reason, the school counseling profession has called for counselors to redefine their roles in terms of advocacy, leadership, and collaboration (House & Martin, 1998). However, school counselors may lack training or feel unprepared for their role as collaborators, especially when it comes to working with families (Holowiak-Urquhart & Taylor, 2005; Magnuson & Norem, 1998).

In fact, school counselors have historically received mixed messages about the appropriateness of this aspect of their role, although the consultation aspect of the position has been consistently endorsed as it relates to helping parents with academic, social, and behavioral concerns about their children (Campbell, 1993; Holowiak-Urquhart & Taylor, 2005; Magnuson & Norem, 1998; Mathias, 1992; Murphy, 1999; Ritchie & Partin, 1994; Strother & Jacobs, 1986). Inadequate training may thus pose one more barrier to healthy collaboration, and so we urge counselor educators to expand the focus in their programs on skills needed for collaboration and consultation.

Teacher Norms of Isolation

Lortie (1975) argued that unique patterns develop in an occupation such as teaching because of the structure of the job and the particular meaning that teachers assign to their work. When professional socialization pressures are strong, the values that people hold will mix with those of the school culture. In contrast, when these pressures are weak, individuals' personal values and beliefs will remain the salient factors in professional socialization (Lortie, 1975).

Norms for teachers include working in isolation without asking for help or discussing teaching practices with others (Little, 1990; Lortie, 1975; Sarason, 1982). In other professions, where there is more of a sense of a common language and culture, the burden on the individual is lessened (Lortie, 1975). Most professions have a shared language, whereas teachers lack this technical language and must construct their own individual ways of understanding what is important in the school setting. There is less collegiality among teachers because of this isolation, which means less professional support during the course of induction (Lortie, 1975). The isolation commonly found in school settings contributes to the tendency for beginning teachers to attempt to solve problems on their own without or before asking for assistance from others. That teachers are socialized to work in isolation from each other makes it even more of a stretch to encourage them to consult with school counselors, parents, or students.

Alienation of Parents

Parents, especially minority parents and those from urban areas, also suffer from their own experiences of socialized isolation. They often feel left out of the decision-making process regarding their children's education (Fusick & Charkow Bordeau, 2004). Cutler (2000) traced a history of "disdain" among educators (including school counselors) towards African American and immigrant families, as well as those from lower socio-economic strata, back to the early 1900s. Whitfield (2004) described the way in which school systems came to exclude parents and grandparents from participating in the education of their children as follows:

> The advent of schools as separate institutions took these intergenerational processes out of the hands of the whole community and placed them in the hands of specialists whose job was teaching school. The arena for education moved from the whole community

into the schoolhouse. This came about as society became more and more specialized and fragmented. The social division of labor must have seemed to require it. We can lament the fact that this took place but it remains a fact. It tends to explain some of the social and economic problems that our society has. Those who would be shoemakers are taught by those who have never made a shoe. We wonder why some young people find it so difficult to fit into their communities in a healthy and wholesome way when they are instructed in civics by those who hold their communities in contempt and who are not familiar with its realities. More and more, most adults feel alienated from the process of the education of children. We have accepted too limited a role because we are not the experts, the educators, the teachers and the school administrators. This leaves education barren and often abstract—disconnected from life and community, and not serving the children well in their transition to adulthood. (p. 28)

Giles (2005) outlines three "narratives" used by counselors and others to conceptualize the role of parents within the school system. The first one, the "deficit narrative," takes the position that parents from lower socio-economic strata are either manipulative or uninvolved. Negative perceptions of parents within this model refer to the notion that these parents are working against the goals of school personnel, and that they are irresponsible and cannot be trusted. The second narrative, "in loco parentis," is also characterized by a negative attitude towards parents, though in this model the fundamental belief is that it is the job of school personnel, and not of the parents, to educate children. These first two narratives serve to alienate parents. However, the third perspective, the "relational narrative," offers a more positive view of relationships with parents. In this model, "educators work *with* parents, rather than *for* them" (Giles, 2005, p. 232). Educators and parents are seen as experts within their own "fields," and each brings various strengths to the educational process.

Negative attitudes toward parents are historically rooted in racist and classist belief systems, and they pose one of the most serious obstacles to collaboration. Parents tend to adopt their roles within the school system based on the messages they receive from school personnel (Giles, 2005; Murphy, 1999). Magnuson and Norem (1998) and Holowiak-Urquhart and Taylor (2005) urge school counselors to improve their competence in working effectively with parents, even if it means pursuing additional training in family systems theory, and to attempt to build good consultative relationships with community agencies that could serve as referral sources for families seeking additional help.

Exclusion of Students

Students are rarely consulted about their views on schooling, and they are rarely included as participants in the change process (Fullan, 1991). Student perspectives are typically ignored, yet they are the primary recipients of school change. Students are directly affected by the school climate, and directly and indirectly affected by the communication that occurs between and among the adults in the school setting. Students tend to become engaged in learning when they experience school as a consistent environment that is relevant to their lives, understand what is expected of them, and feel connected to the environment and supported by the adults (Fullan, 1991). The value that students attach to school is directly related to the quality of human interactions they have at school (Corbett & Wilson, 1995).

Fine (1995) made the following comments about the ways in which schools exclude students:

> . . . public schools . . . effectively paper over power asymmetries in the broader culture. Social problems are justified or taught through primarily individualistic explanations. . . these schools limit the kinds of literacies that young people can attain from official schooling practices. Discourses on individualism and meritocracy inhibit students' questions and writing. . . [and suffocate] critical consciousness when voiced – forcing those at the bottom to develop a "double consciousness". (p. 201-2)

If school counselors are to be successful collaborators, they cannot ignore the central role of students within this process. After all, it is because of students that our jobs exist.

Strategies to Overcome Barriers to Collaboration

Improved mutual and self-understanding and communication may help to deepen awareness, sensitivity, and connections between and among school personnel, parents, and students; and may, in turn, help to improve the functioning of the school and openness toward change. As described by Fullan (1991), an effort toward any type of school change should focus on helping "schools accomplish their goals more effectively by replacing some structures, programs and/or practices with better ones" (p. 15). Kruse and Louis (1995) outlined the five critical elements that enhance the strength of the professional community in a school as: (a) reflective dialogue; (b) de-privatization of practice; (c) collective focus on student learning; (d) collaboration; and (e) shared norms and values.

There is much that a "culturally competent" counselor can do to remove barriers, but there are also some serious barriers affecting student personal growth, academic achievement and career choices such as underfunded schools and increasing numbers of non-living wage jobs, that cannot be removed by an individual. Those barriers can only be removed in the next social movement (Anyon, 2005). In the meantime, school counselors who work with "underserved and marginalized students" can become truly "culturally competent" by making a serious commitment to deepen their understanding of the history of social inequality and how race, class, and sex have been used to create and perpetuate such inequality, especially the history of testing and tracking. In this section, various strategies are described to help school counselors become better collaborators.

Achieving Multicultural Counseling Competence

Fusick and Charkow Bordeau (2004) underscore the importance of not being "color blind," as this attitude denies the real impact of the history of racism upon relationships today. Holcomb-McCoy's (2005) survey of school counselors' perceived multicultural counseling competence included questions regarding definitions of racism, prejudice, stereotypes, and White racial identity development, as well as awareness of one's own cultural identity and the role of culture in choosing counseling interventions. This type of questionnaire provides a useful tool for counselors to assess their own competence. Counselors should be specifically aware of the history and dangers of standardized testing as described above (Emery, 2002; Emery & Ohanian, 2004) and should resist efforts to define students based on a single test score (Carlson & Lewis, 1993; Popham, 2001).

Understanding the ways in which American cultural mythology ("pull yourself up by your bootstraps," and "anyone who works hard enough can be a millionaire") serves to disempower people of color by ignoring the true impact of institutional racism can enable the school counselor to remove these blinders and work to effect change. Similarly, recognizing the role of "the collective" for minority students is an important tool. As Weis (1985) argued, we must understand why:

> [working class minority students might] create a cultural form that unmasks an ideology which offers everyone an opportunity to attain elite status while simultaneously justifying an unequal distribution of rewards . . . . [S]tudent cultural form makes a discernment of the difference between individual and group logics . . . while the individual may succeed in the college and may ultimately escape the urban underclass, the group can never follow. The college cannot possibly work for blacks as a collectivity . . . in the case of the urban poor, the collective enables survival, and it offers literally the only form of security the urban poor have . . . it is only the community that has enabled black Americans to live with some decency in the face of a white nation which would deny them this right….it is not a community from which the individual separates easily. (p. 136)

As mentioned previously, training in multicultural counseling competence can involve formal coursework as well as experiential activities, some of which should occur in the counselor preparation program. However, we recommend that counselors consider this task to be lifelong and to actively pursue opportunities for additional training, whether formal or informal, in sensitivity to diversity and multicultural competence. Furthermore, we argue that if schools were to approach education from a truly collaborative perspective, involving and valuing equally the contributions and priorities of all constituencies (students, parents, teachers, administrators, staff, counselors, and members of the community), the need for specialized training in multicultural counseling skills would actually diminish as competence would naturally emerge from these ongoing, real and mutual interactions.

Increasing Self-awareness

Self-awareness is repeatedly mentioned within the literature as an essential tool for counselors who wish to work in a more collaborative fashion and as a key component in multicultural competence (Constantine, 2002; Fusick & Charkow Bordeau, 2004; Giles, 2005). Constantine's research (2002) on school counselors' self-reported levels of multicultural counseling competence indicated the importance of both training and self-awareness. Multicultural counseling competence usually involves developing a self-concept within the contexts of race and culture, meaning that the counselor understands him/herself as a racial and cultural being. In addition, this type of training involves educating counselors about the realities of White privilege and helping them to let go of their defensiveness regarding these unearned privileges (McGoldrick, 1998; McIntosh, 1998). Examining one's own assumptions is central to becoming more able to work effectively with others who are from different backgrounds.

Tools for cross-cultural competence that specifically relate to self-awareness include the following: (1) being open and letting go of defenses; (2) not insisting there is no problem or "I'm not part of the problem"; (3) not insisting that "We're all the same"; (4) understanding that we are all affected by racism, sexism, classism, etc., as these "isms" limit our ability to be close to one another; (5) for White counselors especially, acknowledging areas of privilege and the unearned benefits of White privilege; (6) understanding that others have stories that are different from ours; (7) being willing to truly listen to others and to become informed about differences; and (8) being willing to offer support and to surface issues related to racism.

Building Relationships

Holowiak-Urquhart and Taylor (2005) posit that key qualities for counselors include flexibility, objectivity, and relationship-building skills. They highlight the fact that school counselors are called upon to communicate with multiple individuals and to navigate their way through various systems. School counselors' training in human development, behavior, and relations assists them as consultants. Consultation can occur with teachers on matters of classroom management, with school personnel in the form of in-service training, with parents on behalf of their students, and with administrators regarding curriculum and policy matters (Borders & Drury, 1992). Finally, because of their expertise in communication and relational skills, school counselors represent an obvious answer to the question, "Who should do the work of building

collaborative relationships within the school community?"

Working Effectively with Administrators

In the relational narrative described by Giles (2005), administrators adopt an intentional policy of considering parents as powerful and trustworthy allies, and this policy is clearly communicated to teachers. The doors of the school offices and classrooms are open to parents, and there are regular opportunities for input and communication, key qualities in healthy collaborative relationships (Giles, 2005; Murphy, 1999). Cooperative and collaborative relationships tend to foster a greater sense of ownership and responsibility among all participants (Murphy, 1999). School counselors can work collaboratively with administrators to instill a school culture in which the relational narrative replaces the more passive, blaming narratives of deficit and in loco parentis.

Working Effectively with Teachers

The ASCA National Model (ASCA, 2003) also focuses on the importance of collaboration with teachers. School counselors can conduct in-service training for teachers and other school personnel to raise awareness of racism and stereotyping (Fusick & Charkow Bordeau, 2004). Counselors can support teachers, instead of buying into the "blame game" that is unfortunately common these days (Emery & Ohanian, 2004). They can assist teachers by understanding the norms of social isolation and not asking for help (Lortie, 1975), and by reaching out to teachers to support them with appropriate, useful counseling interventions with students on academic, social/emotional, and career-related concerns (Campbell & Dahir, 1997).

Working Effectively with Parents

Strong relationships with parents are highly correlated with successful school reform efforts and with improvements in student achievement (Bemak & Cornely, 2002; Bryk & Schneider, 2002; Giles, 2005; Henderson & Mapp, 2002; Hoover-Dempsey & Sandler, 1997). Counselors can strive to understand the points of view of "underserved and marginalized students" and their parents and learn how their experiences have led to those views. Counselors can engage in "deep conversations" with parents and students and help them successfully develop a "double-consciousness." The "deep conversations" can allow counselors to better understand the values, priorities, and issues that parents and their children have in their communities, which they bring to school. This understanding can then help the counselor explain the difference between the culture of the school and the culture of the home and neighborhood. "Double-consciousness" is developed when parents and students understand how to move within the school culture without giving up their home culture or feeling that their home culture is inferior or lacking because it is different from the school culture. This is particularly difficult when educational policy reformers and pundits continue to explain the "achievement gap" as a result of the deficiencies in the culture of low-income and minority students. This is only one way in which counselors can learn why some parents of color feel alienated from the school system, and the ways in which educational systems have historically perpetuated that alienation. Finally, making home visits is another recommended way to reach out to parents and families and to express an interest in making connections with them (Fusick & Charkow Bordeau, 2004).

Including Students

School counselors can facilitate groups for students to help foster a sense of ethnic and racial identity, to bond peer groups and promote belonging within the school community. Training peer mediators to work with students is a specific tool that counselors can use to enhance and expand collaboration in a school setting (Fusick & Charkow Bordeau, 2004). Including students in this process increases their sense of control, empowerment, and involvement in their own education. Since the ASCA National Model (2003) depicts the counselor's role in terms of helping students to acquire knowledge and skills for understanding themselves and others, this approach is consistent with the current recommendations for school counselors.

Working Towards Systemic Change at the School Site Level

As mentioned previously, systemic change at a school is difficult to realize within a school because of the conscious and unconscious acceptance of the "deep structure" and the associated norms that assist in maintaining that structure (Elmore, 1995; Oakes, 1992; Tye, 1987). Yet, community groups with expertise in urban reform initiatives can be particularly useful in helping to alter the power structure within a school (Gold, Rhodes, Brown, Lytle, & Waff, 2001). Or, as Murphy (1999) notes, change is "part of the daily fabric

of schools" (p. 364); those who work in schools, then, need to have an operative approach to change. Murphy (1999) argues that the following steps must be taken in order to effect organizational change: (1) conducting needs assessments; (2) analyzing strengths and barriers within the system;(3) planning and implementing interventions based on the outcome of steps 1 and 2; and (4) evaluating these interventions in a systematic manner. This basic framework can be adopted and adapted by school counselors interested in forging change within their school systems with the overarching goal of creating a more collaborative and mutually empowering school community.

Working Toward Systemic Change at the District and State Level

There is only so much individuals can accomplish, even when working in concert with groups within and without the school sites. This reality has led Jean Anyon (2005) to conclude that:

Macroeconomic policies like those regulating the minimum wage, job availability, tax rates, federal transportation, and affordable housing create conditions in cities that no existing educational policy or urban school reform can transcend . . . . *macroeconomic mandates continually trump urban educational policy and school reform* . . . . How can a successfully reformed urban school benefit a low-income student of color whose graduation will not lead to a job on which to make a living because there are not enough such jobs, and will not lead to the resources for college completion? New curriculum, standardized tests, or even nurturing, democratic small schools do not create living-wage jobs, and do not provide poor students with the funds and supports for enough further education to make a significant difference in their lives. Only government policy can mandate that jobs provide decent wages; and adequate family income or public provisions (such as the 1944 GI Bill ...) are necessary to guarantee funds for college degrees to the millions of urban poor who want, and need, them. (pp. 2-3)

Anyon argues that to change city, state, and federal policies so as to eliminate the debilitating effects of poverty that make educational opportunity impossible, individuals must not only continue to make a difference in their daily lives, but join together into a group of "hundreds of thousands of citizens who are 'street marching mad,' and who voice their demands for change" (p. 5). In other words, she calls for a social movement and believes that public educators are currently in a position to "call groups in other movements to the table to work toward unity" (p. 5). Many school counselors might balk at extending the definition of collaboration to this degree. Although, if true collaboration results in finding common cause in a common good, the next social movement may be closer than we think.

Conclusion

If a school counselor sets out to develop collaborative relationships among parents, students, teachers, administrators, and members of the larger community, it behooves the counselor to understand the interests of the members of each of these groups. School counselors are expected by ASCA to develop programs that enlist the cooperation and support of parents, teachers, and administrators in order to promote social skills, academic achievement, and career planning for every student. Under current conditions, this may appear to be an impossible task. Consequently, individual counselors will have to make choices based upon how they define their own interests, their own values, and what kind of future they envision for their community, our nation, and the world. One cannot do this thoroughly without a critical evaluation of the past and its impact on current beliefs and institutions.

Ten Point Summary of Chapter

1. Collaboration among school staff, parents, students, and the larger community can lay the groundwork for effective educational reform.
2. School counselors can play a unique and effective role in fostering collaboration if they are aware of the obstacles to communication among the various groups making up the school community.
3. Many barriers to effecting communication between groups have been created in the past and inherited from generation to generation, so that many people today are unaware of the degree to which their beliefs and actions reinforce those barriers.
4. White, middle class counselors and teachers consciously or unconsciously use the norms and values of their profession, especially their status as "experts" to alienate working class parents of color,

thereby preventing open and honest conversations about educational means and ends.
5. Racism reinforces inequalities that lead to miscommunication, which, in turn, undermines collaboration.
6. As policymakers pressure school sites to increasingly rely on standardized test scores as the sole measure of academic achievement, they increase the distrust and anxiety of students and parents.
7. School counselors need to be provided with adequate training, both in credential programs and throughout their professional careers, in multicultural competencies.
8. School counselors must take responsibility for developing self-awareness through continual practice with the "tools for cross-cultural competence."
9. Academic success cannot be achieved by the individual alone or by the school site alone.
10. School reform that meets the needs of all members of a school community may require educators to join forces with other urban reformers in creating the infrastructure for the next social movement.

Discussion Questions

1. Why is it useful to understand the origins of current educational policies and practices?
2. What is the relationship between communication and collaboration?
3. What has typically prevented middle class White school staff from working easily and comfortably with working class parents of color?
4. Describe an instance of miscommunication involving a discussion over educational philosophy or practice. Are there any aspects to that instance that illustrate or contradict any of the arguments made in this chapter?
5. In what ways have you been led to believe that you must solve the professional dilemmas in your life on your own? What prevents you from seeking help, or more help than you sought? What or who has encouraged you to or discouraged you from seeking the help of school staff, parents, students, or local urban reform organizations?
6. Describe a problem or issue you have had in school, either as a student, parent or staff member, in which you hesitated to communicate about it. What norms, values or assumptions did you call upon to help you decide to whom you talked to and to what extent?
7. How do power inequalities undermine collaboration?

8. What changes can school site members make to a school? What changes can they not make?
9. Describe what authentic collaboration would look like between parent(s) and teacher(s); administrator(s) and teacher(s); teacher(s) and student(s); or parent(s) and administrator(s).
10. Describe a situation in which you could practice one or more of the eight "tools for cross-cultural competence."

References

American School Counselors Association. (2003). *The ASCA national model: A framework for school counseling programs.* Alexandria, VA: Author.

American School Counselors Association (1981, September). ASCA role statement: The practice of guidance and counseling by school counselors. *The School Counselor,* 7-12.

Anyon, J. (2005). *Radical possibilities: Public policy, urban education, and a new social movement.* New York: Routledge.

Axelson, J. A. (1999). *Counseling and development in a multicultural society.* Pacific Grove, CA: Brooks/Cole.

Bemak, F., & Cornely, L. (2002). The SAFI model as a critical link between marginalized families and schools: A literature review and strategies for school counselors. *Journal of Counseling and Development, 80*(3), 322-331.

Berlak, A., & Moyenda, S. (2001). *Taking it personally: Racism in classrooms from kindergarten to college.* Philadelphia: Temple University Press.

Borders, L. D., & Drury, S. M. (1992). Comprehensive school counseling programs: A review for policymakers and practitioners. *Journal of Counseling and Development, 70,* 487-498.

Brown, D., & Trusty, J. (2005). School counselors, comprehensive school counseling programs, and academic achievement: Are school counselors promising more than they can deliver? *Professional School Counseling, 9*(1), 1-8.

Bryk, A .S., & Schneider, B. (2002). *Trust in schools: A core resource for improvement.* New York: Russell Sage Foundation.

Campbell, C. (1993). Strategies for reducing parent resistance to consultation in the schools. *Elementary School Guidance & Counseling, 28,* 83-91.

Campbell, C. A., & Dahir, C. A. (1997). *Sharing the vision: The national standards for school counseling programs.* Alexandria, VA: American School Counselor Association.

Carlson, J., & Lewis, J. (Eds.). (1993). *Counseling the adolescent: Individual, family, and school interventions* (2nd ed.). Denver, CO: Love Publishing Company.

Constantine, M. G. (2002). Racism attitudes, White racial identity attitudes, and multicultural counseling competence in school counselor trainees. *Counselor Education and Supervision, 41,* 162-174.

Constantine, M. G., Erickson, C. D., Banks, R. W., & Timberlake, T. L. (1998). Challenges to the career development of urban racial and ethnic minority youth: Implications for vocational intervention. *Journal of Multicultural Counseling and Development, 26,* 83-95.

Corbett, D., & Wilson, B. (1995). Make a difference with, not for, students: A plea to researchers and reformers. *Educational Researcher, 24*(5), 12-17.

Corey, G., Schneider-Corey, M., & Callanan, P. (2007). *Issues and ethics in the helping professions* (7th ed.). Pacific Grove, CA: Brooks/Cole.

Cutler, W. (2000). *Parents and schools: The 150-year struggle for control in American education.* Chicago: The University of Chicago Press.

Delpit, L. (1995). *Other people's children: Cultural conflict in the classroom.* New York: The New Press.

Durodoye, B. A. (1998). Fostering multicultural awareness among teachers: A tripartite model. *Professional School Counseling, 1,* 9-13.

Elmore, R. F. (1995). Structural reform and educational practice. *Educational Researcher, 24*(9), 23-26.

Emery. K. (2002). *The Business roundtable and systemic reform: How corporate-engineered high-stakes testing has eliminated community participation in the development of educational goals and policies.* Retrieved March 26, 2008, from http://www.educationanddemocracy.org/ED_emery.html

Emery, K., & Ohanian, S. (2004). *Why is corporate America bashing our public schools?* Portsmouth, NH: Heinemann.

Fine, M. (1995). Silence and literacy. In V. L. Gadsden & D. A. Wagner (Eds.), *Literacy among African American youth* (pp. 201-227). Cresskill, NJ: Hampton Press.

Fullan, M. G. (1991). *The new meaning of educational change* (2nd ed.). New York: Teachers College Press.

Fusick, L., & Charkow Bordeau, W. (2004). Counseling at-risk Afro-American youth: An examination of contemporary issues and effective school-based strategies. *Professional School Counseling, 8*(2), 109-115.

Giles, H. C. (2005). Three narratives of parent-educator relationships: Toward counselor repertoires for bridging the urban parent-school divide. *Professional School Counseling, 8*(3), 228-235.

Gilyard, K. (1991). *Voices of the self.* Detroit, MI: Wayne State University Press.

Gold, E., Rhodes, A., Brown, S., Lytle, S., & Waff, D. (2001). *Clients, consumers, or collaborators? Parents and their roles in school reform during Children Achieving, 1995-2000.* Philadelphia: Consortium for Policy Research in Education.

Gopaul-McNicol, S., Reid, G., & Wisdom, C. (1998). The psycho-educational assessment of Ebonics speakers: Issues and challenges. *The Journal of Negro Education, 67*(1), 16-24.

Greenberg, P. (1969). *The devil has slippery shoes: A biased biography of the Child Development Group of Mississippi.* London: Macmillan.

Heath, S. B. (1983). *Ways with words: Language, life, and work in communities and classrooms.* Cambridge, England: Cambridge University Press.

Helms, J. E. (1984). Toward a theoretical explanation of the effects of race on counseling: A Black and White model. *The Counseling Psychologist, 12*, 153-165.

Helms, J. E. (Ed.) (1990). *Black and White racial identity attitudes: Theory, research, and practice.* Westport, CT: Greenwood Press.

Henderson, A. T., & Mapp, K. L. (2002). *A new wave of evidence: The impact of school, family and community connections on student achievement.* Austin, TX: Southwest Educational Development Laboratory.

Hobson, S. M., & Kanitz, H. M. (1996). Multicultural counseling: An ethical issue for school counselors. *The School Counselor, 43*, 245-255.

Hodgkinson, H. L. (1985). The changing face of tomorrow's student. *Change, 17*, 38-39.

Holcomb-McCoy, C. C. (2005). Investigating school counselors' perceived multicultural competence. *Professional School Counseling, 8*(5), 414-423.

Holowiak-Urquhart, C., & Taylor, E. R. (2005). When theory collides with practice: One day in the life of a middle school counselor. *Professional School Counseling, 9*(1), 88-92.

Hoover-Dempsey, K. V., & Sandler, H. M. (1997). Why do parents become involved in their children's education? *Review of Educational Research, 67*(1), 3-42.

House, R. M., & Martin, P. J. (1998). Advocating for better futures for all students: A new vision for school counselors. *Education, 119*(2), 284-291.

Johnson, L. S. (1995). Enhancing multicultural relations: Intervention strategies for school counselors. *The School Counselor, 43*, 103-113.

Joint Committee on Testing Practices. (2004). *Code of fair testing practices.* Retrieved March 26, 2008, from http://www.apa.org/science/fairtestcode.html

Kruse, S., & Louis, K. S. (1995). Teacher teaming: Opportunities and dilemmas. *Brief to Principals, No. 11* (pp. 1-6). Center on Organization and Restructuring of Schools, University of Wisconsin.

Lee, C. C. (1995), School counseling and cultural diversity: A framework for effective practice. In C. C. Lee (Ed.). *Counseling for diversity: A guide for school counselors and related professionals* (pp. 3-17). Needham Heights, MA: Allyn & Bacon.

Little, J. W. (1990). The mentor phenomenon and the social organization of teaching. In C. B. Cazden (Ed.), *Review of research in education* (pp. 297-351). Washington, DC: American Educational Research Association.

Lortie, D. C. (1975). *Schoolteacher: A sociological study.* Chicago: University of Chicago Press.

Magnuson, S., & Norem, K. (1998). A school counselor asks: "Am I prepared to do what I'm asked to do?" *The Family Journal: Counseling and Therapy for Couples and Families, 6*(2), 137-139.

Mathias, C. E. (1992). Touching the lives of children: Consultative interventions that work. *Elementary School Guidance & Counseling, 26*, 190-201.

McGoldrick, M. (Ed). (1998). *Re-visioning family therapy: Race, culture, and gender in clinical practice.* New York: Guilford Press.

McIntosh, P. (1998).White privilege : Unpacking the invisible knapsack. In M. McGoldrick (Ed.), *Re-visioning family therapy: Race, culture, and gender in clinical practice.* (pp. 147-152). New York: Guilford Press.

Mitchell, G., Udow, G., Downs, L. L., McMaster, S., DeWitt, K., Parres, S. L., & Stevenson, M. (2002) *Do inland southern California schools meet American school Counselor Association national standards: A Qualitative Study.* (ERIC Document Reproduction Services No. ED467345)

Murphy, J. J. (1999). School-based change. In M. A. Hubble, B. L. Duncan, & S. D. Miller, *The heart and soul of change: What works in therapy* (pp. 361-386). Washington, DC: American Psychological Association.

National Association for College Admissions Counseling. (2006). *Annual state of college admission report.* Available at: http://www.nacacnet.org/Member Portal/ProfessionalResources/Research/SOCA.htm

Oakes, J. (1992). Can tracking research inform practice? Technical, normative, and political considerations. *Educational Researcher, 21*(4), 12-21.

Orfield, G. (2001). *Schools more separate: Consequences of a decade of resegregation.* Retrieved March 26, 2008, from http://www.civilrightsproject.ucla.edu/ research/deseg/separate_schools01.php

Perry, T., & Delpit, L. (Eds.) (1998). *The real Ebonics debate: Power, language, and the education of African-American children.* Boston: Beacon Press.

Popham. J. (2001). The truth about testing: An educator's call to action. *Association for Supervision and Curriculum Development.* Selected chapters available at: http://www.ascd.org/portal/site/ascd/ index.jsp/

Ritchie, M. H., & Partin, R. L. (1994). Parent education and consultation activities of school counselors. *The School Counselor, 41,* 165-170.

Sarason, S. (1982). The principal and the use of "the system." In S. Sarason, *The culture of the school and the problem of change* (2nd ed.) (pp. 163-178). Boston: Allyn & Bacon.

Sink, C. A. (2005). Comprehensive school counseling programs and academic achievement: A rejoinder to Brown and Trusty. *Professional School Counseling, 9*(1), 9-12.

Smith, S. (2000). *Making cities black and poor: The hidden story.* Retrieved March 26, 2008, from http://www.prorev.com/blackcities.htm

Strother, J., & Jacobs, E. (1986). Parent consultation: A practical approach. *The School Counselor, 33,* 292-296.

Sue, D. W., Arredondo, P., & McDavis, R. J. (1992). Multicultural counseling competencies and standards: A call to the profession. *Journal of Multicultural Counseling and Development, 20,* 64-68.

Sue, D. W., & Sue, D. (1999). *Counseling the culturally different: Theory and practice* (3rd ed.). New York: Wiley & Sons, Inc.

Thorndike, R. M., & Lohman, D. F. (1990). *A century of ability testing.* Chicago: Riverside Publishing Company.

Tye, B. B. (1987, December). The deep structure of schooling. *Phi Delta Kappan,* 281-284.

U.S. Department of Housing and Urban Development. (1998). *The state of America's cities: Finding #2.* Retrieved March 26, 2008, from http://www. huduser.org/publications/polleg/tsoc98/part1-2.html

Weis, L. (1985). *Between two worlds: Black students in an urban community college.* Boston: Routledge and Kegan Paul.

Whitfield, E. (2004). *What diversity left out.* Jubilee Pre-Print Series #3. Retrieved from http://www. educationanddemocracy.org/Resources/Ed_Whitfie ld.pdf

Chapter 9

Assessing Readiness to Implement the
ASCA National Model for School Counseling Programs

John C. Carey, Natalie Kosine, Brian W. Mathieson, and Jason Schweid

Abstract

Implementation of the ASCA National Model can be facilitated by an assessment of the district readiness on a range of important factors. The determination of factors that predispose towards successful implementation, or which may impede successful implementation, can be accomplished through the use of self-assessment instruments. Potential problem areas can be anticipated and resolved before they derail implementation. This chapter reviews both readiness factors and readiness instruments and suggests strategies to assess readiness.

Introduction

School counselors across the nation are currently attempting to implement the National Model for School Counseling Programs (ASCA, 2003) in a wide variety of contexts. The National Model for School Counseling Programs (National Model) is an ambitious attempt to enhance the practice of school counseling and the position of school counseling in public education. By refocusing the objectives of school counseling on the academic achievement of all students, the National Model explicitly connects school counseling with contemporary movements in education reform. The National Model also represents a massive change effort; specifically, The National Model supports a comprehensive, developmental guidance approach (Gysbers & Henderson, 2000) to organizing and delivering services and includes a foundation, a management system, and an accountability system. The foundation ensures that school counseling programs are aligned with national standards along with district and building standards in an effort to educate all students. The management system ensures that the school counseling program engages in effective planning and tracking of activities, including interventions and initiatives. The accountability system ensures that school counseling programs evaluate the impact and effectiveness of interventions and uses results to bring about improvement.

The implementation of the ASCA Model represents a systemic departure from past practices.

Schools looking to start the implementation are, in many ways, committing to undertake profound organizational change. It is important to know what factors determine whether the ASCA National Model will be successfully implemented in a specific school or district.

The United States has a strong tradition of local control of education. This tradition situates much of the decision-making authority for public education at the local level. School boards, superintendents, principals, and parents have great influence over the roles of school counselors, the nature of school counseling programs, and the level of support available for school counseling programs. Ultimately, the ASCA National Model will be implemented one district at a time.

Several factors related to the Model itself will impact the likelihood that it will be implemented locally. First, implementation will be more likely if local decision-makers believe that adopting it will lead to valued outcomes. In the present high-pressure public education climate, tying school counseling activities to student achievement is likely to positively dispose decision makers. Research documenting the impact of implementing a National Model program on student achievement is needed to provide support for the major "selling point" of the Model. In addition, effective marketing of the Model to local decision makers is needed to ensure that they are operating from accurate and timely information about the Model and its potential benefits. Finally, local implementation will be facilitated if state departments of education adopt its principles in the formulation of state school counseling models and provide needed implementation supports—that is assuming that local decision makers are likely to want to implement a state-sanctioned model that is connected to increased resources to facilitate implementation.

While all these factors are important, we believe that they do not provide sufficient conditions for implementation of the National Model. This is due to the fact that, in general, factors exist within districts and schools that determine whether educational innovations are likely to be adopted and to what extent. In addition, we believe that more specific factors exist within districts that determine whether the specific innovations related to the National Model are likely to be adopted. Furthermore, we believe that it is possible to measure the existence of district "readiness factors" and identify impediments to Model implementation. Measuring school readiness across a range of variables is an important first step in implementing the National Model because it will allow school counselors to identify and address those factors that may exist that facilitate and/or impede implementation in their district.

Readiness to Implement Educational Innovations

A good deal of research exists regarding implementation of school programs and school innovations. Although many factors are credited for the success or failure of change efforts, it is effective leadership, stakeholder mindset and attributes, and past experience in advocating and negotiating change that stand out as bellwether variables (Berends, Grissmer, Kirby, & Williamson, 1999; Bodilly, 1998; Elmore & Rothman, 1999; Fullan, 1991; Grissmer & Flanagan, 1998; Keltner, 1998; McLaughlin, 1990).

For instance, case studies (Berends et al., 1999; Bodilly, 1998) have revealed that higher levels of implementation were found in districts that had 1) stable district leadership, 2) leadership that placed a high priority on effort, 3) the absence of budget crises, and 4) a history of trust between central office and schools. In the *Implementation of Performance in New American Schools* (2001), Berends, Nataraj-Kirby, Naftel and McKelvey identified teacher characteristics that affect implementation, such as: the ability to cope with simultaneous pressures and demands, commitment to change, experience, attitudes, orientations, and characteristics that affect attitudes. Similarly, the authors suggested that school size and school level may also be related to implementation. Finally, Berends et al. (2001) suggest that if staff receive financial resources, professional development, materials to support implementation, and the time to plan and develop the program, it is likely that implementation will deepen over time. It has been widely observed that when resources decrease or disappear, the likelihood of success of change efforts also diminishes (Glennan, 1998; Montjoy & O'Toole, 1979).

Readiness to Implement Comprehensive Developmental Guidance

Similarly to general education reform efforts, several key factors have been identified that help predict readiness to change within school counseling programs. Not surprisingly, factors such as, commitment, support, and inclusion, dovetail with all education reform efforts. These factors, seemingly, coalesce upon stakeholder perception.

Engel, Castille, and Neely (1978) suggest a number of conditions as prerequisites for successful implementation of a school guidance program. These consist of: 1) counselors who are committed to program improvement; 2) counselors who are committed to change; 3) counselors who are committed to formulating specific goals; 4) visible support for the program coordinator from administration and counseling staff; 5) funding for in-service training; and 6) backing from the local school board in the initial stages as well as throughout the program.

Soon thereafter, Gysbers and Moore (1981) provided a very similar list: 1) all staff members are involved; 2) all staff members are committed to the common objective of totally integrated development of individual students; 3) the administration is committed to the comprehensive approach and is willing to negotiate (trade off), helping staff members identify current activities that do not contribute to priority outcomes and supporting staff members' abandonment of such activities in favor of those that do contribute to priority outcomes; 4) all staff members see the comprehensive systematic counseling and guidance program as a function of the total staff rather than the exclusive responsibility of the counselor; 5) counselors are willing to give up such "security blankets" as writing lengthy reports of their contracts with counselees or seeing counselees individually on matters better addressed in a group; 6) counselors are interested in acquiring competencies; 7) staff development activities are provided to help staff members acquire competencies needed for successful implementation of comprehensive program; 8) time is made available for planning and designing the program and the evaluation, with all interested groups participating; and 9) program developers design an incremental rather than abrupt transition that could ignore the need for continuing many current activities.

Placing their attention on actual counselor readiness, Sink and Yillik-Downer (2001) conducted a nationwide survey of school counselors' concerns and perceptions regarding their Comprehensive School Counseling Programs (CSCPs). Practicing school counselors (*n* = 1,033) from eight states within three regions of the United States were surveyed using a revised version of the Stages of Concern Questionnaire, which was originally designed to measure teachers' readiness to change (Hall, George, & Rutherford, 1998; Hord, Rutherford, Huling-Austin, & Hall, 1987). In addition, they completed the Perceptions of Comprehensive Guidance and Counseling Inventory (PCGCI), which identifies school counselors' perceptions of CSCPs at three phases of program development: planning and designing, implementing, and evaluating (Gysbers & Henderson, 2000). Of the 1,033 PCGCI surveys that were returned by the participants, 20% described their programs as being in the planning and designing phase, 60% in the implementing phase, and 18% in the evaluating phase. Counselors in the planning and designing phases indicated significantly more concerns about collaboration, task, and impact than did respondents who were either in the implementation or evaluating phases. Sink and Yillik-Downer stated that, "While a causal direction cannot be determined from this study, we speculate that the more counselors value their Comprehensive Developmental Guidance Program (CGCP), the higher their level of engagement." (p. 285) Furthermore, they echoed the call to better equip school counselors to implement comprehensive programs (Borders & Drury, 1992; Gysbers & Henderson, 2000; Myrick, 1997). High school counselors reported higher task concerns than did elementary school counselors (Sink & Yillik-Downer, 2001). Also, high school counselors spent far more of their work time performing clerical-type duties than did elementary school counselors (e.g., Gysbers & Henderson, 2000; Schmidt, 1999; Wittmer, 2000). Sink and Yillik-Downer emphasize the need for CGCP leaders and school administrators to work conscientiously with secondary school counselors to eliminate non-guidance activities (Gysbers & Henderson, 2000).

Lehr and Sumarah (2002) sought to assess the factors that contribute to the successful implementation of CSCP in Nova Scotia. Using a 21-item survey distributed to 72 school counselors, the researchers sought to assess counselors' perceptions of what helps or hinders successful implementation. The researchers also conducted in-depth interviews with eight counselors who had returned surveys. Their survey analyses as well as the interview findings suggested that the key factors in the implementation of a CSCP were: support and involvement of others, adequate time and resources, leadership, and commitment. Although the counselors felt personally supported by their school boards, they also expressed a desire for more tangible support for their programs. Additionally, the researchers found that high school counselors found it more difficult than elementary and junior high counselors to enlist the support of teachers.

Measuring Readiness to Implement the ASCA National Model

The development of statewide versions of the ASCA National Model has provided ample ground for research into understanding variables that affect implementation of counseling reforms at the local level. This research has also led to the creation of several surveys that assess readiness to implement such reforms locally.

Mathieson (2005) developed a survey to measure the preconditions for successful implementation of the Arizona Comprehensive Competency Based Guidance Model—a precursor to the ASCA National Model. The majority of the items on the survey instrument were derived from the National Model's (ASCA, 2003) chapter on implementation. Twenty-six pre-conditions are listed under the subheadings of *program, staff, budget, materials, supplies and equipment, facilities,* and *technology.* Fifteen of the survey items were taken from the National Model's pre-conditions and were slightly modified. Minor modifications were made to the language of 11 items selected from the National Model's preconditions and four other items were revised extensively. Item 1, for instance, was split into two separate items (one and eight) because in the National Model the original item addressed both "a supportive work environment" and "an adequate budget." The author revised Item 20 because the 250-to-1 student-to-counselor ratio recommended by ASCA is not in line with the present student-to-counselor ratio in Arizona of 742-to-1 (ASCA, 2002). Originally Item 23 included four sub-questions about the Internet, word processing, student database systems, and presentations in its stem. The revised version of item 23 broadly asks the respondents about their use of technology. Finally, item 17 was revised because the author felt the precondition listed in the National Model was unnecessarily vague. The author included a parenthetical phrase to clarify whether a school counselor's role should be determined by the program or the principal. The remainder of the items (7, 16, 18, 19, & 26) reflected the top ten "critical issues" identified by Henderson and Gysbers (2002). Three of the twenty-eight items were created from implementation issues identified in Maliszewski (1997).

For example, while Maliszewski briefly mentions a K-12 linkage (item 13), he directly talks about the need for a guidance leader and partnering with local higher-education institutions.

TABLE 1: Survey of Preconditions of CSCP Implementation (Mathieson, 2005): Abbreviated Survey Items with Subscales

Survey Items	Subscale
1. Program should operate in a supportive environment	Program Support
2. Staff should understand and support goals	Program Support
3. Administrators should support program	Program Support
4. Central office personnel should support program	Program Support
5. Superintendents should support the program	Program Support
6. Department of Education should provide leadership	Program Support
7. Parents should be involved in the program	Program Support
8. A budget should be established	Program Support
9. Counselors have files, telephones and computers	Facilities
10. Facilities should be accessible and provide space	Facilities
11. School counselors should have private offices	Facilities
12. Access should be provided for meetings with groups	Facilities
13. The school counseling program has K-12 linkages	Collaboration
14. Program should have a relationship with a university	Collaboration
15. Guidance leader identified and given responsibility	Collaboration
16. Counselors and teachers should work together	Collaboration
17. Responsibilities defined by the program	Program/Counselor Expectations
18. Counselors should not be engaged in non-guidance	Program/Counselor Expectations
19. School counselors should not be administering tests	Program/Counselor Expectations
20. A student-to-counselor ratio of 350 to 1 is desirable	Program/Counselor Expectations
21. Counselors should hold state certification	Program/Counselor Expectations
22. Counselors should be members of their professional associations	Program/Counselor Expectations
23. School counselors should use technology daily	Technology Use
24. Counselors should use technology to help students	Technology Use
25. Counselors should use data to improve achievement	Program/Counselor Expectations
26. Counselors should be able to respond to all cultures	Cultural Competency
27. Counseling programs should be held accountable	Program/Counselor Expectations
28. School counselors should be held accountable	Program/Counselor Expectations

Mathieson (2005) grouped the 28 items into 6 subscales (see Table 1) including: Program Support (8 items), Facilities (4 items), Collaboration (4 items), Program/Counselor Expectations (9 items), Technology Use (2 items), and Cultural Competence (1 item). Based on data from 89 Arizona school counselors, three scales were determined to have adequate reliability characteristics for subsequent analyses, these included: Program/Counselor Expectations (α = .782), Collaboration (α = .748), and Program Support (α = .859). Only the Program/Counselor Expectations scale was found to be significantly correlated with the degree to which the Arizona Comprehensive Competency Based Guidance Model was purportedly implemented in respondent's schools. Respondent ratings suggested that the following items were considered as the most important preconditions for implementation: counselors should be able to respond to all cultures; programs should operate in a supportive environment; access should be provided for meeting with groups; school counselors should have a private office; counselors require files, telephones, and computers; school counselors should not be administering tests; counseling programs should be held accountable; counselors should not engage in non-guidance activities; a student-to-counselor ratio of 250 to 1 is desirable; and school counseling programs should have a relationship with a university. Respondents recognized the importance of cultural competencies in a quality program and they tended to focus on very tangible manifestations of adequacy of facilities, resources, work roles, and working conditions.

Carey, Dimmitt, and Harrity (2005) developed the *ASCA National Model District Readiness Survey* as a measure of school district factors affecting ASCA National Model implementation. The authors surveyed the literature on CGCP implementation (Gysbers & Henderson, 2000; Gysbers, Hughey, Starr, & Lapan, 1992; Hargens & Gysbers, 1984; Lehr & Sumarah, 2002) and the National Model in order to identify conditions deemed necessary or important for successful implementation. They identified school counselor skills required to perform functions specified in the National Model (e.g., using data to plan interventions) that are not uniformly addressed in counselor education training programs. Conditions that logically would need to be in place in a school district for successful implementation (e.g., the ability of the district to provide the data upon which data-based decision-making is centered) were also identified. Finally, they used their experience in

evaluating school counseling programs and in helping districts transition to CGCPs to supplement literature reviews and logical extrapolation. Items were developed related to seven readiness domains:

1. Community Support (e.g., "The School Board recognizes that School Counseling is an important component of all students' public education") was defined as a cluster of indicators of readiness related to the extent to which significant members of the school and local community are prepared to support National Model implementation.

2. Leadership (e.g., "The School Counseling Program has a full-time, district level leader who is respected by the superintendent, principals, and school counselors") was defined as a cluster of indicators of readiness that that are related to the availability, knowledge, beliefs, and skills of district leaders whose stewardship and support are necessary for successful implementation.

3. Guidance Curriculum (e.g., "The School Counseling Program operates from a set of student learning objectives that have measurable student outcomes") was defined as a cluster of indicators of readiness reflecting the presence and use of a formal National Standards-based guidance curriculum as specified in the National Model.

4. Staffing/Time Use (e.g., "School Counselors spend at least 80% of their time in activities that directly benefit students") was defined as a cluster of indicators reflecting school counselor workloads and time use that are conducive to effective National Model implementation.

5. School Counselors' Beliefs and Attitudes (e.g., "In general, School Counselors believe that they should be responsible for helping all students achieve academically") was defined as a cluster of readiness indicators reflecting the consistency of school counselors' beliefs and attitudes with the goals and modes of practice suggested by the National Model.

6. School Counselors' Skills (e.g., "School Counselors can measure how students are different as a consequence of their interventions") was defined as a cluster of readiness indicators that reflect skills needed by school counselors to enact activities specified in the National Model Delivery, Management, and Accountability systems.

7. District Resources (e.g., " The District provides School Counselors with regular institutional data

reports [disaggregated student achievement, attendance, and school climate data] in user-friendly form in order to facilitate monitoring students and defining problems") was defined as a cluster of readiness indicators that reflect the district's ability to provide resources, materials and support necessary for National Model implementation.

After the initial set of clustered readiness indicators was developed, one researcher spent three days observing the National Model implementation in the Tucson Unified School District. The Tucson Guidance Director (who is a co-author of the National Model) and district school counselors were interviewed about the process of implementation. Existing indicators were revised and additional indicators were added. Next the revised instrument was reviewed by both authors of the National Model (Bowers and Hatch) and, again, the

indicators were revised. Finally, the instrument was field tested on a group of 20 school counselors at the 2003 Massachusetts School Counselors Association conference to check for clarity, readability, logical consistency, and perceived usefulness. Minor revisions in items were made.

The instrument (see Table 2) was designed so that raters are asked to make judgments about their district (rather than about a specific school). A simple response format for each indicator was used. Raters are asked to note whether each statement is "Like My District," "Somewhat Like My District," or "Not Like My District." The instrument minimizes the use of technical language related to the field of counseling so that the instrument can be used by a variety of people (e.g., principals, superintendents, and school board members) who might not be familiar with the vernacular of the school counseling profession.

Table 2. ASCA National Model District Readiness Survey Readiness Indicators
by Cluster (Carey, Dimmitt, & Harrity, 2005)

Cluster	Item
Community Support	1. The School Board recognizes that School Counseling is an important component of all students' public education.
	2. The School Board believes that School Counselors can play an influential role in closing the achievement gap.
	3. Parents understand the intended benefits of the School Counseling Program.
	4. Parents support the School Counseling Program.
	5. Students believe that the School Counseling Program is an important resource.
	6. Teachers at all levels appreciate the importance of the School Counseling Program.
	7. Teachers at all levels collaborate with School Counselors in meeting School Counseling Program goals and objectives.
	8. School Counselors are recognized by teachers for their expertise in issues that impact learning and teaching.
	9. Parents from all racial/ethnic and socioeconomic backgrounds believe that the School Counseling Program can be an important source of help for all students.
	10. Influential business and community leaders are familiar with and support the School Counseling Program.
	11. Community leaders would be eager to be active participants on a School Counseling Advisory Board.

Table 2. Continued

Cluster	Item
Leadership	1. The Superintendent believes that the School Counseling Program is an essential component of the district's educational mission.
	2. The Superintendent believes that the School Counseling Program can help support students' academic achievement.
	3. The School Counseling Program has a full-time, district-level leader who is respected by the superintendent, principals and school counselors.
	4. The Superintendent commits resources to support School Counseling Program development.
	5. The district's School Counseling Program Leader knows the principals of standards-based reform and can communicate the relationships between School Counseling activities and student learning outcomes.
	6. The district's School Counseling Program Leader knows how to initiate and coordinate systemic change in the School Counseling Program.
	7. The majority of Principals believe that School Counselors ought to be engaged in developmental and preventative activities.
	8. The majority of Principals believe that School Counselors ought to be involved in helping students achieve academically.
	9. The majority of Principals would be receptive to redefining School Counselor activities.
	10. The majority of Principals would be receptive to creating yearly plans with School Counselors.
	11.The majority of principals would be willing to commit resources to alleviate School Counselors from routine clerical/administrative duties so that they can devote at least 80% of their time to activities that directly benefit students.
Guidance Curriculum	1. The School Counseling Program operates from a set of Student Learning Objectives that have measurable student outcomes.
	2. The School Counseling Program operates from a set of Student Learning Objectives that are grouped by grade or grade cluster.
	3. The School Counseling Program operates from a set of Student Learning Objectives that are grounded in both the ASCA National Standards and local norms.
	4. The School Counseling Program operates from a set of Student Learning Objectives that are connected to the district's academic curricula.

Table 2. Continued

Cluster	Item
Staffing/Time Use	1. School Counselor workload is consistent with needs of a National Model Program (e.g., 300 students/elementary counselor; 200 students/middle school-high school counselor)
	2. School Counselors spend at least 80% of their time in activities that directly benefit students.
	3. School Counselors spend at least 25% of their time in educational activities that promote student development and prevent problems.
	4. School Counselors spend less than 30% of their time responding to crises, emergencies and delivering mental health counseling.
	5. School Counselors do not spend an inordinate amount of time on routine clerical tasks.
School Counselors' Beliefs and Attitudes	1. In general, School Counselors are open to change.
	2. In general, School Counselors believe that it is important to adopt the ASCA National Model.
	3. In general, School Counselors believe that they should be responsible for helping all students achieve academically.
	4. In general, School Counselors believe that it is important to demonstrate how students are different as a consequence of school counseling interventions.
	5. In general, School Counselors believe that it is important to collect outcome data in order to be able to modify interventions.
	6. In general, School Counselors agree on a mission statement that establishes the School Counseling Program as an essential educational program that is designed to serve all students.
	7. In general, School Counselors are willing to devote the time to learn new skills.
	8. In general, School Counselors believe that it is important that they serve as advocates for underserved students.
School Counselors' Skills	1. School Counselors are competent in a wide range of interventions (whole school, classroom guidance, small group, and individual counseling).
	2. School Counselors understand the individual and systemic factors associated with poor academic achievement and the achievement gap.

Table 2. Continued

Cluster	Item
School Counselors' Skills	3. School Counselors are familiar with the principles of standards-based educational reform and can identify the relationships between school counseling activities and student performance.
	4. School Counselors can identify evidence-based interventions that enhance academic achievement, career development and personal/social development.
	5. School Counselors know how to be effective advocates for underserved students.
	6. School Counselors can measure how students are different as a consequence of their interventions.
	7. School Counselors can use institutional data (e.g., achievement, attendance, school climate surveys) to describe current problems and set goals.
	8. School Counselors use technology effectively to access needed student data.
	9. School Counselors use technology effectively to accomplish routine clerical tasks efficiently.
	10. School Counselors use technology effectively to communicate with students, parents and colleagues.
	11. School Counselors are recognized as leaders in their schools.
	12. School Counselors can establish goals and benchmarks for school counseling in their own schools.
	13. School Counselors can document their impact on students for Principals, School Committees, and the Community.
	14. School Counselors can query student information systems for needed data and information.
District Resources	1. The District's School Counseling Program has developed or adopted a set of instruments, referenced to the Student Learning Objectives, to measure student change in academic development, career development, and personal/social domains.
	2. The District provides School Counselors with regular institutional data reports (e.g. disaggregated student achievement, attendance, and school climate data) in user-friendly form in order to facilitate monitoring students and defining problems.
	3. The District has a School Counselor Performance Evaluation System that evaluates counselor effectiveness in a broad range of activities (e.g., whole school, classroom guidance, small group, and individual counseling).

Table 2. Continued

Cluster	Item
District Resources	4. The District has a School Counselor Performance Evaluation System that is based upon professional performance standards. 5. The District has a School Counselor Performance Evaluation System that is connected to meaningful professional development. 6. The District has a system for ensuring that all School Counselors have access to developmental supervision to improve practice. 7. The District is committed to providing professional development to help School Counselors develop skills necessary for the implementation of the ASCA National Model. 8. The District School Counseling Program Leader has implemented a system for monitoring the ongoing outcomes and continuously improving programs in each school. 9. The District School Counseling Program Leader has implemented a system for periodic program evaluation for the entire School Counseling Program. 10. The District School Counseling Program Leader has implemented a system for coordinating School Counseling Program activities (e.g., a master calendar). 11. The District School Counseling Program Leader has implemented a system ensuring good communication and information sharing across the School Counseling Program.

The National Center for School Counseling Outcome Research developed a web-based version of the *ASCA National Model District Readiness Survey* (www.CSCOR.org) based on national norms that are continuously updated. A free interpretative report is generated for each respondent. This report identifies readiness areas that need to be addressed and suggests approaches to addressing these areas. In interpreting scores on the *ASCA National Model District Readiness Survey*, Carey, Dimmitt, and Harrity (2005) suggest that special attention be paid to low scores on items that have been identified as critical readiness indicators (see Table 3).

Table 3. Critical Readiness Indicators

Cluster	Item
Community Support	1. The School Board recognizes that School Counseling is an important component of all students' public education.
	2. The School Board believes that School Counselors can play an influential role in closing the achievement gap.
Leadership	1. The Superintendent believes that the School Counseling Program is an essential component of the district's educational mission.
	2. The Superintendent believes that the School Counseling Program can help support student's academic achievement.
	3. The School Counseling Program has a full-time, district-level leader who is respected by the superintendent, principals and school counselors.
	7. The majority of Principals believe that School Counselors ought to be engaged in developmental and preventative activities.
	8. The majority of Principals believe that School Counselors ought to be involved in helping students achieve academically.
	9. The majority of Principals would be receptive to redefining School Counselor activities.
Guidance Curriculum	1. The School Counseling Program operates from a set of Student Learning Objectives that have measurable student outcomes.
School Counselors' Beliefs and Attitudes	1. In general, School Counselors are open to change.
	2. In general, School Counselors believe that it is important to adopt the ASCA National Model.
	3. In general, School Counselors believe that they should be responsible for helping all students achieve academically.
District Resources	7. The District is committed to providing professional development to help School Counselors develop skills necessary for the implementation of the ASCA National Model.
	11. The District School Counseling Program Leader has implemented a system ensuring good communication and information sharing across the School Counseling Program.

Based upon the work of the Center for School Counseling Outcome Research, several factors have surfaced that should be addressed in order for readiness for change to occur. For example, a district needs to have the school board and the superintendent recognize the potentially important impact of the school counseling program on student achievement (even though they may be dissatisfied with current models and practices). Principals need to be supportive of school counselors providing preventative services and proactive interventions in order to most effectively impact student achievement. Principals need to be willing to redefine roles so that school counselors can be more effective. The district needs a school counselor program leader to facilitate and direct the change process. A guidance curriculum should be in place to guide practice. School counselors need to be knowledgeable and supportive of the National Model, be open to change, and to recognize the importance of focusing on academic achievement. The district needs to be committed to supporting relevant professional development activities centered on guidance issues. Finally, the district needs a system that supports good communication within the school counseling program (e.g., regular meetings, a Web site, E-mail distribution of information) as a prerequisite to implementation. If the self-study identifies problems in any of these areas, immediate attention is warranted.

Immediate attention and/or action may come in different forms as related to a district's particular needs. For example, many small districts do not have any district-level school counseling program leadership. In these cases, principals are often free to develop building-specific approaches to school counseling, and there may be little, if any, coordination of services district-wide. In such districts, alternative ways to achieve district-level leadership and coordination need to be developed in order to promote the ASCA National Model implementation. Successful strategies may include: 1) the designation of an assistant superintendent as the school counseling program director who is expected to develop needed expertise to perform this duty; 2) the designation of a lead counselor (with adequate release time) to serve as the school counseling program director; and 3) the development of a school district-university school counseling program partnership composed of school counselors and counselor educators that serve some of the leadership, education, and advocacy functions of the program director.

It is not unusual for the self-assessment to highlight an entire cluster that is problematic. In one district's profile, for example, all the guidance curriculum readiness indicators were rated "Not Like My District." If a district is operating without a formal district guidance curriculum, a focus on the development of learning objectives with measurable student outcomes that is based on the ASCA National Standards and referenced to state-mandated curriculum frameworks is warranted in order to achieve school counseling program coordination across levels and in coordination with the academic curriculum.

In some instances, the self-assessment reveals one or two readiness indicators within a cluster that are consistently rated "Not Like My District." In the Community Support cluster, for example, a school counseling program may have good support from within the district (school board, administrators, and teachers) but may not have the support of parents and community leaders. In this case, an action plan focused on parent and community outreach would be clearly warranted. Likewise, in the Staffing/Time Use cluster, appropriate workload and distribution of activities with school counselors may still be burdened by an inordinate amount of routine clerical tasks. Here, an action plan focused on developing alternative ways of getting the necessary clerical work done (e.g., paraprofessional school counseling aides) and securing the support of principals for these changes would be warranted.

Assessing School Counselor Time Use and Workload

A central theme elicited through research on reform efforts is that of school counselor time use and workload. In addition to assessing readiness factors directly, it is often helpful to assess school counselor time use and workload as part of a readiness assessment. Typically, moving to the ASCA National Model will require a reallocation of school counselor time, and it is helpful to have an accurate description of time use and duties to help pinpoint problematic areas. Gysber's and Henderson (2000) suggest using a time log to obtain an accurate estimate of school counselor time use in the specific well-defined categories such as guidance, counseling, consultation, coordination, assessment, program management, professionalism, and appropriate/inappropriate activities. Gysbers and Henderson's process samples representative days over an entire school year in order to achieve an accurate picture of time use. Often, a quick overall analysis of time use is helpful at the early stages of ASCA National Model implementation in order to identify the potentially most problematic time use issues.

The *School Counselor Activity Rating Scale* (SCARS)(Scarborough, 2005) is a useful way to collect time use and workload data. School Counselors can use the SCARS to rate the frequency with which they are currently engaged in a wide range of appropriate (e.g., conduct classroom lessons on conflict resolution) and inappropriate activities (e.g., perform hall, bus, cafeteria duty) that are grouped by functional area (e.g., curriculum activities). Counselors can also rate their preferred frequency of each activity. Thus, it is possible to obtain a useful picture of time use and workload across a wide range of activities through the identification of activities that are unrelated to role and by identifying discrepancies between current time use and how school counselors should be able to use their time. If school counselors are knowledgeable about and committed to the implementation of the ASCA National Model, then their responses should reflect the activities needed for implementation and should help target needed areas for time reallocation and workload adjustment. The SCARS can be downloaded for free from the National Center for School Counseling Outcome Research website (www.CSCOR.org).

Readiness Assessment Process

The assessment of readiness to implement of the ASCA National Model is best conducted in the context of a serious self-study. Ideally, this self-study is conducted by a team chaired by a district's guidance leader. A helpful first step is to obtain district-level readiness information by having representative groups of school administrators and school counselors complete the ASCA National Model District Readiness Survey (Readiness Survey) in either the paper/pencil or web-based form. Comparing the ratings of administrators and school counselors across buildings can be informative. Special attention should be paid to critical indicators, such as low scores on subscales or low item ratings within subscales. The web-based form of the Readiness Survey provides automatic feedback for individual survey-takers. Comparing and contrasting the survey feedback and individual item responses between administrators and school counselors should result in a helpful, comprehensive picture of conditions that will favor and/or impede implementation. Those collecting and analyzing results should pay attention to impeding conditions before proceeding with implementation of the National Model.

Next, the team should gather information on school counselors' perceptions of the presence of specific conditions favoring implementation. The *Survey of Preconditions of CSCP Implementation* is an efficient way to gather this information. This particular instrument yields valuable information regarding counselor's beliefs of what needs to be put in place in order to support program implementation.

Finally, the team needs data on school counselor time use and workload in order to determine how time and work should be reallocated to achieve implementation. The *SCARS* is a useful way to gather data simultaneously on current time use and preferred time use profiles. It is helpful to ensure that counselors are knowledgeable about the ASCA National Model and support model implementation so that their preferences reflect time reallocations needed for model implementation rather than idiosyncratic modes of practice or personal preferences.

Which Is the Chicken, Which Is the Egg?

In assessing school counselors' readiness to implement the ASCA National Model it is rare to find a district where all the preconditions to successful implementation are fully in place. Few districts show optimal implementation conditions. Most districts show gaps—often in resources and ratios. It is tempting for school counselors in these districts to conclude that implementation of the ASCA National Model is impossible unless ratios are lowered and inappropriate out-of-role activities are eliminated. In such instances, it is helpful to remember that the ASCA National Model is intended as a way for school counselors to increase their centrality and effectiveness and to demonstrate their impact on students in order to justify their positions and their right to define their own work. Improved school counselor working conditions are an outcome of the National Model implementation. It is helpful to remember that in assessing readiness, the goals are to determine whether implementation is possible and what conditions need to be addressed in order to maximize the likelihood of success. The presence of optimal conditions is not a prerequisite for National Model implementation. In fact, an important outcome of Model implementation is the achievement of optimal conditions.

Future Directions and Interdisciplinary Perspectives on Assessing Readiness

While it is tempting to focus on the specific problem of assessing a district's readiness to adopt the ASCA National Model, we believe that it is fruitful to look more broadly at the issue of how other organizations deal with the adoption of innovations and the factors that affect productive organizational change. Researchers working in organizational management, organizational theory, and change theory purport that often times the success of reform efforts can be viewed, and ultimately predicted, through observation and understanding of change related factors described here (Armenakis & Bedeian, 1999;Beer and Eisenstat, 1996; Huff, Huff, & Thomas, 1992; Lewin, 1947).

Content, context, and process have long been established as the three main aspects of change efforts surrounding organizational thought (Armenakis & Bedeian, 1999; Beer & Nohria, 2000; Burke & Litwin, 1992). In an extensive review of change theory literature from the 1990's, Armenakis and Bedeian (1999) point to four dominant themes that research identifies as *change readiness*. These consist of: 1) *content issues*, defined as the substance of organizational change; 2) *context issues*, the conditions existing within an organization's external and internal environment; 3) *process issues*, the actions undertaken during the enactment of an intended change effort; and 4) *criterion issues*, dealing with the outcomes commonly assessed in organizational change. In using the aforementioned factors to understand how overall changes will be received, stakeholders would need to accept the importance of each micro-change the National Model offers. The actual individuality of each implementation site, the mode of implementation, and the very method of judging the effectiveness of implementation of a new guidance program will ultimately dictate the meaning of each and every organizational shift.

In a study exploring employee response to reform initiatives, Devos and Buelens (2003) explored several assumptions related to organizational readiness to change that can be applied to organizational structures within schools. They hypothesized that: 1) organizational change that brings about job loss will lead to lower levels of change openness in the workplace. 2) When employees display higher levels of trust in executive management and supervisors, then higher levels of openness to change begin to emerge within the organization (trust in executive management and trust in immediate supervisor's openness to change interrelate, in that an employee's trust for executive management is higher when employees display trust for their immediate supervisor(s), and vice versa). 3) Participation in the change process directly relates to one's openness to change. 4) Content, context, and process factors are directly related to openness to change both

independently and collectively. 5) Finally, higher levels of trust in executive management and a successful history of change are related to higher levels of openness to change within the organization.

In the Devos and Buelens (2003) study, professionals from several fields (n = 836) responded to a series of hypothetical organizational change initiatives revolving around the above-mentioned hypotheses. The questions raised were then broken down into three themes: dominant content, context, and process. Devos and Buelens report that non-threatening organizational change, trust in upper and lower management, and a positive track record of change and opportunities for employees to participate in the change process facilitate an openness to change. Devos and Buelens found a significant relationship (p = .04) between locus of control and openness to change. For example, organizations with a high level of internal locus of control demonstrated a high level of openness to change. That said, a significant relationship was also shown, (F (1.799)=15.11, p< .001) between one's hierarchical level within the organization and their openness to change, demonstrating that those with more power were more open to change.

Devos and Buelens (2003) point out that "even when organizational changes bring about severe job losses, people will not necessarily feel entirely reluctant about change" (p. 16). This directly challenges the notion that organizational changes that bring about job losses will lead to lower levels of change openness than organizational changes that do not bring about job losses. Another major impact of this study is the apparent relationship between trust in management and historical change. Trust only leads to more openness to change when there is a negative history of change. They also posture that if both factors are negative, willingness to change stays consistently low. These findings build off prior work documenting the importance of an organization's past experiences negotiating change (Beer & Nohria, 2000; Huff et al., 1992; Sastry; 1997).

The Devos and Buelens (2003) findings, placed in the context of school-counseling reform, speak to the need for an honest appraisal of each school's history in negotiating change efforts. The findings also speak to a need to broaden current implementation efforts, that focus on guidance leaders, to include school counselors as critical players in accepting and, ultimately, driving a change toward the ASCA National Model. With the dovetailed influences of strong, trusted-leadership and workers who accept reform, readiness to change moves away from individual school issues to the internal relations of a school counseling staff, their leaders, their relationships with one another, and their beliefs and values in the change process. Therefore, if a school counseling staff believes in the changes proposed by the ASCA National Model and trusts in their leaders, then they will be well positioned to change.

Summary

A strong effort has been made at the national level, through ASCA, to standardize and enhance the practice of school counseling. The need for this is best summarized by a statement found in the Foreword of *The ASCA National Model: A Framework for School Counseling Programs*, in which the author(s) state, "The profession [school counseling] has suffered from a lack of consistent identity, lack of basic philosophy, and consequently, a lack of legitimization" (ASCA, 2003, p. 1). The American School Counselor Association National Model is an attempt to fill these gaps. In order for this transformation to come into effect, however, school counselors, school districts, and communities must be willing to participate in the change process. Nevertheless, implementation at the local level is seen as a challenge to many within the school counseling profession; because not only does it require a change in how we look at the school counseling profession, it changes the philosophical foundation of school counseling, in that school counselors are asked to play a pivotal role in increasing the academic achievement of students (ASCA, 2003). This is a major shift for school counselors, who up to this point have played primarily supportive roles in aiding students in their academic achievement and have instead focused on more individualized support services.

With the ever-changing landscape of the school counseling profession coming into full view, we must first determine where we are in order to navigate how to get where we need to go. The process of finding out where we are consists of examining our readiness to change. As has been outlined in this chapter, readiness to change can be measured at the school counselors' personal level and at the larger district level. This is the starting point in determining where changes need to occur and the extent to how "ready" both individuals and districts are to see changes occur.

Once readiness to change has been examined, it is important to examine the conditions that are in place that both help and hinder the change process. As with any profession, we cannot expect the road to change to be without bumps, swerves, and hills. However, as was stated earlier, the ASCA National Model is intended as a way for school counselors to increase their centrality and effectiveness and to demonstrate their impact on students in order to justify their positions and their right to define their own work. Therefore, assessing readiness allows school counselors to determine at what level the implementation of the National Model is possible within their school and assessing readiness helps in determining what conditions need to be addressed in order to maximize the likelihood of success. With this in mind, we often have to look to others to provide direction and inspiration for change. In this chapter we looked at organizational models that demonstrated to us that change can occur if there is trust in the process and trust in the change makers.

Finally, if we review the main purpose of the ASCA National Model, we are reminded that the basic principle of the model is to ensure that every student experiences academic success. This is an immense task that requires strong leadership and well-defined goals. School counselors are the leaders, community-builders, and change-agents who guide this journey; the National Model is the road map we are following; and the first step of the journey is to assess the readiness of ourselves and of others who we need to bring along with us so we can begin.

Discussion Questions

1. What factors are traditionally thought to positively facilitate school reform initiatives?
2. Why are traditional factors in predicting success not enough to ensure successful School Counseling Model implementation?
3. What are the three "bellwether" variables that are thought to predict successful educational reforms?
4. Engel, Castille, and Neely (1978) and Gysbers and Moore (1981) suggest certain overlapping factors that contribute to successful implementation of school counseling programs. List six.
5. What are the school counselor skills that have been shown to correlate with successful program implementation? Why do you think these skills help facilitate reform?
6. What community factors have been shown to correlate with successful program implementation?
7. What are the district or structural characteristics that support program implementation?
8. How would you, as a school counselor, help create the aforementioned structural characteristics?

9. How can school counselors better account for their use of time? Why should they?
10. Describe the process outlined in this chapter for assessing readiness to change.
11. Why are optimal conditions not necessary to begin the implementation process?
12. List examples of each of the following issues in school counseling reform: content issues, context issues, process issues, and criterion issues.
13. How does an organization's historical experience effect organizational change?

References

American School Counselor Association. (2002). *State-by-State Student-to-Counselor Ratios (2001-2002)*. Retrieved May 18, 2004, from http://www.schoolcounselor.org/library/ratios.pdf

American School Counselor Association. (2003). *The ASCA National Model: A framework for school counseling programs* (2nd ed.). Alexandria, VA: Author.

Armenakis, A. A., & Bedeian, A. G. (1999). Organizational change: A review of theory and research in the 1990s. *Journal of Management, 25*, 293-315.

Beer, M., & Eisenstat, R. (1996). Developing an organization capable of implementing strategy and learning. *Human Relations, 49*, 597–619.

Beer, M., & Nohria, N. (2000). *Breaking the code of change*. Boston: Harvard Business School Press.

Berends, M., Grissmer, D. W., Kirby, S. N., & Williamson, S. (1999). The changing American family and student achievement trends. *Review of Sociology of Education and Socialization, 23*, 67–101.

Berends, M., Nataraj-Kirby, S., Naftel, S., McKelvey, C. (2001). *Implementation of performance in new American schools*. Santa Monica, CA: Rand Corporation.

Bodilly, S. J. (1998). *Lessons from new American schools' scale-up phase: Prospects for bringing designs to multiple schools* (MR-1777-NAS). Santa Monica, CA: Rand Corporation.

Borders, L. D., & Drury, S. M. (1992). Comprehensive school counseling programs: A review for policymakers and practitioners. *Journal of Counseling & Development, 7*(4), 487-489.

Burke, W. W., & Litwin, G. H. (1992). A casual model of organizational performance and change. *Journal of Management, 18*, 523-545.

Carey, J. C., Dimmitt, C., & Harrity, J. (2005). The development of a self-assessment instrument to measure a school district's readiness to implement the ASCA National Model. *Professional School Counseling, 84*, 305-312.

Devos, G., & Buelens, M. (2003). Openness to organizational change: The contribution of content, context, and process. *Vlerick Leuven Gant Management School Working Paper Series*. Annual Meeting of the Academy of Management, Washington, DC.

Elmore, R., & Rothman, R. (Eds.). (1999). *Testing, teaching, and learning: A guide for states and school districts*. Washington, DC: National Academy Press.

Engel, E., Castille, R., & Neely, J. (1978, March 23). *Why have a traumatic time creating an accountable developmental guidance program when somebody else had that particular nervous breakdown?* Report on an ESEA Title II Project, APGA Convention, Washington, DC.

Fullan, M. G. (1991). *The new meaning of educational change*. New York: Teachers College Press.

Glennan, T. K. (1998). *New American schools after six years: A status report* (MR-945-NASDC). Santa Monica, CA: Rand Corporation.

Grissmer, D. W., & Flanagan, A. (1998). *Exploring rapid achievement gains in North Carolina and Texas*. Washington, DC: National Education Goals Panel.

Gysbers, N. C. & Henderson, P. (2000). *Developing and managing your school guidance program* (3rd edition). Alexandria, VA: American Counseling Association.

Gysbers, N. C., Hughey, K., Starr, M., & Lapan, R. T. (1992). Improving school guidance programs: A framework for program, personnel, and results evaluation. *Journal of Counseling and Development, 70*, 565-570.

Gysbers, N. C., & Moore, E. J. (1981). *Improving guidance programs*. Englewood Cliffs, NJ: Prentice-Hall.

Hall, G. E., George, A., & Rutherford, W. (1998). *Measuring stages of concern about the innovation: A manual for use of the Stages of Concern Questionnaire*. Austin, TX: Southwest Educational Development Laboratory.

Hargens, M., & Gysbers, N. C. (1984). How to remodel a guidance program while living in it: A case study. *The School Counselor, 32*, 119-125.

Henderson, P., & Gysbers, N. C. (Eds.). (2002). *Implementing comprehensive school guidance programs: Critical leadership issues and successful responses.* Greensboro, NC: ERIC/CASS.

Hord, S. M., Rutherford, W. L., Austin-Huling, L., & Hall, G. E. (1987). *Taking charge of change.* Alexandria, VA: Association for Supervision and Curriculum Development.

Huff, J., Huff, A., & Thomas, H. (1992, Summer). Strategic renewal and the interaction of cumulative stress and inertia. *Strategic Management Journal, 13*, 55–75.

Keltner, B. (1998). *Resources for transforming new American schools: First year findings.* Santa Monica, CA: Rand Corporation

Lehr, R., & Sumarah, J. (2002). Factors impacting the successful implementation of guidance and counseling programs in Nova Scotia. *Professional School Counseling, 5*(4), 292-297.

Lewin, K. (1947). Frontiers in group dynamics. *Human Relations, 1*, 5–41.

Maliszewski, S. (1997). Developing a comprehensive guidance program in the Omaha Public Schools. In N. C. Gysbers & P. Henderson (Eds.), *Comprehensive guidance programs that work, part II.* Greensboro, NC: ERIC/CASS.

Mathieson, B. (2005). *Pre-Conditions for successful school counseling implementation in Arizona with implications for school principals.* Unpublished doctoral dissertation. Arizona State University, Tucson.

McLaughlin, M. W. (1990). The RAND change agent study revisited: Macro perspectives and micro realities. *Educational Researcher, 19*(9), 11–16.

Montjoy, R. & O'Toole, L. (1979). Toward a theory of policy implementation: An organizational perspective. *Public Administration Review*, 109, 465–476.

Myrick, R. D. (1997). Developmental guidance and counseling: A practical approach (3rd ed.). Minneapolis, MN: Educational Media Corporation.

Sastry, M. (1997). Problems and paradoxes in a model of punctuated organizational change. *Administrative Science Quarterly, 42*, 237–275.

Scarborough, J. L. (2005). The School Counselor Activity Rating Scale: An instrument for gathering process data. *Professional School Counseling, 8*, 274-283.

Schmidt, J. J. (1999). Two decades of CACREP and what do we know? *Counselor Education & Supervision, 39*(1), 34-36.

Sink, C. A., & Yillik-Downer, A. (2001). School counselors' perceptions of comprehensive guidance and counseling programs: A national survey. *Professional School Counseling, 4*, 278-288.

Wittmer, J. (2000). *Managing your school-counseling program: K-12 developmental strategies* (2nd ed.). Minnesota, MN: Educational Media Corporation.

Chapter 10

The Support Personnel Accountability Report Card (SPARC): A Practitioner and Consultant Share Perspectives

Bob Tyra and Bill Welcher

Abstract

The Support Personnel Accountability Report Card (SPARC) is an open source, continuous improvement document that focuses on student support services accountability at a school site. A SPARC enables a school counseling program to demonstrate on an annual basis how a cohesive team supports academic success and school safety. The creative dialogue in this chapter between Bill Welcher (BW), high school counselor, and Bob Tyra (BT), school counseling consultant for Los Angeles County Office of Education, emphasizes the development of a SPARC to assist a high school in defining its school counseling program.

BW: When I first arrived at my new position as a high school counselor in the fall of 1999, I was shocked by the lack of available data to support many of the counseling programs being offered. The school population of 2,100, 9th through 12th grade students, reflected almost 60% free and reduced lunch participants. About 90% of the students qualifying for 4-year college entrance were the first in their families to attend college. Many students arrived at our school with little or no English background. The counseling activities had no data to support the activities and programs offered. Did they work? Did the students or parents like what was happening? I began to ask questions about the validity of a particular counseling program or policy. I was met with "Well, we have always done it this way" and "We think this is working because it feels good."

BT: Bill's questions and experience reflect much of what I heard when I was an American School Counselor Association (ASCA) National Standards trainer. As I worked with school counseling programs throughout California, counselors assured me that they were addressing the National Standards, but evidence of that work was hard to find or non-existent. The idea of being able to provide tangible documentation of National Standards implementation to not only the education community but also the general public became a topic of conversation at our monthly Los Angeles County Guidance Advisory Committee meetings.

BW: Having a background in science and athletics, I was used to the idea of using data as a matter of course. In science, I had to learn the scientific method, which taught you to develop a hypothesis and then provide experiments to collected data to either support or contradict your hypothesis. In my twenty-five years as a science teacher, I strove to tap into the natural curiosity that I believed my students had by having them investigate the world they lived in through the use of many laboratory exercises. They collected wonderful bits of information from these lab activities and learned that the process of collecting data actually gave them concrete information from which they could make a statement about the particular problem I had posed for them to solve. As a baseball coach, most of my personnel changes during the course of a game resulted from data I had collected concerning either key player match-ups or key game situations. If I had data telling me the hitter's last three at bats resulted in base hits on outside fastballs, you can bet I would tell my pitcher to throw the ball inside!

BT: Bill is a member of our Advisory Committee, and his background in science and athletics certainly helped us as we worked with the concepts of data and accountability. Our group includes graduate students, administrators, counselors, and counselor educators. We made our goal the design of a report card that was "do-able" for the working school counselor and the student support team at a school site. In keeping with the Tactics of Innovation as detailed by futurist Joel Barker (1998), it had to be true to the "seemingly simple, small steps" strategy of implementing a successful innovation. The Support Personnel Accountability Report Card (SPARC) was the result of our work. A very important feature of the SPARC was the inclusion of a "Focus for Improvement" section. We believed this section could prove to be an essential element in the development of a continuous improvement philosophy and an annual accountability report.

BW: In my third year at Sierra Vista High School, the Western Association of Schools and Colleges (WASC) Accreditation Committee recommended that my high school develop and implement a 4-year graduation plan.We were not sure if our plan for graduation was working, and furthermore, we were being asked to redesign it. Working with a colleague of mine in the information services department at the school district, we put together a 4-year graduation plan. It provides for career pathways in a format that allows for individual changes for any student at any time. This document allows for the registration of students and movement of data from the operating system directly to the plan. This is also a continuous improvement document, and like the SPARC, it has undergone many changes in the two years since its inception.

BT: There is no school counseling or student support program that can say that it has all the answers. Whether it is a 4-year plan, the implementation of a new program, or technology, the nature of working with our students and families requires adaptability. As Bill mentioned, the SPARC itself goes through a yearly review and is revised according to feedback we receive from administrators, counselors, counselor educators, and our public audience. We are currently in the first year of a two-year university research project to further help us with the continuous improvement of our report card.

BW: Without the SPARC as a document to provide me with an example of what an accountability document could be, I don't think that we could have put together such a program as the four-year plan. I truly get the idea of the importance of a rubric that asks counselors to evaluate their program based upon data that provides them with feedback about the validity of what they are doing. Informal reactions regarding our 4-year plan have been very positive. The SPARC kept us honest about our 4-year plan implementation. The public, teachers, students, and parents all have accepted our progress with our plan, and we have had validation for our efforts by our peers. Continuous improvement was built into the process. Each year as the counselors and administrations sit together to take a look at this document, there is a steady flow of ideas concerning ways to make this document even better.

BT: A large part of the success of the SPARC in California has been the incorporation of a statewide peer review and awards process. Schools that want to participate in an awards ceremony submit their report card on March 1 every year. Our scoring judges review each of the 10 sections of a report card to judge how well a school has met the demands of a scoring rubric. Every school counseling and student support program that passes receives an "Academy Award." In 2002, we had 63 schools in 2 California counties submit their report cards for review. In 2006, we had 143 schools in 17 California counties submit their report cards for review. California's two Recognized ASCA Model Program (RAMP) award winners, Brea Olinda High School and Sequoia Middle School have both been SPARC participants.

The creation of our SPARC network has even reached our state legislature. School counseling programs that have received Academy Awards for five consecutive years receive California State Senate Resolutions honoring their commitment to public accountability and continuous improvement.

Summary Conclusion

What is a SPARC?

The SPARC is a continuous improvement document that gives a school counseling and student support program an opportunity to demonstrate effective communication and a commitment to getting results. Modeled after the School Accountability Report Card (SARC), the Support Personnel Accountability Report Card (SPARC) has been developed by an advisory group of Los Angeles County counselors and consultants, counselor administrators, counselor educators, and California Department of Education consultants.

What do you do with a SPARC?

The SPARC will be useful in:
- Presenting a self-evaluation of your student support system;
- Promoting your program to your school administration, school board, community partners, and businesses and parents/guardians;
- Preparing reports for school accreditation, grants or award recognition, and;
- Implementing the American School Counselor Association (ASCA) National Standards and the National Model for School Counseling Programs.

S.P.A.R.C.

Support Personnel Accountability Report Card

A continuous improvement document sponsored by the California Department of Education and Los Angeles County Office of Education for the year 2006

Sierra Vista High School
3600 Frazier Street, Baldwin Park, CA 91706
Phone: (626) 960-7741 **Fax** (626) 856-4050
Website: www.svdons.com

DISTRICT: Baldwin Park Unified School District
GRADE LEVELS: 9-12 **ENROLLMENT:** 2096
SCHOOL YEAR: Traditional
PRINCIPAL: Jackie White

HOME of the DONS

Principal's Comments

The Sierra Vista High School student support team is the heart of the Sierra Vista family. The student support team plays a significant and strategic role in fostering a safe and secure campus and in improving the academic achievement of all students.

Sierra Vista offers a comprehensive guidance program driven by the National Standards for School Counseling. The student support team has received the National Counseling Standards Academy Award for four consecutive years. Last year, SVHS was honored as "Best in the West." Our SPARC is an accurate reflection of the success of our school student support programs and has been integrated into the school site plan.

The student support team ensures the following are accessible to ALL students and their parents: a) identification of students' academic, personal, college and career skills and needs b) referrals to appropriate school support staff, alternative programs and community resources c) continuous guidance in planning students' post high school education and careers.

Student Support Personnel Team

Student support is a team effort. The counselors design, implement, collaborate, and coordinate programs for the academic, career, and personal/social growth of all students. Collaboration through coordination with other support team members is an ongoing and invaluable process.

Team Member	Education Experience	Team Member	Education Experience
Principal	18	Welfare & Attendance Workers (2)	59
Asst. Principals (3)	8	Career Clerk	4
Counselors (4)	13	Attendance Clerks (2)	17
School Psychologist	19	Data Entry Clerk	11
School Nurse	29	Campus Security Aides (3)	11
Speech Therapist	29	Home Liaison	19
Career Counselor	29	Counseling Interns	3
Counseling Secretaries (2)	53	School Police Officers (2)	3

Student support team members have over 330 years of experience in education. Educational qualifications of the team members include: 17 Master's degrees, 10 teaching credentials, 5 administrative credentials, 1 Child Welfare & Attendance certificate, 2 school psychology credentials, 1 neuropsychological certificate, 1 school health credential, a translation certificate and 1 legal secretary certificate. All student support team members belong to their appropriate professional organizations. All counselors hold Pupil Personnel Services Credentials.

School Climate and Safety

At Sierra Vista, we believe students achieve academically and benefit socially when students and their families receive the services they need. The student support team takes an active role in maintaining a positive learning environment in which students feel safe and supported. Counselors develop, implement, and maintain a variety of programs for students including group and individual counseling, tutoring, and group guidance presentations related to academic, career, and post secondary plans. Student support team members also provide ongoing individual and interpersonal guidance and counseling. In addition, our student support team holds conferences with at-risk students and their families in order to refer them to a variety of school and community programs and services. Our student support team members also monitor the campus to make sure students are safe. As a result, the Sierra Vista High School climate is a positive one and the students' safety is not compromised.

Four years ago, the counseling staff identified a need for student services in the personal/social domain. We responded by creating and implementing an on-campus student support program. Counselors recruit, train, and supervise interns in counseling at-risk students, both individually and in small groups, in regards to academic, personal, and college and career issues.

Three Interns assisted 45 at-risk students and positively impacted school climate and safety by helping those students increase their communication and coping skills. They learned to resolve conflicts in a peaceful and effective manner. The effectiveness of this program is demonstrated by the student-reported results in the chart below. Ninety-eight percent of students receiving conflict resolution reported counseling helped them a great deal, in avoiding harmful behavior, such as fighting.

This is the sixth year of operation of the school-wide tutoring program. This year, counselors referred over 300 students to the program. The program, developed and implemented by the student support team, has proven its effectiveness in improving student grades as shown below. Data gathered on average Grade Point Average demonstrates this improvement.

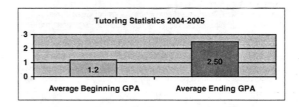

Tutoring provides academic support to students. As their knowledge and skills improve, students gain confidence in their academic abilities, become more academically motivated and improve their grades. When students are more engaged in the learning process, they also feel more connected and are less likely to be disruptive in and out of the classroom.

Student Results

The following results are examples of the student support team's efforts to implement a National Counseling Standards-based comprehensive guidance program and effectively address the students' needs.

Career Domain: Due to outreach efforts by the student support team, in collaboration with the math and science teachers, the number of students participating in career related, yearly and summer programs has increased significantly. The average number of participants has increased from 33 per year to 95, almost a 200 percent increase. Students have completed course work that has aligned their career interest with a summer academic enrichment program in math, science, engineering and health.

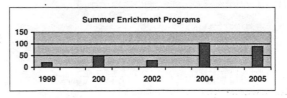

Academic Domain: Sierra Vista's Academic Performance Index has shown marked improvement over the past 7 years. The Sierra Vista Student Support Team impacts the API scores by utilizing proactive and intervention methods with at-risk students, thus meeting students' needs and promoting a climate of personal and academic responsibility and higher achievement. Individual conferencing with academically at-risk students is an integral part of this process.

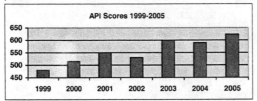

Personal - Social Domain: Weekly group counseling, implemented by the student support team, has helped assist students in coping more effectively with their personal and family problems. Examples of how much this personal support has helped students with their problems are depicted in the graph below. Ninety-eight percent of students receiving coping skills counseling reported that they were better equipped to resolve one or multiple issues.

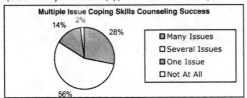

Major Achievements

Our student support team works to implement the National Counseling Standards and has received many accolades. Among them are:

The National Standards Academy Award 2001, 2002, 2003, 2004 Received for successful implementation of the National Counseling Standards and for ongoing development of the Support Personnel Accountability Report Card.

An electronic 4-year plan Developed in conjunction with the Information Services Department. This program allows for electronic 4-year and post-high school planning, as well as data gathering in reference to college choice.

Participation in monthly parent meetings As a result of increased advertising efforts the number of parents attending monthly meetings has doubled to 170. Counselors attend regularly, presenting valuable information.

Recognition by the Department of Education One of the top 10 Career Counseling Programs in 2002.

American School Counselor Association Award of Merit Received for development and implementation of the school-wide tutoring program in 2000.

Junior High Transition Activity Program Informative lessons are delivered by a high school counselor 5 times a year regarding the transition to high school, graduation and four-year college requirements and planning.

Career Pathway Information Each student will have an appropriately identified career pathway, based on interests and aptitudes, on their 4-year plan.

The student support team successfully addressed both items from last year's SPARC *1.* Counselors made classroom presentations and brought in community college representatives to speak to the students personally about their post-secondary plans. *2.* Counselors met individually with all students to discuss their post-secondary plans as a part of the electronic registration process.

Measurements

The student support team gathers information and interprets testing results to better assist in the management and responsiveness of the program. The following are some of our measurements.

Academic

- Preliminary Scholastic Aptitude Test (PSAT) - This test is given every year to our 10th & 11th grade students. Our counselors interpret the PSAT results for students.
- California English Language Development Test (CELDT) - Students with limited English are assessed for proper class placement.
- Scholastic Aptitude Test (SAT) – Students are encouraged to take this college entrance examination.
- Advanced Placement (AP) Exams – Students can earn college credits by taking and passing AP exams in many subject areas.
- Stanford Achievement Test 9th edition (SAT 9) - All 9th, 10th, and 11th grade students take this test to identify those students in need of additional support.
- California High School Exit Exam (CAHSEE) – Test results are used to identify and place academically at-risk students into English and Math support classes.
- Special Education Assessments – The school psychologist provides assessments for students with special needs, which allows for placement according to individual educational plans.

Career

- Armed Services Vocational Aptitude Battery (ASVAB) - Students receive information concerning career interests and personal aptitudes.
- California Occupational Preference System (COPS) - Students' career interests, aptitudes and abilities, as well as their personality and learning styles are identified for proper class placement and post-secondary planning.
- Career Choices - A computer-based program allows for students to investigate possible careers based on their interests.

Personal/Social

- Health Screenings – Our school nurse conducts health screenings to identify health barriers to academic success.
- California Healthy Kids Survey – This survey assesses a wide range of personal and social issues for our students.

Community Partnerships/Resources

The student support team interacts with many agencies and programs in order to meet the personal and social needs of the students. Our work with community partners supports and enhances the delivery of our program. Individual and family counseling, parent support groups, medical assistance, mental health services, and college preparation are among the many services that are provided by our community partnerships/resources.

Academic

Advancement Via Individual Determination (AVID) Citrus College, Rio Hondo College, Mt. San Antonio College, California State University Educational Talent Search, University of California Early Academic Outreach Program (EAOP), Adult Education, Princeton Review, Los Angeles County Office of Education (L.A.C.O.E.).

Career

Regional Occupational Program (ROP), Work Experience, Boy Scouts Explorers, Armed Services, Career Partners, U.C. Office of the President, Cal State University L.A., Modern Math and Health Opportunities, Kaiser Permanente Work Prep, INROADS.

Personal/Social

Project Sister, the Baldwin Park Teen Center for individual and family counseling, the Baldwin Park Police Department's Boot Camp Program, the Baldwin Park Family Service Center for parent support groups, and the East Valley Community Health Center for medical assistance.

Volunteer Involvement

Our student support team invites parents to be partners in their children's education. Parents provide invaluable support for the Sierra Vista student support program. One parent provides suggestions as a member of School Site Council. Parent volunteers assist with the planning and implementation of the annual Career Fair. Once again, our parent group is developing a newsletter to address specific issues and concerns including student support issues common to parents of Sierra Vista High School students. Interested parents and guardians should contact William Welcher at (626) 960-7741 ext 2021 or email wwelcher871@bpusd.net.

Focus On Improvement

The student support team is strongly committed to continuous improvement. Utilizing data and feedback from financial aid application completion and data from AP grades; the following improvement needs have been identified, prioritized, and aligned to the school improvement plan.

1. Counselors identified a need to provide more financial aid outreach to students and parents and will develop a plan to provide for this need.

2. Counselors identified a need for more classroom academic student support and will develop a system pairing AP students with core subject teachers.

Keeping you Informed

The student support team is dedicated to keeping the school and community informed. Because the support team is sensitive to home language needs, documents are sent home in both Spanish and English. Other translation is provided as needed. Listed below are some of the ways we communicate with our educational community.

- The SPARC is distributed to The Board of Education, administration and faculty.
- Phone Calls and home visits are conducted by the home liaison and the two attendance and welfare officers.
- Evening parent meetings are held monthly to provide valuable guidance information; also there is an 8th grade parent night, financial aid night, etc.
- Workshops are held for students interested in attending community colleges and four-year colleges.
- A monthly newsletter is distributed to all seniors.
- Student handbooks, which cover all school policies and procedures, are given to each student in the fall of each year.
- The high school Website is www.svdons.com
- Class visitations are conducted at each grade level at least once per year to provide pertinent guidance information.
- 10th grade conferences provide parents and students with the opportunity to have an evaluation of their progress towards H.S. graduation and fulfilling their post-secondary plans.

Discussion Questions

1. How does the use of data make a difference in a school counseling program?
2. How did Bill's work on the 4-year plan relate to his experience working with the SPARC?
3. Visit the www.sparconline.net website and review elementary, middle, and high school SPARCs. What are the similarities and what are the differences?
4. Why would a school counseling program choose to write and publish a SPARC?
5. Why would a peer review of a SPARC be an important element of a continuous improvement document?

Reference

Barker, J. (1998). Tactics of innovation. [DVD]. Available at http://www.starthrower.com/joel_barker.htm

Resources

For additional information about RAMP Award winners, view the American School Counselor's Association (ASCA) website at www.schoolcounselor.org

To review more than 80 SPARCs in California, the current scoring rubric, research reports, and the growth of accountability report cards across the country, please visit www.sparconline.net.

Chapter 11

From Planning to Practice:
Instituting Effective Professional Development

Brenda L. Melton and Janice S. Gallagher

Abstract

Instituting professional development for school counselors is a course of action to provide sustained growth and life-long learning. The 21st century role of the school counselor as agent of systemic change begins with professional development as part of the practice, supporting the school counseling program. Through collaboration, effective professional development must be relevant to the participants and based on needs assessments and data-driven programs. In this chapter, the authors address current research, resources, and practices from the perspective of a practicing school counselor and a counselor supervisor/educator.

Introduction

The *American School Counselor Association National Model* (ASCA, 2003, p. 43) includes system support activities in the Delivery System component that establish, maintain, and enhance the total school counseling program and promote systemic change. Professional development, as part of the system support component, ensures school counselor skills are updated in areas of curriculum development, technology, and data analysis through in-service instruction in school counseling curriculum and other areas of special concern to the school and community.

The 21st century role for counselors in education reform includes professional development as a process of collaboration, leadership, advocacy, and systemic change. Through professional development, *systemic change* may be achieved as counselors develop skills and advocate for school counseling program improvement. *Collaboration* generates enthusiasm and helps participants learn new techniques for reinforcing and developing accountability measurements in their program and supporting school reform (Lester, 2003). School counselors serve in *leadership* roles on campuses, attend to staff development, and subsequently provide staff development to other counselors, administrators, and educators. Through professional development, counselors advocate for student access and success and systemic change for strengthening school

counseling programs and the profession. As a benefit, effective staff development is part of the practice that adds depth and understanding.

Why Is It Important?

In *The ASCA National Model: A Framework for School Counseling Programs* (2003), system support includes "designated program and staff leadership, and program and staff development" (Gysbers & Henderson, 2006, p. 76). The ASCA National Model references three areas for updating and sharing professional knowledge and skills: 1) inservice training; 2) professional association membership; and 3) post-graduate education.

Planning and instituting staff development that is meaningful and relevant helps:
- To introduce new information about current trends
- Participants assume the role of learner if the learning is valuable to them.
- Job-embedded activities that originate from collaborative professional development planning sessions engage counselors as active participants in their learning.
- New strategies and ideas enhance counselors' expertise and best practices in the school counseling program (Lester, 2003).

Staff development is a critical factor in the implementation of an effective school counseling program. School counselor responsibilities regarding professional development include:
- Identifying resources
- Gaining access to resources
- Ensuring the utilization of resources
- Evaluating, including follow-up activities

Professional development needs to be approached as to how it will impact student learning. For example, if data shows that students are not performing well on assessment due to test anxiety or other factors, then counselors will advocate for professional development to improve interventions.

Brief Review of Empirical and Experiential Research

Counselors often are resource brokers that use data as a foundation for professional practice to identify resources, gain access to resources, and ensure the utilization of resources, which provides a clear direction to counselor action and a framework for accountability and advocacy (Colbert & Kulikowich, 2006). Professional development must be data-driven. Most states have in place an educational accountability system for measuring student academic success and progress. For example, Texas' Academic Excellence Indicator System (AEIS) provides a profile of school districts and campuses and disaggregates data into student groups (SES, ethnicity, age, gender, and special programs). Emerging research indicates effective professional development includes an action plan that participating educators use to bring positive change in student performance (Garet, Porter, Desimone, Birman, & Yoon, 2001). Through careful data analysis, professional development addresses student needs, achievement, and discipline indicators. In addition, equity and access discrepancies and barriers may be identified, which are referred to as "closing the gap" action plans in the ASCA National Model (2003).

As districts move toward new models that feature learning opportunities and topics suggested by research to improve professional skills, the implementation of collaborative action plans increases the acceptance of continuing professional improvement (Darling-Hammond, 1995). Information from this study indicates that educators are anxious to learn about best practices and willing to try new ideas and techniques for accountability in promoting student success.

Garet et al. (2001, p. 935) found that "sustained and intensive professional development is more likely to have an impact... than is shorter professional development". Lester states, "An effective professional development program involves a system of continuing dialogue to survive in a hectic school environment" (2003, p. 50).

School reform has prompted the development of learning communities, or small groups or teams with similar goals and interests that result in positive professional development and higher levels of learning for everyone involved, according to the National Staff Development Council's *Standards for Staff Development* (2001). Although most professional development

continues in face-to-face situations, technology has added dimensions by providing access to resources and a multitude of ways to facilitate electronic learning (e-learning), which may include videotape, audiotape, computer-aided instruction, tutorials, online courses, and Web-based videoconferencing. In addition to immediacy and access, professional development using e-learning offers more diverse learning experiences that are personalized, job-embedded, and less costly. The similarities between traditional professional development and e-learning are significant. Requiring the same level of support and resources to ensure effectiveness, both use many of the same learning processes, including collaboration, inquiry, dialogue, and reflection. Both modes seek the same outcome—to increase student achievement (National Staff Development Council, 2001, p. 7).

Professional Development Best Practices

Best practices are based on data from participants in the planning and follow-up stages and from expert experiences. Professional development entices and stimulates further exploration into areas of previous dogmas. Often times, counselor professional development has been "fun and games," but we must strive for a higher level of learning by integrating research into practice. Professional development must include partnerships with practicing school counselors and those who are deeply involved in behavioral research, action research, and program outcomes. Ideally, the efficacy of school counseling could be isolated from the work of others in improving student achievement. In reality, school counselors lead and collaborate with others to provide a comprehensive counseling program to meet the needs of all students.

Characteristics of quality professional development are high standards, content focus, and in-depth learning opportunities. Collaboration is effective in planning with the explicit goals to improve student success, thus measuring outcomes. School counselors must learn more about the student competencies (academic, career, personal/social), which they teach and about how students master these competencies. Continual deepening of knowledge and skills is an integral part of any profession.

In planning a professional development activity on guidance curriculum, the collaborative process would begin by collecting data about the topic choices. Study groups may form and develop guidance curriculum on different topics of interest. The study groups would

A Comparison of Professional Development Formats

	Traditional Format	Reform Format Lester (2003), Garet et al. (2001), National Staff Development Council (2001)
Type	Institutes, courses, conferences, workshops	Study groups, collaboratives, internships, peer observation. Networks/committees, resource centers, mentoring, coaching. On-going seminars and courses of study tied to practice; school-university partnerships-collaborative research, formal/informal learning opportunities; e-learning (Web-based) includes self-study and collaborative models using technology
Location	Away from school; outside the school environment	During the school day; during the process of activities
Duration	Same effects with same duration	Same effects with same duration
Leader/Group	Outside Expert(s) Group- passive learners	Peer leaders Collective participation at same school. Work together- more likely to discuss concepts, skills, problems; share common curriculum materials, course offerings, and assessment requirements
Schedule	Formal times	Self-determined
Core features	Content, interests	Professional Action Plan: content, active learning, and coherence
Outcomes	Immediate; may provide new information	Easier to sustain over a period of time; may change practice; more responsive to students' needs and goals Better outcomes of a longer duration Has student achievement increased as a result of the professional development activities? Are professional growth goals being met?
Responsiveness	May or may not be relevant	Meet immediate needs on an ongoing basis
Connections	Connected with conference theme, specific topic	Connected with school counselor activities
Technology	Utilize technology- PowerPoint; overheads. boards	May be more involved- Web-based; e-learning
Evaluation	Post session evaluation Less accountability Emphasis on the product	On-going participation, implementing practices and follow-up Emphasis on the process- reflection, reviewing, and planning

review the literature and curriculum and develop an action plan that includes goals and objectives, activities, and a timeframe for implementation and expected outcomes. The guidance curriculum study groups would meet at regularly scheduled times in an accommodating environment with a high level of participation. After implementing the guidance curriculum, participants would evaluate the effectiveness of the lesson or program. Through reflection, the participants would also develop best practices and share their experiences. The ongoing review of the process and outcomes would be an integral component of the professional development process (Lester, 2003).

Key Components of the Professional Development Process

According to Lester (2003), the professional development process involves three stages: (1) collaborative planning; (2) implementing; and (3) evaluating. Collaborative planning begins with a needs assessment and data analysis to generate topics for professional development. Study group members are selected with consideration of their level of expertise and involvement in the process. Objectives and outcomes are created using measurable, concrete terms with a timeline and assigned responsibilities. Activities and a timeframe for implementation are then developed to provide the learning opportunities to accomplish the expected outcomes. The logistics of professional development are found in the implementation stage. Examples are determining meeting times, the environment, and the level of participation (active or passive). Evaluation is an ongoing process as collaborative group members contribute by providing feedback on the effectiveness of the activities and reflecting on the content and the process.

Strategies for Implementing a Professional Development Program

In planning professional development, the process includes the following:
• Conducting a needs assessment

A needs assessment is a means through which counselors may share areas of concern, topics of interest, and aspects of the topic; help in designing the program with specific learning experiences; address specific needs and requests; and take ownership of the learning process. Participants are thus more open to trying new approaches and new ideas (Lester, 2003).

• Data analysis

Data may include academic, behavior/discipline, attendance, course distribution, and stakeholders' perceived needs and interests. The Counseling Program Advisory Council may be involved in the evaluation and environmental survey to recommend relevant professional development.

• Knowing your audience

The planning stage includes consideration of the most appropriate level of professional development (beginning, intermediate, or advanced). In addition, logistics, such as time, room arrangement, location, and resources need to be considered.

• Developing objectives and outcomes

Based on data analysis and needs assessment, the professional development objectives and projected outcomes are created using measurable, concrete terms with a timeline and assigned responsibilities.

Barriers and Challenges to Implementation and How to Address Them

Administrative support is essential in instituting professional development at a relevant and meaningful level of competency. Administrative support means being open to new ideas and providing the resources, time, and commitment to instituting professional development and systemic change. Without administrative support, change cannot occur.

Another challenge is breaking the mold of the "status quo"—doing what we have always done; we'll get what we've always gotten. Challenges voiced by single entities must be addressed or they will thwart the outcomes. You need to listen to the dissenters and incorporate their concerns into the professional development. By taking note of criticism and responding to individual or group concerns, the challenges of providing high-quality professional development are addressed.

Short and Long Term Benefits

Short-term benefits include immediate mental rejuvenation, and sparking enthusiasm. New ideas and techniques prompted by peer support add dimension to professional development. Sustained and intensive professional development is more likely to have significant impact than shorter professional development.

Professional development that focuses on content, provides active learning, and is integrated into the daily life of the school is more likely to produce long-term benefits of enhanced knowledge and skills. Monitoring, for example, identifies effective processes and mechanisms for professional development over time and across learning communities.

Conclusion

Instituting professional development for school counselors is a course of action to provide sustained growth and life-long learning. The 21st century role of the school counselor as agent of systemic change begins with professional development as part of the practice, supporting the school counseling program. School counselors as professional development team leaders can create consensus, promote shared values, ensure systematic collaboration, encourage experimentation, model commitment, provide one-on-one professional development/mentoring, offer purposeful professional development programs, promote self-efficacy, and monitor the sustained effort as evidenced by student success.

To be effective, school counselors should perceive professional development as relevant and based upon the needs as indicated by data-driven decision-making. Professional development creates a culture of readiness for change, promoting the vision, providing the necessary resources, ensuring the availability, maintaining checks on progress, and providing the ongoing assistance necessary for change to occur smoothly.

School counselors must translate what is learned in professional development and visualize its viability in practice. In other words, they must turn theory into reality. Professional development is a means to advocate for the professional status of the school counselor, as an expert in mental health as well as an educator on many different levels, with our publics- administrators, teachers, parents, school board members, community-at-large, and most importantly, students.

Discussion Questions

1. To what degree have stakeholders (e.g., students, educators, administrators, parents, counselors) been included in the study, analysis, and decisions regarding professional development?
2. How will technological/e-learning professional development be viewed in comparison to more traditional, face-to-face professional development?
3. What role does professional development play in your school or district?
4. How can professional development promote collaboration and group problem solving on issues of student achievement?
5. To what degree do school and district administrators understand and value counselor-led professional development?
6. Does the program measure results in terms of learners' outcomes and performance?
7. How much time is provided within the educators' calendar for professional development?
8. What steps will be taken to ensure that counselors have time for appropriate professional learning?
9. Is professional development considered essential in the school's improvement plan?
10. Is there a comprehensive professional plan to coordinate the integration of research and practice?
11. What forms of on-going follow-up are available to ensure implementation?
12. Do professional development participants have multiple opportunities to participate in real-time collaboration and social interaction?
13. Does the professional development environment allow for participants to learn about each other personally and professionally?
14. How is follow-up support sustained beyond the length of the program?
15. To what degree do the professional development strategies align with the intended outcomes, needs, and content?

Note: Special thanks to Beth Bourgeois, University of Texas at San Antonio, for her assistance on research.

References

American School Counselor Association. (2003). *The ASCA National Model: A framework for school counseling programs.* Alexandria, VA: Author.

Colbert, R., & Kulikowich, J. (2006). School counselors as resource brokers: The case for including teacher efficacy in data-driven programs. *Professional School Counseling, 9*(3), 216-222.

Darling-Hammond, L. (1995). Policies that support professional development in an era of reform. Phi *Delta Kappan, 76*(8), 597-604.

Garet, M., Porter, A., Desimone, L., Birman, B., & Yoon, K. (2001). What makes professional development effective? Results from a national sample of teachers. *American Educational Research & Journal, 38*(4), 915-945

Gysbers, N., & Henderson, P. (2006). *Developing and managing your school guidance and counseling program* (4th ed.). Alexandria, VA: American Counseling Association.

Lester, J. (2003). Planning effective secondary professional development programs. American *Secondary Education, 32*(1), 49-61.

National Staff Development Council. (2001). *Standards for staff development.* Retrieved March 25, 2006, from http://www.nsdc.org/library/authors/e-learning.pdf

Recommended Resources

Best Practices Center. (2006). *Rubric for evaluation.* Retrieved March 25, 2006, from http://www. bestpracticescenter .org/pdfs/sarubric.pdf

Desimone, L. Porter, A., Birman, B., Garet, M., & Yoon, K. (2002). *How do district management and implementation strategies relate to the quality of the professional development that districts provide to teachers?* Teachers College Record, 104(7), 1265-1312.

DuFour, R., & Eaker, R. (1998). *Professional learning communities at work: Best practices for enhancing student achievement.* Bloomington, IN: National Educational Service and Alexandria, VA: Association of Supervision and Curriculum Development.

Garmston, R., & Wellman, B. (1999). *The adaptive school: A sourcebook for developing collaborative groups.* Norwood, MA: Christopher-Gordon Publishers, Inc.

Guskey, T. (2000). *Evaluating professional development.* Thousand Oaks, CA: Corwin Press Inc.

Haslam, B. (1997, Fall). How to rebuild a local professional development infrastructure. *NAS Getting Better by Design.* Arlington, VA: New American Schools.

Hord, S. (1997). *Professional learning communities: Communities of continuous inquiry and improvement.* Austin, TX: Southwest Educational Development Laboratory.

Killion, J. (1999). *What works in the middle: Results-based staff development.* Oxford, OH: National Staff Development Council.

Kirkpatrick, D. (1994). *Evaluating training programs.* San Francisco: Berrett-Koehler Publishers.

Little, J. (1997, March). *Excellence in professional development and professional community* (Working paper, Benchmarks for Schools). Washington, DC: Office of Educational Research and Improvement.

Riel, M., & Fulton, K. (2001, March). The role of technology in supporting learning communities. *Phi Delta Kappan, 82*(7), 518-523.

Rényi, J. (1996). *Teachers take charge of their learning: Transforming professional development for student success.* Washington, DC: National Foundation for the Improvement of Education.

Senge, P., Kleiner, A., Roberts, C., Ross, R., Roth, G., & Smith, B. (1999). *The dance of change: The challenges to sustaining momentum in learning organizations.* New York: Doubleday, Inc.

Sergiovanni, T. (1994). *Building community in schools.* San Francisco: Jossey-Bass.

Sparks, D., & Hirsh, S. (1997). *A new vision for staff development.* Alexandria, VA: Association for Supervision and Curriculum Development and National Staff Development Council.

U.S. Department of Education Professional Development Team. (1994). *Building bridges: The mission and principles of professional development.* Washington, DC: U.S. Department of Education.

What matters most: Teaching for America's future. (1996). New York: National Commission on Teaching & America's Future.

Chapter 12

Response to Intervention:
What School Counselors Need To Know

John Brady and Jackie M. Allen

Abstract

An outcome of the Individual with Disabilities Education Improvement Act of 2004, Response to Intervention (RTI) is a three-tiered model of a cooperative process between general and special education designed to provide more students with early intervention to promote achievement and school success. This chapter explains RTI and the important role that school counselors can play in the process.

What Is Response to Intervention?

The new federal legislation reauthorizing the Individual with Disabilities ACT (IDEA) includes provisions for states to set up a new process, Response to Intervention (RTI), for helping children with learning problems. RTI is a cooperative process between general and special education that is designed to serve the academic, social, and behavioral needs of school children through a three-tiered model of service delivery. These tiers are designed and implemented by both general and special education staff and teachers.

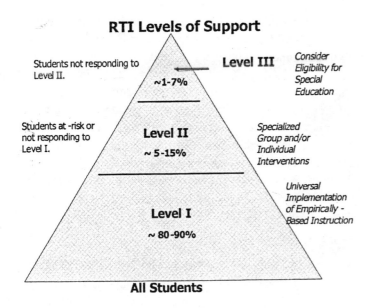

RTI Levels of Support

Students not responding to Level II.

Level III ~1-7%

Consider Eligibility for Special Education

Students at -risk or not responding to Level I.

Level II ~ 5-15%

Specialized Group and/or Individual Interventions

Level I ~ 80-90%

Universal Implementation of Empirically - Based Instruction

All Students

Figure 1. RTI levels of support adapted from Tilly (2006, p. 4)

At Tier I, all students in the school are screened for academic, social, behavioral, or emotional problems. At this tier, based on the screening, adjustments are made to the general education program (e.g., parent conferences, classroom grouping, homework contracts). Those children whose Tier I intervention does not result in enough progress in the targeted area(s) move on to Tier II interventions. In Tier II, the interventions are often based on specific individual or small group processes, such as a reading comprehension instructional group or a homework skills training group. Those students whose Tier II intervention did not result in significant progress are then referred for Tier III services. At Tier III, students are most often considered for special education services.

This new three-tier process emphasizes a collaborative effort between general and special education in which the school counselor can play a large role. In the past, students who had significant academic or behavioral/social needs would be referred for special education services, evaluated, and then served within the special education system. General education staff had little connection with or responsibility for them past that point, and often, prior to a special education referral, there were few other interventions to which a school could refer the child.

Under this new model, the student will be able to receive services at two levels, Tier I and Tier II interventions, within the general education system before consideration for special education services. School counselors will have an opportunity to help provide services to these children in the first two tiers and, if successful, students will avoid being referred to special education at Tier III.

School counselors already track and help at-risk students in their schools. These new RTI programs will provide extra resources for their work with these at-risk students. As noted above, the first resource will be a school-wide process for screening all children for academic, social, and behavioral concerns. In many schools, this has been left up to an informal process of teacher or parent referral and has often missed the needs of some children. Under the new program, schools will set up a coordinated and universal screening process that considers such factors as grades, test scores, teacher concerns, and parent concerns to determine who may need extra support. This screening process will determine which students need classroom support and help. In tracking their progress in the Tier I, supports that are general education classroom-focused, such as seating arrangements, will be made before going on to Tier II and Tier III interventions.

What School Counselor Skills Facilitate Response to Intervention?

The school counselor is uniquely qualified to be a significant participant in the RTI process in that he or she brings a number of important skills to the process. First, the counselor's central position in the school as a hub or resource broker for the whole school experience/environment is crucial in the implementation of RTI. The school counselor's relationships with parents, students, teachers, and staff are critical to making this new integrated general and special education program work.

Second, the school counselor has been trained in and uses communication and consultation skills in much of his or her daily work in the schools, and these skills are critical to an effective RTI process. Because this process creates opportunities for individual and small group interventions outside of special education the number of staff and parents who focus on student needs is expanded through the RTI process. Many more general educators are involved in the process, especially at Tier I and Tier II. This means there are more opportunities for the process to break down, either from a lack of communication or from conflict between the parties.

Participants who understand how to work in groups and get things done are needed to make the RTI process successful. An African proverb states, "It takes a whole village to raise a child," and sometimes it is necessary for elders to prod the other members of the village to assist in the important task of raising a child. Thus, school counselors will act as catalysts to facilitate the RTI process. School counselors' skills in collaboration, problem solving, and consultation will be in high demand to keep everyone focused on student needs and the development of effective interventions.

Third, RTI will not be limited to interventions in academics. It also will focus on children who have social, emotional, or behavioral concerns. The school counselor's knowledge of child development and the field's emphasis on working with the whole child will be invaluable. The American School Counselor Association (ASCA) National Standards, presented in the Foundation section of the *ASCA National Model: A Framework for School Counseling Programs, Second Edition* (2005), emphasize the three domains of academic, career, and personal/social in the nine content standards for students, listed below:

1. Students will acquire the attitudes, knowledge, and skills that contribute to effective learning in school and across the life span.
2. Students will complete school with the academic preparation essential to choose from a wide range of substantial postsecondary options, including college.
3. Students will understand the relationship of academics to the world of work and to life at home and in the community.
4. Students will acquire the skills to investigate the world of work in relation to knowledge of self and to make informed career decisions.
5. Students will employ strategies to achieve future career success and satisfaction.
6. Students will understand the relationship between personal qualities, education, and training and the world of work.
7. Students will acquire the attitudes, knowledge, and interpersonal skills to help them understand and respect self and others.
8. Students will make decisions, set goals, and take necessary action to achieve goals.
9. Students will understand safety and survival skills.

Many children with academic problems also have difficulties in the social, emotional, or behavioral areas of development. These are sometimes overlooked in efforts to help them academically. As noted above in the content standards, the use of career development and career counseling not only motivates students to achieve, but also adds the reality of the world of work and postsecondary education to the achievement of academic goals. The school counselor is in a good position to be the one who reminds the team to look at other areas of potential need and to help the team develop appropriate interventions.

The School Counselor's Role in Each of the Three Tiers of RTI

The Tier I of RTI focuses on ensuring that the child's instruction in the general education classroom is as appropriate and effective as possible. It is also the place that children are screened for progress, so that those needing extra help can be identified. The counselor's role at this level can take several forms: helping the teacher design and implement more effective classroom strategies for learning and behavior, helping students who are failing because of homework problems develop better skills, helping parents and teachers communicate about a student's deficiencies, and developing a comprehensive screening process for all students to determine who needs help (Figure 2).

Role of the School Counselor	
Tier I	Screening for at-risk students
	Member of School Study Team
	Interventions and behavioral strategies
	Home-school partnerships
	Consultation and collaboration
Tier II	Individual, group, and career counseling
	Monitoring of student progress in the interventions
	Data analysis of Tier I interventions
	Suggestions for more intensive interventions
Tier III	Referrals for special education assessment
	Participation in IEP meetings
	Participation in ITP career planning
	DIS counseling
	Facilitation of problem-solving and decision-making

Figure 2. **The school counselor's role in each of the three tiers of RTI**

Tier I of RTI is designed to provide students who are not doing well with classroom-based interventions. The school counselor is in a good position to help teachers with their students. Interventions such as seating placement, increased attention from the teacher, homework checking, peer tutoring, and checking for accuracy are some recommendations that school counselors could provide when asked for help with a student's classroom learning.

Other students do not perform well due to their behavior in the classroom. The school counselor can work with these students on self-monitoring of attending, responding, and note taking. The counselor also can work with the teacher on classroom rules, reinforcement for appropriate behavior, clarifying behavioral expectations with the student, and other behavior strategies that will make classroom learning more effective.

Another major role for counselors at Tier I is developing home-school partnerships for children who are having academic difficulties. Often, parents are either not aware their child is not doing well or do not know what to do to help their child. The school counselor is skilled in taking the lead in bringing students, parents, and teachers together. This can result in clarified expectations and in helping parents develop skills to assist their children with homework completion.

In addition to the direct involvement in academic skill building at Tier I, the school counselor can be a member of the team that develops and utilizes the screening process so that students in need of academic or social/behavioral help are identified early. School counselors, as members of Student Success Teams or Student Study Teams (SSTs), already work with students through general school referrals, state assessment results, and direct referrals from teachers. They are in a good position to help systematize the data so that they are looked at holistically and examined for gaps, where some students may fall through the cracks. The revised and improved screening process should attempt to screen all children in the relevant areas. The school counselor, in collaboration with other SST members, is in a good position to set up a systematic recording of screening results to ensure that direct services are provided to students. Mentoring, tutoring, cross-age teaching, individual or group counseling, study buddies, study skills classes, and peer counseling are some of these direct services.

Tier II of RTI helps those children who have not had their needs met in Tier I programs with more targeted interventions (i.e., the regular classroom with adjustments and other direct services). These interventions could include such services as specialized study groups, homework clubs, and individual behavior plans. The school counselor's role in Tier II interventions begins with the analysis of the screening data and the results of Tier I interventions. The counselor, in conjunction with the other learning specialists at the school, would regularly review the student performance data to identify students who are either very far behind their peers or who have had a Tier I intervention that was not effective. These students are then placed in Tier II intervention programs for approximately 10 to 12 weeks and monitored for progress.

At this level, the counselor, in addition to being involved in the screening, helps develop the interventions (e.g., creating a homework club). More intensive individual, group, or career counseling may be used at this point to assist the student in setting and attaining academic goals. In addition, the school counselor will help monitor the student's progress in Tier II and will help the student and staff integrate the Tier II interventions with the student's general education program. For instance, a student in a small group reading comprehension program may need to be reminded by the counselor to focus his or her practice on the content of his or her classes through weekly meetings or a progress report.

Tier III is often special education placement. As a counselor of the at-risk student, he or she will attend the Individual Education Program planning meeting and make suggestions regarding the need for mental health or Designated Individual Services (DIS) counseling or other special education interventions. At Tier III, counselors can be instrumental in facilitating communication and problem solving between general educators and special educators, facilitating the best placements in general education classes and activities for the student, as well as helping with specific plans for such things as career choices/planning and community resources.

School Counselor Efficacy in the RTI Process

School counselors already have a number of skills that make them effective in this model and that are critical to the success of the model. They are skilled in group dynamics and productivity, they deal with the whole organization and the whole child, and they regularly work collaboratively with parents. In addition to these existing skills, school counselors will need to know a range of research-based interventions, be good at collaborative problem solving, intervention implementation processes, and understand where they can be effective in the special education process.

The RTI model is based on the process of providing the student with help though a three-tiered system of increasingly intensive supports. Each tier of supports has its own set of interventions to support learning. These range from general classroom-based strategies to small group or individual interventions. A fundamental requirement of this intervention process is that it is based on interventions that have been demonstrated through research to be effective and that progress can be directly measured. The school counselor will need to be familiar with a range of effective interventions in all relevant student outcome areas (i.e., academic, social/emotional, behavioral). There is an extensive body of knowledge in this area (Deshler & Schumaker, 2006; Rathvon, 1999; Shinn, Walker, &

Stoner, 2002) from which schools may choose interventions. Although the school counselor does not have to be knowledgeable about all possible interventions, he or she must evaluate those that are proposed for a child by asking:

1. Is the intervention research-based and appropriate for this student?
2. How will progress be measured over the next several weeks/months to ensure that the intervention is working and not wasting student and staff time?
3. Is the school staff committed to providing the appropriate support to make the suggested intervention work?
4. Will there be flexibility in the recommendation of intervention(s)?
5. Will there be proper evaluation of the results of the intervention(s)?

For optimal effectiveness, as noted above, the school counselor also will need excellent collaborative consulting skills, in that the three-tier process is based on staff teams working across several complex systems: the family, general education, and special education. Effective group problem solving skills are needed to hold the process together and keep it focused. The counselor is uniquely qualified to provide leadership in this group problem solving process. The counselor maintains relationships with all the parties, as well as a view of the child as a whole. Collaborative consultation is based on solving problems utilizing each group member's unique contribution to the discussion of the problem. The school counselors' skills in this area can keep the process focused on effective problem solving.

Along with having knowledge of interventions and skills in collaborative consultation/problem solving, the school counselor needs to participate as an active member of the special education IEP team. Once a student has been involved with Tier I and Tier II supports, and they have not worked well, the student often will be considered for the more long-term help and modifications that the special education program can provide (normally this will be considered Tier III). In the past, general education staff has not been very involved at this level; however, in the RTI process, their involvement in Tier III or special education becomes an extension of their work in the two previous levels. The staff that has worked with the child, including the counselor, will have a lot of background and data on the child that will be helpful in planning the interventions at this level. The school counselor, through knowledge of such things as vocational education alternatives, counseling for students who need to explore alternative education paths, community resources, etc., should play an important role in the development of long-term plans, additional interventions, and Individual Transition Plans for students receiving special education services.

Conclusion

Response to Intervention can be a powerful process to help students develop academic, social, and behavior skills. RTI is a true prevention model, linking regular education and special education. Working together as a team, all educators need to act as a "village" and raise each child to be a productive and responsible citizen. In this RTI process, school counselors need to play a key role.

Discussion Questions

1. Has your school instituted the Response to Intervention Model?
2. What do you see as your role in the RTI process?
3. Do you have the skills necessary to assist in the RTI process? If not, what skills to you still need to acquire?
4. Are you a part of the Student Study Team at your school? What is your role?
5. Do you participate in Individual Education Program planning meetings? What is your contribution?
6. Do you work with your school psychologist, teachers, and other staff to facilitate student learning at your school? Explain how.
7. What area some interventions you might suggest for Tier I, Tier II, or Tier III?

References

American School Counselor Association. (2005). *The ASCA national model: A framework for school counseling programs* (2nd ed., p. 33). Alexandria, VA: Author.

Deshler, D. D., & Schumaker, J. B. (2006). *Teaching adolescents with disabilities: Accessing the general education curriculum*. Thousand Oaks, CA: Corwin Press

Rathvon, N. (1999). *Effective school interventions*. New York: Guilford Press

Shinn, M. A., Walker, H. M., & Stoner, G. (2002). *Interventions for academic and behavior problems 11: Preventive approaches and remedial approaches* (2nd ed.). Bethesda, MD: National Association of School Psychologists.

Tilly, W. D. (2006). Response to intervention: An overview. *The Special Edge, 19 (2)*, p. 4.

Section III.
Skill Building:
School Counselors as Practitioners

Chapter 13

Expanding the Therapeutic Repertoire of School Counselors: Family Systems Counseling with Children and Adolescents in Educational Settings

Charleen Alderfer and Mark S. Kiselica

Abstract

Over the course of the past two decades, there has been a growing movement to expand the traditional domain of school-based family services from consultation with parents and parent education to family systems counseling with students and their families. This chapter provides school counselors with an overview of a school-based, family systems approach to counseling students and their families. The central principles of family systems counseling are highlighted, and the process of making systemic interventions with individual students and school-based systemic interventions with families is described.

Historically, school counselors have provided therapeutic services to the families of students. Traditionally, their role has been to help families by serving as consultants to parents with respect to the behavior and development of their children (Wallace & Hall, 1996). For example, it is common for school counselors to offer parents advice regarding the development of educational plans for children and to hold periodic conferences with parents for such purposes (Thompson, 2002). School counselors also have regularly assisted families through the provision of ongoing parent education, utilizing structured, educational strategies with predetermined curriculum materials to teach parents particular skills (Wallace & Hall, 1996). An example of this service is a parent group-training program, which was developed by Cunningham and Brown (1990) and involved teaching single parents a variety of effective child rearing practices.

Over the course of the past two decades, however, there has been a growing movement to expand the traditional domain of school-based family services from consultation with parents and parent education to family systems counseling with students and their families. This movement has been prompted, in part, by calls for educational reforms that include new models of student success involving collaboration among schools, families, and communities (Taylor & Adelman, 2000). For example, Bilynsky and Vernaglia (1999) argued that school counselors must become adept at identifying children whose school adjustment difficulties are linked to dysfunctional family interactions and must know how to work with families to find solutions to the child's problems. Similarly, Carpenter, King-Sears, and Keys (1998) proposed that school counselors must work more closely with educators and families to create trans-disciplinary teams in order to serve students with disabilities more effectively. Dryfoos (1994) proposed that collaboration between parents and schools must involve contributions by community agencies to address the many needs of school students; and Holcomb-McCoy (2001) noted that school counselors are being called to play important roles in school-family-community (SFC) partnerships.

Numerous authorities on school counseling have proposed that the incorporation of family systems interventions into the domain of school counseling will strengthen attempts by schools to create better SFC partnerships (Fine & Carlson, 1992; Kraus, 1998). Ho (2001) suggested that family-centered counseling can be infused into the counseling, large group guidance, consultation, and coordination services of school counselors as a means to better serve students and their families. Mullis and Edwards (2001) described the fundamental concepts of family systems models and some of the basic techniques of family counseling (e.g., tactics for joining with families and strategies for focusing families on their strengths) as part of their vision for an expanded role of school counseling. Davis (2001) reported a case study in which a student's disruptive behavior in school was addressed by making structural changes in the student's family system. The purpose of this chapter is to extend the ideas of these authors by describing how school counselors can make systemic interventions with individual students and in-school systemic interventions with families.

We propose that the provision of family systems counseling in schools is consistent with the responsive services component of the *ASCA National Model: A Framework for School Counseling Programs* (American

School Counselor Association, 2006), which emphasizes counseling to address the crucial events and situations in students' lives for the purpose of enhancing student development and academic achievement. Accordingly, in this chapter we have included two brief case studies illustrating how school counselors successfully employed family systems principles to respond to urgent family-related matters that were adversely affecting the adjustment of students in school.

School-Related, Family Systems Counseling

School counselors must be prepared to use different forms of family systems counseling. In some instances, the counselor must work systemically with an individual student and not his or her family because either the school does not permit the counselor to see families or a family refuses to participate in counseling. In other cases, the counselor will work directly with families in the school.

In-School Family Systems Counseling with Individual Students

There are models of family counseling in which the individual is the focus of treatment. Among these are Bowen's natural systems theory (Bowen, 1978; Kerr & Bowen, 1988), solution-focused, (de Shazer, 1985), and early communications models (Watzlawick, 1983). In each model, the individual is the client who is seen by the counselor; but the family dynamics are the focus of the treatment. Counselors following Bowen's model are likely to work on developing a genogram, the symbolic depiction of at least three generations of one's family of origin, to determine the client's place in the generational patterns and behaviors. A solution-focused counselor will work to help the client discover existing ways to deal with the problem by focusing on the positive rather than negative aspects. When the solution-focused model is used with adolescents, the family is likely to be of central importance; but it also may be the peer group. The early communication models were the forerunners of post-modern narrative models, both of which emphasize telling the story of the problem with consideration of multiple perspectives – an approach that often appeals to adolescents. The retelling of the story focuses on understanding situations more positively, which allows the client to have different feelings in relation to the problem. Any of these models is useful when it is not possible or against school policy to see the family as the client. The systemically-oriented counselor can use both his/her training and established models to work with the adolescent.

In the following case example, the school counselor has knowledge of systems theory, which she can use in working with her student even though school policy does not permit her to do ongoing counseling with families. She elects to work with the student by following Bowen's natural systems theory, a model of treatment that allows her to work with the student with a family perspective.

Jenna is a 16-year-old, upper-middle-class, white female who is a junior in high school. She is bright, involved in Shakespearean theater, and plays several instruments very well. She has always had some difficulty fitting in with her peers partly due to her so called off beat intellectual interests, her lack of athleticism, and her weight problem. She has been in several different schools, all catering to her intellectual needs. After a serious bout of depression that left her hospitalized, her present private school refused to take her back. She has been forced to go to a public school because no other private school would take her in mid-semester. The adjustment has been traumatic and image shattering. Her school counselor, Marie, is trying to facilitate the transition, and, at the same time, adhere to the school policy of "fixing the student" as quickly as possible.

The administration in this school district believes that counselors in the high school are hired primarily to help the students find and be accepted by appropriate colleges. Providing counseling to students with emotional problems is a small part of their job description. However, policy does allow counselors a limited amount of time to work with students before referring them to an outside counselor or therapist. Marie is aware that Jenna's parents have just divorced. The impact of that event and the years of unhappiness in the family described by Jenna inform the structure of Marie's treatment plan. She knows the policy will not allow her to work with Jenna and her parents together, so she proceeds with Jenna alone. Marie realizes she needs more information to help Jenna through her depression and anxiety, not only in relation to school, but with her family issues as well. She learns from Jenna's description of family life that she has always been her mother's ally and confidante and, although she loves her father, is afraid to show it for fear that she will hurt or alienate her mother. This rigid and fixed triangle has been her life story.

Marie is trying to place Jenna in honors classes so that she will feel better about herself, but Jenna's fear of disappointing one or both parents is interfering with the process. As Jenna tries to be acceptable to a peer group that has been together for nearly four years, she finds that her talents are respected by a precious few and they tend to be what the school has labeled "alternative kids." Marie continues to work within the parameters of the school policy, so all her information comes from Jenna's perception of her parents rather than Marie's direct experience of them. Jenna's grades remain high because of her superior intellect;, but, because she needs a peer group, she has become a part of the drinking and drugging group. This leads her to be seen by school personal as a bad influence. It will take more than finding the right classes to help her survive in this setting.

With family systems training, the counselor is alert to the triangulation and boundary problems that continue to affect Jenna's mood and her performance in school. Without ever conducting a family counseling session, Marie uses these principles to work with Jenna. She constructs a genogram with Jenna to help her see patterns of behavior through the generations, areas of over-connection and of cutoff, and relationships where triangles have existed in other areas of the family (McGoldrick, Gerson, & Shellenberger, 1999). To help Jenna think about her place in the family structure, she uses her understanding of the enmeshed boundary indicating over-involvement between Jenna and her mother and the seemingly disengaged boundary indicating under-involvement between Jenna and her father (Minuchin, 1974). The task of this stage of family development is separation and leaving home. Marie addresses this task with Jenna and helps her to see that separation is a normal process at this age. She uses examples of the importance of being cared for physically as a child and psychologically as an adult. She and Jenna use an enactment by role-playing a problematic event between Jenna and her mother or father, thus increasing her ability to see a different way of relating to her parents. This is an especially difficult intervention for Jenna because she has been entwined in her parents' relationship for her whole life.

Because Marie sees only Jenna for treatment, her therapeutic role is shaped by the nature of their relationship. Marie serves as a transitional attachment figure while Jenna moves toward the development of the emotional independence she previously had not been able to enjoy. Marie is aware of the developmental stages

of both Jenna and her family. Clearly, the divorce has interfered with a successful pattern of leaving home, even though college has always been a part of the plan for Jenna. Now, both parents feel the need to have her nearby to help them through their difficult transition. At the same time, they want her to go to an excellent college. It is impossible for her to fulfill the desires of each of her parents. It is also necessary for Marie to be aware of the importance of a peer group and the disruption Jenna has had in that area. It is highly unlikely that, in a few months, she will find a group comparable to the one she had in her other school. Her need for attachment to a group of people her own age with values similar to hers will not be satisfied easily or quickly. It is not surprising that a desire for acceptance led her to the "wrong crowd." In spite of this, Jenna was able, through the guidance of her counselor, to reconnect with a friend from grade school who was in her present class. This gave her at least one support in addition to Marie's unwavering concern.

The counselor with an understanding of family systems is able to assess the patterns of behavior that have become rigid and destructive as well as those that are functional and supportive. She can determine the student's role in the family and assess how this is affecting the observable behavior, which has been labeled symptomatic. By understanding the life cycle of the family, she can help the student to more effectively work through the tasks of that stage of development (Carter & McGoldrick, 1999). As a more holistic picture of Jenna emerges, the counselor with systemic training is more fully equipped to work with her even without the family present for treatment. The presence of the whole family in treatment most certainly would have expedited the entire process towards a more effective and efficient outcome.

In-School Family Systems Counseling with Families

Recognizing the importance of seeing the student in the context of her or his family and not an entity acting alone, some schools have begun to hire school counselors with systems training (Fine & Carlson, 1992; O'Callaghan, 1993; Silvestri, Steinberger, & Scambio, 1996). In a recent segment of 60 Minutes (CBS-TV), the principal of the Molly Stark School in Bennington, Vermont, instituted a program in which family therapists were a part of the school staff. They worked with children and their families in family counseling over a period of time. Marked positive changes were noted at the end of treatment in terms of the child's behavior in the school setting and reports by parents of improved behavior at home.

School districts that hire school counselors with a family systems orientation may face some roadblocks in the process. When local teachers' unions determine policies for teachers, those policies often apply to the counselors as well. This can create problems, particularly in the determination of flexible time. Usually counselors can see families only after school hours, but policies permitting that to happen are often not in place. Therefore, a principal or superintendent needs to be committed to family counseling in the schools and be willing to take the issue to the next level.

A second identified problem is the determination of the kind of work that is done by a school counselor on the secondary level. Often, their job descriptions include far more administrative and disciplinary duties and college placement counseling than mental health counseling. Therefore, there is little, if any, time to see students, let alone to see families. Job descriptions may need restructuring so that counseling and working with families are seen as equally important as administrative work.

A third area of potential difficulty is confidentiality. It is common practice for teachers, administrators, and counselors to discuss students' problems and progress. When the family becomes the client, the protection of confidentiality is dependent on the ability of all those involved to respect the boundaries of the therapeutic relations. Ideally, the counselor gives information about students to school personnel only with the proper consent forms signed by those involved. Information about the family is not given to school personnel except when the family requests that it be given. In reality, it is a difficult situation for the counselor who is a part of the school staff and has been, for the most part, accustomed to sharing information about students with school staff. It would behoove school personnel to have careful and thoughtful discussions about the issue of confidentiality before initiating the practice of family counseling in the school. It should not be incumbent only on the counselor to maintain boundaries, but also on the staff.

If the difficulties can be addressed and remedied as much as possible, the benefits of instituting the practice of family counseling in the schools are many. About the use of systems theory, Fine states, "Mental health professionals, whether school or community based, can utilize this frame of reference to precipitate changes that have the potential to be lasting" (Fine & Carlson, 1992, p. 15). The possibility of lasting change

is certainly an incentive to include families in the treatment of their children. In the paradigm of systems theory, working with the individual creates first order change and is temporary, while working with the family creates second order change which affects the whole system and tends to create a more stable system that will support that change (Watzlawick, 1983). Frequently, the student having the most difficulty in school, behaviorally or educationally, has parents who are uninvolved with the student in relation to the school. By including them in the treatment, second order change can be effected not only in the family, but also in their relationship to the school. As the family situation improves, parents become more able to deal with the school personnel and feel less threatened by issues that arise in school.

The following case is an example of cooperation between an elementary school counselor and a secondary school counselor, both of whom are trained in family systems theory. The case included both school counselors because it involved an elementary and a middle school student from the same family. Although the initial focus was on the elementary school student, it soon became clear to the counselors that the identified client was not the younger sister, but rather the adolescent and her mother. Fortunately, the school district in which they worked was supportive of family systems work as a part of the counselors' job. Their decision was to allow the elementary counselor to see the family since the younger child was referred to her and, with the consent of the mother, the two school counselors kept in touch about the progress of the family. Teachers were informed that treatment was in progress, but they could only get reports if the mother agreed. When counseling ended, each followed up with their respective student and had a good understanding of the family's dynamics.

Carrie is a second grade white female who was sent to the elementary counselor by her teacher. She had been crying in class and saying she hated her hair, which had just been cut, and that she "wanted to die." The teacher reported that she was often either distracted or hyperactive in class. After speaking with the child, the counselor decided to call and invite the family for a session to determine more about what was happening in the family. Beth, Carrie's mother, Carrie, and Mary, Carrie's 14-year-old sister, joined Carrie for the session. The parents had been divorced three years ago, and the girls saw their father on a regular basis.

After introductions, the therapist, whose model

of working is Bowenian, asked the family to construct a genogram (McGoldrick, Gerson, & Shellenberger, 1999). Beth described her early life in Ireland and explained that at age fourteen, her mother came to the states and brought her youngest daughter, but left Beth and her sister with their dad in Ireland. It was not until Beth was nineteen that she came to the states. Even then, she felt cut off from her mom, who has since died. She describes her relationship with her ex-husband as having "the usual ups and downs," but also states that she is still very close to her father and her sister.

Carrie began to talk about Mary and how much she liked to be with her. Mary agreed, but tried to act unconcerned, not unusual for an adolescent. Mary also talked about having only a few friends in school. As the focus quickly turned to Mary, she began to cry. When the therapist intervened with an enactment by asking Beth what she did when Mary cried and to do it now, Carrie played quietly by the therapist's side. After some time of Mary and Beth talking, Mary said quietly, "I thought you didn't love me when Carrie came along." More talking and reassurances began a conversation about Beth's disconnection from her mother and her fears and difficulty about becoming too close to her daughter for fear of losing her. Carrie continued to play and watch out of the corner of her eye. At the end of the first session, the therapist congratulated Carrie for bringing her mother and sister to counseling.

Treatment continued with the elementary school counselor keeping the secondary school counselor apprised of the progress. If scheduling had allowed, they could have worked as co-therapists with the family. In lieu of the ideal situation, they spoke after each session in the language of family systems, one each of them understood.

In this case, assessing the information in the genogram and discovering the family projection process was a key component of understanding the present behavior of Mary and Beth (Bowen, 1978). Developmentally, Beth had left home in a premature and destructive separation from her mother. Now that Mary was at that same age, the fear of a painful separation happening again was alive in the family unconscious. Carrie was the only one able to signal the problems, which she perceived existing between her mother and sister. She became the symptom bearer and drew attention to a potentially volatile family problem (Haley,

1980). Beth's separation from her mother when she was fourteen was not resolved as she continued to be cut off from her mother who was now deceased. There was no way to work this out face-to-face, and a replay of those feelings occurred as Mary was now the same age as Beth had been when she experienced being abandoned. Mary's fears of being sent to live with her Dad were activated, as she was aware of the family history. The projection process, which puts the hopes and fears of one generation onto the next generation, was not a part of the family awareness. This dynamic could only exacerbate Mary's feelings of potential upcoming abandonment. Pulling Carrie closer and pushing Mary out was not a rational response, but it was the only one Beth had experienced with her own mother. These systems interventions created a better understanding between the two and allowed Carrie the freedom to be a little girl again and dispense with the care taking of her mother and sister. As the school year wore on, there were fewer complaints about Carrie from her teacher; and the secondary school counselor, who continued to see Mary every other week, reported that she was more outgoing and seemed to be developing a peer group with whom she was comfortable. Because of the counselor's awareness of the family dynamics, she was able to include discussion and intervention based on her theory of families in general and on this family in particular.

Discussion

In response to demands that school counselors be prepared to carry out interventions that involve one or more members of a student's family (Baker & Gerler, 2004) and contribute to the mission of school-family-community (SFC) partnerships as a part of the educational reform movement (Holcomb-McCoy, 2001; Taylor & Adelman, 2000), we have described two approaches to doing family systems counseling with middle school and high school adolescents and their families. Consistent with the ASCA National Model (American School Counselor Association, 2006), we demonstrated how family systems counseling fits within the domain of responsive student services. Two case studies were provided, which illustrated how school counselors used systemic interventions to enhance the school adjustment of two troubled students.

We recognize that the degree to which school counselors practice family systems counseling and the type of family systems counseling that is employed will be determined by the needs and requirements of community boards, state regulations, and parental demands. These requirements vary greatly from school district to school district, so school counselors must understand and accommodate to the rules that shape counselor roles in their school district. The approaches to family systems counseling discussed in this article provide school counselors with two options for doing family systems counseling in response to these external requirements. School counselors who are limited to counseling with students only can use family-systems concepts to help individual students to explore the relationship between family dynamics and personal and school adjustment. Counselors employed in districts providing more flexibility to work with families can engage families in counseling in schools.

Two other approaches to school-related family counseling, which were beyond the scope of this chapter, can also be practiced. First, school counselors can make home visits and conduct family counseling with students in their home. Second, counselors employed in schools with a SFC partnership utilizing the services of outside agencies on school grounds can develop a cooperative arrangement with those agencies to furnish family systems counselors as consultants to the school. The degree to which counselors do these latter forms of family counseling will be determined by school policies and resources for such services.

In some school districts, there may be strong opposition to school counselors doing any type of family systems counseling. We recommend that school counselors who find themselves in this position take proactive measures to define family systems counseling as an appropriate service within the domain of school counseling. Related to this idea, Bryan and Holcomb-McCoy (2004) urged counselor educators to teach school counseling students how to advocate for SFC partnerships that include services for families. School counselors interested in redefining their roles to include providing assistance to families in schools will find useful suggestions for transforming school counseling in Gysbers and Henderson (2000).

Although it is possible that some school districts will oppose the provision of family systems counseling, it is encouraging to note that family counseling in schools has gained wider acceptance by school administrators, teachers, parents, and counselors (Boyd-Franklin & Bry, 2000; Merrill, Clark, Vavril, Van Sickle, & McCall, 1992; O'Callaghan, 1993; Silvestri et al., 1996). In addition, school counselor training programs have begun to include family systems training in their curricula (Terry, 2002). So, both the school counseling profession and school systems appear to be on the verge of embracing family systems counseling. Related to this trend, the senior author of this article is the coordinator of a post-master's degree program in marriage and family therapy. Most of the students in the program are school counselors who have sought specialized training in marriage and family therapy. They have been highly committed to learning about family systems theory and techniques; and they have applied their knowledge about family systems approaches in their schools, exemplifying that the ideas described in this article can enhance the work of school counselors. Given the complex and varied needs of families in contemporary American society, we believe that other school counselors will find family systems models helpful as they assist students to maximize their personal development and academic achievement.

Discussion Questions

1. How does the practice of family systems counseling expand the traditional work of school counselors with students and their families?
2. Describe how a counselor can use a family systems approach during individual counseling with a student?
3. What are some of the potential roadblocks that might prevent school counselors from doing family systems counseling with families in schools?
4. How can family systems counseling enhance student academic achievement?
5. In this chapter, school-based family counseling with either individual students or students and their families was emphasized. What are two other approaches to school-related family counseling?

References

American School Counselor Association. (2006). *The ASCA National Model: A framework for school counseling programs.* Alexandria, VA: Author.

Baker, S. B., & Gerler, E. (2004). *School counseling for the twenty-first century* (4th ed.). Upper Saddle River, NJ: Pearson.

Bilynsky, N. S., & Vernaglia, E. R. (1999). Identifying and working with dysfunctional families. *Professional School Counseling, 2,* 305-313.

Bowen, M. (1978). *Family therapy in clinical practice.* New York: Jason Aaronson.

Boyd-Franklin, N., & Bry, B. (2000). *Reaching out in family therapy: Home-based, school and community intervention.* New York: Guilford Press.

Bryan, J., & Holcomb-McCoy, C. (2004). School counselors' perceptions of their involvement in school-family-community partnerships. *Professional School Counseling, 7*, 162-171.

Carpenter, S. L., King-Sears, M. E., & Keys, S. (1998). Counselors + educators + families as a transdisciplinary team = more effective inclusion for students with disabilities. *Professional School Counseling, 2*, 1-9.

Carter, B., & McGoldrick, M. (1999). Overview: the expanded family life cycle: Individual, family, and social perspectives. In B. Carter & M. McGoldrick, *The expanded family life cycle: Individual, family, and social perspectives* (p. 2). Needham Heights, MA: Allyn & Bacon.

Cunningham, N. J., & Brown, J. (1990). A parent group training program for single parents. In E.R. Gerber, J. C. Ciechalski & L. Parker (Eds.), *Elementary counseling in a changing world* (pp. 54-62). Ann Arbor, MI: ERIC Counseling and Personnel Services Clearinghouse.

Davis, K. M. (2001). Structural-strategic family counseling: A case study in elementary school counseling. *Professional School Counseling, 4*, 180-186.

deShazar, S. (1985). *Keys to solution in brief therapy.* New York: W.W. Norton.

Dryfoos, J. G. (1994). *Full-service schools.* San Francisco: Jossey-Bass.

Fine, M., & Carlson, C. (1992). *The handbook of family-school intervention: A systems perspective.* Needham Heights, MA: Allyn & Bacon.

Gysbers, N. C., & Henderson, P. (2000). *Developing and managing your school guidance program* (3rd ed.). Alexandria, VA: American Counseling Association.

Haley, J. (1980). *Leaving home: The therapy of disturbed young people.* New York: McGraw-Hill.

Ho, B. S. (2001). Family-centered, integrated services: Opportunities for school counselors. *Professional School Counseling, 4*, 357-361.

Holcomb-McCoy, C. (2001). *Examining urban school counseling professionals' perceptions of school restructuring activities.* (ERIC Document Reproduction Service No. ED452451)

Kerr, M., & Bowen, M. (1988). *Family evaluation.* New York: Norton.

Kraus, I. (1998). A fresh look at school counseling: A family-systems approach. *Professional School Counseling, 1*, 12-17.

McGoldrick, M., Gerson, R., & Shellenberger, S. (1999). *Genograms: Assessment and intervention* (2nd ed.). New York: Norton.

Merrill, M., Clark, R., Vavril, C., Van Sickle, C., & McCall, L. (1992). Family therapy in the schools: The pragmatics of merging systemic approaches into educational realities. In M. Fine & C. Carlson (Eds.), *The handbook of family-school intervention: A systems perspective.* Needham Heights, MA: Allyn & Bacon.

Minuchin, S. (1974). *Families and family therapy.* Boston: Harvard Press.

Mullis, F., & Edwards, D. (2001). Consulting with parents: Applying family systems concepts and techniques. *Professional School Counseling, 5*, 116-123.

O'Callaghan, J. (1993). *School based collaborations with families: Constructing family-school-agency partnerships that work.* San Francisco: Jossey-Bass.

Silvestri, K., Steinberger, C., & Scambio, E. (1996). Collaboration and reform: A model for MFT in the schools. *Family Therapy News, 27*, 22-23,27.

Taylor, L., & Adelman, H. S. (2000). Connecting schools, families and communities. *Professional School Counseling, 3*, 298-307.

Terry, L. (2002). Family counseling in the schools: A graduate course. *The Family Journal: Counseling and Therapy for Couples and Families, 10*, 419-428.

Thompson, R. A. (2002). *School counseling: Best practices for working in the schools.* (2nd ed.). New York: Brunner-Routledge.

Wallace, W. A., & Hall, D. (1996). *Psychological consultation: Perspectives and applications.* Pacific Grove, CA: Brooks/Cole.

Watzlawick, P. (1983). *The language of change.* New York: Basic Books.

Chapter 14

Working with Students of Deployed Family Members

Kelly Collins and Gerald Chandler

Abstract

Working with families during times of deployments is not an easy task. This chapter provides useful information regarding the stages of deployment and outlines possible emotional issues students may experience during each stage. Activities that professional school counselors can employ with affected students and families are provided along with helpful websites and print resources.

Why Is This Topic Important?

September 11, 2001, changed the world's view on many things. For students, this tragedy brought about a reality, which they believed, only existed in their history books—war. Oates (2002) states, "In the period from September 14 through 30, 2001, 29,000 military personnel were deployed to the conflict region on brief notice and approximately 17,000 reservists were called to active duty." Consequently, professional school counselors are faced with the challenge of assisting students in dealing with the effects caused by deployment. Deployment doesn't affect just the military family; it affects the school and community as a whole. While the military does much to take care of their own, the soldiers, it is those left behind that the professional school counselor must assist. "The role of the professional school counselor during this time is that of ally: ally for the student, ally for the affected family, and ally for the staff who work with these students on the 'front lines'" (Collins, 2005).

Research on the effects of deployment on students is rare. However, much research exists on stress, anxiety, and fear in children and adolescents. Professional school counselors can draw on this vast amount of research to work with students who have a deployed family member or members.

The Deployment Sequence

When using the term "military," the authors are referring to all branches of the military: Air Force, Army, Coast Guard, Marines, National Guard, and Navy. This includes the National Guard and Reserve Forces as well as the regular military services. Deployment can be best defined as the time when military personnel are required to serve temporary tours of duty (TDY) and cannot take the family (Military Child Education Coalition, 2004). The area where the soldier is called to serve can be a state or an ocean away from the family. No matter where an individual is called to serve, deployment is a time of transition with unique issues at every step.

Stages of Deployment

Deployment is best illustrated in three stages: pre-deployment, deployment, and reunion (Military Child Education Coalition, 2003). The initial stage, pre-deployment, is the time prior to deployment. This period can last from months or weeks to just hours. During this stage, families attempt to adjust to the idea of one parent being away for an extended period of time. Maladjustment may occur when this stage happens rapidly, and the student is not given adequate time to adjust to the loss of a family member. Stress is often high during this time period.

The second stage is deployment. During this period, a family member is physically gone on a temporary duty assignment. Remember, this assignment may be across an ocean, in a dangerous circumstance, or right around the corner. In some instances, there may be a rapid deployment or a deployment without warning. Thus, the child is thrust into the second stage without the adjustment time allowed during the pre-deployment stage. For example, a child may have breakfast with their parent and arrive home from school only to discover that mom or dad has been deployed. This is often complicated when the parent is in a unit that is deployed with a great deal of secrecy such as not knowing where or what the mission is. This stage can further be complicated if the deployed individual is a single parent or if both parents are being deployed. This situation forces the child into another home life with grandparents or other guardians who may or may not live near where the child currently lives.

The final phase is reunion. Reunion is best described as the time when families are reunited after deployment. This phase carries with it some very distinct characteristics such as readjustment to family life for the soldier and an additional parental figure for the child. Although each phase of the deployment cycle has its own unique issues and concerns, which can be handled separately, school is the one constant in the student's life. Therefore, the most important thing for the professional school counselor to foster during this time is communication for the student and family.

Issues That May Arise During the Deployment Cycle

Issues arising during the varied parts of the deployment cycle will vary not only from child to child but also between age groups. In addition, they may overlap.

Pre-deployment

During pre-deployment, commonly seen issues that span all age groups are anxiety, shock, and disbelief (Collins, 2005). One key consideration for the professional school counselor to remember during this time is that these students believe the safety and security of their lives is gone due to the parent's leaving. The stress level in many homes rises dramatically as a parent make plans that most civilian, non-military individuals, take for granted (Kennedy, 2004). For example, the deploying individual must ensure that finances are in order so that bills can be paid during the absence, that a will is drawn up, and required paperwork is completed. Furthermore, the individual must make sure that practical things like home leases and automobile maintenance are taken care of before leaving. Add the emotional toll of leaving your family, hoping that you will have a means of communicating with them while you are away, and that they will have a strong support system while you are deployed, it's easy to see why these children need the support of everyone to adjust during this difficult time.

Deployment

When the parent or, in some cases, parents deploy, many students struggle with feelings of loss and grief. They work through the five stages of grief (denial, anger, bargaining, depression, and acceptance) that individuals who have experienced a death or catastrophic event undergo (Kubler-Ross & Kessler, 2005). In sharp contrast, some students have strong coping skills and face this time with resiliency (OSD staff, n.d. a). Regardless of how students and their families begin the

deployment cycle emotionally and cognitively, most find a way to cope and adjust to a "normal" way of life without the deployed parent or spouse. However, their "normal" may be completely dysfunctional.

Looking for the best way to see how a student is coping? Ask. Most students are waiting for an adult who isn't their parent to show an interest in them during this time. When asked how it felt when his dad was deployed, one student responded, "It really wasn't any big deal. My dad goes TDY a lot, so I am used to it." Another teenage girl responded: "I was really scared. My dad goes TDY a lot, but I always know where he is going and what day he is going to be home. This time was different. I knew my dad might have to go to war, but I didn't think it would really happen. He talked to my sisters and me a lot about it and made sure that we knew he might have to go, but couldn't tell us where he was going or when he would come home. One day I came to school and when I got home; he was gone. He wasn't able to call us for almost two weeks. Every day I watched the television to see if he was on it. When he did finally call, he only got to talk to us, my sisters, mom, and me, for five minutes. I was glad he was okay, but we didn't know if he would be able to call us again. So, I started watching the television to see if he was on it" (Collins, 2005).

A conversation the author (K. Collins, personal communication, Fall 2005) had with a mother who has two teenage daughters focused on discipline. She said, "The girls just don't mind me when their dad is gone. They walk all over me. I don't know what to do about it." These examples are but a brief view into the world of students with deployed family members and the issues that may arise.

Reunion

When a family is made aware that their loved one is returning, the emotional rollercoaster begins again. This time anticipation replaces anxiety as the most commonly reported emotion (OSD Staff, n.d. b). Students wonder how their parent will look when they return. They question whether the parent has changed or wonder if mom or dad will know who they are. Some students report being upset that their parent is returning. One young man stated, "Now that my dad is coming home, I won't get to be the man of the house anymore." Another young man declared, "My dad is really strict. I won't get to play my video games as much now that my dad is coming home" (Collins, 2005). The majority of the focus on behaviors during deployment is negative.

However, there are some positive behavioral changes that may occur. Deployment can promote maturity, facilitate personal growth, foster independence, and increase flexibility. Additionally, deployment can help students build abilities for dealing with separations and losses later in life. Finally, and perhaps most importantly, it helps strengthen family bonds (Military Child Education Coalition, 2001).

Behaviors to Look for During Deployment

Many of the behaviors discussed do not appear within specific age boundaries. Therefore, for the purpose of this chapter, the authors will not break them down within the specific cycle stages, but will list the general school age categories and the corresponding concerns.

Preschool – Elementary Children: Anxiety; anger outbursts; confusion; regression in behaviors like thumb-sucking; overly concerned about losing someone else; overly cautious; clinging; and fear of things that they were not afraid of prior to deployment.

Middle School - Junior High: Anxiety; anger outbursts; quick temper; depression; withdrawal from normally enjoyed activities; change in relationships with same-age friends; and choosing adults over friends.

High school: Eating difficulties; sleeping difficulties (may include nightmares); psychosomatic complaints of headaches, stomach aches, or other illnesses; irritability; and increase in school problems such as grades or attendance, and behavioral changes.

At all levels changes in a child or adolescent's normal behavior should be monitored. Although behaviors have been broken into specific school ages, remember that symptoms can cross age boundaries depending on the maturity of the individual.

Activities to Support Students During Times of Deployment

The following activities have been used successfully by professional school counselors in assisting students. The authors have chosen to divide the activities into school age categories; but all activities can be modified to be used across the age span.

Pre-School and Elementary School:
- Create a bulletin board devoted to parents who have been deployed.
- Allow each student to bring a picture and write something about their parent (Collins, 2005).
- Encourage teachers to incorporate deployed parents into their lesson plans.
  1. A math lesson could include figuring the distance from your city to where parents are deployed.
  2. English lessons could utilize letter writing on a regular basis, and stories could be incorporated that show children overcoming conflict through problem solving skills.
  3. Geography lessons could include a study of the cultures of the various locations.
  4. Art lessons could include creation of an "All About Me Book."

Middle School through High School:
- Create a "Hall of Stars" where stars are made out of cardboard, then decorated and hung in a special section of the school with the service member's information and the student's information. This would allow the entire student body and faculty to offer support and encouragement (Hockstader, 2005).
- Faculty can become involved within their specialty areas.
  1. Individuals in language arts could incorporate reports or papers that focus on the area of deployment. In addition, this department could encourage students to keep a journal with happenings and things to share with deployed family members upon their return. After Desert Storm several returning veterans at Ft. Bragg indicated that such a journal or scrapbook helped them to reconnect with their family. This was particularly true where their children were going through various developmental changes (G. Chandler, personal communication, 1992).
  2. The social studies department could focus on map reading and geographical facts.
  3. The mathematics department could discover equations necessary for travel to deployment areas within a specified amount of time.
  4. The family and consumer sciences and foreign language departments could host an International food fair featuring cuisine from the deployment area.
- All faculty should encourage students to get more involved in school activities.

How the Professional School Counselor Can Help

The best place to begin with any type of program

is to conduct a survey. The survey does not need to be elaborate; it simply needs to gain required information to assist the professional school counselor in determining the most appropriate services (See Figure 1). Be sure to include staff members in your survey; they may be directly affected, too.

Instructions: Please answer the questions below. This information is being collected from all students and faculty. It will be used to offer assistance to those who are concerned about the present military situation.

1. Is someone you personally know in the military deployed overseas or called to active duty for service in the U.S.?

   _____ yes   _____ no (If "no" go to question 4.)

2. If "yes", who is this person?

   _____ your mother _____ your father _____ your brother/sister
   _____ other relative _____ a friend

3. How do you feel about the safety of this person?

   _____ Extremely concerned and anxious
   _____ A little concerned and anxious
   _____ Not at all concerned

4. What are your feelings about the current situation in the United States since the events of September 11, 2001?

   _____ Extremely concerned and anxious
   _____ A little concerned and anxious
   _____ Not at all concerned

Figure 1 – Sample Survey Form
(Adapted from Oates, 2002)

Services that should be implemented in all situations are individual and group counseling. Individual counseling may be more beneficial during the middle school through high school years, depending on the various student needs. At the elementary level, small group counseling with students on problem-solving skills, grief, and communication may be extremely valuable. In addition, classroom guidance activities can also focus on these issues (Oates, 2002).

Educate staff members about how to deal with these students. Provide your staff with information and handouts about how to respond to traumatic events. Also, provide them with handouts on how to help students handle stress and how to help them handle their own stress. Encourage your staff to be sensitive to students and each other during this time. They should closely monitor what is shown in their classroom. News reports should be kept to a minimum. In the event watching newscasts is part of the curriculum, encourage the creation of an alternate assignment for those students for whom watching might do more harm than good. Also, advise staff members to watch voicing their personal opinions about what is going on—even when they think no students are listening. You never know just how good their hearing might be! For instance, a student told the author (K. Collins, personal communication, September 2005),

I always thought my dad was doing the right thing by choosing the military as his career until we were discussing the war in one of my classes. The teacher disagreed with what my dad was doing and said some really terrible things about soldiers and the war. It made me wonder if what my dad did was really making a difference. It was the first time I didn't see my dad as the hero.

Resources Available

An abundance of resources are available to assist the professional school counselor in helping students and families deal with deployment. These resources range from books and pamphlets to websites. Each service branch has a family support center on their military installation as well as a website which deals with issues specific to their branch of service and their preferred coping mechanisms. Make sure to have a point of contact at the family support center closest to you in the event a student or family needs assistance beyond what you can give them. This individual can also assist the professional school counselor in obtaining items and services offered by the military that would otherwise be unavailable. The Military Child Education Coalition is another great resource. This organization was formed to support military children during times of transition.

You can find outstanding publications for download and Website links at http://www.militarychild.org. In addition, the guidance channel, part of The Bureau for At-Risk Youth, has numerous publications to assist military families at a minimal cost. Their Website is http://www.MilitaryFamily.com. Another excellent resource that both authors have used is http://www.militarystudent.org. This site is designed especially for students of all ages and the issues they face being military. It even includes scholarships available only to military dependents.

Professional organizations can also serve as a great resource. The American School Counselor Association has links and downloads available at http://www.school counselor.org. The American Counseling Association also has resources available at http://www.counseling.org. You can use group exercise books to assist in developing activities that work for your clientele. Another wonderful resource is the *Skill* streaming series by McGinnis and Goldstein, which focus on pro-social skills. Finally, utilize the Internet. A simple Google search will provide thousands of links for you to explore.

Professional School Counselors Can Make a Difference

As a professional school counselor, you are required to wear many different hats. When working with families during times of deployment, you do not need to have all the answers. You should have knowledge about the deployment cycle, issues that may arise, and signs to look for in affected students. With this information in hand, try various activities to assist

affected individuals. Patience, persistence, and personal contact are what the professional school counselor must remember. Ultimately, these families are a puzzle; and you must help them work at finding the pieces that connect to make their picture complete. Many of them cannot do it without some assistance from the professional school counselor. You don't have to work wonders. A bottle of puzzle glue will work just fine.

Discussion Questions

1. What are your views on the military?
2. How will your beliefs impact the way you work with children whose parent(s) are in the military and in particular those whose parent(s) have been deployed?
3. In the event of a parent death while he/she is deployed what should be the role of the school counselor in assisting the student?
4. Should outside groups be allowed to demonstrate at the above funeral? What are the pros and cons of this issue?
5. How many in your graduate class grew up in a military family? What was it like for them being a military dependent? Look for patterns of similarity and difference in their experience.
6. If there are no graduates who grew up in a military family, seek out several adults who were military dependents as well as children who are currently dependents and interview them. Look for patterns of similarity and difference in their experience.
7. After interviewing/discussing these issues have your perceptions changed? If so how and why?

References

Collins, K. (2005, March/April). Dealing with deployment. *The ASCA School Counselor*, 11-14.

Hockstader, L. *War shadows school near fort hood.* Retrieved January 5, 2005, from http://www. militarystudent.org

Kennedy, A. (2004, June). Emotion cycle of deployment information for civilian counselors about the military family. *Counseling Today*, 1, 12, 45.

Kubler-Ross, E., & Kessler, D. (2005). *On grief and grieving: Finding the meaning of grief through the five stages of loss.* New York: Simon & Schuster Ltd.

Military Child Education Coalition. (2004). *How communities can support the children and families of those serving in the National Guard or Reserves.* [Brochure]. Harker Heights, TX: Author.

Military Child Education Coalition. (2003). *How to prepare our children and stay involved in their education during deployment.* [Brochure]. Harker Heights, TX: Author.

Military Child Education Coalition. (2001). *Working with military children: A primer for school personnel.* [Brochure]. Harker Heights, TX: Author.

Oates, M. (2002). Meeting the needs of adolescents with a family member recently deployed for military duty. *TCA Journal, 30*(2), 68-75.

OSD Staff. (n.d. a) . *How to cope.* Retrieved January 5, 2005, from http://www.militarystudent.org/teens

OSD Staff. (n.d. b). *Getting ready for the return.* Retrieved January 5, 2005, from http://www.military student.org/kids

Chapter 15

Brain-based Learning

Jackie M. Allen

Abstract

The decade of the 1990s was declared "the decade of the brain." Neuroscience has provided the educator with an abundance of knowledge about the development and function of the human brain. Now in the 21st century brain research demands a new approach to traditional pedagogy. Reading, writing, and mathematics abilities all are seated in the interrelationships of brain functions. Learning styles have changed and challenge educators to approach learning in new ways. School counselors, as part of the educational team, can make a difference in student success by employing the knowledge from brain-based learning research.

Introduction

In the past decade, advances in neurology and application of that knowledge to education have resulted in the development of brain-compatible or brain-based learning. Researchers have suggested that the scientific-inquiry has developed to the point of providing evidence-based techniques for working with learning disabled students in a brain-compatible way (Bender, 2002).

The brain is a marvelous organ and perhaps the most complex machine ever constructed, about which we are just beginning to learn. "The brain is also the basis of our interactions with the world. Indeed, it is the organ responsible for realizing there is a 'me' and there is a world that is different from me" (Dubin, 2002, p. 1). Our growing understanding of how we learn is all there in brain anatomy and how the brain learns. Communication, alertness, attention, memory, problem solving, emotionality, visualization, movement, and creativity all are aspects of brain functioning.

Eric Jensen (2000) challenges us to come out of the "Dark Ages" and view learning from a new perspective; "Present problems cannot be solved with the same level of thinking or with the same tools that created them" (p. xii). Wolfe (2001) explains that learning is a process of building up neural networks to make curriculum meaningful through problem-solving, simulations, and role play. Matching instruction to how the brain learns is resulting in the confirmation of some well-established principles of learning such as repetition and multimodal approaches as well as paving new paths in memory, attention and behavior, areas crucial for the success of the learning disabled (LD) child. For example, accessing the episodic, procedural, automatic, and emotional memory lanes and developing episodic memory strategies facilitates learning (Sprenger, 1999).

Background

I remember when I first started my career as a school psychologist in the early 80's and the Resource Specialist was testing students using the Frostig and the Illinois Test of Psycholinguistic Abilities, including both fine and gross motor activities in the assessment. If the student did not meet the age level norms, perceptual motor training was recommended. At that time, learning disabilities were described as "minimal brain dysfunction." When such approaches failed to mediate the learning disabilities, the profession turned to behavioral approaches to work with learning disabilities and still did not find a satisfactory solution for working with LD students. After 30 years of empirical research supporting a biological basis for the majority of childhood disorders, once again we are returning to the brain to understand and explain learning disabilities and behavioral disorders (Miller, 2007). Feifer and DeFina have done extensive research on the neurobiological connections to reading disorders (2000), written language disorders (2002), and mathematical disorders (2005). Feifer and Della Tofallo expanded previous research linking cognitive neuropsychology, Response to Intervention, and a scientific approach to reading disorders (2007). Attention Deficit Hyperactivity Disorder and pervasive developmental disorders are explained as having their etiology in brain-based abnormalities (Kolb & Whishaw, 2003).

Numerous articles, books, and papers have emphasized the importance of brain research and neurological findings on the development of learning in children. The decade of the brain was the 1990s. For example, Sylwester (2006) writes about the Tween Brain, the brain development between infancy and adulthood. Malcolm Gladwell, drawing on both neuroscience and psychology, explores new frontiers of decision-making in *Blink: The Power of Thinking Without Thinking* (2005).

Training programs in neuropsychology have mushroomed in the last 5 to 10 years. The Fielding Institute in Santa Barbara, California, was one of the early programs to develop a certificate in Clinical Neuropsychology. The American Board of School Neuropsychology announced a national school neuropsychology training program in 2005, held the first national conference for school neuropsychology in 2006; and currently there are 195 diplomates across the United States. The Association for Supervision and Curriculum Development produced a series of educator-friendly books, videotapes, and online resources on brain research around the beginning of the 21st century.

The Need for a New Approach

Dropout rates have skyrocketed, as much as 40% to 50% in many urban school districts. Employers demand literacy in reading and also in technological skills. Learning styles have shifted from a predominantly auditory processing society to a majority of today's students preferring visual stimuli and kinesthetic learning. Visual learning preference is now 46%, kinesthetic tactile-35%, and auditory –19% (Swanson, 1995; Sousa, 1997). Notable legislative influences upon education have come fast and furious in the past six years. First the No Child Left Behind Act (NCLB) of 2001, than the Rethinking Special Education for a New Century Report (Finn, Rotherham, & Hokanson, 2001) for the Thomas B. Fordham Foundation and the Progressive Policy Institute, the Report of the President's Commission on Excellence in Special Education (2002), Minority Overrepresentation in Special Education (Donovan & Cross, 2002) for the National Research Council, Learning Disabilities Roundtable Report (2002), and the reauthorization of Individuals with Disabilities Education Act in 2004—Individuals with Disabilities Education Improvement Act (IDEIA) with the Response to Intervention model. Student needs have also prompted a new approach to learning and particularly for those students who are having difficulty learning.

Old methods of determining learning deficiencies used the discrepancy model in which the student's Full Scale IQ measured; and intelligence was compared to achievement in reading, mathematics, or written language. This method of determining a learning disability and eligibility for special education has been

described as a "wait and fail" method. The new method of Response To Intervention holds promise, but also has been described as "failure to respond" (Fagan, 2007). A new approach must be preceded by knowledge of the relationship between the function of the brain and its relation to learning.

Brain Function and Academic Performance

Sophisticated scientific imaging tools have made it possible to actually track and measure brain activity. Computer-Assisted Tomography (CAT) scans and Magnetic Resonance Imaging (MRI) provide structural imaging. Electroencephalography (EEG), Event-Related Potentials (ERPs), and Evoked potentials (Eps) are used in tracking electrical activity in brain waves at rest and during tasks. Positron Emission Tomography (PET) scans and functional MRIs use blood flow to do functional imaging. With these advanced scientific methods, it is possible to understand not only the structural areas of the brain affected by learning disabilities, but also the functional aspects of brain activity through the measurement of electrical activity and blood flow moving to and from various regions of the brain. (Berninger & Richards, 2002, p. 64).

Out of these biological and physiological research studies, we are beginning to understand how a child learns to read, do mathematical calculations, and write language using symbols. The next step is to incorporate that knowledge into our pedagogy, into our counseling techniques, and into our skills as educators to assist students in the learning process.

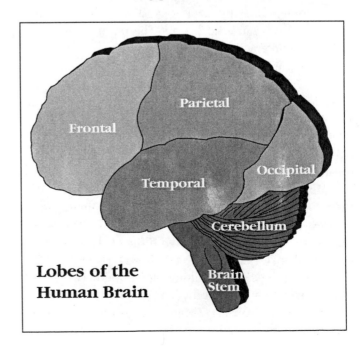

The four major lobes of the brain are the frontal lobe, the parietal lobe, the temporal lobe, and the occipital lobe (Figure 1). Hale and Fiorello (2004) divide up the functions of cortical structures in the following way: the frontal lobe as the motor area with the function of praxis-drawing, writing; the parietal lobe as the somatosensory area with the function of gnosis-feeling/texture/pressure; the temporal lobe as the auditory area with the function hearing-understanding/memory; and the occipital lobe as the vision area with the function of seeing-objects/words/faces. The frontal lobe includes Broca's area, the source of expressive language, the "brain director" in charge of executive function, working memory, self-monitoring, decision-making, behavioral and emotional regulation, and cognitive flexibility. The temporal lobe contains Wernicke's area, the receptive language area, which receives auditory information and is important in language comprehension. The parietal lobe is the primary processor of somatosensory information processing touch, pressure, pain and temperature and is also associated with spatial perception and sense of oneself in the environment. The occipital lobe is associated with visual processes including color, location, orientation, contrast, and motion.

A simplistic view of brain function would link human behavior to one region of the brain and assign a task such as reading or writing to the function of one lobe of the brain. We know, for a fact, that no complex human behavior can be linked to one specific brain area. In order to understand brain-behavior relationships, it is important to examine interrelated brain networks. Differences in brain organization and function may be greater in a single individual than differences between individuals (Hale and Fiorello, 2004)

Learning and academic tasks such as reading, mathematics, and writing involve the coordination of many brain functions. Sousa (2007, p. 84) concludes, "Reading is the most difficult task for the young brain to do." It begins with phonemic awareness and moves to reading comprehension. For the effective reader, three neural networks must coordinate: auditory processing, cognitive processing, and visual processing involving the visual cortex, the angular gyrus, and Broca's and Wernicke's areas. Reading impacts every aspect of learning, and problems in reading are the most common difficulties for school age children. Dyslexia has been used as the generic term to describe reading difficulties. In actuality, there are many types of dyslexia, from Dyslexia with Dysgraphia ("Deep Dyslexia"), the severest form of reading disability, to Dysnemkinesia

Dyslexia, minimal dysfunction in letter formation frequently evidenced in letter reversals, such as d for b, and p for q. (Pierangelo and Giuliani, 2006) Learning to read is a process utilizing attention and executive function as well as short and long-term memory. The student who is unable to read suffers greatly from lack of self-esteem and lacks confidence in the ability to do other types of schoolwork.

Like reading, writing requires the coordination of multiple neural networks. The parietal, occipital, temporal, and frontal lobes as well as the limbic system are all involved in writing. Attention, fine motor coordination, memory, visual processing, language, and higher-order thinking are all part of learning to write. The simultaneous processing of writing starts with visual input and moves to orthographic analysis, graphemic output, and motor output (Wing, 2000). Dysgraphia is "the inability to perform motor movement…extremely poor handwriting" (Pierangelo & Giulianai, 2006, p. 48). Dysorthographia describes difficulty in spelling. Even in the computer age, writing difficulties frustrate students and may cause students to avoid learning. Inventive spelling can lead to permanent memory of misspelled words (Sousa, 2001). In the elementary grades where written assignments are required, poor writers and poor spellers may give up and refuse to turn in any assignments.

Mathematics, the third "r" in "Reading, wRiting, and aRithmetic," requires phonological working memory abilities, visual-spatial abilities, and central executive system cognitive abilities. Feifer and De Fina (2005) emphasize the importance of executive functioning and math. Sustained attention, planning skills, organization skills, self-monitoring, and retrieval fluency are all necessary to develop math skills. Dyscalculia is the impairment in mathematical reasoning or in calculation skills. A number of mathematical disorders are frequently seen in students with dyscalculia. Basic mathematical skills are built on language skills, working memory, executive functioning skills, verbal retrieval skills, and visual-spatial skills. Mathematics, like reading, involves a series of hierarchical skills that must be developed to master the meaning and understanding of numbers. Brain development, unique in each individual may not provide the readiness for abstract concepts until late teens or early adulthood. The student who attempts algebra too early may experience failure until his/her brain is developed to handle abstract thinking.

Student support professionals (counselors, psychologists, and social workers) have increasingly been charged with providing services for all children to promote academic achievement and school success. Teachers and student support professionals must work together in Student Study Teams to determine what students need to succeed. The American School Counselor National Model (2003) calls for a cross walking of school counselor standards and state standards. Standards have been raised, and accountability has been demanded. No longer can any educator sit in the bleachers and let others on the playing field carry the ball. All educators are cognizant of the enormous responsibility of bringing all students up to the level of meeting academic standards, passing high school exit exams, graduating from high school, and being prepared for post secondary education.

What Can Educators Do?

Berninger and Richards (2002, p. 317) in *Brain Literacy for Educators and Psychologists* summarize *the attributes of brain-based educators:*

1. Acknowledge, tolerate, and celebrate normal variation in students.
2. Recognize that learning is the result of nature-nurture interactions.
3. Understand that learning is a long developmental process from novice to expert
4. and is characterized by alternative learning pathways and different levels of learning outcomes in specific domains and components.
5. Draw on the multiple codes and modes of representation (redundancy) in designing instructional hints and clues and alternative instructional approaches if the current ones are not effective.
6. Recognize that functional systems involve many different components that have to be orchestrated and thus the complexity of the learning process.
7. Use multiple modes of assessment to document and evaluate student progress and keep up to date on research literature.
8. Have patience and "compassionativity".

Counselors, as part of the school's educational team, have the privilege and opportunity to provide many support services for students, consultation to faculty, recommendations for local system change, and leadership in the overall school system. The ASCA National Model indicates the following school counselor themes: leadership, advocacy, collaboration and training,

and systemic change. Eric Jensen in his book, *Brain-Based Learning: The New Science of Teaching & Training* (2000), suggests many ways to enhance learning through brain-based activities that can be used in the school and as a basis for staff in-services. These suggestions have been adapted to assist counselors in developing brain-based learning. The following ideas are divided into four groups: suggestions for school system leadership and change; collaboration and advocacy with teachers; support for parents; and services for students (Allen, 2006).

School System Leadership and Change

- Provide in-service training for staff on Brain-Based Learning.
- Develop each one-teach one-cross age teaching program.
- Start intergenerational tutoring and peer tutoring programs.
- Encourage the school system to keep art, music, and physical education in the curriculum.
- Provide an in-service for teachers on learning disabilities.
- Start a school wide "learners club."
- Help teachers create positive learning environment for all learning styles.
- Support the use of scientifically-based interventions by the Student Study Team and the entire faculty.
- Work with other educators to create a safe, violence free environment where students can learn.
- Serve as an informed, active member of a Student Study Team.

Collaboration and Advocacy with Teachers

- Disseminate information about brain-based learning workshops and lectures to staff.
- Team teach a study skills class including lessons for students on how to ask adults for help and develop coping skills.
- Work with teachers to develop educationally enriching field trips to museums, businesses, etc.
- Encourage teachers to have patience with slow learners and learning disabled and special education students.
- Work with teachers to help students develop problem-solving and decision-making skills.
- Help teachers design learning-style appropriate curriculum for learning disabled and special education students.

Support for Parents

- Assist parents in understanding learning disabilities.
- Provide grief counseling with families to help them adjust to special education qualification and placement for their children with low incidence disabilities.
- Provide parents with information about learning disabilities, study skills, parent-student relationships, school success, etc.
- Encourage parent patience with slow learners and learning disabled and other special education students.

Services for Students

- Recommend student interventions under the Response To Intervention model.
- Recommend student assessment when appropriate.
- Avoid labeling students as "slow learner" or "hyperactive."
- Use memory games, such as Concentration, in individual and group counseling.
- Develop students' unique strengths and skills - every student has some.
- Provide individual counseling to assist students with personal and family problems so that they can focus on schoolwork.
- Help students individually and in small groups work on organizational skills, e.g., organize a notebook, set up a schedule for schoolwork and homework, etc.
- Counsel students to help them understand their learning problem and help them develop coping skills.
- Work with students on building self-esteem.
- Identify students with attitude problems, possibly stemming from learning disabilities.

Summary and Conclusions

School counselors are challenged to inform themselves about new brain research and its application to student learning. Brain-based learning techniques and methods provide the student support services member with insights into individual student needs. Reading, writing, and arithmetic are the basic academic subjects in which all students must achieve mastery in order to transition into postsecondary education and/or the world of work. If no child is to be left behind, all students, including those with learning disabilities, must receive the full services of educators both in the classroom and in the counseling office. There are many ways in which counselors can facilitate the learning process; only a few of them are listed in this chapter. It is the author's hope that this will be just a beginning for more exploration into brain-based learning and increased application of brain-based learning techniques. School counselors can make a difference in the lives of each student by realizing the importance of individual differences, diverse learning styles, brain function and growth, rates of development, and academic abilities.

Discussion Questions

1. Are you familiar with brain-based learning techniques, if not, how can you learn?
2. Do you know your preferred learning style? What is your preferred teaching or counseling style?
3. Are you acquainted with individuals who have learning disabilities? Do you relate to them differently than others? How do you feel about being around individuals with severe handicapping conditions? How might you improve your comfort zone?
4. How would you work with a learning disabled student to assist that student make academic progress?
5. What type of in-service would you design to help your teachers become familiar with and use brain-based learning techniques?
6. How would you work with teachers to assist students make academic progress?
7. How would you help parents to understand the needs of their students who are challenged by learning problems?
8. What other brain-based ideas would you suggest that counselors use in their schools?

References

Allen, J.A. (2006). Workshop presentations at the 2006 International Counselling Conference, Brisbane, Australia.

American School Counselor Association (2003). *The ASCA national model: A framework for school counseling programs.* Alexandria, VA: Author.

Bender, W.N. (2002). *Differentiating instruction for students with learning disabilities: Best teaching practices for general and special educators.* Thousand Oaks, CA: Corwin Press, Inc.

Berninger, V.W. & Richards, T. L. (2002). *Brain literacy for educators and psychologists.* New York: Academic Press.

Donovan, M.S. & Cross, C.T. (2002). *Minority students in special and gifted education. Committee on minority representation in special education.* Washington, DC: National Research Council.

Dubin, M.W. (2002). *How the brain works.* London, England: Blackwell Science Inc.

Fagan, T.K. (2007). Quoted in *From specific learning disability identification within the context of IDEA from theory to practice.* Presentation by Dawn P. Flanaga at the California Association of School Psychologists Conference Los Angeles, CA, March8, 2007.

Feifer, S. & De Fina, P. (2000). *The neuropsychology of reading disorders: Diagnosis and intervention workbook.* Middletown, MD: School Neuropsych Press, LLC.

Feifer, S. & De Fina, P. (2002). *The neuropsychology of writing: Diagnosis and intervention.* Riverside, CA: RET Center Press.

Feifer, S. & De Fina, P. (2005). *The neuropsychology of mathematics: Diagnosis and intervention.* Riverside, CA: RET Center Press.

Fifer, S. & Della Toffalo, D. ((2007). *Integrating RTI with cognitive neuropsychology: A scientific approach to reading.* Middleton, MD: School Neuropsych Press, LLC.

Finn, C.E., Rotherham, A.J., & Hokanson, C.R. (Eds.), (2001). *Rethinking special education for a new century.* Washington, DC: Thomas B. Fordham Foundation and the Progressive Policy Institute.

Gladwell, Malcolm (2005). *Blink: The power of thinking without thinking.* New York: Little, Brown, & Company.

Hale, J. & Fiorello, C. (2004). *School neuropsychology: A practitioner's handbook.* New York: The Guilford Press.

Jensen, R. (2000). *Brain-based learning: The new science of teaching & training.* San Diego, CA: The Brain Store.

Kolb, B. & Whishaw, I.Q. (2003). *Fundamentals of human neuropsychology* (5th ed.). New York: Worth Publishers.

Miller, Daniel C. (2007). *Essentials of school neuropsychological assessment.* Hoboken, NJ: John Wiley & Sons, Inc.

Pierangelo, R. & Giuliani, G. (2006). *Learning disabilities: A practical approach to foundations, assessment, diagnosis, and teaching.* Boston: Pearson Education, Inc.

Sprenger, M. (1999). *Learning & memory: The brain in action.* Alexandria, VA: Association for Supervision and Curriculum Development.

Swanson, L.J. (1995). *Learning styles: A review of the literature.* ERIC Document NO. ED 387 067.

Sousa, D. (1997). Sensory preferences of New Jersey students, grades 3 to 12. Unpublished data collected by graduate students at Seton Hall University, 1994-1997.

Sousa, D. (2007). *How the special needs brain learns.* 2nd edition. New York, NY: Corwin Press.

Sylwester, R. (2006, March & April). *The Tween brain: Midway between infant dependency and adult autonomy: Part I & II.* Retrieved April 11, 2006, from http://www.brainconncection.com/content/228_l/printable.

Wing, A.M. (2000). Mechanisms of motor equivalence in handwriting. *Current Biology, 10,* R245-R248.

Wolfe, P. (2001). *Brain matters: Translating Research into classroom practice.* Alexandria, VA: Association for Supervision and Curriculum Development.

Chapter 16

Suicide Prevention: Things the Counselor Must Know

Deborah Kimokeo, Rosemary Rubin, and Nancy Schubb

Abstract

Suicide is the third leading cause of death in America for 10-24 year olds. This chapter addresses the problem of youth suicide in the United States from an ecological model. The ecological model addresses multiple systems (personal, family, school, work, and community) that are involved in emergence, development, and maintenance of suicidal behavior. Protective and risk factors associated with youth suicide are presented, as well as barriers and challenges to school-based suicide prevention. Evidence-based suicide prevention programs, implementation strategies, and postvention procedures are described, to be used as tools for the new and seasoned school counselor.

Introduction

Youth suicide is the third leading cause of death in the United States among youth ages 10-19 years old (Anderson, 2002). The literature confirms that the school and the school counselor have critical roles in the prevention of suicide. On average, one out of every three school districts loses a student to suicide each year, yet only one in ten schools has a plan to address this problem (Portner, 2000). Educators have moral responsibilities to help ameliorate this problem through education and identification of at-risk students. School districts are also experiencing increased legal accountability to prevent youth suicide and inform parents whenever there is cause to believe a student may be suicidal or experiencing serious mental health problems (Milsom, 2002).

There has been an increase in the number of federal initiatives calling for pro-active responses to the problem of youth suicide. The *Surgeon General's Call to Action to Prevent Suicide* (U.S. Department of Health & Human Services [DHHH], 1999) and its companion volume, *National Strategy for Suicide Prevention* (NSSP) (DHHH, 2001) are two strongly written federal initiatives addressing youth suicide that assign specific roles and responsibilities to schools and their leaders. These efforts call for schools to participate in suicide reduction as part of a wider national effort.

The research on school-based suicide prevention continues to grow. Below is a synopsis of key points from the youth suicide prevention literature, both from statistical and ecological prevention lenses.

Statistics

The incidence of suicide among adolescents and young adults nearly tripled between 1952 and 1995 (Centers for Disease Control & Prevention [CDC], 2002). Teen suicide rates demonstrated a drop of 26 percent between 1993 and 2000 in the year 2000 (Child Trends, 2002); but suicide remains the third leading cause of death for 10-24 year olds (Hoyert, Heron, Murphy & Kung, 2006).

The suicide rate of children 10-14 years of age is growing faster than any other demographic, nearly doubling in the past few decades (National Institute of Mental Health [NIMH], 2000). In the year 2000, 1.5 per 100,000 children in the 10-14 year age group took their own lives (CDC, 2002).

Hispanic students (12.1%) were significantly more likely than black or white students (8.8% and 7.9%, respectively) to have attempted suicide (Grunbaum et al., 2002). American Indians and Alaska Native adolescents have the highest rates of suicide, being more than twice as likely to commit suicide as other racial/ethnic groups (Borowsky, Resnick, Ireland, & Blum, 1999; CDC, 1999).

Female students (11.2%) were significantly more likely to have *attempted* to kill themselves than male students (6.2%) (Grunbaum et al., 2002). Nearly five times more 15-19 year old boys actually commit suicide than females (MacKay, Fingerhut, & Duran, 2000).

Ecological Theory of Suicide

In looking at youth suicide prevention from the framework of ecological theory, the risk factors most strongly associated with completed youth suicide are, in decreasing order: prior suicide attempts; depression; substance abuse (including alcohol); and conduct disorder (Bell & Clark, 1998; Brent, 1995; Moscicki, 1997).

The vast majority of experts agree that suicide is a

multi-dimensional problem. The ecological model addresses multiple systems (personal, family, school, work, and community) that are involved in emergence, development, and maintenance of suicidal behavior (Bronfenbrenner, 1979). An effective ecological approach to school-based suicide prevention serves to reduce suicide rates which must include all of those multiple levels and is implemented carefully and with diligence to best practice (Henry, Stephenson, Hanson, & Hargett, 1993; Shagle & Barber, 1995; Motes, Melton, Simmons, & Pumariega, 1999).

The guidelines, programs, and procedures for school-based suicide prevention should target and reduce risk factors most strongly associated with completed youth suicide (Borowsky, Ireland, & Resnick, 2001; Burns & Patton, 2000). They should also identify and enhance protective factors related to youth suicide prevention and resilience (Borowsky et al., 2001; Burns & Patton, 2000).

Suicide must be viewed from a psychiatric illness model, rather than a stress model as many studies verify nearly 90% of those completing suicide suffer from a diagnosable mental illness that needs to be identified and treated (Beautrais, 2001; Brent, Baugher, Bridge, Chen, & Chiappetta, 1999; Shaffer et.al.1996). Emphasis on identification, diagnosis, and treatment of the underlying psychiatric disorder are the most critical pieces of suicide prevention (Beautrais, 2001; Brent et al., 1999; Shaffer et al., 1996).

Risk Factors for Youth Suicide

There are many personal characteristics that place youth at greater risk for suicide. Psychopathological disorders (particularly mood disorders, schizophrenia, anxiety disorders, certain personality disorders, alcohol & other substance abuse disorders) are serious risk factors (Beautrais, 2001; U. S. Department of Health and Human Services [DHHS], 2001). Cognitive and personality factors such as skill development delays, emotional difficulties, apathy, hopelessness, school problems, and poor interpersonal problem-solving ability (Russell & Joyner, 2001) also are risk factors. Biological factors, e.g., major physical illness, abnormalities of serotonin function, (Arango, Underwood, Boldrini, et al., 2001; DHHS, 2001) add to the danger of youth suicide. Shaffer et al. (1996) cite prior suicide attempts as a critical risk factor. Sexual orientation (homosexual, trans-gender, bisexual) have also been reported to increase the risk for youth suicide (Blake et al., 2001; McDaniel, Purcell, & D'Augelli, 2001).

There are family characteristics that place youth at greater risk for suicide. These include family history of suicidal behavior (Agerbo, Nordentoft, & Mortensen, 2002; Gould, Fisher, Parides, Flory, & Shaffer, 1996) and parental psychopathology (Gould et al., 1996).

Protective Factors for Youth Suicide

Just as there are risk factors that increase the danger of youth suicide, there are protective factors that increase the safety of young people from suicide. Involvement in sports and physical activity and high academic achievement are examples of protective factors (Jessor, Van Den Bos, Vanderryn, Costa, & Turbin, 1995; King, Vidourek, & Davis, 2002; Resnick, Harris, & Blum, 1993). Emotional wellness is especially protective for adolescent girls (Borowsky et al., 1999). Statistically, being female is more protective than being male (Kaslow, McClure, & Connell, 2002; Maris, 2002).

Ethnicity comes into play as a protective factor. Overall, the rate of suicide is lower in ethnic minorities, as a whole, than whites (Maris, 2002); although there are some individual minority group exceptions (i.e., Native Americans). European-Americans were 1.8 times less likely than Mexican-Americans to die by suicide (Rew, Thomas, Horner, et al., 2001). Suicide attempts are 19.3% higher among Latina girls than in many other ethnic-gender groups (Rew et al., 2001).

Religious faith and practice has been shown to be a protective factor (Fernquist, 2000; Forman & Kalafat, 1998; Foster, 2001; Maris, 2002). Greater religiosity has been touted as the reason for the historically lower suicide rate among African-Americans (Glowinski et al., 2001).

Barriers and Challenges to School-Based Suicide Prevention

There are a number of barriers that one may encounter in implementing a suicide prevention program. These include stigma attached to mental health services and the lack of resources, system priority, and application of empirical research into a viable prevention program. Each of these barriers is addressed below.

School counselors are faced with the dilemma of providing a suicide prevention curriculum while addressing the stigma attached to mental health in general, and suicide prevention specifically. Consequently, the stigma attached to suicide *prevention programs* has been the cause in some instances for schools to avoid researching or implementing a suicide prevention program (Johnson, 1999; Minois, 1995). There are many common misconceptions about suicide that have led to some myths. For example, a common myth is that discussing suicide actually causes it (Johnson, 1999).

Budget and time constraints often prohibit the implementation of effective prevention programs or staff education. With the current focus being primarily on results-based testing, there is little time for critical programs like suicide prevention. As change agents in schools, counselors have an obligation to educate the school community that, in fact, youth suicide *IS* a public health concern.

Currently, there is a growing body of research about school-based suicide prevention; however, schools must be careful to adopt research-based programs and implement them with fidelity (Elias, 1997; Kalafat & Elias, 1995; Orbach & Bar-Joseph, 1993). Even with a quality suicide prevention program adopted, without proper training and administration, harm may occur despite a school counselor's best intentions.

Research reports that youth suicide is at crisis proportion (American Association of Suicidology, 1999), and school counselors must help address and bring down barriers to school-based suicide prevention with research-based programs. Schools must find means to provide suicide prevention programs that reach all students, not just those at highest risk. Proactively addressing the mental health needs of students will better enable them to focus on academic achievement.

Research-Based Suicide Prevention Programs

The goal of school-based suicide prevention programs is to reduce incidents of suicide through identification, education, and referral of youth who may be at risk. The National Strategy for Suicide Prevention (DHHS, 2001) is very adamant that schools must employ evidence-based youth suicide prevention programs and best practices. In response to the National Strategy for Suicide Prevention (DHHS, 2001) and its call for schools to provide evidence-based suicide prevention, the former National Registry of Effective Programs (NREP; Screening for Mental Health, Inc., 2002) was developed. Since January 2005, the NREP has been discontinued and subsumed by the newly formed National Registry of Evidence-Based Programs and Practices (NREPP), administered under the Substance and Mental Health Services Administration (SAMHSA). The NREPP is also a voluntary rating and classification system for mental health and substance abuse prevention and treatment programs. The new NREPP Web site is under construction and is expected to be in place soon. Its address is http://www.nationalregistry.samhsa.gov.

Table 1 (see next page) identifies the programs currently identified as either effective or promising by the old NREP, giving a school district a good place to begin as it seeks to employ research-based suicide prevention methods in its pursuit to help students and staff prevent suicide until the new NREPP is up and running. Both suicide prevention and a screening program were evaluated. Screening programs can range from formal depression inventories to comprehensive self-administered mental health evaluations. The purpose is to identify diagnosable mental disorders that are highly correlated with suicide (e.g., depression). Existing assessments aim to predict suicidal behavior and suicidal ideation, measure suicidal intent and the lethality of suicidal intent, and measure hopelessness.

Resilience based suicide prevention programs also exist. Their primary goal is to develop the resilience skills of social competence, individuation/differentiation, problem solving, and sense of purpose and future in order to prevent youth from ever considering suicide as an option. In Table 2 (see page 149) one such well-researched program is defined (Scales & Leffert, 2004).

As a school counselor, one may be expected to be competent in providing suicide prevention information for age appropriate classroom presentations, teacher in-service, and parent education. It is, therefore, important that the school counselor become thoroughly knowledgeable about suicide prevention and effective prevention programs

Implementation

As a student advocate, the school counselor will be expected to collaborate with district personnel in creating a school-wide suicide prevention program. This includes securing district mandates for suicide prevention curriculum, intervention and postvention education, regular training, and teacher in service. The goal is to reduce incidence of suicide as well as other risk behaviors. A school based suicide prevention program should be developmentally appropriate, supported by the school district, and consistent with best practices. The school counselor should be one of the leaders in the education and implementation of a suicide prevention policy and program at the school site and within the district. A suicide prevention program will be most effective if implemented as part of a broader risk prevention program or health promotion program.

Table 1: Evidence-Based Suicide Prevention Programs Used in Schools

Programs	C-Care/CAST	SOS: Signs of Suicide	Columbia Teen Screen©
Authors	Thompson, Eggert, Randell, & Pike, 2001	Aseltine & DeMartino, 2004	Shaffer, Scott, Wilcox, Maslow, Hicks, Lucas, et al., 2004
Description	A school-based intervention for students at risk for suicide. It combines one-to-one care (C-Care for Counselors Care) with a series of small group sessions (CAST for Coping and Support Training).	This program uses a two-prong approach by combining a suicide awareness curriculum and a brief depression screening. Addresses suicide from a mental illness model, rather than simply a reaction to stressful circumstances. First to empirically demonstrate significant reductions in self-reported suicide attempts. (Spanish version)	This program seeks to newly identify youth at risk for suicide and those who are suffering from mental illnesses using screening instruments.
SPRC Classification	Effective	Promising	Promising
Target Age	14-18	14-18	11-18
Gender	Male & Female	Male & Female	Male & Female
Ethnicity/Race	Multiple	Multiple	Multiple
Level of Intervention	Selective, Indicated	Universal	Universal
Increased Protective Factors	Skills in problem solving, conflict resolution, and non-violent dispute resolution	Easy access to variety of clinical interventions and support for help seeking, cultural and religious beliefs that discourage suicide and support self-preservation, and strong family and community support.	Easy access to clinical interventions and support for help-seeking.
Decreased Risk Factors	Mental disorders, particularly mood disorders, schizophrenia, anxiety and personality disorders, hopelessness	Alcohol and substance abuse disorders. Mental disorders, particularly mood disorders, schizophrenia, anxiety disorders and certain personality disorders, impulsive and/or aggressive tendencies. Relational or social loss.	Barriers to accessing health care, particularly mental health and substance abuse treatment.
Cost	Not specified	$100 per set of materials per school.	ColumbiaTeenScreen© is currently offering materials and consultation for free.
Contact Info	Reconnecting Prevention Research Program Phone: 206-543-8555; Email: elainet@u.washington.edu; Elaine Thompson, PhD, RN Psychosocial & Community Health Campus Box 357263 UW School of Nursing - Seattle, WA 98195	SOS Suicide Prevention Program for Secondary Schools: One Washington Street, Suite 304 Wellesley Hills, MA 02481 Web site:www.mentalhealthscreening.org/sos_highschool Email: highschool@mentalhealthscreening.org Phone: 781-239-0071; Fax: 781-431-7447	Columbia TeenScreen© Program 1775 Broadway, Suite 715 NY, NY 10019 Phone: 1-800-TEENSCREEN (833-6727) Email: teenscreen@childpsych.columbia.edu Web site: www.teenscreen.org

Table 1: Evidence-Based Suicide Prevention Programs Used in Schools (pg. 2)

Programs	Lifelines	Reaching Youth Class	Zuni Life Skills Development
Authors	Kalafat & Elias, 1995	Eggert, Thompson, Herting, & Nicholas, 1994	LaFromboise, 1995
Description	School-based program made up of four 45-minute lessons of suicide prevention awareness material. It also includes model policies and procedures for schools to adopt, as well as gatekeeper presentations for educators and parents/guardians.	This program targets students in grades 9-12 who are achieving poorly, potential for drop out, and other at-risk type behaviors. It endeavors to build resiliency skills against risk factors, give social support and life skills training, and reduce substance abuse and depression/aggression issues.	This program is based on social cognition theory, is culturally tailored to American Indian youth, and seeks to develop competency in a range of life skills.
SPRC Classification	Promising	Promising	Promising
Target Age	12-17	14-18	14-18
Gender	Male & Female	Male & Female	Male & Female
Ethnicity/Race	Multiple	Multiple	Native American
Level of Intervention	Universal	Selective, Indicated	Selective
Increased Protective Factors	Easy access to variety of clinical interventions and support for help-seeking. Strong family and community support connections.	Strong family and community support connections. Skills in problem solving, conflict resolution, and nonviolent handling of disputes.	Easy access to a variety of clinical interventions and support for help-seeking. Skills in problem-solving, conflict resolution, and nonviolent handling of disputes.
Decreased Risk Factors	Stigma associated with help-seeking behavior.	Alcohol and substance abuse disorders. Mental disorders, particularly mood disorders, schizophrenia, anxiety disorders, and certain personality disorders, impulsive and/or aggressive tendencies. Relational or social loss.	Hopelessness.
Cost	Varies depending on number staff/students. Manual $40.	Curriculum Guide - $300; 10 Student Workbooks - $212; RY Training (8 participants/1 trainer) $3000; Other materials vary.	Life Skills Curriculum Text - $30.00; Other materials vary.
Contact Info	John Kalama, Rutgers University Graduate School of Applied & Professional Psych 152 Frelinghuysen Road Piscataway, NJ 08854 Phone: 732-445-2000 x121; FAX: 732-445-4888 Email: kalafat@rci.rutgers.edu	RY Program Information & Scheduling Ms. Beth McNamara Phone: 425-861-1177 FAX: 206-726-6049 Email: beth.mcnamara@comcast.net	Teresa D. LaFromboise, PhD, Associate Professor of Education Stanford University – Cubberley 216, 3096 Stanford, CA 94305-3096 Phone: 650-723-1202; FAX: 650-725-7412 Email: lafrom@stanford.edu

Table 2: Example of a Research-Based Resilience-Based Program Used in Schools

Program	40 Developmental Assets
Author	Search Institute
Description	The 40 Developmental Assets are concrete, common sense, positive experiences and qualities essential to raising successful young people. The Developmental Asset framework is categorized into two groups of 20 assets. External assets are the positive experiences young people receive from the world around them. These 20 assets are about supporting and empowering young people, about setting boundaries and expectations, and about positive and constructive use of young people's time. External assets identify important roles that families, schools, congregations, neighborhoods, and youth organizations can play in promoting healthy development.
Type of Program	Resilience-based suicide prevention program
Target Age	0-18
Gender	Male & Female
Ethnicity/Race	Multiple
Level of Intervention	Universal
Increased Protective Factors	Developmental assets also promote thriving behaviors, such as valuing diversity, maintaining good health, and succeeding in school, among young people from all racial/ethnic groups.
Decreased Risk Factors	Developmental assets protect youth from all racial/ethnic groups studied from engaging in 10 different high-risk behaviors, including violence, alcohol use, and illicit drug use.
Cost	Varies depending on number staff/students and materials ordered.
Contact Info	Search Institute The Banks Building 615 First Avenue NE, Suite 125 Minneapolis, MN 55413 612-376-8955 or 800-888-7828 www.search-institute.org

Steps to implement the program (Based on the *Guidelines for School-Based Suicide Prevention Programs*, American Association of Suicidology [AAS], 1999)

1. **Discuss the need for suicide prevention with district leaders, school principals, educators, and possibly a parent group.** This dialogue will be helpful in determining specific needs, resources, and implementation challenges in one's community.

2. **Obtain administrative support.** District approval is paramount to the long-term continuation of a program, although the principal's support may suffice. Principals also have the ability to motivate staff, allocate resources, and make organizational changes to facilitate the program (Aos, Lieb, Mayfield , Miller, & Pennucci, 2004). Research what other districts offer as a way of endorsements for your program. As with any program, be clear on your goals and objectives and be able to quantify how the students are different because of your suicide prevention program.

3. **Create a suicide prevention policies and procedures document, if not already in existence.** This may include educating all staff regarding suicidal students, the crisis response team's intervention role, and postvention steps.

4. **Be sure that there is access for students at risk to community referrals when adults are not available.** For example, publishing telephone crisis and referral service phone numbers.

5. **Initiate gatekeeper training.** Gatekeepers are any adults who have direct contact with your students (e.g., teachers, janitors, bus drivers). Education is necessary for them to identify and refer students. Initiate gatekeeper training that is research based. An updated list of these programs is available at http://www.sprc.org.

6. **Confirm a crisis response team is in place.** Check with your immediate supervisor to clarify your role in the crisis response team.

7. **Provide parent education.** This would be sharing suicide prevention information with parents, including "means restriction strategies," which could be accomplished in parent meeting venues.

8. **Offer student education.** According to the AAS, lesson plans should be research-based, meaningful to the student, age appropriate, interactive, and implemented with fidelity.

9. **Final implementation steps should include the necessary intervention and postvention.**

Intervention

The following guidelines are designed to assist in intervention with a suicidal student. Everyone working in a school system that comes into contact with children should be knowledgeable about suicidal risk factors, warning signs, and how to respond to a suicidal student. The foundation of this is the assumption that suicide is preventable and that preventing it requires administrator and school staff commitment (Lieberman, Poland, & Cowan, 2006).

A. **Basic steps that any staff member can follow with a suicidal child:**

1. Be supportive of the child. Let the child know that you are concerned and that you care. Remain calm.
2. Acknowledge feelings of the child, listen, and be empathic. Resist the urge to tell the student he or she should not feel that way.

3. Supervise at all times.
4. Do not promise secrets and confidentiality.
5. Immediately refer to a trained school mental health professional.

Prevention and intervention go hand in hand. In order to be able to intervene successfully with a possible suicidal child, all members of the school community need to understand the significance of their respective roles in the process.

B. **Roles and responsibilities.**

1. *Students* often tell other students of their suicidal ideation long before an adult is informed. Therefore students need:
   a. Education in the warning signs of suicide.
   b. To understand that in the case of suicide, secrets cannot be kept.
   c. To know those in the school and the community who can be a source of help.
2. *Parents/guardians* should be:
   a. Educated in the depression, risk factors, and warning signs of suicide.
   b. Knowledgeable about ways to be supportive.
   c. Informed as to where to seek help in the school and community.
3. *School and district staff* should be:
   a. Educated in the risk factors and warning signs.
   b. Clear there is no confidentiality with suicidal students.
   c. Knowledgeable about the school or district's referral process for assistance with suicidal students.

A trained team member should follow an intervention process. The process for a school-based suicide intervention program has been identified and includes the following steps:

C. **Intervention Process.**

1. *Rapport.* Establish rapport and follow good counseling techniques.
2. *Risk Assessment.* Gather information related to warning signs. Use risk factors as a guide, especially in examining areas of loss and stress.
   a. Risk Factors adapted from the National Strategy for Suicide Prevention: Goals and Objectives for Action (DHHS, 2001) are:

1) Mental disorders
2) Alcohol and other substance disorders
3) Loss (e.g. death, divorce, transience, romance, humiliation)
4) History of trauma or abuse
5) Presence of firearms
6) School crisis (disciplinary, academic)
7) Family crisis (e.g. domestic violence, running away, argument with parents)
8) Suicide in community

b. Warning signs from a Youth Suicide Prevention Program Training manual (Lieberman & Rubin, 1999) are:
1) Threats, both explicit and implicit (e.g. "world better off without me")
2) Plan and attempts to secure means
3) Previous attempts
4) No support and resources
5) Depression
6) Giving away prized possessions
7) Changes in relationships, behavior, and academics
8) Effort to hurt self (see section on self injury)
9) Death and suicidal themes

c. Questions to ask a suicidal child. Below are important questions to include. (It is a myth that these questions will cause or prompt a student to suicide.)
1) Do you have a plan to kill yourself?
2) What do you plan to do?
3) Do you have access to ___ (means)?
4) Do you know someone who has attempted suicide or died by suicide?

d. Degree of risk. The following reference guide has been developed to assist trained staff in determining how critical the need is for immediate outside assistance (e.g. psychological evaluation and hospitalization). While using this as a guide, continue listening to hear if what the child is saying may elevate the risk factor.
1) Lower risk. Ask the student questions pertaining to:
   a) Current thought
   b) Past thought (more than six months)
   c) Non-verbal warning sign (writing/drawing)
2) Moderate risk: Ask the student questions pertaining to:
   a) Previous attempts/gestures

b) Previous trauma (abuse, victimization, loss of parent)
c) Previous hospitalization
d) Current medication (Currently there is some concern that some of the depression medication for children and adolescents can lead to suicidal feelings)

3). Higher risk. Ask the student questions pertaining to:
   a) Method. What would you do or use? Assess for lethality of method.
   b) Firearms mentioned
   c) Refusal to sign no-harm agreement*
   d) Threaten violence to others

* No harm agreements are useful techniques when combined with other assessment information in establishing an overall protection plan for the student. The agreement does not take the place of contacting the parent or guardian and providing referrals to mental health agencies. In school situations, a no harm agreement is an agreement between the student and a trained team member (e.g., school counselor, school psychologist, school nurse, or school social worker) not to harm him or herself. It also is used to identify adults on campus who the student would feel comfortable going to in the case of a problem. This helps to increase the students coping abilities.

3. *Contact.* Consider developing a list of contingencies regarding parent contact (e.g., when parent or guardian is unavailable for contact in an emergency).
a. The parent or guardian must be contacted regardless of degree of risk unless there is an open case of child abuse or by doing so it is felt that the child's life may be in danger. (Remember that a suicidal student may not be thinking clearly.)
b. If the parent or guardian is not contacted, referral should be immediately made to child protective services or law enforcement.
c. School district policy and parent or guardian will determine whether a low risk child may remain on campus for the remainder of the day.
d. When contacting parents, (preferably in person if at all possible), explain what has happened and the reason for concern.
   1) Reassure the parent that the child is currently safe.

147

2) If appropriate, explain need to restrict access to lethal means.

3) Work to develop a plan of action, which includes follow-up care.

4) Parents often need to be educated so that they will follow-up with their child.

5) Educate parents to understand depression in children.

    a) Address the statement, "Just doing it for attention." Remember that statement is not always said, but should be discussed anyway. A sample answer might be: "Yes, they are doing it for attention. Your child is attempting to tell you that something is seriously wrong. If we do not pay attention, he or she might take the next step, and it might be fatal."

    b) Help them to focus on the child.

    c) Help to take the blame off the parent or guardian. Often times they feel that the school is blaming them for this problem. Help them to understand that this is happening to the child. It is about the child, not them.

4. *Referral.* At the beginning of each school year, a referral list should be developed or updated following school district or school site guidelines for referrals to mental health agencies and hospitals in the community.

    a. Refer family to agencies on resource guide. If a parent or guardian has private insurance or HMO, in most cases family should be referred back to the insurance company or doctor.

    b. If a child is considered a higher risk, it is important to refer to a hospital or agency that is capable of taking appropriate action. With parent permission, a hospital, agency, or doctor can be contacted and assessment information given.

5. *Follow-up/Documentation.*

    a. Contact parent or guardian regarding follow-up appointments with doctor or agencies.

    b. Assist the family in keeping appointments and understanding the necessity of receiving appropriate help.

    c. Stress the fact that one or two appointments may not be enough to work through problems.

    d. Empower the parent or guardian to understand that if they are unhappy with a therapist, rather than not receive help, they may request a different therapist.

    e. Document all work related to the suicidal student. This documentation should not be part of the student's cumulative record and should be maintained in a separate confidential file.

D. Related topics.

1. Suicide Attempts on campus.

    a. If there is a medical emergency, deal with the medical issues before dealing with suicidal issues.

    b. If the attempt does not require medical attention, follow procedures for dealing with a suicidal student.

    c. If a student shares that they attempted suicide before or went to the emergency room for an attempt, contact the parents and explain the situation. Help them to follow up with appropriate referrals if needed.

    d. If the attempt is high profile, follow the above and be sure to provide crisis counseling for students who witnessed the event and friends of the student.

2. Returning from Mental Health Hospitalization.

    a. If possible have a school release of information form signed prior to the student's return, thus allowing someone from the school or district to communicate with the doctor.

    b. From the doctor, obtain information regarding medications the student may be on, especially if administered at school, and any suggestions regarding the student's ability to handle the school day and classes.

    c. A member of the team should re-admit the student to school and assist the student with the transition. Some sample suggestions are:

    6) Discuss his or her feelings concerning the return to school.

    7) Identify a network of adults that the student can see in the event that she or he is having a problem.

    8) Help the student anticipate questions from peers and some appropriate responses.

3. Self-injury

Students who self-injure are not necessarily suicidal. It is important to ask the following assessment questions:

  a. Are you attempting to hurt yourself?

  b. Are you attempting to kill yourself?

A suicidal student will answer yes to both questions, while someone who self harms will answer no to wanting to kill his/her self. Note that some students can be both self-injurious and suicidal. In this case, follow the above guidelines for responding to a suicidal student. It is important to respond by offering help, contacting the parent or guardian, and providing referrals. For the most part, the actions are not life threatening. Be sure that any wounds receive medical attention. With self-injurious students, contact the parent or guardian, provide referrals, and work with them to get help for the student. Those who self-injure have a multitude of needs that this complex problem fulfills. The following are suggested responses:

  a. Do not react with shock or disgust at what the student has done. This may feed into the poor self-image the student may have.

  b. Do not discourage self- harm. If one does, they may find another place to self-injure, and that may not be visible.

  c. Do help the student substitute communication skills and other help-seeking (coping skills) behaviors.

  d. If there is contagion, do the following:

    1) Separate students.

    2) Respond to each student individually.

    3) Contact parents or guardians and provide referrals along with encouragement to seek help for their child.

For further information on counseling students who self injure, see Chapter 17.

Postvention

As with any crisis, it is no longer a question of if something will happen, but when. Since suicide among 10 to 24 year olds (Hoyert et al., 2006) is the third leading cause of death, schools need to be prepared for a suicide on campus and in the school community. A suicide might be of a student or a staff member.

Below are suggestions for dealing with the aftermath of a suicide. For the most part, standard crisis postvention activities are followed. However, due to the contagious nature of suicide, especially for youth, some changes need to be made.

A. If a suicide occurs on campus:

  1. Treat this as a medical emergency. In addition to notifying emergency medical personnel, contact law enforcement at the same time.

  2. If possible, an administrator and school counselor should accompany law enforcement when the victim's family is informed. Be sensitive to the wishes of the family if the family asks that the word suicide not be used to notify the students and staff. The school needs to decide what is in the best interest of the students at school. (Note: The findings of the coroner or medical examiner is a matter of public record.)

B. If a suicide occurs off campus:

  1. Confirm that the suicide occurred by contacting the law enforcement or the medical examiner or coroner. Make a home visit to offer condolences and support. (See A.2 above)

C. In the aftermath of a suicide on campus or off:

  1. If media become involved, direct requests to media spokespersons and restrict media access to campus. Be familiar with the recommended guidelines for *Reporting on Suicide: Recommendation for the Media* prepared by the American Foundation for Suicide Prevention (2001).

  2. Provide grief work through individual and group counseling. Identify students who are most at risk for suicidal behavior, close friends, those who may have seen the victim as a role model, or may be at risk because of other life situations. These students may be in need of outside counseling. Continue to work with the students to ensure that they receive the help needed and to support them on campus.

  3. Emphasize that no one is to blame. There is no one cause of suicide as it is a complex issue.

  4. Make note of birthdays and anniversary dates of the deceased and provide counseling as needed at that time.

D. Need to avoid contagion:

  1. In the aftermath of any suicide, there should be no memorial or dedication on campus or sidewalks around campus due to the contagious nature of suicide. One does not want to do anything to romanticize and glorify suicide. It is appropriate to do positive things such as to collect money for the family, donate to charity, donate to a suicide prevention hotline, or print up helpline cards for students.

2. Have a parent meeting to discuss their concerns. During the meeting, discuss risk factors and warning signs, as well as ways to help children.
3. In the aftermath, the staff should receive an in-service session highlighting risk factors and warning signs as well as procedures to follow should warning signs be observed. This should occur as soon as possible after the initial postvention has occurred.

Conclusion

There are important long and short-term benefits to employing evidence-based suicide prevention programs. These programs help shape problem-solving and help-seeking behavior. Delivering in-service training about youth suicide prevention to all school employees (called "gatekeeper training") is important in the identification of students at risk for suicidal behavior. Mental health screening for young people is also helpful in the identification of at risk students. Students who enjoy greater mental health are better able to successfully access learning opportunities and to advance their emotional development. School counselors share an important leadership function in the development, implementation, and institutionalization of suicide prevention initiatives and must be well versed in the current literature of best practice in this arena.

Discussion Questions

Research

1. What sources could a school counselor cite or access to be better informed about school-based suicide prevention?
2. What research data could a school counselor present to school administrators and staff to demonstrate the need for school-based suicide prevention?
3. What are the risk factors most strongly associated with completed youth suicide and how can they be ameliorated?

Barriers and Challenges

4. In the absence of funding, what can school counselors do to facilitate suicide prevention education?
5. What are critical barriers to overcome in educating others about suicide prevention? Why?

Prevention

6. What are reasons that administrative support for school-based suicide prevention is essential?
7. What is the role of a school counselor in implementing a school-based suicide prevention program?

8. List and discuss elements of at least two research based suicide prevention programs that can be used in schools.

Intervention

9. During a suicide assessment process, what are key questions to ask?
10. If a parent indicates to the school counselor that a child threatening suicide is "doing it for attention," how should a school counselor respond?
11. If a child is considered "high" risk for suicide, what should be the school counselor's plan of action?
12. What are the key differences between a child who is suicidal and one who self-injures?

Postvention

13. If a family denies a suicide occurred, yet law enforcement has confirmed that it has, as a school counselor how do you handle this announcement at school when notifying students and staff about the death?
14. If one wishes to avoid suicide contagion on campus, what steps should be taken?
15. How and why is a suicide handled differently than other deaths in the school community?

References

Agerbo, F., Nordentoft, M., & Mortensen, P. B. (2002). Familial, psychiatric, and socioeconomic risk factors for suicide in young people: Nested case-control study. *British Medical Journal, 325*, 74.

American Association of Suicidology, Prevention Division. (1999). *Guidelines for school-based suicide prevention programs.* Washington, DC: Author.

American Foundation for Suicide Prevention, American Association of Suicidology, & Annenberg Public Policy Center. (2001). *Reporting on suicide: Recommendation for the media.* Retrieved January 15, 2007, from http://www.afsp. org/index.cfm?fuseaction=home.viewpage&page_id=7852EBBC-9FB2-6691-54125A1AD4221E49

Anderson, R. N. (2002). Deaths: Leading causes for 2000. *National Vital Statistics Reports, 50*(16). Hyattsville, MD: National Center for Health Statistics.

Aos, S., Lieb, R, Mayfield, J., Miller, M., & Pennucci, A. (2004, July 12). *Benefits and costs of prevention and early intervention programs for youth.* Olympia, WA: Washington State Institute for Public Policy.

Arango, V., Underwood, M. D., Boldrini, M., et al. (2001). Serotonin 1A receptors, serotonin transporter binding and serotonin transporter mRNA expression in the brainstem of depressed suicide victims. *Neuropsychopharmacology, 25*, 892-903.

Aseltine, R. H., & DeMartino, R. (2004). An outcome evaluation of the SOS suicide prevention. *American Journal of Public Health, 94*(3), 446-452).

Beautrais, A. L. (2001). Child and young adolescent suicide in New Zealand. *Australian and New Zealand Journal of Psychiatry, 125*, 355-373.

Bell, C. C., & Clark, D. C. (1998). Adolescent suicide. *Pediatric Clinics of North America, 45*, 365-380.

Blake, S. M., Ledsky, R., Lehman, T., Goodenow, C., Sawyer, R., & Hack, T. (2001). Preventing sexual risk behaviors among gay, lesbian, and bisexual adolescents: The benefits of gay-sensitive HIV instruction in schools. *American Journal of Public Health, 91*, 940-946.

Borowsky, I. W., Ireland, M., & Resnick, M. D. (2001). Adolescent suicide attempts: Risk and protectors, *Pediatrics, 107*(3), 485-493.

Borowsky, I. W., Resnick, M.D., Ireland, M., & Blum, R. W. (1999). Suicide attempts among American Indian and Alaska Native youth: Risk and protective factors. *Archives of Pediatrics and Adolescent Medicine, 153*(6), 573-580.

Brent, D. A. (1995). Risk factors for adolescent suicide and suicidal behavior: Mental and substance abuse disorders, family environmental factors and life stress. *Suicide and Life-Threatening Behavior, 25*(Suppl.), 52-63.

Brent, D. A., Baugher, M., Bridge, J., Chen, T., & Chiappetta, L. (1999). Age- and sex-related risk factors for adolescent suicide. *Journal of the American Academy of Child and Adolescent Psychiatry, 38*, 1497-1505.

Bronfenbrenner, U. (1979). *The ecology of human development.* Cambridge, MA: Harvard University Press.

Burns, J. M., & Patton, G. C. (2000). Preventive interventions for youth suicide: a risk factor-based approach. *Australian and New Zealand Journal of Psychiatry, 34*, 388-407.

Centers for Disease Control & Prevention. (1999). *Wonder, mortality* (compressed data set). National Center for Health Statistics. [Online database]. Retrieved October 10, 2003, from http://wonder.cdc.gov

Centers for Disease Control & Prevention. (2002). *CDC surveillance summaries: Youth risk behavior surveillance-United States, 2001.* MMWR 51(SS-4), 1-64. Atlanta, GA: U.S. Department of Health and Human Services.

Child Trends. (2002). *Child Trends databank indicator: Suicidal teens. Tables 1 and 22, Homicide, suicide, and firearm death among youth ages 15-19.* (Original data from the National Vital Statistics System administered by the National Center for Health Statistics, Centers for Disease Control & Prevention.) Retrieved February 14, 2003, from http://www.childtrendsdatabank.org/tables/70_Table_1.htm

Eggert, L. L., Thompson, E. A., Herting, J. R. & Nicholas, L. J. (1994). A prevention research program: Reconnecting at-risk youth. *Issues in Mental Health Nursing, 15*(2), 107-135.

Elias, M. J. (1997). Reinterpreting dissemination of prevention programs as widespread implementation with effectiveness and fidelity. In R. P. Weissberg, T. P., Gullotta, R. L., Hampton, B. A., Ryan, & G. R. Adams (Eds.), *Enhancing children's wellness* (pp.253-289). Thousand Oaks, CA: Sage.

Fernquist, R. M. (2000). Problem drinking in the family and youth suicide. *Adolescence, 35*(139), 551-558.

Forman, S., & Kalafat, J. (1998). Substance abuse and suicide: Promoting resilience against self-destructive behavior in youth. *The School Psychology Review, 27*(3), 398-406.

Foster, T. (2001). Dying for a drink: Global suicide prevention should focus more on alcohol use disorders. *British Medical Journal, 323*(7317), 817-818.

Glowinski, A. L., Bucholz, K. K., Nelson, E. C., Quiang Fu, P., Madden, A. F., Reich, W., et al. (2001). Suicide attempts in an adolescent female twin sample. *Journal of the American Academy of Child and Adolescent Psychiatry, 40*, 1300-1308.

Gould, M. S., Fisher, P., Parides, M., Flory, M., & Shaffer, D. (1996). Psychosocial risk factors of child and adolescent completed suicide. *Archives of General Psychiatry, 53*(12), 1155-1162.

Grunbaum, J., Kann, L., Kinchen, S., Williams, B., Ross, J., Lowry, R, et al. (2002). Youth risk behavioral surveillance- United States, 2001. *Morbidity and Mortality Weekly, 51*(SS-4): Tables 40-41, pp. 57-58.

Henry, C. S., Stephenson, A. L., Hanson, F., & Hargett, W. (1993). Adolescent suicide and families: An ecological approach. *Adolescence, 28*, 291-308.

Hoyert, D. L., Heron, M. P., Murphy, S. L. & Kung, H. C. (2006). Death: Final data for 2003. *National Vital Statistics Report, 54*(13). Hyattsvile, MD: National Center for Health Statistics. (DHHS Publication No. (PHS) 2006-1120)

Jessor, R., Van Den Bos, J., Vanderryn, J., Costa, F., & Turbin, M. S. (1995). Protective factors in adolescent problem behavior: Moderator effects and developmental change. *Developmental Psychology, 31*(6), 923-933.

Johnson, W. Y. (1999). *Youth suicide: The school's role in prevention and response.* Bloomington, IN: Phi Delta Kappa Educational Foundation.

Kalafat, J., & Elias, M. (1995). Suicide prevention in the education context. *Suicide and Life-Threatening Behavior, 25*, 125-133.

Kaslow, N. J., McClure, E., & Connell, A. (2002). Treatment for depression in children and adolescents. In I. H. Gotlib & C. L. Hammen (Eds.), *Handbook of depression* (pp. 441-464). New York: Guilford Press.

King, K. A., Vidourek, R. A., & Davis, B. (2002). Increasing self-esteem and school connectedness through a multidimensional mentoring program. *The Journal of School Health, 72*(7), 294-299.

Lacourse, E., Claes, M., & Villenueve, M. (2001). Heavy metal music and adolescent suicidal risk. *Journal of Youth and Adolescents, 30*(3), 321-332.

LaFramboise, T., & Howard Pitney, B. (1995). The Zuni life skills development and curriculum: Description and evaluation of a suicide prevention program. *Journal of Counseling Psychology, 42*(4), 479-486.

Lieberman, R., Poland, S., & Cowan, K. (2006) Suicide prevention and intervention. *Prinicpal Leadership.* 7(2), 11-15.

Lieberman, R., & Rubin, R. (1999). *Youth Suicide Prevention Program Training Manual* (unpublished).

MacKay, A. P., Fingerhut, L. A., & Duran, C. R. (2000). *Adolescent health chartbook: Health, United States, 2000.* Hyattsville, MD: National Center for Health Statistics.

Maris, R. W. (2002). Suicide. *The Lancet, 360*, 319-326.

McDaniel, J. S., Purcell, D. W., & D'Augelli, A. R. (2001). The relationship between sexual orientation and risk for suicide: Research finding and future directions for research and prevention. *Suicide and Life-Threatening Behavior, 31*(1) (Suppl.), 84-105.

Milsom, A. (2002). Suicide prevention in schools: Court cases and implications for principals. *National Association for Secondary School Principals (NASSP) Bulletin, 86*, 24-33.

Minois, G. (1995). *History of suicide: Voluntary death in western culture.* Baltimore, MD: The Johns Hopkins University Press.

Moscicki, E. K. (1997). Identification of suicide risk factors using epidemiological studies. *Psychiatric Clinics of North America, 20*, 499-517.

Motes, P. S., Melton, G., Simmons, W. E. W., & Pumariega, A. (1999). Ecologically oriented school-based mental health services: Implications for service system delivery. *Psychology in the Schools, 36*(5), 391-401.

National Institutes of Mental Health. (2000). *Child and adolescent violence research at NIMH.* Washington, DC: Author.

Orbach, I., & Bar-Joseph, H. (1993). The impact of a suicide prevention program for adolescents with suicidal tendencies, hopelessness, ego identity, and coping. *Suicide and Life-Threatening Behavior, 23*, 120-129.

Portner, J. (2000). Suicide: Many schools fall short on prevention. *Education Week, 19*(32), 1, 20-22.

Resnick, M. D., Harris, L. J., & Blum, R. W. (1993). The impact of caring and connectedness on adolescent health and well-being. *Journal of Pediatrics and Child Health, 2* (Suppl 1), S3-9.

Rew, L., Thomas, N., Horner, S. D., et al. (2001). Correlates of recent suicide attempts in a triethnic group of adolescents. *Journal of Nursing Scholars, 33*, 361-367.

Russell, S. T., & Joyner, K. (2001). Adolescent sexual orientation and suicide risk: Evidence from a national study. *American Journal of Public Health, 91*, 1276-1281.

Scales, P. C., & Leffert, N. (2004). Developmental assets: *A synthesis of the scientific research on adolescent development* (2nd ed.). Minneapolis, MN: Search Institute.

Screening for Mental Health, Inc. (2002). *High school suicide prevention program reduces suicide attempts.* Wellesley Hills, MA: Author.

Shaffer, D., Gould, M. S., Fisher, P., Trautman, P., Moreau, D., Kleinman, M., et al. (1996). Psychiatric diagnosis in child and adolescent suicide. *Archives of General Psychiatry, 53*, 339-348.

Shaffer, D., Scott, M., Wilcox, H., Maslow, C., Hicks, R., Lucas, C. P., et al. (2004). The Columbia Suicide Screen: Validity and reliability of a screen for youth suicide and depression. *Journal of the American Academy of Child and Adolescent Psychiatry, 43*(1), 71-79.

Shagle, S. C., & Barber, B. K. (1995). A social-ecological analysis of adolescent suicidal ideation. *American Journal of Orthopsychiatry,* 65,114-124.

Suicide Prevention Resource Council. (2004). *Suicide Prevention Resource Council & American Foundation for Suicide Prevention release the online registry of evidence-based practices in suicide prevention.* Newton, MA: Education Development Corp., Inc. Retrieved April 5, 2005, from http://www.sprc.org/whatweoffer/ebp.asp

Thompson, E. A., Eggert, L., Randell, B. P., & Pike, K. C. (2001). Evaluation of indicated suicide risk prevention approaches for potential high school dropouts. *American Journal of Public Health*, 91: 5, 742-752.

U. S. Department of Health and Human Services (DHHS). (1999). *The Surgeon General's call to action to prevent suicide.* Washington, DC: Author.

U. S. Department of Health and Human Services (DHHS). (2001). *National strategy for suicide prevention: Goals and objectives for action.* Rockville, MD: Author.

Organizational Resources

- American Association of Suicidology (AAS)
  www.suicidology.org
  Phone: 202-237-2280
- American Foundation for Suicide Prevention (AFSP)
  http://www.afsp.org
- Centers for Disease Control (CDC) and Prevention
  Phone: 1-800-311-3435
  www.cdc.gov
- National Institute of Mental Health (NIMH)
  Phone: 301-443-4513
  www.nimh.nih.gov (NIH)
- Office of the Surgeon General
  National Strategy for Suicide Prevention (NSSP)
  www.mentalhealth.org/suicideprevention
- Substance Abuse and Mental Health Services Administration (SAMHSA)
  Phone: 1-800-487-4890
  www.samhsa.gov
- Suicide Prevention Advocacy Network (SPAN)
  www.span-california.org
- www.suicidology.org
- Suicide Prevention and Research Center (SPRC)
  www.sprc.org

Chapter 17

Self-Injury: Understanding and Providing Assistance to Students Who Self-Mutilate

Chris Simpson, and Samuel K. Bore

Abstract

The phenomenon of self-injurious behavior (SIB) is an issue that has fostered confusion and concern for professionals in school settings. The purpose of this chapter is to offer an overview of self-injury among school age populations. Included is a conceptualization of self-injury that may empower the school counselor to offer support and make appropriate referrals. Additionally, a working definition is outlined which involves a means of identifying types of SIB. Common myths about the behavior are explored. Means of addressing the behavior are also discussed, as well as potential challenges to treatment. The aforementioned components are highlighted in a case example of a school counselor's experience with a self-injuring student.

Introduction

Self-injury has become a topic of intense study and controversy in clinical and school settings. Controversy exists from treatment techniques to descriptive terminology. An extensive review of the existing literature reveals that several terms exist to define the behavior (e.g., self-cutting, self-destructive behavior, self-harm, self-mutilation, and parasuicide) (Laye-Gindhu & Schonert-Reichl, 2005; Stanley, Gameroff, Michalson, & Mann, 2001; Suyemoto &MacDonald, 1995; Zila & Kiselica, 2001). As Laye-Gindhu and Schonert-Reichl (2005) point out, little consensus exists among practitioners and researchers on how to define and conceptualize the phenomenon. This fact adds confusion when deciding how to provide assistance to a self-injuring child, adolescent, or teenager.

With few exceptions, mainstream North American/European culture typically has viewed self-injury as a maladaptive behavior. No lineage of self-injurious behavior for the purpose of advancing or celebrating this culture exists. The concept of cutting, burning, or otherwise injuring one's own body can conjure feelings of confusion and even disgust. In school settings, similar confusion exists with teachers and other school professionals. The school counselor is often asked to manage this baffling phenomenon. The purpose of this chapter is to offer a conceptualization of self-injury that may empower the school counselor to offer support and make appropriate referral.

The Importance of Understanding Self-Injury

School counselors and fellow school professionals have reported that self-injury in the school environment has grown at an alarming rate. In 1995, Suyemoto and MacDonald reported 1,800 out of 100,000 adolescents and young adults were participating in self-injurious behavior. In a sample of 143 high school students, Lloyd (1997) found that 39% of the sample reported committing some form of self-injury over the course of one year. More recently, one study indicated that 13.9% of 440 adolescents sampled participated in self-injurious behavior (Ross & Heath, 2002). Furthermore, accounts of school counselors discovering the behavior in their own schools are increasing (Jeffery & Warm, 2002). While statistics vary, the prevalence of self-injurious behavior in schools and among the adolescent population raises concerns for those who must work with the behavior.

A variety of theories for the increase in this behavior exist. The depiction of self-injury in popular media, the increase in "cutting" chat rooms, the influence of peers who participate in the behavior, continued evidence of childhood abuse, and perceived loss of significant relationships have all been assigned some blame for the perceived increase in self-injury among school populations (Conterio & Lader, 1998; Laye-Gindhu & Schonert-Reichl, 2005).

The phenomenon is easily misunderstood and often difficult to identify. Ineffective techniques of dealing with the self-injuring student can ultimately result in wasting the counselor's time and damaging the relationship with the student. With this said, accurate conceptualization is imperative if healing is to be facilitated (Coy & Simpson, 2002).

Approaches to Intervention

Definition

To work with self-injury, a single definition of the phenomenon is important. Conterio and Lader (1998) define it as "the deliberate mutilation of the body or body part, not with the intent to commit suicide but as a way of managing emotions that seem too painful for words to express" (p.16). Self-injury is performed through a variety of methods and instruments including, but not limited to, knives, the burning end of a cigarette, scratching the skin, pulling the hair, self-biting, self-hitting, scalding, and the use of sharp objects such as a beltbuckle, sharp glass, screwdriver, and razorblades (Conterio & Lader, 1998; Kettlewell, 1999; Levenkron, 1998; Simpson, 2001; Warm, Murray & Fox, 2002).

Moderate or superficial self-injury is performed with intent. The person committing the act seeks out the pain associated with self-harm. Additionally, self-injury is a means of managing feelings. The self-injurer specifically intends to avoid inevitable feelings of fear, anger, anxiety, shame, guilt, or any other feeling that might be perceived as negative. Those concerned and hoping to provide assistance to a person who commits self-injury must understand this component of the phenomenon if care is to be administered.

Types of Self-Injury

In defining self-injury, it is important to note that different types exist. Favazza and Rosenthal (1993) identify three types of self-injury: stereotypic, major, and moderate.

Stereotypic. Stereotypic self-injury is associated with stereotypic movement disorder. This includes hand waving, rocking, head banging, self-biting or self-hitting. This form of self-injury is often associated with severe mental retardation (American Psychiatric Association, 2000, *Diagnostic and statistical manual of mental disorders*).

Major. Favazza and Rosenthal (1993) identify major self-injury as most frequently associated with DSM-IV-TR (2000) diagnoses such as schizophrenia. This form of self-injury involves the amputation of digits, limbs, or even the genitals. The individual who commits acts of major self-injury would be rare in a school setting and likely would require treatment beyond that described in this writing.

Moderate. Moderate/superficial self-injury is the most common type of self-injury in school settings. Spanning social class, gender, ethnicity, and race, this form of self-injury is one in which the individual cuts to avoid painful or intolerable feelings. A variety of diagnoses may be consistent with this form of self-injury including personality disorder, eating disorders, and posttraumatic stress disorder (Conterio & Lader, 1998; Favazza & Rosenthal, 1993).

A connection has been identified between self-injury and sexual, emotional, and/or physical abuse in childhood. There does appear to be a strong correlation between the existence of abuse in the individual's background and the use of self-injury. However, when conceptualizing the self-injurer, it is important to note that other possibilities for the behavior may exist (Conterio & Lader, 1998; Levenkron, 1998; Strong, 1998). Levenkron (1998) suggests a means of dividing the behavior into two dimensions: nondissociative and dissociative. The author goes on to say that self-injurious behavior often stems from events that occur in the first six years of a child's development.

The nondissociative self-injurer usually experiences a childhood in which she is required to provide nurturance or support to the parent or caretaker. Appropriate rebellious affect, normally placed on the parent or caretaker, is perceived by the child to be unacceptable. This environment may exist in a home in which the parent or caretaker is dealing with a physical, emotional, or mental limitation (i.e., clinical depression, alcoholism, debilitating stroke, or heart attack) or when the parent or caretaker simply may not be present in the home. The child who experiences this reversal of dependence perceives that she/he can only express anger toward herself/himself. In this dimension, the individual does not dissociate when committing the act of cutting or burning. The individual experiences a sense of calm or relief after cutting.

Dissociative self-injury is often precluded by the individual experiencing cruelty by the parent or caretaker during childhood or adolescence. Related to the dissociation that often occurs during an abusive act, dissociation occurs prior to the occurrence of negative feelings. In this instance, cutting or otherwise self-harming serves to center the person or assist her in feeling present or awake. In both dimensions, the self-injuring individual often reports feelings of relief or reduction of tension after committing the act. In any case, self-injury serves to reduce feelings of frustration, anger, or anxiety (Levenkron, 1998; Rosen, Walsh & Rode, 1990; Stanley et al., 2001).

Much of the literature links self-injury to eating disorders (e.g., anorexia nervosa, bulimia, or compulsive overeating; Conterio & Lader, 1998; Favaro & Santonastaso, 2000; Zila & Kiselica, 2001). Eating disorders and self-injury appear to possess many of the same psychological roots. Strong (1998) reports that both serve as means to have some control over experienced trauma.

Common Myths about Self-injury

Failed suicide attempt. While suicide and self-injury appear to possess the same intended goal of pain relief, the desired outcome of each of these behaviors is entirely different. The individual who self-injures commits the act with the hope of escaping impending anxiety or attaining some level of focus. The sight of blood or the pain of the wound serves to accomplish this goal. Following the act, the typical self-injurer will report feeling a sense of calm, or feeling awake and alive, whereas a suicide attempt does not provide any sense of relief (Simpson, 2001; Zila & Kiselica, 2001).

Attention-seeking. Those who self-injure are often accused of attempting to gain attention (Conterio & Lader, 1998; Levenkron, 1998; Pembroke, 1994; Walsh & Rosen, 1988). While self-injury is certainly a means of communicating feelings, the act itself is often completed secretly and privately. The typical self-injurer will often attempt to conceal wounds by wearing clothing that will cover cuts or burns, or the individual may self-injure in areas not easily seen by others (e.g., inner thigh, around the breast, between the toes). Since cutting serves to alleviate inner anxiety and discomfort, drawing attention to the behavior is not typically desired (Simpson, 2001).

Strategies for Implementation

Conterio and Lader (1998) consider the treatment of self-injury as a long-term prospect for practitioners. With many responsibilities and time constraints, it is unrealistic to expect the school counselor solely to dedicate the required time and effort to treatment of a self-injuring student. However, the counselor can facilitate the student moving into therapy and remaining an instrumental part of the student's support system. For this to occur, the counselor must possess certain empathic qualities. Additionally, some techniques may be proposed to promote the student's health and movement toward treatment.

Empathic Relationship

A trusting and sharing relationship with a student who self-injures may be difficult to develop (Levenkron, 1998). Communicating an understanding that the behavior is a means of managing feelings is essential. The counselor may, at least partially, communicate this understanding by reflecting feelings and assisting the student in verbally communicating feelings. For example, if a student revealed a recent cut along the forearm accompanied by the comment, "My teacher just makes my life miserable and this is the only way to feel better," the counselor might reflect to the student, "You were really angry and hurt with your teacher and you believed that this was the only way to express it." If the counselor can empathically communicate a level of understanding and acceptance followed by a mutually decided upon means of alternative expression, a greater chance of facilitating assistance exists (Jeffery & Warm, 2002).

Therapeutic Techniques

For self-injury to decrease in frequency or cease all together, non-hurtful alternatives must be introduced and practiced (Conterio & Lader, 1998; Zila & Kiselica, 2001). The following are commonly used techniques for assisting the self-injurer better manage feelings and thoughts.

Alternatives List

Helping the student develop a list of coping strategies may be helpful when the student feels the compulsion to self-harm. These safe alternatives to cutting should be activities that can be done almost anywhere or anyplace. The student may pick as many activities as she/he likes. Conterio and Lader (1998) recommend five alternatives to cutting. Below is an example of a list of possible alternatives:

Alternatives List
1. Taking a walk
2. Drawing on a sketch pad or some other art activity
3. Writing in a journal
4. Sitting down and allowing yourself to experience feelings
5. Talking and listening to a trusted friend or caretaker

Journaling

Those who self-injure typically experience difficulty sharing and verbalizing feelings. A means of becoming more comfortable with verbally expressing feelings is through journaling. This activity can assist the individual in organizing thoughts and becoming more self-aware. The counselor may encourage the student to write in her journal at specific times each day (e.g., after waking in the morning, before going to bed at night, mid-day, or whenever the urge to cut may arise). The counselor and the student may take some time each week to discuss journal writings. Writing a brief (or detailed) autobiography, describing how she sees herself, identifying emotions she experienced during the course of the day, describing when she feels most angry, sad, or lonely are all possible journal entries for the student who reports difficulty in what to write (Conterio & Lader, 1998; Levenkron, 1998; Strong, 1998).

Working Together to Find a Therapist

The school counselor will likely experience difficulty providing all of the therapeutic needs of the self-injuring student. Consequently, after a trusting relationship has been established with the student, a primary focus should be on finding a therapist outside of the school environment. Finding a therapist that promotes an environment of healthy expression of emotions and patience is of the utmost importance (Simpson, 2001; Strong, 1998; Zila & Kiselica, 2001).

Many students may experience concern about trusting a potential caregiver outside of the current relationship. The school counselor may ask the student to write in his journal all of the desired qualities of a potential helper. The counselor and student may discuss these qualities and develop an interview sheet for the potential therapist. This exercise allows the student to experience power in the decision-making process and some form of control in those relationships in which he chooses to participate (Conterio & Lader, 1998; Strong, 1998).

Classroom Guidance

Classroom guidance activities may be a useful tool in working with self-injury. Since students who self-injure struggle with experiencing affect perceived as negative, classroom guidance activities that specifically address affect can be beneficial. A variety of topics would be appropriate. Some appropriate topics for classroom guidance range from feelings in general to divorce, grief, death of a loved one, avoiding abusive situations, identifying abusive situations, alcohol/ drug use, and, of course, self-harm. The constant thread through each of these topics is expression of and alternative measures of managing emotions (Warm, Murray, & Fox, 2002).

Successful classroom guidance can be enhanced through cooperation between the teachers and the counselors. Counselor and teacher collaboration allows students to experience the two as teammates who mutually facilitate learning and discussion, thus fostering the development of effective curricula that stresses personal life skills as well as academic growth (Hall & Rueth, 1999; Paternite & Johnston, 2005). Moreover, the collaborative approach may allow the teacher to provide a safe and open atmosphere even in the absence of the counselor. Frequent counselor presence in the classrooms will enable students to put a face with a name and title, and students will see the counselor as caring and understanding their everyday challenges and experiences. Consequently, it would be easier for students who may have been reluctant to seek help, like most self-injurers, to feel at ease contacting the counselor.

For the classroom guidance approach to be effective, it is imperative that teachers embrace the idea. This requires the counselor's fervent promotion of the school's counseling program preferably through faculty trainings. In these faculty meetings, the counselor can emphasize the importance of counseling and its impact on enhancing the students' social, mental, and emotional wellbeing. Faculty trainings are forums for the counselor to train teachers on basic listening and reflecting skills that can facilitate students' openness. In addition, information and resources on various topics such as self-injury and intrapersonal development can be shared. Also, this would be an opportune occasion to educate the staff on the referral process and the importance of confidentiality.

Challenges to Treatment

Breaching Confidentiality

The nature of the self-injuring student is that of lack of trust. Consequently, breaching confidentiality without weighing the ramifications is full of potential pitfalls. Counselors must clearly outline the limits of confidentiality with students and parents to avoid any misunderstandings or violations of trust (American School Counselor Association, 2004; Froeschle & Moyer, 2004). The student's age, capability, consequences of disclosure on the therapeutic relationship, and legal and ethical policies within each school district should be considered when deciding to violate confidentiality. If referral to an outside resource is to be done, it may be necessary that parents/guardians be informed and efforts be made to ensure minimal interruption of services during transition (American School Counselor Association, 2004). In weighing these factors, consulting with fellow school professionals is recommended.

Setting Boundaries

To avoid frustration and promote healthy boundaries, the counselor must avoid offering that which cannot be provided. Making promises like, "I will be here whenever you need to talk," "You can call me at home if you need to," or "I promise I will never talk about this with anyone," are unreasonable demands of the counselor. On the contrary, the counselor should schedule specific meeting times in which you discuss the proposed techniques to encourage the student to learn to appropriately express feelings and thoughts. In addition to preserving the counselor's ability to provide assistance, setting appropriate boundaries will ultimately promote trust and learning of new coping skills for the student.

Tip Sheet

1. Try to see the pain behind the behavior.
2. Offer acceptance and support.
3. Communicate understanding that behavior is a method of coping.
4. Offer observations and statements instead of too many questions.
5. Assure the individual that she/he is not "bad" or "insane".
6. Reflect and/or talk about feelings.
7. DO NOT offer that which you are not capable of delivering.
8. Set appropriate boundaries.
9. Get help from a counselor outside of the school setting.
10. Seek consultation before breaking confidentiality.

A Case Example

The following is a school counselor's account of an interaction with a middle school student named Brenda:

Brenda was a new student at X middle school. She had been at the school for only two months, having moved from Kansas City, Missouri. Brenda kept to herself and did not share much. Even as summer approached, she wore long sleeved tops. She even wore a light long sleeved t-shirt to the gym. Brenda's grades were sinking and she seemed to struggle with low self-esteem. She often stated that she did not know how to complete her assignments regardless of her teacher's attempts to work with her. Brenda's English teacher became concerned when she noticed some cuts on her right wrist. She voiced her concern with the school counselor.

Before calling Brenda to her office, the counselor hoped to gather more of the teacher's observations. The counselor learned of Brenda's tendency to wear clothing that concealed her skin and her apparent lack of confidence in the classroom. The counselor also noted that Brenda was new to the school and did not have many friends. All of these factors contributed to the counselor's conceptualization that Brenda might be experiencing grief. Furthermore, the cuts and Brenda's attempts to conceal them assisted the counselor in understanding that Brenda may be using this behavior to manage her grief.

Possessing this basic conceptualization, the counselor asked Brenda to meet with her. In her initial meeting with Brenda, the counselor pointed out that she was concerned about Brenda. She mentioned Brenda's newness to the school and her teacher's concern about Brenda's school work. The counselor was careful to cultivate some trust with Brenda before addressing her self-injurious acts. Initially, Brenda dwelt much on her moving from Missouri to Texas. She reported adjustment difficulties as she struggled to get used to Texas.

It took several sessions before Brenda would share about cutting herself. As Brenda mentioned the behavior, the counselor made the observation, "It seems like cutting helps you manage your frustration." Brenda concurred and began to tell her story. She shared that she had lived with her grandparents in Missouri before her mother brought her home. Brenda was the youngest of three children. Her brother was a decorated soldier, and her sister owned her own catering business.

Brenda disclosed that she felt that her mother loved her brother more than Brenda or her sister. Though on the surface this seemed a very plausible reason for her self-injuring behavior, the issue was much deeper. Brenda revealed that her grandfather had sexually abused her. As her relationship with Brenda continued to solidify, the counselor investigated Brenda's willingness to attempt some techniques to assist managing feelings that prompted cutting herself. Brenda voiced that she was skeptical, but willing to try alternatives. At this point, the counselor suggested that Brenda write in a journal at least once a day. When

Brenda asked what and when she should write, she and the counselor identified the circumstances and time when she was most likely to cut. Brenda stated that she typically cut in the afternoon after she came home from school. The counselor then suggested that before she cut, Brenda was to write what was happening with her before she cut. After one week of diligently completing the activity, Brenda reported that while journaling did not keep her from cutting completely, the frequency of her cutting did decrease. Successful completion of the activity served to increase trust between Brenda and the counselor.

With Brenda's consent, her mother was called in. With the support of her counselor, Brenda shared the truth about her grandfather's abuse. Initially, Brenda's mother appeared shocked and remorseful. The counselor suggested that Brenda and her mother attend Youth and Family Services for counseling. However, Brenda's mother didn't want to follow up with the referral. She contended that Brenda just wanted attention. The counselor was able to share with the mother that she believed Brenda's self-injurious behavior was more than a ploy to gain attention. In fact, her behavior was used to manage a myriad of feelings that she was unable to express. Consequently, she cut herself. After initial hesitance, the mother agreed to follow-up with the referral for counseling with her daughter.

Summary and Conclusions

While self-injury is not a new phenomenon, confusion and controversy still surround it. It is imperative to understand that the act of self-injury is not the focus of treatment, but rather providing alternative and facilitative means of sharing underlying feelings. When the student learns to meet her needs through alternative expression of feelings and thoughts, only then will she be able to avoid the compulsion to self-injure. In the school setting, where reports of the behavior increasing abound, new approaches must continue to be developed to not only manage existing cases of student self-injury, but to provide preventative measures for students who have yet to exercise the behavior.

Preventative measures like classroom guidance activities and essential services like individual and group counseling must continue to be researched in order to provide students with alternatives to this phenomenon.

Discussion Questions

1. How do you define self-injury?
2. What are the primary objectives for a school counselor faced with a self-injuring student?
3. What are some techniques for working with self-injury in a school setting?
4. What are some salient topics for classroom guidance activities aimed at the topic of self-injury?
5. What are some ethical considerations in the school setting when working with a student who self-injures?
6. What must be considered when introducing an "alternatives list" to a student who self-injures?
7. How can you assist a student in finding a therapist outside of the school setting?
8. What qualities must a therapist possess who works with a self-injuring client?
9. How do you involve parents/guardians when a student is self-injuring?
10. What is the best way to support students who self-injure?
11. How different is self-injury from suicide attempt/threat?
12. What is the value of using journaling to explore highly personal experiences?
13. What limits to confidentiality may arise when working with a student who self-injures?
14. What would a counselor do if he/she discovers that a student self injures and is moving to another school?
15. How can a school counselor provide support to other school personnel when addressing self-injury?

References

American Psychiatric Association. (2000). *Diagnostic and statistical manual of mental disorders-Text revision* (4th ed.). Washington, DC: Author.

American School Counselor Association. (2004). *Ethical standards for school counselors.* Alexandria, VA: Author.

Conterio, K., & Lader, W. (1998). *Bodily harm: The breakthrough healing program for self-injurers.* New York: Hyperion.

Coy, D. R., & Simpson, C. (2002). Kids who cut. School *Counselor, 40*(1), 16-19.

Favaro, A., & Santonastaso, P. (2000). Self-injurious behavior in anorexia nervosa. *The Journal of Nervous and Mental Disease, 188*, 537-542.

Favazza, A. R., & Rosenthal, R. J. (1993). Diagnostic issues in self-mutilation. *Hospital and Community Psychiatry, 44*, 134-140.

Froeschle, J., & Moyer, M. (2004). Just cut it out: Legal and ethical challenges in counseling students who self-mutilate. *Professional School Counseling, 7,* 231-235.

Hall, S. E., & Rueth, T. W. (1999). Counselors in the classroom: A developmental approach to student well-being. *NASSP Bulletin, 83,* 603-630.

Kettlewell, C. (1999). *Skin game.* New York: St. Martins Press.

Jeffery, D., & Warm, A. (2002). A study of service providers' understanding of self-harm. *Journal of Mental Health, 11,* 295-303.

Laye-Gindhu, A., & Schonert-Reichl, K.A. (2005). Nonsuicidal self-harm among community adolescents: Understanding the "whats" and "whys" of self-harm. *Journal of Youth and Adolescence, 34,* 447-457.

Levenkron, S. (1998). *Cutting.* New York: W.W. Norton and Company.

Lloyd, E. E. (1997). *Self-mutilation in a community sample of adolescents.* Unpublished doctoral dissertation, Louisiana State University and Agricultural and Mechanical College.

Paternite, C. E., & Johnston, T. C. (2005). Rationale and strategies for central involvement of educators in effective *school*-based mental health programs. *Journal of Youth and Adolescence, 34*(1), 41-49.

Pembroke, L. (1994). *Self-harm: Perspectives from personal experience.* London: Survivors Speak Out.

Rosen, P. M., Walsh, B. W., & Rode, S. A. (1990). Interpersonal loss and self-mutilation. *Suicide and Life-Threatening Behavior, 20,* 177-184.

Ross, S., & Heath, N. (2002). A study of the frequency of self-mutilation in a community sample of adolescents. *Journal of Youth and Adolescence 31*(1), 67-77.

Simpson, C. (2001). *Self-mutilation.* Greensboro, NC: ERIC/CASS.

Stanley, B., Gameroff, M. J., Michalson, V., & Mann, J. J. (2001). Are suicide attempters who self-mutilate a unique population? *American Journal of Psychiatry, 158,* 427- 432.

Strong, M. (1998). *A bright red scream: Self-mutilation and the language of pain.* New York: Penguin.

Suyemoto, K. L., & MacDonald, M. L. (1995). Self-cutting in female adolescents. *Psychotherapy, 32*(1), 162-171.

Walsh, B. W., & Rosen, P. M. (1988). *Self-mutilation: Theory, research, and treatment.* New York: Guilford Press.

Warm, A., Murray, C., & Fox, J. (2002). Who helps? Supporting people who self-harm. *Journal of Mental Health, 11,* 121-130.

Zila, L. M., & Kiselica, M. S. (2001). Understanding and counseling self-mutilation in female adolescents and young adults. *Journal of Counseling & Development, 79,* 46-52.

Recommended Resources

Conterio, K., & Lader, W. (1998). *Bodily harm: The breakthrough healing program for self-injurers.* New York: Hyperion.

Kettlewell, C. (1999). *Skin game.* New York: St. Martins Press.

Levenkron, S. (1998). *Cutting.* New York: W.W. Norton and Company.

Young People and Self-Harm. www.selfharm.org.uk/

Self-Injury Information and Resources. www.self-injury.info

American Self-Harm Clearinghouse Website. http://selfinjury.org

Chapter 18

Working with the Victims of Extreme Crises

Cheri Lovre

Abstract

When crises overwhelm the usual coping strategies of individuals and systems, specific measures can make a difference. The dynamics of individual and group recovery are a cycle of interaction – children will recover as well as the adults around them, adults must do good self-care to be able to provide an environment that supports recovery for students, and the environment and safety needed must be sanctioned and supported by administrators. Providing case studies and examples, this chapter illustrates how counselors are the only school staff who have the knowledge and skill to influence all levels of the recovery process.

Extreme Crises and Overwhelming Events

It is critical for us to look at both the dynamics of how overwhelming crises impact students and the school and to recognize that they also have a much more deleterious effect on counselors and mental health specialists than we might realize when we're in the midst of it. While we know at some level that crises and tragedies will touch the lives of our students and impact the school environment, we each have our own view or expectation of what that might entail. Fortunately, for many school counselors, the everyday kinds of losses will be what we experience. Some of us, however, are in districts that suffer impact due to natural disaster, major chemical spills, or human-caused disasters, such as Oklahoma City and New York after 9/11, which experienced the effects of terrorism and unbridled violence.

Self-Care and Our Innate Stability

Perhaps the most important place to start this discussion is to look at the importance of self-care on an ongoing basis. We can only call to our aid those supports we had in place prior to going into the event; and in the case of our own survival, it is crucial to look at what sustains us in crisis. We need to practice what sustains us on an everyday basis or it is not in place for us when we most need it. For instance, some people respond to "What sustains you?" with comments about their faith. Others find a belief in the goodness of humankind to be inspiring. Still others talk about the importance of family. It doesn't appear to be so crucial *what* it is one believes, but *that* one has something to cling to in journeys through turbulent waters.

So one place to begin is to take time for a few minutes to really consider what it is that sustains you and how you practice your connection to that sustenance on a daily basis. Think about the ways you reinforce its presence in your daily life, and ways you might want to improve that part of your life. Don't go on reading for now. Just set the book down and ponder this for a moment. Realize that this may be the time for you to make a new, sustained effort at creating or enhancing your relationship with what it is that supports you when all else falls away.

Determinants of Children/Youth Trauma and Recovery

One of the many important reasons to address this first and foremost is that, in general, children do as well as their parents and caregivers do – as well as those adults around them on whom they depend. In many ways, the degree to which a child has traumatic reactions that could move into full-blown Post Traumatic Stress Disorder (PTSD) is at least as much dependent on the degree to which the adult appeared to be rendered helpless or powerless, much more than the actual degree of danger to life or limb. A child can suffer terribly if a parent is hysterical about something relatively minor, and a child can survive more dangerous things remarkably well if they are not separated from their parents or caregivers and are able to have trust in competent adult support.

For instance, in the bombing blitz of London during WWII, some Londoners sent their children to live with relatives outside the danger zone of the city in order that they be safe. One might think that would also shield them from traumatic symptoms. But it was found, perhaps surprisingly, that those children who remained with their parents in the city suffered less residual trauma because they had their most trusted adult support with them, and they knew what to do when the sirens went off. Run to the shelter. Run with the parents to the shelter. As long as the parents maintained some modicum of ability to support the child, and as long as the parents themselves didn't dissolve into panic and hysteria, the children remained remarkably able to cope with the devastation of the city as it fell all around them. (Van der Kolk, 1997).

System-Wide Issues

Another area of concern is to examine what it is that your district and your building have in place for responding to overwhelming events. As the school counselor, you are in the best place to determine weaknesses in the school plan with regard to meeting the emotional needs of students and parents in the aftermath of critical events. Several issues come into play here:

- How clearly do your administrators see the tie between prevention and school climate? In a recent episode, a "Columbine-like event" was planned by a core group of around a dozen middle school students. The planning went on for months, with the date of execution planned for the anniversary of the shooting at Columbine. One student in that core group, at the last minute, involved adults who were able to intervene, undoubtedly saving many, many lives. The disturbing fact, however, was that upon further investigation, it was discovered that upwards of 100 students knew enough about the plan to know it was in the works, feasible, likely, and the date it was to occur. The fact that so many students knew and didn't tell is frightening. But also, it only takes one student coming forward to save all of those lives. In this aspect, school climate can be influenced by the school counselor if s/he has the support of site administration. There is no better use of a counselor's time!

- How do you educate parents ahead of time about what you will do should you have to evacuate the school and reunite parents with their children in another location? Letting them know ahead of time can greatly reduce chaos, which keeps hysteria down. In some districts, instead of having one big "here is all you need to know about crisis in our district," every newsletter gave parents more and more insights and information about this. In that way, parents recognize that your school safety and crisis response plans are really integrated into the larger system, which gives parents greater confidence in your district.

- How do you mitigate inducing fear by the kinds of drills your school holds? Some districts do life-like drills about shooters being in the building. But really, what puts your students at greatest risk? Although we lose about 11 students a year to school violence including shootings, we lose 11 students a day in the United States to gun-related incidents that happen outside of the school setting. We lose more people to being struck by lightning than we do to school shootings, yet most of our schools have no policy or procedure for responding to or avoiding lightning deaths on athletic fields. It is important not to introduce unnecessary psychological fears about events that are least likely to occur for our students. Counselors can help reinforce this concept. In many cases, the best lock-down drills, for the sake of avoiding the psychological anxiety it brings about for many students and staff, is to instead modify similar drills (such as weather-related drills, or shelter-in-place drills related to a chemical spill) and practice lock-down drills with only staff in the building on inservice days.

- How well apprised is your administration of the importance of maintaining environmental structure while providing time and the means for teachers to help students process the event? An example of this is to continue with the bell schedule and students moving from class to class while giving teachers permission to suspend curriculum and lead discussions about the event. School counselors are critical in bringing this awareness to teaching and administrative staff. In the weeks following the deaths of several students from a private, parochial school while on an all-class climb on Mt. Hood, it was so critical for students to be able to gather together that day that students brought sleeping bags and stayed in the dorms with the residential students for several nights. During the day, the bells rang, and students went from class to class, but there was no question that students had to grieve, to gather, to mourn, to share memories, and to struggle together to give the deaths meaning. It was helpful for the bells to ring and for students to go from class to class in order to see who was there and what desks were empty. Not that they didn't know which students had died, but the movement from class to class made it more real for them and gave them the opportunity to grieve the losses in the configurations of the classes in which they knew the peer, at least for one important part of their process.

- Do you have handouts and flyers ready to go for events outside the realm of the ordinary? It is helpful to have guidelines for teachers and parents on how to help students cope after overwhelming events, and it saves critical time when things are unfolding if you have those written and ready to go. In the aftermath of hundreds of school events, a one-page flyer has been on the back of the letter that went home telling parents what happened and what the school did to manage a tragedy or crisis. Parents appreciate the support at a time when they are sometimes feeling out of their comfort zone, and children do as well as the adults around them. These suggestions pay great dividends.

- Follow-up after critical events has everything to do with how well students and staff will adjust. Often we forget that students will only do as well as the adults around them, so the school counselor's input to administration, to the school plan, and to all plans for follow-up will be important in assuring that needs are met. This also has to do with how students are involved as well as how adults gain information from students on what will really make a difference.

In the aftermath of Columbine, one principal called an assembly and stood before the student body, acknowledging that what had happened at Columbine was shocking, overwhelming, and more than he could manage on his own. But, he went on to say, it wasn't bigger than all of them if they worked together. He implored students to help come up with a plan that would address school climate in their building.

Within a couple of days the students had come up with the plan. It was for students to devise a seating chart for lunch time that would make every table have students who would never talk to one another – in the students' words, "One jock, one nerd, one pierced lip, one purple hair, one gay kid, somebody in a dance class, and a skater." For several days, students hardly spoke to one another. But within a week, conversation was rippling about at the tables, and over time they witnessed their first food fight in this new configuration. The principal actually saw that as a great sign – that they were behaving – or misbehaving – in a very normal fashion!

By the end of the school year, two brothers went to see the principal to reinforce their belief that it was important to continue this practice into the next school year – they had a little brother who would be coming into the high school and, "He really needs this!" One of the popular girls came in to the principal

to say that she'd noticed that now that she was talking to the pierced lip at her lunch table, she was also talking to the pierced eyebrow in the locker next to hers. Although these students' reactions have a delightful quality to them, they also have a significance in a far deeper way. These are the kinds of insights counselors can bring to administrators who might otherwise lean on discipline as the lead response to some things in which a different technique might bring much greater pay-off for the school.

Issues of Trauma

Trauma is fundamentally different from grief, yet few school counseling programs clearly separate the two and give specific skill-building on how to help students and staff cope with the distressing symptoms that commonly follow traumatic events. Although it is beyond the scope of this chapter to deal with trauma as a psychological challenge, this is an area that bears focus for all school counselors.

Understanding how to help students and staff in the aftermath of traumatic events is not just critical to the possibility that you'll face such an event in your school. It is critical because you will have students daily who come to you with symptoms of trauma or with ongoing hyper-arousal, which results from the mobilizing biochemistry of the traumatic response. This biochemical presence in the body has deleterious effects on the student's ability to concentrate, lodge information into memory, and the side effects of the high level of adrenaline leave students irritable, on edge, and easily provoked. It is well worth taking time to learn much more about the impact of trauma and how to help students mitigate the symptoms (Sapolsky, 2004).

An example of this irritability was very evident following the death of a student to a heart attack one evening after an extracurricular activity. About a dozen students were in the parking lot and tried to administer CPR. The ambulance eventually transported the student to the hospital, but it wasn't possible to save his life.

The next day the school crisis response team set aside a place for students who knew the boy (or who had other losses) to grieve or process the death. Those students who had been on the scene and had tried to help save him were throwing spit wads, teasing other students, and were impossible to manage or bring into acceptable behavior. By mid-morning a time and space was created to provide trauma intervention to those who had been on the scene, and when they returned to the Safe Room following that opportunity, they moved directly into grieving and were very caring, compassionate, and appropriate in their responses.

Although it is well beyond the usual training of school counselors to be able to provide that level of trauma intervention (it is a unique and specific skill usually learned outside of the school counselor's college curriculum), counselors are often those best equipped to take that training and lead those interventions. This is one of the most fundamental—and frequent—trainings done by Crisis Management Institute.

A few of the determinants of likelihood that students and staff will suffer trauma include:
- Proximity to the event
- Degree of surprise
- Level to which adults were rendered powerless, helpless
- Magnitude of the event in its impact across the community/population
- Degree of gore, pain, suffering of the victims and what kinds of things bystanders witnessed
- Whether the child had a personal relationship with the victim(s)
- Length of time from onset of crisis to arrival of effective help
- Past history of these kinds of events for your community and for each individual
- Ability to reunite with family as soon as possible
- Level of stability or contagion experienced by children from their parents, caregivers
- Availability of adequate help for students in terms of trauma intervention (debriefing) if indicated

There are many other determinants as well, but these are crucial. It is also important to note here that many schools are using Critical Incident Stress Management (CISM) techniques for students, staff, and parents in the aftermath of these events. While that model is very effective for emergency workers, for whom it was designed, it is crucial that we recognize that it is not necessarily an appropriate model for use in school settings, with children, or with "civilian" (non uniformed) populations. There have been scores of lawsuits levied in New York post 9/11 because so many people rushed in with Critical Incident Stress Debriefing (CISD) or CISM to settings other than those for which it was designed (Yandrick, 2003).

In order to work in the aftermath of trauma with victims, witnesses, children, and non-uniformed people, counselors need to use a model that is designed for this population and this need. Remember, not all children on the scene of an event will be traumatized. There are

many factors that contribute to the development of Post Traumatic Stress Disorder (PTSD), some of which appear to be the existing levels of cortisol in the brain prior to the event. That means each child will be vulnerable based on inherent biology that we can't know or measure. Thus, we must be certain not to make assumptions that all students on the scene of an accident or incident need the same kind of follow-up. Too, it means that school counselors need to learn skills other than or at least in addition to CISM in order to meet this need.

Working with Students in the Aftermath of Extreme Crisis

There are two critical elements in looking at working with students in the aftermath of extreme crisis. One is looking at meeting the needs of the student, and the other is considering the steps that need to be taken to stabilize the environment as a whole. Counselors are critical in both areas.

Meeting the needs of the students as individuals is dependent on the environment being stabilized. A student cannot begin to process the impact and meaning of an event until s/he feels safe. Feeling safe depends on the level of stability perceived by the student toward the adults around them, including parents, teachers, and caregivers. As mentioned above, one major determinant of the level of impact is the degree to which children perceive that the adults around them were rendered helpless or powerless. The role of the school counselor in this aspect is multi-dimensional:
- To help administrators understand trauma and the system-wide measures that can be put in place to aid recovery;
- To both educate and support teachers and school staff in their understanding of trauma, the impact of traumatic events on themselves and on students, and what can be done to support them and mitigate the residual effects on students;
- To help align messages to parents so crucial information is released hand-in-hand with insightful suggestions that will help parents assist their children in recovery;
- To help students deal with the crisis and normalize their school experience through trauma intervention, grief counseling, referrals for PTSD, etc.

The Use of Local and National Experts

In the aftermath of these events, it is common for do-gooders to ooze out of the woodwork. People with an amazing array of skills *and illusions of skills* appear at the doorstep of the school. It is critical that schools realize that those who have effectively helped others deal with major crises will be able to help you predict what will unfold over the next days and weeks, and any ability to take out the element of surprise will be very helpful. At the same time, it is crucial to screen people carefully and to ascertain their intent.

In the aftermath of one major event (a school shooting), when the trauma training was held for the many "incoming" counselors who were going to provide support, one woman who attended was clear and open in sharing that it was her intent to bring in tarot cards and do palm readings to reassure students that, because the "life line in the palm of their hands" was long and uninterrupted, they could return to school without fear of another such incident. There are many kinds of approaches, some proven, some not. Some appropriate, some not. It isn't that one would always turn away people who have a skill that is ineffective, but one might use caution in the kind of placement that person is given. Some approaches that are quite effective might still be inappropriate for a given setting or community culture. Getting too far afield from something that looks like a norm in terms of responding to crises can engender mistrust or wariness on the part of students, staff, and parents.

It is important, though, not to just circle the wagons. Outsiders with expert experience can bring insights and ideas that you can weigh out and decide whether to implement or not. Generate long lists of ideas and select those that appear most helpful. Inviting others in for support doesn't have to mean turning the response over to them. Check out their experience base. Call references from past events. Prepare a list of reliable mental health practitioners in the community to have available in time of crisis. Counselors can be instrumental in helping administrators make good decisions on how to screen and train those who are invited to provide support in overwhelming crises.

The Need to Gather

Recovery from trauma is dependent on social support. Intuitively we know this, but clinically this is critical. The first crucial social support is for the students to reunite with their families, and to find the safe haven that home provides. Thus, the process the school uses for evacuating, relocating, and reuniting is crucial. Plan ahead to have handouts ready for parents on how they can help their children in the first days after a traumatic event. If it is possible for parents to gather at the site with a counselor who can be providing support while also educating the parents that their own reactions will greatly influence their child's recovery, there will be much good that will come of this.

Once that safe haven of home and family has been re-established for the child, the next critical social need is to reunite with those with whom one survived. So it is important to facilitate a means for students to be invited to an all-school gathering as soon as possible. It is fine to use an armory, another school, or some other site large enough for the gathering; in fact, depending on the nature of the tragedy and the degree to which the school site was damaged, it may be very helpful to have the first gathering away from the place that will cause re-experiencing of the trauma for those closely involved.

In these early days, be careful about requiring that students separate from their parents. They need both the comfort of family and the opportunity to gather with peers. In many cases, this first gathering is best organized to give students the choice of sitting with their parents or with peers. A gathering can be organized such that the initial part is with all of them together, and then provide the opportunity for parents to gather in small, facilitated groups to be able to voice their concerns and find support, and for the students to gather in groups knowing that their parents are still in the building so the separation is temporary and they are not without a lifeline.

Any ways you can begin to re-establish group identity and belonging are encouraged. For instance, students may sing songs, some songs may be sung to them by individual students, cheerleaders may lead a couple of cheers that reunite school spirit, the principal needs to speak to reaffirm all that students did well in responding and to set the first stone in place for the foundation of recovery. Have some of their favorite staff address the group. Physical activity is very helpful and important. Dancing, movement with cheers, and creating something in groups work, but especially effective are activities like basketball and running and using large motor skills in bilateral movement. It is why daddies pace when moms are having babies. Bilateral movement is calming (Van der Kolk, 1997).

In keeping with this – the need to self-regulate and be able to calm oneself - counselors can work with students, with teachers and with parents on teaching a variety of methods for self-soothing. It is worth taking a few minutes of class time to help students relax, to help students learn self-regulation of emotion, and to find some of their own best ideas for calming.

Re-Visitation of the Site: An Example for Elementary Schools

If the scene of the event or the location of the student during the survival of a terrifying event was the school building itself, this, too, then, becomes another hurdle to overcome. Returning to the scene of a traumatic event will be a trigger for many to re-experience all of the biochemistry of the fight or flight response, and flashbacks and arousal symptoms will likely be magnified. In these cases it is extremely important for schools to give students the opportunity to gather together once the locale has been restored (i.e., remodeled, cleaned up) and to have some time with parents at the site (Van der Kolk, 2007).

Following the shooting at Thurston High School (Springfield, Oregon, May 1998) this was planned for the day before school would resume. The cafeteria in which the shooting had occurred had been cleaned, repaired, and needed areas repainted. Media was not allowed on school grounds during the three-hour visitation in which students were invited to come to the school with their parents in order to, for the first time since the shooting four days earlier, re-enter the cafeteria.

When providing these times of re-entry to the scene, a few guidelines are helpful. One is to allow students to come, stay, and leave in the company of their parents. Thus, it is most helpful for this to be on a day prior to the first day back at school. It is crucial to have media away from the site so families can come and go without being hounded by reporters, both for their own sakes and in order to keep the media coverage from continuing the invasion of the privacy of student grief. At Thurston High School, the school and cafeteria were open spanning a three-hour period of time, with people coming and going, staying as long as they felt they wanted. It doesn't have to be an organized "event" like an assembly. That kind of organization works well for the first gathering, which has likely already happened. The visitation to the site works well after that initial gathering.

Have activities for students to do once in the space. In an elementary school, it might work well to structure time by starting the gathering in a room other than the room of the event, if that is possible (for instance, if there were intruder and student injuries or deaths, begin the gathering somewhere other than that room). One such case occurred in an elementary school when a deranged man with a machete entered a kindergarten classroom. Although no one died and adults were more viciously attacked than children, the likelihood of high anxiety and re-experiencing the trauma upon returning to the scene was certainly high.

Because the traumatic elements of the event occurred in the classroom, the students and their parents gathered first in the library. Because their teacher and principal had been seriously injured and taken from the scene via helicopter med-evacuation, they were introduced to their substitute teacher and the interim principal in the library. Some welcoming discussion by staff familiar to the students ensued. One might consider including people such as the library staff, clerical staff, PE teachers, and others known to all of the students in this initial gathering. The principal stepping in to see the school through this crisis was a recently retired principal from that school, so many parents were familiar with her, which was helpful.

Empowerment is crucial at these times. One of the hallmarks of trauma is the inability to move or effectively respond in the midst of terror. Thus, one step in recovery is for the students to regain their sense of control and experience mastery. In this case, while still in the library, one of the school staff whom students all knew made note of how the new teacher would not know how they did calendar and weather activities during rug time first thing in the morning. One obvious way of empowering students during the return to their classrooms was to invite them to show the teacher how they do rug time and start the day with their usual routine. Students and their parents walked down to the classroom where, as they entered, each student received a teddy bear from the substitute. Students sat in their seats first, were gathered to rug time, and then were invited to demonstrate with the calendar and the weather chart, how they made note of those elements at the beginning of each day.

The teacher, who was still to be hospitalized for some time, had recorded on tape an encouraging message for the students, so that was played. Students made cards for both the principal and teacher, and a few activities that involved action were included. Because movement and rhythm are part of re-establishing a sense of group connection and of internal self-calming, using music, singing, drumming, dance, or movement will be very helpful at such times (Lovre, 2005).

Students enjoyed a snack, and then were able to leave with their parents. At no time on this first visit were children expected to separate from their parents. Anticipating the first school day and putting some clear parameters on parent presence in the classroom is helpful. Many want to hang on in the classroom, which makes it difficult for the "new" teacher to establish his/her leadership in the room without the parent fears and needs contaminating the process. For that reason, it was determined that parents would be able to come in, help their children settle into their desks, and could watch the first morning's calendar and weather activity. They would then leave.

In order to help them with their own anxiety, consider having coffee and light refreshments in a room where they can gather to have some informal social support around the level of trauma, fear, or anxiety they are continuing to re-experience. This is also a wonderful time to reinforce that students will only do as well as their caregivers and parents do, so parents will do well to deal with their fears without visiting them upon their children. Those discussions need to occur outside of earshot of the youth.

High School Re-Visitation

Following the shooting at Thurston High School, the cafeteria was cleaned, repaired, and prepared for the revisiting. Students came with their parents. But just standing around in a hollow room would allow students to focus only on the shooting and their memories. Here are some activities that could be useful:

1. Consider taping huge pieces of butcher paper on the walls with suggestions of things to write on each; titles such as "Something I look forward to…" "Someone who is there for me…" "Something people did that was helpful was…" "Next year we will…" and other ideas or sentence starters.
2. Provide big buckets of flowers donated by local florist shops and—if gardens are producing—flowers that staff and students bring in. Ask for donations of vases that don't need to be returned, and let students create beautiful flower bouquets to take to some of the classrooms.
3. Have tables set up with some common Safe Room activities, such as creating colorful cards and letters for those injured or families of those who died in the event (Lovre, 2005).

Knowledge is Power; Understanding Is the Beginning of Mastery

Find ways to educate staff, parents, and students about trauma. Normalize the human range of reactions at times such as these. The school counselor plays a critical role in organizing what kinds of information will be helpful and how best to disseminate that information. Fear is often based in lack of understanding or lack of clear information, so several elements come into play here:

- Clear information about what occurred;
- Predicting how the response will now unfold;
- Reinforcing those behaviors and activities that will help rebuild a sense of trust in the school;
- Collaboration with all engaged agencies, organizations, and response efforts;
- Letting all know where they will continue to get updates and helpful information;
- Giving an open line for all to voice concerns and needs;
- Providing a means for all concerned to give some level of input into recovery efforts and organization – getting information on needs to those who will organize the response.

Start-Up in the Aftermath

Counselors should carefully consider what might be done to facilitate the return to school. First in that list is to re-establish trust on the part of students, parents, and staff for a sense of safety in the building. Sometimes, though, administrators leap to the assumption that this will mean having uniformed security or police on site in great numbers. Remember, to find out what will help people feel safe, you have to ask the people!

As an example, in a rural school there was a brutal homicide of one student by another in a park behind the school on a Sunday. On Monday when students arrived, the yellow barrier tape was still in place and the investigation was still under way. The principal assumed that having metal detectors at the doors, a show of police cars in the parking lot, and uniformed police and security in the hallways would bring a sense of safety.

However, when asking the students what would help, a very different solution emerged. The students didn't feel at threat when at school. Staff members are there, and great numbers of people gave the sense of safety that groups can provide. The most helpful step that was taken was to ask students in the Safe Room what they most wanted or needed to feel safe. The girls wanted self defense taught in PE. Their fear was, if this student, whom they knew and trusted, could kill one of their classmates, they were all at risk; and the risk was greatest when they weren't with a group. Hiring a martial arts instructor to lead girls' PE for a few weeks was much less expensive than all of the security that was being considered. It was also much more effective, because it met the students where their fears existed and empowered them with some level of mastery.

In any event, the school counselor will be a key player in eliciting insights from students on what will help them feel safe and how best to address these initial efforts.

Meeting the Needs of Parents

Counselors need to remember that students only do as well as the adults around them. That makes it at least as important to work with parents as it is to work with students regarding the recovery and rebuilding of trust. Schools often err on the side of calling too few parent meetings, sending home flyers only when there are major numbers of new issues or details, or in response to parent requests and concerns.

Sometimes we forget that, unless media coverage is exactly the message we wanted parents to hear, many of our families' perceptions of how we handled the response will be only what the media report. Controlling the message means the school needs to adopt a two-pronged approach—to continue giving your own "spin" to the story as you give information to reporters and to send ample information home to parents. Included in this is the importance of providing the means for parents to voice their concerns and needs to the district, so providing "one number to call" goes a long way in rebuilding home/school trust.

Further, educating parents on how best to support their children pays dividends to the school recovery efforts. You can do the best job possible in working with students while they're with you, but when they get home, just one disparaging comment from a parent can disintegrate all you've built up in your efforts.

It is sometimes said that in the aftermath of critical events, students need counselors and parents need experts. That, however, sells short the importance of the counselor's role in two ways – in actively joining in the parent response efforts and in giving insights to those experts who will be addressing parents at some times. There is nothing like a familiar face that emanates both compassion and understanding to help a parent move toward the school with trust.

Anticipating Long-Term Triggers and Re-Emergence of the Event

If your district or community suffers a major event, whether a hurricane, shooting, accident, or other kind of incident, it is likely that there will be similar events in the national or regional news in the future. That people expect. What is sometimes a surprise is that, for years, your local news stations will follow that lead story with a reminder of your own event. So it is likely that if you have a school shooting in your district, for years to come, each time there is a school shooting anywhere in the U.S., the follow-up story to that will be, "And this comes just eleven months after… just two years after… the school shooting at our own River City High School."

There are also many natural times of re-visitation of the event into the current moment. One is when the students who died would have graduated. Often their friends want to have a posthumous diploma given to the parents or some other mention made. This isn't inappropriate, but the caution here is not to let the graduation ceremony become a Life Tribute or Memory Event. One way to do this is to have a special gathering a few days before graduation to give this special attention, but keep it from being too much of a focus for the graduation day ceremonies. Counselors can help students find ways of meeting their needs and to feel validated in the process, while perhaps steering some of those efforts away from graduation itself.

The Anniversary of the Event

It is worth taking time prior to the anniversary to look at how to meet student and staff needs without this becoming a huge deal again. At the Thurston shooting anniversary, it was decided that students would not be required to attend school, that school would be held but that any student who decided not to attend would be excused, no questions asked. They had about 50% turnout for that day. It was also decided that they would not allow another memorial wall to be created, so students were told this ahead of time, and any flowers or memorabilia left at the fence was removed immediately by staff who were stationed outside.

There is no one "right" way to do any of this, but it is really helpful for counselors to both validate the need to mark the anniversary while also keeping the acknowledgement of the anniversary from becoming a major event itself, gauging carefully how much is enough, and how much creates more drama. Gather people together a few weeks before the anniversary and begin listening early on so people aren't pressured at the last minute to agree to something hastily devised.

Providing Ongoing Support

In the aftermath of the shooting at Thurston, the district received a grant that provided two full-time counselors in the school who did nothing but provide individual and group sessions for the entire following school year. The year after that they funded one full time position, and after that, counseling fees were covered for students who continued to need services and were referred to local mental health providers.

Administrators are Equally Vulnerable to Trauma

Find ways to educate administrators in the rudimentary brain function and reaction to trauma, both so they allow for the psychological recovery needs of the students, but also, frame it in ways that help administrators realize the toll this has taken for them as well. Administrators tend to have the least collegial support within their buildings because of their positions of leadership and how that sets them apart. Counselors can be crucial in educating administrators about these issues as well and providing some of that support.

School-wide steps to take in the aftermath:
- Provide great support up front in order to get the foundation for recovery established.
- Do all you can to keep clear information flowing to the people who will benefit. The unknown breeds fear. Lack of information breeds rumors.
- Provide the means for memory events, life tributes, and vigils.
- Maintain structure and routine for the most part while suspending curriculum so students have the opportunity to talk together about what happened, how well people coped, and what will help them feel safe.
- Use people with expert experience in trauma to help determine needs of individuals and the district as a whole.

Remember that recovery will depend on students and staff being able to self-regulate arousal, which means that feeling safe is the first step. Giving people whatever kinds of support will allow them to feel a sense of control is helpful. Reinforcing the importance of self-care and self-nurturing is critical. Giving staff the opportunity to take "well days" and not have to be actually sick in order to re-establish their own strength and wellness is advised. Providing the opportunity for social gatherings was facilitated after the Thurston High School shooting when the school board provided staff with a barbecue, and the board members provided the meal, ran the barbeque, and served the staff.

Handling Media in the Aftermath of School Crises

Although handling media is not the role of the school counselor, s/he can be critical in helping administrators and public information officers be effective in their efforts. There are several things to remember. Parents' perceptions will be greatly formed and influenced by media coverage. You can do the best job imaginable with parents and students, but if the media coverage is not favorable, it can easily undermine your good work. Here are some things counselors can do to make a difference:

- Help your administrator understand that, should you ever need to evacuate your building and relocate students for reuniting with their parents, it is likely that you'll also need to keep streets adjoining your school open for ingress and egress of emergency vehicles. Plan for that now. Then should such an event unfold, be sure that the first message that local media give out is clear information to parents on what streets to use and which to avoid in order to safeguard the lives of students and facilitate the efforts of emergency workers. As an example,

    "Coreyville School District acknowledges the unfolding of a critical event at JFK High School. We need the help of parents and the public in keeping J and Paramount streets open for emergency vehicles. We will be transporting all students to St. Timothy's Lutheran Church on Elm and D Streets to reunite with their parents."

- Help your administrator or district public information officer to craft messages that give parents the most important details and give the story your spin. As an example:

    "JFK High school staff acknowledges the deaths of three students yesterday following the tragic shooting on campus. Our hearts and prayers are with the families at this time. While we are reviewing our school safety plans and other policies related to prevention and response to such events, we also recognize that violence is not specifically a school problem; it is a societal problem, a cultural problem, a challenge to our entire community. We at Coreyville District and JFK High School look forward to the support of our loving parents and understanding community as you help us recover at the school level. We appreciate that in recognition of the community-wide nature of this event, churches and civic groups have donated time, help, and resources for our students and families."

This kind of message makes clear that violence is, indeed, not a school problem per se, it is a much larger problem and that, yes, sometimes it visits our schools. This kind of message is also crucial for consideration with administration, as this is the kind of message that can help lessen the likelihood of litigation as the blame is not focused on the school, but shared by the larger community (Lovre, 2006).

- Have flyers, handouts, and resources ready for parents before you need them. These would include an educational flyer on the nature, reactions to and needs of children in the aftermath of traumatic evens, flyers on grief, on prevention, intervention and response to suicide, on helping students attend a funeral for the first time and much more. Many of these can be downloaded from the Crisis Management Institute website at www.cmionline.org or are included in CMI materials.

- Determine how you will provide counseling support at the relocation site in times of confusion as a school is evacuated and counselors are needed at both ends. Parents will benefit from counselors being able to work with them as they wait for their children. They need to understand that their own reactions will greatly influence their child's recovery, so appearing in control, using restraint emotionally when talking with their children, and finding adult support for their own anger or frustration will be healthiest for their children.

- Work at helping reporters understand that dramatic coverage and interviewing those who make inflammatory or dramatic statements only further endanger your students. Put some of the responsibility of your recovery at their feet and give them suggestions and guidelines they could publish that would be helpful for parents and those who work with youth.

- Continue to work at getting positive coverage long after the event; so over time, the disaster shrinks into becoming history of the school rather than the identity of the school.

In the aftermath of the shooting at Thurston High School, Springfield, Oregon, May 1998, the school public information officer teamed up with the public information officer from the mayor's office. They provided one number for parents, community members, and media representatives to call for information. This greatly reduced confusion, facilitated getting congruent information out to all, and brought down fear. Once that phone line was in place, people could once again get through to 911, to local mental health agencies, to the hospital, and to many other phone lines that had become jammed with desperate parents looking for information. Even the neighboring school district's phones were overwhelmed with parents hoping for information.

Over time it was evident that giving the media the school district's "spin" (that violence is not a school problem, it is a societal problem, and that today it visited school) greatly mobilized the community to support rather than criticize the school. It remains one of the only mass casualty shootings on school grounds in which there were no lawsuits toward either the school district or agencies by bereaved parents of those whose students were injured. Every one of those Thurston families received multiple calls from attorneys who had successfully won suits on behalf of parents in prior school shootings, and not one family in Springfield said "yes" to those offers. That is a great accomplishment, given that there were 26 students shot that day, two of whom died (Lovre, 2006).

The counselor's role in this crisis is to help administrators recognize that the way to avoid litigation is to be forthright, open, to release information, and most of all, to meet the emotional needs of parents, students, and staff. If families feel well taken care of, they're much less apt to sue. The role of the school counselor in helping administrators see how best to do this cannot be overstated.

Tying This All in with the ASCA National Model

There are several areas of cross-over between mobilizing and responding to critical events and the American School Counselor Association (ASCA) National Model (2003). Under "Appropriate Counseling Responsibilities" is listed "Assisting the school principal with identifying and resolving student issues, needs and problems." Certainly, in the aftermath of crises and tragedies, there are a myriad of student issues, needs and problems that are directly related to the counselor's field of responsibilities. Another area listed is "Collaborating with teachers to present proactive prevention-based guidance curriculum lessons." Although there are ready-made programs and materials available from a variety of sources, there are a number of national events every year that provide a "teachable moment" for teachers within the classroom. The loss of the astronauts, school shootings, and a wide range of kinds of deaths and circumstances provide times when counselors could provide an outline of discussion ideas for teachers to use in the classroom. A number of those can be found on the Crisis Management Institute Web site at www.cmionline.org in the "free downloadables" section.

Under "Personal Social Development," it is listed that students will acquire the knowledge, attitudes, and interpersonal skills to help them understand and respect self and others. Again, although there are materials available to address these issues, counselors can be very effective in helping teachers learn the language and learn skills in leading classroom discussions at opportune moments in order to reinforce these concepts and attitudes. Although produced materials can be helpful, if students receive them much the same as they receive other curricula, it is just another lesson. But if teachers can become leaders and models for students in these very attitudes, school climate begins to change.

The ASCA National Model states that students will understand safety and survival skills. Counselors would have wonderful insights on issues that strike close to home for children based on their own specific communities, and the kinds of stresses, prejudices, and rifts that exist in a given district or school. Counselors can play a major role in creating activities for teachers to use in the classroom to explore these issues with students.

Conclusion

While much of what we might examine here could be seen as specific to counseling, this is also an opportunity for counselors to have input into the whole system—the philosophy of the school—in order to use the teachable moments provided by tragedies and crises to teach respect, compassion and acceptance of others, to reinforce the importance of the common good and in students being responsible in their behavior toward others. Although school safety planning is often left up to those who are in the department of school safety, there is clearly only one sure insurance policy against school violence, and that is school climate. The only insurance against a school shooting is by creating an environment in which students who know critical plans and information feel free to come forward to share that information with adults who can intervene and make a difference. In this way, counselors can play a critical role in curbing school violence and in prevention of overwhelming, tragic events.

Discussion Questions

1. How do your administrators demonstrate and reinforce their understanding of the connection between school climate and prevention? What needs to be done and how might you influence this?
2. How well is your building and the greater crisis response team prepared to meet the needs of students and staff suffering from a traumatic response to a critical event? What alternative do you have to Critical Incident Stress Management for interventions for those suffering the aftereffects of trauma?
3. How consistently do your teachers use the "teachable moments" that national crises provide in order to teach empathy and compassion?
4. A climate in which students will tell what they know is crucial. Has your school done a comprehensive questionnaire for both students and staff to compare perceptions and address issues of bullying, race relations, harassment and other issues that become evident?
5. Responding to a major event is likely to destabilize your entire district. How have you involved people beyond your district in your entire crisis team training so you have a pool of people on which to draw when your own coping strategies are overwhelmed?
6. You cannot create a support system for yourself in the midst of crisis. How carefully have you examined what sustains you and integrated practices into your daily life to create that safety net to catch you when all else falls away?
7. Follow-up is often our downfall. Look back over the past events to which you've responded, either for school-wide responses or individuals who have suffered losses. How would you rate the follow-up that was afforded those most impacted? What improvements could be made?
8. What flyers or materials do you already have ready to distribute to parents in the aftermath of critical events?

References

American School Counselor Association. (2003). *The ASCA national model: A framework for school counseling programs.* Alexandria, VA: Author.

Lovre, C. (2004). *The catastrophic events resource manual* (rev. ed.). Salem, OR: Crisis Management Institute.

Lovre, C. (2005). *The crisis resource manual* (rev. ed.). Salem, OR: Crisis Management Institute.

Lovre, C. (2006). *Media relations for schools.* Bloomington, IN: Solution Tree.

Sapolsky, R. (2004). *Why zebras don't get ulcers: The acclaimed guide to stress, stress-related diseases, and coping.* New York: Owl Books.

Van der Kolk, B. (1997). Speech presented in Seattle, WA.

Van der Kolk, B. (2007, January 26). *New frontiers in trauma treatment.* Workshop hosted by the Institute for the advancement of human behavior, Seattle, WA.

Yandrick, R. M. (2003). *Traumatic event debriefings getting second thoughts.* Retrieved January 28, 2006, from http://www.cmiatl.com/news_article59.html.

Chapter 19

Crisis Intervention and the School Counselor: A Case Study

Michael Pines, Brandon Dade, and Samar Yassine

Abstract

School counselors have responded to crises on school campuses for decades, but in recent years crisis intervention practices have become refined and evidence-based. Just as schools have improved the organization and planning for crisis intervention, increased attention is being paid to the role of the school counselor and the competencies required. This chapter provides a case example illustrating the unique and complex demands of school counselors in response to a crisis on campus.

Introduction

". . . and grief counselors are on the scene." The all-too familiar words from a news anchor are intended to re-assure her television audience that events are under control. Just moments before, she reported all of the lurid details about a shooting incident that occurred on a local school campus. In the competitive sound-bite world of television news coverage, few viewers pause to ponder, "Who are these 'grief' counselors? Where did they come from? Where did they learn how to do that kind of work?"

Today, crisis training is required in most graduate programs; but this is a recent development, and many practicing school counselors are not formally trained. This article offers a brief overview of school crisis intervention and the responsibilities of school counselors. The crisis intervention team approach is introduced as a tool to crisis recovery. The impact and response of school crisis is presented with examples from schools in the nation's most populous county, Los Angeles County. Finally, the experience of one school district engaged in planning, training, and responding to crises is punctuated by a hands-on account from counselors that responded to the recent death of a popular student. Crisis intervention is a responsive service provided by school counselors.

A Brief History of Crisis Intervention in Schools

Four major influences led to the development of crisis intervention: warfare, disasters, first responders, and law enforcement psychology. After returning from armed combat in Viet Nam, service members exposed to battle frequently exhibited symptoms of post-traumatic stress. Studies confirmed the value of early intervention to prevent the exacerbation of symptoms into mental disorders including post-traumatic stress disorder and major depression. Military psychologists began to understand and treat these symptoms. These practices were also found to be effective in helping those responding to and witnessing large-scale catastrophic events in civilian life.

Emergency personnel who responded to major disasters such as hurricanes and air disasters also began to develop similar stress-related symptoms. Burnout and attrition were commonplace. This phenomenon was to become known as compassion fatigue. The brief interventions used by military psychologists were found to be helpful in preventing symptom escalation among these responders.

Jeffrey Mitchell, a former firefighter/paramedic and psychologist, developed a standardized intervention model for firefighters and other first responders, including medical personnel (Mitchell, 1983). Mitchell's Critical Incident Stress Management contains many interventions, the most well known being Critical Incident Stress Debriefing. It has been adopted by emergency responders including fire service and law enforcement personnel throughout the nation. These interventions are designed for the responder who witnesses and supports victims of numerous catastrophes.

In schools, crisis intervention has been practiced as long as schools have existed. How many teachers have hugged a child who was injured on the playground? Such support is commonplace. Since the 1990s, however, with an increase in media coverage of large critical events affecting large numbers of students and staff, there has been pressure to develop formalized and effective practices in response to very visible situations where many students and staff are exposed to trauma. School practitioners have had to take individual crisis intervention to a larger scale so that effective practices could be expanded school-wide.

School practitioners turned first to the emergency responders for guidance. Educators asked emergency workers to equip them with skills and practices to aid students and staff with recovery from traumatic experiences. Experts, such as Mary Schoenfeldt (1998, p. 12), urged educators to adopt these crisis intervention practices. "The concepts and strategies of Critical Incident Stress management should be an integral part of any safe school crisis intervention plan to provide support for trauma among students and staff in the wake of a crisis." It was assumed that the needs of students and staff witnessing school violence are similar to those of soldiers and air disaster survivors. The effectiveness of these practices was documented by anecdotal testimony of survivors, teachers, administrators, and crisis team responders.

Recent studies of crisis intervention practices, however, have concluded that some of the practices used by emergency personnel may not be appropriate for the school environment. Pynoos and his associates (1987) conducted an extensive evaluation of debriefing practices used throughout the country and concluded that they lacked evidence of effectiveness in preventing post-traumatic stress disorder. Even more disturbing was their finding that some of the practices were harmful. While more research is needed, the University of California at Los Angeles studies paved the way to the development of a cognitive behavioral approach to school crisis intervention that was recently released (National Child Traumatic Stress Network and National Center for Post-tramatic Stress Disorder [PTSD], 2005). The Center's *Psychological First Aid: Field Operations Guide* provides guidelines to responders in many situations, including school crises.

The National Association of School Psychologists (NASP) has taken the lead in disseminating information about effective crisis intervention practices in schools. *Best Practices in School Crisis Prevention and Intervention* (Brock, Lazarus, & Jimerson, 2002) continues to be the definitive collection of articles on theory, primary prevention, secondary prevention, tertiary prevention, and long-term treatment for traumatized individuals. A special NASP task force is currently developing and field-testing a multi-disciplinary model for training school personnel in effective crisis intervention practices. This model includes interventions proposed in the manual developed by the National Child Traumatic Stress Network and National Center for PTSD.

A plethora of highly publicized accounts of violent attacks at school have given many citizens the impression that school violence is on the increase. This perception is inaccurate and misguided. National statistics tell us that schools continue to be safe havens for children. School violence at school has declined dramatically since 1994. The annual rate of serious violent crime in 2003 was less than half of the 1994 rate (DeVoe, Peter, Noonan, Snyder, & Baum, 2005, Table 2.2). Counselors have a responsibility to set the record straight and educate parents, faculty, and school personnel.

It has been said that there are two kinds of schools: those that have experienced a crisis and those that will. A National Education Assistance Team has responded to many highly publicized incidents. All educators need to prepare to respond to the worse case scenario; still, few educators will ever be called upon to help with crises on that scale. By preparing for the unspeakable, we will be able to respond quickly and appropriately. Administrators need to have plans in place to support individual schools with additional resources whenever the need arises.

Since 1998, the School Mental Health Center at the Los Angeles County Office of Education has labored to increase the capacity of school personnel and mental health partners to respond to traumatic events. The Center assists and trains school policy makers, administrators, and practitioners including school counselors, school psychologists, school nurses, and community mental health providers. Legislation requires that school plans are consistent with the other school emergency response procedures. The Center also plays a critical role in dispatching and coordinating school mental health resources for assignments to other schools whenever a crisis overwhelms any one school district. The Center maintains an Internet site that contains timely bulletins and a downloadable copy of the *School Mental Health Crisis Intervention Team Manual: A Companion to SEMS for Schools* (Los Angeles County Office of Education, 2002) with guidelines for organizing district and school-site mental health crisis teams. Finally, the Center plays a critical role in crisis notification in cases where rapid notification is critical to crisis team mobilization.

Crisis Intervention and School Counselors

School counselors are not unfamiliar with crisis intervention. One would need to look far and wide to find a school counselor who has not had to drop everything to address a student emergency such as a family tragedy or a personal emotional challenge. The responsibility to respond to crisis is addressed prominently by the American School Counselor Association (ASCA). The ASCA Framework for School Counseling Programs addresses the delivery system component of "Responsive Services." Crisis counseling activities are described in this component.

Crisis counseling provides prevention, intervention and follow-up. Counseling and support are provided to students and families facing emergency situations. Such counseling is normally short term and temporary in nature. When necessary, referrals are made to appropriate community resources. School counselors can provide a leadership role in the districts intervention team process (ASCA, 2003, p. 42).

In the last ten years, crisis intervention competencies have been recognized and codified. A school-wide crisis has the ability to seriously disrupt the educational process. When a crisis impacts an entire school community, appropriate response activities must be woven into an integrated fabric with others on the crisis team to ensure sound management. Crisis team responders often include school staff from other disciplines (e.g., administrators, school psychologists, school nurses). Sometimes responders from government agencies, neighboring schools, and community-based services may also be involved. All need to work together to stabilize the situation and return the campus to the educational routine as quickly as possible.

School districts and private schools develop crisis response plans. In California, schools are required to incorporate a crisis response plan into a mandated school safety plan that is reviewed and updated annually. Not all schools, however, have incorporated school counselors into those plans. School counselor involvement varies considerably from school to school and district to district. School counselors must be represented on planning committees that are responsible for drafting procedures, developing training, and evaluating those plans.

School counselors are a pivotal component of the school crisis team. This reality is documented in an unpublished survey conducted annually by the School Mental Health Center of the Los Angeles County Office of Education. Since 2001, the Center has a unique partnership with the Los Angeles County Department of Coroner, and it assists in the timely notification of schools about the death of school-age children and youth. In July, the Center asked school districts that received notifications during the 2005-06 period about the impact of the child's death and the response activities

that were required. Among the 22 school districts that responded to the survey, school counselors provided assistance in 70.1% of those incidents (Los Angeles County Office of Education, 2006).

For a detailed example of the crisis intervention planning, training, and response, the experience of the Alhambra Unified School District, a medium size school district of about 20,000 in the San Gabriel Valley in Los Angeles County, will be presented. An account of the historical involvement of school counselors will be followed by a description of the activities of school counselors during the response of a crisis that impacted Alhambra High School in 2005.

The Alhambra School Crisis Intervention Model

In 1999, the Deputy Superintendent requested assistance from the Los Angeles County Office of Education (LACOE) to improve their plan for school crisis management. Although every school had a mandated school safety plan on the bookshelf, few staff really understood what each plan contained and that not many schools employees were clear about their responsibilities. Our first task was to gather documents from every school site and compare the written plans against their actual needs. In addition, district office administrators were not clear about how to best support the efforts of each school site. LACOE was given a unique opportunity to work directly in the development of planning and training with the hopes of developing a model that is useful for other medium and small school districts in the county.

We concluded that the staff most frequently utilized in past crisis events were those responsible for recovery and mental health needs. Mental Health team organization and training was the district's highest priority. As a result, additional staff training activities were planned for 2000-2001.

A preliminary activation protocol was developed by LACOE Pupil Services Division, and staff was invited to attend a two-day training workshop conducted jointly by staff from LACOE and the Los Angeles County Department of Mental Health Emergency Outreach Bureau. As misfortune would have it, however, the training experience was suddenly tailored to allow trainees to respond to an actual school emergency. At the end of training on Day 1, a sixth grade student collapsed during class and died in the presence of classmates, his teacher, a school psychologist, and instructional aids. Day 2 training plans were immediately scrapped, and the team was pressed into action with an impromptu version of on-the-job training.

At the time of the initial training, the district team was staffed with district administrators, school nurses, and school psychologists. The team reacted immediately and performed effectively at the elementary school crisis that day. Unfortunately, the elementary school had no counselors, so no counselors were included in the crisis team. The following year, a district crisis response at a high school made district administrators aware of the problems associated with the failure to include school counselors. The district team responded to a high school after a student died from a self-injury prank in a classroom. Talented high school counselors that might have provided valuable support to the team were marginalized. The oversight was quickly recognized and additional training was organized for counselors later that year. Since 2002, school counselors have been included in the training and response activities of the district response team.

Since the initial years of the team formation, each year the Alhambra Unified School District (Alhambra USD) Mental Health Crisis Intervention Team has responded to an average of six incidents on their own campuses. In addition, at the request of LACOE's School Mental Health Center, Alhambra USD staff has responded to school crisis incidents in several other school districts and area private schools. An Integrated School Mental Health Services federal grant from the Office of Safe and Drug Free Schools has given the district the tools to improve their crisis intervention preparedness.

A Mental Health Crisis Intervention Team Field Operations Guide is currently being developed. This portable manual also includes valuable resources to increase cultural competency. In addition, the district staff and LACOE established and provided training to a network of nearby districts and private schools in the San Gabriel Valley Public Private School Crisis Partnership. Crisis response protocols help increase the capacity of the area schools to re-deploy mental health staff to provide mutual aid when disaster strikes. The LACOE School Mental Health Center has the responsibility to activate and coordinate the mutual aid activities. Finally, the effectiveness of each response is evaluated with input from multiple stakeholders.

Case Study: Crisis at Alhambra High School

The District Crisis team received aid from other districts in response to an incident involving a student from Alhambra High School during the first week of the Fall semester in 2005. The following first person account by co-authors Brandon Dade and Samar Yassine, who responded to this crisis, illustrates the complexity of needs and competencies required. (Note: The real identity of the student is being protected by the use of the fictitious name of Monica.)

Sunday

We received a call from the Assistant Principal of Guidance on Sunday morning notifying us that there had been a fatal accident Saturday night involving some of our students. She told us that all of the facts were not yet clear but here is what she knew: A car carrying at least three Alhambra High School students hit the side of the freeway late Saturday night and Monica, a cheerleader, was killed. We were asked to report to the school Career Center that would be the "Command Center" at 7:30 am sharp for organizing and briefing the Crisis Response Team on Monday.

We also assisted with preparation on Sunday so that the Team would be "ready to roll" Monday morning. Immediately, we looked up a photo of Monica so that we could put a face to the student. When we arrived at the high school on Sunday morning, we were surprised to find that we were not alone - a number of school support staff members were busy preparing for the following day's events. One individual called every staff member, including over 150 teachers to inform them about the tragedy. Another manned the school football team phone lines. Already, concerned parents and students were telephoning for information. Substitutes were contacted to stand in for teachers who would be unable to continue with their regular duties upon hearing the news.

The District Crisis Team Coordinator was in communication with local authorities to sort out fact from fiction. A letter was written and translated in multiple languages to go home with students discussing the incident. Folders were created for members of the Crisis Team. These folders included the following essentials:

1. Maps of the school
2. A school bell schedule
3. A class schedule of students known to have been in the vehicle
4. Photos of the students known to have been in the vehicle
5. A list of other students who were currently undergoing grief counseling for a loss in their lives

6. Assignment lists for team members
7. A list of locations that would be used by each team

Monday

The following day we met at the Command Center as planned. The counselors who had worked with Monica checked with one another to be sure that each of us was dealing with the loss and able to continue with our work. Other members of the crisis team included school psychologists, nurses, and other counselors from the Alhambra Unified School District. We were told that we would receive assistance from staff from neighboring school districts the following day. At the initial briefing, facts were clarified, and team members were assigned responsibilities.

Some team members visited Monica's classrooms and the other students involved to discuss the incident and identify students who were having a difficult time coping with the loss. Other team members met with these students individually. Some members of the team manned the telephones, while other team members waited in the office for teachers to refer students for counseling. Each student seen by a crisis response member was given a note to take home to their parents letting them know they had spoken with a crisis counselor. The counselors also made notes about each student they spoke with and indicated those who might need additional counseling. This information was collected and organized at the Command Center. The names of students needing follow up were given to other crisis team members. These students included those who had recently experienced a personal loss. A team of Alhambra High School Counselors and Psychologists were assigned to the "Safe Room," where students and staff wanting to speak to a counselor could just drop in.

We were informed that a group of cheerleaders and football players were sitting together in the quad; these students were truly unable to go to class. The athletes and cheerleaders were the students most affected by Monica's death. We were assigned to work with this group of approximately 20 students in the school library. The Library became their "safe room" for the remainder of the day. Little did we know that by the end of the day this group would grow to more than 50.

It was clear from the beginning that many of the football players and cheerleaders were in shock. Very few words were spoken. The look of pain on their faces spoke for itself. Our first task was to encourage the students to talk about it. We formed a large group and allowed students to just say anything they wanted. We asked them what they knew and what they thought Monica would have wanted. This was an open forum for discussion where the students consoled one another. In the next phase, we asked students to form groups of 4-6 around individual tables. Each small group had one crisis response member as well. We asked them to try to find words to describe their feelings, and we listed them on a large board for all to see. Next, we asked specific questions designed to elicit from each student the sequence of events from when they first learned about the death up to the present time. This is when the students really began to open up. It was in the privacy of their chosen groups. Whenever necessary, we took individual students aside and provided them individual support.

Following that activity, students shared positive words to describe Monica. The positive feelings were contagious and lunch had to be brought in because these students did not want to break away from the group to eat. Finally, the students planned and worked on projects to honor Monica. These included preparing special banners to be displayed at the football game and converting the upcoming pep rally into a celebration of her life. This had powerful healing benefits for the students, as they were able to channel their energy into positive action. As the school day came to a close, the coaches met with their teams (football and pep). They also discussed what had occurred and decided to play and cheer in Monica's honor.

In summary, the students were encouraged to express their thoughts and emotions in many different ways in the safe room. It was a place where they could console one another and share their feelings, fears, and memories with the guidance of trained crisis team members.

Later that week

In the following days that week, the crisis team remained active. Students who were identified on Monday were followed up in individual meetings. Counselors assisted them with preparations for the Friday assembly. On Friday morning, the school auditorium was filled. Hundreds of students sat silently in respect for the life and memory of Monica while her family and friends celebrated her life. Monica's aunt and nieces also attended but did not speak at the assembly. Crisis Team members were also present to distribute tissue and hugs to students and to one another. Teenagers are extremely resilient, and most were able to move forward without further counseling while a few others continued to meet individually with counselors and team members in the weeks to come.

Conclusion

Crisis intervention is an indispensable tool in the bag of competencies of the professional school counselor. It has been said that there are two kinds of schools – those that have had a crisis and those that will. With well-prepared and practiced school counselors ready to assume leadership in these tragic events, schools throughout the nation will be better prepared to respond to the unspeakable.

Discussion Questions

Please discuss the following questions as they apply to a given school site.

1. Is crisis intervention addressed in the school safety plan?
2. Are school counselors included in the safety plan?
3. Are school counselors represented on the safety planning committee?
4. What are the responsibilities of school counselors in the safety plan?
5. Have counselors received training to perform crisis intervention duties?
6. Have you personally been a member of a crisis intervention team? What responsibilities did you have? How did you feel about being a crisis intervention team member?
7. If you are a crisis team member, do you feel prepared to deal with a crisis? If not, what would have helped you to be better prepared?

References

American School Counselor Association. (2003). *The ASCA natonal model: A framework for school counseling programs.* Alexandria, VA: Author.

Brock, S., Lazarus, P. J., & Jimerson, S. R. (Eds.). (2002). *Best practices in school crisis prevention and intervention.* Washington, DC: National Association of School Psychologists.

Los Angeles County Office of Education. (2002). *The school mental health crisis intervention team: A companion to SEMS for schools*: Downey, CA: Author. Retrieved October 13, 2006, from www.lacoe.edu/smh

Los Angeles County Office of Education. (2006). *The Impact of student fatalities on schools in Los Angeles County* (Unpublished). Downey, CA: Author.

Mitchell, J. (1983). When disaster strikes: the critical incident stress debriefing process. *Journal of Emergency Services, 8,* 36-39.

National Child Traumatic Stress Network and National Center for PTSD. (2005, September). *Psychological first aid: Field operations guide.* Los Angeles: Author. Retrieved May 28, 2006, from www.nimh.nih.gov/publicat/NIMHviolence.pdf.

Pynoos, R. S., Frederick, C., Nader, K., Arroyo, W., Steinberg, A., Eth, S., Nunez, F. & Fairbanks. L. (1987). Life threat and post traumatic stress in school-age children. *Archives of General Psychiatry, 12,* 265-272.

Schoenfeldt, M. (1998, Fall). Support students, staff in crisis recovery. *School Safety.* 9-12.

DeVoe, J. F., Peter, K., Noonan, M., Snyder, T. D., & Baum, K. (2005). *Indicators of school crime and safety:2005* (NCES 2006–001/NCJ 210697). Washington, DC: U.S. Government Printing Office.

Chapter 20

School Counseling and Technology: An Overview

Russell A. Sabella and Theresa Stanley

Note: Parts of this chapter were adapted from or originally published in Sabella, R.A. (2007). School counseling and technology. In J. Wittmer, *Managing and implementing a K-12 guidance and counseling program* (3rd ed). Minneapolis, MN: Educational Media Corporation. Reprinted by permission.

Abstract

Technology continues to pervade and influence every aspect of our society at a dizzying pace. School counselors are working to meet the challenges of learning how to leverage appropriate technologies to help make them more effective and efficient in their work. This chapter comprehensively describes technological literacy, proposes an organizational schema including four categories (Information/ Resource, Communication/Collaboration, Interactive /Productivity Tools, and Delivery of Services) for how counselors use technology, and provides practical examples for each category.

Introduction

Progressively powerful computers, software, electronic gadgets, and expanding networks are rapidly changing traditional school counseling approaches and standards of performance. Although no one is truly certain if or when the exponential growth of technology will taper, it is well recognized that we are immersed in a new age of information, communication, and collaboration. For better or worse, computers are changing the ways in which we conduct our work, interact, and especially make decisions. Counseling professionals must adapt to new ways of interfacing with technology and the people that use them in a way that promotes the goals and objectives of their work (Sabella, 2003). Even as far back as a decade ago (McClure, 1996), it was recognized that no aspect of society or economy can function effectively and compete without such tools. Information and networking technologies are now essential tools for manipulating ideas and images and for communicating effectively with others – an important component of the counselor's job. In the 21st century, our ability to harness the power and promise of leading-edge advances in technology will determine, in large measure, our national prosperity, security, and global influence, and with them the standard of living and quality of life for all. School counselors that decide to "opt out" of information technology would be working with students who perceive them to live in a world that no longer exists (Sabella, in press).

This chapter provides a practical overview of the current practice and future potential for using high-tech tools in our work as school counselors. To better conceptualize the extremely broad topic of technology, Sabella (2003) provided a useful categorization scheme, which can help you manage how you think about and implement technology. Technology can help counselors in one or more of four areas:

1. *Information/Resource*: In the form of words, graphics, video, and even three-dimension virtual environments, the Web remains a dynamic and rapidly growing library of information and knowledge.
2. *Communication/Collaboration*: Chat rooms, bulletin boards, virtual classroom environments, video conferencing, online conferences, electronic meeting services, e-mail – the Web is now a place where people connect, exchange information, and make shared decisions.
3. *Interactive/Productivity Tools*: The maturing of software and Web based programming has launched a new level of available tools off the shelves and on the Net. These high-tech tools can help counselors build and create anything ranging from a personalized business card to a set of personalized Web site links. Interactive tools help counselors to process data and manipulate information such as calculating a GPA or the rate of inflation, convert text to speech, create a graph, or even determine the interactive effects of popular prescription drugs.
4. *Delivery of Services*: Most controversial, yet growing in popularity, is how counselors use the web to meet with clients and deliver counseling services in an online or "virtual" environment.

In fact, technologically literate counselors use an array of technologies in two or more of the above areas to most effectively and efficiently accomplish their goals.

The Case for Counselor Technological Literacy

Imagine the frustration of suddenly living in a new country where you cannot effectively and efficiently communicate or interact with others, you are not able to decipher road signs, or navigate basic living tasks because you are unfamiliar with the country's language and customs. Children watch you in amazement and find it difficult to believe that you live in such a place without these basic capabilities. Increasingly so, such might be the experience in any developed country, especially here in the U.S., for counselors who do not have a basic level of technological literacy. For now, some people still take refuge by being able to live their lives in a relatively low-tech manner although this lifestyle is becoming more difficult every day. Americans understand the rapid progress in the development and integration of technology through every day experience and have thus embraced technological literacy as the "new basic" for today's world, along with reading, writing, and arithmetic (Tyler & Sabella, 2004).

Today's children find it difficult to imagine a life as we lived it not so long ago - without compact discs, high powered computers, and palm-sized appliances such as cell phones, iPods, game devices, and personal digital assistants. It is likely that our future counselors, now in grade school and even college, will not hesitate to integrate high-tech tools in their work. They will merely continue along an already well established path of learning to use and apply new technologies as they become available, probably assisted by the technologies themselves. The majority of today's counselors grew up learning and practicing counseling in a very different environment. We used index cards instead of spreadsheets; typewriters instead of word processors; reference books instead of online journals and the web; overheads in lieu of multimedia presentations; and we waited until class to communicate with the professor and our classmates instead of sending e-mails or conversing in chat rooms.

Many of today's counselors acknowledge the usefulness of computers and the need for keeping up with the rapidly changing times yet remain frozen in the fear generated by an unknown frontier. "I feel intimidated by technology" has been a common comment by counselors, who even after training, sometimes revert to more traditional procedures. The customary statements, "My kids know more about computers than I do" and "I'm not a technical person" suggest that although counselors may be interested or even intrigued, they frequently feel awkward and uneasy with computers and their operations (Myrick & Sabella, 1995). My (RS) own experience, luckily, is that once such counselors are exposed and begin to truly learn how to use technology in their work, they quickly become excited and adept. Many of my older students at the university who are forced to learn high-tech tools in my courses often tell me that they receive many kudos from their own children who perceive their moms or dads to be "more with it." Their more highly technologically literate friends and partners share in their delight and also get excited about new shared interests. And the students themselves bask in the pride they take in working with contemporary tools.

What Exactly is Technological Literacy?

Many people have written on the subject of technological literacy. Hayden (1989), after a literature review, takes the position that technological literacy is having knowledge and abilities to select and apply appropriate technologies in a given context. While not revealing the source of his thoughts, Steffens (1986, p. 117-118) claims that technological literacy involves knowledge and comprehension of technology and its uses; skills, including tool skills as well as evaluation skills; and, attitudes about new technologies and their application. This insight is similar to that of Owen and Heywood (1988) who say there are three components to technological literacy: the technology of making things; the technology of organization; and, the technology of using information. Applying a Delphi technique to opinions expressed by experts, Croft (1991) evolved a panel of characteristics of a technologically literate student. Those are: abilities to make decisions about technology; possession of basic literacy skills required to solve technology problems; ability to make wise decisions about uses of technology; ability to apply knowledge, tools and skills for the benefit of society; and, ability to describe the basic technology systems of society (Waetjen, 1993).

A theme among various attempts to define technological literacy is that technology has evolved to become a powerful medium - not only a set of high-tech tools. If technology functioned merely as a set of tools, as the pervasive mechanical, user-in-control view of technology holds, the problem of advancing technological literacy would not be so challenging. A few more required courses or conference training sessions, and more specialists to teach them, could simply be added. But technology has become more than a set of devices to be picked up and used when a person decides he or she needs them. It has become a required medium that mediates experience in most aspects of peoples' lives (Fanning, 1994). Broadly speaking, technological literacy, then, can be described as the intellectual processes, abilities and dispositions needed for individuals to understand the link between technology, themselves, and society in general. Technological literacy is concerned with developing one's awareness of how technology is related to the broader social system, and how technological systems cannot be fully separated from the political, cultural, and economic frameworks which shape them (Saskatchewan Education, 2002). These definitions, together with one provided by the International Technology Education Association (2000) have provided the foundation for a definition of counselor technological literacy developed by Tyler and Sabella (2004):

> The intellectual processes, abilities and dispositions needed for counselors to understand the link among technology, themselves, their clients, and a diverse society so that they may extend human abilities to satisfy human needs and wants for themselves and others.

This means that counselors who have adequate levels of technological literacy are able to:

- understand the nature and role of technology, in both their personal and professional lives;
- understand how technological systems are designed, used, and controlled;
- value the benefits and assess the risks associated with technology;
- respond rationally to ethical dilemmas caused by technology;
- assess the effectiveness of technological solutions;
- feel comfortable learning about and using systems and tools of technology in the home, in leisure activities, and in the workplace; and
- critically examine and question technological progress and innovation.

How are Counselors Already Using Technology in their Work?

Counselors who have used computers to assist them in their work have done so in many areas such as computer-assisted live supervision (Froehle, 1984; Neukrug, 1991); discussions of counseling issues with other counselors (Rust, 1995); supervision (Myrick & Sabella, 1995); advocacy (Stone & Turba, 1999); counselor training (Cairo & Kanner, 1984); school counseling program promotion (Sabella & Booker, 2003); as part of counselor interventions with children (D'Andrea, 1995; Glover, 1995; Shulman, Sweeney, & Gerler, 1995) and counseling simulations (Sharf & Lucas, 1993). Probably the most extensive use of computers in counseling so far has been in the area of career development and guidance (e.g., Bobek et al., 2005; Chapman & Katz, 1983; Friery & Nelson, 2004; Haring-Hidore, 1984; Harris, 1972; Katz & Shatkin, 1983; Kivlighan, Johnston, Hogan, & Mauer, 1994; Pyle, 1984). Career counselors need to amass and process a great deal of information about various careers, the career decision-making process, and a diversity of client personal and professional characteristics. Computers do a splendid job of compiling such data and helping individuals select the best fit among working environments, required aptitudes, interests, values, and other human qualities.

In May of 2005, I (RS) conducted an informal survey among the over 18,000 subscribers to my SchoolCounselor.com eNewsletter (which focuses on advancing tech-literacy among counselors) about how they currently use technology in their work (Sabella, 2005). I was pleased to receive 49 responses that included descriptions of a variety of innovative and creative ways that school counselors were using technology to help them manage, deliver, or otherwise support their counseling programs. The range of responses included using technology to connect mentors and students; developing databases to manage student information not included in the districts database system; conducting online surveys; chart data; automate forms; translate documents from one language to another; maintain student services Web sites; conduct career development activities; communicate with parents and other stakeholders; and develop television and other multimedia broadcasts.

In general, computers and the Internet can be especially helpful in a variety of ways including as technologies for information and resource retrieval, communication, collaboration, productivity (interactive tools), and intervention delivery.

Technologies for Information & Resource Retrieval

The Internet could be described as the world's largest library and the availability of counseling-related bibliographies, abstracts, full-text journal articles, lectures, research projects, and funding sources is currently a "mouse click" away from your desktop. Counseling organizations, associations and individual professionals are creating Web sites every day and access to authoritative information on specialized topics is current, convenient, and almost limitless (Jackson & Davidson, 1998). Following are descriptions of various sources of information and resources that school counselors would probably find useful:

The World Wide Web

The World Wide Web continues to be mostly used as a source of rich, diverse, and highly current information in the form of text, graphics, sounds, video, and some animation. Many times when I (TS) write grants I use search engines such as Google and Yahoo. For instance, recently I wrote a grant that aimed to increase students' skills and interest in reading by purchasing children's books that were written by celebrities. It was called The Read, Write and Invite Grant. Students read the books and then wrote to the celebrity authors and invited them to come to our school. When preparing the grant, I needed to produce a list of celebrity-authored children's books. The local bookstores had a limited list but when I searched on the Web I found the information I needed. I was able to identify more than enough books for the grant. I also found summaries that were helpful in deciding which books to purchase as well as price information to ensure I was getting competitive rates.

The Web, however, has evolved into a medium that includes tools and functions which could easily cut across all four areas of technology previously mentioned (information/resource, communication/collaboration; interactive tools, intervention delivery). The key to effectively and efficiently using what the Web makes available is finding specific sites or pages that can best help you. Basically, there are four methods to do this (in order of increased sophistication):

1. *Know the URL.* Each site on the Web has its own unique, case-sensitive, electronic address called a Universal Resource Locator (URL) that points a computer to the Web page's location. Users who discover a useful site might communicate to others, probably via electronic mail, the page's URL. Once known, a user can simply enter the URL into his or her Web browser and go directly to the intended site. Once at the site, a counselor can then place an electronic "bookmark" that will allow him or her to point and click on a description of the site without ever again having to recall the URL. This form of finding information on the Web is quickest and easiest.

2. *Surf the Web.* A second method for finding information is to rely on the hypertext feature of the Web and "jump" from page to page using related links. Moving from one link to another is affectionately known as "surfing the Web." As a counselor surfs the Web, he or she might bookmark and essentially create his or her own compilation of valuable Web sites. The advantage of surfing the Web is that it gives the user control over what sites are deemed valuable. The disadvantage is that such a search is less than systematic and can be very time consuming.

3. *Consult Directories.* Third, you might consult an Internet directory, which categorizes Web sites into various hierarchies of information: a vast collection of categories and sub-categories, some created by people and others created by computers. By browsing the directory, you can have in front of you a pretty good (although not complete) listing of all the sites that cover a particular subject. For instance, check out the Yahoo! Guidance and Counseling Directory at http://dir.yahoo.com/Education/K_12/Guidance_Counseling/ or the Google Counseling and Guidance directory at http://www.google.com/Top/Reference/Education/K_through_12/Counseling_and_Guidance/. For example, last year I (TS) researched "Bully Prevention" on both Google and Yahoo and their Guidance and Counseling directories. I found that Yahoo's Guidance and Counseling directory produced more than Google's. Different topics seem to produce varied results depending on how the directory is prepared.

4. *Use Search Engines.* A search engine is a program designed to help find information stored on a computer system such as the World Wide Web, or a personal computer. The search engine allows one to ask for content meeting specific criteria (typically those containing a given word or phrase) and retrieves a list of references that match those criteria. Search engines use regularly updated indexes to operate quickly and efficiently. Without further qualification, search engine usually refers to a Web search engine, which searches for information on the public Web. Other kinds of search engine are enterprise search

engines, which search on intranets, personal search engines which search individual personal computers, and mobile search engines. Some search engines also mine data available in newsgroups, large databases, or open directories like DMOZ.org. Unlike Web directories, which are maintained by human editors, search engines operate algorithmically (Search Engines, n.d.). Using unique search terms and search conditions can narrow the results from hundreds of thousands of possible sites to a more manageable number in a matter of seconds. Literally hundreds of search engines exist although several popular ones stand out and include http://www.google.com, http://www.yahoo.com, http://www.lycos.com, http://www.dogpile.com, http://www.excite.com, http://www.alltheweb.com, http://search.msn.com, http://a9.com, and http://www.av.com.

It seems there is no topic that cannot be entered into a search engine that will not result in at least a few sites being found. For many topics, the number of sites runs into the thousands or tens of thousands. And, the availability and popularity of electronic books or e-books, which can be instantly downloaded, is steadily increasing. Like so much in technology, this creates challenge as well as opportunity. The challenge lies in sorting through the available information to find that which is of high quality and targets your particular needs. Many counselors, while technologically capable, may not have the skills necessary to evaluate a site or the information provided. Lacking any sort of review or oversight, anyone can put any information they choose on the Web. With basic technology skills (or the money to purchase assistance) a site can be created that looks quite polished. Without adequate knowledge and skills to evaluate sites, counselors may be drawn to sites that appear professional and are easy to understand, rather than sites that contain accurate and current information which may be slightly more difficult to understand and navigate. School counselors can save a great deal of time and increase their productivity by advancing their expertise in searching and navigating the Web (e.g., see http://www.schoolcounselor. com/cd/). Also, familiarizing yourself with criteria for evaluating any Web site or page (e.g., see http://www.schoolcounselor.com/Web site-evaluation.htm) will help you become a smart consumer of web based information/resources.

Full-Text Electronic Databases

The number of journal, magazine, and newspaper titles available online has grown rapidly in recent years. Many databases are only accessible by paying a fee although, often, schools and local universities provide free access to anyone while on campus. Some databases are designed for individual users and are more reasonably priced. Finally, other full-text databases have been provided for free as a government service or by the incredible generosity of individuals and organizations. Following are examples:

Larger and More Expensive Databases Typically Subscribed to by Institutions

1. CollegeSource® Online features over 33,550 college catalogs in complete cover-to-cover original page format including 2-year, 4-year, graduate, and professional schools. http://www.collegesource.org/
2. Congressional Universe is a web-based indexing and abstracting service for Congressional committee publications, including hearings (testimony), committee prints, reports, documents, and public laws. It also includes the full text and status of bills, selected testimony, regulations, and two periodicals, National Journal and Congress Daily. Additional features include Member directories and campaign contributions and a guide to creating citations. The publisher, Congressional Information Service, is an affiliate of LEXIS-NEXIS, so much of the full text is identical to material found in the LEXIS on-line data base. http://web.lexis-nexis.com/congcomp/
3. EBSCO Information Services provides information access and management solutions through print and electronic journal subscription services, research database development and production, online access to more than 150 databases and thousands of e-journals, and e-commerce book procurement. EBSCO has served the library and business communities for more than 60 years. http://www.ebscohost.com/
4. IngentaConnect allows subscribers to search over 19 million articles, chapters, reports, and more. http://www.ingentaconnect.com/
5. LexisNexis® provides authoritative legal, news, public records, and business information; including tax and regulatory publications in online, print or CD-ROM formats. http://www.lexisnexis.com/
6. Online Computer Library Center (OCLC) is a nonprofit, membership, library computer service, and research organization dedicated to the public purposes

of furthering access to the world's information and reducing information costs. http://www.oclc.org

7. Ovid is a Platform-independent access to bibliographic and live full text databases for academic, biomedical, and scientific research. http://www.ovid.com/

8. ProQuest® online information service provides access to thousands of current periodicals and newspapers, many updated daily and containing full-text articles from 1986. Deep backfiles of archival material are also expanding daily as they digitize 5.5 billion pages from their distinguished microfilm collection. http://www.proquest.com/

9. ReferenceUSA contains more than 12 million U.S. businesses; 102 million U.S. residents; 683,000 U.S. health care providers; 1 million Canadian businesses; and 11 million Canadian residents. http://reference.infousa.com/

Inexpensive Full-Text

For those that do not have access to expensive full-text databases provided by schools or other institutions, HighBeam Library Research (http://www.highbeam.com/library/) has an extensive archive of more than 35 million documents from over 3,000 sources – a vast collection of articles from leading publications, updated daily and going back as far as 20 years. As of this writing, a monthly subscription is $19.95 or $99.95 for an annual subscription.

Another example of an inexpensive full-text database ($11.95 per month) is the Encyclopedia Britannica online (http://www.britannica.com/) which includes the complete encyclopedia as well as other resources such as dictionary, thesaurus, and newsletters.

Free Full-Text

Following are examples of various full-text resources which are freely available online:

1. National Center for Research in Vocational Education (NCRVE) is the nation's largest center engaged in research, development, dissemination, and outreach in work-related education, and is funded by the Office of Vocational and Adult Education of the U.S. Department of Education. The Center's mission is to strengthen school-based and work-based learning to prepare all individuals for lasting and rewarding employment, further education, and lifelong learning. http://vocserve.berkeley.edu/fulltext.html

2. Maintained by an individual, this page links to Web sites containing full-text state constitutions, statutes (called codes or compiled laws in some states), legislation (bills, amendments and similar documents) and session laws (bills that have become laws). http://www.prairienet.org/~scruffy/f.htm

3. The Education Resources Information Center (ERIC), sponsored by the Institute of Education Sciences (IES) of the U.S. Department of Education, produces the world's premier database of journal and non-journal education literature. The ERIC online system provides the public with a centralized ERIC Web site for searching the ERIC bibliographic database of more than 1.1 million citations going back to 1966. More than 107,000 full-text non-journal documents (issued 1993-2004), previously available through fee-based services only, are now available for free. ERIC is moving forward with its modernization program, and has begun adding materials to the database. http://www.eric.ed.gov/

4. A list of free (29 titles at the time of this writing) free full-text journals on the Web and maintained by the Lesley College Library are located at http://www.lesley.edu/faculty/kholmes/libguides/cpfulltext.html

5. The Journal of Technology Education provides a forum for scholarly discussion on topics relating to technology education. Manuscripts should focus on technology education research, philosophy, and theory. In addition, the Journal publishes book reviews, editorials, guest articles, comprehensive literature reviews, and reactions to previously published articles. http://scholar.lib.vt.edu/ejournals/JTE/

6. The Journal of Technology in Counseling publishes articles on all aspects of practice, theory, research, and professionalism related to the use of technology in counselor training and counseling practice. The Journal accepts manuscripts that respond to the full scope of technology interests of its readers. The Journal recognizes that modern technology has surpassed traditional ways of presenting information to readers by encompassing learning methods that go beyond the two-dimensional page. Authors are encouraged to use the full range of available Web resources when submitting manuscripts including hyperlinks to other Web resources, audio, graphics, video clips and video-streaming. http://jtc.colstate.edu/

7. FindArticles. Search millions of articles from leading academic, industry and general interest publications. http://www.findarticles.com/

8. Technology Horizons in Education (T.H.E.) is a free magazine for educators dedicated to technology solutions in education. http://www.thejournal.com/

9. Edutopia Magazine gives practical, hands-on insight into what works, what's on the horizon, and who is shaping the changing future of education. http://www.edutopia.org/

Technologies for Communication/Collaboration

Over the Net, counselors can communicate and collaborate with students, teachers, administrators, parents, other counselors, and community members with continually greater convenience and efficiency. While you are reading this, thousands of school counselors enjoy the convenience of corresponding and consulting with each other via e-mail, listservs, bulletin boards, chatrooms, instant messaging, and more.

Collaboration is a process by which people work together on an intellectual, academic, or practical endeavor. In the past, that has meant in person, by letter, or on the telephone. Electronic collaboration, on the other hand, connects individuals electronically via the Internet using tools such as e-mail, or through access to sites on the World Wide Web. This Internet-based work allows collaborators to communicate anytime, from anywhere to any place. People from different parts of a building, state, country, or continent can exchange information, collaborate on shared documents and ideas, study together, or reflect on their own practices.

Most counselors are used to short-term professional development seminars and workshops that provide finite information. Electronic collaboration — because it can be done at any time, from anywhere — allows for a sustained effort where participants can propose, try out, refine, and shape ideas themselves. The potential to communicate with others from all over the world provides a pool of resources and professional companions that counselors might not find within their own school walls. It can also provide them with a sense of belonging, a sense of identity within a larger community. Using high tech tools to collaborate, counselors actively and interactively contribute to exploring innovative ideas. With electronic collaboration, the adage "two heads are better than one" could just as well be "two hundred heads are better than

one." One person's provocative question can lead to many creative, exciting solutions. By sharing what they know with others, participants advance their own knowledge and the collaborative community's knowledge.

E-Mail

I (TS) have worked as a school counselor at the elementary, middle, and high school levels. At every level and at every school, e-mail was a cornerstone of communication. Indeed, one cannot hardly be effective without the use of e-mail in business, industry, or in education. Beyond day-to-day internal communications, e-mail offers counselors the same kind of advantage that it offers those involved with distance learning education – it forms the basis of a network that conveniently connects counselors and others (e.g., supervisors, community members, parents, and students) individually and in groups (Myrick & Sabella, 1995). The advantages of electronic mail have contributed to its pervasiveness and popularity and include:

- the convenience of corresponding at any time of the day or night;
- being able to think through a communication before making it;
- not having to rely on a mutual time to communicate as one would with a phone conversation;
- saving money in long distance charges when having to make only brief comments;
- instantaneously communicating the same message to multiple people on a distribution list;
- diminished inhibitions that face-to-face conversation may present;
- that, whereas spoken words must remain in memory and are sometimes lost in a quick exchange, written e-mail messages can be reviewed; and
- large files, especially documents, can be instantly sent to others via e-mail which can save precious time and money as compared to printing and shipping the document via traditional postal carriers.

However, anyone who uses e-mail as a staple form of communication, can readily tell you about the disadvantages of e-mail communication which would include that:

- for some, typing can be slow and tedious;

- the absence of nonverbal communication such as gestures, facial expression, or tome of voice can sometimes lead to mistaken interpretations of an e-mail message;
- although relatively very secure, sending an e-mail over the Net is sometimes like sending a postcard through the mail – others whom desire to do so might intercept and read an e-mail. Therefore, issues of confidentiality and privacy are central to communicating sensitive information;
- if not careful, counselors can receive too many e-mail messages which may lead to time and organizational management challenges. In this sense, counselors must be smart consumers of information and determine how much one reads, digests, discards, and to which messages one should respond.

Many school counselors take the opportunity to participate in an electronic network that enables participants to share professional ideas and information. It offers counselors a unique and valuable opportunity for supervision and consultation. For example, Myrick and Sabella (1995) wrote about how they used e-mail as a supplement to practicum and internship supervision which they called cybervision. In this case, the student counselors, during group supervision, first learned how to access the Internet through computers in their schools or with their own personal computers and modems at home. They could also access the system through computer stations at various locations on campus. Each person had his or her own e-mail address, which was known to the supervisor and other group supervision members. Using e-mail, a student-counselor could send written messages to a supervisor asking for information or describing a case. When appropriate, the case was forwarded to other group members for their interest and reactions. The group supervision members discussed the best way to send an e-mail case. It would include (a) a brief description of the counselee; (b) the presenting problem, including the referral source; c) the observed behaviors related to the problem or concern; (d) the counselor interventions to that point; and (e) any concerns or questions that were evolving. The authors concluded that e-mail supervision supplements the traditional modes of face-to-face meetings, telephone conferences, and fax transmissions. An on-going group experience, it can take place in remote and diverse locations. Although the common once-a-week group meeting has its own value, group members felt that they were always within reach of assistance or encouragement. They felt closer to one another, and e-mail created a special bond that also enabled them to be more open about their situations.

I (TS) found e-mail to be especially helpful when I was going through the National Board for Professional Teacher Standards (NBPTS) certification process. I knew I wanted feedback from someone who had already experienced the process and could provide timely advice. But, there was no one in my locale who completed this rigorous certification process at that time. So, I used the NBPTS Web site to locate and then e-mail National Board School Counselors in my state and in other states throughout the country. E-mail allowed me to communicate with others, some of whom became my mentors, from hundreds and thousands of miles away. E-mail afforded me a priceless support system of professional colleagues. Another example of how e-mail, when used appropriately, can help a counselor be more effective and efficient is when I (TS) read about using Microsoft Outlook™ for voting in the SchoolCounselor.com eNewsletter (SchoolCounselor.com eNewsletter, 2005). I had never used Outlook in this fashion but I thought it might be useful. In one instance, I had a video tape called Bud and Dud on loan for a month from the company. Bud and Dud was a video series in which a dog gave tips for taking tests to students via 5-minute clips shown during the morning announcements. The deadline for making a decision was quickly approaching and our school budget, like many, was very tight. We needed to decide if we should buy the program or send it back. Many of the students and teachers seemed to love it but one person was outspokenly against it. I wasn't sure if we should buy it because it was a "talking-dog-thing and seemed a little corny" – but I didn't want to make the decision without more concrete feedback. So, I used the Microsoft Outlook voting feature, which allows the user to send a survey-type messages with voting buttons to a group of recipients. By clicking a button, each respondent can express a preference and generate a response message to vote. Outlook logs vote messages to the original message's tracking page (visit http://support.microsoft.com/?kbid=197420 for more details). The results were impressive. Over 95% of the respondents were in favor of purchasing and using the film. The principal saw the data and decided to purchase the program. The students and staff loved it and ask for it each and every year. Interestingly, the person that was originally against purchasing the program later told me that her students took a surprising liking to it. The Microsoft Outlook voting process was a simple feature that summarized the data in a matter of seconds. What would have required several hours otherwise only took seconds with this technology, a true positive impact on my productivity.

Yet another benefit to using productivity software (in my case, Microsoft Outlook) is that I (TS) can keep a calendar and quite efficiently manage a busy schedule. It enables me to realistically set meetings and plans. Further, others at the school can view my calendar to see when I may be available. Frequently I use it to schedule appointments and meetings with other staff. With a couple of clicks I can send reminders so that everyone remembers to attend.

List Servers

List servers are programs that allow an administrator to create lists of e-mail addresses and attach them to a single e-mail address (called the listserv address). All messages that are e-mailed to the listserv are distributed, again via e-mail, to all subscribers, sometimes by a "moderator" who reads them first (in a "moderated list") or more typically in an automated manner (or "unmoderated list"). Some list servers require an administrator to add people to the list. In others, anyone who wishes can automatically subscribe (or unsubscribe) by either sending an e-mail message to the program which resides on a server or by completing an online form. List server programs can provide some security by allowing only authorized users to post to the list or by using a moderator to approve messages before they are posted to the list. Counselors can also set up their listserv to act more like a mailing list for those who simply want to receive reminders, newsletters, or announcements. This is called a post-only listserv. Creators (or "owners") of these listservs are usually the only people who can send an e-mail via the listserv. Any one else who tries is humbly and automatically rejected. Try subscribing to two different types of listservs, a post only newsletter listserv and a full fledged discussion listserv, respectively. The Scout Report is the flagship publication of the Internet Scout Project. Published every Friday both on the web and by e-mail, it provides a fast, convenient way to stay informed of valuable resources on the Internet. The report is developed by a team of professional librarians and subject matter experts who select, research, and annotate each resource. Visit http://scout.wisc.edu/mailman/listinfo/scout-report, and complete the form. Next, you will be sent an e-mail requesting confirmation to prevent others from gratuitously subscribing you (this is called a double opt-in list). Second, the International Counselor Network (ICN) is a network for counselors working in all specialty areas. Topics range widely, including such issues as self-esteem, multicultural issues, program development, career planning, play theory, professional

issues and more. Complete the online form at http://listserv.utk.edu/cgi-bin/wa?SUBED1=icn&A=1 and you will once again receive an e-mail with instructions for how to confirm your identity.

List servers are an efficient way of sending e-mail to large and/or specific groups and are ideal for disseminating timely information, such as announcements of conferences, pointers to new Web sites of interest, and descriptions of print resources. Anyone on the list can be a source of information. List servers are well-suited to groups of users who regularly use e-mail and who need to receive information in a timely way. They are less effective for extended or lengthy discussions, because participants may not be able to remember all the previous entries when they respond to a particular item. Another disadvantage is that mailing list servers can be inconvenient for recipients, filling their e-mail in-boxes when they're busy with other things. Two of the most commonly used mailing list server programs are Majordomo (http://www.greatcircle.com/majordomo/) and Listserv (http://www.lsoft.com).

There are primarily two methods for learning about available listservs of interest. First and most popular, a specific listserv of interest may be announced in relevant professional or related publications such as journals, magazines, newsletters, or newspapers. Second, you may seek for listservs of interest by conducting a basic web search using keywords such as "counseling listserv" which should take you to web pages that describe the listserv and provide instructions for subscribing. Remember, however, not all listservs are open to the public, some are private and require administrative approval. Creating your own listserv is not always easy although definitely doable. The best thing to do is work with your school's technology people to see if they can do it for you. Or, you can use a free online mail list service such as http://www.coollist.com. Otherwise, read up on how to do this yourself by visiting web pages such as http://www.librarysupportstaff.com/4creategroup.html and http://lists.gurus.com/creating.html.

Chat Rooms

E-mail is a great way to communicate electronically although this method suffers from the lack of real-time interaction between one person and with others whom he/she would like to communicate. Historically, real-time communication has occurred either in face-to-face conversation or over the telephone. The use of chat software, especially over the Internet, makes it possible to electronically converse in real time.

Following the metaphor for which this technology is named, imagine yourself entering a room in which you can converse with other users you will find there. You can see on screen what each user is typing into the conversation, and when you type something, the other users in the room can see your message as well.

Chat environments have progressed from simple text-based interactions to full blown graphical user interfaces (GUIs). Today's chatrooms allow users to personalize their communications by posting their photos or a close facsimile (sometimes a computer generated likeness) next to their text communications. Other programs also allow for sending to members of the chatroom audio files that contain music, sound effects, or the users own recorded voice. One of the most popular chat clients (not be confused with the clients with whom we work, software that resides on our computer and acts as the recipients of server programs are also called clients) is a program called mIRC available for download at most shareware sites or directly at http://www.mirc.com/. However, many chats are now conducted over the web, which eliminates the need to download any software. Simply visit the site, choose your chat community, log in, and begin chatting (e.g., see http://chat.msn.com or http://chat.yahoo.com). You should know that, like anything else on the Net, some chatrooms are not intended for the easily offended. Not all, but many of the rooms are "R" to "X" rated because they contain inappropriate and/or pornographic communications including text, sound, and sometimes graphics. Also, users of chatroom can easily maintain anonymity and, even worse, pose as someone they are not. To create a chat room for your very own special gathering, you could use a free online service such as http://www.chatzy.com/, http://www.userplane.com/, or http://chatshack.net/.

Instant Messaging

Instant messaging (IM) requires the use of a client program that hooks up an instant messaging service and, similar to chat rooms, conversations are then able to happen in realtime. What IM has that chat rooms do not have are extra abilities such as a presence information feature, indicating whether people on one's list of contacts are currently online and available to chat. This may be called a "Buddy List". Other features include voice and video transfer, file transfer, the ability to play games with other users, and application sharing (such as working together in real time on a spreadsheet or document). Popular instant messaging services on the public Internet include Qnext (http://www.qnext.com/), MSN Messenger (http://messenger.msn.com/), AOL Instant Messenger (http://www.aim.com/), Yahoo! Messenger (http://messenger.yahoo.com/), Google Talk (http://www.google.com/talk/), Jabber (http://www.jabber.org/) and ICQ (http://www.icq.com/). These services owe many ideas to an older (and still popular) online chat medium known as Internet Relay Chat (IRC) (*Instant Messaging*, n.d.).

WebBoards

One drawback of e-mail, listservs, and even instant messaging is that they organize discussions chronologically. This type of organization is fine for many short discussions or written materials, but most discussions aren't linear and well-organized. One comment can generate ideas on many different tangents. In this case, you may want to organize the discussion by topic. But that doesn't always work well; what if one message in a discussion has ideas that relate to several different parts of the discussion? Topic-oriented and threaded discussion systems, oftentimes called Bulletin Board Systems or WebBoards, attempt to respond to this problem by keeping an archive and allowing different ways of organizing the discussion. Because of the creative, inventive, and nonlinear nature of human conversation, it's difficult to develop an ideal method of organizing records of conversation. The information in a threaded discussion system is organized and displayed hierarchically, so you can see how the messages are related. Each posting (or "article") in a threaded discussion has a topic or subject. Users can comment on the topic, see what others have to say about it, and reply to questions or other people's comments. All of the comments, replies, and discussions on a single topic are collectively called a "thread." The difference between topic oriented and threaded discussions is a matter of format and organization. Usually messages in topic oriented discussions are listed chronologically on a single topic page, messages in threaded discussions are organized in an outline format with replies indented and listed directly under the message to which they are a reply (Koufman-Frederick, Lillie, Pattison-Gordon, Watt, & Carter, 1999). As a member benefit, the American School Counselor Association provides various bulletin boards (e.g., organized by grade level) to facilitate communication and collaboration among its members.

Blogs

You've probably heard the term blog more than once, most likely used on television or print news media. However, you may still not exactly understand what a blog is. According to the Webopedia (Blog, n.d.), a blog, short for "web log," is a web page that serves as a publicly accessible personal journal for an individual. Typically updated on a daily basis, blogs often reflect the personality of the author. Google owned Blogger.com describes a blog as, "A blog is a personal diary. A daily pulpit. A collaborative space. A political soapbox. A breaking-news outlet. A collection of links. Your own private thoughts. Memos to the world." Creating a blog is simple and free. It only takes a few minutes by entering your name, e-mail address and a few other pieces of (usually personal) information. You select "the look" (template) for your blog from a set of standard options, click a few buttons, and another blog has been added to the "blogosphere." Once the blog is set up, you can post text, links, audio, video, and more to your hearts delight. From your computer or cell phone, you can say or show anything and everything. With a bit of know-how, you can even syndicate to other blogs and Web sites. Syndication is a process by which the latest content from a blog, or from any other web page, can be made available for re-publication in another Web site or in some other application. And millions of people (including children) are doing it.

As compared to dynamic Web sites, blogs feature several unique characteristics (*How Blogs Work*, n.d.) such as:

- A blog is normally a single page of entries. There may be archives of older entries, but the "main page" of a blog is all anyone really cares about.
- A blog is organized in reverse-chronological order, from most recent entry to least recent.
- A blog is normally public – the whole world can see it.
- The entries in a blog usually come from a single author.
- The entries in a blog are usually stream-of-consciousness. There is no particular order to them. For example, the blogger sees a good link; he or she can throw it in his or her blog. The tools that most bloggers use make it incredibly easy to add entries to a blog any time they feel like it.
- A typical blog has a main page and nothing else. On the main page, there is a set of entries. Each entry is a little text blurb that may contain embedded links out to other sites, news stories, etc. When the author adds a new entry, it goes at the top, pushing all the older entries down. This blog also has a right sidebar that contains additional permanent links to other sites and stories. The author might update the sidebar weekly or monthly.

The technology that allows individuals to write one's own blog is so relatively simple and inexpensive that it is no surprise that blogs have proliferated the Web as fast as they have. Any counselor can create a basic blog for free, and most of these toolsets have additional features available for a price. Here are just a few of the services available.

- Blogger is a free, automated weblog publishing platform in one easy to use Web site. http://www.blogger.com/
- bBlog is a powerful, elegant personal publishing system written in PHP and released as free, Open Source software under the GPL. It is a flexible but simple way to blog that works for blogging beginners, and can grow into a more advanced user's needs. http://www.bblog.com/
- Xanga is a community of online diaries and journals. http://www.xanga.com/
- TypePad is similar to blogger, another blogging service although this one has a minimal cost. http://www.sixapart.com/typepad/
- LiveJournal is free although users can choose to upgrade their accounts for extra features. http://www.livejournal.com/
- Moveable Type is another popular web publishing platform. http://www.sixapart.com/movabletype/
- MySpace.com is actually a hybrid site that allows people to post their personal interests, write blogs, put up video and set up ways to communicate with their friends. http://www.myspace.com/

Consumers of blogs, in this case, our stakeholders, have several ways that they can learn about new updates or additions to your blogs. First, they can periodically visit your blog and look for any updates which is easy to do since entries are listed in chronological order. Second, if your blog allows it, they can sign up to receive e-mail notification of any new information. Or third, you can subscribe to the blog if the blog host offers RSS (Real Simple Syndication) feed capability. In this case, you simply copy the Web site address of the feed into a feed reader or aggregator (e.g., see http://blogspace.com/rss/readers). Anytime the blog is updated, you automatically receive a copy of it right in your reader.

Podcasting

Podcasting, in its basic form, is creating audio files (most commonly in MP3 format) and making them available online in a way that allows users to automatically download the files for listening at their convenience (i.e., subscribing to the podcast). After subscribing to the podcast, future "broadcasts" automatically download to your computer, which can then be transferred easily to a handheld such as a Palm OS Handheld, a Pocket PC, or an iPod - hence, the name Podcast. In essence, anyone with a computer, Internet access, free software, and a microphone can turn their computer into a personal studio and produce their very own radio show/program [see Valesky & Sabella (2005) for a more detailed description of how this technology works].

Podcasting is clearly in its infancy although shows great potential for disseminating information in a timely and efficient manner. The potential of podcasting stems from several advantages to using this relatively new medium. For one, it's cheap. Podcasting requires no more hardware or software than a typical computer user has. Second, the MP3 files and accompanying text, which are served over the World Wide Web, are supported among virtually all operating systems (i.e., podcasting works across many platforms). As a result, these types of files have become quite pervasive. Third, given the difficulties and intricacies of using computer technology sometimes, podcasting is surprisingly simple to do. Only three steps are required (create the MP3 file, upload the file, and update your RSS feed) to broadcast any content you would like. Fourth, podcasting further removes barriers of space, pace, and time by allowing the consumer to download and listen to broadcasts at his or her convenience (sort of like the Tivo® of radio). And, the consumer may listen to a broadcast using various devices such as computers, as, MP3 players, CD players (after burning the files to a CD), personal digital assistants (PDA's), Bluetooth or USB enabled call our radios, and eventually cell phones. Finally, I have found that podcasting is just plain fun.

Several disadvantages that accompany podcasting do exist, some of which are related to the use of any technology:

1. Podcasting is still in its early stages of development and so finding those that are valuable and meaningful to you may be somewhat difficult. Relatedly, although the number of podcasts is growing in leaps and bounds, many are personal and amateurish which will probably not be useful to you other than for entertainment purposes.

2. Like everything else on the Web, podcasts are not regulated. Pornographers, bigots, bullies, and others have also discovered podcasts as a powerful method for disseminating information. This information is currently limited to audio although video podcasts or v-casts are already in development. Anyone who has the knowledge, including children, can easily access a range of smut or obscene matter.

3. Technology, computers, and the Internet seem to have become a ubiquitous component of life in the United States, yet there still exists a digital divide among the "haves" and the "have-nots." High speed Internet connections, computers, MP3 players, microphones, etc. do cost money which may prevent the economically disadvantaged from benefitting from this promising emerging technology.

4. Lastly, the development of podcasting emphasizes once again the importance of media literacy among youth and adults alike. Evaluating, choosing, and using information presents challenges that, if not managed, can leave us unbalanced, unfocused, and in a state of deterioration.

The potential for how podcasts can become a useful tool for mass communication in the school counseling profession is only beginning. For instance, school counselors can share best practices with each other, essentially having access to "on-demand professional development." Consider the motivational effects of students developing their own podcasts. Students could create a series of podcasts specifically for their parents that describe their learning experiences and inform them of school activities. Busy parents could listen to the podcasts on their commute to work. Imagine a peer helper model where K-12 students develop a podcast series to which other students listen and learn more about how to advance their competencies in key guidance and counseling areas delineated by the ASCA National Model® (ASCA, 2005). Try your hand by listening to CouselorAudioSource.Net (CAS; http://www.counseloraudiosource.net/), a weekly podcast designed for practicing counselor's personal and professional development. The CAS Podcast typically features a 20-40 minute interview with a practicing counselor or counselor educator on a topic relevant to the support and growth of the practicing counselor.

Internet Conferencing

With the increased proliferation of high speed Internet access, more powerful computers, and the need to work on a more global scale comes an increasing popularity in the use of Internet conferencing technology. These programs or services provide users with multi-point data conferencing, text chat, audio/video chat, whiteboard, file transfer, as well as application sharing. The Internet conferencing environment is similar to a live conference which allows a presenter to speak, present multimedia slides, conduct polls, allow for questions and answers, share handouts (in the form of files), point to Web sites, and share other visuals from his or her computer. In most cases, participants can also interact among themselves via a simultaneous phone conference. The cost of these programs range from free to 39¢ per minute per participant. Following are a few of the more popular online conferencing tools:

- Microsoft NetMeeting (http://www.microsoft.com /windows/netmeeting/).
- Microsoft Office Live Meeting (http://www.microsoft .com/office/rtc/livemeeting/)
- GoToMeeting (http://www.gotomeeting.com)
- WebEx (http://www.webex.com/)
- Macromedia Breeze (http://www.adobe.com/products /breeze/)

Social Networking

In addition to professional development, counselors who attend conferences report that "networking" with others is another reason why they attend these meetings. Face to face networking provides counselors with new ideas, opportunities for partnering and collaborating, support, and usually inspiration. Until now, these networks were primarily designed for use among adults for both professional and personal fulfillment. For business and industry, social networks connect buyers and sellers, employers and prospects, and otherwise facilitate the sharing of business opportunities and contacts. For example, sites such as http://openBC.com, http://spoke.com, http://ryze.com, and http://zerodegrees.com help a user to set up their own Internet space to store contacts, invite others to join his/her own network, and ultimately search across the extended network for individuals and organizations that can help the user achieve his/her business, career and/or personal goals.

These networks can grow very quickly and be quite effective at making important business contacts. For example, on the Spoke Web site, a user completes a simple personal profile (e.g., name, title, company, contact information) and then clicks a button marked "build network." A program is then downloaded from the Spoke Web site that mines the user's Outlook e-mail and contact database for information about who he/she knows and how frequently he/she maintains contact with them. In a few minutes, the user's new, online "Spoke book" is populated not only with the hundreds or thousands of contacts he/she had manually entered into his/her Outlook contacts list, but also with everyone she/he had ever exchanged e-mail with from that e-mail account. Spoke also rates the strength of these relationships based on how often and how recently the user e-mailed with each person, as well as whether he/she was the only recipient of a message or was simply part of a larger distribution list.

Social networking technologies can help counselors network all year around, perhaps as a supplement to live networking. For instance, one of the most popular social networking services is MySpace (http://myspace.com). At MySpace, a counselor can create a private community and share photos, journals, e-mails, classifieds, music, start/join interest groups, blog, discuss issues, and share events with a growing network of mutual colleagues and/or friends. Other similar social networks of interest include Friendster (http://www.friendster.com/), LinkedIn (http://www.linkedin. com/), Xanga (http://www.xanga.com), Yahoo! 360 (http:// 360.yahoo.com), and Face book (http://www.facebook. com/).

Social Bookmarking

Social bookmarking is an online process that allows users to save and categorize a personal (or professional) collection of bookmarks or favorites and share them with others. Users may also take bookmarks saved by others and add them to their own collection, as well as to subscribe to the lists of others. This means that we can use our collective judgment to "pool" what we deem as valuable Web sites. One social bookmarking site, del.icio.us (http://del.icio.us/), has become very popular because of its ease of use, tagging abilities (i.e., one can sort bookmarks using different tags or categories), and sharing features.

Technologies as Interactive Tools

The types of interactive tools that professionals are most typically interested are those that help us to be more productive. Most counselors would agree that they perceive themselves as having to meet increasing work loads with either the same or reduced resources – that is, they are having to "do more with less." Thus, the common cry among counselors, "How can I provide quality services and programs (i.e., continue to be effective) for my students in a more efficient manner?" High-tech interactive tools allow us to input certain data which is processed or manipulated and then returned to us in a more meaningful or valuable format. Word processing, data processing (e.g., spreadsheets and data bases), desktop publishing, audio/video editing, calculators, web browsers, multimedia development, etc. are all examples of interactive tools. Tools usually come from software which we download or purchase and run on our computers or other electronic devices, or they can be run on the Internet. In addition to the readily available productivity suites (e.g., Microsoft Office), following are descriptions of selected interactive tools that the school counselor would find helpful:

Data and Accountability

School counselors are responsible for knowing and keeping track of all sorts of information such as student records, student contacts, parent conferences, case notes, counseling schedules, accountability data, list of tasks, and sometimes grades. Without the help of technology, counselors may feel overwhelmed, unorganized, or lost as a result of the sheer quantity of information. Consequently, effectiveness and motivation could suffer. Yet, measuring outcomes or using the current research to help inform school counselors of the nature of their efforts is an important task for ensuring the viability of a school counseling program. Technology can make the process more efficient, accurate, and automated.

Database and spreadsheet programs are designed and intended to help users store, organize, and retrieve data. This function can be especially helpful as counselors feel the effects of the "information age." In addition to managing information, database programs can also be used to facilitate decision making. For instance, Sabella (1996) wrote about how school counselors can use a database program to use existing data collected by his/her school to identify and assign students to small groups for counseling. Using a database program for small group assignment is especially helpful when group membership is contingent on traits such as age, race, and sex (e.g., balancing groups by race and sex while perhaps keeping age uniform). The key to this procedure lies in how the data are identified, sorted (also known as indexed), and processed.

Current database and spreadsheet programs allow counselors to collect data and conduct basic analyses such as monitoring changes in student test scores or attendance rates throughout the year. Once a data query is initially set up and run, all a counselor needs to do next time is press a button which conducts the same procedure over any data set. The savings in time over the long run can be quite significant. Relatedly, database/spreadsheet programs do a very good job of seamlessly integrating with word processors and other programs so that a counselor can then glean any data from a spreadsheet, for instance, and insert it in appropriate places in a counseling report. Sabella (1996) gave several examples of how school counselors use the integration of database and word processing programs to collect, process, and use data in various documents:

- In consultation with the Dean of Students and the district database person, a counselor obtained a file containing a list of students who had not been referred for discipline problems that year. It was requested that the list be sorted by home room teachers, who were also included in the data file. The Dean and the counselor created an award on the computer and merged the names of each student on the award. The certificates printed in the same order that they appeared in the file--by home room teacher. After each certificate printed, all that had to be done was deposit them in the home room teachers' mailboxes, which were also in alphabetical order. This process required 30 minutes to set up and 90 minutes to print the approximately 600 awards. A nearby student assistant was responsible for refilling the printer with paper when it ran out.

- A counselor who conducted an outdoor adventure field trip at the beginning of each semester asked her district office to send her a file with the names, lunch numbers, last semester grade point averages (GPAs), and home room teachers for all students at her school. She also asked that the list be sorted by GPA, race, and sex. The counselor was then able to identify students with the lowest GPAs and print out a list balanced by race and sex. Then, she merged a list of names with lunch numbers to give to the cafeteria staff who provided lunches for the trip. Using the data and her word processor, the counselor was also able to generate certificates, permission letters, and a list of participants that would be used for gathering post intervention data. At the end of the year, she had the district office provide GPAs for the same students so that she could compare them against GPA's at the beginning of the year.

- For an annual career day, an elementary school counselor maintained a database of speakers and other participants. He merged this information into standard invitations, confirmations, brochures, and thank-you letters.

- Another counselor used the merge capability of her word processor while working closely with a program designed for students who were not successful in the regular classroom environment. These students were self-contained with only 15 other students and a teacher with advanced training. The counselor worked with the students, their parents or guardians, and juvenile case workers. She maintained information about each student in a database file to help her manage each case. She then used these files to complete already formatted reports for the juvenile justice department, drop-out prevention office, district office, and parents. All she had to do was indicate to the computer which report she wanted to complete and for which child or group of children. The computer and printer did the rest.

- Using a spreadsheet program, a counselor maintained an activity log which included time spent in various categories of tasks (e.g., consulting with parents, individual counseling, large group guidance, peer helper training, and professional development to name a few). With one click of the mouse each quarter, he could print out a report which he provided to his principal complete with textual descriptions and bar graphs.

By far, the most prevalent interest in data processing in school counseling right now is how it applies to data-driven decision making and accountability. I (TS) use spreadsheets to collect, disaggregate, compare, and summarize student achievement data. For example, I developed an incentive plan designed to increase students' knowledge of addition facts. I wanted the students to know that, with more focused effort, they could indeed improve their math scores. I first identified the students by reviewing their state achievement test math scores, talking to their teachers and giving them an addition pre-test. Next, I met with the students for three sessions and taught them ways to increase the retention of their facts. Then, I gave them a post-test and inputted all the data into a spreadsheet. I used a simple formula of subtracting the pre-test number from the post-test number to calculate the growth. Using the spreadsheet allowed me and the students to visually and vividly witness progress. Rather then analyzing who had the most or least correct I could see how each individual student had grown. Using a

spreadsheet allowed me to access, in real time, specific information about each student and the group as a whole.

Another example of how I (TS) used a spreadsheet (e.g., Microsoft Excel™) was when I disaggregated and analyzed students' scores on our state achievement test, the Florida Comprehensive Achievement Test (FCAT) Reading test. Specifically, I reviewed the scores for 3rd grade students who were retained at grade level because of low scores on the test (yes, a student is retained in the same grade if he or she does not pass the state achievement exam). By inputting the raw data from specific categories of the test (e.g., Cause & Effect, Main Idea, and Reference Research) I was able to see which areas had the highest and lowest percent correct. As a school counselor, I found this process quick and amazingly helpful for then creating customized lessons. I also shared the data with the students, their parents, and teachers so we could better assist them in a more collaborative and systematic approach. Additionally, I continue to use Microsoft Excel™ to help our 3rd grade students by analyzing their Reading scores according to various categories or subgroups such as Exceptional Student Education (ESE), Limited English Proficiency (LEP), and 504 plan status. This procedure provides me with important information about how well we as educators reach different subgroups. Once disaggregated, I then create visual displays to summarize salient points. For example, I used Excel's chart function to create a column graph to compare each student's 2004 FCAT score to their 2005 FCAT score. This process made it much easier to see the various gains. I also used the pie graph function to display the percentage of students with an ESE, LEP, and 504 plan that did not pass the FCAT as a proportion of the total student population. Once again, this provided an instantaneous visual representation of the data which makes determining achievement gaps much easier. Using basic options such as sorting and filtering, I was then able to delve more deeply into the data and make other comparisons such as how gender, age, and ethnicity relate to scores. One thing to keep in mind is that data processing in this way actually takes less time the more you do it because of continued practice, and because formulas and functions can be copied from one spreadsheet to another for future use.

I (TS) plan to continue using Microsoft Excel™ to assist students in all domains including academic, personal/social, and career. Within the career domain, for instance, I will have students chart various characteristics associated with effective job performance. They will rate themselves on items such as being on time, having good communication skills, being a team player, and others. The data will be collected and used to help them prioritize which skills to address. Within the personal/social domain, I am using a the Solution Focused Scaling approach (see Sabella, 2006) in combination with Excel to help students track self-perception ratings regarding classroom behavior before, during, and after a large group guidance intervention. Thus, the data collection serves as both part of the intervention and as part of an effort to determine the intervention's impact or results. In addition, I (TS) use this basic Solution Focused scaling approach and spreadsheet software to help students address other questions such as "How would you rate your effort today in class?" or "How would you rate your support for other students?" Creating graphs to depict responses is useful for demonstrating change (before & after) and comparing categories (such as, "How did the students collectively rate Mondays versus Thursdays?").

In addition to off-the-shelf software, customized software for counselors is becoming increasingly available. For instance:

- EZANALYZE is a computer program designed to enhance the capabilities of Microsoft Excel™ by adding "point and click" functionality for analyzing data and creating graphs. It works on both Macs and PC's. http://www.ezanalyze.com/
- SCAATAP provides school counselors a quick and easy way to record activities and create daily, weekly, monthly, quarterly, and annual reports. The data generated by these reports will provide the "process" accountability that administrators and policy-makers desire. The reports will help answer the question "What do school counselors do?" http://www.scaatap.com/
- TheraScribe® 4.0 Counseling Record Management Software eliminates hours of time-consuming paperwork. You can quickly enter all the necessary information about a client including personal, diagnostic, treatment plans, medical information and much more. http://www.4ulr.com/products/counseling/therascribesoftware.html
- CounselingSurveys.org is a not-for-profit Web site created to promote quantitative research in the Counseling profession by sponsoring electronic surveys free of charge for researchers and practitioners. (This site does not offer services to the general public.) http://www.counselingsurveys.org/.

Multimedia

One popular technology tool for persuasive communication is multimedia presentation (MMP) software. A multimedia presentation (MMP) is created by a computer program and incorporates a series of projected images called slides. Slides may incorporate animated text, graphics, pictures, audio and video clips, graphs, tables – and any other electronic representations – in an integrated series (Sabella, 1998). Effective comprehensive school counseling programs/services include a diversity of stakeholders, which include students, principals, teachers, staff, parents, community members, and others. Helping stakeholders to advance their knowledge and understanding about your work and how they may become involved can be a tough task. A method which is highly expedient and yet effective is needed. Technology such as multimedia presentations is one tool that can effectively and efficiently proliferate a message about your work among many important people. Also as important, multimedia software may be a feasible answer to the question, "How can I provide others training that will help them better cope and succeed in realizing developmental milestones?"

Specifically, coupled with the power of the Internet, using multimedia software can help counselors:

1. Communicate a message that is rich with sound, animation, clip art, photos, graphs, data, and other elements;
2. Provide information that is highly up-to-date and easily accessed anytime of day or night;
3. Present to others without having to be present at a conference or meeting. This advantage has the benefit of also being quite cost and time effective;
4. Tailor information to each specific audience without building a new presentation from scratch. Existing MMPs can be altered and saved under a new name;
5. Collaborate with others more efficiently by enhancing the democratic process; and
6. Communicate to others that they are knowledgeable and capable of using desirable technology skills, which can respectably be modeled for the clients they serve. In this case, the medium is the message.

Perhaps the most important use of electronic tools for communicating with important others is the ability to shift time and location. No longer are counselors required to be present for collaborating and communicating with others. A multimedia presentation can be stored on various devices to accommodate a wide variety of recipients' needs. Using the Internet to share presentations allows counselors to literally cultivate the message across a global audience within a matter of seconds. Once a presentation arrives, target audience members can access and view the presentation at their own convenience and at their own pace. Because today's multimedia software allows the counselor to easily include narration and timed slide transitions, an audience member can listen to and learn from a presentation, almost as if the counselor were present. And, if the recipient chooses, he or she may study the information as frequently as desired, pass along the information to others, or respond to the counselor for further inquiry or feedback.

How might counselors use multimedia presentations in their work? Sabella and Booker (2003) wrote specifically about counselors have and could use MMPs to enhance the impact of their work:

1. Counselors can enhance multicultural competencies by sharing rich MMP with others around the world. For example, D'Andrea (1995) wrote about several activities which include music, art, food, and photos that can foster both multicultural appreciation and technological literacy among elementary school students;

2. Scan in the work of clients, such as art projects, and share with appropriate others (e.g., faculty, parents, other consulting counselors);

3. Create a MMP that describes the counselor's work so that others such as teachers, administrators, parents, and community members may better understand and increase their involvement for facilitating client progress;

4. MMPs can also offer suggestions for how others may choose to support the school, refer clients, and otherwise contribute needed resources;

5. Similar to distance learning, MMPs can be used as professional/personal development delivery systems to help others learn important skills, knowledge, and attitudes to do their part in the client's progress (e.g., academic, personal, social, and career achievements); and

6. School counselors can (a) conduct a very large group guidance for all students at the same time. After a MMP is created, it can be transferred to video and then shown on the school's television network. For classes that have computers, the counselor can use the Internet to conduct a live chat about the topic. For classes that do not have a computer, the counselor can

follow up that day and conduct live discussions; (b) provide teachers-as-advisors with a MMP to use with students thus insuring that they are presenting consistent and accurate information to students; and c) provide peer helpers (e.g., peer mediators) MMPs for learning relevant helping skills and attitudes as part of a homework assignment.

Other forms of multimedia electronics such as digital cameras and video recorders seem to be increasingly integrated into the work of school guidance and counseling. Although prices are falling, these tools can still be expensive and require alternative methods of funding. This past year, I (TS) obtained a grant to purchase a video camcorder, which was used in a variety of ways. First, I was able to record and provide to other counselors in the district a local training on Solution Focused Brief Counseling provided by Russ Sabella. We recorded, burned several sets of DVDs for checkout, and also used the audio portion to create CDs which counselors could also listen to at home, in their cars, or on their iPods if they wanted to. When using the video recorder with students, I noticed that they enjoyed being both in front of and behind the camera. What I did not anticipate, however, is how implementing the camera would increase their motivation to read. The students wanted to be on "TV" or at least behind the scenes, and they wanted to make sure that they sounded "smart" when they were on. Many students who were previously not interested in reading, pronunciation, fluency, and appearance were now eager to enhance their communication and related literacy skills. Yet another way that I used the video camera in my work was to have students develop and broadcast public service announcements that promoted (and demonstrated) positive student behavior. For example, the science teacher and I collaborated with students to create a video on "I Messages" and positive communication. The data is still coming in although, anecdotally, teachers tell me that they are noticing some improvement.

Personal Information Managers

Personal information managers (PIMs) are a type of software application designed to help users organize random bits of information. Although the category is fuzzy, most PIMs enable you to enter various kinds of textual notes – reminders, lists, dates – and to link these bits of information together in useful ways. Many PIMs also include calendar, scheduling, and calculator programs. The usefulness of this type of software lies in its ability to integrate data and provide feedback in the form of potential scheduling conflicts and event reminders. Microsoft Outlook, one of the most "mature" PIMs, allows users to integrate e-mail, calendars, coordination of meetings, notes, alerts, and much more. Several online PIM's such as My Yahoo! (http://my.yahoo.com/) and MSN Hotmail (http://www.hotmail.com) allow you to automatically import events that others manage (e.g., educational programming on television) as well as information from other PIMs such as Microsoft Outlook. Finally, your personal information can be synchronized with other portable devices such as your cell phone, handheld computer, or Ipod which makes access to the data highly convenient.

Technologies for Intervention Delivery

When you think of conducting counseling with your students, you probably envision you and your client(s) in your office, in the classroom, or perhaps even on a "walk and talk." However, others may also have a mental image of a counselor who sits in front of the computer and conducts counseling over the Internet. WebCounseling is the attempt to provide counseling services in an Internet environment. The environment may include connecting with your clients via e-mail, chatrooms, instant messenger, or Internet video conferencing. The practice of WebCounseling, also referred to as cybercounseling, cybertherapy, e-therapy, e-counseling, and online counseling to name a few, began slowly although it is rapidly finding popularity among both counselors and clients. Among counseling professionals, WebCounseling has created somewhat of a debate about the utility and effectiveness of this new medium and whether "cybercounseling" even really exists. Moreover, those involved in traditional counseling ethical and legal issues are wondering how such matters relate to the Internet environment.

Some counselors would say that defining the nature and practice of webcounseling is futile and misleading. Counselors and others in this camp believe that webcounseling is a term which leads people to erroneously believe that the work of professional counselors can effectively and appropriately be conducted in an electronic or "virtual" environment such as the Internet. They argue that, although noteworthy attempts are currently in progress, empirically supported counseling theories and techniques have not yet been adequately tested in the virtual environment. Thus, we cannot confidently assume current approaches have the same effect or, even worse, do not have unanticipated negative effects for online clients. This group further argues that these online services cannot be considered counseling unless and until they can be demonstrated to be effective. Similarly, an important question has remained unanswered: Is counseling in cyberspace so different from traditional face-to-face counseling that it requires special training and certification?

Many counselors wonder if the therapeutic alliance can reliably be established without ever working with the client in person. Even if the counseling relationship could be developed in cyberspace, they wonder if the online personality with whom you are working is the same as the "real world" personality of the client. Finally, it is unknown if potential growth or progress made during online sessions will generalize to life in the real world as we would expect to happen in face-to-face counseling. Counselors who view cybercounseling as more of a potential than an existing counseling modality may be optimistic about how developing technology can help counselors do their work in alternative environments and media. However, for now, they caution us that traditional or face-to-face counseling is not well understood by the general public, notwithstanding its much longer history and exposure via public relations, and that discussing WebCounseling as if it exists stands to confuse the practice of counseling even more. This group wants the public to understand the difference between the special relationship a counselor and client share, as compared to the relationships established in other related helping activities such as advising, mentoring, coaching, and teaching. These counselors argue that "cybercounselors" who believe they are counseling in cyberspace are more accurately providing cyberadvice, cybercoaching, cybermentoring, and distance learning. While each of these is important and valuable, none are adequate substitutes for professional counseling.

Other counselors have adopted a more "middle of the road" belief about cybercounseling. They espouse that cybercounseling is not counseling per se but an effective means to supplement live counseling sessions. They believe that technology has not yet developed tools to effectively create an environment that can substitute for a live setting although tools do exist to help counselors (and clients) be more effective and efficient in meeting their goals. Such counselors may indeed call themselves cybercounselors or e-therapists, for instance, but only insofar as it describes their use of computer and Internet technologies as a part of their face-to-face work with clients. These counselors affirm the role that technology plays throughout the process of counseling, including collaboration and communication, and continue to explore how such tools can enhance the probability of successful live interaction (Tyler & Sabella, 2004).

On the other side of the continuum reside counselors and researchers who view the Web as a new delivery and management system for doing the work of professional counseling. These cybercounselors celebrate the latest tools provided by computers and networking technologies as providing the means to work with clients whom, without these tools, they could never connect. With some adaptations, they posit that they can effectively use their counseling knowledge and skills to provide counseling services in cyberspace.

Many future possibilities and potential problems in the delivery of counseling services exist. Following is an overview of each:

Possibilities

* Delivery of counseling services: Walz (1996) noted that the information highway "allows counselors to overcome problems of distance and time to offer opportunities for networking and interacting not otherwise available" (p. 417). In addition, counseling over the Net may be a useful medium for those with physical disabilities whom may find even a short distance a significant obstacle. And yet for others who are reticent in meeting with a counselor and/or self-disclosing, the Net may prove to be an interactive lubricant which may very well foster the counseling process.
* Delivery of information resources: The Internet is a convenient and quick way to deliver important information. In cybercounseling, information might be in the form of homework assignment between sessions or bibliocounseling. Also, electronic file transfer of client records, including intake data, case notes (Casey, Bloom, & Moan, 1994), assessment reports, and selected key audio and video recordings of client sessions, could be used as preparation for individual supervision, group supervision, case conferences, and research (Sampson, Kolodinsky, & Greeno, 1997).
* Assessment and evaluation: Access to a wide variety of assessment, instructional, and information resources, in formats appropriate in a wide variety of ethnic, gender, and age contexts (Sampson, 1990; Sampson & Krumboltz, 1991), could be accomplished via Web and FTP sites.

* Communications: Especially via e-mail, counselors and clients can exchange messages throughout the counseling process. Messages may inform both counselor and client of pertinent changes or progress. E-mail can provide an excellent forum for answering simple questions, providing social support, or to schedule actual or virtual meeting times.
* Marriage and family counseling: If face-to-face interaction is not possible on a regular basis, marriage counseling might be delivered via video conferencing, in which each couple and the counselor (or counselors) are in different geographic locations. After independent use of multimedia based computer-assisted instruction on communication skills, spouses could use video conferencing to complete assigned homework (e.g., communication exercises; Sampson et al., 1997).
* Supervision: Anecdotal evidence has shown that e-mail is an enhancing tool in the process of counselor supervision and consultation, It provides an immediate and ongoing channel of communication between and among as many people as chosen (Myrick & Sabella, 1995).

Potential Problems

* Confidentiality: Although encryption and security methods have become highly sophisticated, unauthorized access to online communications remains a possibility without attention to security measures. Counselors whom practice on the Net must ethically and legally protect their clients, their profession, and themselves by using all known and reasonable security measures.
* Computer competency: Both the counselor and client must be adequately computer literate for the computer/network environment to be a viable interactive medium. From typing skills to electronic data transfer, both the counselor and client must be able to effectively harness the power and function of both hardware and software. Similar to face-to-face counseling, counselors must not attempt to perform services outside the limitations of their competence.
* Location-specific factors: A potential lack of appreciation on the part of geographically remote counselors of location-specific conditions, events, and cultural issues that affect clients may limit counselor credibility or lead to inappropriate counseling interventions. For example, a geographically remote counselor may be unaware of traumatic recent local

events that are exacerbating a client's reaction to work and family stressors. It may also be possible that differences in local or regional cultural norms between the client's and counselor's community could lead a counselor to misinterpret the thoughts, feelings, or behavior of the client. Counselors need to prepare for counseling a client in a remote location by becoming familiar with recent local events and local cultural norms. If a counselor encounters an unanticipated reaction on the part of the client, the counselor needs to proceed slowly, clarifying client perceptions of their thoughts, feelings, and behavior (Sampson et al., 1997).

❖ Equity: Does the cost of Internet access introduce yet another obstacle for obtaining counseling? Does cybercounseling further alienate potential clients whom might have the greatest need for counseling? Even when given access to the Net, could a client competently engage cybercounseling without possibly having ever had a computer experience? WebCounseling seems to exacerbate equity issues already confronting live counseling.

❖ Credentialing: How will certification and licensure laws apply to the Internet as state and national borders are crossed electronically? Will counselors be required to be credentialed in all states and countries where clients are located? Could cybercounseling actually be the impetus for a national credential recognized by all states? Will we need to move towards global credentialing? Who will monitor service complaints out-of-state or internationally?

❖ High Tech v. High Touch: How can counselors foster the development of trusting, caring, and genuine working relationships in cyberspace? Until video transmission over the Web makes telecounseling a reality, cybercounseling relies on a process devoid of non-verbal or extraverbal behavior. Even if we were able to conduct real-time counseling over the Net via video, can this medium help us to communicate so as to foster the counseling core conditions? Further, Lago (1996) poses a key question: "Do the existing theories of psychotherapy continue to apply, or do we need a new theory of e-mail therapy?" (p. 289). He then takes Rogers' (1957) work on the necessary and sufficient conditions for therapeutic change as his starting-point and lists the computer-mediated therapist competencies as: the ability to establish contact, the ability to establish relationship, the ability to communicate accurately with minimal loss or distortion, the ability to demonstrate understanding and frame empathic

responses, and the capacity and resources to provide appropriate and supportive information. This proposal begs the question as to whether such relationship conditions as outlined by Rogers can be successfully transmitted and received via contemporary computer-mediated telecommunications media.

❖ Impersonation: A famous cartoon circulated over the Net depicts a dog sitting in front of a computer. The caption says, "The nice thing about the Internet is that nobody knows you're a dog." Experienced Internet users can relate to the humor in this cartoon because they know that there are many people who hide behind the Net's veil of anonymity to communicate messages they ordinarily would not communicate in real life. Messages that convey unpopular sentiments and would ordinarily be met with castigation. Others rely on anonymity provided by the Net to play out fantasies or practical jokes. Who is your cyberclient, really? Does your client depict himself/herself as an adult and is actually a minor? Has the client disguised their gender, race, or other personal distinctions that may threaten the validity or integrity of your efforts.

❖ Ethics: How do current ethical statements for counselors apply or adapt to situations encountered online? For the most part, counselors can make the leap into cyberspace and use current ethical guidelines to conduct themselves in an ethical fashion. However, problems exist. The future will inevitably see a change in what it means to be ethical as we learn the exact nature of counseling online.

The Ethics of WebCounseling

In 1995, the National Board for Certified Counselors (NBCC) Board of Directors appointed a WebCounseling Task Force to examine the practice of online counseling and to assess the possible existence of any regulatory issues NBCC might need to address. The task force established a listserv composed of more than 20 individuals who had specific knowledge, expertise, skills, and opinions regarding the practice of what is herein referred to as webcounseling. Soon it became apparent that counseling had a diverse presence on the Internet, from Web sites that simply promoted a counselor's home or office practice, to sites that provided information about counseling and others which actually claimed to offer therapeutic interventions either as an adjunct to face-to-face counseling or as a stand alone service. Some sites were poorly constructed, poorly edited and poorly presented. Others were run by anonymous individuals, individuals with no credentials or fraudulent credentials, and some sites were operated by individuals with appropriate credentials and years of professional experience. However, these credentials were all based on education and experience gained in face-to-face counseling, and the relevance of these credentials to the practice of WebCounseling is unknown. No one knew if the lack of visual input made a difference in the outcome of the counseling process. No one knew about the legality of counseling across state or national boundaries. No one knew if there was any relevant research in any field of communication, which could shed light on these questions (Bloom, 1998). As a result of the Task Force's work, a set of standards, the Standards for the Ethical Practice of WebCounseling, were developed and are now included online at http://www.nbcc.org/.

Ethical and Legal Use of Technology

Computer, electronic networking, and other technologies provide vast power, especially as a medium for communication, collaboration, and intervention delivery. With this freedom, however, comes an important responsibility to use technology, especially the Internet, in a manner which is safe, secure, ethical, and contributes to the overall welfare of all involved. Counselors should dedicate themselves to becoming aware of the dangers involved in using computers and the Internet. For instance, Sabella (2003) wrote about counseling related issues that computer and Internet technology have spawned and includes: Internet addiction, equitable access, pornography, online sexual harassment, security, and safety. With increased awareness, counselors can more effectively make decisions about their computing and online behavior. In addition, Tyler and Sabella (2004) dedicated a chapter in their book, *Using Technology to Improve Counseling Practice: A Primer for the 21st Century*, about the legal and ethical issues involved in counseling technology. They reviewed precautions for protecting confidentiality such as using encryption methods for communication, file passwords, and electronic file shredders. The authors also included tips for keeping one's personal computer secure from threats such as spyware and viruses which could compromise sensitive information.

The Future of School Counseling and Technology

Technology poses either opportunities or threats to the development of our work as school counselors and to our profession, depending upon how it is used. Focusing on the parts that are helpful and avoiding those which are not can be a difficult task because of the vastness and morphological nature of technology. As part of ongoing professional development, school counselors are wise to stay informed of new technological developments and how they are being applied to our work. Technologies currently under development and becoming more pervasive (and thus usually less expensive) merit special attention:

1. Digital cameras allow for counselors to take pictures and instantly use them in a variety of ways. Some are posting photos of evidence of their work on counseling Web sites or electronic portfolios as a matter of public relations and accountability. Others are using digital cameras, both video and still, to help clients capture and describe "their world" in the form of electronic collages or journals which are then used in the counseling process.

2. Voice recognition software allows for humans and machines to interact in more meaningful ways than ever before considered. Counselors can dictate their words into various applications as well as issue computer voice commands that will further increase efficiency and effectiveness.

3. As bandwidth (the capacity of copper and fiberoptic wires to move data) increases, we will see the proliferation of Internet videoconferencing and online full-length videos, which will further enhance efforts in communication, collaboration, consultation, distance education, and intervention delivery. Websites will become more dynamic, offering virtual three-dimensional worlds. In addition, wireless high-speed access to the Internet throughout the country is becoming a reality.

4. Computer scientists are making rapid gains in developing what is known as natural language so that computers can better "understand" human questions or commands and more appropriately respond.

5. Massive data warehouses and mining applications will provide educators with an early warning alert system to better help identify students who perform outside of expectations. These systems will also help counselors to maintain sophisticated student profiles and design customized guidance lessons, perhaps even electronically deliver those lessons.

6. Computers are breaking capacity and speed barriers every day. As they become faster, smaller, and are able to store more data, computers will help us to perform and manage tasks with unprecedented proficiency.

7. The rapidly advancing gaming technology (e.g., Xbox, Playstation) will advance how counselors can create and deliver "virtual reality" experiences as part of guidance and counseling interventions.
8. Social networking technologies will help school counselors share, collaborate, and support each other in all aspects of the profession.

The experience and world views of our clients and stakeholders have been profoundly impacted by the rapid evolution of computer technologies. We sit at the edge of an electronic frontier without knowing for certain what lies ahead. The journey, with its extraordinary potentials and realistic pitfalls, is exciting and oftentimes frightening. Careful and purposeful practice, however, can help us to stay connected and competent amidst chaotic transition. This chapter sought to provide readers with an introduction and overview of technology and its special meaning to school counselors. As an agent of change and advocacy, it is your job now to explore how technology best works for you so that you may work best for your clients.

Summary/Conclusion

No counseling professional is immune to the significant impact technology has made on how we practice, communicate, manage, and measure the outcomes of our work. In addition, technology is also changing the types of counseling issues presented by our clients within the various systems in which they live and work (e.g., family, peer, society). The message is clear: Opting out of technological literacy and implementation in today's high-tech world reduces effectiveness and efficiency while increasing the risk of unethically practicing beyond one's competency. On the other hand, counselors who march along with the progress of high-tech tools and electronic media stand to enjoy the benefits and temper the potential dangers that prevail. Technological literacy and implementation is not merely a response to a problem, but an important and life-long part of professional development and training. For better or worse, the availability of various technologies and how we apply them will continue to change. Changes will be pleasant or unpleasant, in large part determined by our familiarity and abilities to adapt.

Discussion Questions

1. How is maintaining minimal levels of technological literacy an ethical and/or legal issue for school counselors?

2. What future technology would you invent that school counselors would find invaluable in their work?
3. How has technology created problems, issues, or challenges for the profession (e.g., accountability, student records, planning)?
4. How has technology introduced undue stress for the school counselor? As a school counselor, what will you need to do to mitigate this potential problem?
5. How do common technologies such as e-mail, database management, multimedia, and information resources apply to each of the parts of the ASCA National Model?
6. What are the implications of the "digital divide" for modern day school counseling?
7. How else can you use technologies (e.g., podcasting, blogs, and video) to facilitate academic achievement within a comprehensive school counseling program?
8. How do you know when the work to learn a new technology (e.g., financial and human resource expenditures) has an appropriate Return on Investment (ROI) in your work?
9. How does technology allow you to "replicate" your services and you?
10. Which technologies would you deem time wasters instead of time savers?

References

American School Counselor Association. (2005). *The ASCA National Model: A Framework for School Counseling Programs* (2nd Ed.) Alexandria, VA: Author.

Blog. (n.d.) Retrieved December 11, 2005, from http://www.webopedia.com/TERM/b/blog.html.

Bloom, J. W. (1998). The ethical practice of webcounseling. *British Journal of Guidance and Counselling, 26*(1), 53-59.

Bobek, B. L., Robbins, S. B., Gore, P. A., Harris-Bowlsbey, J., Lapan, R. T., Dahir, C. A., & Jepsen, D. A. (2005). Training counselors to use computer-assisted career guidance systems more effectively: A model curriculum. *Career Development Quarterly, 53*(4), 363-371.

Cairo, P. C., & Kanner, M. S. (1984). Investigating the effects of computerized approaches to counselor training. *Counselor Education and Supervision, 24*, 212-221.

Casey, J. A., Bloom, J. W., & Moan, E. R. (1994). Use of technology in counselor supervision. In L. D. Borders (Ed.), *Counseling supervision.* Greensboro,

NC: ERIC Clearinghouse on Counseling and Student Services. (ERIC Document Reproduction Service No. ED 372 357)

Chapman, W., & Katz, M. R. (1983). Career information systems in the secondary schools: A survey and assessment. *Vocational Guidance Quarterly, 32*, 165-177.

Croft, V. (1991). *Technological literacy: Refined for the profession, applications for the classroom.* Unpublished paper presented at the 1991 Annual Conference of the International Technology Education Association.

D'Andrea, M. (1995). Using computer technology to promote multicultural awareness among elementary school-age students. *Elementary School Guidance & Counseling, 30*(1), 45-55.

Fanning, J. M. (1994). Integrating academics and technology: Uncovering staff development needs. In J. Willis, B. Robin, & D. A. Willis (Eds.), *Technology and Teacher Education Annual, 1994* (pp. 331-334). Washington, DC: Association for the Advancement of Computing in Education.

Friery, K., & Nelson, J. G. (2004). Using technology to develop a high school career awareness workshop: The REACH program. *TechTrends: Linking Research & Practice to Improve Learning, 48*(6), 40-42.

Froehle, T. C. (1984). Computer-assisted feedback in counseling supervision. *Counselor Education and Supervision, 24*, 168-175.

Glover, B. L. (1995). DINOS (drinking is not our solution): Using computer programs in middle school drug education. *Elementary School Guidance & Counseling, 30*, 55-62.

Haring-Hidore, M. (1984). In pursuit of students who do not use computers for career guidance. *Journal of Counseling and Development, 63*, 139-140.

Harris, J. (1972). *Computer-assisted guidance systems.* Washington, DC: National Vocational Guidance Association.

Hayden, M. (1989). What is technological literacy? *Bulletin of Science, Technology and Society, 119*, 220-233.

How blogs work. (n.d.) Retrieved December 21, 2005, from http://computer.howstuffworks.com/blog.htm

Instant messaging. (n.d.) Retrieved December 20, 2005, from http://en.wikipedia.org/wiki/Instant_messaging

International Technology Education Association. (2000). *Standards for technological literacy: Content for the study of technology.* Retrieved March 31, 2008, from http://www.iteaconnect.org/TAA/PDFs/xstnd.pdf

Jackson, M. L., & Davidson, C. T. (1998). The web we weave: Using the Internet for counseling research; Part I. *Counseling Today, 39*(2).

Katz, M. R., & Shatkin, L. (1983). Characteristics of computer-assisted guidance. *The Counseling Psychologist, 11*(4), 15-31.

Kivlighan, D. M., Jr., Johnston, J. A., Hogan, R. S., & Mauer, E. (1994). Who benefits from computerized career counseling? *Journal of Counseling & Development, 72*, 289-292.

Koufman-Frederick, A., Lillie, M., Pattison-Gordon, L., Watt, D. L., & Carter, R. (1999). Electronic collaboration: *A practical guide for educators.* Providence, RI: The LAB at Brown University.

Lago, C. (1996). Computer therapeutics. *Counselling, 7*, 287-289.

McClure, P. A. (1996, May/June). Technology plans and measurable outcomes. *Educom Review, 31*(3).

Myrick, R. D, & Sabella, R. A. (1995). Cyberspace: New place for counselor supervision. *Elementary School Guidance & Counseling, 30*(1), 35-44.

Neukrug, E. S. (1991). Computer-assisted live supervision in counselor skills training. *Counselor Education and Supervision, 31*, 132-138.

Owen, S., & Heywood, J. (1988). Transition technology in Ireland. *International Journal of Research in Design and Technology Education, 1*(1).

Pyle, K. R. (1984). Career counseling and computers: Where is the creativity? *Journal of Counseling and Development, 63*, 141-144.

Rogers, C. R. (1957). The necessary and sufficient conditions of therapeutic personality change. *Journal of Consulting Psychology, 21*, 95-103.

Rust, E. B. (1995). Applications of the International Counselor Network for elementary and middle school counseling. *Elementary School Guidance & Counseling, 30*, 16-25.

Sabella, R. A. (1996). School counselors and computers: Specific time-saving tips. *Elementary School Guidance & Counseling, 31*(2), 83-96.

Sabella, R. A. (1998). Practical technology applications for peer helper programs and training. *Peer Facilitator Quarterly, 15*(2), 4-13.

Sabella, R. A. (2003). *SchoolCounselor.com: A friendly and practical guide to the World Wide Web* (2nd ed.). Minneapolis, MN: Educational Media Corporation.

Sabella, R. A. (2005). *What are school counselors doing with technology?* Retrieved March 31, 2008, from http://www.schoolcounselor.com/pdf/counseling-technology-activities.pdf.

Sabella, R. A. (2006). *Scaling towards success.* Retrieved August 1, 2006, from http://www. guidancechannel.com/default.aspx?M=a&index= 1326&cat=15

Sabella, R. A. (2007). School counseling and technology. In J. Wittmer, & M. A. Clark, (Eds.), *Managing your school counseling program* (3rd ed). Minneapolis, MN: Educational Media Corporation.

Sabella, R. A., & Booker, B. (2003). Using technology to promote your guidance and counseling program among stake holders. *Professional School Counseling, 6*(3), 206-213.

Sampson, J. P., Jr. (1990). Computer-assisted testing and the goals of counseling psychology. *The Counseling Psychologist, 18*, 227-239.

Sampson, J. P., Jr., & Krumboltz, J. D. (1991). Computer-assisted instruction: A missing link in counseling. *Journal of Counseling & Development, 69*, 395-397.

Sampson, J. P., Kolodinsky, R. W., & Greeno, B. P. (1997). Counseling on the information highway: Future possibilities and potential problems. *Journal of Counseling and Development, 75*(3), 203-213.

Saskatchewan Education. (2002). *Understanding the common essential learnings: A handbook for teachers.* Regina, SK, Canada: Author.

SchoolCounselor.com eNewsletter, Issue #33.(2005, March 10). Retrieved March 10th, 2005, from www.schoolcounselor.com/newsletter.

Search engines. (n.d.) Retrieved December 19, 2005, from http://en.wikipedia.org/wiki/Search_engine.

Sharf, R. S., & Lucas, M. (1993). An assessment of a computerized simulation of counseling skills. *Counselor Education and Supervision, 32*, 254-266.

Shulman, H. A., Sweeney, B., & Gerler, E. R. (1995). A computer-assisted approach to preventing alcohol abuse: Implications for the middle school. *Elementary School Guidance & Counseling, 30*, 63-77.

Steffens, H. (1986). Issues in the preparation of teachers for teaching robotics in schools. In J. Heywood & P. Matthews (Eds.), *Technology, society and the school curriculum.* Manchester, England: Roundthorn Publishing.

Stone, C., & Turba, R. (1999). School counselors using technology for advocacy. The *Journal of Technology in Counseling, 1*(1).

Tyler, J. M., & Sabella, R. A. (2004). *Using technology to improve counseling practice: A primer for the 21st century.* Alexandria, VA: American Counseling Association.

Valesky, T., & Sabella, R. A. (2005). *Podcasting in educational leadership and counseling.* Paper presented at the Southern Regional Council on Educational Administration Conference (SRCEA), Atlanta, Georgia, October 27-30. Retrieved March 31, 2008, from http://coe.fgcu.edu/edleadership/podcasting.pdf

Waetjen, W. B. (1993). Technological Literacy Reconsidered. *Journal of Technology Education 4*(2).

Walz, G. R. (1996). Using the I-Way for career development. In R. Feller & G. Walz (Eds.), *Optimizing life transitions in turbulent times: Exploring work, learning and careers* (pp. 415-427). Greensboro, NC: ERIC Clearinghouse on Counseling and Student Services

Chapter 21

Staying Current: Using Cybertools to Reach More Students

Sally Gelardin and Marilyn Harryman

Abstract

Today's students are adept at using cell phones, e-mail, and the Internet. They get their information from television and radio programs and talk shows. Counselors who take advantage of the new "cybertools" can use these methods to more effectively reach all of their students, including the shyest and those disenfranchised from adults and the mainstream. This chapter describes various cybertools and presents examples of how to make the most of each tool to reach students in ways that speak directly to their interests. Additionally, the authors discuss how to enhance counseling programs and strengthen communication with students, staff, and parents.

Introduction

Cyber- or computer-mediated communication is transforming school counselor education in curriculum delivery, supervision, and professional development... (Wilczenski & Coomey, 2006, 1).

The chaotic cyber-world is influencing the direction of the school counseling profession, forcing us to consider new ways to do our work that can be useful and interesting to students and meet our own needs as well. Much has changed even since we began writing this chapter. Although some of what we suggest may have become commonplace by the time you read this, by staying current with the Internet and media tools, many challenges to the school counseling profession can be overcome, such as the following:

- Students who receive the most counseling attention are those who excel and those who are the most academically challenged.
- Most students (those in the middle) are often "lost in the shuffle" to fend for themselves without a counselor to help make informed decisions about their future.
- School boards often eliminate counseling programs to save money because they see counseling as adjunctive instead of as essential to student achievement.
- School counselors are often burdened with excessive administrative responsibilities; and therefore their specialized skills are under-utilized.

Currently, telephone and e-mail are the most popular tools used to counsel through distance. In this chapter, we will explore additional "cybertools" and discuss how we can use them in school counseling, as well as consider potential problems that may arise. We shall also discuss how you can enhance your counseling program and strengthen communication with students, staff, and parents. In general, the advantage of employing distance tools in your counseling practice is that they save time, transportation, and other costs, and may even allow you to do your job more effectively than in person.

The American School Counselor Association (ASCA) emphasizes the importance for school counselors to provide a comprehensive school counseling program encouraging all students' academic, career, and personal/social development and helping all students in maximizing student achievement (ASCA, 2006). By becoming more familiar with distance learning tools, we can learn how to take advantage of information that much of the millennial generation is already using and better insure that they receive timely career and academic information, as well as tips on how to handle difficult personal/social issues. By providing new ways for students to access their school counselor, we can reach more students and enable reluctant students to feel more comfortable seeking help.

What Do Students, Parents, and Administrators Need From Us?

As advocates for our students, we also are responsible to administrators, parents, staff, school boards, and even the community. Each of these groups has unique needs and preferred forms of communication. At the end of this chapter, we have provided a "Table of Distance Delivery Tools" that contains definitions and examples of the new cybertools available for communicating with these groups.

Students

They have them, they use them! Most students are already proficient with cell phones, text messaging, computers, MP3 files, and IPods. Portfolios are often required for graduation, and electronic portfolios (e-portfolios) are already becoming requirements for many college and graduate programs. In addition, an increasing number of potential employers are requiring applicants to fill out e-profiles and/or submit electronic resumes (e-resumes) instead of submitting traditional paper resumes.

Raised in an era of e-mail and texting, many youth shun conversation, preferring the "authentic" voice of electronic delivery systems (Zinko, 2006). The new generation in secondary schools and on college campuses today has been referred to as "Millennials," "Echo Boomers," and the "Net Generation." They are often more comfortable talking on their cell phones, text messaging, and blogging than communicating with those in the same room, while their younger siblings are glued to their PlayStations, DVD games, and TiVo, (a consumer video "time shifting" device that allows users to capture television programming to internal hard disk for later viewing). Many are proficient multitaskers, doing homework and instant messaging (IMing) at the same time. Rather than being confined to the time constraints of home and local community, the Millennial generation's community is the world community, and they can often have what they want at a more convenient time for them. These individuals are typically more interested in living fully in the present than planning for the future.

Richard Florida describes how progressive companies are trying to fit in with their possible future employees, more than young people trying to fit in with an employer. He writes:

As I walked across the campus of Pittsburgh's Carnegie Mellon University one delightful spring day, I came upon a table filled with young people chatting and enjoying the spectacular weather. Several had identical blue T-shirts with "Trilogy@CMU" written across them---Trilogy being an Austin, Texas-based software company with a reputation for recruiting our top students. I walked over to the table. "Are you guys here to recruit?" I asked. "No, absolutely not," they replied adamantly. "We're not recruiters. We're just hangin' out, playing a little Frisbee with our friends." How interesting, I thought. They've come to campus on a workday, all the way from Austin, just to hang out with some new friends. (Florida, 2002)

In a pre-publication flyer, best-selling career author Richard Bolles (2007) says, "The most dramatic change in the past year has consisted in the various new forms that information has taken: blogs, podcasts, Web sites, RSS feeds, TiVo, satellite radio, Webcasts, etc., supplementing the older and more familiar forms."

In the 1960s, when author Sally's mother was a high school English teacher, she introduced journaling into the English curriculum. Students wanted to understand themselves in the 1960s, not just go through society's expectations of them. Now, in the 21st century, students are expressing their needs again. This time, they are searching, not only to understand themselves, but also to connect with other young people in the virtual community and to create value in work and life. Online journals are becoming commonplace among today's students who may have their own Web sites and blogs where they communicate with friends. One student's well-organized site, complete with archives, announces "Rants and Ravings, Pictures, and Otherwise Useless and Amusing Information." Dated topics are as varied as "Cleaning and organizing," "I hate emergency rooms," "The concert that wasn't," "Things are not always as they seem," etc. Very creative and insightful!

In the *Chronicle of Higher Education* (Carnevale, 2006), we learned that because students are ignoring their campus e-mail accounts, many colleges are trying new ways of communicating including cell phone text messages, instant messages, and even MySpace and Facebook to reach students. "These students are walking spam filters," says Paul Lehmann, the director of student activities at Utica College. "They are masters of multiple forms of communication and have perfected the skill of cutting through the multiple forms of communication that they are bombarded with to find what they are interested in and want to reply to" (Lehmann, cited in Carnevale, 2006, section 4).

School counselors can tap into this need for connection by learning new ways to communicate with students, even using MySpace (http://www.myspace.com). Teachers are already using Internet-based platforms, such as Blackboard (http://www.blackboard.com) and WebCT (http://www.Webct.com) to teach students. Because school counselors often have responsibility for several hundred students, tools such as those found on Web platforms (some of which are free) are becoming another way to effectively connect with students, parents, administrators, staff, and community

Parents/Administrators/Staff/Community

Unlike the younger generation, parents, administrators, staff, school boards, and community are often not comfortable with emerging ways of receiving and sending information. The amount of information coming in through television, print media, and computers is overwhelming. Unlike their children, who function well in a cyber-world of computers and cell phones, parents are primarily concerned with supporting the family and maintaining a certain standard of living.

Parents expect a great deal from the schools to help their children develop into secure, self-supporting adults. They understand that the Internet has a great potential for helping their kids, but they are also worried by it. They see their kids talking on the phone, "texting" and then at home "IMing" on the computer. Administrators are wary and often restrict cell phone use to prevent in-class cheating and chatting. Therefore, the current environment is one where counselors need to figure out how to meet various, and sometimes conflicting needs of students, staff, and parents.

How Do You Choose Which Cybertools to Use?

"If you want to keep earning, then you must keep learning"

Melvin Grade, former Governor of New Jersey

Living in a fast-moving culture, with an over-abundance of information churning around us on IPods, blogs, text messages, podcasts, and other high tech communication systems, we need to learn how to manage these distance tools, rather than be overwhelmed by them. Education and training can be delivered through a variety of methods.

Considering the ways both you and your students learn best would be a good place to start. For example, if you prefer to listen to music more than watch television, you may prefer audio-taped instruction or teleconferencing. If you like to read brief copy, connect with others through the Web, and use a keyboard, text messaging or online courses might work best. If you like to watch movies and talk with others, hosting or serving as a guest speaker on an educational television show or creating digital stories with your students could be effective and fun. Cable TV and video or DVD can be engaging ways to involve students, staff, and community in dealing with timely information and issues. Next are examples of how distance delivery tools can bring energy to your counseling program.

Radio, Video/DVD, or Cable Television

In Oakland, California, the original show, CCC LIVE! "The Counselor Community Connection" (KDOL Cable Channel 27), has aired a variety of lively discussions and video clips (short videos of an event or interview) related to student achievement. With live, call-in capabilities, the show has been effective in engaging a broader community audience. In addition to rebroadcasts two to three times a week, videotapes have also been used in after-school programs and for classroom discussion. Students, families, and friends tune in to see and listen to themselves and each other (Harryman, 1994-2008).

If your school or educational institution has a radio or television station and student media classes, there may be opportunities to reach a targeted audience with your counseling information while developing and showcasing the talent of students, staff, and guests from outreach and other community programs. To make your program more interesting, you or your students can videotape local events, interview people on location, and edit the tape into one or more video clips. Using a studio editing tool such as Final Cut Pro (Macintosh) or other programs (both for fee and free) to edit, with practice, the video clips can seamlessly capture the essence of the event in one to five minutes from a master tape of 20 minutes to an hour. Students will often do a better job of finding the essential information to include in the clip, but it is important that you view them first to make sure they haven't missed something. Your district probably has a specific confidentiality release form that you should use to document those interviewed for the clips. If your program will be broadcast, call all the people that you interviewed prior to the show to remind them to watch.

The following school-year schedule for CCC Live! relates to what middle and high school counselors are typically dealing with during specific times of year and may stimulate your own ideas for topics that can be featured with cable TV or other distance tools and resources. For example, if attendance is a problem in your school or district, you might focus on how students perceive the situation and what they would do about it. The December program on grief issues came directly from students who were deeply upset about the death of a friend and family members. Their title, "Are Your Spirits Low? Here's Help," expressed how they felt as they worried about separation and sadness during the long winter break. In November, with anxiety about passing the college entrance assessment tests as well as state required tests, there are many approaches you can use to inform parents and students including professional videos or resources that companies may provide. A performance coach who likes to work with students and will volunteer his/her services could also add interest to your program while increasing confidence in test taking.

With experts on a panel, sensitive issues such as bullying, racism, and families of divorce, could also be explored. You will think of those that best fit the needs of your students and community.

School Year Schedule for CCC Live! The Counselor Community Connection (Harryman, 1994-2008).

JULY/AUGUST/SEPTEMBER: Rebroadcasts - Summer Opportunities; Scholarship Winners: and/or **What's Going on This Summer!** A live show which highlights positive summer programs. Clips: School-to-Career training, internships, summer jobs.

AUGUST/SEPTEMBER: Welcome to Best High. Create a short video on how classes are scheduled, how classes can be changed. Insert background footage (b-roll) showing students and/or parents going through the process. (This could keep complaint lines short.)

OCTOBER: College, Making it Happen for You!! College Fairs, planning your academic coursework, outreach programs. Clips: college fairs, visits to past graduates on college campuses – their classes, dorms.

NOVEMBER: Improving Your Test Taking Performance - Preparing for Success! High School Exit Exam, PSAT, ACT, SAT I, SAT II, Talk with a Performance Coach. Clips: interviewing students and teachers on campus about test taking.

DECEMBER: Are You Present? Conversation about what keeps students in school. Student leaders, students, and representatives from successful programs to keep students connected. Clips: site interviews with staff and students about problems with attendance.

Alternate: **Are Your Spirits Low? Here's Help.** Conversations about grief issues and holiday blues. Clips: students on campus. Good time for "call in" problems to discuss.

JANUARY/FEBRUARY: Funding Your Future, Cash for College!!! Scholarships, Expert help with FAFSA and Financial Aid. Clips: interviews and/or commercial videos.

MARCH: Charting Your Path to the Future! (Career Awareness Fair) What are your dreams, and what are you doing now to support them? Career days, taking charge of your high school or middle school program. Clips: career day, student interviews, and apprenticeship programs.

APRIL: After School, What Then? What's Going On After School To Support Academic Achievement? Mentoring/after school programs, or Post Secondary Options- Outreach Programs such as Upward Bound, Gear Up, etc. Clips: various programs on location.

Alternate: **Athletics/ Academics! What Does It Take To Compete In Local and NCAA College Athletics?** Clips: school events, coach interviews, former Olympic, professional, college athletes from the community.

MAY: Summer Opportunities for Oakland Youth! Summer school, public libraries, parks and recreation, fine arts, summer jobs/internships. Clips: employer and site visits.

JUNE: Conversations with Scholarship Winners Feature graduating seniors and scholarship providers. Clips: awards banquets and assemblies.

Online Assessment Tools and Information Resources

Schools can access a wide variety of educational resources and assessment instruments electronically at school and at home. Many require licensing agreements, but there are also free resources and assessment tools available on the market, some of which are provided by the U.S. Government. Some may require a personal pin number for students to access the program. Therefore, you will need to make sure that each student knows how to use it. As an educator, you may also be given access to monitor and use student responses. Overview free and for-fee online assessment tools by linking to the following Web sites: http://www.jobhuntersbible.com/counseling/ctests.shtml#jhsds or http://www.quintcareers.com/career_assessment.html.

The Association of Computer-based Systems for Career Information, http://www.acsci.org, lists Career Information Systems (CIS) offered in each state, such as EUREKA, http://www.EUREKA.org, which provides the following:

- **Career Information** – Employment resources to develop a plan to get started on any career-track. Access Occupational Descriptions on thousands of careers and jobs.
- **Career Assessment** - Use online tools to unlock hidden skills and discover your true personality through True Colors. Match results to promising career options.
- **Colleges and Financial Aid/Scholarships** - Filter through 2,000+ colleges, majors, programs of study, and 6,300+ scholarships and financial aid awards.

Through these resources, educators, jobseekers, students, parents, and agencies can find information on the following topics: career decision-making, choosing a college, researching career descriptions, finding college enrollment levels, discovering your personality traits, and how they relate to others, finding scholarships or college grants, and reviewing job openings.

The free demo of the first lesson of The Job Juggler electronic course, http://www.jobjuggler.net/students.html, contains links to many free and for-fee career and academic assessment tools, as well as career information resources available online. This job search and employability skills course is available for students from high school age on up.

Academic and Career Guidance through Electronic Learning (e-Learning)

Michigan became the first state in the U.S. to require students to successfully complete an online course or learning experience under new legislation signed into law on April 20, 2006. This action was part of a comprehensive legislative package to revamp Michigan's high school graduation requirements, beginning with incoming eighth graders in the fall of 2006.

Our online learning requirement makes Michigan a leader among all the states in using the power of the Internet to create learning opportunities in the classroom, the home and the workplace. In a world that demands lifelong learning, we are giving our students and our state a competitive advantage when it comes to landing the good-paying jobs of the 21st Century economy.
(Governor Jennifer Granholm, cited by Fisher, 2006)

The importance of requiring all students to take an online course today can be compared to the efforts to teach young people how to use print resources in a public library 50 years ago. (Michael Flanagan, State Superintendent of Public Instruction and member of the Michigan Virtual University (MVU) Board of Directors, cited by Fisher, 2006)

In this decade of information overload, e-learning provides an opportunity for students to learn at their own pace and in their environment of choice. Many schools have a Web platform, such as WebCT/Blackboard, where you can design your own curriculum. Alternatively, your school may choose to license an electronic course (e-course) on some aspect of career or life planning that is automated and that requires partial or no instructor intervention. An example of an e-course that offers both options to school counselors is The Job Juggler, http://www.jobjuggler.net. Students can go through the e-course entirely by themselves or you can overview their progress on the e-course by viewing their responses to progress, review, and discussion questions, as well as a final quiz (Gelardin, 2003-6).

By taking an e-course, students become aware that they have mastered a set of skills, such as job search strategies. School counselors will be called upon to become distant educators and distant advisors because of the quantity of students for whom they are responsible.

In Michigan, schools and teachers have options to meet requirements, develop their own online course, or add online components to their coursework curriculum. E-learning is here. Counselors can take the lead!

209

Discovering Your Web Presence and Helping Students Discover Theirs

"According to a recent survey of 100 executive recruiters by ExecutNet, 77 percent of recruiters reported using search engines in an attempt to find information on candidates" (C-Cubed Career Consulting and Coaching, n.d.).You may have an Internet presence and not be aware of it. When your students start looking for jobs or internship experiences, they should be aware of their Web presence.

Search for your name in the following Web addresses on the Internet. Each may have different results and possible surprises.

- http://www.google.com
- http://www.zoominfo.com
- http://www.ask.com
- http://myspace.com

You could also ask your students to search for themselves with these or other search engines. Each search engine has its own way of finding out information about you and may differ from one search engine to another. If you (or your students) don't have a Web presence, then you (and they) can create one. If you already have an Internet presence, you can influence what the search engines show about you.

Managing Your Web Presence

To begin managing your Web presence, set up your own electronic profile (e-profile) on an interactive Internet platform to document your professional development and/or to recruit and communicate with your students. Include the features of "restricted access" and ability to modify your profile at any time. That way, you have more control over your Web presence. Optimally, on an interactive Internet platform, you would have the ability to restrict access to one or more of the following: (a) just yourself, (b) one student and you, (c) a group of students and you, (d) a group of colleagues, (e) a group of individuals who have interests similar to yours, or (f) the whole world.

In addition to setting up your e-profile on the Web, an Internet platform is a good place to communicate with teachers and administrators within your school system through an interactive blog. Your school may be able to provide this capability through its technology services.

Edit this profile | Change site picture | Page help |

Who am I?

As a career professional and educator, my mission is to support you in managing your career and life, two closely closely related concepts. Career used to include just those work activites that produced something of economic value or of service to others, but now it is considered the progression of purposeful activites that you engage in throughout your life, including school years and retirement. Living life fully is a career in itself!

Click on the following links to learn about my counseling/educational services that will empower you in both work and life.

|Services
|New Clients
|Career Practitioners
|About
|Brief Vita
|Communities
|Products, Publications, Presentations
|Contact

–NOTE–

If you ARE interested in joining one of my **Owned communities**, first REGISTER by clicking on "Welcome Guest" or "[Log in]" in the upper left corner of this page.

Join one of the **communities** that I started.

Brief description

| Products | Communities | Career Counseling Services | New Clients | About |

Sally Gelardin
RSS | Tags |
Resources

| Products |
Communities |
Career
Counseling
Services | New
Clients | About |
Contact | Sally's
Mailbox

Recent Activity

View your activity

Owned communities

Lifework Book Clubs

Entrepreneur

ACAeport

JobJuggler

Global Career Development Facilitator (GCDF)

Family Influences

JJBusiness

Creativity

eCDF

If your school does not have this capability, or if you would like to learn about communicating on the Internet with other professionals, parents and community members outside of your school environment, a good place to start is the Lifework Planning Services Web platform (LWPS) http://www.lifeworkps.com. LWPS is based on the same technology as Blackboard and WebCT, the most frequently used college and university Web platforms for communication with students and online course development. On the LWPS Web-learning platform, view http://www.lifeworkps.com/sallyg (See Web site on the preceding page). Browse through the communities listed in the menu on the right side of the page. After you have registered to join LWPS and set up your e-profile, you are welcome to link to http://www.lifeworkps.com/acaeport/ and participate in this e-portfolio community with other counseling and career professionals.

Networking and Blogging

A recent study by the Pew Internet & American Life Project showed that one in five children between the ages of 12 and 17, about 4 million, keep a blog (Web log). About twice that many regularly read them. Some young people use blogs for class assignments, thoughtful journals, or outlets for creativity (Pew Internet, 2006).

If your school has a Web site, you can set up a counselor blog – a Web page journal with words, photos, sound, and art created by an individuals or a group. Blogs may be exclusive postings or an interactive form of communication that welcomes readers to contribute comments or links. Professional blogs or online forums allow you to interact with other career and counseling professionals in an ongoing discussion, generating the feel of a "live" community. A blog is often free.

Some blogging features that would be helpful for communicating with your students are the following:

- Restricted access – allows you to blog exclusively with your students or to set up a blog that is restricted to a community of students, or that is open to the entire school community.
- Keywords – provides way for users to connect with other users who are interested in the same topic that they are.
- HTML links – enables you or your students to link word documents, pictures, movies, sound, and other media from the Web to your blog.

Through online or electronic networking (e-networking), you can create a virtual community of contacts who can provide valuable academic, scholarship, and occupational information, job leads, educational opportunities, industry trends, and potential job and internship/apprenticeship openings.

E-portfolios

An e-portfolio is a personal digital collection of information describing and illustrating a person's learning, career, experience, and achievements. E-portfolios can be used for the following purposes: (a) self-reflection to help students make academic and career decisions; (b) learning to demonstrate how skills have developed over time; and (c) professional use to demonstrate that one has met program or certification requirements, to present skills and accomplishments for employment, and to review professional development for career advancement.

Students usually are required to write essays for college and scholarship applications. Many college applications are electronically delivered. Students from ninth grade on up, and even earlier, can set up e-portfolios, making it easier for counselors and teachers to give students feedback and have more information about the students to write letters of recommendation. If your students have been entering information into their e-portfolio throughout their school experience, it will be easier for them to cut and paste this information into a college e-profile application and employment applications.

You can begin to help more students in this process by learning how to use your school's technology or by encouraging your school to provide platforms on which students can set up e-portfolios, and then guiding students in the use of e-portfolios. For examples of online high school e-portfolios, view http://www.electronicportfolios.com/hs/index.html. More information on e-portfolios can be found in the references section of this chapter (Barrett, n.d.; Gelardin, 2005; Gelardin & Harryman, 2006; Meyer & Lumsden, 2006; Tran, Baker, & Pensavalle, 2006).

Electronic Mailing (E-mailing)

If you are frustrated with disconnected home phones or constant busy signals, and if some students are too timid to discuss something confidential with you in person, then e-mail is another way to provide counseling services to students. Here is an idea. At the beginning of the year, when you visit classrooms, bring a questionnaire that will help you know your students better. Following are a few questions that you might ask:

- What is your name, nickname, home phone, cell phone, and e-mail address?
- What would you like me to know about you?
- What kind of help do you need from your counselor?
- Do you use e-mail or IMing to regularly communicate with your friends?
- What are your favorite Web sites or blogs?
- Would you like to be able to communicate with me through e-mail?

At the end of the questionnaire, write: "What you share will be kept confidential unless I determine what you share will be dangerous to yourself or to someone else." By viewing students' handwriting and content, you also have an idea of where they are academically to assist you in programming their classes.

To make yourself visible and accessible to students, consider creating a business card or brochure, including your picture, and handing it out during your classroom visit. Include your name, school phone, office address, and a special e-mail address for students and parents to contact you.

Text Messaging and Instant Messaging

Text messaging is a rapidly growing communication tool. Read this phrase aloud:

HRU RUOK

Did you understand this phrase (Hint: "H" stands for "How")? Text messaging and instant messaging (IMing) are technology tools that have captured the attention of young people. Have you ever watched students rapidly text messaging on their cell phones or computers? The advantage of IMing on a computer is that in contrast to e-mail or phone, the parties know whether their peer is online.

It behooves parents and educators to pay attention to their children's text messaging to protect them from more than embarrassment and gossip. Cyberbullying can be serious, even lead to suicide. Author Marilyn Harryman's first experience with text messaging, as counselor coordinator for a large district, was most dramatic and poignant when a student was killed in a gang-related murder the night before. Marilyn recalls:

I was immediately called to support staff and students at the local high school. Working closely with the assistant principal, girls were brought together who knew the young man. In our time together, I became keenly aware of their cell phone calls and rapid

fingers. Somehow I gained their trust, and to my surprise, they willingly shared with me the messages sent by the boys off campus. The immediate, real time connections they made, sharing fears, love and concern for each other, deeply touched me. I am forever grateful to them for opening that world. They opened up and were also empowered because they were teaching/sharing something in a safe place. I was empowered to better gain trust and to understand and penetrate the broader circle of influence in this case, possibly forestalling further violence.

Forever changing, text messaging lingo can be found at http://www.Webopedia.com/quick_ref/textmessagea bbreviations.asp

Keeping up with the times, using an instant messenger such as those found on Google Talk, Yahoo, AOL, and MSN Messenger to respond directly to patron's questions, librarians in Livermore, California, have put themselves in the online, instant messaging (IMing) "hot seat" from 3 p.m. to 5 p.m. four days a week. Because IMing is a major means of communication among school-age children, those hours are good ones for doing homework (Blevins, n.d.). Why not for counseling? When a counselor is at the computer at specified times anyway or when offices are typically closed, an instant message from a student with a quick question or needing support could be answered with little disruption for the counselor. Students in danger of harming themselves or others might decide to "talk" to you first. Frequently asked questions could be quickly answered with a "cut and paste" if responses were in the computer, already prepared ahead of time for a flier or a Web site.

No longer in the future, technology is here for "Wiffiti", wireless graffiti in which text messages can be projected on a wall. "Mobile devices are in a unique position to enable new forms of communication within groups and crowds." Already used in cafes, Wiffiti can ultimately give people a way to stay engaged with each other instead of disconnecting from society by plugging into games and music ("The Writing on the Wall," 2006). Perhaps schools and counselors can take advantage of this as well.

Problems that May Arise In Cyber-Communication

LOUISVILLE, Ky. -- MySpace.com is wildly popular. It started up back in January of 2004 and now claims more than 47 million registered users. But some local schools are sending home notes telling parents beware . . . "Think about it -- there are predators out

there. And we're putting children in harm's way. Why would we do that?" Tom Robbins, director of counseling for Louisville's Catholic schools, says "MySpace.com should be off limits to anyone under 18." (Flanagan, 2006)

A new challenge for counselors and administrators is to teach students and parents "netiquette." Students are usually not aware of the consequences of some of their online posts; their comments may be viewed by thousands beyond the one or few they initially intended. Many educators regularly check MySpace and other Web sites to discover what their students are saying to help protect them from potential harm.

Deborah Finlay, guidance director at a middle school in Virginia, first tuned into the dangers of blogging when a student committed suicide. Cyberbullying appeared to be a big factor. Her goal is to raise awareness about the dangers of the Internet, one child at a time. Finlay pointed out that many students have two blogs -- "a nice one, and a bad one." "The way I deal with it is to find kids' blogs online and alert the parents," Finlay said. "I'll call and say, 'I would like Susy to show you her blog'." Noting that students are "sophisticated with technology but socially immature," she and other guidance staff conduct regular "netiquette" sessions with every class on safety and bullying and also educate parents who in many cases, are "just as naive as the kids" (Finlay, 2006a).

Bernard Piel, a history teacher and assistant to the dean at Norman Thomas High School in New York, talked to a student who posted provocative photos. Consider sharing his approach with your students. Piel said to his student, "I want you to imagine that you're 24 years old, you're trying to get a job somewhere, Human Resources does a background check, and these things come up" (Finlay, 2006b).

Students can receive threatening e-mail, have their password changed, and be signed up for embarrassing pornographic Web sites without their permission. With counselor awareness, classroom presentations can prepare students for the dangers, as well as the fun. Here are safety tips from the National Center for Missing and Exploited Children that you can use for your presentation. You can copy and paste it from the Web site http://www. missingkids.com/missingkids/servlet/PageServlet?Languag eCountry=en_US&PageId=207 (Magid, 1998).

Internet-Related Safety Tips for Teens

1. Don't give out personal information about yourself, your family situation, your school, your telephone number, or your address.

2. If you become aware of the sharing, use, or viewing of child pornography online, immediately report this to the National Center for Missing & Exploited Children at 1-800-843-5678.

3. When in chatrooms, remember that not everyone may be who they say they are. For example a person who says "she" is a 14-year-old girl from New York may really be a 42-year-old man from California.[1]

4. If someone harasses you online, says anything inappropriate, or does anything that makes you feel uncomfortable, contact your Internet service provider.

5. Know that there are rules many Internet Service Providers (ISP) have about online behavior. If you disobey an ISP's rules, your ISP may penalize you by disabling your account, and sometimes every account in a household, either temporarily or permanently.

6. Consider volunteering at your local library, school, or Boys & Girls Club to help younger children online. Many schools and nonprofit organizations are in need of people to help set up their computers and Internet capabilities.

7. A friend you meet online may not be the best person to talk to if you are having problems at home, with your friends, or at school - remember the teenage "girl" from New York in Tip number three? If you can't find an adult in your school, church, club, or neighborhood to talk to, Covenant House is a good place to call at 1-800-999-9999. The people there provide counseling to kids, refer them to local shelters, help them with law enforcement, and can serve as mediators by calling their parents.

8. If you are thinking about running away, a friend from online (remember the 14-year-old girl) may not be the best person to talk to. If there is no adult in your community you can find to talk to, call the National Runaway Switchboard at 1-800-621-4000. Although some of your online friends may seem to really listen to you, the Switchboard will be able to give you honest, useful answers to some of your questions about what to do when you are depressed, abused, or thinking about running away.[2]

(1) Adapted from *Teen Safety on the Information Highway* by Lawrence J. Magid. Copyright© respectively 1994 and 1998 National Center for Missing & Exploited Children (NCMEC). All rights reserved.

(2) Adapted from *Children Online: The ABCs for Parenting: When Is Your Child Ready* by The Children's Partnership. Reprinted with permission of The Children's Partnership. http://www.childrenspartnership.org

Conclusion

Here are a few suggested strategies that you might use to connect with students through distance delivery systems:

1. Survey all of your students for best ways to contact them by distance. Ask for their personal cell phone number and e-mail addresses. Give them an e-mail address you have set up just for them to contact you. A student can help you set up an e-mail database. Monitor it every day.

2. Ask how many students regularly use cell phones, text messaging and e-mail. Ask permission to contact them this way in your survey to clarify potential problems. Be aware that there may be a major divide between students who have the computers, cell phones, iPods, and those who don't.

3. Develop a counseling page on your school site and/or district's Web site, if not already in existence. Explain in faculty meetings and update the site regularly, so staff and students can view it at their convenience.

4. Devote part of your day/week to monitor and to deliver essential messages to students/staff and parents who use e-mail regularly. Consider setting up designated instant messaging hours for students needing a quick response from a counselor.

5. Familiarize yourself with current communication systems available and possibilities for use, which can include the school's media class and/or cableTV/radio station. Instant messaging, virtual support groups, blogs, virtual job clubs, e-portfolios, podcasting, digital story-telling, e-forums, online courses (as well as cyber-high schools), career/college information Web sites, and online assessment tools.

6. If you decide to have a forum for students on a designated Web site, someone needs to monitor it. Students in trouble, as well as those prone to bullying, can sometimes be identified and appropriately counseled.

7. Support students who are on independent study, short day, out for long-term illness, or out of the country. For foreign-born students who must leave with their parents at inconvenient times, you might be able to connect with a school in their community and provide credit instead of the student losing a whole semester's work because of missed exams and reports.

8. Develop new skills and earn continuing education units (CEUs) for your professional development. Below are five distance counseling and training programs for you to consider for your professional development:

- *Cybercounseling: Going the Distance for Your Clients* (Bloom, Walz, & Ford, 2003).
- *Job Search Practitioner Training* (Gelardin, 2003).
- *Distance Credentialed Counseling Training Program*, (ReadyMinds, 2003).
- *eLearning Career Development Facilitator Training* (National Career Development Association, 2008).
- *eCDF Career Development Facilitator Training* (Floyd & Gelardin, 2008).

The authors' recommendation is to "Just do it!" It is possible to expand your counseling program and effectively support students "from a distance." Our intent has been to stimulate thinking on how you can enhance your program, as well as provide more opportunity for "real-time" attention to those who need you most. We would love to hear comments from you and learn about your efforts to use new cybertools in your counseling program.

Note: If you would like an electronic copy of this chapter to more easily access references and resources, please contact one of the authors. If you have trouble accessing any of the specific Web site locations, a strategy would be to access the Web site and do a search within the Web site for the particular article or topic. For example, if you want to find "Blog Beware," then link to the following URL: http://www.missingkids.com/missingkids/servlet/ResourceServlet?LanguageCountry=en_US&PageId=2361. If this doesn't work (probably because it has so many letters and numbers, that it is easy to make a mistake), try the abbreviated version: http://www.missingkids.com. Then, once you are on that Web site, click on "site search" at the bottom of the page, and do a search for "Blog Beware."

Table of Distance Delivery Tools

Delivery	Definition	Examples
Audio	Audio communication delivered over the Internet (streaming) or downloadable onto handheld devices.	Career Expert Audio Interviews http://www.jobjuggler.net/careerexpertaudios.html Balancing Career with Caregiving http://www.AskDrSal.com
Blended delivery	A mixture of in-class and distance learning.	Job Juggler's Global Career Development Facilitator (GCDF)Training http://www.jobjuggler.net/careerprofessionals.html
Bio-Optic Organized Knowledge device (BOOK)	BOOK is constructed of sequentially numbered sheets of paper (recyclable), each capable of holding thousands of bits of information.	http://www.jumbojoke.com/the_biooptic_organized_knowledge_device_490.html
Blog, (Web log)	A type of Web site where comments much like a journal or diary are made and displayed in a reverse chronological order.	http://www.networkworld.com/allstar/2006/092506-open-source-saugus-union-school-district.html
CD (Compact Disc)	CD: a disk used to store audio digital data.	World Wide Web Boot Camp for School Counselors – CD http://www.schoolcounselor.com/cd/
DVD (Digital Video Disc or Digital Versatile Disc, DVD-Rom)	Disk storage media format that can be include movies with high video and sound quality. They look the same as CD's but they are encoded in a different format and at a much higher density.	DVD Surviving Trauma & Tragedy: Lessons For Future Physicians & Mental Health Professionals. A wonderful tool for educating and sensitizing medical students to the issues of trauma. How to assist them in recovering their strength, dignity and resiliency. Description and Clips at http://www.giftfromwithin.org, Contact JoyceB3955@aol.com (207) 236-8858.
CATV (Community Antenna Television, Cable)	System of providing television, FM radio programming and other services to consumers via radio frequency signals transmitted directly to people's televisions through fixed optical fibers or coaxial cables as opposed to the over-the-air method in traditional TV broadcasting.	KDOL, *CCC Live! The Counselor-Community Connection* Contact author at marilynhar@aol.com for sample tapes and more information.
Cyber counseling	Counseling through distance technology, such as Internet, e-mail,	Bloom, J., Walz, G., & Ford, D. (2003). *Cybercounseling: Going the Distance for Your*

	Webinar, and teleconferencing.	*Clients.* Retrieved July 15, 2008, from http://www.counseling.org/AM/Template.cfm?Section=CONTINUING_EDUCATION_ONLINE#online. NBCC approved.
Digital storytelling	Tools of digital media to craft, record, share, and value the stories of individuals and communities, in ways that improve all our lives.	http://www.storycenter.org/
Educational TV on the Web	ETV's educational Web portal, a collection of fun, interactive Web sites for K-12 students, teachers and parents.	http://www.knowitall.org/
Electronic newsletter	Newsletter delivered over the Internet.	http://www.schoolcounselor.org/
e-Book	Books in digital form that can be read online or downloaded onto an electronic device such as an iPod.	http://www.jobjuggler.net/Practitioner_Manual_demo.pdf
e-Portfolio	Online portfolio – Personal digital collection of information describing and illustrating a person's learning, career, experience and achievements. E-portfolios are privately owned and the owner has complete control over who has access to what and when.	http://www.electronicportfolios.com Croonquist, C. Portfolios = portable proof! (2004). *Career Convergence.* Retrieved July 15, 2008, from http://www.ncda.org. Search within Web site for "Croonquist."
IM (Instant Messaging) IChat	A form of real-time communication between two or more people based on typed text conveyed via computers connected over a network such as the Internet.	http://www.teachingtechie.typepad.com/learning/2004/09/iming_revolutio.html http://www.jcmc.indiana.edu/vol11/issue2/bryant.html http://www.Webquest.org/bdodge/2002/09/iming-with-a-boy.html
iPod	A brand of portable media player which can also serve as an external data storage device when connected to a computer.	Software used for transferring music, photos and videos is called iTunes, http://www.en.wikipedia.org/wiki/ITunes . The most recent version of iTunes has photo and video synchronization features.
Mentor or mentoring	Person or program that facilitates the personal and professional growth of others.	http://www.mentors.ca/mentorprograms.html
MP3 files	A digital format for people to collect, listen to, and distribute music.	http://www.howstuffworks.com/mp3.htm
Online course	Course that is administered and graded on the Internet. May be self-paced, with built-on online assessment to measure learning outcomes.	• *Cybercounseling: Going the Distance for Your Clients* (Bloom et al., 2003). http://www.counselor.org . • *Job Search Practitioner Training* (Gelardin, 2008).

		reader you choose will have instructions for how to subscribe to RSS feeds.
Teleseminar	Audio communication delivered electronically in real time.	http://www.jobjuggler.net/careerexpertaudios.html http://www.lifeworks.com/tele
Text messaging	A service on most digital mobile phones, a Pocket PC, or desktop computer that permits the sending of short messages (also known as text messages, texts or even txts) between mobile phones and/or computers.	http://www.innovateonline.info/index.php?view=article&id=219 . View Global Nomads Group (GNG) http://www.Webopedia.com/quick_ref/textmessageabbreviations.asp.
Videotape	Electronic tape used to record sign and sound for subsequent playback on TV monitors.	http://www.beneficialfilmguides.com/. Learn to recognize mental health disorders from Hollywood movies. NBCC approved.
Video Webcast	Video communication delivered over the Internet (streaming) or downloadable onto handheld devices.	http://www.counseling.org. Link to Gore/Lewis keynote speeches. http://www.innovateonline.info . Open access e-journal published by the Fischler School of Education and Social Services at Nova Southeastern University. These Webcasts are produced as a public service by ULiveandLearn.
V-log, Videoblog	A blog that includes video or video link with supporting text and images.	Using a digital camera, video footage can be inserted in a blog. Upload your own video to include or send to a site that features private videos.
Webinar	Online meeting and presentation tools used for conferencing on the Internet.	http://www.bridges.com/us/training/index.html
Web site	In addition to school Web sites, your state department of education may have a comprehensive Web site of resources.	http://www.ed.sc.gov/
Wiffiti	Digital graffiti. Using a computer or cell phone, text and instant messages can be projected on a wall in any public place.	http://www.Wiffiti.com

		reader you choose will have instructions for how to subscribe to RSS feeds.
Teleseminar	Audio communication delivered electronically in real time.	http://www.jobjuggler.net/careerexpertaudios.html http://www.lifeworks.com/tele
Text messaging	A service on most digital mobile phones, a Pocket PC, or desktop computer that permits the sending of short messages (also known as text messages, texts or even txts) between mobile phones and/or computers.	http://www.innovateonline.info/index.php?view=article&id=219 . View Global Nomads Group (GNG) http://www.Webopedia.com/quick_ref/textmessageabbreviations.asp.
Videotape	Electronic tape used to record sign and sound for subsequent playback on TV monitors.	http://www.beneficialfilmguides.com/. Learn to recognize mental health disorders from Hollywood movies. NBCC approved.
Video Webcast	Video communication delivered over the Internet (streaming) or downloadable onto handheld devices.	http://www.counseling.org. Link to Gore/Lewis keynote speeches. http://www.innovateonline.info . Open access e-journal published by the Fischler School of Education and Social Services at Nova Southeastern University. These Webcasts are produced as a public service by ULiveandLearn.
V-log, Videoblog	A blog that includes video or video link with supporting text and images.	Using a digital camera, video footage can be inserted in a blog. Upload your own video to include or send to a site that features private videos.
Webinar	Online meeting and presentation tools used for conferencing on the Internet.	http://www.bridges.com/us/training/index.html
Web site	In addition to school Web sites, your state department of education may have a comprehensive Web site of resources.	http://www.ed.sc.gov/
Wiffiti	Digital graffiti. Using a computer or cell phone, text and instant messages can be projected on a wall in any public place.	http://www.Wiffiti.com

Discussion Questions

1. How could you become more accessible to students through distance communication?
2. What are two or three distance communication systems that you have never used before?
3. What local resources can you identify to take advantage of distance opportunities to support student achievement and planning for the future?
4. What strategies can you use to connect with students and parents through distance?
5. How can you discover and manage your own Web presence?
6. How can you use text messaging to be available to students at specified times when you or they are otherwise unavailable?
7. What challenges might you encounter with cyber-communication?
8. What are some problems your students might encounter?
9. How can you protect a student from cyber bullying?
10. How can you employ distance communication to support students who are on independent study, long-term illness, or out of the country?
11. What are some ways you might develop new communication skills while earning continuing educational units for your own professional development?

References

The American School Counselor Association. Retrieved June 7, 2008, from http://www.schoolcounselor.org/

Barrett, H. (n.d.). *Electronic Portfolio Development and Digital Storytelling*. Retrieved June 7, 2008, from http://www.electronicportfolios.com

Blevins, L. (n.d.). *Librarians are just a click away. Livermore: New instant-messaging service helps those with questions get a quicker response.* Retrieved June 7, 2008, from http://www.contra costatimes.com

Bloom, J., Walz, G., & Ford, D. (2003). *Cybercounseling: Going the distance for your clients.* Retrieved June 7, 2008, from http://www.counseling.org/AM/Template.cfm?Section=CONTINUING_EDUCATION_ONLINE#online

Bolles, R. (2007). What color is your parachute: A practical manual for job-hunters and career changers (Pre Publication Flier). Berkeley, CA: Ten Speed Press. Retrieved June 7, 2008, from http://www.jobhuntersbible.com/articles/article.php?art_item=013

Carnevale, D. (2006). E-Mail is for Old People, As students ignore their campus accounts, colleges try new ways of communicating [Electronic version]. *The Chronicle of Higher Education.* Retrieved Retrieved June 7, 2008, from http://chronicle.com/free/v53/i07/07a02701.htm

C-Cubed Career Consulting & Coaching. (n.d.). *Before you look for a job, you better google yourself.* Retrieved June 7, 2008, from http://www.newsletter@ccubedcareer.com/

Croonquist, C. (2004). *Portfolios = portable proof!* Retrieved June 7, 2008, from http://www.ncda.org (Search Croonquist)

Finlay, D. (2006a). *News from the dangers of blogging and our kids... Did you know...* Retrieved June 7, 2008, from http://www.spotsylvania.k12.va.us/News/School%20Board/cyberbullying/did%20you%20know.pdf

Finlay, D. (2006b, Spring, 29). *A lot more the school can do.* Retrieved June 7, 2008, from http://www.tolerance.org/teach/magazine/features.jsp?p=0&is=38&ar=653&pa=2

Fisher, K. (2006). *Michigan to require "online courses" for high school graduation.* Retrieved September 1, 2006, from http://www.arstechnica.com/news.ars/post/20060423-6657.html

Flanagan, M. (2006). In Seymour, T. *Growing concern over Myspace.com.* Retrieved June 7, 2008, from http://www.whas11.com/education/stories/WHAS11_TOP_MySpace.11ea4141.html

Florida, R. (2002). *The rise of the creative class.* Retrieved June 7, 2008, from http://www.washingtonmonthly.com/features/2001/0205.florida.html

Floyd, R., & Gelardin, S. (2008). *eLearning Career Development Facilitator Training.* Retrieved June 7, 2008, from http://www.lifeworkps.com/eCDF

Gelardin, S. (2008). *Job Search Practitioner e-course.* Retrieved June 7, 2008, from http://www.jobjuggler.net/jsp/1jumpstart.html

Gelardin, S. (2006). *The Job Juggler's Web-based job search and employability program for career practitioners and their clients.* Retrieved June 7, 2008, from http://www.jobjuggler.net

Gelardin, S. (2004). *Career Assessment eMaps.* (sal@jobjuggler.net; Based on Chritton, S., Career Assessment Maps. SLC4PWAYS@aol.com)

Gelardin, S. (2005). ePortfolio presentation. Retrieved June 7, 2008, from http://www.jobjuggler.net/NCDA_ePort.pdf

Gelardin, S., & Harryman, M. (2006). *ePortfolios are replacing resumes: Are you ready?* Paper presented at American Counseling Association 2006 Convention, Montreal. Retrieved June 7, 2008, from http://www.counselor.org (view http://www.lifeworkps.com/ACAePort)

Harryman, M. (2008). *CCC LIVE! The Counselor Community Connection*, KDOL 27. (Contact: marilynhar@aol.com)

Magid, L. J. (1998). *Teen safety on the information highway.* National Center for Missing & Exploited children (NCMEC). Retrieved June 7, 2008, from http://www.missingkids.com/missingkids/servlet/PageServlet?LanguageCountry=en_US&PageId=207.

Meyer, K., & Lumsden, J. (2008). Online career portfolios: Reactions from users and employers. *Career Convergence.* Retrieved June 7, 2008, from http://www.ncda.org (Search "Meyer" or "Lumsden")

National Career Development Association. (2008). *Career development facilitator training.* Retrieved June 7, 2008, from http://www.ncda.org (Click on "Credentialing Programs")

Pew Internet & American Life Project (2006). Retrieved June 7, 2008, from http://www.csmonitor.com/2006/0202/p01s04-stct.htm http://www.Webopedia.com/quick_ref/textmessageabbreviations.aspA3

Readyminds. (2003). Distance Credentialed Counselor Training. Retrieved June 7, 2008, from http://www.readyminds.com

Tran, T., Baker, R.; & Pensavalle, M. (2008). *Designing eportfolios to support professional teacher preparation.* Retrieved June 7, 2008, from http://209.85.173.104/search?q=cache:B8gkiz4sSv8J:www.ascilite.org.au/conferences/sydney06/proceeding/pdf_papers/p108.pdf+Tran,+T.,+Baker,+R.%3B+%26+Pensavalle,+M.+Designing+eportfolios+to+support+professional+teacher+preparation&hl=en&ct=clnk&cd=1&gl=us&client=firefox-a.

The Writing on the Wall. (2006). *The Economist. Economist Technology Quarterly*, p. 18.

Wilczenski, F. L., & Coomey, S. M. (2006). Cyber-Communicating: Finding its place in school counseling practice, education, and professional development. *Professional School Counseling, 94*, 327-331.

Zinko, C. (2006). Why tlk whn u cn txt? - Many raised in era of e-mail and texting shun conversation. They call electronic voice 'authentic' [Electronic version, September 22, 2006]. *San Francisco Chronicle.*

Additional Resources

Bloom, J., Walz, G., & Ford, D. (Eds.) (2005). *Cybercounseling and cyberlearning: Strategies and resources for the millennium.* American Counseling Association (Corporate Author). Caps Inc. (Corporate Author), and Eric Counseling and Student Services Clearinghouse (Corporate Author). Retrieved September 1, 2006, from http://www.counseling.org

Cyber Safety for Children. Retrieved October 30, 2006, from www.cybersafety.ca.gov

ELGG. Free hosted service and open Web source; fully-featured electronic portfolio, Weblog and social networking system, connecting learners and creating communities of learning. Retrieved September 1, 2006, from http://www.elgg.net

ePort Consortium. Association of individuals and higher education and IT commercial institutions interested in the development of academic ePortfolio software systems. Retrieved September 1, 2006, from http://www.eportconsortium.org/

Gelardin, S. (2005). Professional Development Institute #1 Presentation *Bringing Career Development Home: Traditional and Electronic Ways the Family Can Support Career Decision-Making.* National Career Development Association 2005 Conference.

Gelardin, S. (2004, December). Career practitioner as distance educator: A personal perspective. *Career Convergence.* Retrieved June 8, 2008, from http://www.ncda.org. Search for "Gelardin."

Hubbard, P. Lifework Planning Services for virtual space on the Internet where users can manage their personal and career development over their lifespan. Retrieved June 8, 2008, from http://www.lifeworkps.com

Jackson, L. *A techtorial: Education World. E-Porfolio Fever.* : http://www.educationworld.com

Myspace, an online community for creating profile, personal network, search other members. Retrieved June 8, 2008, from http://www.myspace.com

National Career Development Association. *Guidelines for the use of the Internet for provision of career information and planning services*. Retrieved June 8, 2008, from http://www.ncda.org. View "Guidelines"

Paulson, A. (2006, February 02 edition). *Schools grapple with policing student's online journals*. Retrieved June 8, 2008: http://www.csmonitor.com/2006/0202/p01s04-stct.html

Printable Resources for Parent and Kids from Web Wise Kids. Retrieved June 8, 2008, from http://www.wiredwithwisdom.org/parent_resources.asp

Sabella, R. *SchoolCounselor.com 2.0: A friendly and practical guide to the World Wide Web*. Retrieved June 8, 2008, from http://www.schoolcounselor.com

Web Wise Kids – Equipping Today's Youth to Make Wise Choices. Retrieved June 8, 2008, from www.wiredwithwisdom.org/

Zoominfo, a targeted search engine that enables user to set up own eportfolio, find others who may or may not be members of platform; create or add to existing ePortfolio. Retrieved June 8, 2008, from http://www.zoominfo.com

Chapter 22

The Impact of Cyber-Communication on the
Personal, Social, and Emotional Growth of Today's Youth

Marie A. Wakefield and Cynthia J. Rice

Abstract

Cyber-communication has become an integral part of the culture of today's youth. Through cyberspace, such venues as emails, text messaging, chat rooms, and blogging provide the means for unlimited information shared instantaneously over great distances. However, the extraordinary growth of electronic media is not without concern. This chapter briefly explores the pros and cons of various communication modalities that may have significant outcomes on personal, social, and emotional growth. The authors also discuss some initial indicators that are emerging and provide strategies and interventions that counselors can use to assist youth in the cyber-communication age of today.

Introduction

Although the Internet is useful for educational, career, and entertainment purposes, adults are fearful of its influence on today's youth. Research done by the Pew Internet and American Life Project (Lenhart, Rainie, & Lewis, 2001) found that the Internet has a pivotal role in the lives of American teenagers (see Appendix A). It has been found that 87% of the youth of today go online (Weiss, 2005b), representing 21 million youth. Teens go online to chat with family and friends, kill boredom, expand their knowledge, and follow the latest trends. The advances in technology that provide opportunities for our youth to reach out to new sources of knowledge and cultural experiences are not without challenges. Conversations may range from the mundane to the emotionally charged events of the day. A set of hieroglyphics and lists of abbreviations, text messaging, instant messaging, chat rooms, and personal Web sites increase the speed of multiple, simultaneous interaction. However, as we embrace the rapidly changing modes of communication in the new millennium, there is a need for school counselors to assist parents and school personnel in protecting their students from harm and victimization.

According to the latest research presented in a special issue of *Developmental Psychology* published by the American Psychological Association (APA Press, 2006), spending a lot of time on the Web can have both positive and negative effects on youth. This chapter will discuss some initial indicators that are emerging and provide strategies and interventions that counselors can use to assist youth in the cyber-communication age of today.

Cyber-Communication Influences Youth in the Personal Domain

According to Webopedia, the online encyclopedia dedicated to computer technology, cyber is a prefix used to describe new experiences spread by the use of computers or the Internet (Webopedia, 2006). In the personal domain, there are several factors, which contribute to issues related to the use of cyber-communication, a major factor in how children communicate.

Cyber-communication provides unlimited access to information for our young people. In day care centers and preschool programs, facilities are outfitted with cameras, so parents may see their child at any time of day from a computer at work. Elementary students access current information for educational reports and counseling resources. According to Educator Peter Carey (1997), the Internet is acclaimed by many as heralding a new era in global information sharing and becoming a more active rather than passive resource for information. On the secondary level, teachers are using the Internet as a vehicle to receive reports and essays with date and time. Additionally, teachers can check online for plagiarism and validity.

There is an ever-increasing plethora of communication devices that have become indispensable parts of our children's daily lives (Seel, 1997). This has created the growing phenomenon of cyber-tasking, Internet multitasking (Bradley, 2005), where children work with several computer screens to access information from many different sources. Cyber-communication offers opportunities for valued learning, responsibility, and independence. Students can learn to manage time and resources effectively; master the art of accessing and processing skills gained in a meaningful context, and communicate this information clearly to the intended audience. Integrating the Internet with communication allows students to share personal perspectives, knowledge and experiences, and structure discussions for debate.

Access to grades is available on Web sites for parents and students at all times. For post-secondary counseling, students can take virtual tours of any college campus, complete all college applications, and retrieve scholarship availability.

The negative side of cyber-communication is the access to personal information. With the press of a button, you can find out where someone lives, a phone number, even directions to someone's house. It is becoming increasingly hard to protect children from unsafe access to their personal information. Children use chat rooms as vehicles for communication which are places where sexual predators can make contact with children. Myspace.com and similar Web sites offer a personalized platform for exchanging messages with "friends" (Payne, 2006). In most cases kids are safe maintaining a profile on Myspace or other social networks; however, one in five youth ages 10 to17 received unwanted sexual advances online (Olsen, 2006). Nearly half of the offenders were other youth and there are a large number that go unreported (Wolak, Mitchell, & Finkelhor, 1999).

Some sites expose personal blogging to others, illegal videoing of children, and the techniques for acts of violence. Youth are also exposed to pornography and illegal Web sites popping up on their computer screens. Twenty-five percent of youth indicate they were exposed to unwanted pornography (Fleming & Rickwood, 2004). The number of pornographic Web pages jumped from 14 million in 1998 to 260 million in 2003 (Weiss, 2005a). Although the unlimited access to information is a positive, now it is increasingly difficult to keep children safe from giving information with unwanted consequences or being exposed to harmful information. Although school counselors routinely provide interventions to balance personal, social, and emotional growth, interacting through cyber-communication is creating a new dimension.

Cyber-Communication Influences Youth in the Social Domain

With the use of cellular phones, text messages, e-mails, and instant messaging, we are communicating more and more through the written word or our voice more than fact-to-face contact. For example, youth have adopted instant messaging (IMing) and text messaging rather quickly because these technologies are more convenient, less expensive, and faster than the traditional methods of communication. The ability to time-shift and talk at non-traditional times are added incentives (Bryant, Sanders-Jackson, & Smallwood, 2006).

Communicating through the Internet has expanded the social circle. Youth are actively using the Internet as an important form of social interaction (Brignall & Valey, 2005). Some research results have reported an improvement of relationships with friends (Freeman-Longo, 2000; Lenhart et al., 2001). No longer does the social circle have to be limited to geographic locations. There is a "virtual" rather then "physical" presence (Pankoke-Babatz & Jeffrey, 2002). Many chat rooms, featuring instantaneous responses, are selected by topics of interest. Young people geographically remote, disabled, or housebound due to illness may find online chat an important form of communication (Fleming & Rickwood, 2004).

Cyber-communication today is not face-to-face, although video conferencing and Webinar access are forthcoming for youth. Thus, it helps children, who might not otherwise be confident, to communicate quite well over the Internet. Many youth feel that they can be themselves online and that looks don't count (Globus, 2002). Brignall & Valey (2005) in their article, "The Impact of Internet Communications on Social Interaction," stated that a fundamental position is that online social interaction is one form of role play, thus an element in the development of self.

Due to increased use of cyber-communication, a feeling of being autonomous also exists. There is less direct human contact. Families talk less face-to-face. Teenagers would rather text a neighbor than go next door to talk in person. Passing notes in class is now done via text messaging. Social isolation for adolescents and the impact on family relations is a concern (Littlefield, 2004).

Gender, stage in the life cycle, cultural milieu, social economic status, and offline connections are all factors that are part of online interaction. Many children have several on-line identities and because of the inability to connect the cyber-name with a real person, they write things that they might not otherwise express. They use "digital disguises" (Rudman, 2006). There are no social boundaries or social contracts and very few know proper "netiquette," the rules for Internet use.

Research suggests that there are differences between relationships formed through computer-mediated communication (Bryant et al., 2006). There is increasing freedom to harass and use put-downs because there are no repercussions personally. The views are expressed anonymously, and with the lack of non-verbal cues, a great amount of cyber-communication may lead to inappropriate behavior (Ybarra & Mitchell, 2004). This creates cyber-bullying, cyber-stalking, cyber-harassment conversations, or "flaming," a public personal attack, where people demonstrate verbal aggression. One of the recognized instances in cyber-bullying occurred when Eric Harris, one of the killers in the Columbine High School massacre, put up a Web site where he discussed murdering fellow students. Other observed differences include the open display of group norm violations such as racism, sexism, and homophobia (Brignall & Valey, 2005).

Discussions of suicide, self-mutilation, harming oneself or someone else are prevalent on the Internet. Using a search engine, suicide Web sites can be found in seconds (Becker, Mayer, Nagenborg, El-faddagh, & Schmidt, 2004). We, as counselors, have control over creating a safe environment in schools, but with more youth communicating through cyber-space, we no longer are able to directly help youth with social interactions.

Another consequence of forming a cyber relationship is the possibility of encountering a pedophile. One in five young people reported receiving a sexual solicitation or approach over the last year, and one in 30 received an aggressive solicitation (Weiss, 2005a). Cyber-guidance lessons are vital in our deliverance today of "stranger danger." Teaching children safe ways to deal with cyber-communication in order to create healthy social relationships is a key role in our counselor, parent, and student interactions.

Cyber-Communication Influences Youth in the Emotional Domain

The increased use of communication and entertainment technologies through search engines on the Internet has created the potential for negative experiences. The Internet is increasingly being accessed as a key resource for issues relating to anything from abuse to self-help. It is also used as a vehicle for youth to express themselves. Now, many students access healthy resources like suicide hotlines, support groups, information on medical conditions, and contact with appropriate organizations. This interaction helps to give them a support system outside of their immediate environment to assist them in dealing with emotional issues.

The Internet is being used as a vehicle for expression by youth. Middle and high school students have a great interest in "social networking" through such sites as Myspace.com, Xanga, Facebook, and Live Journal. They are using blogging as a place to write journals, diaries, and poems. Students, who won't write anything during journal writing time in a classroom, write pages of self-expression on the Internet. As educators, we need to start using this form of expression as a part of our curriculum.

On the negative side, this ability to find resources regarding the emotional domain can be harmful. There are hemlock (suicide) societies on-line. There is information on how to build bombs, self-mutilate, be sexually active, participate in drug use, and many other illegal and illicit activities (Payne, 2006). Youth find Web sites through search engines in seconds to find out information on harming themselves or someone else. Thirty percent of all adolescents have suicidal thoughts, and over half of them use the Web (Becker et al., 2004). Lisa, 17, visited suicide Web forums, where she researched reliable methods, contacted an anonymous user, and purchased substances. Children are exposed to unhealthy emotional ideas and outlets that they otherwise would not be aware of until a more mature age normally (Becker et al., 2004).

Cyber-bullying and online harassment are a major source of negative emotional exposure to youth. A study done in 2005 found that one-third of youth reported being victimized online (Wikipedia, 2006). Cyber-bullying occurs more often; because first, electronic bullies can remain "virtually" anonymous, and second, electronic forums lack supervision (Wikipedia, 2006). A notable example was the Stars Wars kid whose classmates uploaded illegally obtained video footage of him posing as Star Wars character Darth Maul onto Kazaa in 2003. The footage was downloaded extensively and modified causing the subject extensive embarrassment resulting in treatment at a psychiatric hospital (Wikipedia, 2006). Camera phones are being used to send, copy, edit, and post nude photos of fellow students (United Educators, 2004).

Knowledge of students talking online about harming themselves and someone else is not readily available. To access this information in order to help students, counselors rely on other youth who visit the same chat rooms, Web spaces, or blogging sites. It is the counselor's role to assist youth with their emotional stability. For example, when there was a death, a crisis plan was designed to help the faculty and students deal with their shock and grief. Now, when there is a death, students are e-mailing and texting their feelings.

Strategies and Interventions for Counselors Dealing with Cyber-Communication

There are many strategies and interventions counselors can use today to deal with cyber-communication and helping youth. We have to change our focus on dealing with youth and their needs if we are to be effective in the 21st century. We must become Cyber-Counselors and use the Internet as an increasingly effective source of information. It is a great resource for educational, emotional, and post-secondary information. If we are to stay current with our information, it is vital that we use the Internet as a resource and teach our students to use the Internet as a healthy resource of information. A counselor's knowledge of cyber vocabulary/terminology is key to understanding communication on the Internet (see Glossary of Cyber Terms, Appendix B).

Cyber-Safety is an important aspect of counseling today. It is important that we train parents and children to be aware of cyber-safety and to avoid victimization, including sexual solicitations and harassment. Teachers can integrate instruction into the curriculum and the classroom to address plagiarism, cheating, and other forms of unethical communication methods.

Cyber-Lessons are vital in the classroom and in the counselor's office. Those lessons may include: critiquing an instant/text message or an email to understand the message/messenger, discussing "netiquette," reviewing appropriate use of MySpace.com, reading various pieces written for expression of poetry or other literary forms on blogs, and demonstrating the use of software with positive benefits (see examples of MySpace.com, instant messaging, text messaging, & blogging in Appendices B, C, D, & E). We need to take advantage of those "teachable moments" (Freeman-Longo, 2000). It is important that children understand safe use of the Internet, proper etiquette when communicating (Szofran, 1994), how to prevent cyber-bullying or harassment, and how to use the Internet to find reliable sources. Following are examples of teenagers' instant/text messaging and blogging:

Example 1. Instant Message Conversation

redwingsbabe2 (11:30:30 AM): hey how r u doing?
prepPn14 (11:30:51 AM): im doing pretty good
prepPn14 (11:30:54 AM): what about u?
rewingsbabe2 (11:31:15 AM): doing good, what r u diong tonight?
redwingsbabe2 (11:31:19 AM): doing*

prepPn14 (11:32:18 AM): im going to hit the mall hard. They wont know whats coming
rewingsbabe2 (11:32:26 AM): lol
rewingsbabe2 (11:32:52 AM): can I come wit u
prepPn14 (11:33:24 AM): sure if u bring some HAWTIES
redwingsbabe2 (11:33:39 AM): ok will do, call u late
prepPn14 (11:33:51AM): alright ttyl
(IM & Text message shorthand: lol-Laughs out loud, ttyl-Talk To You Later)

Example 2. Text Messages Recorded on a Cellular Phone Used for Cheating

Received from My Baby 6:45 a.m.:
Nomas mi amor kiero de te concentren bien haciendolo ok mi amor te deseo mucha suerte y vas aver ke lo vas a pasa mi baby.
(My love I just want you to concentrate and do a good job. I wish you much luck and know you will pass.)
Sent to My Baby 8:06 a.m."
Bebe me puedes decir k se significa think a piece of clothing that is important to u or was at some time in your time
(Baby, can you tell me what this "quote/question in English means?"
Received from My Baby 8:06 a.m.:
Ke pienses en una ropa ke es especial para ti o una ke fue especial para ti en un tiempo.
(Translation of the test question in English)
Sent to Lupe 8:10 a.m.:
Wey k ld pue do poner think of a time when u had to face a challenge, something that was difficult for u to do
(Hey ass, what can I write for "question"?)
Received from My Baby 8:13 a.m.:
As de cuenta como una camis oun sueter.
(Think about a shirt or sweater.)
Sent to Barbara 8:43 a.m.:
Com 6 le pongo todos me voltaiaban a ver o me distingia en medio de todos
(How do I write "Everyone turned to see me or I stood out from everyone else?)
Received from Edith 12:16 a.m.:
Sorry! K no t marke ayer esk tube una ermergensia
(Sorry! I didn't get in touch yesterday I had an emergency.)
Received from Gustavo 2:30 p.m.:
Good afternoon mr counselor can u please give the

cell phone back to my friend Mia. If u do I will bring us a good garnachas Mexican food but please give her the cell phone thank u and have a nice day scincerely Gustavo Barajas Jimenez my friend needs her cell phone now?

Example 3. Teenage Blogging for Expression

Blog.myspace.com/xxxxx
Friday, February 24, 2006

as I wake

Current mood: lonely

every morning as the sun cracks through the unshut window
my eye awake to greet the morning
but my thoughts have other ideas
they think I am alone
worthless of ever living
feeling guilty in everything i do
nothing is ever good enough
for those who I have learned to trust
but who dont trust in me
live is nothing but a game
where you never win
fore your components are your judges
having no faith in you
because of their prejudgements of you
nevermind the impossible
nevermind the unpredictable
always your way or the highway
as I wake in the morning
life just seems the more abandoned

(permission given by Brandon Harding for publication)

Cyber-Helpers are an essential part of counseling for today and in the future. The Internet provides an unlimited source of information. It is not possible to monitor all of the social interaction and communication that happens on the Internet or cellular phones. It is the children who have access and are exposed to the communication going on outside the school walls on a daily basis. Students are a great network resource for informing school personnel if someone talks about suicide, harming others, or is participating in cyber-bullying. Training is essential for establishing a partnership between the counselor and students.

Additional support may include:

1. Addressing the local media or services providers to use public service announcements that educate young people of potential hazards with cyber-communication.
2. Ensuring that administrators, teachers, parents, and students are familiar with the applicable legal framework and school policies on acceptable uses of the computer networks
3. Consistently engaging in dialogue that gives current information on cyber-communication (see questions, references, and Web site resources). It is important to teach and model for our youth to get "Unplugged." In this age of ever increasing electronic usage from cellular phones to computers to ipods to video games, it is vital to bring back the human social interaction. Balancing the "virtual" world with the "real" world can be the greatest gift of all.

Conclusion

Our youth are plugged into the online universe. Activities range from homework research, making plans with friends and family, downloading music, viewing trends, creating multiple identities, meeting strangers, or victimization. A review of current literature about online interaction and educational use reveals that a significant number of youth are engaged online. Research studies report that 21 million teens go online at least once, daily. Weiss (2005b) gave the following statistics: 12th graders-94 percent, 11th graders-94 percent, 10th graders-90 percent, 9th graders-87 percent, 8th graders-85 percent, 7th graders-82 percent, and 6th graders-60 percent. Online interactions occur from home, school, a friend's house, a library, a community youth center, or a place of worship. Of particular relevance is the impact of the Internet on the personal, social, and emotional well being of our youth today.

Cyber-communication is interactive, bridges the distance, reaches the masses, and provides opportunities to connect with others of similar interests and values. This digital life style provides access to a world of resources. Anonymity promotes self-expression; however, the Internet can be fertile territory for risky, toxic, or criminal behavior.

Cyber-communication may change many aspects of our lives- private, social, cultural, economic, and intellectual. However, with proper instruction, guidance, and supervision, there is the potential for the impact of positive, personal growth.

Discussion Questions

1. How can today's youth/school counselors/parents be prepared for safer Internet use?
2. What are the benefits for appropriate Internet use?
3. What are the risks for over access of the Internet?
4. Do school counselors feel prepared to address the challenges of student's Internet use?
5. How will parents and counselors detect signals of distress?
6. Are there any guidelines or limitations restricting materials from being placed on the Internet?
7. Is there an increase in youth changing their personal identity when engaging in online relationships?
8. How will we maintain humanization in our relationships as technology use expands?
9. What do we know about the characteristics of youth who form online relationships?
10. Is the Internet becoming an addictive behavior requiring a treatment plan?
11. Does language in code exist among a particular age group as they attempt to converse confidentially?
12. As a result of Internet use, do youth become more socially isolated or resort to more anti-social behaviors?
13. Are relationships developed on line likely to be more superficial than genuine?
14. Is there such a thing as "Web-rage"?
15. Does online sexual behavior/activity predispose some children and teens to act out sexually and/ or engage in sexually abusive behavior?
16. What effect does solitary or peer group use have on youth's interpretation and internalization of Web messages?

References

APA Press. (2006). *Internet use involves both pros and cons for children and adolescents, according to special issue of developmental psychology.* Retrieved July 17, 2006, from http//www.apa.org/ releases/youthwww0401.html .

Becker, K, Mayer, M., Nagenborg, M., El-faddagh, M., & Schmidt, M. H. (2004). Parasuicide online: Can suicide websites trigger suicidal behaviour in predisposed adolescents?. *Nord J Psychiatry, 58*(2),111-114.

Bradley, A. (2005). Media-use study finds youths increasingly multi-tasking. *Education Week, 24*(27), 4.

Brignall, T.W., III, & Valey, T. V. (2005). The impact of internet communication on social interaction. *Sociological Spectrum, 25*, 335-348.

Bryant, J. A., Sanders-Jackson, A., & Smallwood A. M. K. (2006). Iming, text messaging, adolescent social networks. *Journal of Computer-Mediated Communication, 11*(2), article 10.

Carey, P. (1997, June). Wired for learning. *Youth Studies Australia, 16*(2), 26.

Fleming, M., & Rickwood, D. (2004). Teens in cyberspace. *Youth Studies Australia, 23*(3).

Freeman-Longo, R. E. (2000). Children, teens, and sex on the internet. *Sexual Addiction and Compulsivity, 7,* 75-90.

Globus, S. (2002, February). The good the bad and the Internet. *Current Health* 2, 28(6), 13.

Lenhart, A., Rainie, L., & Lewis, O. (2001, June 20). *Teenage life online: The rise of the instant-message generation and the internet's impact on friendships and family relationships.* Washington, DC: Pew Internet and American Life Project.

Littlefield, L. (2004, November 3). *Psychosocial aspects of mobile phone use among adolescents.* Melbourne: The Australian Psychological Society.

Merriam-Webster. (2006). Retrieved July 17, 2006, from http://www3.merriam-webster.com/open dictionary/

Morris, S. (2004). *The future of netcrime now: Part 1-threats and challenges. Home office crime and policing group.* Retrieved July 17, 2006, from http://www.crimereduction.gov.uk/internet01.htm.

Olsen, S. (2006). *Keeping kids safe on social sites.* Retrieved July 17, 2006, from http://CNET News.com.

Pankoke-Babatz, U., & Jeffrey, P. (2002). Documented norms and conventions on the internet. *International Journal of Human-Computer Interaction, 14*(2), 219-235.

Payne, J. W. (2006, July 4). Invitation to harm. *The Washington Post*, F-1.

Rudman, G. (2006). The techno-flux effect. *Brandweek, 47*(14), 22-23.

Seel, J. (1997). Plugged in, spaced out, and turned on: electronic entertainment and moral mindfields. *Journal of Education, 179*(3), 17.

Szofran, N. (1994). *Internet etiquette and ethics.* Speech delivered at the CODI National Conference, Provo, Utah, Feb. 27-28, 1992.

United Educators. (2004). Cyberbullying: Protecting children in the school domain. *Public School News, 1,* 1-11.

Webopedia (2006). Retrieved on July 17, 2006, from http://www.webopedia.com/TERM/clcyber.html.

Weiss, D. L. (2005a, August 11). Children and pornography online. *Focus on the Family.*

Weiss, D. L. (2005b, August 11). Youth & the Internet. *Focus on the Family.*

Wikipedia (2006). *Cyber-bullying.* Retrieved on July 17, 2006, from http://enwikipedia.org /wiki/cyberbullying.

Wolak, J. Mitchell, K. J., & Finkelhor, D. (2003). Escaping or connecting? Characteristics of youth who form close on line relationships. *Journal of Adolescence, 26*, 105-119.

Ybarra, M. L., & Mitchell, K. J. (2004). Youth engaging in online harassment: associations with caregiver-child relationships, internet use, and personal characteristics. *Journal of Adolescence, 27*, 319-336.

Web Site Resources

http://www.blogsafety.com/index.jspa
http://www.chatdanger.com
http://www.netsmartz.org
http://yahooligans.yahoo.com/parents
http://www.nypl.org/admin/pro/pubuse.html
http://www.nsbf.org/safe-smart/full-report.htm
http://www.getnetwise.org
http://www.safekids.com/
http://safechild.org/internet.htm
http://safeonlineoutreach.com/
http://www.haltabusekdt.org/
http://www.cyberbullying.org/

Appendix A. Activities on the Web

What teens have done online

The percentage of youth with Internet access aged 12 through 17 who have done the following activities online:

Send or read email	92%
Surf the Web for fun	84%
Visit an entertainment site	83%
Send an instant message	74%
Look for info on hobbies	69%
Get news	68%
Play or download a game	66%
Research a product or service	66%
Listen to music online	59%

Visit a chat room	55%
Download music files	53%
Check sports scores	47%
Visit a site for a club or team that they are a member of	39%
Go to a Web site where they can express opinions about something	38%
Buy something online	31%
Visit sites for trading or selling things	31%
Look for health-related information	26%
Create a Web page	24%
Look for info on a topic that is hard to talk about	18%

Source: Pew Internet & American Life Project Teens and Parents Survey. Nov.-Dec. 2000. Margin of error is + 4%.

Note - These statistics are from 2000, these percentages are much higher today.

Appendix B. Glossary of Cyber Terms

Acme Auteurs: The term for teens customizing their personal Web space with commercial enhancement (Rudman, 2006).

Blog: A Web site that contains an online personal journal with reflections, comments, and often hyperlinks provided by the writer (Merriam-Webster, 2006).

Brain Blur: When someone does multiple tasks at once and is unable to give full attention to any one activity (Rudman, 2006).

BRB: Text messaging shorthand for "Be Right Back".

Cellular telephone: A mobile phone that is wireless.

Chat Rooms: A real-time online interactive discussion group (Merriam-Webster, 2006).

Chill-challenged: Teens that are unable to exist without using technological devices at times (Rudman, 2006).

Computer: A programmable usually electronic device that store, retrieve, and process data (Merriam-Webster, 2006).

Cyber: Relating to or involving computers or computer networks (Merriam-Webster, 2006).

Cyber-Bullying: The willfull and repeated harm inflicted through the medium of electronic text (Wikipedia, 2006).

Cyber-Communication: Communicating through computer or electronic devices.

Cyber-Counselor: A counselor who assists others using the Internet (Wakefield, 2007).

Cyber-Helpers: The use of students to help assist counselors in accessing others who might be in crisis or need help or assistance as expressed on the Internet (Wakefield, 2007).

Cyberkids: A term used for today's youth who use technology.

Cyber-Lessons: Guidance lessons regarding safe and helpful use of the Internet (Wakefield, 2007).

Cyber-Patrol: One of many forms of Internet blockers for parents to use with children for safety purposes.

Cyber-Relationship: A relationship that is developed on the Internet.

Cyber-Safety: Making sure that there is safe use of the Internet.

Cyber-Stalking: Stalking through the Internet or some other form of technological device used for communicating.

Cyber-self: A screen name or identity used on the Internet.

Cyberspace: An online world of computer networks and especially the Internet (Merriam-Webster, 2006).

Cyber-tasking: Multitasking on the Internet (Wakefield, 2007).

Dataddiction: Teens' dependence on the Internet as a source of stimulation and information (Rudman, 2006).

Digital Disguise: A person's online screen name and identities (Rudman, 2006).

E-Mail: A means or system for transmitting messages electronically (as between computers on a network) (Merriam-Webster, 2006).

Emoticon: A group of keyboard characters (as :-)) that typically represents a facial expression or suggests an attitude or emotion and that is used especially in computerized communications (as e-mail) (Merriam-Webster, 2006).

Flaming: A public personal attack on the Internet (Pankoke-Babatz, 2002).

Friends: The title Myspace.com uses for personal e-mail contacts.

IJunkies: Teens' need for instant gratification and information at a bush of a button (Rudman, 2006).

**IM-
Instant Messaging:** The act of sending dialogue over the computer between people in real time.

**Information
Superhighway:** A telecommunications infrastructure or system (as of television, telephony, or computer networks) used for widespread and usually rapid access to information (Merriam-Webster, 2006).

Internet: An electronic communications network that connects computer networks and organizational computer facilities around the world (Merriam-Webster, 2006).

IPOD: An electronic device that holds a vast amount of music or auditory information.

Kill: To role-play a death on an online game (Pankoke-Babatz, 2002).

Life Caching: When the brain uses memory indexing to store locations of where information is (Rudman, 2006).

LOL: The online abbreviation for "Laugh out loud".

MP3 Players: A computer format for playing music and/or other information.

MUD: Multiuser Dungeons or Multiuser Domains where more then one person participates online at the same time. (Pankoke-Babatz, 2002).

MySpace.com: One of many free Web sites that allow people to set up their own Web sites and profile pages for communication.

Neighbornet: The world where teens communicate socially in cyberspace (Rudman).

Netcrime: Criminal or otherwise malicious activity utilizing or directed towards the Internet and/or information technology applications (Morris, 2004).

Netiquette: Customs and protocols of online behavior (Globus, 2002).

Online: Connected to, served by, or available through a system and especially a computer or telecommunications system (as the Internet) (Merriam-Webster, 2006).

Screen Names: The fictitious name used on the Internet to communicate via e-mail, chat rooms, message boards etc.

Simcity: A computer game where one is put in charge of creating one's own world (Seel, 2006).

SIT: Socially Interactive Technologies (Bryant, 2006).

Spamming: Posting long and frequent messages or sending large amounts of postings to hundreds of e-mail addresses (Pankoke-Babatz, 2002).

Techno Flux Effect: The state of flux experienced by teens who are constantly upgrading their personal operating systems (Rudman, 2006).

Technobling: The interest of teens in the style factor of gadgets (Rudman, 2006).

Technomadism: Where teens with their wireless laptops, cell phones, Ipods, cameras, video games are walking access points of the information pipeline (Rudman, 2006).

Text Messaging: Sending messages through text on phones rather then by voice.

Text Messaging Shorthand: Abbreviations used when text messaging

TTYL: The online abbreviation for "Talk to you later".

Video Game: An electronic game played by means of images on a video screen and often emphasizing fast action (Merriam-Webster, 2006).

Virtual Reality: An artificial environment, which is experienced through sensory stimuli (as sights and sounds) provided by a computer and in which one's actions partially determine what happens in the environment (Merriam-Webster, 2006).

Unplugged: To be without all electronic devices.

User friendly: Any text or message that is easy to read.

Web Site: A group of World Wide Web pages usually containing hyperlinks to each other and made available online by an individual, company, educational institution, government, or organization (Merriam-Webster, 2006).

World Wide Web: A part of the Internet accessed through a graphical user interface and containing documents often connected by hyperlinks (Merriam-Webster, 2006).

Chapter 23

Career Development:
Foundation for Student School Success and Postsecondary Transition

Linda Kobylarz and Martha Russell

Abstract

School counselors have the skills and knowledge to assume a leadership role in designing and implementing comprehensive, developmental guidance programs that support student school success and a smooth transition from high school to postsecondary education or employment. This chapter emphasizes the role of career development as a foundation for student success and encourages the inclusion of career development experiences as part of an effective comprehensive program beginning in the elementary grades and extending through high school and beyond.

Introduction

In recent years, there have been numerous studies and reports about the state of American education and the American workforce. They suggest that education must continue to keep pace with the new and more demanding knowledge and skills required in the emerging workplace. Schools are expected to deliver a revised curriculum that is both more relevant and more rigorous for all students. National, state, and local initiatives seek to meet the challenge of preparing students to be successful in the highly competitive global economy. The No Child Left Behind (NCLB) legislation sets imperatives for improving the quality of education. The response from school districts across the country includes an ambitious agenda for school improvement and rigorous career/technical education based on a career clusters and career pathways approach.

The role of school counselors in school reform initiatives must not be overlooked. School counselors have the skills and knowledge that position them to assume a leadership role in designing and implementing a comprehensive, developmental guidance program that supports student school success and a smooth transition from high school to postsecondary education or employment. Career development activities and interventions must be key components of successful school guidance programs.

What is Career Development?

The concept of career development encompasses much more than resume writing and exploring occupations. Consider this holistic approach to career development. Dr. Edwin Herr (2004), a nationally known expert in the field of career development, considers career development a lifelong process comprised of many tasks that arise in conjunction with exploring, choosing, and implementing decisions about educational, occupational, and related life roles. He further comments that career development is that aspect of human development which includes how individuals incorporate their values about work, their beliefs about their own interests and abilities, their decisions about education, the ways they negotiate transitions into and out of work experiences and their unique interactions between work and other life roles.

Dr. Donald Super (1976) defined career development as "the sequence of occupations and other life roles, which combine to express one's commitment to work in his or her total pattern of self-development." It follows then that career development is the process by which we develop and refine our self-identity as it relates to many life and work roles, including those involving occupations, education, social responsibility, and leisure.

We can see that career development is a lifelong process, but what is a career? Put simply, a person's career is the sum total of the work (both paid and unpaid) that he/she does throughout life. Each person has one lifelong career journey that may include several jobs or positions (usually for pay), numerous occupations (the type of work we do such as nurse or diesel mechanic), volunteer work, schoolwork, and work in the home. Even in our leisure time we are doing "work" when we produce goods or provide services for others or ourselves.

Over the lifespan a person must make many career-related decisions. Examples include: identifying career interests; deciding what subjects to take in high school; what postsecondary education/training route to follow; what job to take; when to change jobs; and when to retire or retrain for another stage of life. To keep on track, a person must manage his/her career; and that is not an easy task at any stage. Ongoing career development activities, beginning in elementary school and continuing though high school and beyond, provide experiences for students to help them gain valuable knowledge of themselves and the world of work and to learn the skills needed for effective career planning, preparation, and career management.

Career Development Guiding Principles

Career development experiences should be delivered as part of a comprehensive program that begins in the elementary grades and extends through high school and beyond. These experiences are guided by the following principles:

1. Career development is a lifelong process for all people.
2. Career development experiences should be provided in an equitable manner to all students.
3. Career development is developmental in nature (K-Postsecondary) moving from self and career awareness - to career exploration - to implementation of decisions and plans. The entire development process can be, and usually is, repeated more than once during the life span.
4. The individual freedom of career choice should be enhanced and protected for every person.
5. A person's work values are part of his/her total system of personal values.
6. Work is an integral part of a person's total lifestyle.
7. Both paid and unpaid work is important.
8. The relationship between education and work is recognized and emphasized at all levels of education.

Benefits of Career Development

Much has been written about what promotes academic achievement in our schools. Carey, DeCoster, and Blustein (2004) put forward several assumptions about the connection between career development and academic achievement.

1. Career development interventions positively affect academic achievement by helping students understand the relationship between educational course-taking and career success.
2. Career development interventions enhance academic achievement by developing work-related attitudes and skills that lead to better self-direction and self-management in school.

3. Career development interventions help close the achievement gap by providing disadvantaged students with "in school" opportunities to gain the knowledge, skills, and attitudes that predispose students towards academic engagement and success.
4. Career development interventions positively affect academic achievement by increasing the salience of school and enhancing students' motivation to achieve academically.

Of course, these assumptions are hypotheses that need to be tested. However, career development strategies operating on these assumptions and based on the goals and indicators of the National Career Development Guidelines and the ASCA National Standards are consistent with learning principles associated with the exciting research in neuroscience and brain-based learning (Caine & Caine, 1991). As much of the literature states, the foundation of empirical research supporting the value of career development is sparse and continues to benefit from focused attention to the relationship between guidelines, principles, and practices.

However, there are several studies that can be cited as examples of research based on the cause and effect of the relationships with recommendations for continued professional exploration. One such example is the research by Peterson, Long, and Billups (1999) in which they investigated the impact of three levels of career interventions on the educational choices of eighth grade students as they prepared for their transition into high school. The interventions centered on the completion of a Four Year Trial Program of Study and included three levels of increasingly intensive intervention between the student and the school counselor. The study specifically looked at how the career interventions influenced the choices students made related to high school course selection and students' understanding of the impact of these choices. The authors found that the level of career intervention administered to students had a direct impact upon students' abilities to understand the importance of their educational choices related to postsecondary education and future career choices. The students who had the level three intensive, four-day intervention were most able to make wise and informed decisions related to their course selections. Selections were based on a multi-step process that included exploration of various careers and the educational criteria related to these careers.

A study by Dykeman et al. (2003) states that career interventions lead to increased academic efficacy and motivation, two variables that are known to have a positive relationship to academic achievement and school success. Palladino-Schultheiss, Palma and Manzi (2005) explored childhood career development by examining 4th- and 5th-grade students' career and self-awareness, exploration, and career planning. The purpose of this investigation was to contribute to the theoretical knowledge of childhood career development by using a grounded theory approach and consensual qualitative research methods to explore childhood career development as it naturally unfolds in young children from an underserved urban population. The results support literature attesting to the importance of early career interventions (Magnuson & Starr, 2000). The authors suggest that further research on the process of continued childhood career development and the coordinated efforts to deliver empirically supported comprehensive career interventions in school settings will expand counseling's contribution to developmental and prevention efforts and contribute to the educational development of students.

Baker and Taylor (1998) present a meta-analytic review of twelve studies published between 1993 and 1996, which demonstrated that career education interventions are having positive impacts on academic achievement. This review also points out that there is a need for continued qualified research and an obligation of reporting based on observation and measurable phenomena.

The research must be coupled with focused and directed programs based on needs, policies, and best practices. It is through implementation of these programs that the relationship between career development and academic achievement and transition can gain strength.

Career Development Program Implementation

Implementation concepts that guide the success of each program include:

1. The career development program is competency-based. The National Career Development Guidelines framework of domains, goals, and indicators provides the foundation for clearly stated outcomes at the elementary, middle, high school, and adult levels. (See below for more information.)
2. The career development program is part of the school improvement plan.
3. A scope and sequence of activities reflects the student outcomes and guides students through the career awareness, career exploration, and career planning stages of their ongoing career development.

4. The career development program incorporates the excellent career development activities already in place in the schools.
5. The successful delivery of a career development program involves students, counselors, teachers, administrators, and school specialists working together as a team. In all schools, administrative support at the building level is essential.
6. Career development programs should take advantage of and utilize a wide variety of community resources.
7. Outreach involving stakeholders such as parents, the business community, and students is essential.
8. Ongoing public relations and marketing efforts are crucial.
9. Both product and process evaluations provide valuable information for the long-term effectiveness of the career development program.
10. The career development program supports the goals of No Child Left Behind.

No Child Left Behind (NCLB)

The NCLB legislation, signed into law by President Bush in January 2002, is a driving force for school reform that places great emphasis on academic achievement (especially in reading and math), school accountability for learning results (demonstrated through national, state, and local assessment), high quality teaching, and closing the achievement gap between minority and disadvantaged students and their peers. There is increased support for English language instruction to ensure English proficiency for bilingual and immigrant students. Emphasis is placed on preparing all students for some kind of postsecondary education/training and the necessity of lifelong learning is stressed. Drop-out prevention, safe schools, drug-free schools, and character education programs are also included in the legislation.

Career Development Frameworks

Two frameworks, the ASCA National Standards for School Counseling Programs (ASCA, 2004) and the National Career Development Guidelines (NCDA, 2007) can be used to provide the foundation for K-12 career development programs. Each is described below.

ASCA National Standards

The American School Counselors Association (ASCA) has long been a strong advocate of K-12 career development programs. In 1997, the Association developed the National Standards for School Counseling

Programs (ASCA, 2004). The ASCA Standards provide the foundation for skill, attitude, and knowledge acquisition that enables students (K-12) to make a successful transition from school to the world of work and from job to job across the life career span. Career development, according to the ASCA Standards, includes using strategies that enhance future career success and job satisfaction as well as assisting, understanding of the connections among personal qualities, education and training, and a career choice. As students progress through school and into adulthood, ASCA believes they need to acquire a firm foundation for career development. ASCA urges school counselors to implement activities and strategies related to the content standards for career development to provide K-12 students with the foundation for future career success (Dahir, Sheldon & Valiga, 1998). The ASCA model encompasses Academic, Career and Personal/Social areas with nine standards, including the integration of career development principles throughout the model.

Academic
1. Students will acquire the attitudes, knowledge and skills that contribute to effective learning in school and across the lifespan.
2. Students will complete school with the academic preparation essential to choose from a wide range of substantial post-secondary options, including college.
3. Students will understand the relationship of academics to the world of work and to life at home and the community.

Career
4. Students will acquire the skills to investigate the world of work in relation to knowledge of self and to make informed career decisions.
5. Students will employ strategies to achieve further career success and satisfaction.
6. Students will understand the relationship between personal qualities, education and training and the world of work.

Personal/Social
7. Students will acquire the attitudes, knowledge and interpersonal skills to help them understand and respect self and others.
8. Students will make decisions, set goals, and take necessary action to achieve goals.
9. Students will understand safety and survival skills.

National Career Development Guidelines

The National Career Development Guidelines resource (NCDA, 2007), developed for the U.S. Department of Education-Office of Vocational and Adult Education (OVAE) through funding from Perkins, Section 118 offers a comprehensive framework for career development programs K-Adult that complements the ASCA standards. The Guidelines can help counselors:

- prepare students for the changing workplace by increasing their understanding of the need for lifelong learning and the relationship between education and employment;
- reduce student risks by promoting better understanding if self, improving social adjustment, and enhancing decision-making and planning skills;
- increase program accountability by evaluating program processes and outcomes through regular assessment based on the Guidelines indicators;
- promote program coordination and articulation by defining a sequence of delivery for program activities, reinforcing learning from previous levels, and reducing duplication of services; and
- expand public awareness of the need for and benefits of career development.

(America's Career Resource Network, 2004)

The Guidelines content includes eleven goals that define broad areas of career development competency for Personal Social Development, Educational Achievement and Lifelong Learning, and Career Management as described below.

Personal Social Development
1. Develop understanding of self to build and maintain a positive self-concept.
2. Develop positive interpersonal skills including respect for diversity.
3. Integrate growth and change into your career development.
4. Balance personal, leisure, community, learner, family, and work roles.

Educational Achievement and Lifelong Learning
5. Attain educational achievement and performance levels needed to reach your personal and career goals.
6. Participate in ongoing, lifelong learning experiences to enhance your ability to function effectively in a diverse and changing economy.

Career Management

7. Create and manage a career plan that meets your career goals.
8. Use a process of decision-making as one component of career development.
9. Use accurate, current, and unbiased career information during career planning and management.
10. Master academic, occupational and general employability skills in order to obtain, create, maintain, and/or advance your employment.
11. Integrate changing employment trends, societal needs, and economic conditions into your career plans.

The goals are further detailed by indicators that define the specific career development skills and competencies students need. Visit the America's Career Resource Network Web site (www.acrnetwork.org) or the National Career Development Association Web site (www.ncda.org) for more information about the NCDG and related online activities and resources.

Both the ASCA National Standards and the NCDG provide counselors a framework for organizing their activities and services. Following are examples of career development services that counselors can provide. They are listed under the content domains.

Personal Social Development (ASCA National Standards and NCDG)
- Administer, analyze, and discuss career assessments (e.g., interests, aptitudes, abilities, and work values) with students
- Help students develop conflict resolution skills
- Help students develop behavior management skills for school, social, and work situations
- Provide assistance to students in solving problems at school and work

Academic Development (ASCA National Standards) and Educational Achievement and Lifelong Learning (NCDG)
- Help students identify strategies for improving educational achievement and performance
- Help students identify their learning style and make connections to effective study skills
- Ensure that students know the requirements for graduation, assist them with appropriate course selection, and recommend remedies when graduation is in jeopardy

- Provide information about postsecondary education and training options and financial aid and assist students with the transition process

Career Development (ASCA National Standards) and Career Management (NCDG)
- Assist students with identifying career goals (e.g., career pathway) and developing plans to reach those goals
- Help students develop effective decision-making skills
- Help students identify and learn to use a variety of career information resources (i.e., occupational, educational, economic, and employment) to support career planning
- Help students identify and learn about career pathways
- Provide opportunities for students to explore occupations (including nontraditional) and discuss occupations of interest
- Help students develop job seeking skills (e.g., resume writing and job interviewing)
- Help students identify their general employability skills (e.g., time management, organization, problem solving, critical thinking, and interpersonal)
- Help students understand how employment trends, societal needs, and economic trends can affect their career plans

Implementation Strategies

The establishment of or redesigning of an effective career development program is a team effort. Counselors, career specialists, teachers, administrators, school support staff, parents, business, and the community must join together in partnership to deliver the kind of career development program that will ensure our students are adequately prepared to meet the challenges of today's workplace. The ASCA National Standards and the National Career Development Guidelines provide an excellent foundation for program planning.

Both school-based and work-based approaches have proven effective in the delivery of career development activities. Examples of school-based methods for career development include:
- Guidance curriculum;
- Career clusters and career pathways, Tech Prep, dual credit, and AP;
- Teacher advisory programs;
- Classroom infusion and alignment with the state's learning standards;

- Intentional infusion of employability skills (e.g., workplace readiness skills, SCANS employability skills);
- Career portfolios and senior projects;
- Career development simulation (e.g., The Real Game Series); and
- Computer-based career information delivery systems.

The implementation strategies of guidance curriculum, teacher advisory programs, classroom infusion and alignment with state learning standards, and intentional infusion of employability skills, and career portfolios are further discussed below.

Work-based strategies complement school-based strategies. They include: job shadowing, field trips, internships, cooperative education, youth apprenticeships, mentorships, service learning, school-based enterprises, and career fairs.

School Counseling Program Curriculum

Counselors often take a leadership role in providing direction for career development program activity selection and design ensuring that the developmental needs of students at each grade level are met. A national trend is for all students to have an individual education and career plan by the end of eighth grade. The student, parents, and counselor review the plan annually. Many school counselors meet the challenge of providing services to all of their students by teaming with teachers to deliver guidance activities in the classroom. In some schools, guidance "themes" are identified for each grade (for example, All About Me for third graders, or Exploring Careers for 8th graders, or Setting Goals for 11th graders). Examples of school districts that support strong career development components in their developmental guidance programs include: Tucson Unified School District; Omaha, Nebraska; many districts in Missouri that follow the Gysbers model; Broward County Schools in Florida; Bismarck, Grand Forks, and Fargo, North Dakota; and most districts in Utah. Many state departments of education have developed career guidance activities for school use. A few examples include: South Carolina, North Carolina, Ohio, Maine, Oklahoma, and more.

Teacher Advisory Program

Another approach is the school-wide teacher advisory program, most common at the middle school and high school levels. Usually, a block of time is set aside each day or each week in which teachers cover a curriculum of counseling related topics. Ideally, school counselors play a key role in the creation of the teacher advisory curriculum and have opportunities to coordinate its implementation. This is an excellent way to deliver career development content.

Classroom Infusion and Alignment with State Learning Standards

The NCLB legislation has led to renewed emphasis on state learning standards, assessment, and accountability throughout the country. Understandably, teachers feel great pressure to concentrate on curriculum topics and prepare students to pass state mastery tests. Yet, many career development competencies can easily be infused into classroom instruction. Careful analysis of the curriculum content and state learning standards as well as awareness that career development is more than talking to students about jobs, are required to make the connections.

State learning standards incorporate the knowledge and skills that enable students to be successful in the workplace of their choice, in addition to their roles as citizens, family members, and participants of society. The learning standards also create opportunities to integrate academic and career development knowledge and skills. This approach enhances students' ability to see connections between what is learned and practical applications of that learning. All subject areas can be used as a vehicle to deliver career development related activities. The ASCA National Standards and the National Career Development Guidelines provide a framework for the development of specific classroom lessons. North Dakota and South Carolina are leaders in this approach.

In order for the classroom infusion approach to work, teachers must broaden their understanding of career development content. Staff development workshops that introduce teachers to the career development concepts help to accomplish this. Teachers who review what they already teach in light of the ASCA Standards and the NCDG often find that they make some general connections to career development. With a more intentional approach, they can crystallize those connections for the students and add a new dimension to their lessons.

Lessons that are constructed from the beginning with the purpose of aligning academic and career development standards are even more powerful. For example, students might write business letters to sources for career information or historical figures might be analyzed from the perspective of their employability skills. A contextual learning teaching strategy is very compatible with classroom integration of career development competencies. Contextual learning is that which occurs in close relationship with actual experience. Contextual learning enables students to test academic theories via tangible, real world applications by stressing the development of "authentic" problem-solving skills. Contextual learning is designed to blend teaching methods, content, situation, and timing. Science lab experiments are an example of contextual learning. Two sample classroom infusion activities developed by America's Career Resource Network (2004) are provided at the end of this chapter.

Intentional Infusion of the Employability Skills

Any skills that are used to perform an occupation or that help an individual to be successful in the workplace are employability skills. They can be grouped into three broad categorics: Foundation Skills, Workplace Know-How Skills, and Work Content Skills. The Foundation Skills and the Workplace Know-How Skills are skills that are used in almost every job. They were identified through an extensive survey of hundreds of businesses conducted by the United States Department of Labor and are commonly referred to as the SCANS Employability Skills (Secretary's Commission on Achieving Necessary Skills, 1991).

The Foundation Skills include basic skills (reading, writing, listening, speaking, and arithmetic/ mathematics); thinking skills (e.g., creative thinking, decision-making, and problem solving); and personal qualities (responsibility, self-esteem, sociability, self-management, and integrity/honesty). The Workplace Know-How skills include skills to manage resources (e.g., time and money); interpersonal skills (e.g., teamwork, leadership, and the ability to work with diversity); information acquisition and management skills; skills to work with systems; and technology skills.

Every day, in every class, teachers make reference to some of the employability skills when they encourage students to get their work done on time, to work cooperatively with classmates, to show respect for others, to think critically and creatively, to solve problems, to use technology effectively, and so on. However, the connection between these messages and employability skills is seldom made. When we intentionally point out to students the employability skills they are developing in school, we make their learning more relevant. We must expand student awareness of the broad range of employability skills, help students make connections between schoolwork and employability skills, and provide opportunities for students to document their experience with key employability skills. In so doing, we will better prepare them to successfully discuss their full array of talents in college, financial aid, or job interviews. Character education programs are common. Both Miami-Dade County Schools and Chicago Public Schools have system-wide programs.

Career Portfolios

Career Portfolios are a compilation of students' educational and work experiences, accomplishments, goals, and plans for the future. Used as a structured tool for personal reflection, identification of academic and professional goals, and assessment of accomplishments, it has been instrumental in helping serving as a bridge between educational transition and entry into employment. Career portfolios and other career pathway tools can help students understand how learning goals and objectives connect to the real world. Many states have adopted Career Portfolios as part of the competency and graduation requirements while others have incorporated this process with grade level presentations, standardized career products and other avenues that serve to move students towards academic and personal success. Successful programs have been incorporated in the Chicago Public Schools and schools in Oregon and Washington State (McLain & Thompson, 2001). North Branford Middle School in Iowa is an example of successful implementation.

Implementation Challenges/Barriers

As with many initiatives there are often gaps between the intent of the concept and the program and the implementation. While there may be numerous challenges, it is our responsibility as professionals, as supporters of the process, and as visionaries to take action. That action may include research, designing programs, obtaining the support systems for implementation, and continuing to be advocates for the building of the relationship between career development and student school success and transition.

Next Steps for Counselors and Others

1. Be sure that administrators, teachers, and counselors have a common understanding of career development concepts.
2. Align your career development program with

ongoing school initiatives (e.g., NCLB, drop-out prevention, character education, safe schools, drug abuse prevention).

3. Communicate clearly the benefits of the program to administrators, teachers, counselors, parents, and students.

4. Use a team approach – involve administrators, teachers, and support staff in program design, development, and delivery. Ask for volunteers. Many individuals are equipped to take a leadership role in this area.

5. Provide practical training to counselors, staff, and all team members.

6. Build on success and examine what is already working. Become familiar with best practices, review programs, resources, and strategies.

7. Start small. Be realistic about what can be accomplished and allow adequate time to develop a solid program.

8. Demonstrate the value of accountability and program evaluation by keeping these elements in mind from the very beginning. Take a competency-based approach using the ASCA standards and the NCDG as a framework. Find effective ways to document program outcomes.

9. Share your successes as well as your challenges. Present at conferences, write about your work, and continually improve the process for yourself and others. Be creative.

10. Keep the momentum going. Celebrate success and find solutions to challenges.

Discussion Questions

1. What can you learn from the current initiatives and programs that will assist in adapting to the changes of the future?

2. What role can you and your team play in strengthening the relationship between career development and academic success? How can you continue to link educational development and career development?

3. With multiple issues impacting decision making for young people what programs can you develop using the National Career Guidelines for personal and social development?

4. How can you develop a brief overview in writing or for an oral presentation that will meet the needs and interests of your area? How can you best gain the support you need for your program?

5. How do you role model the integration of successful career development and decision making?

References

American School Counselor Association (2004). *ASCA National Standards for Students*. VA: Author.

America's Career Resource Network. (2004). *National Career Development Guidelines*. Author.

Baker, S. B., & Taylor, J. G. (1998). Effects of career education interventions: A meta-analysis. *Career Development Quarterly, 46*, 376-385.

Caine, R., & Caine, G. (1991). *Making connections: Teaching and the human brain*. Alexandria, VA: Association for Supervision and Curriculum Development.

Carey, J., DeCoster, K., & Blustein, D. (2004). *School-based career development and No Child Left Behind*. Unpublished document developed for the National Training Support Center, Washington, D.C.

Dahir, C., Sheldon, B., & Valiga, M. (1998). *Vision into action: Implementing the national standards for school counseling programs*. Alexandria, VA: ASCA Press.

Dykeman, C., Wood, C., Ingram, M., Gitelman, A., Mandsager, N., Chen, M., & Herr, E. L. (2003). *Career development interventions and academic self-efficacy: A pilot study*. St. Paul, MN: National Research Center for Career and Technical Education.

Herr, E. L. (2004). *Career development: Some perspectives*. Unpublished document developed for the National Training Support Center, Washington, D.C.

Magnuson, C. S., & Starr, M. F. (2000). How early is too early to begin life career planning? The importance of the elementary school years. *Journal of Career Development, 27*, 89-101.

National Career Development Association (2007). *National Career Development Guidelines (NCDG) Framework*. Retrieved May 31, 2008, from http://www.ncda.org/pdf/ncdguidelines2007.pdf.

McLain, B., & Thompson, M. (2001). *Educational opportunities in Washington's high schools under state education reform: Case studies of eight Washington high schools* (Document 01-09-2202). Washington State Institute for Public Policy.

Palladino-Schultheiss, D. E., Palma, T. V., & Manzi, A.J. (2005) Career development in middle childhood: a qualitative inquiry. *Career Development Quarterly, 53*.

Peterson, G. W., Long, K. L., & Billups, A. (1999). The effect of three career interventions on the educational choices of eighth grade students. *Professional School Counseling, 3*(1), 34-42.

Secretary's Commission on Achieving Necessary Skills (SCANS). (1991). *What work requires of schools: A SCANS report*. Washington, DC: U.S. Department of Labor.

Super, D. E. (1976). *Career education and the meaning of work*. Washington, D.C.: U.S. Department of Education.

Resources

America's Career Resource Network (ACRN)

America's Career Resource Network is a grant program established by Section 118 of the Carl D. Perkins Vocational and Technical Education Act. A national office and 59 state and territory entities carry forth the mandates of the grant that include:

a. Supporting career guidance and academic counseling programs to promote improved career and education decision-making by individuals K-Adult;

b. Developing and disseminating occupational and career information;

c. Making available information and planning resources that relate educational programs to career goals and expectations; and

d. Equipping teachers, administrators, and counselors with knowledge and skills needed to assist students with career exploration and with accessing educational opportunities and financing postsecondary education/training.

The National Career Development Guidelines is a major initiative associated with ACRN.

America's Career Resource Network Web Site

America's Career Resource Network Web site (www.acrnetwork.org) is a wonderful tool for keeping up-to-date on resources and research in career development. The materials for counselors, teachers, administrators, parents, and students are downloadable as Word or PDF files. New information is added regularly, so visit the site often.

Web site Highlights:
- Career Decision-Making Tool – interactive process teaches students how to make informed career decisions

- After High School – excellent overview of postsecondary options
- Where the Jobs Are – colorful graphs and charts make understanding employment trends easy
- School Days – outlines essential career/education planning steps for grades 9-12
- Students Activities – interactive exercises and games for enhancing self-knowledge, career exploration, and career/education planning
- Parent brochures – promote involvement of parents/guardians in student career development
- Articles, research, links – No Child Left Behind, academic achievement, career pathways, model programs, and more
- Sample lessons – show how career development concepts can be easily integrated into the core academics and aligned with state learning standards
- Program evaluation – 9-step process for evaluating career development programs
- NCDG framework – complete list of goals and indicators for program development

Internet Resources

American School Counselor Association
http://www.schoolcounselor.org

California Career Resource Network (CalCRN)
http://www.cde.ca.gov/ci/ct/cc/

Chicago Public Schools
http://www.cps.k12.il.us

Miami Dade County Public Schools
http://www.dadeschools.net

National Career Development Association
http://www.ncda.org

New York State Education Department
http://www.nysed.gov

North Carolina Department of Education
http://www.ncpublicschools.org/

North Dakota Career Resource Network
http://www.ndcrn.com/

Oregon Department of Education
http://www.ode.state.or.us/

South Carolina Department of Education
http://ed.sc.gov/

Tucson School District Counseling Program
http://instech.tusd.k12.az.us/counseling/index.asp

Empowering the 21st Century Professional School Counselor

Sample Lessons

The following pages contain two sample lessons which can be used to infuse career development into classroom activities: *Which Road Do I Take?* and *Weather Disasters*. Both were developed in 2004 by America's Career Resource Network, http://www.acrnetwork.org.

TITLE: Which Road Do I Take?

SUBJECT: English/Language Arts | **GRADE LEVEL: 9**

Content Standard	English Standard: Students will read, comprehend, analyze and evaluate literary texts.
	
	• Analyze important ideas and messages in literary texts.
	    —Reflect on or explain personal connections to the text.
	    —Explain the implications of the text for the reader and/or society.

Career Development Domain	Career Management
Career Development Goal	CM2 Use a process of decision-making as one component of career development.
Career Development Indicator	CM2.A2 Demonstrate the use of a decision-making model.

Lesson Objectives

• Students will explain the connection between their personal experience in making decisions and the situation of the speaker in Robert Frost's poem, *The Road Not Taken*.

• Students will use the planful decision-making process to make a decision.

Assessment

1. Students will complete the worksheet: *Which Road Do I Take?* and explain the connection between their personal experience in making decisions and the situation of the speaker in Robert Frost's poem, *The Road Not Taken*.

2. Students will document their use of the planful decision-making process to make a personal decision by completing the worksheet: *Planful Decision-Making*.

CAREER DEVELOPMENT/ACADEMIC LESSON*

*Adapted from: North Dakota Career Development Tool Kit, North Dakota Career Resource Network, 2001. Used with permission.

LESSON ACTIVITIES

Preparation

- Prior Learning — Unit on interpreting and analyzing poetry
- Handouts/Worksheets —*Which Road Do I Take?* and *Planful Decision-Making* worksheets
- Resources: *The Road Not Taken* by Robert Frost
- Time Required — one block (2 hours)

Procedures

- Read and discuss the poem *The Road Not Taken* by Robert Frost.
- Use the worksheet: *Which Road Do I Take?* to help students analyze the poem.
- Encourage the students, through class discussion, to make connections between their personal experience in making decisions and the situation of the speaker in the poem.
- Ask students to brainstorm some decisions that they have to make or have recently made. How do they go about making decisions? Do they talk to others? Do they consider many alternatives? Do they get good information? Do they make a snap judgment?

Career Development Connections
- Explain to students that they will have to make many decisions during high school that will have long-lasting consequences. Ask students to brainstorm what some of those decisions might be about (e.g., career clusters, courses to take, dropping out of school and going to college).
- Give students the worksheet: *Planful Decision-Making*. Introduce the decision-making model shown on the handout as follows:
  1. Identify the decision or problem to be resolved.
  2. Gather information. Be sure that the sources you use will give you accurate, up-to-date, unbiased and complete information.
  3. List all of the possible ways to make this decision (alternatives). Write down all of your ideas, even if they seem almost impossible.
  4. Consider the consequences of each alternative. Ask yourself, "What is likely to happen if I do this?".
  5. Make a decision. Choose what seems to be the best alternative. Remember to consider your personal priorities, beliefs and values in your decision-making.
  6. Follow through and take action on your decision.
  7. Review the results of your decision. Ask yourself these questions:
     - Did I get the results I expected and wanted?
     - Did any new problem arise because of this decision?
     - Is there any further action I need to take?
  8. Make new decisions as needed.
- Take the students through the process using the career choice example described in the handout.
- Take the students through the process again using a typical, but simple decision that a student might have to make.
- Tell the students to select a decision they have to make and follow the planful decision-making model to make their decision. They are to complete the worksheet, documenting each step in their decision-making process.
- Invite students to share their decisions with the class.
- Engage students in a discussion of the planful decision-making process. Do they usually follow all of the steps when they are making a decision? What steps are difficult for them? What steps take a lot of time? For what kinds of decisions would they use the planful decision-making process?
- Remind students they can use the planful decision-making model when they are making important career decisions such as what career cluster they will choose for their high school studies.

CAREER DEVELOPMENT/ACADEMIC LESSON*

*Adapted from: North Dakota Career Development Tool Kit, North Dakota Career Resource Network, 2001. Used with permission.

Which Road Do I Take?

NAME_____ DATE_____

Instructions: In *The Road Not Taken* by Robert Frost, the speaker must make an important decision in his life. Using information from the poem, answer the questions below.

The planful decision-making process can be divided into the following steps:

Define the problem

Gather information

Explore alternatives

Consider the consequences, risks of each alternative

Take action

Review the results

Make new decisions as needed

1. What is the speaker's problem?

_____
_____
_____
_____

2. What are the speaker's alternatives?

_____
_____
_____
_____

3. What consequences might the speaker face along each path?

_____
_____
_____
_____

4. Which path does the speaker decide to take? Why?

_____
_____
_____
_____

5. What effect did the speaker's decision have upon his life?

_____
_____
_____
_____

CAREER DEVELOPMENT/ACADEMIC LESSON*

*Adapted from: North Dakota Career Development Tool Kit, North Dakota Career Resource Network, 2001. Used with permission.

Planful Decision Making

NAME_____ DATE_____

Instructions: In the next few years you will be making some big decisions. The planful decision-making process can help you make an informed decision that you will be happy with. Complete this worksheet using the planful decision-making process. Follow the example provided for you.

EXAMPLE

Define the problem
Choose a career cluster to study in high school

•

Gather information
See counselor, go to orientation, take interest inventory
Choose from 16 clusters

•

Explore alternatives
Learn more about my top two clusters: HealthScience and Hospitality/Tourism

•

Consider the consequences, risks of each alternative
Health Science—lots of jobs, 4-yr.-college plus, good pay
Hospitality/Tourism—fewer jobs, 2 yr. college, less pay

•

Make a decision — select an alternative
Choice—Health Science

•

Take action
Register for classes

•

Review the results
Take classes—see if I like them

•

Make new decisions as needed
Change cluster choice if needed

Now It's Your Turn!

Define the problem _____

_____

Gather information _____

_____

Explore alternatives _____

_____

Consider the consequences, risks of each alternative _____

_____

Make a decision— select an alternative _____

_____

Take action _____

_____

Review the results _____

_____

Make new decisions as needed _____

_____

CAREER DEVELOPMENT/ACADEMIC LESSON*

*Adapted from: North Dakota Career Development Tool Kit, North Dakota Career Resource Network, 2001. Used with permission.

TITLE: Weather Disasters

SUBJECT: Science | GRADE LEVEL: 9

NCDG

Content Standard	Science Standard: Students will identify and describe the atmospheric conditions related to weather systems. • Identify and describe the atmospheric and hydrospheric conditions associated with the formation and development of hurricanes, tornadoes and thunderstorms.
Career Development Domain	Personal Social Development
Career Development Goal	PS2 Develop positive interpersonal skills including respect for diversity.
Career Development Indicator	PS2.A4 Demonstrate the ability to get along well with others and work effectively in groups.

Lesson Objectives

• Students will participate in a cooperative learning project to identify and describe 1) the atmospheric and hydrospheric conditions associated with the formation and development of a specific weather-related disaster such as a hurricane or tornado and 2) report on its consequences.

• After completing the group project, students will document their skills for working in a group and how that affected their academic achievement.

Assessment

1. Students will satisfactorily complete the group research project to identify and describe the atmospheric and hydrospheric conditions associated with the formation and development of a specific weather-related disaster such as a hurricane or tornado and report on its consequences.

2. Students will participate appropriately in the cooperative learning project and complete the two group activity related worksheets.

CAREER DEVELOPMENT/ACADEMIC LESSON

LESSON ACTIVITIES

Preparation

- Accommodations — To adapt this activity for students with special needs, review the *Suggested Accommodations* section below.
- Prior Learning—Unit on Interactions of Hydrosphere and Atmosphere
- Handouts/Worksheets—*Tips for Working in a Group, Working in Groups Question Guide, Group Evaluation* worksheet
- Time Required—90 minutes, time for group presentations and homework

Procedures

- Begin the activity with a discussion of some recent weather-related disasters. What were they? Where were they located? Have you lived through a hurricane or tornado? What weather-related disasters might we face in our state?
- Divide the class into groups of 3-5 students. Give students the *Tips for Working in a Group* handout and review it with them.
- Explain to the class that each group will present a team project that documents a weather-related disaster (hurricane, tornado, or severe thunderstorm). Review the requirements for the project and the resources the students can use for their research.
- Encourage students to use various methods to display their documentation such as: newspaper articles, visuals, written report, the Internet and taped interviews.
- Have each group present its display to the class.

Career Development Connections

- After the project is completed, engage students in a discussion of what makes a team work well. What kinds of behaviors help the team accomplish its task? What kinds of behaviors hinder the work of the team? Is it easier to get a project done as part of a team, or is it easier to work alone?
- Have students discuss how working as a team can improve the quality of a project (e.g., new ideas, different points of view, special talents of each person). Show how the ability to work well on a team can affect academic achievement.
- Have students complete the *Working in Groups Question Guide* and the *Group Evaluation* worksheet.
- Remind students that the ability to work cooperatively in group activities is an important skill for their academic achievement now, as well as an important skill in the workplace.
- Optional: use the *Working in Groups Question Guide* and the *Group Evaluation* worksheet as artifacts in the student's career portfolio.

Suggested Accommodations

Although each situation is different and the student is the best source of information regarding useful accommodations, the following accommodations are typical for a student with specific disabilities. Many of the suggested accommodations are adapted from: *DO-IT*, University of Washington (Copyright © 2001-2004). Permission is granted to copy these materials for educational, noncommercial purposes provided the source is acknowledged. For more information visit http://www.washington.edu/doit/Faculty/Strategies/Universal/.

Typical Accommodations for Students with Asperger's Disorder and High-Functioning Autism

Learning activities that may be particularly challenging for students with Asperger's Disorder (also referred to as Asperger Syndrome) and high-functioning Autism include social interactions, noisy or disordered environments, intense sensory stimulation, and changes in expected routines. Many students with Asperger's Disorder or high-functioning Autism have difficulty using a pencil and paper for writing. Some have difficulty with organization and schedules. The following accommodations are suggested.

CAREER DEVELOPMENT/ACADEMIC LESSON

LESSON ACTIVITIES

- Clearly established and ordered routines
- Warning and preparation when changes are anticipated
- Planning and practicing communication strategies and social routines
- Earplugs or noise canceling headsets when in the hallways or lunchroom
- A quiet area where the student can take a time-out if necessary
- Visual schedules and graphic organizers
- Visual or written, rather than auditory, instructions
- Computer use, especially word processing for writing
- Notetaker

Typical Accommodations for Students with Cognitive Impairments

Cognitive impairments represents a range of students who experience from mildly to severely delayed intellectual functioning. The following accommodations are suggested.
- Seating in the front of the classroom to assist concentration and involvement in the class
- Visual, aural, and tactile instructional demonstrations
- Written supplement to oral instructions, assignments, and directions
- Tape recording lectures
- Notetaker for class lectures
- Unfamiliar vocabulary written on the board or a handout
- Training to use "scan and read" technology to supplement low reading skills
- Instruction presented in small, sequential steps with frequent review

Typical Accommodations for Students with Health Impairments

- Note taker
- Flexible attendance requirements and extra exam time
- Assignments made available in electronic format; use of e-mail to facilitate communication

Typical Accommodations for Students with Hearing Impairments

- Interpreter, real-time captioning, FM system, note taker
- Open- or closed-captioned films, use of visual aids
- Written assignments, lab instructions, demonstration summaries
- Visual warning system for lab emergencies
- Use of electronic mail for class and private discussions

Typical Accommodations for Students with Learning Disabilities

- Note takers and/or audiotaped class sessions, captioned films
- Extra exam time, alternative testing arrangements
- Visual, aural, and tactile instructional demonstrations
- Computer with voice output, spelling checker, and grammar checker
- Writing strategies
- Proofreading strategies
- Color-coded information
- Test-taking strategies
- Time management strategies
- Organizational strategies for reviewing research articles
- Videotaping for self-evaluation
- Role-playing practicum exam questions

CAREER DEVELOPMENT/ACADEMIC LESSON*

*Adapted from: North Dakota Career Development Tool Kit, North Dakota Career Resource Network, 2001. Used with permission.

LESSON ACTIVITIES

Typical Accommodations for Students with Mobility Impairments
- Note taker / lab assistant; group lab assignments
- Classrooms, labs, and field trips in accessible locations
- Adjustable tables; lab equipment located within reach
- Class assignments made available in electronic format
- Computer equipped with special input device (e.g., voice input, Morse code, alternative keyboard)

Typical Accommodations for Students with Psychiatric or Mental Health Impairments
- Notetakers
- Early notification of projects, exams, and assignments to reduce stress
- Flexible attendance requirements
- An encouraging, validating, academic environment
- Alternative testing arrangements in a quiet room
- Assignments available in electronic format
- Web page or electronic mail distribution of course materials and lecture notes

Typical Accommodations for Students with Vision Impairments
- Audiotaped, Brailled, or electronically formatted lecture notes, handouts, and texts
- Verbal descriptions of visual aids
- Raised-line drawings and tactile models of graphic materials
- Braille lab signs and equipment labels; auditory lab warning signals
- Adaptive lab equipment (e.g., talking thermometers and calculators, light probes, and tactile timers)
- Computer with optical character reader, voice output, Braille screen display and printer output
- Seating near front of class
- Large-print handouts, lab signs, and equipment labels
- TV monitor connected to microscope to enlarge images
- Class assignments made available in electronic format
- Computer equipped to enlarge screen characters and images

CAREER DEVELOPMENT/ACADEMIC LESSON*

*Adapted from: North Dakota Career Development Tool Kit, North Dakota Career Resource Network, 2001. Used with permission.

Weather Disasters

Tips for Working in a Group

1. Elect a group leader. This person should be organized, responsible and personable. The leader should encourage all students to participate.

2. Listen to each other. Everyone should have an opportunity to be heard.

3. Be organized. Brainstorm ideas and write them down. Be creative.

4. Research and gather information on your topic.

5. Solve problems in a diplomatic manner. Be fair.

6. Respect the feelings of other people in the group. Try to control tempers.

7. Demonstrate tolerance and flexibility in group situations. Negotiate with each other.

8. Communicate your ideas and feelings with each other.

9. Have a good time.

CAREER DEVELOPMENT/ACADEMIC LESSON

Weather Disasters

NAME_____ DATE_____

Group Evaluation

Instructions: Answer the following questions.

1. What did you learn about working in a group?

_____

_____

_____

2. What did you contribute to your group project?

_____

_____

_____

3. Were there any disagreements within the group? If so, how were they resolved?

_____

_____

_____

4. Do you like working in a group or do you prefer to work alone on a project?

_____

_____

_____

5. Are you satisfied with the performance of your group members?

_____

_____

_____

6. On a scale of 1 to 10, how would you rate your group's performance? Why?

_____

_____

_____

CAREER DEVELOPMENT/ACADEMIC LESSON

Weather Disasters

NAME_____ DATE_____

Working in Groups Question Guide

Instructions: Complete the following.

1. My job was... _____
   _____
   _____

2. As a team member I did... _____
   _____
   _____

3. I liked working with a team because... _____
   _____
   _____

4. I didn't like working on a team because... _____
   _____
   _____

5. The strengths that I brought to the group were... _____
   _____
   _____

6. I found the entire group experience to be... _____
   _____
   _____

CAREER DEVELOPMENT/ACADEMIC LESSON

Chapter 24

How Families Can Become Career Developers

Robert C. Chope

Abstract

Family members, especially parents, clearly influence the career choices of their children. But school counselors may not be taking advantage of this potentially useful counseling material. In this chapter, new approaches are introduced for school counselors to consider when exploring the influence of parents on the career planning process. Thereafter, school counselors are shown how they may use this information to enlist different family members in support of the job seeking strategies of their students. The chapter demonstrates how family members, students, and counselors can support each other as they try new approaches to career and life planning

Introduction

This chapter draws attention to two areas often neglected by school and career counselors alike. The first area concerns how the family of origin affects the process of students' deciding upon their career paths. The second focuses upon the interventions family members might utilize to assist in their relatives' career development. The purpose of the chapter is to provide school counselors with innovative counseling tools and interventions that deepen the entire school, career, and life planning process in efficient and systematic ways. With these new techniques, counselors can understand how family background, history, mobility, support, conflicts, nurturing, and exposure to new ideas or protection from them affect the counseling process. By incorporating a more holistic approach, school counselors can engage family members as partners in a collaborative planning process. As pointed out elsewhere (Chope, 2001) counselors and their clients don't necessarily need to work alone, without a safety net. Bringing in family members to help in the decision making process could be wonderfully beneficial to all the parties concerned.

Why Should This Approach Be Taken Now?

It doesn't take much effort, really, to find examples of the influence of the family on school, career, and life

planning. After all, the career coach Mary Jacobsen (2000) has written how the dreams, even unattained dreams, of parents and caregivers, shape the career choices of their children. Goals, interests, values, and rules are often explicit.

As any school counselor knows, students often become alarmed when they feel as if they disappointed or shamed their family. Wendy Wasserstein's experience illustrates this point. When she won the Pulitzer Prize for *The Heidi Chronicles*; her mother commented with frustration that she wished that she were celebrating Wendy's nuptials instead (Aron, 2003). Comments like that, especially at the celebration of a significant life event, can make anyone feel that no matter the accomplishments, they must be consistent with the family agenda. Children learn early on to hurdle the family acceptability threshold.

Including the family influence in career and life planning interfaces well with the current contextual, constructionist, and relationship approaches to career counseling. Career decision theory and practice have evolved beyond the epistemology of logical positivism developed by early career theorists to include relationship factors. Current career literature now gives greater appreciation to the family as a part of the career counseling process (Niles & Harris-Bowlsbey, 2005)

A Brief Review of Empirical and Experiential Research

Some researchers have focused primarily on the influence of parents on career and educational planning (Niles & Harris-Bowlsbey, 2005). Parents have a lot of sway in the career choices of their children. And, they have a profound influence on the intellectual, social, and emotional components of their children's lives (Peterson & Gonzalez, 2005; Steinberg, 2004). Their guidance is a powerful component in the decision making process but more emphatically, they expose their children to a particular variety of well-intentioned career choices. Brown (2003, p. 332) posits that "...parents exercise more influence than any other adults on the educational and vocational choice of children." Ettinger (2001) suggests that parents can help with the career planning process if they can assist their children in answering questions like: Who am I? Where am I going? How do I get there? Gray and Herr (2000) have recommended a four step career awareness program beginning in the eight grade that includes parent meetings and intensive involvement with objective feedback and individual assistance.

However, recently it's been suggested that the entire family be given more consideration in understanding life planning (Blustein, Walbridge, Friedlander, & Palladino, 1991; Herr and Lear, 1984). Extended family members have been suggested as a source of terrific influence (Schultheiss, Kress, Manzi, & Glasscock, 2001) along with the influence of siblings (Kenny & Perez, 1996). In addition, Blustein (2001) points out that significant cohorts as well as teachers and other mentors also impact the career planning process and should be a source of both research and clinical material.

New Interventions and Approaches

There are a variety of approaches available to school and career counselors wishing to explore the influence of families in career decision making. Career genograms, retrospective questionnaires, and critical incident techniques are samplings of qualitative assessment methods that are applicable to the career and educational planning process.

The Career Genogram

The career genogram (Okiishi, 1987), a type of occupational family tree, is undeniably the most commonly recognized and frequently administered qualitative instrument for gathering information about family context and its influence on individual career decisions. Its is a well defined technique, easily understood by lay people and professionals alike and can readily be completed at home with or without the assistance of family members, although students report enjoying the genogram as a family project.

The genogram can help guide students in the exploration of current as well as historical, multigenerational family career development patterns. The roles, behaviors and attitudes of family members along with unfulfilled goals that specific family members had can be unearthed with this tool. Family patterns of all types can be pinpointed and the pressures of differential family standards can be discussed.

Creating a family genogram requires that the student gather pertinent information from other family members; parents, siblings, cousins, aunts, and uncles can all play a role. Families of origin and extended families can add a rich perspective to a student's particular strengths and weaknesses. Understanding personal development from the perspective of different family members sharing a common ancestry gives a unique view of the evolution of work roles in the family.

The best method of creating a genogram with a student is to first explain the purpose of the genogram and then gather have the student gather the appropriate historical information. The genogram is unstandardized so there are many different ways of constructing one. Currently there are over 8,000 genogram Web sites on the Internet identified by simply "googling" the word genogram. After the genogram is completed a number of questions can be asked to the student by the school counselor. Many of these have been suggested by Dagley (1984):

> What family patterns exist?
> Which family members had a clearly formed work identity?
> Which family member did you most admire?
> Who did you identify with?
> Whose career aspirations are most similar to your own?
> Which person was most influential in the creation of your own career identity?
> What pressures do you feel when you compare yourself to your family?
> What were the dominant values in the family?
> What legends existed?
> Are there any family myths that transcended generations?
> What about family secrets?
> Who was vocal and who was silent?
> What are the pressures that each observes with regard to decision making and economic status and position?
> What is the meaning of success?
> What are the family traditions?
> How did the family balance learning, working, and playing and how were these valued?

As suggested by the questions above, the genogram can elicit a substantial amount of information for future in-depth discussion including power differentials, political beliefs, anger, substance abuse, addictive behaviors, and emotional demands. The information extracted from the genogram permits a continuing exploration of family history, the themes that encompass the family, and how these affect the student.

Genograms can be shared as a classroom activity and can serve as an ice breaker in student workshops as well as career and educational exploration classes. Counseling with the genogram demands a high level of clinical skill and even then, Okiishi (1987) says that it may be cumbersome. Some of the same information can be obtained with good interview questions or retrospective questionnaires which follow below.

Retrospective Questionnaires

Counselors commonly assess family influence through the use of their own retrospective questionnaires. These instruments typically reflect a potpourri of ideas grounded in different theories. The following are representative instruments found both in the literature and made available to the author in unpublished form.

Taylor's Family Work History

Taylor (2003) has created a family history worksheet that she has her students fill out. Her focus is multigenerational; she requests that her students interview six individual family members or close family friends from at least three different generations (cohorts, parents, grandparents) about their work and careers.

The students are guided to gather information about the first paid experiences of the interviewees. Interviewees are also asked to describe their favorite job and to further describe the job tasks, their relationships with others on the job, and why this favorite job was so rewarding. They are also queried about favorite employers along with immediate supervisors and coworkers. Finally they are invited to provide information about their current work status or, as the case may be, their last full time paid experience. To complete the exercise, Taylor suggests that the interviewee give four "tips" or important pieces of advice to the student.

The following information is recorded from the six family members or friends:

Your first work experience–paid or unpaid.
  Your age and approximate year of the
    experience
  Where did you work?
  What did you do?
  Was this full or part time?
  What was the pay scale?

What was your favorite job?
  Where did you work?
  What were the job responsibilities and duties?
  Was this full or part time work?
  What was the pay scale?
What was your favorite company or employer?
  What made this experience your favorite?
What is your current work status?
  Your age and approximate years of the experience
  Where did you work?
  What did you do?
  Was this full or part time?
  What was the pay scale?

For those who are retired, the same questions from the current work status group are asked. A final, mentoring question is asked:

What are four tips or pieces of advice that you would offer to a family member regarding work and career development?

Taylor's history extracts the family's worldview about careers and work. The family work history, like the genogram provides an opportunity for a student to chronicle some of the memoirs that create family myths and legends. The history also provides a template for further information gathering to discover which attributes a client has that may be multigenerational.

Family Constellation Questionnaire

Peterson and Gonzalez (2005) have created a family constellation questionnaire to assist with understanding multicultural family influence while building a career genogram. This instrument can serve as a guide to gather information regarding family contextual factors:

Your racial and ethnic background
Major influences in your career decisions
Mother's occupation, father's occupation
Number of brothers and sisters
Your place in the birth order
Education of parents
Career expectations of the parents for the children
Parents' marital status
Occupations of all four grandparents
How many times have you changed careers?
Are you satisfied with your current career choice?

Peterson and Gonzalez introduce new ideas for constructivist counseling, placing race and ethnic background at the forefront of the information requested. They also include requests for information that can lead to a discussion about the impact of birth order, sibling rivalry, and parental marital status and expectations.

Chope's Family Protocol

Using variables from professional experience as well as relevant research on relational influences (Phillips, Christopher-Sisk & Gravino, 2001; Schultheiss et al., 2001). Chope (2006) developed the following instrument for gathering career development data. The instrument has six primary questions with follow-up inquiries made to questions 1 through 3 and 6 and is used to elicit important information from a client's history. It follows a constructionist strategy for gathering, organizing and understanding family data.

The questions follow, each inviting a different type of exploration.

1. What kind of career related information does your family provide?
   A. Does your family help you generate different possibilities and new experiences?
   B. Does your family suggest alternatives regarding schools, training or careers? How do these affect you?
   C. What is your family's impression of gender roles? How do these affect you?
   D. What family traditions or legends exist?
   E. Is there any "forced guidance", a tendency to push you in a direction more reflective of the family's interests than yours?
2: What tangible assistance is provided and are there any strings attached?
   A. Are tuition, books, and supplies provided?
   B. Is transportation provided to attend school or get to a job?
   C. Is housing provided or made available?
   D. Are incidentals taken care of?
   E. Will health insurance be paid for until the age of 23?
3. What type of emotional support does your family provide?
   A. How certain are you that emotional support will be available, no matter what?
   B. Does the family take a hands-off but supportive approach?

C. Is there subtle emotional pressure to pursue a particular path?
D. Are you told by the family to "just be happy"?
E. Are you told that your plans won't amount to much?
F. Who is supportive and who isn't?

4. Are you concerned about the impact of your school and career choices on the family?
5. What disruptive family events have affected you or other members of your family?
6. What are the actions of family members who were asked to help and actions of those who were not asked to help?
   A. Of those who are involved, which are welcomed and which were not?
   B. Of those who are asked to help, who offer assistance and who do not?

School counselors may notice that these questions point to the projected fantasies of the family and may outweigh the information base and realities of the job market. The questions inform counselors of the family's impressions of particular roles that they wish their children will play both now and in the future.

What is clear from all of the retrospective questionnaires is that hypotheses can evolve from the data and the subsequent client narratives that ensue. It's also clear that the retrospective questionnaire technique demands that the school counselor be well skilled in asking follow up questions. Of course, more in-depth questions can be asked as well that focus on the developmental, interpersonal, psychodynamic, and sociological influences as well as intriguing multicultural and multiethnic, gender and political issues and events. These all shape career choice and planning.

Critical Incidents

Time lines have been a hallmark of developmental career theory (Super, 1990). Using a time line, students, teachers, classmates and counselors can explore the critical public and private incidents that have taken place that could be considered disruptive or enhancing to all of their career paths. Some examples include weather disasters, tragedies like September 11th, excessive relocations, the untimely death of a significant other, separation or divorce, job loss, the closing of a business, or something as simple but traumatic as moving away from the safety of home.

Students may draw a horizontal line and break it

up into three to five year increments with the line going from birth until the present. In each interval, the student can write down critical events that have impacted their lives. These events can be personal and historical. If any students don't have any personal critical incidents, a teacher or counselor could consider current news events as examples.

After enumerating the critical incidents, students can review and comparatively discuss the effect of the critical incidents on their life planning. Uncertainty about the future, self esteem issues, or simple choices about interests and career pursuits can be discussed with this in mind.

Young and Friesen (1992) examined the intentions of parents who wanted to influence the career development of the children, and they found that they could translate over 1,500 critical incidents and parents' responses to them into ten intentions that parents had for the children. These were: skill acquisition; acquisition of values and beliefs; protection from an unwanted experience; increase in independent thinking or action; decrease in sex role stereotypes; moderation of parent child relationships; facilitation of human relationships; enhancement of career development, particularly self esteem and self efficacy; development of personal responsibility; and achievement of parents personal goals. This list of intentions can be framed as a series of questions that counselors may use to explore the intentions of parents.

Strategies for Implementation

So how can school counselors further use the results of the qualitative assessment of family influence? Qualitative family assessment can open new clinical possibilities for counselors. Beyond what is presented here, there are undoubtedly many other unpublished instruments that school counselors have created for themselves to delve into the interaction between family influence and career decisions.

The gathering of family historical data allows for the evaluation and understanding of family interaction patterns and the family's meaning of success. Data may be used to assist clients and other family members to rethink traditional measures of success, and counselors can assist clients to define success with respect to what gives meaning to their lives. Learning about the stories and examples of other family members who have had alternative choices can be encouraging. Supportive family members can help to impart new information to students, material that the client may be oblivious to.

This approach can open up innovative family contributions. The family could be encouraged to serve as a creative "sounding board". A supportive family will teach the possibility of forging new connections and networks. Clients who have developed a sense of connectedness and partnerships through family networking could be in a better position to develop stronger social connections and potential employment networks. The family, by example, assists with this and can work to maintain new and developing relationships to help.

Newcomers to the job market will need all the support that they can muster and that is why the family's so important. It can be the one place where people feel safe discussing their ideas and aspirations. I'd like to briefly offer eight tips for demonstrating how the family can be used in a positive way in career planning.

Mattering

People need to feel that they matter. Mattering has been defined as a perception or belief that people hold onto suggesting that somebody else cares about them, whether that perception is correct or not (Schlossberg, Lynch, & Chickering, 1989). People like to be recognized for who they are. People matter when they are given advice, and they matter when their advice is listened to. School counselors might offer some simple advice. Make your students' family members feel that they count, listen to their well intentioned ideas, and let your students be aware of the concerns of their family.

Group Decision Making

People shouldn't try to make difficult decisions alone and that advice is extended here. Career decisions don't have to be made in a vacuum, and the addition of the support of the family can make the process a more pleasant one. Extended family members can offer all types of practical ideas regarding colleges and universities as well as apprenticeships, volunteering, or part time projects.

Building and Maintaining a Strong Network

Everyone needs to establish and maintain a strong network. Individual connections are a job seeker's most important asset. People obtain jobs by who they know (Bolles, 2001). And the people we seem to know first and foremost are from the family. So, in any job search, people need an up to date e-mail address book, beginning with the immediate as well as the extended family.

In addition to keeping the e-mail contacts, people can let everyone in their family address book know what kind of work they are looking for by sending out a broadcast letter. Activities like these can help a job seeker to be focused and direct with clear objectives honed with concerned family members. If any students or career seekers are unable to name what they're searching for, then they can use the family network to generate ideas or point to new possibilities.

Knowing Talents

Everyone has accrued both specific and transferable skills and should know what these are. Students should practice selling these talents to family members. Resumes and cover letters should be crafted so that these attributes sparkle. This is an arena where the family can be useful both as a source of support and a gentle critic. Family members can spend some time generating ideas about self-promotion. They can also review resumes and cover letters and lend suggestions for improvement.

Relocating

We live in a highly mobile society and among a highly mobile workforce. Part of the difficulty that people have with the workforce is what Putnam (2000) has refereed to as the "repotting hypothesis". Frequent mobility and "repotting" tends to disrupt root systems. But family support can help. Family contact can make people feel less uprooted, freeing them to pursue positions that may be out of the area.

Gathering assistance from family members who have lived in particular locations or states can provide useful information about costs of housing, taxes, economic prospects, and the like.

Regularly Reviewing Decisions

Too often we think of our career decisions as final. Yet they should really be considered transient and subject to periodic review. The Gelatts (2003) have suggested that people need to be focused and flexible in what they do and to treat goals as hypotheses. This suggests a never ending type of decision making model. Families can help with the review process. People are often able to manage their career decisions by knowing which opportunities are the best for them.

Being Creative

In the 21st century, creativity is demanded from everyone. And families can help here, too. Creative questioning is becoming a part of the job search process. Human resources professionals now recommend that job seekers read books like *How Would You Move Mt. Fuji?* (Poundstone, 2003). To evaluate creative thinking and imagination, interviewers are asking questions that seem to resemble brain teasers. Families can help here with practice by suggesting "out of the box" questions.

Maintaining Vision, Flexibility, and Adaptability Along with Realistic Expectations

Maybe this is where the family can offer the most support. The difficult decisions that we all make take us on a journey. Sometimes it takes us where we want to go and other times we end up somewhere else. Ironically, the somewhere else could be the best place for us to be.

Conclusion

This chapter has presented a variety of challenges for the future. It has suggested places where families can help job seekers in appropriate and powerful ways. The family can improve the self esteem of the job seekers by making them feel that they matter. They can offer evaluative assistance and provide well placed contacts from their own network. With the world of work continuing to be in some turmoil, family members can support students and counselors when they try innovative approaches to educational, career, and life planning.

Discussion Questions

1. What benefits would school counselors experience by incorporating family members into the career planning process?
2. Why should the entire extended family be considered in the life planning?
3. What is a career genogram and how should it be used in career and life planning?
4. What types of career related material can be gleaned from retrospective questionnaires?
5. What are critical incidents and how can school counselors use them in educational and career planning?
6. What is a "network" and what role does the family play in establishing and maintaining a strong network?
7. How can parents assist their children in being creative but also inculcating them with realistic expectations about their careers?
8. What structural issues might make it difficult to incorporate the family into the school counseling career planning process?

9. Which clients would probably gain the most advantage by having the family engaged in the career planning process?
10. Why is there so little research exploring the influence of the family in career decision making?

References

Aron, W. (2003, August 25). Every Jewish mother's worst nightmare. *Newsweek*, 14.

Blustein, D. (2001). The interface of work and relationships: Critical knowledge for the 21st century psychology. *The Counseling Psychologist, 29*, 179-192.

Blustein, D. L., Walbridge, M. M., Friedlander, M. L., & Palladino, D.E. (1991). Contributions of psychological separation and parental attachment to the career development process. *Journal of Counseling Psychology, 38*, 39-50.

Bolles, R. N. (2001). *What color is your parachute.* Berkeley, CA: Ten Speed Press.

Brown, D. (2003). *Career information, career counseling, and career development* (8th ed.). Boston: Allyn & Bacon.

Chope, R. C. (2001). *Shared confinement: Healing options for you and the agoraphobic in your life.* Oakland, CA: New Harbinger Publications.

Chope, R. C. (2006). *Family matters: The influence of the family in career decision making.* Austin, TX: Pro-Ed.

Dagley, J. (1984). *A vocational genogram* [Mimeograph]. Athens, GA: University of Georgia.

Ettinger, J. (2001). *A guide to planning and implementating K-12 career development programs.* Center on Education and Work, University of Wisconsin-Madison.

Gelatt, H. B., & Gelatt, C. (2003). *Creative decision making using positive uncertainty.* Menlo Park, CA: Crisp Publications.

Gray, K. C., & Herr, E. L. (2000). *Other ways to win: Creating alternatives for high school graduates* (2nd ed). Thousand Oaks, CA: Corwin Press.

Herr, E. L., & Lear, P. B. (1984). The family as an influence on career development. *Family Therapy Collections, 10*, 1-15.

Jacobsen, M. H. (2000). *Hand-me-down dreams: How families influence our career paths.* New York: Three Rivers Press.

Kenny, M. E., & Perez, V. (1996). Attachment and psychological well being among racially and ethnically diverse first-year college students. *Journal of College Student Development, 37*, 527-535.

Niles, S. G., & Harris-Bowlsbey, J. (2005). *Career development interventions in the 21st Century* (2nd ed.). Upper Saddle River, NJ: Pearson Education.

Okiishi, R. W. (1987). The genogram as a tool in career counseling. *Journal of Counseling and Development, 66*, 139-143.

Peterson, N., & Gonzalez, R. (2005). *The role of work in people's lives: Applied career counseling and vocational psychology* (2nd ed.). Pacific Grove, CA: Brooks Cole.

Phillips, S. S., Christopher-Sisk, E. K., & Gravino, K. L. (2001). Making career decisions in a relational context. *The Counseling Psychologist, 29*, 193-213.

Poundstone, W. (2003). *How would you move Mt. Fuji? Microsoft's cult of the puzzle-How the world's smartest company selects the most creative thinkers.* Boston: Little Brown & Co.

Putnam, R. D. (2000). *Bowling alone.* New York: Simon and Schuster.

Schlossberg, N. K., Lynch, A. Q., & Chickering, A.W. (1989). *Improving higher education environments for adults.* San Francisco, CA :Jossey-Bass.

Schultheiss, D., Kress, H., Manzi, A., & Glasscock, J. (2001). Relational influences in Career development: A qualitative inquiry. *The Counseling Psychologist, 29*, 214-239.

Steinberg, L. (2004). *The 10 basic principles of good parenting.* New York: Simon and Schuster.

Super, D. E. (1990). A life-span, life life-space approach to career development. In D. Brown & L. Brooks (Eds.), *Career choice and development: Applying contemporary theories to practice* (2nd ed., pp 197-261). San Francisco, CA: Jossey-Bass.

Taylor, T. (2003). *Family work history* [Mimeograph]. Livermore, CA: Career Tayloring, Career Counseling & Consulting Services.

Young, R., & Friesen, J. (1992). The intentions of parents in influencing the career development of their children. *The Career Development Quarterly, 40*, 198-207.

Chapter 25

Helping Unfocused and At-Risk Kids with Career Planning

Suzy Mygatt Wakefield and Deborah Crapes

Abstract

The term "unfocused kids", coined by the first author, seeks to capture the essence of teens who cannot connect what they are doing in school with what they are doing outside of school—their "real world." Often, they do not see their time in school as having anything to do with their real lives. This author employs the term "unfocused kids" in an effort to bring more career development support to these teens. This article provides strategies to help teens explore many career opportunities and to develop their own "high school and beyond plan."

Introduction: Who Are Unfocused Kids?

The term "unfocused kids" seems to capture for many people the essence of teens who just cannot connect what they are doing in school with what they are doing outside of school—their "real world." Often, they do not see their time in school as having anything to do with their real lives. They do the minimum to get by, do not connect school work and homework with skills they will really need in the real world, and put little thought into their future plans. Most do at least the minimum to stay on track towards graduation; although dropout statistics tell us that many do not even do that (Thornburgh, 2006). "They tend to be academic underachievers and see little value in career guidance activities" (Wakefield, Sage, & Coy, 2004, p. 8). We now know that one third of ninth graders do not manage to graduate four years later with their class (Greene, 2002).

The Path of Least Resistance

Fritz (1984) has described the path of least resistance as a river and suggests that we are each "like a river" in that we go through life taking the path of least resistance. To change that, one must change the layout (the bedrock) of the riverbed.

If a riverbed remains unchanged, the water will continue to flow along the path it always has, since that is the most natural route for it to take. If the underlying structures of your life remain unchanged, the greatest tendency is for you to follow the direction your life has always taken..." (Fritz, 1984, p. 5)

The metaphor applies to teens who appear unfocused and without much guidance--except to follow their own path of least resistance. Unless there is some sort of intervention, such as an educational program taught by committed educators with specific goals and objectives to help students see life in other ways and with new skill-sets, students tend to continue along the same path. As engineers might excavate a new riverbed, it is important for educators and parents to understand how important it is to redirect disengaged young people to help them take charge of their lives and their education.

The path of least resistance, regarding why students drop out, is illustrated by Bylsma and Ireland (2002, p. 9) in *Graduation and Dropout Statistics for Washington's Counties, Districts, and School Final Report, School Year 2001-2002.* The reasons students drop out include: "expelled or suspended, poor grades, school not for me/stayed home, married and needed to support family, pregnant or had a baby, offered training, chose to work, or other." Although this is a rather dated list of options, probably developed in the 1960s or before, as school attendance is now mandatory in some states until the age of 18, it does capture the typical options taken by students who leave school.

Most students who drop out do so in their senior year, according to Bylsma and Ireland (2002, p. 9). Students often seem embarrassed when they are not able to keep up with their friends in terms of earning credits toward graduation. The senior year is crunch time. Either students are lined up to graduate, with adequate credits, or they are not. Without family pressure not to quit school, it has been this retired high school counselor's impression that a student caught in that bind tends to leave school and move on in the world of work without a diploma, earn minimum wage, and regroup. That would be the path of least resistance. In fact, Hoyt (2001) reported that approximately 22 million of the anticipated 50 million new jobs between the years 1996-2006 would only require two to three weeks of short-term, on-the-job training, so that low-skilled, low wage, and dead end jobs have been plentiful in the American economy. Just look at who is taking your order at Dairy Queen, Jack in the Box, McDonalds, Taco Bell, and so forth. Fast food restaurant wages aren't necessarily bad for teens starting out as they learn responsibility, punctuality, and how to work with the public, but the prospect for managerial and financial growth in the fast food industry, for most, is probably minimal. Their odds of earning a living wage at that job for forty hours a week are minimal; usually they would need to work at least two jobs to make ends meet.

Classroom Behavior

Many students seem unfocused while in school. Teachers often discuss these issues during their lunch hour.

One wonders, when looking in on a typical American classroom, why some students appear focused and purposefully occupied with the teacher and classroom activities, while others seem so unfocused and preoccupied. They may pass notes to their friends, or stare into space, or simply sleep at their desks. In this country of remarkable opportunity, what is going on? How is it that we have so many adolescents in high school who appear so disengaged and unfocused? Even educators with many years of experience appear to be puzzled about this strange phenomenon—the increasing number of unfocused, unmotivated students. (Wakefield et al., 2004, pp. 8-9)

This author has defined *unfocused kids* by indicating that they have the following characteristics: they haven't put much effort into planning for their future and do the minimum to get by; they seem to have no clear sense of educational focus or purpose and lack a focal point; they do not connect what they are learning in school with their lives outside of school; and they do not see success in school as a stepping stone to success in life.

One wonders, "How has this happened?" Steinberg (1996) suggests that through long work hours, participation in multiple activities, not *prioritizing achievement* in school, and just plain too many distractions—including peer influence—students do not take full advantage of their schooling. He further reports

that 25-30 percent of parents are "disengaged" with their kids. They do *not* know how they spend their free time, who they are hanging out with, or even how they are doing in school. He says that these parents have basically "checked out."

Further, European and Asian teens tend to take more difficult academic subjects, take a much longer school day, work very few hours outside of school, and have limited time for socializing. On average, American kids would find these expectations unpleasant, if not downright intolerable. Steinberg adds that the average American student spends *four hours per week* on homework outside of school. In other industrialized nations, the average is *four hours per day!* (Steinberg, p. 184). That is not to say that there are not many highly motivated students in our public high schools, packing in four hours of homework a night, to be prepared for their Advanced Placement and/or International Baccalaureate courses that they take in school each day. But this chapter isn't about them. It's about the unfocused kids who are not taking advantage of the remarkable educational and career exploration opportunities offered in thousands of our public high schools.

College Dropout Rates

Let's take a brief look at college dropout rates. According to Tom Mortenson (2002), editor of the periodical *Postsecondary Education Opportunity*, "*One in four freshmen* at four-year universities does not return for their sophomore year. *One in two freshmen* (48.2 percent) at community/technical colleges does not return for their second year." He draws his statistics from ACT National Dropout Rates (1983-2002) data. But the flip side of this issue is that taking the third year of college-preparatory math (2nd year Algebra or higher) while still in high school can do much to increase one's chances of graduating from college—by 73 percent, according to Trusty and Niles (2004) referencing the National Education Longitudinal Study (NELS). In a longitudinal study of 3,116 students, using the NELS 88 Sample (U.S. Department of Education, 2002), students who were selected in the 8th grade as above average in their reading and math and who indicated that they planned to attend college were found to be 73 percent more likely to graduate from college within 8 years than if they did *not* take Algebra 2 or higher math while in high school. This is an astounding finding and certainly speaks to the need for all students who are math-capable to take as much math as is reasonably possible. Their foreign counterparts in Asia and Europe are prioritizing math, so American students must prepare wisely to compete in the highly competitive global marketplace.

At-Risk Kids

Another category of student is the at-risk student, who may be drug or alcohol involved, from a single parent family, from low socio-economic status, or may even be homeless. Capuzzi and Gross (1989) suggest that young people who make poor choices about their lives often do so as a result of painful personal circumstances beyond their control; consequently, they face a "limited choice repertoire." They just do not see other alternatives so tend to take the first opportunities that come along, whether they are wise choices or not. Capuzzi and Gross add that personal circumstances, over which a teen has little control, may have a profoundly negative impact on their lives and lead to further destructive choices. These circumstances might include: a dysfunctional or destructive/abusive family environment, low family income forcing a student to work long hours, and/or marginal academic ability. Young people in these circumstances tend to choose what gives them immediate satisfaction, thus limiting better choices and options. Adults working with young people in these circumstances can help them to see beyond their immediate problem and to consider more productive coping strategies.

In the Spokane School District, Deb Crapes (Career Specialist and co-author) reports that a number of activities are provided for students to help them expand their options:

- Senior Project and Career Planning Portfolios
- Career Exploration activities—such as the Career Fair or College Fair
- Various Career Assessments—such as the *Washington Occupational Information System/ The Career Information System Interest Profiler and Skills Assessment*
- Mock interviewing
- Informational interviewing, job shadows, and internships
- Volunteer/service learning
- Business and college visits and tours
- Non-traditional and hands-on Career Fairs
- Guest speakers
- Special workshops on specific topics

The Spokane School District offers a variety of workshops on topics including: the job and college application process; writing resumes and cover letters; preparing for a job interview including dressing appropriately; and financial aid and scholarship workshops. Another option offered to students is based on the partnership between the Spokane School District and the local area community colleges, which provides a counselor who visits with high school students once a month—to provide support. The district has been able to secure funding for free college applications and entrance placement testing for juniors and seniors—using the Comprehensive Computer Adaptive Testing System. Last year, over 75 percent of the graduating senior class from the alternative high school, Havermale High School in Spokane, were accepted and registered in the two local community colleges— Spokane Community College and Spokane Falls Community College, with many students receiving complete financial aid packages. These students will be monitored, and additional resources will be provided to help them succeed in the community college.

Other resources include providing the Armed Services Vocational Aptitude Battery (ASVAB) to juniors and seniors and the Junior Achievement programs that provide guest speakers on a variety of topics and participate in their annual Groundhog Day Job Shadow Program. There is a strong coordination of programs between the school district and government service agencies, apprenticeship programs, and local employers to provide students many opportunities to try out their skills and to successfully fit into the World of Work.

Career Development Leadership Provided by ASCA

The American School Counselor Association (ASCA, 2003) has provided great support in the area of career development for *all* students by establishing clear career development standards for comprehensive high school counseling programs. In particular, ASCA has developed three domains, which are "broad developmental areas including standards and competencies and promote behaviors that enhance learning for all students" (ASCA, 2003, p. 32). The three inter-related domains are: academic, personal/social, and career development.

These domains incorporate *standards*, which are "those statements providing a description of what students should know and be able to do at the highest level of expectation", *competencies*, which are "specific expectations that students achieve in the content standard areas", and *indicators*, which describe the "specific knowledge, skills or abilities that individuals demonstrate to meet a specific competency" (ASCA, 2003, p. 32). The ASCA National Model (ASCA, 2003) has done much to provide templates with standards, competencies, and indicators in the area of career development to help school counselors and administrators design their own school-wide and district-wide career development programs. An example is Narragansett High School in Rhode Island, where the school counseling department has developed a career development program for all students incorporating the SCANS competencies, the career development competencies in the *ASCA National Model*, and the National Career Development Guidelines (O'Brien, Pinch, &Shuman, 2006). SCANS is an acronym for the Secretary's Commission on Achieving Necessary Skills, developed by the U.S. Department of Labor in 1991, incorporating both foundation skills (Basic Skills, Thinking Skills, and Personal Qualities) as well as Competencies (Resources, Interpersonal Skills, Information, Systems, and Technology.) The authors indicate, "SCANS connects to everything that counselors do, and it is aligned with the ASCA National Model. Counselors can apply SCANS in a variety of ways without changing their current system. It can be applied individually, in small groups and in larger presentations" (pp. 42-43). In all, it has been found that "students are better prepared to develop career goals based on their awareness and knowledge of skills required for success in particular careers [and] they can answer the question, 'Why do I need to do this (take certain courses, meet certain standards, and participate in career planning)?'" (O'Brien, Pinch, & Shuman, 2006, p. 40). This high school program is an excellent example of collaboration by school counselors with the ASCA National Model, the SCANS Report, and the National Career Development Guidelines.

Working Together to Provide Career Development for All Students

Kuranz (2002) reports that the average student-counselor ratio is 551:1, although strides are being made in some states to lower this ratio. With ratios that high, it is virtually impossible for school counselors alone to provide career development programs for all students, thus necessitating all appropriate educators and community members to collaborate to provide these programs. As stated earlier, ASCA has developed standards in the academic, career, and personal/social development domains, with specific career development standards as part of the *ASCA National Mode: A*

Framework for School Counseling Programs (ASCA, 2003). These standards are very helpful to school counselors when developing school-wide, sequential, age-appropriate career guidance programs with administrators and teachers.

Washington State's "High School and Beyond Plan"

Career development can play an important role in student success. It is best if a mandate for career development for *all* students comes from the state level, so that educators are pulling together. Otherwise, the competition for student time in their academic and technical classes tends to preclude an emphasis on career development as well as releasing students from class to attend career development activities, such as career units, College Fairs, Career Fairs, and so forth. An example of a state mandate for career development comes from the state of Washington. In 2000, the State Board of Education proposed and implemented a new set of graduation requirements for the class of 2008—*Washington State Minimum High School Graduation Requirements*. Students must pass the Washington Assessment of Student Learning (WASL) which is the Washington State proficiency exam, as well as present a culminating project, and complete a "High School and Beyond Plan"—going one year past high school.

For example, in the Spokane School District in eastern Washington, students must complete various career assessments by grade level and save their results to an electronic portfolio. Many districts use WOIS/The Career Information System (see www.wois.org) to guide students through their planning. This career delivery service has career and college information and a variety of career and personal assessments to explore student skills, values, and abilities. The portfolio that the students create through the WOIS system contains many components, including: assessment results, awards/ scholarships/ honors; best works; career research; cover letter and resume management; an educational planner; essays; external links; school involvement; and work/community experience. This is a permanent Internet site where students can keep all of their information in one spot—in their electronic career planning portfolio. This portfolio follows the students through their high school career and can be transferred to a college as they continue on to postsecondary education. This example shows the importance and power of a state mandate to provide career development activities for all students; it is up to each district as to how to meet the mandate.

Therefore, educators must work together with parents and people in the community to provide career guidance for *all* students. The job is too difficult and too demanding for one group to take on the responsibility by themselves. It must be shared! Career guidance for teens is everybody's job—school counselors, teachers, career specialists, administrators, parents, employers and legislators! We all must help! We need to sit down together and work out plans to support each other in our efforts to provide appropriate and meaningful career development experiences for all teens.

Strategies to Help Students Find Career Planning Opportunities

Here are some suggestions to help teens to recognize and act on career exploration and career planning opportunities. First, they need to recognize that there is an opportunity. Otherwise, opportunities are missed. Then they need to act on it. Here are some ways in which teens may enhance their chances to pursue and follow up with some career planning opportunities.

1. *Students need opportunities to explore their strengths and interests*—through firsthand experiences in academic classes, special skills classes such as art and technology, and social and athletic activities. They can also do this by gaining experience, through participation in school activities: career interest testing such as the ASVAB; extracurricular activities; leadership; guest speakers; Career Days; Internet career delivery systems (www.wois.org & www.onetcenter.org); job search skills (resumes, cover letters, thank-you letters); internships; mentorships; and volunteer/service learning. Students can participate in those special experiences (enhancers) that will look good on resumes and teach them more about a particular field (Harris & Jones, 1997). Examples are: a special summer school program; a foreign exchange program; special computer training; a special volunteer experience; a carefully selected part-time job; or an internship. Enhancers can help a student be accepted into college, or be hired for a specific job.

2. *Students also need to be encouraged to acknowledge their weaknesses and dislikes.* It is important to note the feedback from experiences that do not work out. Learning what one does not like is as important as learning what one does like! Both experiences have great value in guiding future decisions.

3. *Students need to be encouraged to seek out those adults and peers with whom they can talk about their career plans*—their parents/guardians, teachers, and friends. These relationships are crucial for them—for emotional support, financial guidance, and just plain interest in what they're doing. They need adults and friends who will push them or inspire them to achieve. Many adults remember those special people who made a big difference in their lives.

4. *Students need to learn about a broad range of occupational opportunities*—through the Internet, career exploration units, class projects, job shadow experiences and internships, and part-time jobs. Teens need to get out there and find out what's going on. They need to ask others about their jobs and how they got them—and what they like and dislike about them! Informational interviews can provide useful information and contacts.

5. *Students need to write down their Education and Career Plan*; in Washington State, this is called a "High School and Beyond Plan." Components may include: required and elective courses grades 9-12; extracurricular activities; career areas to explore; long and short-term goals; part-time jobs; field experiences including volunteer/service learning, job shadows, and internships; and tentative career choices and educational plans after high school.

6. *Students need to organize their Personal Career Planning Portfolio*, as a place to keep all of this information. Components may include: Education and Career Plan; career search information; career interest inventory results; self-assessment results; postsecondary education and training information; best works—essays and projects; cover letters and job applications; resumes; hobbies; extracurricular activities; and a journal.

7. *Students need to complete a Culminating Project (Senior Project)*. Many school districts require that teens to do a culminating project—that may be based on a career interest. This usually involves 60 documented hours by the student, oversight by a teacher advisor, a research project, a presentation before a panel, and often an internship. In many districts, this is a graduation requirement. In Washington State, it is required for graduation for the class of 2008.

8. *Students need to build a network of contacts—* friends, neighbors, relatives, business contacts, college contacts, and employers. Teens need to keep track of their contacts through their telephone or computer address book, and find a good place to keep business cards so that they can follow up later, if needed.

9. *Students need to learn job search skills—*how to write resumes, cover letters, and thank you letters; how to interview effectively—through mock interviews; and how to dress and speak appropriately.

10. *Students need to do a job shadow, internship, volunteer/service learning experience, or take a real part-time job.* They need to find out what the job is really like, and to find out what the people are like who go into this field, and what the pay and conditions are like. Teens need to find out what they like and what they don't like about this field.

11. *Finally, students need to evaluate where they are.* Are they satisfied with their choices? Do they like their course of action? If not, they need to go back to Step One: *Explore their strengths and interests. Take a closer look.* Exploring their strengths and interests is the key to effective educational and career planning and to their ultimate career satisfaction. If teens find something they truly enjoy, they will work very hard to find a way to be successful. It is our job as adults, educators, parents, employers, and other community members to find and create as many meaningful career exploration and career planning opportunities as possible for our kids!

Discussion Questions

1. You have read the author's definition of an "unfocused kid." In your experience, how do you characterize "unfocused kids"?

2. Were you aware that the high school dropout rate in our country is one out of three? If so, what steps have you thought about taking to help remedy the situation?

3. Were you aware that one out of four university students, in the aggregate, does not return for their sophomore year? Are you able to get statistics on attrition data from your local colleges and universities? (Have you found this information difficult to acquire?)

4. Were you aware that one out of two community/technical college students, in the aggregate, do not return for their sophomore year (second year)? Are you able to get statistics on attrition data from your local community/technical colleges?

5. If you are able to get college/university attrition data, would that be useful in your current graduate school or work setting? How would you use that data?

6. Were you aware that high school students taking one additional year of college-prep math (2nd year Algebra) are found to be 73 percent more likely to graduate from college? If so, how is this information useful to you—as far as working with students, and as far as working with other educators and school board members?

7. What are some methods with which you are familiar to help "unfocused" and at-risk students with their career planning? Did this chapter add any ideas for you?

8. Does your training program or school setting utilize the ASCA National Model? If so, have you found support with planning for Career Development activities and with acquiring outcome data? Further, have you developed *competencies* and *indicators* based on the three ASCA *domains* (i.e., personal/social development, academic development and career development) and related standards?

9. Have you developed *competencies* and *indicators* based on the three ASCA domains (e.g., personal/social development, academic development, and career development) and related *standards*?

10. Do you believe that counselor-student ratio makes a difference in the quality of school counseling services provided? Explain.

11. In your state, are there overall requirements that *require* an education plan or a senior/culminating project (which, in effect, gives each school district overall support with career development priority for each student)? If not, please contact the Washington State Board of Education website at www.sbe.wa.gov or the Workforce Training Board at www.wtb.wa.gov as resources.

References

American School Counselor Association. (2003). *The ASCA National Model: A framework for school counseling programs.* Alexandria, VA: Author.

Bylsma, P., & Ireland, L. (2002). *Graduation and dropout statistics for Washington's counties,* districts, and schools. *Final report, school year 2000-2001*. Olympia, WA: Office of the Superintendent of Public Instruction.

Capuzzi, D., & Gross, D. (1989). *Youth at risk: A resource for counselors, teachers, and parents*. Alexandria, VA: American Association for Counseling and Development.

Fritz, R. (1984). *The path of least resistance*. New York: Fawcett Columbine.

Greene, J. P. (2002). *Graduation rates in Washington state*. New York: Manhattan Institute for Policy Research. Retrieved December 19, 2002, from www.manhattan-institute.org/html/cr_27.htm

Grossman, L. (2005, January 24). They just won't grow up. *Time, 165*(4), 42-54.

Harris, M. B., & Jones, S. L. (1997) *The parents' crash course in career planning*. Lincolnwood, IL: VGM Career Horizons.

Hoyt, K. B. (2001). Helping high school students broaden their knowledge of postsecondary options. *Professional School Counseling, 5*(1), 6-12.

Kuranz, M. (2002). Cultivating student potential. *Professional School Counseling, 5*(3), 172-179.

Mortenson, T. G. (2002). *ACT National Dropout Rates, 1983-2002*. Retrieved August 22, 2002, from the Postsecondary Education Opportunity Web site: www.postsecondary.org/archives/Reports/Spreadsheets?ACT%20National%20Dropout

O'Brien, S., Pinch, S., & Shuman, R. (2006, March-April). Building the school-to-work connection. *ASCA School Counselor, 43*(4), 39-43.

Steinberg, L. (1996). *Beyond the classroom—why school reform has failed and what parents need to do*. New York: Touchstone.

Thornburgh, N. (2006, April 17). Dropout nation. *Time, 167*(16), 30-40.

Trusty, J., & Niles, S. (2004, September). Realized potential or lost talent: High school variables and bachelor degree completion. *The Career Development Quarterly, 53*, 2-15.

U.S. Department of Education-Office of Educational Research (2002). *National Education Longitudinal Study: 1988-2000 Data Files and Electronic Codebook System* (NCES 2002-322). Washington, DC: Author.

Wakefield, S. M., Sage, H., & Coy, D. R. (Eds.). (2004). *Unfocused kids: Helping sudents to focus on their education and career plans—A resource for educators*. Greensboro, NC: CAPS Press and the American Counseling Association.

Washington state minimum high school graduation requirements (WAC 180-51-061), Effective Fall 2004 for entering ninth graders and in 2008 for graduating seniors. Retrieved December 10, 2002, from www.leg.wa.gov/wac/ (The full set of graduation requirements may be found at the Washington State Board of Education [SBE] Web site at www.sbe.wa.gov)

Chapter 26

The Real Game Series: Helping Students Imagine Their Future

Phil Jarvis and Michael Gangitano

Abstract

Accelerating change in contemporary workplaces is altering the focus of career development from helping people choose career destinations to helping them learn essential career and life management competencies. Among the most effective learning strategies are future-based simulations with role-playing in which learner's imaginations are engaged. This chapter introduces a series of learning resources for teachers and counselors to help students imagine themselves in adult life and work scenarios set in the future. With specific regard to the ASCA national standards in the ASCA National Model, The Real Game Series completely aligns itself with all three domains: academic, career, and personal /social development.

Introducing *The Real Game*

Bill Barry, a teacher, writer, and actor, decided something needed to be done when his 12-year old daughter said she couldn't see any connection between her school subjects and her dreams (Perry, 2004). Bill took it to heart and asked, "What if we could give young people a practice run at being an adult while they're still in school – something that feels like the real world they'll soon be part of?" Bill set out to develop an engaging program that would make learning about careers and work fun and interesting. This was the genesis of *The Real Game*.

There is clear evidence that helping students "make informed and considered career decisions results in improved matches between people and their work. Such matching manifests itself in improved utilization of education and training resources, higher levels of worker satisfaction, preferred patterns of employment stability and mobility, increased income and benefits, and many attendant benefits to families and communities" (Gillie & Isenhour, 2003). It is difficult for educators to find ways to help students make informed career decisions in an era of academic accountability and high stakes testing. Yet, without a vision of their career future, too many students fail to see the personal relevance of their studies, thus lacking motivation to do their best academically. Moreover, it has been the tradition of most academic institutions not to address career issues until students reach high school, if at all. Thus, too many students who enter post-secondary programs or the workforce after high school are ill prepared, have no clear goals, and lack the necessary career management skills to succeed. Opportunities for those who find themselves in these situations are limited at best, which in turn puts enormous pressures on a myriad of other societal institutions, including families.

As we continue to search for ways to address this challenge, we need to keep a watchful eye for any vehicle that can assist us. *The Real Game* is one such program. With its humble beginning, when a father created an experiment in response to his daughter's concerns that what she was learning in school did not connect with her dreams, *The Real Game* has evolved into a series of programs and an international phenomenon (Barry, 2005). Today, millions of children and adults are engaged daily in the programs of *The Real Game Series* (Jarvis, 2000), acquiring critical career management skills they will use all their lives, increasing their awareness of potentially satisfying career opportunities, and gaining hope and confidence about their future.

In the simplest terms, *The Real Game* engages students in a classroom setting around career management issues in such a way that they become immersed in real life, practical adult scenarios in which they learn and practice skills in making career and lifestyle choices (Jarvis & Gangitano, 2004). In our experience, one of the most difficult challenges of the classroom teacher is convincing young people that what they are doing in school is important and will arm them with skills, knowledge, and attitudes that will help them create a successful life for themselves. Far too many students simply fail to see the relevance of their experience in school. With the best of intentions, we endeavor to impart knowledge to our students without helping them understand how this knowledge will touch their lives in real, practical ways that make sense to them "here and now." This is exactly what *The Real Game* does, in a way that is fun and engaging for students, *and for educators*.

The Real Game Series consists of six separate programs, each of which is tailored to a specific range of age and grade levels, as follows:

THE REAL GAME SERIES

PROGRAM	GRADES	AGES
The Play Real Game	3 to 4	8 to 10
The Make It Real Game	5 to 6	10 to 12
The Real Game	7 and 8	12 to 14
The Be Real Game	9 and 10	14 to 16
The Get Real Game	11 and 12	16 to 18
Real Times, Real Life	Post-secondary	Adults

The programs are packaged in three-ring binders that include all facilitator and student materials (including overhead transparencies, posters, and reproducible masters) needed to implement the programs for as many participants as desired, year after year. The series is highly flexible, allowing customization of the lessons to fit almost any institutional framework and schedule. These programs are used in K-12 schools, colleges, universities, one-stop career resource centers and employment service sites, vocational rehabilitation and workers' compensation offices, human resource offices, correctional institutions, military settings, summer camps, faith-based groups, and other settings across the United States, Canada, the United Kingdom, France, The Netherlands, Ireland, Germany, Hungary, Australia, and New Zealand.

The series incorporates increasingly challenging concepts and vocabulary which students learn by taking on real life and work roles in the safety of the classroom. The learning objectives and performance measures are deliberately aligned with state department of education academic and career and technical education learning standards, as well as with the National Career Development Guidelines, the American School Counselor Association (ASCA) National Model for School Counseling Programs, and the Secretaries Commission on Achieving Necessary Skills (SCANS) Employability Skills.

With specific regard to the ASCA national standards in the *ASCA National Model* (ASCA, 2005), *The Real Game Series* completely aligns itself with all three domains: academic, career, and personal /social development. The lessons do a wonderful job of linking the importance of academic success with future work and life realities. It also focuses significantly on what would be considered the "soft skills" (e.g., respect for self and others, teamwork and collaboration, personal responsibility, and many others). As a school counselor, the author has come to view this resource as invaluable for engaging students and a vehicle to place them in the right environment to explore their futures and acquire the vital skills they will need on their personal journeys.

Career Management Principles

Five career management-guiding principles called the "High Five" are incorporated into all six programs in the series. They are:

1. *Change is Constant "We change constantly and so does the world around us."*

The day has long past when one could enter the work force after high school or other post secondary programs, find one or two jobs, retire at the end of one's working life, and predictably expect a pension. Today's students will likely encounter a succession of jobs, occupations, and even industry sectors during their careers, including some that do not yet exist. They need to understand that constant change is now the norm, and they need to be able to find the opportunities and new possibilities in change.

2. *Learning is Lifelong – "Graduating from high school or college does not mean the end of learning."*

Because change is constant, learning must be ongoing. We will never really be "finished" learning. Any number of opportunities / circumstances could arise that would require us to learn something new or different in our career journeys.

3. *Focus on the Journey – "Traveling through life is like going down a road: Pay attention to the journey, with all its roadblocks and opportunities."*

This principle perhaps best illustrates the shift in thinking in career planning in a changing world. The old question, "What would you like to be when you grow up?" has now been replaced with new questions like, "Who are you now? What do you enjoy doing? Who needs what you like doing?" We now focus on the journey itself, rather than the destination, paying attention to the opportunities, relationships, and situations we encounter on every step of our journey. Jobs are now stepping stones, not destinations.

4. *Access Your Allies – "The journey of life is not taken alone. Family, friends, and teachers can help you decide what steps to take on life's path."*

Now more than ever, we need to identify those in our lives, on our journey, who can help us achieve our goals and dreams. Collaboration and teamwork skills are crucial in the 21st century work environment. We also must be willing and able to be a good ally to others in helping them on their journey.

5. *Follow Your Heart – "Know yourself, believe in yourself, and follow your heart."*

Dreaming can lead to an understanding of what we really want in life. Knowing what you want and keeping it in the forefront of your mind can give you the motivation needed to deal with life's challenges. The more we can clearly imagine the dreams with which our heart resonates, the more we naturally move towards their fulfillment. Students need to get in touch with their hearts and begin to dream in technicolor about their future.

The Real Game Programs

Below is a synopsis of the six programs that are divided into two-year grade level programs and an adult program.

The Play Real Game: Grades 3 & 4

The Play Real Game introduces basic life/work concepts and vocabulary for 8- to 10-year-olds as they play the roles of adults who create neighborhoods, find jobs for themselves and others, and work together as town citizens. While having fun with maps and career roles in any community, students learn the value of community, the joys and responsibilities of teamwork, the importance of essential employability and life skills, and how education relates to career and life choices.

The Make It Real Game: Grades 5 & 6

The Make It Real Game takes 10- to 12-year-olds on a simulated journey into the global economy while reinforcing the importance of teamwork and cooperation. Playing adult roles, each with a unique personal history, students form companies that research and develop creative international projects, which are presented to an audience at the conclusion of the program. Language arts and social studies abilities are developed as students discover for themselves that there are many different career possibilities in any community and that everybody's work is important.

The Real Game: Grades 7 & 8

The Real Game gives 12- to 14-year-old students the opportunity to explore adult realities such as taxes, living expenses, workplace environments, and unexpected emergencies. Students role-play adults in randomly assigned occupational roles and see how schoolwork relates to occupational choices and, therefore, to lifestyle and income. Delving deeper into their roles, students learn how to budget time and money and see the value of a balanced lifestyle, community involvement, and lifelong learning. By the end of the game, students realize that satisfaction in work is a priority issue in life and that it is an outcome that they can achieve by making choices that are right for them.

The Be Real Game: Grades 9 & 10

The Be Real Game shows 14- to 16-year-old students how a person's career is built with everyday choices and decisions, starting in childhood and encompassing every area of life including family, friends, education, leisure and lifestyle choices, community involvement, and dealing with changing labor market conditions. As they role-play an experienced adult worker in a variety of employment, unemployment, and family situations, students explore in-depth the importance of transferable skills, self-knowledge, lifelong learning, and career planning. They are exposed to dozens of career possibilities and encouraged to formulate and actively pursue their own dreams.

The Get Real Game: Grades 11 & 12

The Get Real Game enables students in their last years of secondary school to simulate a five-year school-to-work transition to their current occupational goal. In-depth factual information is supplied for each role so students can realistically explore different possible gateways to their goals, including postsecondary education, various forms of on-the-job-training, workplace experience, internship or apprenticeship, military service, volunteer and community work, entrepreneurship, and self-employment. As they pursue their personal occupational goals, students learn how to budget their time, research their options, define their goals, plan a course of action, and present themselves well in an interview.

Real Times, Real Life: Adults

Real Times, Real Life helps adult learners to put their lives in perspective, relieving the negative self-image that often comes with unemployment so that they can begin to plan their future with confidence. Role-playing as workers from 1900 to the present day, participants learn that change is constant and inevitable, develop an understanding of the modern labor market, and see how skills acquired in one area of life are transferable to another. Working in teams, participants learn how to assess their situations and create realistic action plans and where to get help when they need it.

Implementation of *The Real Game* at Lee Middle School

To see what these programs entail, what follows is a glimpse into the middle school program, with specific reference to its use for the past five years by Michael Gangitano at Lee Middle School in Woodland, California. *The Real Game* begins with students dreaming about the lifestyle they would like as adults. They choose housing, transportation, entertainment, travel, pets – whatever lifestyle items they dream of in their future. Each choice has a price tag, but the students are initially told to ignore cost. Then each student is randomly assigned an occupation from a set of role profiles that represent the diversity of work roles one would expect in any community, from untrained to highly skilled professionals. Students must step out of their egos and engage their imaginations to step into the future, where they take on the role of an adult character with a specific occupation for the duration of the game.

Each role profile contains basic information about the occupation – gross monthly income, usual vacation allowance, education/experience requirements, licenses or certifications needed, transferable skills, and a job description. With their roles, students receive unique "Day in the Life" descriptions of what their character encounters on a typical day. This also serves as a language arts lesson, introducing vocabulary specific to the occupation. Players become "experts" on their assigned occupation, create business cards for themselves, and describe their roles to other students. Through "meet and greet" scenarios, like a high school reunion for example, players meet old classmates and answer the usual question, "What are you doing now?" Participants do research and become creative as they use their imagination to describe and answer questions on their occupation. Other activities follow that help students to see the range of requirements and financial rewards of different occupations.

They choose their housing and transportation options and then must figure out how they are going to make ends meet, just like their parents have to do. They are required to balance their monthly budgets. Because the average salary varies greatly depending on what job

a student has, some students must make very difficult decisions on what they are willing to part with in order to balance their budget.

What! You mean I don't get to bring home what I make? It's not fair.

— 8th grade student

Then, of course, there are those lifestyle plans. What are the payments on the house you chose? The car? The boat? Every adult knows that monthly payments are only the beginning – all require upkeep, maintenance, insurance, etc. Of course, we also have to eat and wear clean clothes and maybe have a little fun along the way.

I thought my parents didn't like me because they kept saying no to the Reeboks. Now that I'm playing The Real Game, I can't understand how they have been able to say yes so often.

— 7th grade student

Budget adjustments are made as students face reality—maybe select a smaller house, without acreage, get a less expensive car, and postpone plans for the boat for a while. These are individual decisions, based on individual values. The only requirement is that the budget must balance.

Now I know why my father grumbles under his breath when I see him pay the bills at the end of the month.

— 8th grade student

Then students face the challenge of time management, "So much to do and only 168 hours in a week to do it all!" They learn that time, like money, must be budgeted. Work, commuting, sleep, meals, shopping, cleaning, etc., are necessities, but there should also be some leisure time. How will that time be spent and what will be the cost (budget implications)?

Now the class, which has been divided into neighborhood groups, is ready to plan a vacation. Each neighborhood is to plan a group vacation and must not only agree on the destination but also on the cost and length of the vacation. Another reality strikes home – those with the money may not have the time, and those with the time may not have the money. Innovative problem solving is encouraged – as long as it is legal. Bartering is rampant, and the credit card and loans may show their dangerous faces (budget implications). Amazingly, decisions are made, and everyone has learned a bit about the give and take of teamwork.

No occupational road is completely smooth. Players learn that changing technology, economic recession, environmental catastrophe, and resource depletion are some of the causes of layoffs and cutbacks. A worker in each neighborhood receives a pink slip. Their services are no longer needed. After the initial shock, the neighbors rally. Various solutions are considered – networking, retraining within the industry or in a new occupation, relocating, self-employment, and entrepreneurial pathways are explored. This is when all the students learn how to create a resume, using their transferable skills as one tool they will need in their career journey.

As students progress through the lessons of *The Real Game*, they begin to understand and appreciate the complexity of adult life in ways they never imagined. They have an opportunity to closely examine how they would like their adult lives to be. They truly begin to draw connections between what they are learning in school now and how it will impact them tomorrow, as well as twenty years from now. It is simply amazing how this phenomenon unfolds before their very eyes.

Because this curriculum is activity based, hands on, and very practical, it is easily adaptable to students from varied backgrounds and ability levels. Students strong in certain skills such as math, become very helpful to those who are not through the team building aspect of the curriculum. Students become good collaborators and are able to identify who their allies are and how to access them. The curriculum can easily be introduced into a language arts class, social studies, mathematics, or science class because it addresses real life skills that need to be mastered in those classes. As the students approach the end of the game, they link their past, present, and future lives through the activity— "circle of life." They are now able to use the information and experience from the class to establish a road map, one that comes with a myriad of skills they can use to negotiate on their journey through life.

The Real Game offers many more activities than outlined here but these illustrate why students, teachers, administrators, and parents enthusiastically receive The Real Game. In addition, we have seen the community business members come on board to be the latest partners in the collaboration. They recognize the need to have their future workforce equipped with the skills taught in The Real Game. This program becomes the bridge to bring all the stakeholders together sharing a vested interest in improving the lives of all our students.

The following is an excerpt from a proposal submitted to a local Rotary Club by its president in support of *The Real Game*:

- *The Real Game* is a structured curriculum that makes real the reasons for math, social studies, and language subjects being taught.
- It augments and correlates with adult-world reality.
- It stresses and makes obvious the need to stay in school and advance.
- It has continuity with Real Game programs taught in earlier and later grades.
- It reinforces through repetition prior class material through exercises and role-playing.
- It introduces for the first time concepts of cost of living, wages, job application, work ethics, the nature of money, how to make it, and how to lose it.
- It can open up dialogue and discussion with parents who, to students' surprise, are using this material every day. It is, indeed, "REAL." (Baker, 2003)

A development model with extensive piloting was a key factor in the success of the Real Game Series. At least 100 pilot sites from across the United States and Canada tested every session in each program in the series. Over 5,000 students, teachers, parents, and community members were involved in over 125,000 hours of focus testing over three to four months for each program and provided extensive suggestions for improvements. This process was repeated 12 times in 6 programs, both English and French over an 8-year period. This resulted in extensive post-pilot fine-tuning before any program was launched.

The overall reaction to *The Real Game* from teachers, parents, and students has been overwhelmingly positive from the outset. As one teacher said, "From this resource came a realization that secondary school studies have a direct impact on their future lifestyle, an aspect that can only have a positive impact on school retention rates."

Students, too, echoed the lessons learned. As one student said, "I liked TRG (The Real Game) because it made me realize that being grown up is harder than it looks."

Even parents were enthused about the program. Here are samples of two parent responses: "At last school subjects can be seen to relate to real life and provide a reason for learning." "She has learned that to gain most of her dreams, she has to work hard along the way."

The following areas of student competency are identified in the National Pilot Feedback Summary (Baran & Baran, 1997) as usually improving through exposure to *The Real Game*:

- Understanding about the world of work
- Increased vocabulary relating to the world of work and other aspects of adult life
- Literacy/numeric (mathematics) skills
- The importance of budgeting and managing money
- Working in groups
- Prioritizing what is important in life
- Researching and exploring issues
- Problem-solving and negotiating skills
- Communication skills
- Using technology
- General knowledge
- Interpersonal skills
- Awareness of different ways of earning income
- Knowledge about a variety of jobs
- Awareness of relative earning capacities

By engaging students' imaginations to visualize possible future life and work scenarios, they more clearly see the relevance of their school experience to future career success. In my experience at Lee Middle School, one teacher reported, "I have had several students in my Real Game classes who would be classified as at risk of leaving early. *The Real Game* helps these students realize that having dreams and aspirations is necessary, and that education is a key to helping them achieve their dreams."

Conclusion

The Real Game Series is an excellent series of learning resources for anyone searching for a key to unlock the mystery of how to make education relevant and connected to the "real world" for all students, including those with specials needs of learning, behavioral, and physical challenges. It is a magical experience for those who are willing to climb on board, focus on the journey, and follow their hearts. In a perfect world, these programs would be team-taught, with counselors, academic subject teachers, peer facilitators, volunteers from the local business community, and parents all involved. It takes some organization to implement these programs, but the materials are exceptionally teacher-friendly, and once the programs are up-and-running, they tend to take on a life of their own, impacting the entire school in positive ways.

Note: The National Life/Work Center and Real Game Inc. partner with career development organizations across the United States. For further information visit www.realgame.org. The California Career Resource Network (CalCRN) has adapted *The Real Game* specifically for students in California. For more information on *The Real Game California* visit: www.californiacareers.info. Programs in The Real Game Series are being used in over 10,000 schools and community agencies in virtually every state and territory in the United States.

Discussion Questions

1. Is relevance of schoolwork an issue in your teaching/counseling experience? If so, how have you addressed this?
2. Are students motivated to research career options on their own, and can they identify career options congruent with their school subjects?
3. In your experience, do students understand the impact of personal attitudes, behavior, and character on their potential for career and life success?
4. Would you have benefited from a safe and fun dress rehearsal of adult life while you were still in school?
5. Do you think you could convince administrators and other educators to support you in implementing *The Real Game*?
6. What obstacles / challenges would need to be addressed in order to implement a program such as this?
7. Most educational institutions do not address career planning with students until high school, if at all. *The Real Game* strongly advocates starting much earlier. Do you agree with this philosophy? Why or why not?
8. Please reflect on the significance of the "High Five" principles of *The Real Game* in relation to your personal / professional career journey.

References

American School Counselor Association. (2005). *National model: A framework for school counseling programs* (2nd ed.). Alexandria, VA: Author.

Baker, C. (2003). *The Real Game career management training program proposal*. Unpublished proposal submitted to Woodland Sunrise Rotary, Woodland, CA.

Baran, D., & Baran, P. (1997). *The Real Game national pilot feedback summary: United States and Canada*. Memramcook, New Brunswick, Canada: National Life/Work Centre.

Barry, B. (2005). *The Real Game facilitator's guide.* St. John's, Newfoundland, Canada: Real Game Inc.

Gillie, S., & Isenhour, M. G. (2003). *The educational, social and economic value of informed and considered career decisions.* Alexandria, VA: America's Career Resource Network Association.

Jarvis, P.S. (2000). *The Real Games Series: Bringing real life to the classroom.* Memramcook, New Brunswick, Canada: National Life/Work Centre.

Jarvis, P. S. (2006). *Talent ...opportunity: A nation's prosperity depends on connecting the dots.* Memramcook, New Brunswick, Canada: National Life/Work Centre.

Jarvis, P.S., & Gangitano, M. (2004, January). Educators use games to teach lifelong career management skills. *Techniques: the Journal of the Association of Career and Technical Education, 34-37, 48.*

Perry, N. (2004). The Real Game: A real hook to involvement. In S. M. Wakefield, H. Sage, & D. R. Coy (Eds.), *Unfocused kids: Helping students to focus on their education and career plans,* (pp. 371-382). Greensboro, NC: CAPS Press.

Additional Resources

Curriculum Corporation. (2001). *Evaluation of The Real Game 12-14: Final report.* Commonwealth of Australia: Training and Youth Affairs, Department of Education.

Edwards, A., Barnes, A., Killeen, J., & Watts, A.G. (1999). *The Real Game: Evaluation of the UK national pilot.* NICEC Project Report. Cambridge, England: CRAC.

Gangitano, M. (2004). Best practices: The Real Game Series in action. *The California School Counselor, 3*(3), 8-9.

Jarvis, P. S. (1988, December 2). *A nation at risk: The economic consequences of neglecting career development.* Paper presented at the Annual Conference of the Association of Computer-Based Systems for Career Information (ACSCI), St. Louis, MO.

Jarvis, P. S. (2003). *Career management paradigm shift: Prosperity for citizens, windfalls for governments.* Memramcook, New Brunswick, Canada: National Life/Work Centre.

Jarvis, P. S. (2005). *The Real Game Series* [Brochure]. Memramcook, New Brunswick, Canada: National Life/Work Centre.

Jarvis, P. S., & Keeley, E. S. (2003). From vocational decision making to career building: Blueprint, Real Games and school counseling. In Career Development and the Changing Workplace, a special issue of *Professional School Counseling, 64,* 244-251.

Chapter 27

School Counselors Are in Charge of Learning

John D. Krumboltz and Stephanie Eberle

Abstract

This chapter discusses the Happenstance Learning Theory, which asserts that people encounter innumerable learning experiences, planned or unplanned, and make interpretations from them that may be correct, partially correct, or wrong. The authors propose that the counselor's job is to understand each student's view of the problem and to engage in a mutual dialog so that the student can learn what next step can be taken to begin solving the problem. It is further suggested that helping students learn is the counselor's job as well as the teacher's job and that the counselor's role is one of providing support, generating options, and offering hope.

Introduction

Ellen is walking down the hallway between classes in her high school. She sees her classmate, Janet, walking toward her. Ellen says, "Hi." Janet, her eyes focused straight ahead, passes by saying nothing.

A learning experience has just occurred within three seconds. Ellen observed that Janet did not acknowledge her greeting. Janet observed that Ellen's greeting could be ignored. It was a learning experience that neither girl had planned in advance. How important was that learning experience? The importance depends on the interpretations each girl creates. Ellen might generalize thoughts like this: "Janet hates me." Or, "Everybody thinks they are better than I am." Or, more charitably, "Janet is probably suffering from one of her severe migraine headaches today."

Janet's generalizations might resemble one of these: "My math test is next period. I have to pass it. I can't think about anything else." Or, "That uppity Ellen thinks she can join my friends. I'll keep her in her place." Or, "Mom thinks I tune people out. I wonder if that's true."

Which generalization is correct? We don't know. Neither girl knows what the other is thinking. However, each believes that her own assumption is correct. The consequences may appear in the school counselor's office. Ellen may be in tears sobbing "Everybody hates me." Janet may be plagued with anxiety, "I'm so afraid

I'm going to flunk math and my parents will never forgive me."

Every day students, teachers, and counselors have an uncountable number of learning experiences. From these experiences they form generalizations about themselves and others. Some of these generalizations may be correct; others may be completely wrong. However, each person assumes that her/his own generalizations are correct.

The Happenstance Learning Theory (HPL) is an explanation for why people act the way they do and what counselors can do to help them. It asserts that people encounter innumerable learning experiences, planned or unplanned, and make interpretations from them that may be correct, partially correct, or wrong. They may or may not modify their interpretations on the basis of subsequent learning experiences. They act, appropriately or inappropriately, on the basis of what they currently believe to be true, whether it is or not.

Students come to counselors with their problems. The counselor's job is to understand each student's view of the problem and to engage in a mutual dialog to figure out what step the student might take next to begin solving the problem. The student should leave the counselor's office with a clear idea of some next action step toward resolving the problem. Helping students learn is the counselor's job as well as the teacher's job.

The Lucile Packard Foundation for Children's Health sponsored a study on the emotional and behavioral health of preteens and available services for them (Katz, 2005). Family-related problems, stress, and anxiety were the most pressing problems identified. Bullying, depression, and academics posed other significant issues. The study recommended an increase in the number of school counselors and the inclusion of social and emotional health education as part of the regular school curriculum.

When John Lennon first said, "Life is what happens while you're busy making other plans," he may have been referring to the notion that, more often than not, unplanned events seem to have more impact on our lives than do planned ones. School counselors know well that unplanned events can affect what you do next. However, rather than bemoaning the fact that your plans for the day have to be changed, the HPL would help you celebrate your open-minded ability to adapt quickly and effectively to changing circumstances. In this chapter, we are expanding an earlier article (Krumboltz & Eberle, 2006) by presenting additional examples of how the HPL might be applied in the work of the school counselor.

The Student Who Could Not Read

Jose was in the Special Education class in the 8th grade at the middle school where Sue is a counselor. One day she saw him sitting in the Principal's office. She went in and sat down beside him.

"What happened?" Sue asked.
"I got in a fight with some kid."
"How did that happen?"
"We were playing flag football. He hit me hard. So I hit him harder. Then someone told the principal on me."
"Did you tell the principal the truth?"
"Yeah, and then she called my home."
"Well, let me know what happens next," Sue said as she had to leave.
"Where's your office?" Jose asked.
"Near the front door."

Later Sue spotted him walking slowly by the door to my office.

"Jose," she called to him, "What happened?"
"I have to go home. I got suspended."
"For fighting?"
"Yeah, but I don't care."
"Well, I care."
"Why do you care?"
"Because I think you have the ability to be a good student here and I hate to see you get into trouble."
"You don't have to care. The principal said I was acting like a bully."
"Do you think you're a bully?"
"I don't know."
"I don't think you are a bully."
"You don't even know me."
"No, I don't know you, but I sure know your family."
"How do you know my family?"
"I had your sister and brother as counselees."
"You know Juardo?"

"Yes."
"Juardo is bigger than I am but someday I'm going to be bigger than he is."
"Sounds like Juardo may not be treating you well."
"He calls me stupid."
"So Juardo is mean to you, and you are mean to others. Is that what is happening?"
"You'd be mean too if you were the only Mexican in the class, and the kids make fun of you all the time."
"That must really make you feel bad."
"Yeah, but I decided that if I was meaner to them, they would stop teasing me."
"So you learned how to be a better bully?"
"Yeah," he said smiling.
"How are you doing in school?"
"Don't you know about me?"
"I'm learning more about you. What do you want me to know?"
"You were at my meeting."
"You mean your IEP?"
"Yeah."
"I remember that people said you were interested in geography."
"Yeah."
"How did you develop an interest in geography? In school?"
"No."
"How did you learn about it?"
"I watch the Discovery channel and the History channel and Nova. They have some good programs on those channels."
"Aren't you reading about Egypt right now in your social studies class?"
"Don't you know I'm a zero?"
"What do you mean, a zero?"
"Didn't you look at my tests?
"What tests?"
"Reading. I can't read."
"Then I think that you want to read more than anything in the world."
(There was a long silence.)
"Jose," Sue said, "I don't want you to be a bully any more. I want you to learn how to read. I want you to know how smart you really are. I want to help you make that happen."

Sue interviewed Jose's social studies teacher. She knew Jose was a poor reader, but didn't know how poor. Sue asked her if she could help him learn how to read.

She replied, "No, that's not my job. He should have learned to read in elementary school. He never turns in any homework." Sue then contacted a special education teacher who agreed to help Jose learn how to read. Over the next few months, Jose made good progress in his reading and seemed to have higher expectations about his own potential.

One day Sue asked him, "Jose, what do you want to do after high school?"

"My uncle has a lawn service. I'll work for him. But first I want to travel around the world."
"Which country would you like to visit first?"
"Mexico."
"Then where?"
"I don't want to see every place, but I do want to know about the whole world."

Subsequently, Jose was enrolled in a social studies class with an engaging teacher. Almost every day Sue would see him in the hallway. She always gave him support. However, when he was required to submit written work in his social studies class, he wanted to drop the class. Sue wouldn't let him drop it and told him she would talk with the teacher.

"Jose, I just want you to sit and listen. When you can participate, I want you to participate."
"Yes, but I can't pass tests."
"But if you learn the stuff, you can tell the teacher about it, can't you?"

Sue arranged for the test to be administered by a special education teacher verbally, and Jose demonstrated that he clearly understood the material. Later he said to Sue, "Thanks for making me take classes I didn't want to take."

By the time Jose approached the end of the eighth grade, he was far above being a "zero" and was reading at the fourth grade level. Sue arranged a school service project for him as an aide to a special education teacher who worked with developmentally delayed students. Jose worked with those students more effectively than the hired aide.

Sue asked him, "Have you ever thought about a job of helping kids?"

"I'd have to go to college for that, wouldn't I?"
"Yeah. Just an idea, but you might enjoy college. You'd make a heck of a social studies teacher!"

Sue's last communication with Jose was just before he graduated from middle school. He was not planning to attend the party after graduation. Sue said to him, "You'd better go. I got a ticket for you." She had ordered a ticket for him. He went to the party where Sue was a chaperone. She noticed that he was dancing with a girl and seemed to be having a good time. He took Sue aside at the party and said, "I guess I'll be going to high school soon. I can read now. If you hadn't helped me, I'd still be stuck in my old rut. You really helped me a lot. You believed in me."

The counselor here took the initiative after an unplanned event—spotting Jose in the principal's office. The HPL emphasizes the importance of being alert to significant unexpected events. She engaged him in a conversation, empathized with his situation, and let him know she cared about what happened to him. She happened to spot him walking past her office (perhaps that was not unplanned!) and called him in. She arranged some special reading instruction. She placed him with a social studies teacher who was open to new ways of dealing with special education students. She made sure that he would be included in social activities also. There may not be time in the day to provide all these services for every student, but some students need it more than others. Some schools may not have the staff and facilities to provide individual attention, but counselors must make do with whatever resources they have or can scrounge.

The Student Who Would Not Go to College

Kelly is a school counselor at a large, California high school. Kelly's student, Geoff, had decided he wanted to attend college "after all." What is most significant, however, is that he had not planned to do so until now, his junior year. Geoff had always planned to be an artist and, as such, wanted to go to art school in San Francisco. As a result, his grades were very bad and his SAT scores were worse. Geoff had always been a "C student with potential" as his teachers put it, but he just did not want to get a college degree.

This troubled Kelly who all along had encouraged him to try "just in case." So, she wanted to try something new. She encouraged him to: (a) take summer classes to boost his GPA; (b) take an SAT prep course; and (c) get involved in the local community. She also warned him that he may not be able to get into a four-year college right away.

Geoff followed her advice and raised his scores and grades a little. However, his community service helped most. He became involved in a local theater, making scenery. In the same production was a woman faculty member at a local liberal arts college. The faculty member was impressed with Geoff's work, and they began to talk over lunch. The relationship was very genuine. Geoff never thought of the faculty member as a possible future reference. However, when it came time to apply to colleges, the faculty member encouraged him to apply to schools he had not considered, such as the one at which she worked. His grades were not the best, but Geoff's reference letter from the faculty member was the best the committee had ever read. He plans to attend that college next September.

A key idea in Happenstance Learning Theory is that one can create desirable unexpected events. Kelly encouraged Geoff to take three kinds of actions. We don't know how much the first two paid off, but his involvement in the local community theatre was crucial. Kelly did not know that a college faculty member was also working at that theatre nor that Geoff and the faculty member would begin talking with each other. Geoff deserves credit for creating this unplanned beneficial connection too. He must have displayed some desirable social skills and taken some initiative in building the relationship.

The HPL can support school counselors in encouraging students to engage in a variety of potentially interesting activities. Some activities may have great benefits; others may have none. However, even learning what you don't like to do is valuable.

The Boy with Multiple Girlfriends

Derek is a high school counselor who is sometimes asked to settle disputes between students. Jill and Jennifer have come to trust him and want his advice on a dispute they are having. Jill and Jennifer are tenth graders, but have been best friends since the 6th grade. Now their friendship is on the rocks because each says the other one is a liar. They both like Billy who is a popular senior athlete in their school. In spite of the multiple demands on Derek's time, he decides he will try to help Jill and Jennifer work out the dilemma, hopefully enabling them to be friends again.

Jill's initial statement is something like this: "I have been best friends with Jennifer since sixth grade, but now I hate her because she is such a liar. I have been dating Billy for a few weeks now, and we really like each other. He even told me that he loves me, and we had sex last night. It was my first time and really special to me. I think we will get married after high school. Jennifer (who used to be my best friend) says he calls her too, but I know she is lying because she is jealous that I have a boyfriend."

Jennifer's response can be summarized like this: "Sure, Jill and I have been best friends since sixth grade, but now I hate her because she is such a liar. Billy and I really like each other. He even told me that he loves me. We hang out after school a lot. He wants to have sex with me, but I want to wait. Jill says Billy likes her and brags that they even have done 'stuff' together, but I know she is lying because Billy loves me."

To use the Happenstance Learning Theory, Derek first used all his good active listening skills to understand and empathize with the feelings of both Jill and Jennifer. When he sensed they each felt fully understood, he summarized their situation like this: "What I hear is that both of you value your long friendship together and wish it could continue. Each of you says that Billy loves you and believes that the other of you is mistaken. Now I personally don't have the slightest idea who Billy loves. But I'm wondering, how could we find out?"

Then some brainstorming of ideas took place. Certainly Billy was the only one who could answer the question. Because neither one of them wanted to confront Billy directly, they both wanted Derek to inquire about Billy's intentions. He agreed to call Billy in for a private conference.

Billy told Derek, "I talk to a lot of girls. I just like to call them up and have long conversations on the phone. I don't have a girlfriend. Jill, Jennifer, Justine, and Samantha are some of the girls I am talking to right now. I don't know if they know about each other or not. I don't worry about stuff like that."

Clearly, there were major misconceptions afloat, and some direct and honest communication was needed. Options to be considered by all three parties might include the following:

- Arranging a meeting with Derek, Billy, Jennifer and Jill;
- Teaching Jill and Jennifer how to confront Billy directly;
- Teaching Billy how to make his true feelings known; or
- Contacting another student to mediate the dispute.

The unhappiness and hostile feelings that Jill and Jennifer were experiencing with each other were based on a misconception that each was Billy's sole object of affection. Clearly, neither one was. The counselor's job was to transform this tragedy into a valuable learning experience for all three. Billy needed to learn the importance of honesty in his interpersonal communications. Jill and Jennifer needed to learn to be skeptical of words that may only be intended to seduce. They all needed to learn about the dangers of jumping to conclusions without checking out all the facts.

The essential point from Happenstance Learning Theory is that some action needed to be taken by the people involved. Derek as the counselor could facilitate that action by helping the participants to brainstorm possibilities, teach needed skills, and/or arrange a suitable environment for the needed communication to take place.

When Stellar Kids Experience Failure

Kim is a counselor at one of the top public high schools in the country. It is not uncommon for the teachers with whom she works to have PhDs and/or be educated at elite universities from around the world. Her students are equally impressive. Every year she can expect to see SAT scores which hit the highest percentile, a few may even have perfect scores, and about 98% will continue their studies at a four-year university.

The problems many school counselors face are unfamiliar to Kim. She sees very few behavioral problems, and her students' parents are highly involved in the educational process. What worries her most about her students is not lack of motivation. Rather, it is the amount of stress and anxiety experienced by such highly motivated students. In addition to their involvement in team sports, clubs, and community service, they are pressured to achieve 4.0 GPAs to gain admission to top tier colleges after graduation. The pressure does not just come from parents and teachers. The pressure is internal and generates largely unstated competitiveness among classmates.

One of Kim's students, Noi, was the first in her family to be born outside of Thailand and the first to have the opportunity to attend college. She was known by most of her teachers as a diligent, intelligent student who did not say much in class. Her GPA was a 3.5 and her SAT scores were above average. In addition, she had an impressive history of community service experience. Compared to many students nationwide, she was, perhaps, ideal. Compared to her peers, however, she was average.

In Noi's senior year of high school, Kim began meeting with her regularly to review her college applications. While supportive of Noi's plan to apply to only top tier schools, Kim encouraged her, to no avail, to research and apply to other top, though not "elite" schools as well. When acceptance letters started coming to all of her classmates, Noi received only one letter stating she'd been placed on a waiting list; the remaining denied her admission. She was sick for an entire week and a half after the final rejection letter.

Kim knew that psychosomatic symptoms were common in her student population: "They blame themselves; they stay up all night; they cry; they literally worry themselves sick." When Noi came into Kim's office, she was crestfallen and asked how she could have done "everything right" and still be rejected. In essence, this was her first major rejection experience and she seemed to feel that she no longer had options.

The counselor's role in this situation is one of providing support, generating options, and offering hope. Two weeks later an unexpected event occurred. A brochure arrived inviting interested students to apply for an international research fellowship. Out of fear of not knowing what else to do, Noi begrudgingly applied and was excited to learn she had been accepted into the program. Noi spent the next two years after graduation working with HIV positive people in Myanmar (formerly Burma). The experience led to acceptance into the university of her choice when she returned home.

Think about just one of the unplanned events in this story - "a brochure arrived." Someone had to write that brochure. Someone had to mail it. Somehow the brochure had to be delivered to Kim at just the right time. She had to take time to read it and to be alert to the possibility that the fellowship program described in that brochure might be an attractive possibility for Noi. She had to initiate a conversation with Noi to tell her about it. Noi had to take all the actions necessary to apply. The selection committee had to see Noi as a good candidate. All of this could not have been planned in advance. Yet Kim's actions, Noi's actions, and the actions of many people running the fellowship program combined to produce a result perhaps even more beneficial than a college admission.

Noi and Kim still keep in touch, and they both seem to believe that Noi's current successes, ironically, come from the initial rejection from the colleges to which she originally applied. Had this not occurred, Noi would not have considered the fellowship program. Due to Kim's effective actions and support, Noi will start medical school in September.

When the Disciplinarian and Counselor Are the Same Person – Role Conflict in School Counseling

"When I was first hired 20 years ago, I also played the role of Truancy Officer," Jim, a school counselor in a rural community in the Midwest, explained. Whether because of low funding sources, school policies, or staff shortages, school counselors may find themselves in conflicting roles: one of trust and support and one of discipline.

Throughout the school year, Jim noticed that two brothers stayed home due to sickness quite often. The peculiar fact was that when Maurice was sick, Max would be at school and vice versa. They were never at school at the same time. He had spoken to both of them several times and they confided that their father had recently died, so they both worked late nights and rarely saw their mother in between her two jobs. Jim always listened empathically, and the students always left with promises to improve.

The truant behavior continued, and Jim decided to investigate. He and an officer knocked on the door on one of the days Max stayed home. Max answered the door in an old pair of boxer shorts. His mother was not home, and he did not look sick. "He knew right away why I was there," Jim told me. Max's explanation was predictable. Their mother worked late nights in a factory, and the two boys worked as late-night janitors in spite of the fact that they were not yet sixteen. While Jim tried again to be empathic, he explained that truancy is illegal, no matter what.

Max continued, "We don't have the money to go to school." Later, Jim realized what he meant. Maurice and Max had one work uniform and one school uniform between them. On some days, Max would go to school in the school uniform and stay home to do both his and his brother's homework for the next day. On those days, Maurice would go to work. They would clean the house during the day, and their mother cleaned clothes when she could.

After finding social service resources for the family, Jim took the following happenstance approach: "I independently met with Maurice, Max, and their mother and asked them, "What is the one thing you need most now?" Their mother's biggest concern was money and making sure her children were respectable. Max and Maurice, however, primarily spoke of missing their father and their mother now that she was always working. "I knew that social services would help financially so that each could own his own school uniform and work uniform. However, I knew I would still need to monitor their attendance," Jim said. "Yet, I wanted to make sure they had some sort of guidance or mentor."

Jim's next step was to find a program to help. He worked with social services and even the police department to find a mentoring program for children who were missing a father figure in their lives. As he explained: "I ended up using my dual role to my advantage by making it a condition of their 'punishment' for skipping school to attend the program." Max and Maurice attended and did not like it at first, but they eventually started sharing their experiences with their assigned mentors and group members. They started going to programs on their own and began taking leadership roles within it.

Jim had applied the HLT approach by using his dual role both to enforce the rules and to open up a new learning opportunity for both students. While it was difficult to arrange, Jim was pleased with the result. Today, Max runs his own mentoring program and Maurice is a school principal.

Happenstance Implications for School Counselors

In applying the HLT, school counselors understand that the best laid plans can be changed as new events unfold and new opportunities arise. Therefore, they do not insist that every student declare a future occupation. Instead of describing themselves as "undecided," students would be able to label themselves as "open-minded." The emphasis would be on trying a variety of activities and keeping eyes and ears open for new opportunities.

When life changes and unplanned events happen, seeing them as opportunities as opposed to tragedies is a shift in thinking. It allows students to grow comfortable with change and gives them the self-confidence to adapt to the inevitable unexpected events that the future will bring.

The actions school counselors take with their students and the actions they encourage their students to take provide the foundation for change. While making plans for the future can be reassuring, more important is teaching ways to anticipate opportunities arising from unplanned events. Planting the seeds for change and teaching the methods for coping with such change are important tasks for school counselors. The case studies here are intended to illustrate a helpful theoretical framework for accomplishing such tasks.

A book about the Happenstance Learning Theory that school counselors and their students might find valuable is entitled *Luck Is No Accident: Making the Most of Happenstance in Your Life and Career* (Krumboltz & Levin, 2004). It contains stories, cartoons, quotes, exercises and references that may help further clarify how to create and benefit from unexpected events.

Discussion Questions

1. What unplanned life events have affected what you are doing now?
2. How have you seen unexpected happenstance events playing out in the lives of your students, colleagues, and relatives?
3. You have probably been asked many times, "What are you going to be when you grow up?" How would you want your students to respond to that question?
4. What are the advantages and disadvantages of trying to forecast your future career?
5. How is the Happenstance Learning Theory applicable with people from different ethnic, religious, racial, gender, socio-economic, and sexual orientation backgrounds?
6. A common misunderstanding of Happenstance Learning Theory is that it encourages passive waiting. How would you convince someone that, on the contrary, one must be involved in taking action to make things happen?

References

Katz, C. (2005). *School-based counseling for preteens in San Mateo County: A study of key issues affecting the emotional and behavioral health of preteens and an examination of available services.* Available at : http://lpfch.org/informed/preteens/counselor study.pdf

Krumboltz, J. D., & Eberle, S. (2006, Winter). How school counselors can use happenstance theory. *The California School Counselor, 5*(2), 1,5,8.

Krumboltz, J. D., & Levin, A. S. (2004). Luck is no accident: *Making the most of happenstance in your life and career.* Atascadero, CA: Impact Publishers.

Chapter 28

Career Education for Special Education Students

Jackie M. Allen

Note: This article first appeared as Allen, J. (2007). Career education for special education students. Counselling, Psychotherapy, and Health, 3(1), 33-41. A few minor changes have been made, and the sections on Additional Resources–Web sites and Discussion Questions have been added. Reprinted by permission.

Abstract

This article discusses the importance of career education for special education students. Special education students need career education as much or more than regular education students. One aspect of the school counselor role, the Individual Transition Plan process, is discussed in greater detail. It is argued that the key to a special education student's success in K-12 and postsecondary pursuits and in transition to life and the world of work is often dependent upon the assistance the student and his/her family receive from the school counselor and student support personnel during the early years of education.

Introduction

...elementary schools are creatively integrating general and special education programs; parents are being given a legitimate voice in policy decision-making; and more disabled children are in regular schools than ever before. Yet there are still many obstacles toovercome before a truly equitable system is achieved.

Madelon Cloud (1999, p. 9)

One of the remaining challenges for full integration of general and special education programs for special education students is the full implementation of career education programs into the curriculum for all children. Special education students, those students receiving accommodations in the regular classroom or program modifications with placement in special education classes, must be included in the mainstream of career counseling and career development programs from kindergarten through twelfth grade. The future of many special education students depends on the participation of these students in post secondary training programs.

School counselors need to work with the parents of special education students to increase awareness of the educational opportunities available for their children. Career education will prepare special education students for fulfilling and successful lives and instill in them the desire for life long learning.

The Needs of Special Education Students

In California, there has recently been a renewed interest in Career Technical Education, in part, to meet the needs of employers and also to motivate students who are dropping out of school. Dean Gabriel Meehan asserts: "Face it, instant gratification is not going away. Provide students with interesting activities and hands on projects and it is guaranteed they will learn." (Kruk, 2005). Certainly if the regular curriculum is in need of career education, the special education programs are even more in need of viable career education for their students. Special education students need normalizing experiences, and inclusion in career education programs is definitely a means of demonstrating to these students and their parents the value of considering their post secondary education and future. The American School Counselor Association (ASCA) National Standards for Counseling Programs and the *ASCA National Model for School Counseling Programs* (2005) call for academic, career, and personal/social counseling for all students.

Special education students may need extra help with exploring interests and determining strengths. What better person is there to provide that extra help than the school counselor with the aid of a career technician? Sacramento State University in California trains career counselors, teaching them how to utilize career resources, create career counseling programs, and train classified personnel to assist them with career programs for all students.

Robert Chope, in his recent book *Family Matters* (2006), has made the case for the importance of the involvement of family members in the career planning process. Family members often know the strengths and challenges that their special education children face. Parents need to be acquainted with available resources for post secondary training designed especially to assist special education students. Parents can also be enlisted to support maximizing the potential of their special education student. Preconceived ideas about the future of their child who has special needs and grief at the loss of a "normal" child are also areas in which counseling is extremely helpful for families of special education students.

Laws Guiding Special Education in the United States

In the United States, four specific federal pieces of legislation dictate the parameters of funding and qualifications for special education: The No Child Left Behind Act (NCLB) of 2001, The Individual With Disabilities in Education Act (IDEA) 2004, Section 504 of the Vocational Rehabilitation Act of 1973, and the Carl D. Perkins Vocational and Technical Education Act. Reauthorization of the Elementary and Secondary Education Act providing funding for education became the No Child Left Behind Act of 2001. NCLB made schools accountable for student learning through the use of assessment with the goal to ensure that at-risk youth were "not left" behind academically. Accountability was measured through an annual yearly progress report (AYP) required by states in order to maintain federal support.

At the local level, schools were required to make local education plans (LEAP) for the implementation of scientifically-based programs and the spending of education dollars. Sanctions were imposed on local schools if test scores failed to improve, and the consequences were: cuts in funding, mandates for increased academic support services, replacing staff, or eventually restructuring, privatizing, or state takeover of school districts. An assessment rate of 95 percent student participation was required, and participation rates and assessment data could be averaged over a 3-year period for reporting AYP results. All students, including those with disabilities, were to be tested annually; provisions for assessment accommodations for special education students were to be included in the Individual Education Program documents. Alternative achievement standards were allowed for those with significant cognitive disabilities in approximately two percent of the total student population. For alternative assessment measures, teachers could use observation, samples of student work, or criterion referenced tests of specific student competencies. Assessment must be in line with state curriculum standards (U.S. Department of Education, 2005b).

Although alternative assessment measures are permitted in a small percent of the special education population, there are concerns about testing disabled students. Dollarhide and Lemberger (2006) cited a 2004 public opinion poll of 1,050 voters in which 57% disapproved of requiring the same tests for disabled students and non-disabled students.

Special education, in part, is funded through the Individual with Disabilities in Education Act (IDEA), reauthorized in 2004 (U.S. Department of Education, 2006). School districts are to initiate scientifically based early reading programs, positive behavioral interventions and supports, and early intervening services to address the learning and behavioral needs of children. IDEA 2004 has made some significant changes in rules and regulations for special education in the United States. One of the major changes is that states can no longer require districts to consider an IQ/achievement discrepancy as a criterion for learning disabled eligibility. Scientific, research-based intervention response is part of the evaluation procedures for severely learning disabled (SLD) students. Teachers are receiving additional training to become "highly qualified" to provide special education and inclusion in regular education classes.

Response to Intervention (RTI) is the new alternative to the discrepancy method used to determine if and how students respond to specific changes in curriculum and instruction. Problem solving models such as the "three-tiered model" are being used to provide a larger group of students with intervention to improve learning and test scores. Tier I is primarily early intervention for at-risk students in the general education classroom, using all available school supports and evaluating student progress. Tier II consists of more interventions and ongoing evaluation. For students who are not making progress consistent with standards, remedial services and instructional additions and/or modifications to regular classroom instruction are used. If success has not been gained in the previous tiers, Tier III provides access to referrals for psychoeducational assessment for learning disabilities (Christo, 2006). More specific and intense remedial instruction, through special education as well as regular classroom instruction with modifications, are initiated at this level. Individual Education Plans (IEP) and Individual Transition (career) Plans (ITP) are written for special education students and constitute legal documents between the school district or other interagency service provider(s) and the parents. ITP plans will be discussed in detail later in this chapter.

Other options open to students with disabilities not eligible for special education classes are provided through Section 504 of the Vocational Rehabilitation Act of 1973. This act requires accommodations to be made within the regular curriculum for qualifying individuals. The requirements for eligibility for 504 accommodations are:

1. A mental or physical impairment which substantially limits one or more major life activities which include, but are not limited to caring for one's self, performing manual tasks, walking, seeing, hearing, speaking, breathing, learning, and working.
2. A record of such impairment as described above.
3. The individual is regarded as having such an impairment as previously described.

(U.S. Department of Education, 2003)

No extra money or legal protections are offered through this legislation. A student with a 504 plan, due to a permanent leg injury from a car accident, may have an accommodation for longer breaks between classes in order to walk from one class to another class.

For Career Technical Education, the Carl D. Perkins Vocational and Technical Education Act, Public Law 05-332, provides funding and guidelines through the Office of Vocational and Technical education for state basic grants. Career counseling and guidance are included in the funding and defined as:

… a comprehensive, developmental program designed to assist individuals in making and implementing informed educational and occupational choices. A career guidance and counseling program develops an individual's competencies in self-knowledge, educational and occupational exploration, and career planning.

(U.S. Department of Education, 2005a, p.1

Professional Association Leadership

The National Career Development Association (NCDA), a division of the American Counseling Association (ACA), has teamed with the Association of Career Resources Network (ACRN), federally funded through Carl Perkins monies, to update and produce the National Career Development Guidelines (NCDG) Framework (America's Career Resource Network, 2005). The framework is organized in three domains: Personal Social Development (PS), Educational Achievement and Lifelong Learning (ED), and Career Management (CM). The eleven goals are coded numerically and by domain.

Three indicators (Knowledge Acquisition-K, Application-A, and Reflection-R) or learning stages are derived from *Bloom's Taxonomy* and no longer tied to an individual's age or educational level. An example of the NCDG Framework coding system follows:

PERSONAL SOCIAL DEVELOPMENT

- **KNOWLEDGE ACQUISITION**-PS1.K2 **Identify** your abilities, strengths, skills, and talents
- **APPLICATION**- PS1.A2 **Demonstrate** use of your abilities, strengths, skills, and talents.
- **REFLECTION**- PS1.R2 **Assess** the impact of your abilities, strengths, skills, and talents on your career development.

The American School Counselor Association, the largest division of ACA, developed standards for school counseling programs. The National ASCA Standards for School Counseling Programs include three developmental domains: academic, career, and personal/social. These standards have guided school counseling programs for almost 10 years. Recently ASCA published *The ASCA National Model; A Framework for School Counseling Programs-Second Edition* (2005) and the *ASCA National Model Workbook* (2004) with the standards as a foundation for counseling programs, adding the 21st century emphasis on accountability and organizational structure. The theme of the ASCA model is systematic change in the way school counseling programs are organized, implemented, and evaluated. The basic themes of the model are counselor leadership and advocacy, system change, and collaboration. The delivery system, based on the Gysbers and Henderson model, advocates for school guidance curriculum, individual student planning, responsive services, and system support. The management system employs agreements; advisory councils; and use of data, action plans, and time calendars. Accountability is measured in student outcomes using performance standards, program audits, and results reports.

An example of an ASCA National Standard in the Career domain is:

Standard 4: Students will acquire the skills to investigate the world of work in relation to knowledge of self and to make informed career decisions.

(ASCA, 2005)

In intersecting this standard with the more extensive National Career Development Guidelines Framework domains and stages, the above examples of PS1.K2, PS1.A2, and PS1.R2 are essential skills for accomplishing ASCA Career Domain Standard 4. Thus the two professional association guidelines can be integrated into a comprehensive counseling and guidance program.

School Counselor Role

Career education in the United States has a rich legacy of national and professional association regulations and guidelines. What then should be the school counselor role in providing career education for special education students? The school counselor as a service provider for special education students is both an integral part of a comprehensive counseling and guidance program and an important member of a student support services team (Allen & La Torre, 1998). ASCA (2004), in the revised school counselor role position statement, recommends the following roles for school counselors:

- Providing assistance with transitions from grade to grade as well as post-secondary options
- Consulting and collaborating with staff and parents to understand the special needs of these students
- Advocating for students with special needs in the school and in the community
- Assisting with the establishment and implementation of plans for accommodations and modifications
- Advocates for students with special needs and is one of many school staff members who may be responsible for providing information as written plans are prepared for students with special needs.

Allen (2004) has outlined the program areas, roles, and functions of a school counselor in the career development domain of a comprehensive counseling and guidance program. The school counselor is a member of the integrated services team of student support personnel, with a responsibility to raise awareness of the team to career development needs of special education students. On the IEP team, the school counselor is the case manager for career education and development, which includes the Individual Transition Plan (ITP) process for the special education student. As coordinator of the comprehensive counseling and guidance program the school counselor coordinates the program, counsels students, provides career guidance lessons in the classroom, and evaluates the overall program including the career guidance components. In the school system, the school counselor as staff member provides in-service presentations on the importance of career education, advocates for the rights of special education students for inclusion in the career education program, and leads and coordinates the career program throughout the school. The school counselor acts as coordinator and collaborator with community agencies developing linkages for career education, vocational training, and work experience programs.

Individual Transition Plan Process

As stated above, the school counselor serves as the advocate for special education students, which means representation at Student Study Team Meetings, Individual Education Program planning meetings, 504 meetings, and ITP meetings. Allen (2004) discusses the unique function of the school counselor in the Individual Transition Process. Under IDEA 2004, transition plans must be developed and in place by the time the special education child is 16 years old. The ITP, like the IEP, is a legal document. Key areas of the transition plan are:

- Employment Skills
- Community Living Skills
- Training/Education
- Living Arrangements
- Community Recreation/Leisure
- Social Emotional Needs
- Financial/Economic Needs

In preparation for an ITP meeting, key questions that a school counselor might ask a student with the assistance of the parent include:

What are your strengths?
What skills do you need to develop to transition from school to adult life?
What kind of a job or career do you envision in the future?
Do you want to attend a college or community college?
Do you want to prepare for a job through career and technical training?
Do you want to continue to live at home or do you want to live on your own?
How will you earn money to support yourself if you live on your own?
What kind of recreation and leisure activities do you want to participate in?

Are you aware of special programs and resources for special education students?

The ITP meeting focuses on the needs of the special education student and the creation of a purposeful, organized process (the plan) to produce the desired outcomes that will enable the special education student to transition from school to employment and then to a quality adult life. Many educators as well as community specialists may meet to work with the family and student to review relevant data, summarize current functioning and previous goals achieved, develop transition goals and objectives based on identified needs and student preferences and interests, and decide on appropriate interagency linkages. ITP members include special education teacher(s), school counselor, parent and student (when appropriate), administrator, career specialist, regular education teacher(s), school psychologist and/or other student support specialist(s), and community agency liaisons that may be providing specialized services for the student.

When a high school student has completed an ITP, that student should have a plan for transition to the work world and life. It must be stressed that this is not an end, but just a beginning. For the last two years of high school, the school counselor working with regular and special education teachers, family members, and other specialists must carefully monitor the progress of the special education student. Some students will leave high school ready to continue formal education, others will embark upon specialized training programs in shelters; some may choose to live at home; others may try independent living; and some may need residential placement depending upon their individual needs.

Conclusion

There is no question that there is a need for career education for special education students. Federal and state laws and professional association guidelines define the career education path for special education students; the school counselor is the guide and mentor along the way. There are many programs designed to assist learning disabled students to make their way in the world. Parents must be informed of these resources and programs, such as the special section on Programs and Services for Students with Special Needs in the *Life After High School* student guide (Allen & Hansen, 2006). Parents often need help to access this information that is so important in making their student's life more successful. The school counselor has an important role

to play throughout the educational process and career education. It very well may be the most important service a school counselor can provide for special education children and their families.

Discussion Questions
1) What is the school counselor role in career education?
2) What are you doing about career education for special education students in your school?
3) Who serves on the Individual Transition Plan meetings in your school district?
4) Discuss how you would find funding for career and technical education programs.

References

Allen, J. (2004). Career education for special education students. In S. M. Wakefield et al., *Unfocused kids: Helping students to focus on their education and career plans* (pp. 455-467). Greensboro, NC: CAPS Press.

Allen, J., & Hansen, R. (Eds.) (2006). *Life after high school.* Downey, CA: Los Angeles County Office of Education.

Allen, J., & LaTorre, E. (1998). What a school administrator needs to know about the school counselor's role with special education. In C. Dykeman (Ed.), *Maximizing school counseling program effectiveness* (pp. 117-122). Greensboro, NC: ERIC/CASS Publications.

American School Counselor Association. (2004). *The ASCA National Model Workbook.* Alexandria, VA: Author.

American School Counselor Association. (2005). *The ASCA National Model: A Framework for School Counseling Programs* (2nd ed.). Alexandria, VA: Author.

America's Career Resource Network. (2005). *National Career Development Guidelines Framework.* Retrieved August 24, 2006, from www.acrnetwork.org/ncdg.htm

Christo, C. (2006). *School psychologists and response to intervention* (CASP Position Paper adopted by the Board of Directors 2/15/06). Retrieved August 15, 2006, from http://www.casponline.org/

Chope, R. C. (2006). *Family matters: The influence of the family in career decision making.* Austin, TX: Pro-Ed, Inc.

Cloud, M. (1999) IDEA implementation: Successes, problems, and solutions. *The Special Edge,* 12(3), 9.

Dollarhide, C., & Lemberger, M. (2006). "No Child Left Behind": Implications for school counselors. *Professional School Counseling, 9*(4), 295-303.

Kruk, L. (2005). Career technical education in the 21st century. *The California School Counselor, 4*(2).

U.S. Department of Education. (2003). Part 104—Nondiscrimination on the basis of handicap in programs or activities receiving federal financial assistance. Retrieved August 10, 2006, from http://www.ed.gov/policy/rights/reg/ocr/edlite-34cfr104.html

U.S. Department of Education. (2005a). Career guidance and counseling programs. Retrieved August 31, 2006, from http://www.ed.gov/about/offices/list/ovae/pi/cte/cgcp.html

U.S. Department of Education. (2005b). *Spellings announces new special education guidelines, details workable, "common-sense" policy to help states implement No Child Left Behind.* Washington, DC: Author: Retrieved August 31, 2006, from http://www.ed.gov/news/pressreleases/2005/05/05102005.html

U.S. Department of Education. (2006). *IDEA 2004 news, information, and resources.* Retrieved August 30, 2006, from http://www.ed.gov/policy/speced/guid/idea/idea2004.html

Additional Resources-Web Sites

IDEA 2004 News, Information, and Resources
http://www.ed.gov/policy/speced/guid/idea/idea2004.html
No Child Left Behind
http://www.ed.gov/nclb/landing.jhtml
National Career Development Guidelines (NCDG) Framework www.acrnetwork.org/ncdg.htm
The Carl D. Perkins Vocational and Technical Education Act, Public Law 105-332
http://www.ed.gov/offices/OVAE/CTE/perkins.html
The Carl D. Perkins and Career Guidance and Counseling Programs
http://www.ed.gov/about/offices/list/ovae/pi/cte/cgcp.html

Using Student Study Teams and School Attendance Review Boards to Improve Attendance, Graduation Rates, and Academic Performance

David Kopperud, Betty Collia Ibarra, and Steve McPherson

Abstract

To respond to low graduation rates and alienated or disengaged youth, a combination of school and district level teams must be organized to provide safety nets for students with persistent needs or problems that interfere with their ability to learn. The role of school counselors in planning, implementing, and evaluating these teams is crucial. This chapter looks at the substantial work of student study teams and School Attendance Review Boards (SARBs) in improving school attendance, high school graduation rates, and the academic performance of students on the margins of the educational system.

Results-Based Attendance Teams

The school dropout crisis in America has been recognized as social dynamite to the future of the country, and school counselors must lead the charge in a team approach to address the crisis. Margaret Spelling (2005), the U.S. Secretary of Education, has stated: "We wouldn't tolerate 5 out of 10 planes going down. We wouldn't tolerate 5 out of 10 heart surgeries failing. And we shouldn't tolerate 5 out of 10 city students dropping out of high school!" It has never been more urgent to implement results-based attendance teams to meet the needs of at-risk youth.

In a March 2006 report by Civic Enterprises in association with the Bill and Melinda Gates Foundation, dropouts were surveyed to determine why they dropped out and what assistance they needed. Although there was no single reason given for dropping out of school, most respondents reported a lack of connection to the school environment, a perception that school is boring, and a lack of motivation. These problems with school are not insurmountable, and a team of adults led by a school counselor could have successfully intervened when students first began to miss classes. According to *The Silent Epidemic: Perspectives of High School Dropouts*, "The central message of this report is that while some students drop out because of significant academic challenges, most dropouts are students who could have, and believe they could have, succeeded in school" (Bridgeland, DiIulio, & Morison, 2006).

Every year nearly a third of our nation's students slowly disappear from the educational system, and researchers have noted that attendance interventions are often not attempted. Recent reports from the Manhattan Institute for Policy Research (Greene & Winters, 2004), the Education Testing Service (Barton, 2005), the Civil Rights Project at Harvard (2005), and the Education Trust (Hall, 2005) have estimated that nearly one half of all African Americans, Hispanics, and Native Americans end up leaving school entirely before high school graduation.

The National Center for Educational Statistics estimates that the average U.S. graduation rate is 73.9 percent, while Jay Greene, a senior fellow at the Manhattan Institute, and subsequent researchers, place the national graduation rate between 64 and 71 percent (Greene & Winters, 2004). Even if the highest estimates of the graduation rate are accurate, it is clear that more intensive interventions are needed to keep students in school. The school counselor's expertise in planning, implementing, and monitoring student support programs is invaluable in the operation of a results-based school attendance program. Just as there is no single reason why students drop out, there is no single type of intervention to keep these students in school. Of course, it is not always necessary to assemble a team for every student attendance problem. However, persistently irregular school attendance is a precursor to dropping out, and a team approach is often required to combine the necessary expertise and resources these students need. School counselors need to work collaboratively with other members of the team to analyze each individual's situation and implement a plan to overcome the barriers to specific truancy problems.

To handle the variety of attendance problems found in public schools, two different types of collaborative teams depend on school counselor leadership:

1) School-level teams, often called Student Study Teams or Student Success Teams (SSTs) or School Attendance Review Teams (SARTs);
2) District-level teams, such as the School Attendance

Review Boards (SARBs) (used when the normal avenues of SST intervention do not resolve the problem).

An excellent resource for developing effective school-level teams is the *SST: Student Success Teams* publication, developed by the California Department of Education in conjunction with the Sacramento City Unified School District (California Department of Education, 2002b). The book is available through the Education Alliance and can be purchased with a compact disk containing SST forms and tools. An excellent resource for the district- level teams is the *School Attendance Review Boards Handbook* (California Department of Education, 2002a).

The composition of the school-level team should include the school counselor, at least one teacher, at least one school administrator, any other necessary school staff, the student, and the parent. The district level team should be more extensive and also include representatives from the district office, law enforcement, social services, mental health, probation, and any other appropriate youth service agencies.

Mission of the Results-Based Attendance Teams

The mission of the school-level team is to use all the normal avenues of truancy prevention, such as counseling and school-family conferences, to ensure regular school attendance of every student. When the resources of the school-level team are exhausted, it becomes the mission of the district level team to resolve the most persistent school attendance problems, which may include severe problems such as chemical dependency or mental illness. Increasing school attendance and graduation rates are essential components to the school's mission of improving academic performance. Even when students with irregular school attendance do manage to graduate, their poor attendance affects their academic performance. In a 2003 study titled *Determinants of Student Achievement: New Evidence from San Diego* conducted by the Public Policy Institute of California, Betts , Zau, and Rice found that absence was the most consistent negative predictor of gain in math and reading. Therefore, the teams will start by attempting to improve Average Daily Attendance by 2% above the baseline with the expectation that this will contribute to both better graduation rates and better academic performance; therefore, it is important to obtain data of attendance for each one of the students every day.

Using Data to Analyze the Team's Results

The first step in a results-based school attendance program is to analyze available data to determine the strategies that will be used by the school and district-level teams. The Wilder Research Center's review of effective truancy prevention and intervention (August 2003) found that every approach to improving attendance requires ongoing, accurate data to measure the impact of the program. Analyzing the data will enable team members to determine which students need more help. Data can be disaggregated by gender, race, ethnicity, or in multiple other ways to identify student groups with the greatest need for intensive guidance. A sample format for a *District/County SARB Annual Summary Report* is available on the California Department of Education Web site and disaggregates school-level and district-level team data by grade level, sex, nature of problem, outcome after meeting, legal requests, and referrals to agencies. The report template can be downloaded at http://www.cde.ca.gov/ls/ai/sb/documents/sarbform.doc In California, the *District/County SARB Annual Summary Report* is sent to the county superintendent so that a countywide strategy can be developed for attendance improvement and dropout reduction (*California Education Code* Section 48273).

Developing and Maintaining an Inventory of Resources and Educational Options for Team Referral

In addition to good data to drive intervention decisions, teams need to have the right resources and educational options for the students referred to them. At River City High School in West Sacramento, California, the Outreach Counselor Steve McPherson has helped develop an inventory of resources for the high school students referred (due to irregular school attendance) to his School Attendance Review Team (SART). The team consists of the outreach counselor, an assistant principal, another counselor, the school resource officer, a representative from Job Corps, a district administrator, and a representative from a community group helping with violence prevention called People Reaching Out. In many cases, a cultural liaison is also invited who can speak to the parents in their native language, in order to explain to them the importance of daily attendance.

A national study made by Wong Fillmore found that the inability to communicate with parents, as well as to understand their cultural, moral, and ethical values, can lead to truancy, gang membership, and higher rates of incarceration of their children (1991, p. 343). Parents need to be able to communicate with their children and school staff, in order to understand society's rules. The staff also needs to understand the student's emotional and sociocultural needs, and ways to stimulate their academic and social development. It is also important to inform the parents, in their own language, about the state regulations and the importance of daily attendance. In fact, in the U.S., the educational needs for students from other cultures are not being met satisfactorily. Many students leave school in frustration during the middle and high school years (Berliner & Biddle, 1995).

The SART can make referrals for gang prevention, gang intervention, drug counseling, anger management, parenting classes, tutoring, a required extra period for study hall, programs that provide instructional and non-instructional services to non-English speaking students, weekly grade checks, and/or daily attendance checks. The outreach counselor pays especially close attention to students who may need referral to the SART in their first semester of high school. Ninth grade students with low grades in eighth grade who appear to be struggling may be assigned to a ninth grade opportunity program for extra help.

The SART looks at many factors that may be affecting the student's attendance, as well as the student's individual needs, interests, and strengths. The SART may discuss social influences, specific circumstances in the home, language and cultural barriers, lack of basic necessities, and possible medical conditions or learning disabilities. The SART also attempts to identify student strengths that may motivate the student in school. The SART can use this student information to develop a plan, which may include counseling, tutoring, mentoring, differential instruction, and other special programs.

Students who exhaust the resources of the local school SART are referred to a district level SARB team that may transfer students to alternative schools or refer students and parents to court. In California, continually and willfully failing to respond to directives of the SARB or services provided, results in the filing of a criminal complaint. SARBs may also make recommendations for the improvement of needed student resources or for the creation of new resources or programs where none exist. SARBs are involved in expanding the choices students have and in developing appropriate support structures that will enable all students to be better prepared for their futures.

The success of the SARB team relies on the strength of the educational options available to students referred to the team. Steve McPherson, coauthor in a personal communication, noted that with a successful transition to an alternative program, SARB court referrals are not necessary: "Through alternative educational options, many high school students will find the individual attention and more tailored standards-based instruction they need to graduate. Many students are drowning in the regular high school, and the continuation high school and other options provide the right setting for them to earn a high school diploma."

Programs that include English as a second language, native language arts, and core classes, as well as other services like home visits, curriculum development, parenting classes and parent participation have demonstrated a bigger connection with school, as well as better attendance rates, test scores, and participation (Cochran & Schulman, 1983). Instructional and supported services provided to the students and their families, not just improve the students' connection with school, academic performance, and socialization skills but avoid antisocial behaviors, dropt outs, and underperformance in school.

As a result of a culturally grounded ESL program called "Horizontes" at the Metropolitan Campus of Cuyahoga Community College in Cleveland, Ohio, implemented in fall 1992 and winter 1993, "an overall quarter completion rate of 89% was achieved and persistence was high compared to anecdotal accounts of prior cohorts. In addition, 80.7% of students had a 90% or better attendance rate..." (Marsiglia & Guy, 1993).

A continuation school counselor and comprehensive high school counselor are essential members of the SARB. The continuation school counselor can begin serving as an advisor to prospective continuation students at the SARB meeting. The comprehensive high school counselor can introduce the continuation school counselor to the student, and the continuation school counselor can begin developing a relationship with the student and by discussing the pace of course completion possible at the continuation high school. Although most students referred to the SARB are initially disengaged or angry, the continuation school counselor can guide students on the journey to graduation in the new setting and help the student make a plan for life after high school.

Another educational option for the SARB to consider as an alternative to comprehensive classroom instruction is independent study. Independent study program models vary from district to district and state to state, but many school districts offer this alternative for credit-deficient students. Some school districts offer large independent study high school programs with over 1,000 students enrolled at multiple small sites throughout the district. Fontana Unified School District in Fontana, California, offers this alternative in different high schools. Each site provides two to four credentialed teachers and two or three teacher's aides that meet with students individually twice each week to check work in progress and assign new contracts. Many of the independent study students are pregnant or parenting teens or students who are already working regular jobs. These students may develop a more productive and meaningful relationship with the independent study staff than they had with the staff at the comprehensive high school.

Other educational options that SARBs may recommend include community day schools, magnet schools, dropout centers, pregnancy-maternity centers, home and hospital instruction, juvenile court schools, adult education schools, charter schools, and opportunity education programs. There is no one-size-fits-all model for high-risk students, and it takes a diverse and dedicated team to find the best programs to meet the needs of the student. Information about these and other school and program alternatives that provide students with the environment and support systems they need is located at http://www.cde.ca.gov/sp/eo/

Educating All Stakeholders

All the members of the school-level and district-level team, as well as other members of the school community, should be educated about results achieved by the teams in attendance improvement. In California, this data may be used for a Student Personnel Accountability Report Card (SPARC) that shows how the counselor with the rest of the team contributed to the mission of the school and to student success (Los Angeles County Office of Education, 2006). The SPARC provides an opportunity for student support staff to show the impact of various programs with disaggregated data, student outcomes, and major team achievements. Qualifying SPARC programs receive recognition at annual ceremonies of the California Association of School Counselors. The SPARC format can inform school boards, the community, and other stakeholders about accomplishments in improving school attendance and other essential elements of student support. To learn more about the SPARC, see Chapter 10 in this book and visit the SPARC Web site at www.sparconline.net.

Conclusion

Due in part to the staggering national dropout crisis, the school counseling and student support professional staff need to develop and implement teams for a results-based attendance improvement program. A standards-based curriculum and instruction program is not enough to ensure the education of the millions of students who disappear from the nation's education system, especially in schools with large Latino and African American student populations. Drawing these students out of the shadows with accurate early identification and effective team interventions is the first step to keeping them in school through to their graduation. One of the key roles the counselor can play in this team effort is to ensure strong adult-student relationships within the school and improve communication between parents and the school. It is essential to American education that teams be conscientious about tracking student attendance and using this data strategically for developing individual interventions. We are losing too many students before graduation, and only a team effort will meet the intense and urgent needs of these young people.

Discussion Questions

1. Why is a standards-based curriculum and excellent standards-based instruction not enough to ensure the education of every child?
2. What is the estimated percentage of students who do not graduate from high school?
3. What types of teams are needed in a school attendance improvement program?
4. What are three of the educational program options for students who are not successful in the comprehensive school?
5. What are some of the strategies used by school-based teams to meet the academic or social-behavioral needs of students?
6. What are some of the strategies used by district or county level teams to assist high-risk students?
7. What are prevalent reasons students give for dropping out of school?
8. Why is accurate, ongoing data collection essential to an attendance improvement program?

References
Barton, P. E. (2005). *One-third of a nation: Rising dropout Rates and declining opportunities.* Princeton, NJ: Educational Testing Service. Available at www.ets.org/research/pic

Berliner, D. C., & Biddle, B. J. (1995). *The manufactured crisis: Myths, fraud, and the attack on America's public schools.* Reading, MA: Addison-Westley.

Betts, J., Zau, A., & Rice, L. (2003). *Determinants of student achievement: New evidence from San Diego.* San Francisco, CA: Public Policy Institute of California.

Bridgeland, J. M., DiIulio, J. J., Jr., & Morison, K. B. (2006.). *The silent epidemic: Perspectives of high school dropouts.* Washington, DC: Civic Enterprises. Retrieved January 20, 2007, from http://www.civicenterprises.net/pdfs/thesilentepidemic3-06.pdf

California Department of Education. (2002a). *School Attendance Review Boards handbook.* Sacramento, CA: Author. Retrieved January 20, 2007, from http://www.cde.ca.gov/ls/ai/sb/documents/sarb02.pdf

California Department of Education (2002b). SST: *Student success teams.* Soquel, CA: The California Dropout Prevention Network. California Education Code (Section 48273). Retrieved January 15, 2007, from http://www.leginfo.ca.gov/cgi bin/calawquery?codesection=edc&codebody=&hits=20.

Civil Rights Project at Harvard University. (2005). *Confronting the graduation rate crisis in California. Executive Summary.* Cambridge, MA: Author.

Cochran, E. P., & Schulman, R. (1983). *Morris High School new directions for bilingualism. O.E.E. Evaluation Report, 1982-1983.* Brooklyn, NY: New York City Board of Education. (ERIC Document Reproduction Service No. ED247334)

Fillmore, W. L. (1991) When learning a second language means losing the first. *Early Childhood Research Quarterly, 6,* 323-346.

Greene, J. P. & Winters, M. A. (2004). *Public high school graduation and college- readiness rates: 1991-2002.* Education Working Paper, No. 8. New York: Manhattan Policy Institute for Policy Research.

Hall, D. (2005, June). *Getting honest about grad rates: How states play the numbers and students lose.* Washington, DC: The Education Trust.

Los Angeles County Office of Education. (2006). *Student personnel accountability report card.* Retrieved January 20, 2007, from http://www.lacoe.edu/orgs/1077/index.cfm.

Marsiglia, F. F., & Guy, T. (1993). Horizontes: *A culturally grounded English as a Second Language college entry project for a Latino students (Fall-Winter 1992-1993 Pilot Phase).* Cleveland, OH: Cuyahoga Community College. (ERIC Document Reproduction Services No. ED376906)

Spelling, M. (2005, September 28). Remarks at the National Association of Manufacturers Meeting, Washington, DC. Retrieved January 20, 2007, from http://www.ed.gov/news/pressreleases/2005/09/09282005.html

United States Department of Education. (2004). *Dropout rates in the United States: 2001.* Washington, DC: National Center for Education Statistics.

Wilder Research Center. (2003, August). *Effective truancy prevention and intervention.* Saint Paul, MN: Author.

Other Resources

Balfanz, R., & Legters, N. (2005). *The graduation gap: Using promoting power to examine the number and characteristics of high schools with high and low graduation rates in the nation and each state.* Baltimore, MD: John Hopkins University Center for Social Organization of Schools.

California Department of Education. (2000). *School attendance improvement handbook.* Sacramento, CA: Author. Retrieved January 20, 2007, from http://www.cde.ca.gov/ls/ai/cw/documents/schoolattendance.pdf.

Felter, M. (1989). School dropout rates, academic performance, size, and poverty: Correlates of educational reform. *Educational Evaluation and Policy Analysis, 11*(2).

National Governors Association. (2005). *Redesigning the American high school: Graduation counts: A report of the NGA Task Force on State High School Graduation Data.* Washington, DC: Author.

Student Accountability Report Card information now available on www.sparconline.net

Swanson, C. B., et al. (2003). *Who graduates? Who doesn't? A statistical portrait of public high school graduation, Class of 2001.* Washington, DC: The Urban Institute.

United States Government Accountability Office. (2005). *No Child Left Behind Act: Education could do more to help states better define graduation rates and improve knowledge about intervention strategies.* Washington, DC: Author.

WestEd. (2004, May). *California's graduation rate (2004): The hidden crisis.* San Francisco: Author.

Section IV.
Self Care: Care for the Caregiver

Chapter 30

Spirituality and School Counseling

Lee J. Richmond and Deborah R. Margulies

Abstract

The experiences that cause fear, boredom, and confusion can lead to a general lack of well being and cause depression and/or hostility in students. Helping students connect that which is deepest inside of them to that which is perceived to be greatest outside may lead to a sense of meaning and create well being. As such, it is a spiritual endeavor in which school counselors can and do engage. This chapter contains case studies and helpful activities designed to assist professional school counselors who wish to incorporate spirituality into their practice.

Introduction

She came to the office at nine on a rainy autumn morning. She was a tenth grade student who had lived in six different foster homes over her brief lifetime. She had attended nine different schools before entering her present school. The whereabouts of her birth mother were unknown to her. Her "real" father had recently died of AIDS. She had no chance to say goodbye to him. She told her counselor that she has difficulty learning. She expressed the sentiment that what she was learning in school seemed to have no connection to the realities of her everyday life.

He knew that his older sister had always wanted to fly jet airplanes, and when he was a little kid he thought her smart and courageous to join the United States Air Force. Now that she was flying in and out of Iraq, he wondered if she were not crazy to have enlisted. In his thinking, fighting wars was not work for women. He wasn't sure this particular war was even worthwhile. Underneath it all, he was worried about his sister's welfare. In fact, he was very worried! He said that his teacher had sent him to the office because he fell asleep in class. When questioned, he told his school counselor that he had been having difficulty sleeping at night. He stopped watching the news at night because it terrified him.

The two students described in the vignettes brought different issues to their professional school counselor. Each situation has an underlying problem. They are both impaired in their ability to learn because of circumstances in their lives. Neither circumstance could, nor should, be addressed in the classroom. However, unless there is somewhere in the school that problems such as these can be properly addressed, both young people are in danger of failure, not because of incompetence or lack of intelligence on their part. The underlying dynamic is that both students face issues concerning meaning. When students face a crisis in meaning, they cannot make sense of the world in which they live. Confusion replaces clarity and learning is impossible. It is not within the scope of the school curriculum, nor is it the job of the classroom teacher to address personal problems. However, it is the task of the school counselor to do so. When severe issues effecting individual students are not addressed somewhere, there is a danger that the outcome will escalate and affect the entire school community.

It has long been known that experiences such as those described in the vignettes interfere with learning. Holt (1964) described the kinds of experiences that cause young people to fail. These experiences fall into three categories: fear, boredom, and confusion. Fear of failure, fear of humiliation, fear of being hurt, and fear of being left or left out are the common problems that cause anxiety in young people. Boredom, caused by lack of meaningful activity, or by the repetitive practice of seemingly meaningless tasks, frequently leads to vacuous inactivity and/or daydreaming. Confusion, when caused by a seeming contradiction between what has been taught to adolescents by elders and what is actually practiced by those elders, can lead to outright hostility (Lorenz, 1970). These major blocks to student well being and to learning can be effectively addressed by employing meaning-making activities. School counselors have long facilitated students' growth by reflecting statements that seem significant, or by asking questions about purpose. Reflective responding and purposeful questioning, the kind that lends to clarity, have been frequently used in school counseling. These activities are called techniques. They are rarely thought to be spiritual practices. Yet, when they lead students to meaning and help students make sense of their lives they are, indeed, spiritual activities.

Defining Spirituality and Recognizing Its Importance in School Counseling

Allen and Coy (2004) have discussed the growing awareness of the importance of spirituality within the education system and have applied the Council for the Accreditation of Counseling and Related Educational Programs (CACREP; 2001) competencies relating to spirituality in school counseling. These competencies involve becoming aware of one's personal spiritual perspective, understanding and valuing the spiritual perspectives of others, relating spirituality to intervention strategies, and understanding the importance of spirituality in the counseling process. Within a school, these competencies help counselors build a climate of understanding, and hopefully reduce the potential for conflict and violence. But what is spirituality and how is it practiced within a school setting?

There are many definitions of spirituality. Some, but not all, include religion or religiousness. Because public school counselors must be able to work with people from varying religious traditions, or none, a broad definition applicable to all students is recommended (Lonborg & Bowen, 2004). A definition of spirituality that is consistent with the Ethical Standards of ASCA and helps students make sense of their world is required. Such a definition incorporates the crying need and developmental task of adolescents to discover who they are and what is their purpose in life. This must be accomplished in a world that frequently seems confusing, and less than friendly. In this regard, Bloch and Richmond (1998) have defined spirituality as the connection of that which is deepest within ourselves to that which is greatest outside of ourselves. This definition implies that personal meaning can be found and can be connected to what is meaningful in the world. Thus, "spirituality (can be) loosely defined as humans' expressions of and attempts at 'meaning-making' that are uniquely personal as well as communal or socio-cultural" (Sink & Richmond, 2004, p. 291). For school settings this definition can be made operational by activities designed to help students acquire a sense of personal meaning and purpose in life. Such activities may incorporate broad based values, and may be either developmental or remedial, practiced in individual or group settings, and are well within the scope of professional school counseling practice.

Spirituality and School Counseling Activities

Songs, poems, and artistic creations can be spiritual activities that connect students to the larger world. Literary devices such as the "Ask not" speech of Kennedy, the passionate and uplifting words of Langston Hughes, and the "I have a dream speech" of King can serve to validate dreams of students. Poems such as Renascence and the early short verses of Edna St. Vincent Millay, first silently read by students, and then aloud by the counselor, can evoke meaning, even passion, when students apply what they hear to their own experience and discuss the meaning of their experiences in small group counseling sessions.

Most students are into music, and many listen carefully to the lyrics. Being aware of the current music that students enjoy can help the counselor connect with students in a way that is meaningful. By asking students to download a song and its lyrics, the group involvement is insured. Songs that identify their inner pain, songs that define their relationships, and songs that encourage and motivate are usually at the "fingertips" of students. When the songs are played and listened to within the group, and when the elicited feelings and meaning of the songs are discussed, a connection between the student and his or her world occurs. Opening students' minds by bringing to light what they inwardly know in darkness sometimes helps them realize how much they have to offer to themselves and others.

There is a vast difference between words and music discussed in the classroom and words and music discussed in small group counseling. In class the teacher asks the student to seek the meaning that the author tries to convey. Only secondarily, if at all, is the meaning of the work discussed in terms of the everyday life of the student. In counseling groups, the words of poems, speeches, and music serve as a foil from which to illicit that which is deepest in the life of the student and connect it to that which is most meaningful and important to him or to her in the world outside of self. By doing this, the activity becomes a spiritual one.

Another activity that has spiritual overtones is an activity called "Power Rocks." Power rocks are something that the co-author of this chapter (Deborah) developed to make students think beyond their normal realm of thinking and search for a personal affirmation that will lead them to achieving whatever is their goal. The activity usually begins by the student's selection of a sentence or phrase that expresses what he or she wants to achieve. The sentence or phrase needs to focus on the positive. For instance, the boy's goals in the second vignette at the beginning of this chapter were to be less anxious about his sister, to sleep at night, and to stay awake in class. The sentence that he chose to say over and over again was, "I am a fearless person who enjoys learning." He shortened that into a mantra of three words: "I am fearless." This done, he was then told to look though old magazines (supplied by the counselor) and find a small picture that illustrates the words "I am fearless." The student looked for and found a picture and the actual words. The counselor then supplied rounded clear glass discs, one inch in diameter (usually found in craft shops), scissors, and clear drying glue. The student was told to cut out the illustration and words and glue them to the back of the small round disc. When the disc (power rock) was dry, the counselor asked the student to show it to his group, explain the mantra, and tell how his rock symbolized what he needed to do. He and the other students who made rocks were told that they were to keep the rocks in their pockets for as long as they need them.

The girl described in this chapter's opening vignette also made a power rock. To define what she needed to do, she chose the sentence, "I love learning and find it rewarding." She shortened her sentence to the one word, "learn." On the back of her rock, she glued a picture of a book that she found in a magazine. On the diagonal of her book symbol she glued the one word, "learn," which she had typed and cut out. Later, when it was dry, she showed her power rock to the group and told her story. She carried her rock in her purse for six weeks after the group ended. Then, in individual counseling, she told her counselor she now felt that what was happening in school was part of her inner world. She was doing better in her classes. A friend of hers, however, was not doing well, so she decided to give her power rock to her friend as a gift. The counselor heartily approved, rewarding her for her act of altruism.

Lastly, an activity that connects students to their inner experience is called "My Story, My Place." They are asked to draw a picture of the house in which they live. The counselor then asks the students to think about a favorite room or place within the house and to visualize it. The counselor might ask: Is the place a secret place? Are you there alone or with others? Do you imagine that character heroes from books or movies are there with you? What is your favorite thing to do in that place? What fantasies and dreams do you have while you are there? After thinking about these questions, students are

asked to share the answers to them along with the house picture that they drew. On occasion some students will say that they hate their home. If this happens, they are told that the place that they draw can be outside of the house and then proceed with the same questions. Do not ask why they hate their homes. The purpose of the activity is horizontal, not vertical. The idea is to be expansive and not take the students deeper than what they say when answering the questions.

The activities presented in this chapter are only a few of the many activities that can be used to connect a student to self and self to the world in a way that is meaningful. To engage a student in meaning making is one of the most fulfilling acts that a school counselor can perform. To be effective, a school counselor needs compassion for students, passion for the profession of counseling, and a strong sense of purpose and meaning in one's own life. Counseling models are emerging to describe how spiritual wellness can be incorporated into K-12 school settings. One such model is described below.

Spirituality and Comprehensive Professional School Counseling Programs

Sink (2004, p. 313) described in detail how the ASCA Standards (1998) could involve spirituality when counselors focus on meaning-making. Targeted guidance lessons involving meaning-making activities, as well as small group and individual counseling sessions could, according to Sink, play a role in helping students meet the standards. At the early elementary school age, Sink recommends play-oriented methods that involve artwork. Toys and picture books that "challenge students to create, imagine, and make sense" are recommended, as is dialogue about them (Sink, p. 213). For older children and adolescents, Sink recommends the use of Socratic questions, dilemmas, music videos, and films to "evoke discussion and deeper processing" (p. 314). Most important is Sink's suggestion that meaning making approaches should be comprehensive and systematic, starting with guidance lessons in the teachers' classrooms where students feel safe. Sink recommends proceeding from general classroom instruction to the specific issues of students. Thus, after classroom work, groups can be taken into smaller sections where students can discuss their hopes, dreams, purpose and death: the big "why questions" about which students are concerned (p. 314). Spirituality, integrated with the ASCA Standards (1998) and applied systematically to the guidance program throughout the grades, is recommended.

The middle grades are of particular importance. Adolescence has always been difficult, but today it can be dangerous. The media-saturated American social scene has put inordinate pressure on teens, particularly adolescent girls. They are supposed to be sophisticated and good-looking. They are often sexualized (Bruce & Cockreham, 2004). Nevertheless, during the early teen years, most girls, and boys, think about their futures and struggle to "make a difference". They want to feel connected to something important, something beyond themselves. Erik Erikson (1994) wrote about how teens strive to seek identity and how identity is connected to spirituality. Though they question everything, teens want to relate to that which is larger than self. They seek a place to fit in. In so doing they will follow groups and group leaders that offer an idealistic impact on the world. There are many destructive groups that feign to do this. Often young people cannot separate what is truly good, and good for them, from that which is destructive but parades under a mask of social justice. A guidance program that is focused on meaning-making, and that helps students feel good about themselves can go a long way toward helping youth discover what is of genuine value to self and others (Richmond, 2004).

Classroom guidance that is focused on ethics can be very helpful to high school students. Rayburn (2004) suggests that growth in moral values development has not kept pace with the increase in violence in our culture. She suggests morality education that uses special instruments to test students' perceptions of what is moral and vignettes to present ethical dilemmas. The resolution of the dilemmas is a method for teaching positive values. Testing, the presentation of dilemmas and discussion about the dilemmas, according to Rayburn, should be conducted by school counselors in order to help students behave morally toward peers, parents, and society in general.

The Issue of Violence and Trauma

Studies of traumatic happenings and their effects on young people have been published; findings point to a positive correlation between psychopathology and the experience of traumatic events (Breslau, 2002; Pine, 2003; Steinberg & Avenevoli, 2000). Because the detrimental effects of trauma are both immediate and long term, the facilitation of a "culture of respect" within the school is important (Allen & Coy, 2004).

There is hardly a child over ten who does not have vivid images of airplanes crashing into tall buildings in New York, of sniper shootings in Maryland and Virginia, of suicide bombings in Israel, of war in Iraq, of a tsunami disaster in Asia, and, most recently, of hurricane devastation in New Orleans. Many students are familiar with school lockdowns due to fear of one violent act or another. The value of spirituality as a coping mechanism has had little study. Recently Rayburn and Richmond (2005) developed a 41-item instrument, the Traumatic Experience and Children's Health (TEACH) inventory to discover how children feel after very bad experiences. A pilot study was conducted, and it was found that anger was a reaction for both boys and girls, who reported punching a pillow or going outside by themselves as a way of assuaging anger. Sadness was also reported, as were physical symptoms such as stomach pain and sleeplessness. Crying was not uncommon (Richmond, Kimos, Markowsky, & Natalie, 2005). In another part of the pilot study, Richmond and Wexler (2005) tried to ascertain what role spirituality plays in ameliorating symptoms of anger and depression in high school students who have experienced traumatic events. Questions were asked about whether students turn to religion to find meaning in hard and difficult times, whether they pray more at those times, and what spiritual help they feel that they need at those times. The findings were stark. Students who were religious prayed more; students who were not religious did not. However, all students wanted to be able to come to a place where they could work through their anger, their sorrow, and talk about their fears, anxiety, and confusion. They wanted to make meaning out of what seemed to be a senseless situation. They did not see church, synagogue, or mosque as a place where they could go to work through their issues. Perhaps the school counseling office could be that place.

Spirituality and the Counselor

There is a link between spirituality, defined as a quest for connection and for meaning in life, and counseling, defined as a means by which meaning can be discovered in the daily actions and life situations of individuals. However, for the link to be more than cognitive, it must be intentional on the part of the counselor. This implies that the counselor should approach the counseling situation well aware of his or her own spirituality. Allen and Coy (2004) have described how spiritual development takes place within family, culture, and usually (but not necessarily) within an inherited religious tradition. However, as individuals live and grow, spirituality becomes an intensely personal thing that involves not only one's connection to others but also an inner sense of purpose. People who recognize their own spirituality have a sense of being called to something or some work beyond themselves. School counselors who have a sense of their own spirituality believe that their work is a blessing to themselves and to others and often feel chosen to do the work that they do. These counselors are productive and creative. There is congruence between who they are and what they do. When change is needed, they joyfully work to bring it about in their own lives and in the lives of students.

The quest for unity and purpose is spiritual. Like its sister, empathy, spirituality cannot be taught, but it can be realized in self. If lost, it can be reborn in the recognition that the path through life is a search where people struggle to find the unity between who one is and what one does. Sometimes, when things seem to be coming apart, they are really together because all things are parts of a whole (Bloch & Richmond, 1998). Psychology has called this recognition of wholeness "peak experience" and described it as the highest level of human experience. Stress can destroy one's sense of wholeness; and, without doubt, a school counselor's life can be stressful. However, when stillness is practiced, when one allows for the luxury of getting away from it all for a short period, inner harmony can be restored. Sometimes it takes this brief time away from work to do productive work. When the "time out" period is used as a time to rediscover one's gifts, another word for the interests, skills, and abilities that define one, calling is rediscovered.

To be effective, school counselors need to be open to all forms of spirituality, including their own. This requires them to first hear their own story and sing their own song, and value them, before hearing and understanding the stories and songs of students. Each schoolteacher has curriculum to assist him or her when working with students. The curriculum is like the instrument that each member of an orchestra plays when in concert with others. The counselor has neither curriculum nor instruments when doing counseling. All that he or she has is his or her self. The instrument of the self of the school counselor must therefore be kept in very good tune. The spiritual well being of the school counselor is tantamount to his or her existence, even as it is tantamount to doing fruitful work with students. It should therefore be of primary concern, and time and attention must be given to it.

Conclusion

A fifteen- year old female student asked to see her school counselor. She recently moved to a location far from where she had lived before. She was transitioning to a new school. She said,

I have had to deal with parents in the hospital, the loss of a close friend, a recent move to a different state, and a different school- away from everyone I knew. I watched my best friend tear flesh off her arm. I have seen other kids that were cutters and suicidal. I have looked everywhere for answers. There are so many things I don't understand. But in spite of all of this stuff, I still think that life is good and the world is good.

This young student, like so very many of her peers, is a spiritual person, seeking meaning in the world. Her statement is that of a young woman trying to connect what is best in her to what is greatest outside of self. Bloch (2004) wrote about phase transitions and described fitness peaks. A phase transition occurs when someone or something is thrown into change. During phase transitions the state that will yield the greatest chance of survival is sought. That state is called a fitness peak. The fifteen- year old female student was seeking a fitness peak for herself. She decided to talk to her school counselor. Like the young student, professional school counseling is also in a phase transition, seeking a fitness peak for itself. In the past, spirituality was hardly mentioned in articles about school counseling and texts teaching about how to do it. Today, however, is a new day, and it offers new challenges.

Integrating spirituality into school counseling is on the horizon. Connecting what is deepest and most meaningful within the profession to what is the greatest need outside of the profession is a way of living spiritually within the profession. Sink (2004, p. 315) ended his seminal article with the following statement: "It is my long-term hope that school counselors' work within comprehensive programs will become truly holistic-providing genuine acceptance, respect, and support for students' expressions of spirituality as they negotiate a complex and often disturbing world." We echo this sentiment.

Discussion Questions

1. Do you agree with how spirituality has been defined in this chapter? Why or why not?
2. Can you describe some spiritual activities that can be used in school beyond those that were mentioned in this chapter?
3. How might you use power rocks in your school setting?
4. Do you agree that the issues presented in the vignettes are spiritual issues? Explain your reasoning.

5. What have you done to familiarize yourself with the CACREP Standards as they address the topic of spirituality?
6. How should professional school counselors continue to address the issue of spirituality and school counseling?

References

American School Counselor Association. (1998). *Ethical standards for school counselors*. Alexandria, VA: Author.

Allen, J. M., & Coy, D. R. (2004). Linking spirituality and violence prevention in school counseling. *Professional School Counseling, 75*, 351-355.

Bloch, D. P. (2004). Spirituality, complexity, and career counseling. *Professional School Counseling, 75*, 343-350.

Bloch, D. P., & Richmond, L. J. (1998). *Soulwork: Finding the work you love, loving the work you have*. Palo Alto, CA: Davies Black, p. 18.

Breslau N. (2002). Psychiatric morbidity in adult survivors of childhood trauma. *Seminars in Clinical Neuropsychiatry, 2*, 80-88.

Bruce, M. A., & Cockreham, D. (2004). Enhancing the spiritual development of adolescent girls. *Professional School Counseling, 75*, 334-342.

Council for the Accreditation of Counseling and Related Educational Programs. (2001). *CACREP accreditation manual*. Alexandria, VA: Author.

Erikson, E. H. (1994). *Identity, youth, and crisis*. New York: Norton.

Holt, J. (1964). *How children fail*. New York: Pitman.

Lonborg, S. D., & Bowen, N. (2004). Counselors, communities and spirituality: Ethical and multicultural considerations. *Professional School Counseling, 75*, 318-325.

Lorenz, K. (1970). The enmity between generations and its probable ethological causes. *The Psychonalytic Quarterly, 57*, 333-337.

Pine, D. (2003). The effects of trauma on children: working to define roles for mental health professionals. *International Psychiatry, 2*, 3-5.

Rayburn, C. A. (2004). Assessing students for morality education: A new role for school counselors. *Professional School Counseling, 75*, 356-362.

Rayburn, C. A., & Richmond, L. J. (2005). *Traumatic experience and children's health*. Washington, DC: U.S. Copyright Office.

Richmond, L. J. (2004). When spirituality goes awry: Students in cults. *Professional School Counseling, 75*, 367-375.

Richmond, L. J., Kimos, S., Markowski, M., & Natalie, H. (2005). *Religion and spirituality: helping children cope with hard times*. Paper presented at the meeting of the American Psychological Association, Washington, DC.

Richmond, L. J., & Wexler, B. P. (2005). *Religion and spirituality: Helping children cope with hard times*. Paper presented at the meeting of the American Psychological Association, Washington. DC.

Sink, C. A. (2004). *Spirituality and comprehensive school counseling programs. Professional School Counseling, 75*, 309- 317.

Sink, C. A., & Richmond, L. J. (2004). Introducing spirituality to professional school counseling. *Professional School Counseling, 75*, 291-292.

Steinberg, L., & Avenevoli, S. (2000). The role of context in the development of psychopathology: A conceptual framework and some speculative propositions. *Child Development, 71*, 66-74.

Chapter 31

Time Management and the School Counselor

Doris Rhea Coy and Stephanie Zimmermann

Abstract

The role of the school counselor can be physically and emotionally exhausting and the time pressures can be relentless. With e-mail and cell phones helping counselors juggle projects, multitasking can have many benefits. But it also can have side effects such as impatience, irritability, and inefficiency. This chapter suggests that the counselor is in the position to develop habits that identify time as a resource instead of a threatened commodity. The authors explore the connections between personality and time management and provide suggestions for taking control of time and becoming more efficient.

The role of the school counselor can be physically and emotionally exhausting. The time pressures can be relentless. Yet the counselor is in the position to develop habits that identify time as a resource instead of a threatened commodity. School counselors need to develop time management strategies that permit them to spend the bulk of their time on significant activities that contribute to their role as a counselor (Thompson, 2002).

Franklin D. Roosevelt said, "Never have we had so little time in which to do so much." These words ring true for school counselors balancing time and task. Counselors are expected to perform tasks that are not part of the American School Counselor's National Model (American School Counseling Association, 2002; Baggerly & Osborn, 2006).

The role and function of the school counselor has changed. In the early years of school counseling, the emphasis was on personal/social, academic/educational, and career issues. While those issues are still addressed, time is also spent on individual counseling, group counseling, and classroom guidance. In addition, counselors develop a guidance curriculum that addresses basic life skills such as decision-making and problem solving, goal setting and motivation, as well as self-esteem and self-confidence. They also are responsible for responsive services that keep students in school by teaching coping skills and strategies to address challenges to academic success such as: dropping out, physical, sexual, or emotional abuse, and substance abuse. Individual planning provides guidance for students as they plan and manage their education and career plans by providing information on course selection, post-secondary education and scholarships, and career opportunities. Because the counselor is a vital part of a system, time is also devoted to system support that includes the coordination of additional campus and community resources for student success including parent education, teacher/administrator consultation, and staff development for educators (Texas Counseling Association, 2004).

The professional school counselor impacts the entire learning community by:

a. counseling individuals and small groups of students to meet identified needs,
b. teaching the guidance curriculum to students and school personnel,
c. consulting with parents, teachers, and other staff to address students' needs, and
d. coordinating people and resources in the community to benefit students (Texas Counseling Association, 2004).

Stress

By improving time management, one can decrease stress. The number one tool for managing stress at its sources is probably time management (time-management guide.com, 2005). Stress management increases the school counselor's career satisfaction and career commitment (Baggerly & Osborn, 2006).

One of the results of not developing a sound time management program is stress. Michael W. Smith, M.D. at www.webmd.com provides the following ten tips for reducing stress:

1. Keep a positive attitude.
2. Accept that there are events you cannot control.
3. Be assertive instead of aggressive. Assert your feelings, opinions or beliefs instead of becoming angry, defensive or passive.
4. Learn and practice relaxation techniques.
5. Exercise regularly. Your body can fight stress better when fit.

6. Eat healthy balanced meals.
7. Get enough rest and sleep. Your body needs time to recover from stressful events.
8. Don't rely on alcohol or drugs to reduce stress.
9. Seek social support.
10. Learn to manage your time more effectively. (2004)

Personality and Time Management

Conscientiousness

There is a positive correlation between conscientiousness and time management. Kelly and Johnson (2005) administered the Time Use Efficiency Scale (TUES) to 105 university students and found that:

….higher scores on the scale correlated with less procrastination, a greater sense of purpose in time use, more use of routines and time structure, the use of time management behaviors, setting goals and priorities, self-efficacy, less stress, and an internal local of control. The TUES also has been found to positively correlate with higher grade-point averages among college students. (Kelly & Johnson, 2005)

Conscientiousness, as described in the Five-Factor Model of Personality includes: impulse control, planning, and organization (Kelly & Johnson, 2005).

In a section called, "Managing Your Paper Chase," Thompson (2002) offers a number of suggestions to provide some structure to a person's method of operation. She offers the following suggestions:

a. Follow the OHIO principle ("only handle it once") when managing papers, that is, use it, lose it, or file it away.
b. Have incoming mail screened or sorted by the secretary if possible. If that's not possible, move the trash can under your mailbox and leave the junk mail there. Why let unnecessary mail clutter your workspace?
c. If a brief reply to a letter is needed, write it on the incoming letter or memo, make a copy for your file, and return to sender.
d. Avoid unnecessary paper copies. They waste everyone's time to make, distribute, file, trash, or read. Do not become a disciple of the "fat paper philosophy," induced by "memoitis" and spread by copy machines.

e. Set ahead a regular time each day to do paperwork: no more than an hour a day. Examine how much of your clerical work can be given to a clerical worker. Set aside blocks of time for more detailed concentration. Make sure that the first hour of your day, or the last hour of your day, is a productive one.
f. Read flyers, catalogs, and routine memos at a designated time once a week. Follow the technique of "rip-and-read" (rip out the article that could be used later and throw other irrelevant materials away). Better yet, have a designated reader on the staff that will "rip-and-read" or "clip-and-save" for you.
g. Implement a time truce or quiet hour to frame a large block of uninterrupted time for your most important tasks or deadlines.
h. Have your secretary screen and guard your door. (Thompson, 2002, p. 322-323)

Perfectionism and Procrastination

If taken too far, conscientiousness may hinder efforts. Striving for perfection can undermine efficient time management (George Mason University: Counseling and Student Development Center, n.d.). Perfectionism may underlie procrastination. When the organizational style of the individual is observed, there are indicators for a propensity toward procrastination.

Prioritization and Goals

Prioritization helps in gaining control of organization, and the 80/20 rule of time management is a useful technique. This rule states that "20% of your efforts produce 80% of the results you want…." (Vacarro, 2002, p. 64). With this in mind, identify the areas of work and personal life that are most important and keep a written record of them. Knowing what 20% is most important will help the counselor eschew nonessential matters (Vacarro, 2002).

Setting personal performance goals may also help the counselor in staying focused on important tasks. "Research in goal setting has shown that goals can affect strategy formation and the planning of task behavior, and it has been suggested that goals can exhibit effects by structuring an ambiguous situation" (Galimba, 2001 p. 363-4). When asked to set performance goals, an individual will switch tasks less frequently (Galimba, 2001). The following list is helpful in discernment:
  • Lack of clear goals.
  • Underestimating the difficulty of the task.
  • Underestimating the time required to complete the tasks.

- Unclear standards for the task outcomes.
- Feeling as the tasks are imposed on you from outside.
- Too ambiguous tasks. (time-managment guide.com, 2005)

Technology

Counselors need to increase their use of technology following current trends in our society. The majority of school counselors today "are using technology to carry out their professional duties, and there still exists a need for further technology training for practicing school counselors" (Carlson, Portman & Bartlett, 2006, p. 257). Technology can greatly enhance time management, if one has been properly trained in its use. Tools such as personal digital assistants (PDAs), integrated calendars, MS Outlook, and Plan Plus (Franklin Planner software for MS Outlook), are more effectively used by individuals who have been trained (Hartley, 2004). Knowledge of using the Internet to its fullest potential is critical (Guillot-Miller & Partin, 2003). Training in data collection and analysis is becoming more important in the effective implementation and improvement of programs, as well as supporting counselor effectiveness via documented accountability.

By conducting needs assessments, aligning with school improvement goals, identifying achievement barriers specific to their students, and engaging other educators and stakeholders in the process, school counselors can effectively direct their professional expertise and time to contribute to achievement. (Isaacs, 2003, p. 8)

Carlson, Portman, and Bartlett (2006) surveyed school counselors in three states to determine their current technology training and usage. They found that most school counselors are comfortable using computers; however, more than half were anxious about using a variety of software. The comfort level among school counselors would probably increase with actual hands-on experiential work with the software.

Adams (2001) noted that technology can impede organization and goal attainment, when boundaries are not observed.

It's so American to be excited by the potential in technology –to believe it is an unalloyed good that will improve our lives. Perhaps what is most clear about technology; however, is that it has greatly changed the

pace of our lives, blurring the difference between home and school with e-mail, voicemail, and cell phones. (p. 15)

The school counselor must also be cognizant of using technology in a responsible way, filtering the time-eaters that serve no productive purpose. "One of the foils of work-life balance for many professionals is the nearly continuous stream of e-mail and other electronic media (span, popups, offers, electronic reminders) that bombard us" (Hartley, 2004, p. 27). Prioritizing is beneficial for the school counselor to assess his or her work-life balance to maximize the benefits of technology as related to time management (Hartley, 2004). Hartley makes the following suggestions for the use of technology:

1. Sort all unread mail by subject.
2. Delete any obvious junk mail or spam. Consider setting up rules to handle junk mail so that you minimize the chance of getting the same junk mail repeatedly.
3. With messages sorted by subject, go to the most current message in a common subject thread and read it first. Start from the bottom of the message. This will let you read just one message in the same subject. It also minimizes the chance that you won't put your foot in your mouth by responding prematurely to an issue that may have been addressed by a previous sender.
4. You can delete all same-subject e-mails except the most recent when all of the replies are contained in that e-mail.
5. When possible, set up rules to handle any incoming messages.
6. Use e-mail as it's meant to be used – for short concise messaging, not long diatribes.
7. Consider talking with a co-worker, instead of sending e-mails for short notes, questions, and the like. (Hartley, 2004, p. 28)

Suggested Time Management Techniques

Activity Log

In order to prioritize, you must understand where time is wasted. Blair (n.d.) suggests keeping an activity log for one week to see how time is spent. It is suggested that you look at each work activity and decide objectively how much time spent was worth to you, and compare that with the time you actually spent on it. If you are aware of what the appropriate amount of time is to be allotted for a task, you can work to that deadline – then move on to the next task. Review your log to determine where you delay dull or difficult work, by engaging in distractions.

Monthly Checklists

A useful tool in prioritizing is the organization of counselor tasks required by the district. "Evaluating counselor effectiveness helps school counselors examine their time-use practices, set goals for time-use management and develop strategies for reducing time spent on non-program activities" (Learnmoreindiana.org, 2004). The Learn More Resource Center offers a useful template for this purpose. The template helps the counselor determine what to do so he/she can stay on top of key activities, assessments, deadlines, meetings, and other opportunities throughout the school year and during the summer.

Other Suggestions

How can counselors use their time more wisely and avoid activities that consume large amounts of time? Thompson (2002) suggests that counselors address those areas that may use their time. These include:
   a. telephone interruptions;
   b. drop-in visitors;
   c. meetings, scheduled as well as unscheduled;
   d. crisis situations for which planning ahead was not possible;
   e. lack of objectives, priorities, and deadlines;
   f. cluttered desk and personal disorganization;
   g. involvement in routines and details that should be delegated;
   h. attempting too much at one time and underestimating the time it takes to do it;
   i. failure to set up clear lines of responsibility and authority;
   j. inadequate, inaccurate, or delayed information from others;
   k. indecision and procrastination; lack of clear communication and instruction; inability to say "no";
   l. lack of standards and professional reports; compassion fatigue;
   m. family demands; mail, both "snail mail" and e-mail;
   n. incompetent colleagues. (Thompson, 2002, p. 321)

In her book, Thompson makes reference to Ahrens' (1988) strategies that can be adapted for school counselors. This list includes:

   a. Decide which information to carry around in your head and which to leave on the bookshelf or in the computer.
   b. Decide what paper to keep and what to recycle.
   c. Know when to do paperwork and when to have someone else do it.
   d. Resist the urge to have more than one four-drawer filing cabinet. Organize the one you have. Better yet, give the filing cabinet away and keep all your information organized on computer discs or in one-inch binders.
   e. If you are responsible for a flexible system, be sure it is maximally organized. If you have a tightly controlled system, ensure that it is creatively flexible.
   f. Return all phone calls as soon as possible (setting aside a block of time each day for phone calls is also helpful), and gently but quickly refer those that can be made by others.
   g. Control your appointment schedule. If you don't, it will control you.
   h. Know when to say "yes" and when to say "no." Be assertive by expressing your needs and wants.
   i. Don't do anything for those you counsel that they can do for themselves.

Petrie, Landry, and Edwards (1998) in their book *Achieving Personal and Academic Success* offer several suggestions on ways to make the best use of your time. These include:
   a. Use short and long-term schedules (day planner, "to do list").
   b. Set daily priorities and focus on the most important items.
   c. Do not schedule more than you can handle during any time period.
   d. Do work when you are most alert.
   e. Use the 5 and 10 minutes before a meeting with teachers, parents, or students to review your notes.
   f. Use travel time efficiently and productively.
   g. Keep notes organized and easily accessible.
   h. Keep work area uncluttered.
   i. Begin projects with the intention of completing them and then continue working at least until you have made some progress. Make a note to yourself concerning your progress so you don't cover that material again.
   j. Learn to say "no." Or say, "I can take on this project only if you take another project away."
   k. Avoid interruptions.

l. Do low priority tasks during the times you are least alert.

m. Plan time for relaxation and enjoyable tasks. You will not use your time efficiently if you are tired or stressed.

n. Call ahead whenever possible for directions, reservations, hours of operation. And don't forget to use the Internet such as "mapquest" by Yahoo.com or "maps" by Google.com.

o. Whenever possible, handle any business that you can over the phone or through the Internet.

p. Learn to stay focused and attentive so you do not have to repeat tasks.

q. Run errands efficiently – do not make multiple special trips. Instead, tack errands onto already planned trips. Try to do as many as possible when in a certain area.

r. Prepare the night before for the next day.

While this chapter addresses time management for school counselors, the tips listed are also useful for students, teachers, and parents. Time is a valuable commodity and deserves to be spent wisely. Rosemary Thompson offers many wonderful suggestions for school counselors in her book, *School Counseling Best Practices for Working in the Schools* (2002). This book is a must for your professional library. The other references also offer suggestions on time management and stress reduction.

We each receive 168 hours per week. How do we use those hours efficiently? Effective time management is an experience in self-discipline, and each of us is the key to successfully using the time we are given. We need to be aware of what portion of time we have under our control and decide how it can be handled in a more effective way. For the time that is not under our control, how can we handle it more efficiently? We use time in the manner that we choose, whether it is work, play, or rest.

Discussion Questions

1. What can I do as a school counselor to manage my time better?
2. What can I teach to students regarding time management?
3. What can my school do to better use time?
4. What activities can I delegate to others?
5. What activities can be a joint effort?
6. How can I build in time for self-renewal?

References

Adams, D. (2001). Time out. *Independent School, 60*(3), 14-21.

Ahrens, R. (1988). Minimalism in school counseling. *The School Counselor, 36*(2), 85-87.

American School Counselor Association. (2002). *The ASCA national model: A framework for school counseling programs.* Alexandria, VA: American School Counselor Association.

Baggerly, J., & Osborn, D. (2006). School counselors' career satisfaction and commitment correlates and predictors. *Professional School Counseling, 9*(3), 197-205.

Blair, G. (n.d.). *Personal time management for busy manages.* Retrieved May 29, 2006, from http://www.see.ed.ac.uk/~gerard/Managment/art2.html

Carlson, L., Portman, T., & Bartlett, J. (2006). Professional school counselors' approaches to technology. *Professional School Counseling, 9*(3), 252-256.

Galimba, M. (2001). Managing time: The effects of personal goal setting on resource allocation strategy and task performance. *Journal of Psychology, 135*(4), 357-368.

George Mason University. Counseling and Student Development Center. (n.d.). *Time management tips.* Retrieved May 29, 2006, from http://www.gmu.edu/gmu/personal/time.html

Guillot-Miller, L., & Partin, P. (2003). Web-based resources for legal and ethical issues in school counseling. *Professional School Counseling, 7*(1), 52-57.

Hartley, D. (2004). The intrinsic equation. *American Society for Training & Development*, 26-28.

Isaacs, M. (2003). Data-driven decision making: The engine of accountability. *Professional School Counseling, 6*(4), 288-296.

Kelly, W., & Johnson, J. (2005). Time use efficiency and the five-factor model of personality. *Education, 125*(3), 51-515.

Learnmoreindiana.org (2004). Monthly checklists: Counselor time management. *LearnMore Resorce Center, 1-2.* Retrieved June 6, 2006, from http://www.learnmoreindiana.org/@conselors/counselors-elem/monthly-checklists/index

Petrie, T., Landry, L., & Edwards, K. (1998). *Achieving personal and academic success.*

Smith, M. (2004). *10 Tips for reducing stress.* Retrieved May 7, 2006, from www.webmd.com

Texas Counseling Association. (2004). *Professional School Counselors*. Austin: Texas Counseling Association.

Thompson, R. (2002). *School counseling best practices for working in the schools* (2nd ed.). New York: Brunner-Routledge.

Time-management-guide.com. (2005). *Introduction to stress management*. Retrieved June 6, 2006 from http://www.time-management-guide.com/stress-management.html

Vacarro, P. (2002). Time management tips that work. *Family Practice Management, 9*(3), 64.

Chapter 32

Counseling Abroad: Using Your Skills in the World

Gail E. Uellendahl, Mary Rennebohm, and Lisa Buono

Abstract

School counselors interested in contributing to the field within the global community and developing their multicultural competency might want to consider working abroad. Globalization and technological advances make international collaborations among educators increasingly possible. School counselors have begun to play a pivotal role in such collaborations with plans for increasing involvement on the horizon. In addition to a detailed description based on one author's practical experience working abroad, a case is made about the impact such experiences can have on a the profession and on the school counselor's growth and development.

Although there are a variety of settings where school counselors can hone their skills, perhaps one of the most interesting ways to expand one's experience is to work as a school counselor in a foreign country. Working abroad can add to the counselor's own growth and development while simultaneously serving the broader world community and contributing to the profession through informal exchange and collaboration. Whether serving through a brief exchange opportunity or a longer more formal appointment, counselors can widen their perspective in ways that are unique to immersion in cultures that are different than their own.

As globalization and technological advances make international collaboration in many professions a reality, the profession of school counseling has been following this trend for its own research, practice, and professional development. International opportunities can provide school counselors ways to enhance both their personal and professional development, contribute to the development of the field abroad, and collaborate with others to conduct research that informs theory, education and training, and best practices.

There are a variety of ways that American school counselors can participate in this enterprise. At the basic level, counselors can participate in information exchanges, informally on the Web (in various message boards such as on the American School Counselor Association's Message Board), or more formally through exchange initiatives sponsored by professional organizations. Recently, the Association for Counselor Education and Supervision (ACES) helped initiate an exchange between the National Board for Certified Counselors (NBCC) International staff and U.S. based and international counseling professionals (NBCC, 2005). The goal of this collaboration is to share information and expertise through "conference presentations, scholarly publications, and personal interactions with colleagues" (p. 5).

The American Counseling Association (ACA), in cooperation with the *People to People Ambassador Programs*, has extended this type of collaboration by sending a delegation of school counselors to China in an effort to exchange information and get firsthand feedback about the school counselor's role in the U.S. and the developing field of school counseling, now in its infancy, in China (Rollins, 2006). The idea of a student and/or teacher exchange between the U.S. and China is also being considered. More recently, a delegation was sent to Russia where they were impressed with the integration of school counseling practices throughout the curriculum of the Humanitarian Gymnasium #11, a "high-level school for gifted and talented students" (Kennedy, 2006, p. 27).

Perhaps the most intense yet fulfilling opportunity is for school counselors to participate through a formal exchange with a foreign counterpart or to work abroad on their own. Although these experiences can be rich and meaningful, they can be quite challenging as well. Quite often, an exchange will be made to a job that is not exactly equivalent, in terms of role and function, to a school counseling position within the U.S. (Williamson, 1999). Total immersion into a new culture, particularly as a working professional rather than a tourist, enables the school counselor to observe the similarities as well as to appreciate the differences encountered at their "host" school. The benefits of such experiences can be invaluable to the development of the individual counselor and can have far-reaching effects when they return home.

A popular opportunity for school counselors looking for international experiences is through employment at American-Sponsored Overseas Schools (A/OS). Although there are American students at these schools who represent "military, government and private sectors of the United States" (Rifenbary, 1996), there are also significant numbers of students from host and other countries in attendance, making these schools very multicultural. This phenomenon is due to the desire of students from "host" countries to improve their chances of American college acceptance. Indeed, Rifenbary's study revealed that the college counseling function is prominent for A/OS school counselors, accounting for 40% of their time.

School counselors and counselor educators who participate in international collaborations can additionally contribute to counselor training curriculums here and abroad. Quite often, host countries do not have compatible professional roles or training programs. In these cases, U.S. counselors can provide collaboration and assistance with curriculum development and the establishment of school counselor certification (Rollins, 2006).

The authors (Uellendahl and Buono) have participated in this type of collaboration with Occidental College and University of California at Los Angeles to both design an introductory school counseling curriculum and deliver its on-line courses to school personnel on the Micronesian islands of Yap and Kosrae. The goal of local administrators was to bring counseling activities to their schools to increase the college-going rate of their students. This experience has been both enriching and challenging. One of the biggest challenges has been to craft an educational training program that meets the needs of the secondary school students being served while recognizing that the traditional, western models for counseling and school guidance may not always apply in this nonwestern cultural context. For example, a discussion of confidentiality made it clear that our (U.S.) value of protecting students' privacy does not fit the island's cultural norm of community input into problem solving. This, coupled with the fact that many students, teachers, and other school personnel are related, led to some interesting discussions (R. Roth, personal communication, August 28, 2006).

An additional challenge in crafting the curriculum and delivering the on-line courses was recognizing that while Yap and Kosrae are both a part of the Federated States of Micronesia, their cultures are vastly different from one another, and thus delivery of material needed to be modified significantly for each island—from the way on-line discussions were handled to the types of assignments given. One group of students was very verbal and desired and needed a tremendous amount of contact and interaction about coursework as well as about social matters. Whereas students on the other island were quite independent, desiring little or no interaction except in regards to grades for coursework, in fact, social discussion was discouraged by the students. These challenges served as reminders of the importance of thoroughly investigating cultural differences to ensure effective curriculum development and program delivery.

The following section represents the experience of one American trained school counselor (Rennebohm) working overseas in a variety of countries for more than a decade.

School Counseling Abroad:
A Practitioner's Perspective

One of the options available to American trained school counselors is the opportunity for working overseas. There are a variety of different types of international schools abroad ranging from private, proprietary schools, to military (Department of Defense) schools, to private boarding schools. As an American who has chosen to work overseas, I would like to share with you some of the benefits and challenges that one can expect to encounter from an overseas assignment.

I chose to go overseas in 1991 in order to expand my professional horizons and experience another culture. My first overseas assignment was at a private boarding school in Salzburg, Austria. During this two-year assignment, I held a number of various duties, ranging from daily supervision of teenage girls, to the teaching of a health and wellness class. Boarding schools carry with them the added responsibility of supervision during evenings and weekends. As part of this assignment, I planned, coordinated, and supervised school excursions to various parts of Europe, including Venice, Rome, and Florence, Italy; France; Germany; and Hungary. One of the advantages of living at a boarding school is that the school, on a daily basis, covers your accommodations and meals. However, one also has the added responsibility of evening study hall supervision and dealing with interpersonal difficulties as they develop. The students at this particular school came from Europe, the U.S., Canada, and Asia. As a result of this multi-cultural population, students and staff both were able to gain a greater understanding of various cultures, religions, and lifestyles, thus enhancing one's professional skills as a counselor.

From 1991 to 2006, I had the experience of working in a number of international schools in Europe (the Netherlands, Austria, and Germany), Asia (Singapore), and the United Arab Emirates (Dubai). Each one of these schools provided daily opportunities for growth, learning, and personal enrichment. My most recent school, the Dubai American Academy, had students from 72 different countries, thus creating a truly international experience for myself and my colleagues. One of the challenges of working overseas is the necessity of constant *adaptation* and *flexibility*. It is not reasonable to expect lifestyle, government regulations, school policies, and procedures to be the same overseas as they are in the USA. Some of the qualities that one needs in order to successfully cope with an overseas assignment are the following:

- Sense of humor
- Natural curiosity
- Willingness to change and grow
- Flexibility
- Desire to learn from others
- Ability to deal with ambiguity
- A high degree of tolerance and acceptance of people that are different from one's self (multicultural diversity)
- A sense of adventure

Working overseas is not for everyone. Just as one's students encounter and experience culture shock, homesickness, and difficulty coping with living conditions abroad, these same experiences can affect the American counselor living abroad as well.

Something else to keep in mind about overseas opportunities is the reality of *cultural differences*. These can range from something as simple as different foods and meal times to the absence of public eating for several weeks at a time, due to religious and cultural factors. For example, during the celebration of "Ramadan" in the Middle East, it is forbidden to consume food or beverages in public between sun up and sun down for a period of 30 days. It is also important to recognize that culture dictates how people deal with conflict and adversity. During the seven years that I lived in Asia, I learned that "saving face" or avoiding embarrassment is a high priority for the Asian people. As a result of this cultural value, confrontation is rare, and the development of relationships is seen as necessary, before business can be conducted. It was not uncommon to encounter many westerners who grew frustrated at the indirect approach to dealing with negotiation and contract issues; whereas in American culture, openness and a direct approach to business matters is a more common reality. As a school counselor, it is important to keep in mind that one is a visitor in the host country, and one cannot expect the locals to possess the same mindset or way of thinking as Americans do.

One should also realize that each international school is different and varies in its curriculum, school structure, and administrative style. Some international schools use only the U.S. standard curriculum; whereas others use the International Baccalaureate curriculum, which provides a higher qualification and requires an external assessment in the last two years of high school. Other international schools use the British or Australian curriculum, and some schools use a combination of the above, as well as components of the host country. When gathering information about international schools, it is helpful to keep in mind that the role and function of the counselor can vary tremendously, depending on the priorities of the administrative team and the needs of the individual school.

For those who are interested in working at the secondary level as an international counselor, one needs to have a good background in the fundamentals of college and university admissions, as well as competent Internet skills. A large amount of time for secondary counselors is spent assisting high school juniors and seniors in preparation for the Preliminary SAT/National Merit Scholarship Qualifying Test (PSAT/NMSQT) and SAT and assisting them with the college/university application process. Due to the fact that students in international schools choose to attend universities all around the world, one needs to develop a broader awareness and understanding of the different requirements needed for admission.

As a counselor who has worked both in the U.S. and abroad, I find the *ASCA National Model: A Framework for School Counseling Programs* (American School Counselor Association [ASCA], 2003) and the ASCA National Standards (ASCA, 2003; Campbell & Dahir, 1997) to be useful tools in providing a guideline for services and school support. However, one needs to keep in mind that it would not be realistic to duplicate the ASCA model in a foreign environment due to the differences in school policies, procedures, and culture.

Another difference between U.S. public schools and private international schools is the variance in socio-economic and family backgrounds. In all of the international schools that I have worked in, the majority of parents are university graduates, and many of them possess advanced degrees as well. Many of the fathers of international students work in upper management and hold leadership positions in business, banking, technology, and international relations. Academic expectations tend to be quite high and generally one finds strong parent support when it comes to academics and expectations for respectful and responsible behavior.

Class sizes are usually kept to a minimum, compared to U.S. public schools. Specialist teachers are provided for computers, art, music, physical education, and foreign languages, which are part of the international curriculum. Due to the demands of many of these international jobs, it is not uncommon for fathers to be traveling internationally on a frequent basis. As a result of this, teachers and school counselors are often expected to provide additional support in terms of counseling and guidance.

Something else that motivated me to stay overseas has been the positive and long-term relationships that I have developed with both students and teachers from abroad. As a result of my international experiences, I now have close friends in many countries around the world, and during my school holidays I frequently visit and travel to new places in order to maintain these positive relationships. Another plus for me has been the opportunity to work across various grade levels in the international setting. During the past fourteen years, I have worked with children from the ages of 3 to 18, and I have also had the opportunity to work as a teacher and administrator in several of these positions.

Most overseas assignments provide generous benefits and salary packages that usually include some of the following: furnished housing (or a housing allowance per month), funding for professional development, staff in-services, including computer/technology development, air fare to and from the foreign country, financial compensation for tuition fees for dependent children, retirement/pension plans, and in some cases tax-free salaries. If one is interested in learning more about these opportunities, it is important to do the research necessary in order to find out if your desires and goals would be met by an overseas placement. Listed below are some of the resources that I have found helpful in learning about school positions available for U.S. certified school counselors:

- www.iss.edu
- www.tieonline.com
- www.joyjobs.com
- www.search-associates.com
- www.internationalschoolsreview.com
- www.ecis.org
- www.cois.org

For those individuals who choose to pursue an overseas assignment, I would encourage you to keep an open mind, a willingness to learn from your host country, and a well developed sense of humor. If you would like further information, feel free to contact me at: maryrennebohm@hotmail.com Mary Rennebohm, Certified School Counselor.

Additional Resources for Counselors Abroad

In addition to the resources listed above, the following Web sites house invaluable information for counselors interested in working overseas:

1). International Counseling is a Web site affiliated with The Association for the Advancement of International Education (AAIE). International Counseling hosts a plethora of information for international counselors including important topics in counseling, professional development opportunities, job searches, and other useful links. Additionally, a live chat room is currently under construction.
http://www.aaie.org/AAIE_Counseling/Counseling.html.

2). The Web site for the Association of International Schools in Africa contains many resources and links for international counselors, including information and plans for working with students in the academic, personal/social, and career domains. This site also contains links for guidance resources and materials.
http://www.aisa.or.ke/default/index.htm)

3). The U.S. Department of State's Office of Overseas Schools Web site contains a directory of schools overseas, links to regional education associations, as well as numerous educational projects to improve educational programs in American overseas schools.
http://www.state.gov/m/a/os/

4). The U.S. Department of Education's U.S. Network for Education Information (USNEI) Web site provides information about education in other countries and information about U.S. education. The site houses links to education ministries and embassies throughout the world. Additionally, UNSEI includes links about what one needs to know before departing the U.S., how to get in contact with foreign diplomatic and consular services, important contacts to make overseas, and the procedures for returning home.
http://www.ed.gov/about/offices/list/ous/international/usnei/edlite-index.html.

Summary and Implications for School Counseling

The ASCA *Ethical Standards for School Counselors* (2004) discusses the importance of multicultural competency and the development of self-knowledge in order to address the impact of counselor values and identity on their counselees. This self-knowledge, along with an understanding of the historical, sociopolitical and experiential aspects of diversity, here and in the global community, aids the school counselor in becoming more culturally proficient.

Although the *ASCA National Model: A Framework for School Counseling Programs* (ASCA, 2003) can serve as a guide when working abroad, it is important that school counselors avoid the paternalistic trap of "we know what's best." There are many countries where the profession of school counseling does not exist or is viewed differently than in the United States. Multicultural awareness and competency are critical skills for counselors working here or overseas.

Constantine (2002), in her study and review of the effect of multicultural training on multicultural competency, reports the importance of both didactic and experiential training for school counselors. In accordance with this, many school counselor education programs require candidates to intern at schools that are richly diverse so that they might increase their proficiency in working with a variety of students. Constantine and Gushue (2003) present literature that supports the role that school counselors can play in helping the increasing numbers of recent immigrant populations entering schools throughout the United States.

Constantine and Gushue (2003) point out that multiculturally competent counselors can help these students cope with the difficulties raised when cultural differences impact their well-being. School counselors who have worked abroad may be better able to identify with this experience, and be more empathic and competent in identifying particular stressors and their solutions. The Multicultural Counseling Competencies (MCC), developed by Sue, Arredondo, and McDavis (1992) cite three domains of cross-cultural competency. One of them, *awareness of your own worldview*, can be developed by immersion in a country/culture different than your own.

Counseling and collaborating abroad can serve as an opportunity to build your own cultural proficiency and prepare you to lead others in this effort whether in schools at home or abroad. These skills go beyond efforts to foster awareness and appreciation of diversity within one's school. "Educational leaders who are successful in creating culturally proficient learning communities will enable students to play vital roles wherever they go in the global market" (Lindsey, Robins, & Terrell, 2003, p. 15).

Discussion Questions

1. How might you, as a school counselor/counselor educator, make global connections with others?
2. How might the ASCA National Standards be used in countries with differing worldviews and cultural norms?
3. How do your own values, culture, and background impact your views on education, student learning, and the role of the school counselor?
4. What personal characteristics do you have that would prepare you for work abroad?
5. What challenges do you foresee you might face in an overseas school counseling position?

References

American School Counselor Association. (2003). *The ASCA national model: A framework for school counseling programs*. Alexandria, VA: Author.

American School Counselor Association. (2004). *Ethical standards for school counselors*. Alexandria, VA: Author.

Campbell, C., & Dahir, C. (1997). Sharing the vision: *The national standards for school counseling programs*. Alexandria, VA: American School Counseling Association.

Constantine, M. (2002). Counselor preparation. *Counselor Education and Supervision, 41,* 162-174.

Constantine, M., & Gushue, G. (2003). School counselor's ethnic tolerance attitudes and racism attitudes as predictors of their multicultural case conceptualization of an immigrant student. *Journal of Counseling and Development, 178,* 189-193.

Kennedy, A. (2006, July). ACA leads delegation to Russia. *Counseling Today,* 12-20.

Lindsey, R., Robins, K., & Terrell, R. (2003) *Cultural proficiency: A manual for school leaders.* Thousand Oaks, CA: Corwin Press.

National Board for Certified Counselors. (2005). NBCC International Fellows. *The National Certified Counselor, 22,* 5.

Rifenbary, D. (1996). College counseling in far-off lands. *The College Board Review, 178,* 18-34.

Rollins, J. (2006, February). Unveiling China, *Counseling Today,* 1-27.

Sue, D., Arredondo, P., & McDavis, R. (1992). Multicultural counseling competencies and standards: A call to the profession. *Journal of Multicultural Counseling and Development, 20,* 64-68.

Williamson, L. (1999). Colorado counselor exchanges job with Australian school psychologist, *Professional School Counseling, 2*(3), 189-193.

Chapter 33

Writing for Professional and Personal Enjoyment

Jackie M. Allen and Penelope Black

Abstract

This chapter acquaints the reader with the joys of writing. Writing is described as creativity, communication, collaboration, advocacy, and accountability. The reader will find tips for writing, an explanation of the many opportunities for writing, and where the author's writing can be submitted for publication. A special section provides suggestions for using writing skills at the school counselor's own school. Additional resources to help the school counselor write and publish are included.

Introduction

Writing is a source of creativity, communication, information, advocacy, and enjoyment. Writing can be done in a solitary manner or collaboratively. Writing may be for a personal record of events or experiences, such as in a diary or journal; as part of one's work, such as a report; for expression of the muse, such as a poem or inspirational piece; or for publication in a journal article, book, review, or academic thesis or dissertation. What is most important is that you take time to reflect and write your thoughts, opening up the window of your soul to share with others (Allen, 2006).

Writing is creativity.

What better way to do some creative thinking, open up your mind, think out of the box, envision the future, soar with the eagles, enter the universe of the mind and the stars! When you write, you are the creator of new ideas, the link between the past and the future, the catalyst of change, the innovator of the unimaginable. You can create new worlds, fashion the characters in those worlds, and build the structures that embolden others to follow your fantasies or your lead.

What is really you comes through in your writing. You no longer need to hide those challenging thoughts, those unspoken words, and those unproven theories. You can be real in the present, shedding the trappings of the past, and exploring the possibilities of the future. Through writing you expand your personal horizons, revealing your innermost thoughts and feelings, giving new meaning to both your self and others.

Writing is communication...

Language is said to be the defining characteristic of the human being. The ability to formulate and communicate thoughts through spoken and written language is the gift of the gods to mankind. From the hieroglyphics of the past to the computerized world of the present, humans have communicated their thoughts to their mates, to friends, to colleagues, and to the world. It is the desire of every human being to express their thoughts and feelings, to let others know where they are "coming from" and where they want to go or grow. Through writing you can inform others, share common experiences, report on unique events, communicate plans for the future, and begin to actualize those dreams through the written word.

Writing is collaboration.

Although many may think of writing as a solitary activity, only you and your computer, spell check, and a thesaurus, writing is more than an individual project. You are the accumulation of centuries of collective thought passed down through the ages to your being and your pen. You read the great books, you talk with others, you live in a society full of visual images and the bombardment of a plethora of sounds and smells, you are alive and interact with your environment, you take in more than you know, and you collaborate every day with your world. Why not also formally invite another into your writing space and collaborate with them on a project? The old adage- two brains are better than one- can be realized in your collaboration with another writer who will challenge your thoughts and ideas and bring out the best in you. Those daily experiences and musings may become collective events and stories worth telling. Working together on a project can be very rewarding- new worlds, new ideas, new challenges, and new expressions of the joy of working together on a mutually rewarding project.

Writing is advocacy.

Do you remember the last time you called a friend and told them about the new purchase you made- a trip to Europe, a new car, a new dress, tickets to the opera? Most likely you explained where you got the item, how much you paid, why you choose this particular item, who referred you to the vendor, your impressions of the salesperson, and what you expect the new purchase will do to enrich your life. You were advocating for the particular product even though no one paid you for the free advertisement. When you write, you also are advocating for a philosophy, a theory, an event, or a product. You make sure your reader understands why you think a particular idea is worthy of their attention, you back it up with references from other writers who agreed with you, and you make sure that you elaborate on the various important points, refute the arguments of those who may disagree, and put together a soundproof defense of your opinion. You advocate for what you believe in, value, and want to share with others.

Writing is accountability.

Image your grandchild finding a time capsule left by you 50 years after you died. To that child's delight not only does he find artifacts of your world and time in history but a diary, a group of poems, a story or two, or an entire book about your world. Photographs tell only part of the story of an event; add to that the thoughts and feelings you experienced during that event and you have a memorable piece of history to leave your offspring. Let your offspring know what you valued most, what you loved and cherished, what your desires and ambitions were, what jewels of wisdom you gathered in your life and want to leave for posterity. Writing is the accountability of your life- how you lived it and how you want others to know you and your world.

Writing is enjoyable.

How many times in a day, a week, a month, a year do you get to sit and think- ponder your existence, your universe, your time and place in history, your meaning? Writing can be a quiet time in a quiet place- an opportunity to meditate, to contemplate, to reach inside yourself and experience your marvelous thoughts and feelings, a time to let the world go by and concentrate only on YOU. The Me generation has been accused of being self centered but sometimes in order to live in a fast paced world, you need to center on self, draw out the best from your inner core, give yourself time and space to be soul searching and to be authentic. Self-esteem comes from knowing and loving one's self as a prerequisite to knowing and loving others. Those moments of self-focus can be ever so enjoyable and refreshing to both soul and body. Those moments provide the substance for your writing. You are the excitement in your writing. Your writing is the expression of your self, the being you enjoy and celebrate.

Tips for Writing

Perhaps you are wondering where to start; you have the interest and the time, a computer and computer skills, and have thought of something to say. So let's begin. First, know your topic- have good references, resources, and experiences to communicate to your reader. Focus on what you want to say and the audience you want to reach.

Always be clear and concise in your communication. If you need to practice your writing skills, take an adult education class, attend a seminar, or go to a special workshop on writing skills. A friend of mine attended a workshop for Christian writers and, as a result of the pointers she received and encouragement from experts and other writers, she produced a wonderful book entitled *Missy Fundi Kenya Girl* relating her experiences as a child growing up in Kenya. Every year in New Mexico there is a weeklong workshop entitled *Creativity & Madness- the Psychological Studies of Art and Artists*. There are also several books written on the value of writing as a creative activity. Julia Cameron has written a series of books on creativity and writing. My first personal experience with her work was reading *The Artist's Way* (Cameron, 1992). She counsels the emerging artist with her Rules of the Road:

In order to be an artist, I must

1. Show up at the page. Use the page to rest, to dream, to try.
2. Fill the well by caring for my artist.
3. Set small and gentle goals and meet them.
4. Pray for guidance, courage, and humility.
5. Remember that it is far harder and more painful to be a blocked artist than it is to do the work.
6. Be alert, always, for the presence of the Great Creator leading and helping my artist.
7. Choose companions who encourage me to do the work, not just talk about doing the work or why I am not doing the work.
8. Remember that the Great Creator loves creativity.
9. Remember that it is my job to do the work, not judge the work.
10. Place this sign in my workplace: Great Creator, I will take care of the *quantity*. You take care of the *quality*.
(Cameron, 1992, p. 55)

Find a quiet place where you can let your muse do its work. Do not be judgmental of your work- let it flow. Disregard syntax and concentrate on semantics. Endeavor to get your message across to your reader, then go back and fix up punctuation, grammar, spelling, etc. Let the ideas flow through your pen or your computer- do not stop to evaluate, let it be a singular (your personal) brainstorming session. You may want to organize your thoughts in a different way than initially conceived when you finish so do not let your self expression be hung up on organization. Avoid educational jargon- speak clearly and concisely to your audience; the best writers paint a visual picture in the mind of the reader. Use your visual abilities to envision what you want to say and then describe your thoughts through the written word. Although the basic ideas for this chapter have come from a previous *School Counselor Writer's Handbook* designed for the attendees of a writer's workshop at the California Association of School Counselors, Inc. annual conferences, I find myself accessing new thoughts and ideas and instead of sticking to the original outline, expounding upon what I find most helpful for the reader of this chapter.

Few writers complete a work in one sitting. Whether it be a book review, short story, chapter, or an inspirational piece, give yourself the opportunity to let time pass between your thoughts and expression of those thoughts on paper. Go back to your original ideas and add new thoughts, clarify, change, enhance, and create once again that which you want to communicate to your reader. Throughout the process of writing- enjoy your experience, have fun with your topic, get involved personally with your message, put your passion on the paper.

Like anything, the more you write the better you become. You may start out with something simple like a newsletter article for a professional association and end up editing or writing a whole book. I started writing devotionals when in youth organizations at a young age and enjoyed my experience so much that I vowed one day I would write my own book. My first attempt was editing and writing several chapters of *School Counseling: New Perspectives & Practices* (Allen, 1998) and now I am telling others about the joy of writing in this book for school counselors. I feel like I am just beginning and have more to say; my next step along the journey of writing will be a book of my own inspirational thoughts with my son's photography or a whole book on writing or leadership.

As reader- what do you want to know about, what do you want to share, what are you curious about, what do you have to contribute? Your answers to these questions will form the content of your future writings.

Part of self-care is self-expression. This section of the book is dedicated to taking care of one's self. What better way than getting out those ideas, concepts, hypotheses, and theories you have always wanted to express.

Types of Writing

So now that I have your attention, you may ask, "What could I write?" There are so many opportunities for you to write. Some general suggestions include: a poem, a record in your diary, an inspirational article, an article for a newsletter or magazine, a book report, a chapter for a book, a research article for a journal, a book, a thesis or dissertation, and many more. Letter writing is becoming obsolete with the advent of the computer, but perhaps there is someone you could express your thoughts to in a letter. Who in your daily life could use a note of encouragement? Write them a word or two. Who in your life could use some praise? Write them a few words. How about your family- what type of legacy are you leaving them? Write down some of your experiences, stories, and challenges and give your work as a memento or a gift.

If you are currently working as a school counselor, there are so many ways to develop and use your writing skills. Here are quite a few ideas to get you started, and of course there are many more, as many as you can imagine.

- Begin to write school newsletter articles
- Start a school counseling column in the school newsletter
- Better yet- start an electronic newsletter
- Compile, print, and distribute topical resources, such as suicide prevention
- Submit articles to the local newspaper
- Write letters to senators and assembly members to promote counseling legislation
- Prepare a freshman handbook
- Create a weekly school counselor bulletin
- Put together pamphlets to advertise your counseling program and place them in medical and dental offices in the community and or send them to civic organizations such as Lions Club
- Complete a Student Personnel Accountability Report Card to share with your principal, superintendent, board of education, and community
- Create a Web site
- Write e-blasts for important events, like Scholarship Night

- Provide parents with tips on working with their children
- Summarize scholarship winners for an award night
- Complete student college recommendations
- Compile school counseling tips to share with colleagues
- Promote a career speaker's bureau
- Provide handouts for parent nights and parent teacher association meetings
- Prepare a book review to put in staff boxes
- Develop a survey of student needs and/or counselor effectiveness
- Prepare a grant application for school counseling
- Have a student write their story
- Have students write to the parents or teachers who have lost a child or a student
- Tell your success story- a testimonial of school counselor effectiveness
- Write a comprehensive school counseling program document
- Complete annual school counselor evaluation
- Produce a research report on student results (grades, attendance, group counseling, etc.; Allen, 2006)

Many school counselors would like to write for a journal. There are a variety of types of journal articles: assessment and diagnosis, best practices, book and media reviews, practice and theory, perspectives from the field, profiles, review of literature, research, resource reviews, and trends. Articles may be quantitative or qualitative, historical or theoretical, literature reviews, case studies, practice articles, Web site reviews, Internet articles, or special issues. You definitely have something to contribute after you worked in school counseling. My retired husband, who is admittedly not a writer, was thrilled to see his chapter about his counseling program *The Dream Board—A Visual Approach for Career Planning with At-Risk 8th and 9th Grade Students* (Wakefield, Sage, Coy, & Palmer, 2004) in print. He had the satisfaction of contributing to the ongoing body of material on best practices and resources for school counselors and other educators. Wouldn't you like to see something that you have written in print?

Where Can You Submit Your Writing?

Professional associations offer the opportunity for you to begin to practice your writing skills. The power of a counseling organization to put your ideas in print is remarkable. At a Writer's Workshop in 2005 for the

California Association of School Counselors, Inc. (Allen, 2005), I passed out a one-page summary of some of the opportunities offered by professional associations to mentor writing skills and give a voice for school counseling. These opportunities include:

- Advocacy and drafting legislation
- Assessment reviews
- Book reviews
- Bylaws
- Case Studies
- CD program reviews
- Counseling events
- Editorials
- Letters to editors
- Letters to legislators
- Manuals
- Monograph articles
- Newspaper articles
- Poetry
- Position papers
- Reports of counseling successes
- Research projects
- Stories and vignettes of program successes
- Strategic plans
- Summaries of best practices and counseling programs
- Action research studies of your counseling program
- Surveys of client opinions
- Testimonials and tributes
- Web site and Internet Reviews

Counseling publications are always looking for original work by practicing school counselors. Some of the publications you might consider submitting your work to include: your state school counseling organization newsletter, a special monograph put out by your state association, *ASCA School Counselor, Professional School Counseling, Counseling Today, Journal of Counseling and Development*, and other professional educational publications such as the Association for Supervision and Curriculum Development's *Educational Leadership*. You may be able to accept the challenge of writing a column for your professional newsletter or becoming a member of an editorial board of a journal.

I hope you are convinced and ready to write. There are many resources that will help you prepare to write with correct syntax, semantics, and form. One of the brief popular resources is *The Little, Brown Essential Handbook for Writers* (Aaron, 2000). For inspiration the works of Julia Cameron are amazing. I would recommend starting with *The Artist's Way: A Spiritual Path to Higher Creativity* (Cameron, 1992). Publishing companies, such as Houghton Mifflin, produce guidelines for preparing a textbook proposal or prospectus. Magazines and journals provide tips for authors. The Association for Supervision and Curriculum Development's (ASCD) Tips for Authors outline the top five qualities they look for in ASCD books:

Something to say: The text reflects original thinking and fresh information—it's truly enlightening.

Research-based: Assertions in the text are supported by research as necessary. References are up-to-date, and sources reflect current thought in the field.

Practical guidance: The text provides information and ideas that the reader can use to improve practice.

Specificity: The author has included good examples, illustrations, and anecdotes.

Conversational tone: The text is engaging and avoids jargon.

(ASCD, n.d.)

Professional School Counseling, the journal of the American School Counselor Association (ASCA), contains original manuscripts on school counseling research, practice, theory, and contemporary issues in the field. Feature articles and Perspectives from the Field (1,500-2,000 words) are solicited. ASCA provides author guidelines. In preparation of a manuscript for review the following are suggested:

1. Do not submit material under consideration by another periodical.
2. Manuscripts must conform to the guidelines in the 2001 edition of the *American Psychological Association (APA) Publication Manual* (5th ed.).
3. Refer to the APA guidelines to eliminate bias based on gender, sexual orientation, racial or ethnic group, disability, or age. Avoid using passive voice.
4. ASCA style does not allow footnotes (except in tables and figures) or bibliographies. For reference, endnotes, and in-text citations follow APA style.

5. Keep article titles and headings within the article as short as possible.
6. For the reviewers' benefit, double space all material, including references and quotations, and allow wide margins.

For additional information, consult the back cover of the current issue of *Professional School Counseling* (ASCA, 2006).

For publication style and format assistance the *Pocket Guide to APA Style* (Perrin, 2006), a brief version of the 5th edition of the *APA Manual* (APA, 2001), provides the correct editorial style used in counseling and psychological publications. Other suggestions for writing assistance are included in the resource section at the end of the chapter.

An Example of Meaningful Writing

A popular Writer's Workshop at the annual California Association of School Counselors, Inc. provides prospective writers the opportunity to find out about the personal and professional enjoyment of writing. Dr. Penny Black, high school counselor, participated in the 2006 Writer's Workshop and inspired the attendees by telling about her friend and writing mentor with this inspiring tribute to Dr. Laurie Bottoms.

In the Spring of 1998, happily installed in a cozy cottage in Northern California with children launched in college, I received a phone call from Dr. Laurie Bottoms. Laurie had been the first Director of the Carnegie Center for Learning and Teaching (now the Laurie S. Bottoms Gallery) in Lexington, Kentucky. In 1997 she was appointed Assistant Head of Milken Community High School in Los Angeles. She was looking for a new Math Department Head for Milken and she wanted me to apply.

I remember our first conversation. While open to all, the curriculum at Milken Community High School is designed to help Jewish children understand and value their heritage. I assumed in that initial conversation that Laurie was Jewish and I did not want to explain that I am not. It turned out that she was Episcopalian but I was not to learn that until much later.

I did not even want to go down to Los Angeles for the interview. I told Laurie that I had heard that there was terrible smog in LA and that the freeways were parking lots. I explained that I liked living near a university and in a moderate climate. Laurie, who had lived in the Bay Area, was quick with her answer, "It's the same ocean down here and UCLA is almost as good as Stanford." (I was to laugh about that later while earning my doctorate at UCLA.) Laurie said that if I lived on the west side of LA the climate would be better than in the Valley. I flew down for the interview and, after observing Laurie's enthusiasm about the curriculum at this new school, I took the job and rented a house in Westwood.

Laurie was a magnificent leader. Rather than running meetings about schedules and other trivia, every meeting was about instruction. Laurie was delighted that I assigned essays in math class. Laurie loved writing! In the summer of 1999 Laurie ran a weeklong writing workshop for faculty members. I was the only math person there but I thoroughly enjoyed it. Laurie wrote on a note card evaluation, "I would have loved math if you had been my teacher." I keep that on my school bulletin board.

None of us knew that Laurie was a cancer survivor, nor did we know that the cancer had returned during the summer that she was our teacher. Laurie became ill in the fall of 1999 and died soon thereafter. After that year I left Milken and moved to the Los Angeles public schools; another wonderful friend, the English Chair whom Laurie had hired, moved on as well. On the campus of Milken Community High School a statue with a fountain commemorates Laurie's life; someday I will visit it.

Conclusion

Writing brings meaning to our lives in so many ways as evidenced by the preceding tribute. All you have to do to begin is pick up a pen, or sit at your computer and begin to put your thoughts, wishes, desires, experiences, memories, and stories in writing. Yes, writing is creativity, communication, collaboration, advocacy, accountability, and above all personally and professionally enjoyable. I would like to leave with you the 5P's of Productive Writing (Allen, 2005) that you might also be inspired to write: PASSION, PERSPECTIVE, PLAN, PATIENCE, and PERSISTENCE.

PASSION
- A spiritual experience
- Sharing the window of your soul with the world
- Believe in yourself…believe in your writing
- Your audience wants to know what you care about
- Personal inspiration and experience manifests itself in reader interest
- Creative works come from the heart

PERSPECTIVE
- Your personal opinion is valuable and worthy of sharing
- Writing your perspective enhances your communication skills
- Unique opinions make for interesting reading
- Your major literary contribution may be your personal perspective

PLAN
- Develop a general plan of your project
- Write on a daily basis- exercise the pen
- Plan for warm up time and meaningful breaks
- Provide opportunity for your "creative muse" to be released

PATIENCE
- Writing is a process- perfection takes time and practice
- Personally become part of your creative process
- Give yourself permission to create without judging your work
- Honing your craft takes time and patience

PERSISTENCE
- Keep on going- write often- Write…write…write
- Peak writing periods vary with the individual
- Persist in communicating your thoughts to others
- Enhanced effort provides you with a product you will be proud of

Discussion Questions

1. Sometimes people confuse creativity with artistry. "Creative writing," the course that was offered in high school, is not what we are talking about here. School counselors must exercise creativity to come up with strategies to deal with silent teens, difficult parents, and angry teachers. Write a paragraph describing a situation in which you used your creativity.

2. The chapter describes writing as communication. Write a paragraph in which you (as described in the text) let others know where you are "coming from" and where you want to go.

3. While most of us consider writing to be a solitary activity, this chapter suggests that writing is collaborative. In a paragraph describe a situation in which you worked collaboratively with another person(s). Describe the situation, which required you to work together. Was the outcome successful?

4. If you have taken a course in speech and debate you already have discovered the power of writing for advocacy. If you have had such an experience, write a paragraph describing this experience. If you have not written for advocacy before, define an issue, which means a great deal to you and write a paragraph describing how you could help people to see things your way.

5. Suppose that a time capsule was left by you and opened 50 years later. Write a paragraph describing what items you would leave in such a time capsule and what they would tell about you.

6. If indeed writing is enjoyable, as suggested in this chapter, take five minutes and focus entirely upon yourself. During the five minutes make a list of all of the things that you could write about which would describe how you feel about yourself.

7. Pick one item from the list in the "Types of Writing" and explain, in one paragraph, how you would begin to write about it.

References

Aaron, J. E. (2000). *The little, brown essential handbook for writers* (3rd ed.). New York: Addison Wesley Longman, Inc.

Allen, J. M. (Ed.). (1998). *School counseling: New perspectives & practices*. Greensboro, NC: ERIC/CASS Publications.

Allen, J. M. (2005). Presentation at the Writer's Workshop on March 29th at the California Association of School, Counselors, Inc., Pomona, California.

Allen, J. M. (2006). *School counselor writer's handbook*. Unpublished manuscript.

American School Counselor Association. (October, 2006). *Professional School Counseling*. Alexandra, VA: Author.

American Psychological Association. (2001). *Publication manual of the American Psychological Association* (5th ed.). Washington, DC: Author.

Association for Supervision and Curriculum Development (ASCD). (n.d.) *ASCD's tips for authors*. Retrieved April 6, 2008, from http://www.ascd.org/portal/site/ascd/menuitem.2a4fb56d79bd30a98d7ea23161a001ca/template.article?articleMgmtId=505f0f05c1520010VgnVCM1000003d01a8c0RCRD

Cameron, J. (1992). *The artist's way: A spiritual path to higher creativity*. New York: Tarcher/Putnam.

Perrin, R. (2006). *Pocket guide to APA style* (2nd ed.). Boston: Houghton Mifflin Company.

Wakefield, S. M., Sage, H, Coy, D. R., & Palmer, T. (2004). *Unfocused kids: Helping students to focus on their education and career plans*. Greensboro, NC: CAPS Press.

Additional Resources

Elfreida Abbe, E. (2004). *The writer's handbook 2005*. Waukesha, WI: Kalmbach Publishing Co.

Cameron, J. (1996). *The vein of gold: A journey to your creative heart*. New York: Tarcher/Putnam.

Cameron, J. (1998). *The right to write: An invitation and initiation into the writing life*. New York: Tarcher/Putnam.

Cameron, J. (2002). *Walking in this world: The practical art of creativity*. New York: Tarcher/Putnam.

Davis, K. M. (2001). Navigating the publication process II: Further recommendations for prospective counselors. *Professional School Counseling, 5,* 56-61.

Magnuson, S., Davis, K. M., Christensen, T. M., Duys, D. K., Glass, J. S., Portman, T., et al. (2003). How entry-level assistant professors master the art and science of successful scholarship. *Journal of Humanistic Counseling, Education and Development, 42,* 209-222.

McGowan, A. S. (2002). Publishing in JCD: Some goals and objectives. *Journal of Counseling & Development*, 80, 259-260.

McGowan, A. S., & Scholl, M. B. (2004). Counsel from a former editor and the current editor. Successful research and writing for publication in "The

Journal of Humanistic Counseling, Education and Development." *Journal of Humanistic Counseling, Education and Development, 43*, 4-15.

Mettee, S. B., Hall, D., & Doland, M. (2005). *The American directory of writer's guidelines* (6th ed.). Palatine, IL: Quill Drive Books.

Soml, C.A. (2000). Publication process: Recommendations for prospective contributors. *Professional School Counseling, 3*, iii-iv.

Smaby, M. H., Maddux, D. C., Zirkle, D. S., & Henderson, J. J. (2001). Counselor Education and Supervision: On-line peer review editing, on-line submissions, and publishing articles on the World Wide Web. *Counselor Education and Supervision, 40*, 163-169.

Turner, Barry (Ed.). (2005). *The writer's handbook*. New York: MacMillan.

Chapter 34

Food For Thought: Investigating a School Counselor Career Ladder or Pathways

Robert D. Hansen and William Welcher

Abstract

There is a dearth of literature regarding a school counselor career ladder or pathways. This chapter explores career opportunities for school counselors, including educational administration, school psychology, higher education, and a variety of entrepreneurial pursuits, including consulting and private practice. The authors posit that in an ever changing educational environment, armed with a variety of skills and experiences, school counselors should have no difficulty transitioning to another field if they so desire.

Introduction

Recently, we have received numerous inquiries from both counselor trainees, as well as practioners, regarding the concept of a career ladder or pathways for school counselors. A typical inquiry contained the following question: "If I decide to pursue another career related to school counseling, or need to find a new position, what might I investigate?" (Hansen & Allen, 2004). This is a particularly relevant question since the average person in the United States will make as many as three to five major occupational changes within a lifetime and anywhere from twelve to fifteen job changes (Bolles, 2006). Unfortunately, there is a dearth of literature related to this topic. However, several career opportunities immediately come to mind: (1) leadership positions in educational administration; (2) school psychology; (3) higher education, and (4) a variety of entrepreneurial pursuits, including consulting and private practice.

Changing school demographics in the United States will yield future vacancies in educational positions. According to the U.S. Department of Labor, Bureau of Labor Statistics, there will be a projected increase of 16.6 percent in all occupations within educational services between 2004 and 2014. The need for educational administrators, clinical counseling, and school psychologists will increase by 15.6 percent and 22.2 percent, respectively, during this same time frame. This is due in large part to the increase in school population and anticipated retirements due to the "graying" of the educational work force. For example, almost 59 percent of all administrators are over 45 years of age with many slated for retirement in the near future (U.S. Department of Labor, 2006a). Approximately one-third of all school psychologists in the United States are in the 51 to 60-age bracket and rapidly approaching retirement (Levine et al., 2002). In addition, the school age population in the United States is also expected to grow by over 1.4 million between 2006 and 2014. More than 1 million of this student growth is projected to be in the Western Region of the United States (National Center for Education Statistics, 2005a).

Opportunities in Educational Administration

One option, which counselors should consider, is educational administration. School counselors already possess three important skills, which are transferable to the arena of educational administration: listening skills, conflict management and resolution skills, and problem-solving skills. They also have expertise in networking with various educational agencies and identifying community resources.

Site level leadership positions in school administration, which may be attractive to practicing school counselors, include head counselor or assistant principal in charge of student services/counseling. A district or central level position as director of pupil personnel services, counseling and guidance, or student services may also be of interest. Such positions might include supervising the counseling program, psychological services, or child welfare and attendance. Administrative positions are also available at county offices of education and state-level entities (U.S. Department of Labor, 2006b).

Recent changes in certification laws in some states suggest the enhanced accessibility of training in other educational fields. For example, in California there have been significant changes in the available alternatives for educators to earn an administrative services credential. In addition to the completion of a "traditional" university program, individuals can now receive an administrative services credential on an internship basis before completing all course work, enter an alternative preparation program offered by local educational agencies or universities, or pass the "School Leaders Licensure Assessment" administered by the Educational Testing Services (California Commission on Teacher Credentialing, 2006).

Opportunities in School Psychology

Earning school psychology certification is another course of action, which school counselors may wish to consider. Many of the courses (perhaps as many as 50 percent) have been taken by school counselors during their training and may count toward school psychology certification requirements. In addition, there is a required 1,200-hour supervised internship in school psychology required in most states. Many school psychologists work as part of an interdisciplinary team with at-risk students, provide leadership in crisis response and suicide prevention programs, or conduct assessments for placement of special education students (National Association of School Psychologists, 2006).

School psychologists may specialize in such areas as autism, preschool, bilingual assessment, neuropsychology, or working with emotionally disturbed students. School psychologists can become program specialists, directors of special education, or choose to prepare for private practice.

Opportunities in Higher Education as a Counselor Educator

Due to the anticipated increase in postsecondary enrollments and full-time faculty member retirements, there will be significant employment opportunities in higher education in public and private universities. Currently, adjunct faculty comprises 49 percent of all faculty positions in education departments in the United States (National Center for Education Statistics, 2005b). While tenure track positions in higher education will continue to be competitive, there will be an increased need for adjunct faculty members. Adjunct faculty is attractive to universities since they provide current "real" world experiences, often in specialized areas. They instill new energy, and expose students to a variety of viewpoints, thereby enhancing the scope and quality of the educational program. In addition, since adjunct faculty can be hired at a lower rate of pay than full-time faculty members, who also receive fringe benefits, they are of interest to universities operating in a "tight" budget environment.

School counselors could follow one of several paths in securing a position in higher education. First, existing counselors with Master's level training could apply for adjunct positions at local universities to teach specific courses or supervise fieldwork students. Second, those individuals who have "Plan B" in mind, that is, full-time post K-12 employment options, may in some cases use this pre-retirement adjunct position as a stepping stone in obtaining a full-time faculty position after retirement. This would be particularly true of an individual with a doctoral degree. Some institutions, such as the University of La Verne, actually have steps within the adjunct ranks: adjunct instructor, adjunct professor, and senior adjunct professor depending upon experience and degrees. One of the authors of this chapter successfully chose this path, and is now a tenured full professor. Third, those individuals who wish to have part-time employment after retirement should strongly consider becoming an adjunct faculty member. Retirees often find this to be a refreshing change of pace from working with K-12 students or carrying a heavy caseload. A fourth option for school counselors is enrolling in a doctoral program to become a counselor educator and when completed, apply directly for a full-time faculty position. Universities are looking for individuals who have both doctorates and have been school counselors. Although monetary rewards may initially be less, the prestige, flexibility, and intrinsic rewards of contributing to the profession's body of knowledge, research, and future may outweigh other rewards.

In his book *The Farther Reaches of Human Nature*, Maslow (1971) discusses the higher ends of his hierarchy of needs theory, that is, self-actualization and self-transcendence. It is apparent that by becoming adjunct faculty members, school counselors can further meet these needs by increased self-fulfillment and realization of their potential, as well as helping others find self-fulfillment and realize their potential through graduate training. Being an adjunct faculty member can be both challenging and rewarding, offering a real adrenalin rush, and presenting a built-in vehicle to stay current and hone one's skills. Graduate students are generally highly motivated and grateful for the assistance of faculty members. Experience as an adjunct member is seen by some K-12 school districts as being prestigious, which may be factored in when considering candidates for future promotional opportunities. Most importantly, adjunct faculty members make a vital contribution to the profession of school counseling.

Additional Career Opportunities

In the private sector, many other opportunities exist for the flexible, creative, and entrepreneurial school counselor. Private career and college counseling can be a lucrative part-time or full-time endeavor for many trained counselors. Consulting for other school districts, county offices, or state departments of education can offer career challenges for the experienced counselor. Also, the technology arena offers many possibilities for creating novel software products.

In addition, private practice in mental health counseling and marriage and family therapy is open to school counselors who have state licenses. The field of human resource administration or employee assistance (e.g., outplacement) may provide yet other outlets for career options.

Five Tips to Enhance Your Success

In expanding your options beyond the realm of school counseling, you may wish to consider these five tips:

1. Be open to occupational changes. Most people make three to five changes in a lifetime.
2. Be receptive to additional training (for example, as an administrator, school psychologist, or private therapist).
3. Consider relocating to parts of the United States with high student growth to enhance your employment options.
4. Consider rewarding opportunities in higher education as an adjunct or full-time faculty member in counselor education.
5. Be flexible and creative in seeking out entrepreneurial opportunities, such as private, college and career counseling, consulting, and developing new technology.

Conclusion

The careers on the school counselor career ladder discussed in this chapter, and others yet to be created, certainly provide "food for thought." They offer school counselors a myriad of possibilities in changing times when life-long learning, changing occupations, and individual initiative provide optional pathways to career success and development. In an ever changing educational environment, armed with a variety of skills and experiences, school counselors should have no difficulty transitioning to another field if they so desire.

Discussion Questions

1. Have you thought about making a career change?
2. Are you satisfied in your current career as a school counselor? Why? Why not?
3. What are some roadblocks that you are encountering, in your current career as a school counselor? How are you going to refuel?
4. How long do you intend to work?
5. Have you contemplated "Plan B," that is, full-time post K-12 employment options?
6. Would you be willing to relocate geographically in order to change careers?
7. Would you consider making a career change if it meant going back to school for additional education and/or certification?
8. How would you feel about making a career change to educational administration? School psychology? Part-time or full-time positions in higher education? Entrepreneurial type pursuits? Why? Why not?
9. Are there other career pathways you have contemplated which were not discussed in this chapter?

References

Bolles, R. (2006). *What color is your parachute. A practical manual for job-hunters and career changers*. Berkley, CA: Ten Speed Press.

California Commission on Teacher Credentialing. (2006). *Administrative Services Credential*. Retrieved June 23, 2006, from www.ctc.ca/gov/credentials/ CREDS /admin-svs.html

Hansen, R., & Allen, J. (2004, Winter). Food for thought: Investigating a school counselor career ladder. *The California School Counselor, 3*, 3-4.

Levine, S., Curry, A., Sobel, R., Gilgoff, D., Mulrine, A., Pethokoukis, P., et al. (2002, February 18). Careers to count on. *U.S. News & World Report, 132*, 46.

Maslow, A. (1971). *The farther reaches of human nature*. New York: The Viking Press.

National Association of School Psychologists. (2006). *FAQs—The profession of school psychology*. Retrieved June 21, 2006 from, www.nasponline. org/about_nasp/sp_faq.html.

National Center for Education Statistics. (2005a). Projections of education statistics to 2014. Retrieved June 20, 2006, from http://nces.ed.gov.

National Center for Education Statistics. (2005b). *2004 national study of postsecondary faculty. Report on faculty and instructional staff in fall 2003*. Washington, DC: U.S. Department of Education.

U.S. Department of Labor, Bureau of Labor Statistics (2006a). *Career guide to industries: Educational services.* Retrieved June 22, 2006, from www.bls.gov/oco/cg/cgs034.htm.

U.S. Department of Labor, Bureau of Labor Statistics (2006b). Counselors. *Occupational outlook handbook.* Retrieved June 22, 2006, from www.bls.gov/oco/ocos067.htm.

Additional Resources

- For career information on educational administration view the American Association of School Administrators (AASA) Website at www.aasa.org.

- For career information on school psychology view the National Association of School Psychologists Website at www.nasponline.org.

- For assistance as an adjunct professor, consider:
  Greive, D. (2002). *Teaching strategies & techniques for adjunct faculty* (4th ed.). Elyria, OH: INFO-TEC.

- For help with changing careers, consider:
  Bolles, R. (2006). *What color is your parachute? A practical manual for job-hunters and career changers.* Berkeley, CA: Ten Speed Press.

Chapter 35

Retirement: An Opportunity to Live a "Passion" of Your Life

Mary Honer and Winifred Strong

Abstract

Generally, each generation defines "retirement" for itself. Baby Boomers are fast approaching the retirement stage of their lives and will establish a different concept, reflecting many personal, professional, and psychological implications and issues. Retirement can be a time to stir the soul, kick-start the exploration of new experiences, or turn a long-time dream into a new passion. This chapter explores the challenges and opportunities of the retirement phase and addresses the meaning of retirement for various individuals, factors and challenges to consider when planning for retirement, and the importance of creating retirement options.

Introduction

Indications are that the current generation will not be defined by the same rules used by today's 80 and 90 year old retirees. "Fit and fabulous at fifty" leads to "still young and sexy at sixty" and "suave and smooth at seventy." Magazine articles and news items forecast the arrival of the baby boomer generation as a group unwilling to grow old! The emphasis on staying young gives us botox, ways to avoid sagging jowls, magic pills to continue the ability to perform, and procedures for reduction of skin wrinkles. Advice columns highlight the importance of maintaining a regular exercise schedule, where to find fashions to keep one stylish (with the added feature of comfort), and men reap the benefits of relaxed jeans.

For adults, working at home or employed outside the home, **retirement** is a phase of one's life that will become a reality some time in the future-twenty years, five years, perhaps as soon as six months hence. Now the boomer generation has come of age and is swelling the ranks of older Americans, and we have a new challenge to retirement!

Some of today's boomers seem unwilling to accept the psychological components of growing old and are skeptical about life after retirement, viewing this phase as a sign that life shuts down or will soon end. Thinking and planning for retirement remains a task to be undertaken in the distant future and removed from the reality of the present day. It is easy to grasp the aversion to retire as it is defined in *Webster's Dictionary* (1993) as:

> Retire: verb (1) to withdraw from action; (2) to retreat, fall back, to recede; (3) to withdraw from privacy; (4) to withdraw from one's position or occupation, conclude one's working or professional career; (5) to go to bed.

The Meaning of Retirement

The sober mood expressed by these terms does not generate personal excitement associated with a change in lifestyle! It offers a view that one's life is void of personal empowerment and sense of competence. The inference here is: once past active employment, life becomes meaningless, sterile, and unfulfilling. Thus for many who are very involved in their "working world," retirement can be an emotionally charged term that jeopardizes their "balance of life" and threaten loss of personal identification. Traditional work ethic values continue the pressure to maintain the status quo and resist a major transition to retirement as a valid choice versus gainful employment. Stressors closely associated with retirement include worry about a changing lifestyle and fear of economic hardship, compounded by declining physical health.

For many their personal identity is heavily, and perhaps solely, related to their job or professional status. Retirement may be interpreted as a threat to this real or perceived loss of "being somebody."

For others, who have become disenchanted with their employment or always hated their jobs, retirement is viewed with rose-colored glasses and anticipated as a panacea to all their woes. Now is the time one can sleep in, play all day and/or night without having to worry about getting up to go to work. The reality of the normal stressors of this major life change is overlooked while only the euphoric anticipation reigns. For this type of person the reality is sometimes a bitter pill to swallow. The long awaited respite is not so glorious. In recent generations, emphasis on improved health care and nutrition results in a continued rise in life expectancy. The United States Census Bureau reports show the percentage of the U.S. population 65 years and over has increased from 25 million in 1980 to 35 million in 2000 and is expected to push over 50 million in 2020 (U.S. Census Bureau, 2000). The largest increase appears to be age 85 and older. With anticipated retirement at age 65 (or earlier) and a life expectancy of 85 or 90 years, future retirees are faced with 20 to 30 years beyond the phase of a 40-hour week devoted to work. With retirement attained- what do you do with the rest of life?

Traditional perceptions related to retirement suggest the individual should anticipate a decline of the physical and mental processes as one slides toward death. This concept is a MYTH, old fashioned and obsolete! Upon completion of x number of years in a career, this change can be stimulating and elevate the spirit of adventure and freedom for new and satisfying life experiences! Today a retired person can find interests in many areas and can have more time to pursue them. It takes knowledge, planning, and personal confidence to leave full employment to transition to a different lifestyle. Preparation for this change includes the ability to formulate a plan that addresses critical issues and options for the well-being of a retired person.

Planning for Retirement

Conditions and areas that solicit consideration in advance of retirement include:

1. **Financial factors.** Understanding the effectiveness of financial resources contained in an individual's annual income from pension, social security, annuities, interest and the like are balanced with the annual expected living expense plus additional funds for new options.

2. **Legal issues.** Reviewing the legal and ethical issues that impact on management of healthcare, estate planning, choices for long-term care, and protection of personal assets.

3. **Health and wellness.** Evaluating and selecting a health care system appropriate to the retired individual and family, maintaining the physical and emotional well being for older adults, and establishing a cost and benefits comparison of long-term care require a study of medical plans.

4. **Social relationships.** Recognizing the importance of sharing the planning process with spouse or partner, as well as significant family members, develops an appreciation of changing relationships with former co-workers, the opportunity to expand the circle of friends, and the reality of a new "living togetherness."

5. **Use of time.** Using the 40 hours per week x 50 weeks per year x 30 years= 60,000 hours! What are the implications to the years ahead? Does it begin with anticipating leisure time and the fulfillment of creative and satisfying years OR the alternative- a fear of declining health and ebbing income? Fresh ideas and choices, emerging with expansion of free time, can include cultivating new hobbies or special interests, finding new ways to use present career skills as a volunteer to a community agency, or with a part time job in a related area.

6. **Personal growth and development.** Considering new experiences through travel, hobbies, and emeritus programs can offer more personal exposure and discovery for new talents.

7. **Where to live:** Maintaining status quo or changing locations requires thoughtful consideration. Exploring location alternatives with one's spouse or partner challenges the excitement of the new and untried, with comfort and security of a predictable and settled lifestyle. Although retirement offers freedom from an anchor tied to a former employment site, the change also brings additional readjustment experiences and opportunities. There are many varieties of housing and location possibilities. Beginning with expressed needs, personal interests, and available options, one can assess the important features for a retirement location: climate and environment (desert, mountains, or seashore); city or country; intergenerational or seniors only neighborhoods; recreational or cultural interests and activities; area features; and available medical and shopping transportation. Is the new location affordable? What kinds of fees are already in place and how much may they increase with time? When moving to a new location the potential retiree must evaluate the loss of support groups. Family, friends, and neighbors from a former local area may no longer be easily accessible.

The Challenge of Changes

One must also evaluate the possible time when other changes may occur and assisted living becomes necessary. The loss of one's mate and the inability to drive are two of the myriad of possibilities one may not foresee. Children need to be involved in the decisions. Reevaluation of legal documents such as power of attorney, co-signatures on the checkbooks, and funeral arrangements can create a feeling of comfort and security. Having these issues addressed, rather than being morbid, truly creates a feeling of peace and gives the retiree the freedom to enjoy life from day to day.

Retirement can be a two-edged sword! On the final approach to terminating the work phase of a lifetime, this anticipation may be replaced by apprehension. There is an increase in anxiety often followed by second thoughts- is this the right time? With new decisions to make, a sense of loss and foreboding often accompanies the feeling of release. The retiree may suffer several stages of grief suggested by Elizabeth Kubler-Ross in *On Death and Dying* (1969). The stages are:

Denial and Isolation. When retirement fantasies begin to fade and the "honeymoon is over," the retiree continues to say that everything is perfect while experiencing the terrible feelings of loss of identity, redundancy, and missing old friends and daily routines.

Anger. Retirees may be disappointed with the loss of one's work identity and the discovery that one is out of the loop, as well as a loss of status, income, and/or loss of medical benefits. Disenchanted with the sameness in daily living and the shattered illusions of retirement dreams, a retiree enters the anger phase of grief indicated by irritation and aggravation, often leading to depression. Having to live all day, every day with the same person can bring new meaning to "for better or for worse!" This is also often the stage when the senior begins to drink too much.

Depression. The unhappiness of a dull, daily living routine and separation from the security of past support, sometimes leads to further isolation and mourning. Feelings of uselessness and futility are often exaggerated and crippling.

Bargaining. Fantasies once dreamed can bring a retiree to search for ways one can feel more valued and worthwhile by seeking trade-offs: If I get a face lift I can be young again, or If I work out at the gym I can stay firm and not look so old.

Acceptance. Eventually the stage of acceptance is reached and more realistic ideas and plans for this new phase of life emerge toward adjustments of life goals.

It is not always easy to recognize the best time to say "the end" or "farewell" and to begin the retirement phase. In some instances the desire for change, health issues, age, family members, special offers, and even new opportunities may help nudge a person to the decision making time. On their own, a person needs to acknowledge, first to themselves and then to others, when to call quits to a career and to give others the opportunity to sort out the challenges. Retirement plans must be personalized by the individual with consideration for significant others.

Creating Retirement Options

The past two or three decades gave rise to the freedom of selecting options that range from establishing a small commercial project based on a developed interest or hobby to the volunteer aspect of giving back to the community through using career skills in a different environment.

So, what are these options, and where does one find out about them? One needs only to research the possibilities out there to discover that life after retirement can get so busy that one often hears, "When did I ever have time to work?" With the growing population of seniors, the opportunities for recreational involvement, volunteerism for charity, as well as second careers are innumerable. The Internet has many sites for just such options. The local newspaper is also a good source. The local senior center brings one into contact with others who have found interesting occupations for their newfound freedom.

For the person who has enjoyed his work there may be a possibility of part time employment giving the retiree a chance to phase out of one lifestyle into another. This is also a time when the skills learned while working can be transferred into another setting, thus continuing the pleasure one enjoyed while gainfully employed. For example, teachers can always choose to substitute teach, choosing the days they work and the grade and age level they enjoy. There are opportunities overseas in international schools for two-year assignments. Church affiliated mission schools are always looking for teachers willing to go overseas for periods as short as a year. Short-term missions utilize every kind of skill such as teaching, building, sewing, cooking, athletics, etc. There is hardly a skill known that cannot be used somewhere and in some way. The upside is one gets to travel and to see the world, the downside is that usually these assignments require the individual to pay their own way or to find funding some other way.

Even in the United States there are many opportunities to donate time and efforts for the good of others—driving people to medical appointments, Meals on Wheels, clothing closets where used clothes are sorted and donated to the needy, libraries, hospitals, homes for the indigent, women's shelters, and on and on. Many schools welcome grandmas and grandpas to come each week to read to children or to listen to a child read. Learning new things or honing an interest from art, writing, sewing, languages, quilting, etc., have helped the retiree discover talents often left latent until discovered in later years. Some seniors have used the opportunity to go back to earn a degree that had to be abandoned or delayed while the family was growing up. Travel is one major source of adventure, which can now be done during the off-season while the crowds of children are at school and fares are more reasonable. Elderhostel (see resource list for Web site) offers a combination of travel and learning with the advantage of being with people of comparable age and a guide to care for the travel details. Traveling alone may be daunting, and thus traveling in a group may be much more pleasurable.

Many organizations such as churches and religious organizations, civic and governmental organizations, and private organizations, have many opportunities for individuals not required to punch a time clock. Building, teaching, secretarial, computer literacy, driving, cooking, flower arrangement, and gardening skills are a few of the abilities that can be used. Even the government has opportunities that retirees can take advantage of. Counseling for retirement, estate planning, and funeral arrangements are often done by people as a second career or on a part time basis. Hospitals can use receptionists, people to deliver flowers and gifts, and other activities that are so meaningful to the sick person.

People willing to go overseas for a period of time can teach English as a second language in many Asian countries. In some instances the airfare is paid, a place to reside is provided, and a small salary included. For other seniors the opportunity to rock babies in places like India and to provide the personal touch orphaned babies need is rewarding and gives a sense of satisfaction. Being a dorm parent in a boarding school can be challenging but rewarding. In many places cooks and housekeepers are hired to do the manual work while the "senior parents" do the parenting by assisting with homework, drying tears, and generally being the absentee family.

With all the above options and many, many more that can be found, there is no reason for boredom as long as one has health and strength. Unfortunately the time will come when retirees find themselves forgetting more often; the body doesn't respond as well; and one's "get-up-and-go has got up and went." The hearing goes, the teeth rot, arthritis causes constant pain. Yes, aging is not for sissies. However, one can "live till one dies." Keeping active as long as possible, planning well ahead of time, and having the satisfaction that one has made a contribution to those following along in their footsteps can make the final days more acceptable.

Under normal circumstances within the human spirit there appears to be a final acceptance when one is ready and willing to go that final step. One becomes tired and life on this planet no longer has the hold it once did. The person is willing and sometimes looks forward to moving on to heaven or his/her new dimension. Knowing that one has led a satisfying and rewarding life and put his/her house in order prepares for a smooth transition to this final stage of retirement.

Conclusion

In summary here are some "Do's" and "Don'ts" for retirement:

- DO begin thinking and planning for retirement early enough to make necessary changes. Make sure retirement funds are as secure as possible. A good financial planner may cost you now, but can make the difference between living comfortably and poverty later in life.
- DON'T spend all your money from paycheck to paycheck without planning how you will live after retirement. Social Security may not be there for you and really does not provide a living income.
- DO consider where you want to live upon retirement. For many staying put is the best option. For others moving to a retirement community or locating more affordable housing is necessary.
- DON'T move so far from your children, relatives, church, and other community attachments that you feel isolated and friendless.
- DO get your estate planning in order. Fetterman, Block, and Waggoner in USA Today (2006) list the following things to consider:
  - Review your assets and debts
  - Decide who you want to inherit your assets
  - Draft or update your will
  - Choose an executor
  - If you have dependent children, choose a guardian.
  - Get a durable power of attorney
  - Consider whether you need a trust for your assets
  - Discuss an estate plan with your heirs
  - Write a letter of instruction
- DON'T put off making a will. The state will eat up a big share, and your children or heirs will be left to fight over the rest.
- DO provide your heirs with a list of where things are. They will need to know where your insurance policies are kept, whether you wish to be buried or cremated, and your funeral instructions. Consider a prepaid funeral so your children or other family

members won't have to worry over those finances. (There will be enough details for them to think about.)

- DON'T put off making funeral plans. Fortunately we do not know when we will die, so best we are prepared to make our departure less traumatic for the family.
- DO keep busy and active as long as you can. Keep the mind alert with reading, playing games, and new learning. Keep the body healthy with exercise, proper eating, and health maintenance. Medical appointments for eyes, ears, teeth as well as general health should be faithfully kept. Read up on health issues so you have questions for the physician and can intelligently hear what he/she has to tell you. Take one of your children or friends with you to medical appointments if you have trouble talking to the doctor, can't understand what is being said, or do not remember what the physician told you.
- DON'T neglect your teeth, eyes, and ears, and medications.
- DO, now that all of the above suggestions are taken care of – travel, play, volunteer, and keep busy. Use the rocking chair for rocking your grandchildren, great grandchildren, nieces and nephews, some orphans, or foster children who need your love and caring.
- DON'T sit around in your rocking chair getting fat.
- DO

  Grow old along with me!
  The best is yet to be,
  The last of life, for which the first was made:
  Our times are in His hands
  Who said, "A whole I planned,
  Youth shows but half; trust God: see all, nor
      Be afraid!"

  From Rabbi Ben Ezra

- DON'T forget to enjoy each day! A positive attitude keeps you, as well as others, happy.

Discussion Questions

1. List the stages of grief as identified by Elizabeth Kubler-Ross.
2. Consider how each stage of grief may be related to retirement.
3. In what ways can a recently retired person master personal grief associated with departure from the work place?
4. What areas require personal consideration before the move to retire?
5. Make a list of those things one needs to take care of in order to retire well.
6. What are your major strengths and greatest interests? What retirement options exist that would match your personal strengths and interests?

References

Fetterman, M., Block, S., & Waggoner, J. (2006, June 26). Navigating the 5 phases of retirement. *USA Today*, section B, 5.

Kubler-Ross, E. (1969). *On death and dying*. New York: MacMillan Publishing Co.

U.S. Census Bureau. (2000). *Statistical abstract of the United States*. Washington DC: Author.

Webster's Dictionary (10th ed.). (1993). Springfield, MA: Merriam Webster.

Resources

Agencies and Organizations

Federal Agencies

Department of Health and Human Services	1 (877) 696-6775
Civil Rights Administration (Title VI) Discrimination	1 (800) 386-1019
Housing	1 (800) 569-4287
Medicare Information	1 (800) 633-4227
Social Security Administration	1 (800) 232-1311

National Organizations

American Association of Retired Persons (from age 50)	1 (888) 687-2277
Elderhostel, Adventures in Lifelong Learning (from age 55)	1 (877) 426-8056
U.S., Canada, and International Programs Adventures Afloat	

Publications

Adams-Kaplan, D. (2006, July 11). Vacations with vision. *The Los Angeles Times*.

Bland, W. (2005). *Retire in style: 60 outstanding places across the U.S. and Canada*. Chester, N.J.: Next Decade, Inc.

Harkness, H. (1999). *Don't stop the career clock: Rejecting the myths of aging for a new way to work in the 21st century*. Palo Alto, CA: Davis-Black.

Kaplan, L. (1999). *Retiring right.* Garden City, NY: Avery Publishing Group.

McMacken, R. (2006, August 15). Fifty plus and fabulous. *The Los Angeles Times.*

Petras, K., & Petras, R. (2000). *Age doesn't matter unless you're a cheese.* New York: Workman Publishing.

Savageau, D. (2004). *Retirement places rated* (6th ed.). Hoboken, NJ: Wiley Publishing.

State Bar of California-Office of Media and Information Services. (2006). *Seniors and the Law: A guide for maturing Californians.* San Francisco: Author.

Steele, J. (2004, October 19). Not the retiring type. *The Los Angeles Times.*

Web Site Resources

General

www.aarp.org/bulletin
www.aarpmagazine.org
www.elderhostel.org
www.latimes.com/livingwell

For jobs and service

www.coolworks.com
www.elderhostel.org
www.second50years.com
www.seniors4hire.com
www.2youngtoretire.com

Federal Opportunities

www.usaid.gov   The agency for International Development
www.state.gov   The U.S. Department of State